TRAGEDY
AND
COMEDY

An Anthology of Drama

TRAGEDY AND COMEDY

An Anthology of Drama

SYLVAN BARNET, *Tufts University*
MORTON BERMAN, *Boston University*
WILLIAM BURTO, *State College at Lowell*

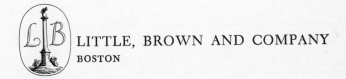

LITTLE, BROWN AND COMPANY
BOSTON

LIBRARY OF CONGRESS CATALOG CARD NO. 67–17723

THIRD PRINTING

Printed simultaneously in Canada
by Little, Brown & Company (Canada) Limited

PRINTED IN THE UNITED STATES OF AMERICA

PREFACE

It would be easy to compile a book, larger than this one, of essays and commentaries on tragedy and comedy, rather than of the plays themselves; and in it one could find, plausibly argued, all sorts of implausible arguments for the superiority of one type over the other, for the rules governing each type, for the uselessness of all rules, etc. And there is value in worrying about the matters that have exercised the insight and ingenuity of a long line of critics. But the plays come first; too often students (and instructors) worry more about the theory than the practice, more about tragedy and comedy than about tragedies and comedies.

Perhaps, however, a few words about this collection will be useful. The PLAYS, arranged chronologically within the categories of tragedy and comedy, cover a range of years and types, but in no case were they chosen only to represent a period or a type. All were chosen because of their dramatic value. Those that were not written in English are represented in the best modern translations. The AFTERWORDS are relatively short. They do not try to explicate the plays, but they do try to make some useful and relevant points, points that will be useful too in connection with other plays. For example, the afterword to *As You Like It* comments on two traditions of comedy, "critical" comedy and "romantic" comedy, but most of this material is relevant to other plays in the book. Similarly, the discussions of farce, in the afterword to *The Matchmaker*, of pathos, in the afterword to *A Streetcar Named Desire*, and of three kinds of laughter, in the afterword to

Henry IV, go beyond the plays in question. The general introduction that begins the book seeks to introduce students to basic concepts and critical terminology, but it may be best to postpone reading it until the students have carefully read at least one tragedy and one comedy. Our own suggestion for beginning is to read *Oedipus the King* and *The Matchmaker;* both are highly readable, and are as representative of the genres as plays can be. The GLOSSARY, drawn in part from the more detailed glossary in our *Aspects of Drama,* is a dictionary of two hundred basic critical and historical terms that are likely to come up in an introductory course. Some of these terms are discussed at length in the commentaries, but they are given again in the glossary itself; no one has to read the commentaries, unless he wants to know the dates of the plays.

Our ideas about tragedy and comedy have been shaped by many playwrights and many critics. Doubtless we are not aware of all of the influences upon us, but we know we are much indebted to Gerald Else, Northrop Frye, Helen Gardner, Richmond Lattimore, Konrad Lorenz, Maynard Mack, D. H. Monro, Rheinhold Niebuhr, and L. J. Potts. If other critics find they have contributed to this book, we hope that they will be as charitable as lovers in a comedy, and will accept our apologies and our thanks.

We have been fortunate in getting permission to print important modern plays and distinguished modern translations of older plays, and we are grateful to the authors, translators, and publishers who have cooperated. We are grateful, also, to Warren Stone, David Giele, and Ellen Silver of Little, Brown, who have never let us get away with anything.

SB
MB
WB

CONTENTS

ix

Contents

INTRODUCTION

Whimsical assertions that all men are Platonists or Aristotelians, or liberals or conservatives ("Nature wisely does contrive/That every boy and every gal/That's born into the world alive/Is either a little Liberal/Or else a little Conservative") reveal a tendency to divide things into two. Two is about right: peace and war, man and woman, day and night, life and death. There may be middle cases; there is the cold war, and Edmund Burke suggested that no man can point to the precise moment that divides day from night — but Burke also suggested that everyone can make the useful distinction between day and night. The distinction between comedy and tragedy may not always be easy to make, but it is usually clear enough. *Hamlet*, which in Horatio's words is concerned with "woe or wonder," is a tragedy; *A Midsummer Night's Dream*, which in Puck's words is concerned with things that pleasingly "befall preposterously," is a comedy.

We are talking, of course, about two aspects of life, or two states of mind, each of which has often been represented in drama. But perhaps first a few words should be given to the term "drama" LYRIC, itself. One way to subdivide literature is to distinguish NARRATIVE, three literary forms or types: lyric, narrative, and DRAMA drama. A lyric is an expression of emotion (examples: the short song, and the long song or ode or hymn); a narrative is a story (examples: the short story, the novel, the epic); and a drama is a representation by means of impersonators. Like a narrative, a drama tells a story, but unlike a narrative it relies on actors (normally aided by costume and scenery) who gesture and speak and

who thus represent, or re-present, some real or imagined happening. At
the beginning of *Othello*, for example, we see and hear two men quarreling. The quarrel had begun before they entered upon the stage;
Shakespeare does not speak in his own person to tell us what they are
quarreling about. We hear them speak of "this," and "such a matter,"
and we see the essence of quarreling men ("Tush! . . . I take it much
unkindly," " 'Sblood, but you'll not hear me"). Shakespeare does not
tell us how they feel; rather, he lets his creations reveal themselves in
lines that call for indignant and placatory gestures. Or look at the beginning of the second scene of *Othello*. Only in the stage direction
does the author speak in his own person.

> *Enter Othello, Iago, Attendants with torches.*

> *Iago.* Though in the trade of war I have slain men,
>   Yet do I hold it very stuff o' th' conscience
>   To do no contrived murder. I lack iniquity
>   Sometimes to do me service. Nine or ten times
>   I had thought t' have yerked him here, under the ribs.
> *Othello.* 'Tis better as it is.

Iago has explained in the previous scene that he serves Othello only "to
serve my turn upon him"; in the speech printed above, when he is
talking to Othello, he hypocritically claims a conscience, and he at the
same time reveals his aggressiveness when he says "Nine or ten times /
I had thought t' have yerked [i.e. stabbed] him here, under the ribs."
Perhaps at "here" Iago touches his own ribs, but probably he more
daringly touches Othello's thus making visible as well as audible his
hatred. The language is fully dramatic: (1) it can be spoken effectively
by an actor (2) it seems to proceed not from Shake-
speare the author but from Iago the treacherous
soldier, and (3) it has an appropriate amount of
tension. One caution: to say that language is drama-
tic does not mean that it necessarily calls for bustling gestures. In
Beckett's *Waiting for Godot*, we get this dialogue and stage direction:
" 'Yes, let's go' (*They do not move.*)"

DRAMATIC
LANGUAGE

The gestures on the stage are, of course, "actions," but they are not
the action of the play in the sense of Aristotle's use of *praxis* or "action"
in *The Poetics*, a fragmentary treatise of the fourth century B.C. that
remains the starting point for most discussions of drama. For Aristotle,
drama is the imitation (i.e. representation, re-presen-
tation, re-creation) by impersonators, of an action.
In tragedy the action is something serious and important, something that matters, done by people who
count (e.g. King Oedipus' discovery that he has killed

IMITATION
OF AN
ACTION

his father and married his mother); in comedy (for Aristotle), the action is done by unimportant laughable people who make mistakes that do not cause us pain. Commonly the tragic action is a man's perception of a great mistake he has made; he suffers intensely and perhaps dies, having exhausted all the possibilities of his life. The comic action often is the exposure of folly and the renewal rather than the exhaustion of human nature. Crabby parents, for example, find that they cannot keep young lovers apart, and so they join in the marriage festivities. Byron jocosely put the matter thus:

> All tragedies are finished by a death,
> All comedies are ended by a marriage.

All tragedies and all comedies do not in fact end thus, but the gist of the idea is right; tragedy has the solemnity, seriousness, and finality we often associate with death,* and comedy has the joy and fertility and suggestion of a new life we often associate with marriage. This concept of *an action* (i.e. an underlying motif, not merely gestures) in tragedy and in comedy makes clear that comedy is not a mere matter of jokes or funny bits of business. It also makes clear what the Greek comic playwright Menander meant when he told a friend that he had composed a play, and now had only to write the dialogue; he had worked out the happenings that would embody the action, and there remained only the slighter task of providing the spirited words. Thornton Wilder, after writing *The Matchmaker*, stepped back from it, so to speak, and described the action thus: "My play is about the aspiration of the young (and not only of the young) for a fuller, freer participation in life." The action or happening dramatized in a tragedy or a comedy may be conceived of as a single course or train of events which is manifested on the stage by a diversity of activities. Think of such expressions as "the closing of the frontier," or "the revival of learning"; each of these might be said to denote an action, though each such action is seen only in its innumerable manifestations. The *Iliad* announces its action in the first line: "Sing, goddess, of the wrath of Achilles." The "action" is not, of course, always explicitly an-

---

* Shakespeare's tragedies all end with the death of the tragic hero, but a good many Greek tragedies do not. In *Oedipus the King* the hero remains alive, but he is blind and banished and seems to have exhausted the possibilities of his life. Some other Greek tragedies have what can reasonably be called a happy ending, i.e., some sort of joyful reconciliation. For example, in Sophocles' *Philoctetes*, the weapon which has been taken from the sick Philoctetes is returned to him, and Heracles, a messenger from Zeus, announces that Philoctetes will be healed. But these tragedies with happy endings, like those with unhappy endings, deal with "important" people, and they are about "serious" things. If there is finally joy, it is a solemn joy.

nounced in a literary work. Among Ibsen's preliminary notes as he worked toward *Hedda Gabler* we find such things as "They [i.e. women] all have a leaning towards sensuality, but are afraid of the scandal," "Men and women don't belong to the same century," and "The play is to be about 'the insuperable' — the longing and striving to defy convention, to defy what people accept (including Hedda)." What Ibsen was trying to do, clearly, was to get hold of his central point and then develop a plot that would reveal it. Shakespeare has left us no such notes, but we can perhaps say that in *Othello* the action is the vulnerability of a man whose generous spirit makes him an easy prey to a schemer; this terrifying and pitiful vulnerability is revealed by a series of occurrences that take place in Venice and in Cyprus, in courts, streets, bedrooms, etc.

A tragic playwright takes some happening, from history (for example, the assassination of Julius Caesar), or from fiction (Shakespeare derived *Othello* from an Italian short story), or from his own imagination, and he makes or shapes or arranges episodes that bring out the nature of the action. He makes (in common terminology) a *plot* that embodies the action or spiritual content. (Even when the playwright draws on history, he makes his own plot because he selects and rearranges the available historical facts.) A glance at a very different kind of drama, now popular, may help to make clear the distinction between a plot that embodies an action or a happening, and mere unconnected activities, happenings, events. In the early 1960's there was a good deal of interest in "Events" or "Happenings" (the latter term was derived from a performance in 1959 of something called *18 Happenings in 6 Parts*), performances in which activities were not connected so as to form a coherent plot that manifested an underlying action. Sample: a girl alternately washes her feet, puts tape over her mouth, dances with a board, sprays paint from a can onto a wall, and finally disrobes. Such a performance may display wit, agility, and other virtues and skills, but it is not a play in the traditional sense, despite its playfulness. Neither would a re-enactment of everything that Julius Caesar did during his last days or hours be a play with an action, for drama is not so much concerned with what in fact *happened* as with some sort of typical and coherent or unified thing that *happens*, a significant action. Sometimes, of course, history provides substantial material for drama, but even Shakespeare's *Julius Caesar* takes frequent liberties with the facts as Shakespeare knew them, and Shakespeare's source, the biographer Plutarch, doubtless had already assimilated the facts to a literary form. At most we can say that history provided Shakespeare with a man whose life lent itself well to an estab-

HAPPENINGS
AND
HAPPENINGS

lished literary form. Not every life does lend itself thus. We are told that Aeschylus, the earliest tragic playwright who has left us any complete plays, was killed when an eagle mistook his bald head for a rock and dropped a turtle on it to break the shell. Aeschylus' death was a great loss, but it did not have the unified significant action required of tragedy. By chance an eagle that had captured a turtle was near to Aeschylus, and Aeschylus by chance (or rather by his chemistry) was bald. There is no relation between these two circumstances; Aeschylus' death (allegedly) happened this way, and we can account for it, but the event has no intelligible unity. (A sentence from Vladimir Nabokov's *Pale Fire* comes to mind: if one is contem-

UNITY   plating suicide, "jumping from a high bridge is not recommended even if you cannot swim, for wind and water abound in weird contingencies, and tragedy ought not to culminate in a record dive or a policeman's promotion.") In tragedy things cohere. The hero normally does some deed and as a consequence suffers for doing it. Actions have consequences in the moral world no less than in the materialistic world of the laboratory. The tragic playwright's solemn presentation of "the remorseless working of things," Alfred North Whitehead pointed out (in his *Science and the Modern World*, 1925), is "the vision possessed by science," and it cannot be accidental that the two great periods of tragic drama, fifth-century B.C. Athens and England around 1600, are periods of scientific inquiry.

This emphasis on causality means that the episodes are related, connected, and not merely contiguous. Generally the formula is to show the tragic hero moving toward committing some deed

THE   that will be a great mistake, he commits it, and then,
TRAGIC   seeing the consequences, he learns the true nature of
HERO   his deed. The plot, that is, involves a credible character whose doings are related to his nature. For Aristotle, in the best sort of tragedy, the tragic hero is an important person, almost pre-eminently virtuous, who makes some sort of great mistake that entails great suffering. Calamity does not descend upon him from above, does not happen *to* him, nor does he consciously will a destructive act; he merely makes a great mistake. The mistake is

HAMARTIA   Aristotle's *hamartia*, sometimes translated as "tragic error," sometimes as "tragic flaw." Probably Aristotle did not mean by *hamartia* a trait, such as rashness or ambition, which the translation "flaw" implies, but simply meant an action based on a mental error, a sort of false step. Oedipus, erroneously thinking that Polybus and Merope are his parents, flees from them when he hears that he will kill his father and sleep with his mother. His action is commendable, but it happens to be a great mistake because it brings him to his real parents. Nevertheless, despite the scholarly elucidations of Aristotle, we can sometimes feel that the erring action proceeds from a particular kind of character, that a person with different traits would not have acted in the same way. The Oedipus that we see in the play, for example, is a self-assured quick-tempered man — almost a rash man, we might say — who might well have neglected to check the facts before he fled from Corinth. There are at least times, even when reading *Oedipus the King*, when one feels with George Meredith (1828–1909) that

> in tragic life, God wot,
> No villain need be! Passions spin the plot:
> We are betrayed by what is false within.

From this it is only a short step to identifying *hamartia* with a flaw, and the flaw most often attributed to the tragic hero is *hybris*, a word that for the Greeks meant something like "bullying,"

HYBRIS   "abuse of power," but in dramatic criticism usually is translated as "overweening pride." The tragic hero forgets that (in Montaigne's words) "on the loftiest throne in the world we are still sitting only on our own rear," and he believes his actions are infallible. Othello, for example, takes it upon himself to execute justice on Desdemona, whom he believes unfaithful, and so he kills her. Macbeth, told that he will be king of Scotland, chooses to make the prophecy come true by murdering his guest, King Duncan; Brutus decides that Rome can be saved from tyranny only by killing Caesar, and he deludes himself into thinking he is not murdering Caesar but sacrificing Caesar for the welfare of Rome.

We have talked of *hamartia* and *hybris* in tragedy; two more Greek words, *peripeteia* and *anagnorisis*, also common in discussions of tragedy, ought to be mentioned. A *peripeteia* (sometimes an-

PERIPETEIA   glicized to "peripety" or translated as "reversal") occurs when the action takes a course not intended by the doer. Aristotle gives two examples: (1) the Messenger comes to cheer up Oedipus by freeing him from fears but the message heightens Oedipus' fears; (2) Danaus (in a lost play) prosecutes a man but is himself killed. The second example, by the way, reminds one of *The Merchant of Venice*, in which Shylock, calling upon the law, in effect demands Antonio's death and finds that his own life may be lawfully taken. A few other examples may be useful: Oedipus fled from Corinth to avoid contact with his parents, but his flight brought him to them; Macbeth kills Duncan to gain the crown but his deed brings him fearful nights instead of joyful days; Othello, seeking to perform an act of justice, performs an unjust act by killing Desdemona. The Bible

— especially the Old Testament — is filled with such peripeties or ironic actions. For example, the Philistines brought Samson before them to entertain them, and he performed his most spectacular feat by destroying his audience. But the archetypal tragic story is that of Adam and Eve: aiming to be like gods, they lost their immortality and the earthly paradise, and brought death to themselves.

The other Greek word, *anagnorisis*, translated as "recognition" or "discovery" or "disclosure," seems to have meant for Aristotle a clear-

ANAGNORISIS
ing up of some misunderstanding, for example, the proper identification of someone or the revelation of some previously unknown fact. But later critics have given it a richer meaning and used it to describe the hero's perception of his true nature or his true plight. In the narrow sense, it is an *anagnorisis* or "recognition" when Othello learns that Desdemona was chaste. In the wider sense, the *anagnorisis* is in his penultimate speech:

When you shall these unlucky deeds relate,
Speak of me as I am. Nothing extenuate,
Nor set down aught in malice. Then must you speak
Of one that loved not wisely, but too well;
Of one not easily jealous, but, being wrought,
Perplexed in the extreme; of one whose hand,
Like the base Judean, threw a pearl away
Richer than all his tribe; of one whose subdued eyes,
Albeit unusèd to the melting mood,
Drops tears as fast as the Arabian trees
Their med'cinable gum. Set you down this.

Similarly King Lear's "O, I have ta'en/Too little care of this," and Hamlet's "There is special providence in the fall of a sparrow," may be called recognition scenes. Here is Macbeth's recognition that his pur-pose has been frustrated, that his deed has been ironic:

My way of life
Is fall'n into the sear, the yellow leaf,
And that which should accompany old age,
As honor, love, obedience, troops of friends,
I must not look to have.

"Troops of friends" abound in comedy. Where tragedy is primarily the dramatization of the single life that ripens and then can only rot,

THE SOCIAL
WORLD OF
COMEDY
that reaches its fullest and then is destroyed, comedy is primarily the dramatization of the renewing of the self and of social relationships. The tragic figure is isolated from society, partly by his different nature, and partly by his tragic act; comedy suggests that

selfhood is found not in assertion of individuality, but in joining in the fun, in becoming part of the flow of common humanity. Where tragedy suggests an incompatibility between the energy or surge of life and the laws of life or the norms of society, comedy suggests that norms are valid and necessary. The tragic hero does what he feels compelled to do; he asserts himself, and is intensely aware that he is a special person and not a member of the crowd. But that his mistake always reveals that he is hybristic is not at all certain. The Greek tragic hero is commonly set against a chorus of ordinary mortals who caution him, wring their hands, and lament his boldness, but these ordinary mortals are always aware that if they are law-abiding men, they are also less fully men than the hero. That they obey society's laws is not due to superior virtue, to the triumph of reason over will, to self-discipline; rather, their obedience is due to a lower vision, or to timidity, and indeed sometimes to a fear of what resides in their own breasts. The tragic hero is, of course, in one way inferior to those about him; his mistake costs him great suffering, and he is thus immobilized as the others are not. But his greatness remains indisputable; the anguish that at times paralyzes Hamlet also makes him greater than, say, Horatio and Laertes. In fact the tragic hero is circumscribed, certainly after the deed, when he is necessarily subject to the consequences (Brutus kills Caesar and finds that he brings to Rome a turmoil that makes him flee from Rome, and ultimately makes him take his own life); even before doing the tragic deed the hero is circumscribed because his action proceeds from something, either from his personality or his circumstances. Still, his action seems to him to be freely his, and indeed we feel that it is an action that a lesser man could not perform. Which is almost a way of saying that it can be argued that a tragic hero may err not so much from weakness as from strength. Why can Iago so easily deceive Othello? Not because Othello is an unthinking savage, or an unsophisticated foreigner, but because (as Iago admits) Othello is of a "loving noble nature," and, again,

The margin labels, aligned left, read: **TRAGIC ISOLATION** and **TRAGIC VIRTUE**.

> The Moor is of *a free and open nature*
> *That thinks men honest* that but seem to be so;
> And will as tenderly be led by th' nose
> As asses are.

Why can Claudius see to it that Laertes murders Hamlet during a fencing match? Not because Hamlet is a poor fencer, or a coward, but because Hamlet,

> being remiss,
> *Most generous, and free from all contriving,*
> Will not peruse the foils.

This is not to say that the tragic hero is faultless, or that he is quite happy with himself and with his action; but he does experience a kind of exultation even in his perception that disaster is TRAGIC JOY upon him. If he grieves over his deed, we sense a glory in his grief, for he finds, like Captain Ahab, that in his topmost grief lies his topmost greatness. At last he sees everything and knows that nothing more can be experienced. He has lived his life to its limits. Othello puts it thus:

> Here is my journey's end, here is my butt,
> And very seamark of my utmost sail.

(In a comedy Shakespeare tells us that "journeys end in lovers meeting," that is, the end is a new beginning.) In "Under Ben Bulben" William Butler Yeats (1865–1939) suggests the sense of completeness that the tragic hero experiences when, under the influence of a great passion, he exhausts his nature and seems to be not a man among men but a partner (rather than a subject) of fate:

> Know that when all words are said
> And a man is fighting mad,
> Something drops from eyes long blind,
> He completes his partial mind,
> For an instant stands at ease,
> Laughs aloud, his heart at peace.
> Even the wisest man grows tense
> With some sort of violence
> Before he can accomplish fate,
> Know his work or choose his mate.

Elsewhere Yeats put his distinction between the tragic hero and the world he is up against thus: "Some Frenchman* has said that farce is the struggle against a ridiculous object, comedy against a movable object, tragedy against an immovable; and because the will, or energy, is greatest in tragedy, tragedy is the more noble; but I add that 'will or energy is eternal delight,' and when its limit is reached it may become a pure, aimless joy, though the man, the shade, still mourns his

* Yeats is rather freely summarizing Ferdinand Brunetière's *La Loi du théâtre*. A translation of Brunetière's treatise is available in *European Theories of the Drama*, ed. Barrett H. Clark.

lost object." And one more passage by Yeats, this one from a play, again calling attention to the revelation of life — joyful to behold — apparent when an impassioned man expresses his fullest nature:

> I would have all know that when all falls
> In ruin, poetry calls out in joy,
> Being the scattering hand, the bursting pod,
> The victim's joy among the holy flame,
> God's laughter at the shattering of the world.

All this is to say splendidly that we sometimes feel admiration for the passionate man, for the man determined to do and to be, and we sense his superiority (as he himself senses it) to the law-abiding men who surround him, perhaps no more so than when his nobility undoes him, i.e. when we see the incompatibility between passionate self-assertion and the laws of life.

But there are contexts and times when we find passionate self-assertion funny (there are contexts and times, too, when we find it vicious, but that is another matter). Much depends on what COMIC is being asserted, and what or who the antagonist is. ASSERTION Recall Brunetière's opinion, or rather Yeat's version of it, that tragedy dramatizes a struggle against an immovable object, comedy a struggle against a movable one. Othello against the diabolic Iago is a tragic figure, but a pedant against a dull schoolboy may be a comic one. The lament of the tragic hero is proportionate to the event, but the effort extended by the comic figure is absurdly disproportionate. Furthermore, as Henri Bergson (1859–1941) pointed out, the comic figure usually is a sort of mechanism, repeating his actions and catch phrases with clocklike regularity in contexts where they are inappropriate. He quotes Latin on every occasion, or he never travels without his pills, or he always wants to know how much something costs, or he is forever spying on his wife. Bergson, who suggested that the comic is "the mechanical encrusted on the living," illustrated his point by telling of the customs officers who bravely rescue the crew of a sinking vessel, and then ask, the moment the shore is reached, "Have you anything to declare?" The mechanical question, inappropriate in the situation, reveals that the officers value trivial regulations as much as they value life itself. Real life, too, affords examples of this sort of comic behavior. Emerson mentions that the biologist Camper, who had spent six months studying hairless water mammals, said he almost began to see people as narwhales, porpoises, and marsouins. This is whimsy, of course, but Emerson goes on to tell of a visit to a dying friend. On his way to the friend, Emerson met the physician, who had just left the patient. The physician, Emerson says, "accosted me in great spirits, with joy sparkling in his eyes. 'And how is my friend, the reverend Doctor?' I inquired. 'O, I saw him this morning; it is the most correct apoplexy I have ever seen: face and hands livid, breathing stertorous, all the symptoms perfect.' And he rubbed his hands with delight."

Emerson's doctor, valuing symptoms rather than life, nicely fulfills Bergson's formula. And in his high spirits — ludicrously out of place in the context — he inadvertently illustrates another aspect of comedy, its prevailing high spirits. The comic world is a world of delight in variety; even its hardships are not lasting. In *As You Like It* when Rosalind, daughter of a banished duke, complains of the frustrations of life, "O, how full of briers is this working-day world," Celia gives the right reply: "They are but burrs, cousin, thrown upon thee in holiday foolery." (But if Celia were to give this answer too often she would become laughable herself.) The comic world seems to be presided over by a genial tolerant deity who enjoys the variety that crosses the stage. The sketchbooks of the Japanese artist Hokusai (1760–1849) wonderfully reveal this comic delight in humanity. There are pages of fat men, pages of thin men (no less engagingly drawn), pages of men making funny faces, and there is a delightful drawing of a man holding a magnifying glass in front of his face so that his nose seems enormous. The comic playwright gives us something of this range of types and grotesques, and he gives us also variety in language (e.g. puns, inverted clichés, malapropisms) and variety in episodes (much hiding behind screens, dressing in disguise). The character, then, who insists on being himself, who mechanically holds to a formula of language or of behavior, is laughably out of place in the world of varied people who live and let live. The thing that comedy does not tolerate is intolerance; it regularly suggests that the intolerant — for example the pedant and the ascetic — are fools and probably hypocrites. Here is the self-righteous Alceste, in Molière's *The Misanthrope:*

COMIC JOY

COMIC
ISOLATION

> Some men I hate for being rogues; the others
> I hate because they treat the rogues like brothers,
> And lacking a virtuous scorn for what is vile,
> Receive the villain with a complaisant smile.
> Notice how tolerant people choose to be
> Toward that bold rascal who's at law with me.

Philinte genially replies, "Let's have an end of rantings and of railings,/ And show some leniency toward human failings./This world requires a pliant rectitude;/Too stern a virtue makes one stiff and rude." Here is the puritanical Malvolio in *Twelfth Night*, trying to quiet down some tipsy but genial revelers:

> My masters, are you mad? Or what are you? Have you no wit, manners nor honesty, but to gabble like tinkers at this time of night? Do ye make an alehouse of my lady's house? . . . Is there not respect of place, persons, nor time in you?

He is aptly answered: "Art any more than a steward? Dost thou think, because thou art virtuous, there shall be no more cakes and ale?" This suspicion of a "virtue" that is opposed to cakes and ale runs through the history of comedy. In Shakespeare's *Love's Labor's Lost*, the young noblemen who vow to devote themselves to study, and to forgo the company of women, are laughed at until they confess their error and accept their bodies and those of the ladies. The celebration of the human body, or at least the good-natured acceptance of it which is present in comedy is well-put by the General in Anouilh's *The Waltz of the Toreadors*. (The life-buoy he refers to is "the ideal.")

> You're in the ocean, splashing about, doing your damndest not to drown, in spite of whirlpools and cross currents. The main thing is to do the regulation breast-stroke and if you're not a clod, never to let the life-buoy out of sight. No one expects any more than that out of you. Now if you relieve yourself in the water now and then, that's your affair. The sea is big, and if the top half of your body still looks as though it's doing the breast-stroke, nobody will say a word.

One way of putting all this is summarized in Horace Walpole's aphorism, "This world is a comedy to those that think, a tragedy to those that feel." Life seen thoughtfully, with considerable detachment, viewed from above, as it were, is an amusing pageant, and the comic writer gives us something of this view. With Puck we look at the antics in the forest, smile tolerantly, and say with a godlike perspective, "Lord, what fools these mortals be!" But in tragedy we are to a greater degree engaged; the tragic dramatist manages to make us in large measure identify ourselves with the hero, feel his plight as if it were our own, and value his feelings as he values them, so that with Othello we may say "The pity of it."* Yeats noticed this when he said that "character is continuously present in comedy alone,"

DETACHMENT
AND
ENGAGEMENT

---

* Bergson's theory that a human being — an organism — is comical when it behaves mechanically requires, as Bergson said, a modification: feelings must be suppressed. A crippled man is not comic despite his mechanical limp, because we feel for him. Comedy requires, Bergson said, an "anesthesia of the heart."

and that "tragedy must always be a drowning and breaking of the dykes that separate man from man. . . . It is upon these dykes comedy keeps house." And Yeats again: "Nor when the tragic reverie is at its height do we say, 'How well that man is realised, I should know him were I to meet him in the street,' for it is always ourselves that we see upon the [tragic] stage."

One consequence of this distinction between tragedy and comedy, between looking-at and feeling-with, is that the comic plot is usually more intricate than the tragic plot, and less plausible. TRAGIC FATE The comic plot continues to trip up its characters, AND COMIC bringing them into numerous situations that allow FORTUNE them to display their folly over and again. The com- IN PLOTS plex comic plot is often arbitrary, full of the workings of Fortune or Chance, and we delight at each new unexpected or unlikely happening. In tragedy, Fate (sometimes in the form that "character is destiny") or Necessity rules, there is the consistency and inevitability, the "remorseless working of things," that has already been mentioned. If Macbeth were struck dead by a falling roof tile while he dozed in the palace after a good meal, instead of dying on Macduff's sword, or if Brutus were to die by slipping in his bath, instead of dying on the very sword with which he killed Caesar, we would have arbitrary happenings that violate the spirit of everything that precedes. But the unexpected letters and the long-lost relatives that often turn up at the close of a comedy are thoroughly in the spirit of the comic vision, which devalues not only rigidly consistent character but rigidity of every sort, even of plot. Tragedy usually follows a straight course, comedy a delightfully twisted one.

The rigid behavior of some of comedy's laughably serious characters (e.g. misers, jealous husbands, stern fathers) is paralleled in the rigid circumstances that often are sketched at the begin- COMIC ning of a comedy. In *As You Like It*, the rightful BEGINNINGS duke has been banished by his usurping brother, and AND ENDINGS (a sort of parallel) an attractive young nobleman has been confined "rustically at home" by *his* brother. The self-satisfied petty tyrannical Horace Vandergelder, known as "Wolftrap" to his employees, begins *The Matchmaker* with "I tell you for the hundredth time you will never marry my niece." Gilbert and Sullivan, to draw on familiar material, afford plenty of examples of comedy's fondness for a cantankerous beginning: *The Mikado* opens with a chorus of Japanese noblemen whose code of etiquette makes them appear to be "worked by strings"; they live in a town where a law ordered that "all who flirted, leered or winked/Should forthwith be beheaded." (Comedy often begins with a society dominated by some harsh law.) Although this law has been suspended, another harsh decree is in effect: the pretty Yum-Yum is betrothed to her old guardian, Ko-Ko. We learn, too, that her appropriate wooer, Nanki-Poo, is a prince who has had to disguise himself as a humble wandering minstrel to escape his father's decree that he marry Katisha, an old and ugly lady of the court. After various doings in a comedy, a new — presumably natural, prosperous, fertile, and free — society is formed, usually centered around lovers who are going to be married. Yum-Yum and Nanki-Poo finally contrive to get married, evading Katisha and Ko-Ko, who make the best of things by marrying each other. The whole business is satisfactorily explained to the Mikado, who affably accepts, and ruffled tempers are soothed:

> The threatened cloud has passed away,
> And brightly shines the dawning day;
> What though the night may come too soon,
> We've years and years of afternoon!
>
> Then let the throng
> Our joy advance,
> With laughing song
> And merry dance,
> With joyous shout and ringing cheer,
> Inaugurate our new career!

The first four of these lines are sung by the young lovers, the remaining six are sung by "All," the new, or renewed, society, free from unnatural law. *H.M.S. Pinafore*, to give a second example from Gilbert and Sullivan, begins with lovers who cannot marry because of disparity in rank, but ends with appropriate shifts in rank so that· there can be "three loving pairs on the same day united."

Another way of putting this is to say that in comedy there is often not only an improbable turn in events but an improbable (but agreeable) change in character — or at least in rank; SELF-KNOWLEDGE troublesome persons become enlightened, find their own better nature, and join in the fun that is commonly symbolized by a marriage-feast. The process of finding one's own nature is common in tragedy, too, but there self-knowledge is co-terminous with death or some death-like condition, such as blindness. *Oedipus the King* ends with a note of finality, even though Oedipus is alive at the end; the fact that twenty-five years later Sophocles decided to write a play showing Oedipus' apotheosis does not allow us to see the earlier play as anything less than complete. The chorus in *Oedipus the King* has the last word:

> This man was Oedipus.
> That mighty King, who knew the riddle's mystery,
> Whom all the city envied, Fortune's favorite.
> Behold, in the event, the storm of his calamities,
> And, being mortal, think on that last day of death,
> Which all must see, and speak of no man's happiness
> Till, without sorrow, he hath passed the goal of life.

Or consider the sense of irreparable loss at the end of Shakespeare's tragedies: "This was the noblest Roman of them all"; "We that are young/Shall never see so much, nor live so long"; "The rest is silence." But comedy ends with a new beginning, a newly formed society, usually a wedding party; the tragic figure commonly awakens to the fact that he has made a big mistake and that his life is over, but the comic figure commonly awakens to his better nature. He usually sheds his aberration and is restored to himself and to a renewed society. In *As You Like It*, for example, Oliver is for much of the play a "most unnatural brother," but he is at last converted by his brother's natural goodness and he gains a lovely wife. Alceste's refusal to change, at the end of *The Misanthrope*, helps to push that comedy toward the borderline between comedy and tragedy. Oedipus learns that his parents were not those whom he had supposed, and he learns that even the mighty Oedipus can be humbled. Othello comes to see himself as a man "that loved not wisely but too well," and, having reached his journey's end, he executes justice upon himself by killing himself. That is, at the end of the play he finds himself, but this finding of the self separates him forever from those around him, whereas the comic figure who finds himself usually does so by putting aside in some measure his individuality and by submitting himself to a partner or to the group.

Thomas Hardy, whose view of life was bleak (it has been said that in Hardy fornication always produces offspring), said:

> Tragedy is true guise,
> Comedy lies.

But the visions of comedy and tragedy are equally true and do not conflict; rather, they are visions of different things and represent different psychological states. And they are equally useful. The tragic vision may have more prestige, but it is no small thing to make men laugh, to call attention amusingly to the follies and joys of life, and to help develop the sense of humor — and humility — that may be indispensable to survival in a world continually threatened by aggressive ideals that demand uncritical acceptance. Infants smile easily, and children laugh often, but growing up is often attended by a frightening seriousness. True, hostile laughter, the scarcely veiled aggressiveness that manifests itself in derision, remains an adult possession, but the laughter evoked by the best comedy is good-natured while it is critical, and it is in part directed at ourselves. We look at bumbling humanity and we recall Puck's words, "Lord, what fools these mortals be." This is not to say that the comic vision is cynical; rather, it attributes to folly what less generous visions attribute to ill-will or to hopeless corruption, and when it laughs it forgives. Analyses of laughter are sometimes funny but more often they are tedious; still, they at least pay the comic spirit the compliment of recognizing it as something worthy of man's best efforts.

TRAGEDY
AND
COMEDY

An Anthology of Drama

Oedipus the King

SOPHOCLES

Translated into English verse by H. D. F. Kitto

Sophocles (c. 495 B.C.–406 B.C.), the son of a wealthy Athenian, is one of the three Greek tragic writers whose work survives. (The other two are Aeschylus and Euripides.) Of Sophocles' more than one hundred and twenty plays, we have seven. The exact date that Oedipus the King *was written is not known, but 430 B.C. is a reasonable guess. Some twenty-five years later, when he was almost ninety, Sophocles wrote* Oedipus at Colonus, *dramatizing Oedipus' last deeds.*

DRAMATIS PERSONAE

Oedipus, King of Thebes
Priest of Zeus
Creon, brother of Iocasta
Teiresias, a Seer
Iocasta, Queen of Thebes
A *Corinthian Shepherd*
A *Theban Shepherd*
A *Messenger*
Chorus of Theban citizens
Priests, Attendants, etc.

2

SCENE

Thebes, before the royal palace

Oedipus. My children, latest brood of ancient Cadmus,
What purpose brings you here, a multitude
Bearing the boughs that mark the suppliant?
Why is our air so full of frankincense,
So full of hymns and prayers and lamentations?
This, children, was no matter to entrust
To others: therefore I myself am come
Whose fame is known to all — I, Oedipus.
— You, Sir, are pointed out by length of years
To be the spokesman: tell me, what is in
Your hearts? What fear? What sorrow? Count on all
That I can do, for I am not so hard
As not to pity such a supplication.
Priest. Great King of Thebes, and sovereign Oedipus,
Look on us, who now stand before the altars —
Some young, still weak of wing; some bowed with age —
The priests, as I, of Zeus; and these, the best
Of our young men; and in the market-place,
And by Athena's temples and the shrine
Of fiery divination, there is kneeling,
Each with his suppliant branch, the rest of Thebes.
The city, as you see yourself, is now

From *Three Tragedies* by Sophocles, translated by H.D.F. Kitto. © 1962 by
Oxford University Press. Reprinted by permission.

3

Storm-tossed, and can no longer raise its head
Above the waves and angry surge of death.
The fruitful blossoms of the land are barren,
The herds upon our pastures, and our wives
In childbirth, barren. Last, and worst of all,
The withering god of fever swoops on us
To empty Cadmus' city and enrich
Dark Hades with our groans and lamentations.
No god we count you, that we bring our prayers,
I and these children, to your palace-door,
But wise above all other men to read
Life's riddles, and the hidden ways of Heaven;
For it was you who came and set us free
From the blood-tribute that the cruel Sphinx
Had laid upon our city; without our aid
Or our instruction, but, as we believe,
With god as ally, you gave us back our life.
So now, most dear, most mighty Oedipus,
We all entreat you on our bended knees,
Come to our rescue, whether from the gods
Or from some man you can find means to save.
For I have noted, *that* man's counsel is
Of best effect, who has been tried in action.
Come, noble Oedipus! Come, save our city.
Be well advised; for that past service given
This city calls you Savior; of your kingship
Let not the record be that first we rose
From ruin, then to ruin fell again.
No, save our city, let it stand secure.
You brought us gladness and deliverance
Before; now do no less. You rule this land;
Better to rule it full of living men
Than rule a desert; citadel or ship
Without its company of men is nothing.

Oedipus. My children, what you long for, that I know
Indeed, and pity you. I know how cruelly
You suffer; yet, though sick, not one of you
Suffers a sickness half as great as mine.
Yours is a single pain; each man of you
Feels but his own. My heart is heavy with
The city's pain, my own, and yours together.
You come to me not as to one asleep

And needing to be wakened; many a tear
I have been shedding, every path of thought
Have I been pacing; and what remedy,
What single hope my anxious thought has found
That I have tried. Creon, Menoeceus' son,
My own wife's brother, I have sent to Delphi
To ask in Phoebus' house what act of mine,
What word of mine, may bring deliverance.
Now, as I count the days, it troubles me
What he is doing; his absence is prolonged
Beyond the proper time. But when he comes
Then write me down a villain, if I do
Not each particular that the god discloses.
Priest. You give us hope. — And here is more, for they
  Are signaling that Creon has returned.
Oedipus. O Lord Apollo, even as Creon smiles,
  Smile now on us, and let it be deliverance!
Priest. The news is good; or he would not be wearing
  That ample wreath of richly-berried laurel.
Oedipus. We soon shall know; my voice will reach so far:
  Creon my lord, my kinsman, what response
  Do you bring with you from the god of Delphi?

[*Enter Creon*]

Creon. Good news! Our sufferings, if they are guided right,
  Can even yet turn to a happy issue.
Oedipus. This only leaves my fear and confidence
  In equal balance: what did Phoebus say?
Creon. Is it your wish to hear it now, in public,
  Or in the palace? I am at your service.
Oedipus. Let them all hear! Their sufferings distress
  Me more than if my own life were at stake.
Creon. Then I will tell you what Apollo said —
  And it was very clear. There is pollution
  Here in our midst, long-standing. This must we
  Expel, nor let it grow past remedy.
Oedipus. What has defiled us? and how are we to purge it?
Creon. By banishing or killing one who murdered,
  And so called down this pestilence upon us.
Oedipus. Who is the man whose death the god denounces?
Creon. Before the city passed into your care,
  My lord, we had a king called Laius.

Oedipus. So I have often heard. — I never saw him.

Creon. His death, Apollo clearly charges us,
  We must avenge upon his murderers.

Oedipus. Where are they now? And where shall we disclose
  The unseen traces of that ancient crime?

Creon. The god said, Here. — A man who hunts with care
  May often find what other men will miss.

Oedipus. Where was he murdered? In the palace here?
  Or in the country? Or was he abroad?

Creon. He made a journey to consult the god,
  He said — and never came back home again.

Oedipus. But was there no report? no fellow traveler
  Whose knowledge might have helped you in your search?

Creon. All died, except one terror-stricken man,
  And he could tell us nothing — next to nothing.

Oedipus. And what was that? One thing might lead to much,
  If only we could find one ray of light.

Creon. He said they met with brigands — not with one,
  But a whole company; they killed Laius.

Oedipus. A brigand would not *dare* — unless perhaps
  Conspirators in Thebes had bribed the man.

Creon. There *was* conjecture; but disaster came
  And we were leaderless, without our king.

Oedipus. Disaster? With a king cut down like that
  You did not seek the cause? Where was the hindrance?

Creon. The Sphinx. *Her* riddle pressed us harder still;
  For Laius — out of sight was out of mind.

Oedipus. I will begin again; *I*'ll find the truth.
  The dead man's cause has found a true defender
  In Phoebus, and in you. And I will join you
  In seeking vengeance on behalf of Thebes
  And Phoebus too; indeed, I must: if I
  Remove this taint, it is not for a stranger,
  But for myself: the man who murdered him
  Might make the same attempt on me; and so,
  Avenging him, I shall protect myself. —
     Now you, my sons, without delay, arise,
  Take up your suppliant branches. — Someone, go
  And call the people here, for I will do
  What can be done; and either, by the grace
  Of God we shall be saved — or we shall fall.

Priest. My children, we will go; the King has promised
  All that we came to ask. — O Phoebus, thou

Hast given us an answer: give us too
Protection! grant remission of the plague!

[*Exeunt Creon, Priests, etc. Oedipus remains*]

[*Enter the Chorus representing the citizens of Thebes*]

STROPHE 1

Chorus.   Sweet is the voice of the god, that
[*mainly dactyls:* $\frac{4}{4}$]*   sounds in the
   Golden shrine of Delphi.
   What message has it sent to Thebes? My trembling
   Heart is torn with anguish.
   Thou god of Healing, Phoebus Apollo,
   How do I fear! What hast thou in mind
   To bring upon us now? what is to be fulfilled
   From days of old?
   Tell me this, O Voice divine,
   Thou child of golden Hope.

ANTISTROPHE 1

   First on the Daughter of Zeus I call for
   Help, divine Athene;
   And Artemis, whose throne is all the earth, whose
   Shrine is in our city;
   Apollo too, who shoots from afar:
   Trinity of Powers, come to our defence!
   If ever in the past, when ruin threatened us,
   You stayed its course
   And turned aside the flood of Death,
   O then, protect us now!

---

* Taking a hint from the French translators for the Budé series I have here
and there added to the lyrical portions a quasi-musical indication of tempo or
mood, on no authority except that of common sense. These may at least serve
to remind the reader, if he needs reminding, that the lyrics were not recited;
they were a fusion of intense poetry, music, and dancing. Of the music we
know nothing; of the dance we can at least infer that its range extended from
grave processional movements to the expression of great excitement, whether of
joy or despair.

STROPHE 2

[*agitated:* $\frac{3}{8}$] Past counting are the woes we suffer;
   Affliction bears on all the city, and
   Nowhere is any defence against destruction.
   The holy soil can bring no increase,
   Our women suffer and cry in childbirth
   But do not bring forth living children.
   The souls of those who perish, one by one,
   Unceasingly, swift as raging fire,
   Rise and take their flight to the dark realms of the dead.

ANTISTROPHE 2

   Past counting, those of us who perish:
   They lie upon the ground, unpitied,
   Unburied, infecting the air with deadly pollution.
   Young wives, and grey-haired mothers with them,
   From every quarter approach the altars
   And cry aloud in supplication.
   The prayer for healing, the loud wail of lament,
   Together are heard in dissonance:
   O thou golden Daughter of Zeus, grant thy aid!

STROPHE 3

[*mainly iambic:* $\frac{3}{8}$] The fierce god of War has laid aside
   His spear; but yet his terrible cry
   Rings in our ears; he spreads death and destruction.
   Ye gods, drive him back to his distant home!
     For what the light of day has spared,
     That the darkness of night destroys.
     Zeus our father! All power is thine:
   The lightning-flash is thine: hurl upon him
   Thy thunderbolt, and quell this god of War!

ANTISTROPHE 3

   We pray, Lord Apollo: draw thy bow
   In our defense. Thy quiver is full of

Arrows unerring: shoot! slay the destroyer!
And thou, radiant Artemis, lend thy aid!
   Thou whose hair is bound in gold,
Bacchus, lord of the sacred dance,
   Theban Bacchus! Come, show thyself!
Display thy blazing torch; drive from our midst
The savage god, abhorred by other gods!

Oedipus. Would you have answer to these prayers? Then hear
My words; give heed; your help may bring
Deliverance, and the end of all our troubles.
Here do I stand before you all, a stranger
Both to the deed and to the story. — What
Could I have done alone, without a clue?
But I was yet a foreigner; it was later
That I became a Theban among Thebans.
So now do I proclaim to all the city:
If any Theban knows by what man's hand
He perished, Laius, son of Labdacus,
Him I command to tell me all he can;
And if he is afraid, let him annul
Himself the charge he fears; no punishment
Shall fall on him, save only to depart
Unharmed from Thebes. Further, if any knows
The slayer to be a stranger from abroad,
Let him speak out; I will reward him, and
Besides, he will have all my gratitude.
But if you still keep silent, if any man
Fearing for self or friend shall disobey me,
This will I do — and listen to my words:
Whoever he may be, I do forbid
All in this realm, of which I am the King
And high authority, to shelter in their houses
Or speak to him, or let him be their partner
In prayers or sacrifices to the gods, or give
Him lustral water; I command you all
To drive him from your doors; for he it is
That brings this plague upon us, as the god
Of Delphi has but now declared to me. —
So stern an ally do I make myself
Both of the god and of our murdered king. —
And for the man that slew him, whether he
Slew him alone, or with a band of helpers,
I lay this curse upon him, that the wretch

In wretchedness and misery may live.
And more: if with my knowledge he be found
To share my hearth and home, then upon me
Descend that doom that I invoke on him.
This charge I lay upon you, to observe
All my commands: to aid myself, the god,
And this our land, so spurned of Heaven, so ravaged.
For such a taint we should not leave unpurged —
The death of such a man, and he your king —
Even if Heaven had not commanded us,
But we should search it out. Now, since 'tis I
That wear the crown that he had worn before me,
And have his Queen to wife, and common children
Were born to us, but that his own did perish,
And sudden death has carried him away —
Because of this, I will defend his cause
As if it were my father's; nothing I
Will leave undone to find the man who killed
The son of Labdacus, and offspring of
Polydorus, Cadmus, and of old Agênor.
On those that disobey, this is my curse:
May never field of theirs give increase, nor
Their wives have children; may our present plagues,
And worse, be ever theirs, for their destruction.
But for the others, all with whom my words
Find favour, this I pray: Justice and all
The gods be ever at your side to help you.

Chorus-leader. Your curse constrains me; therefore will I speak.
   I did not kill him, neither can I tell
   Who did. It is for Phoebus, since he laid
   The task upon us, to declare the man.
Oedipus. True; but to force the gods against their will —
   That is a thing beyond all human power.
Chorus-leader. All I could say is but a second best.
Oedipus. Though it were third best, do not hold it back.
Chorus-leader. I know of none that reads Apollo's mind
   So surely as the lord Teiresias;
   Consulting him you best might learn the truth.
Oedipus. Not even this have I neglected: Creon
   Advised me, and already I have sent
   Two messengers. — Strange he has not come.
Chorus-leader. There's nothing else but old and idle gossip.
Oedipus. And what was that? I clutch at any straw.

Chorus-leader. They said that he was killed by travelers.
Oedipus. So I have heard; but no one knows a witness.
Chorus-leader. But if he is not proof against *all* fear
    He'll not keep silent when he hears your curse.
Oedipus. And will they fear a curse, who dared to kill?
Chorus-leader. Here is the one to find him, for at last
    They bring the prophet here. He is inspired,
    The only man whose heart is filled with truth.

[*Enter Teiresias, led by a boy*]

Oedipus. Teiresias, by your art you read the signs
    And secrets of the earth and of the sky;
    Therefore you know, although you cannot see,
    The plague that is besetting us; from this
    No other man but you, my lord, can save us.
    Phoebus has said — you may have heard already —
    In answer to our question, that this plague
    Will never cease unless we can discover
    What men they were who murdered Laius,
    And punish them with death or banishment.
    Therefore give freely all that you have learned
    From birds or other form of divination;
    Save us; save me, the city, and yourself,
    From the pollution that his bloodshed causes.
    No finer task, than to give all one has
    In helping others; we are in your hands.
Teiresias. Ah! what a burden knowledge is, when knowledge
    Can be of no avail! I knew this well,
    And yet forgot, or I should not have come.
Oedipus. Why, what is this? Why are you so despondent?
Teiresias. Let me go home! It will be best for you,
    And best for me, if you will let me go.
Oedipus. But to withhold your knowledge! This is wrong,
    Disloyal to the city of your birth.
Teiresias. I know that what you say will lead you on
    To ruin; therefore, lest the same befall me too . . .
Oedipus. No, by the gods! Say all you know, for we
    Go down upon our knees, your suppliants.
Teiresias. Because *you* do *not* know! I never shall
    Reveal my burden — I will not say *yours*.
Oedipus. You know, and will not tell us? Do you wish
    To ruin Thebes and to destroy us all?

Teiresias. My pain, and yours, will not be caused by me.
    Why these vain questions? — for I will not speak.
Oedipus. You villain! — for you would provoke a stone
    To anger: you'll not speak, but show yourself
    So hard of heart and so inflexible?
Teiresias. You heap the blame on me; but what is yours
    You do not know — therefore *I* am the villain!
Oedipus. And who would not be angry, finding that
    You treat our people with such cold disdain?
Teiresias. The truth will come to light, without *my* help.
Oedipus. If it is bound to come, you ought to speak it.
Teiresias. I'll say no more, and you, if so you choose,
    May rage and bluster on without restraint.
Oedipus. Restraint? Then I'll show none! I'll tell you all
    That I can see in you: I do believe
    This crime was planned and carried out by you,
    All but the killing; and were you not blind
    I'd say your hand alone had done the murder.
Teiresias. So? Then I tell you this: submit yourself
    To that decree that you have made; from now
    Address no word to these men nor to me:
    You are the man whose crimes pollute our city.
Oedipus. What, does your impudence extend thus far?
    And do you hope that it will go scot-free?
Teiresias. It will. I have a champion — the truth.
Oedipus. Who taught you that? For it was not your art.
Teiresias. No; you! You made me speak, against my will.
Oedipus. Speak what? Say it again, and say it clearly.
Teiresias. Was I not clear? Or are you tempting me?
Oedipus. Not clear enough for me. Say it again.
Teiresias. You are yourself the murderer you seek.
Oedipus. You'll not affront me twice and go unpunished!
Teiresias. Then shall I give you still more cause for rage?
Oedipus. Say what you will; you'll say it to no purpose.
Teiresias. I know, *you* do not know, the hideous life
    Of shame you lead with those most near to you.
Oedipus. You'll pay most dearly for this insolence!
Teiresias. No, not if Truth is strong, and can prevail.
Oedipus. It is — except in you; for you are blind
    In eyes and ears and brains and everything.
Teiresias. You'll not forget these insults that you throw
    At me, when all men throw the same at you.

Oedipus. You live in darkness; you can do no harm
   To me or any man who has his eyes.
Teiresias. No; I am not to bring you down, because
   Apollo is enough; he'll see to it.
Oedipus. Creon, or you? Which of you made this plot?
Teiresias. Creon's no enemy of yours; you are your own.
Oedipus. O Wealth! O Royalty! whose commanding art
   Outstrips all other arts in life's contentions!
   How great a store of envy lies upon you,
   If for this scepter, that the city gave
   Freely to me, unasked — if now my friend,
   The trusty Creon, burns to drive me hence
   And steal it from me! So he has suborned
   This crafty schemer here, this mountebank,
   Whose purse alone has eyes, whose art is blind. —
   Come, prophet, show your title! When the Sphinx
   Chanted her music here, why did not *you*
   Speak out and save the city? Yet such a question
   Was one for augury, not for mother wit.
   You were no prophet then; your birds, your voice
   From Heaven, were dumb. But I, who came by chance,
   I, knowing nothing, put the Sphinx to flight,
   Thanks to my wit — no thanks to divination!
   And now you try to drive me out; you hope
   When Creon's king to bask in Creon's favor.
   You'll expiate the curse? Ay, and repent it,
   Both you and your accomplice. But that you
   Seem old, I'd teach you what you gain by treason!
Chorus-leader. My lord, he spoke in anger; so I think,
   Did you. What help in angry speeches? Come,
   This is the task, how we can best discharge
   The duty that the god has laid on us.
Teiresias. King though you are, I claim the privilege
   Of equal answer. No, I have the right;
   I am no slave of yours — I serve Apollo,
   And therefore am not listed *Creon's* man.
   Listen — since you have taunted me with blindness!
   You have your sight, and yet you cannot see
   Where, nor with whom, you live, nor in what horror.
   Your parents — do you know them? or that you
   Are enemy to your kin, alive or dead?
   And that a father's and a mother's curse

Shall join to drive you headlong out of Thebes
And change the light that now you see to darkness?
Your cries of agony, where will they not reach?
Where on Cithaeron will they not re-echo?
Where you have learned what meant the marriage-song
Which bore you to an evil haven here
After so fair a voyage? And you are blind
To other horrors, which shall make you one
With your own children. Therefore, heap your scorn
On Creon and on me, for no man living
Will meet a doom more terrible than yours.

Oedipus. What? Am I to suffer words like this from him?
Ruin, damnation seize you! Off at once
Out of our sight! Go! Get you whence you came!

Teiresias. Had you not called me, I should not be here.

Oedipus. And had I known that you would talk such folly,
I'd not have called you to a house of mine.

Teiresias. To you I seem a fool, but to your parents,
To those who did beget you, I was wise.

Oedipus. Stop! Who were they? Who *were* my parents? Tell me!

Teiresias. This day will show your birth and your destruction.

Oedipus. You are too fond of dark obscurities.

Teiresias. But do you not excel in reading riddles?

Oedipus. I scorn your taunts; my skill has brought me glory.

Teiresias. And this success brought you to ruin too.

Oedipus. I am content, if so I saved this city.

Teiresias. Then I will leave you. Come, boy, take my hand.

Oedipus. Yes, let him take it. You are nothing but
Vexation here. Begone, and give me peace!

Teiresias. When I have had my say. No frown of yours
Shall frighten *me*; you cannot injure me.
Here is my message: that man whom you seek
With threats and proclamations for the death
Of Laius, he is living here; he's thought
To be a foreigner, but shall be found
Theban by birth — and little joy will this
Bring *him*; when, with his eyesight turned to blindness,
His wealth to beggary, on foreign soil
With staff in hand he'll tap his way along,
His children with him; and he will be known
Himself to be their father and their brother,
The husband of the mother who gave him birth,
Supplanter of his father, and his slayer.

— There! Go, and think on this; and if you find
That I'm deceived, say then — and not before —
That I am ignorant in divination.

[*Exeunt severally Teiresias and Oedipus*]

STROPHE 1

Chorus. The voice of god rang out in the holy cavern,
   Denouncing one who has killed a King — the crime of crimes.
     Who is the man? Let him begone in
     Headlong flight, swift as a horse!
[*anapaests*] For the terrible god, like a warrior armed,
   Stands ready to strike with a lightning-flash:
     The Furies who punish crime, and never fail,
     Are hot in their pursuit.

ANTISTROPHE 1

The snow is white on the cliffs of high Parnassus.
It has flashed a message: Let every Theban join the hunt!
     Lurking in caves among the mountains,
     Deep in the woods — where is the man?
[*anapaests*] In wearisome flight, unresting, alone,
   An outlaw, he shuns Apollo's shrine;
     But ever the living menace of the god
     Hovers around his head.

STROPHE 2

[*choriambics*] Strange, disturbing, what the wise
   Prophet has said. What can he mean?
   Neither can I believe, nor can I disbelieve;
   I do not know what to say.
   I look here, and there; nothing can I find —
   No strife, either now or in the past,
   Between the kings of Thebes and Corinth.

A hand unknown struck down the King;
Though I would learn who it was dealt the blow,
That *he* is guilty whom all revere —
How can I believe this with no proof?

ANTISTROPHE 2

Zeus, Apollo — they have knowledge;
They understand the ways of life.
Prophets are men, like me; that they can understand
More than is revealed to me —
Of that, I can find nowhere certain proof,
Though one man is wise, another foolish.
Until the charge is manifest
I will not credit his accusers.
I saw myself how the Sphinx challenged him:
He proved his wisdom; he saved our city;
Therefore how can I now condemn him?

[*Enter Creon*]

Creon. They tell me, Sirs, that Oedipus the King
    Has made against me such an accusation
    That I will not endure. For if he thinks
    That in this present trouble I have done
    Or said a single thing to do him harm,
    Then let me die, and not drag out my days
    With such a name as that. For it is not
    One injury this accusation does me;
    It touches my whole life, if you, my friends,
    And all the city are to call me traitor.
Chorus-leader. The accusation may perhaps have come
    From heat of temper, not from sober judgment.
Creon. What was it made him think contrivances
    Of mine suborned the seer to tell his lies?
Chorus-leader. Those were his words; I do not know his reasons.
Creon. Was he in earnest, master of himself,
    When he attacked me with this accusation?
Chorus-leader. I do not closely scan what kings are doing. —
    But here he comes in person from the palace.

[*Enter Oedipus*]

Oedipus. What, *you*? You dare come here? How can you find
   The impudence to show yourself before
   My house, when you are clearly proven
   To have sought my life and tried to steal my crown?
   Why, do you think me then a coward, or
   A fool, that you should try to lay this plot?
   Or that I should not see what you were scheming,
   And so fall unresisting, blindly, to you?
   But you were mad, so to attempt the throne,
   Poor and unaided; this is not encompassed
   Without the strong support of friends and money!
Creon. This you must do: now you have had your say
   Hear my reply; then yourself shall judge.
Oedipus. A ready tongue! But I am bad at listening —
   To you. For I have found how much you hate me.
Creon. One thing: first listen to what I have to say.
Oedipus. One thing: do not pretend you're not a villain.
Creon. If you believe it is a thing worth having,
   Insensate stubbornness, then you are wrong.
Oedipus. If you believe that one can harm a kinsman
   Without retaliation, you are wrong.
Creon. With this I have no quarrel; but explain
   What injury you say that I have done you.
Oedipus. Did you advise, or did you not, that I
   Should send a man for that most reverend prophet?
Creon. I did, and I am still of that advice.
Oedipus. How long a time is it since Laius . . .
Creon. Since Laius did *what*? How can I say?
Oedipus. Was seen no more, but met a violent death?
Creon. It would be many years now past and gone.
Oedipus. And had this prophet learned his art already?
Creon. Yes, his repute was great — as it is now.
Oedipus. Did he make any mention then of me?
Creon. He never spoke of you within my hearing.
Oedipus. Touching the murder: did you make no search?
Creon. No search? Of course we did; but we found nothing.
Oedipus. And why did this wise prophet not speak *then*?
Creon. Who knows? Where I know nothing I say nothing.
Oedipus. This much you know — and you'll do well to answer:
Creon. What is it? If I know. I'll tell you freely.
Oedipus. That if he had not joined with you, he'd not
   Have said that I was Laius' murderer.

Creon. If he said this, I did not know. — But I
  May rightly question you, as you have me.
Oedipus. Ask what you will. You'll never prove I killed him.
Creon. Why then: are you not married to my sister?
Oedipus. I am indeed; it cannot be denied.
Creon. You share with her the sovereignty of Thebes?
Oedipus. She need but ask, and anything is hers.
Creon. And am I not myself conjoined with you?
Oedipus. You are; not rebel therefore, but a traitor!
Creon. Not so, if you will reason with yourself,
  As I with you. This first: would any man,
  To gain no increase of authority,
  Choose kingship, with its fears and sleepless nights?
  Not I. What I desire, what every man
  Desires, if he has wisdom, is to take
  The substance, not the show, of royalty.
  For now, through you, I have both power and ease,
  But were I king, I'd be oppressed with cares.
  Not so: while I have ample sovereignty
  And rule in peace, why should I want the crown?
  I am not yet so mad as to give up
  All that which brings me honor and advantage.
  Now, every man greets me, and I greet him;
  Those who have need of you make much of me,
  Since I can make or mar them. Why should I
  Surrender this to load myself with that?
  A man of sense was never yet a traitor;
  I have no taste for that, nor could I force
  Myself to aid another's treachery.
    But you can test me: go to Delphi; ask
  If I reported rightly what was said.
  And further: if you find that I had dealings
  With that diviner, you may take and kill me
  Not with your single vote, but yours and mine,
  But not on bare suspicion, unsupported.
  How wrong it is, to use a random judgment
  And think the false man true, the true man false!
  To spurn a loyal friend, that is no better
  Than to destroy the life to which we cling.
  This you will learn in time, for Time alone
  Reveals the upright man; a single day
  Suffices to unmask the treacherous.

Chorus-leader. My lord, he speaks with caution, to avoid
  Grave error. Hasty judgment is not sure.
Oedipus. But when an enemy is quick to plot
  And strike, I must be quick in answer too.
  If I am slow, and wait, then I shall find
  That he has gained his end, and I am lost.
Creon. What do you wish? To drive me into exile?
Oedipus. No, more than exile: I will have your life.[1]
Creon. ⟨When will it cease, this monstrous rage of yours?⟩
Oedipus. When your example shows what comes of envy.
Creon. Must you be stubborn? Cannot you believe me?
Oedipus. ⟨You speak to me as if I were a fool!⟩
Creon. Because I know you're wrong.
Oedipus.   Right, for myself!
Creon. It is not right for me!
Oedipus.   But you're a traitor.
Creon. What if your charge is false?
Oedipus.   I have to govern.
Creon. Not govern badly!
Oedipus.   Listen to him, Thebes!
Creon. You're not the city! I am Theban too.
Chorus-leader. My lords, no more! Here comes the Queen, and not
  Too soon, to join you. With her help, you must
  Compose the bitter strife that now divides you.

[*Enter Iocasta*]

Iocasta. You frantic men! What has aroused this wild
  Dispute? Have you no shame, when such a plague
  Afflicts us, to indulge in private quarrels?

---

[1] The next two verses, as they stand in the mss., are impossible. Editors are agreed on this, though no single remedy has found general acceptance. The mss. attribute v. 624 [Oedipus' next speech] to Creon, and v. 625 [Creon's next speech] to Oedipus. I can make no real sense of this: the only φθόνος, "envy," that is in question is the envy of his royal power that Oedipus is attributing to Creon; and the words ὑπείξων, "yield," "not to be stubborn," and πιστεύσων, "believe," must surely be used by Creon of Oedipus, not by Oedipus of Creon. Since a translator who hopes to be acted must give the actors something to say, preferably good sense, and cannot fob them off with a row of dots, I have reconstructed the passage by guesswork, putting my guesses within brackets. I have assumed that two verses were lost, one after v. 623 and one after v. 625, and that the wrong attribution of vv. 624 and 625 followed almost inevitably.

Creon, go home, I pray. You, Oedipus,
Come in; do not make much of what is nothing.
Creon. My sister: Oedipus, your husband here,
Has thought it right to punish me with one
Of two most awful dooms: exile, or death.
Oedipus. I have: I have convicted him, Iocasta,
Of plotting secretly against my life.
Creon. If I am guilty in a single point
Of such a crime, then may I die accursed.
Iocasta. O, by the gods, believe him, Oedipus!
Respect the oath that he has sworn, and have
Regard for me, and for these citizens.

[*In what follows, the parts given to the chorus are sung, the rest,
presumably, spoken. The rhythm of the music and dance is either
dochmiac, 5-time, or a combination of 3- and 5-time.*]

STROPHE

Chorus. My lord, I pray, give consent.
Yield to us; ponder well.
Oedipus. What is it you would have me yield?
Chorus. Respect a man ripe in years,
Bound by this mighty oath he has sworn.
Oedipus. Your wish is clear?
Chorus.   It is.
Oedipus.   Then tell it me.
Chorus. Not to repel, and drive out of our midst a friend,
Scorning a solemn curse, for uncertain cause.
Oedipus. I tell you this: your prayer will mean for me
My banishment from Thebes, or else my death.
Chorus. No, no! by the Sun, the chief of gods,
Ruin and desolation and all evil come upon me
If I harbor thoughts such as these!
No; our land racked with plague breaks my heart.
Do not now deal a new wound on Thebes to crown the old!
Oedipus. Then let him be, though I must die twice over,
Or be dishonored, spurned and driven out.
It's your entreaty, and not his, that moves
My pity; he shall have my lasting hatred.
Creon. You yield ungenerously; but when your wrath

Has cooled, how it will prick you! Natures such
As yours give most vexation to themselves.
Oedipus. O, let me be! Get from my sight.
Creon.   I go,
Misjudged by you — but these will judge me better [*indicating Chorus*].

[*Exit Creon*]

ANTISTROPHE

Chorus. My lady, why now delay?
  Let the King go in with you.
Iocasta. When you have told me what has passed.
Chorus. Suspicion came. — Random words, undeserved,
  Will provoke men to wrath.
Iocasta. It was from both?
Chorus.   It was.
Iocasta.   And what was said?
Chorus. It is enough for me, more than enough, when I
  Think of our ills, that this should rest where it lies.
Oedipus. You and your wise advice, blunting my wrath,
  Frustrated me — and it has come to this!
Chorus. This, O my King, I said, and say again:
    I should be mad, distraught,
    I should be a fool, and worse,
    If I sought to drive you away.
    Thebes was near sinking; you brought her safe
  Through the storm. Now again we pray that you may save us.
Iocasta. In Heaven's name, my lord, I too must know
  What was the reason for this blazing anger.
Oedipus. There's none to whom I more defer; and so,
  I'll tell you: Creon and his vile plot against me.
Iocasta. What has he done, that you are so incensed?
Oedipus. He says that I am Laius' murderer.
Iocasta. From his own knowledge? Or has someone told him?
Oedipus. No; that suspicion should not fall upon
  Himself, he used a tool — a crafty prophet.
Iocasta. Why, have no fear of *that*. Listen to me,
  And you will learn that the prophetic art
  Touches our human fortunes not at all.
  I soon can give you proof. — An oracle

Once came to Laius — from the god himself
I do not say, but from his ministers:
His fate it was, that should he have a son
By me, that son would take his father's life.
But he was killed — or so they said — by strangers,
By brigands, at a place where three ways meet.
As for the child, it was not three days old
When Laius fastened both its feet together
And had it cast over a precipice.
Therefore Apollo failed; for neither did
His son kill Laius, nor did Laius meet
The awful end he feared, killed by his son.
     So much for what prophetic voices uttered.
Have no regard for them. The god will bring
To light himself whatever thing he chooses.

Oedipus. Iocasta, terror seizes me, and shakes
     My very soul, at one thing you have said.
Iocasta. Why so? What have I said to frighten you?
Oedipus. I think I heard you say that Laius
     Was murdered at a place where three ways meet?
Iocasta. So it was said — indeed, they say it still.
Oedipus. Where is the place where this encounter happened?
Iocasta. They call the country Phokis, and a road
     From Delphi joins a road from Daulia.
Oedipus. Since that was done, how many years have passed?
Iocasta. It was proclaimed in Thebes a little time
     Before the city offered you the crown.
Oedipus. O Zeus, what fate hast thou ordained for me?
Iocasta. What is the fear that so oppresses you?
Oedipus. One moment yet: tell me of Laius.
     What age was he? and what was his appearance?
Iocasta. A tall man, and his hair was touched with white;
     In figure he was not unlike yourself.
Oedipus. O God! Did I, then, in my ignorance,
     Proclaim that awful curse against myself?
Iocasta. What are you saying? How you frighten me!
Oedipus. I greatly fear that prophet was not blind.
     But yet one question; that will show me more.
Iocasta. For all my fear, I'll tell you what I can.
Oedipus. Was he alone, or did he have with him
     A royal bodyguard of men-at-arms?
Iocasta. The company in all were five; the King
     Rode in a carriage, and there was a Herald.

Oedipus. Ah God! How clear the picture is! . . . But who,
 Iocasta, brought report of this to Thebes?
Iocasta. A slave, the only man that was not killed.
Oedipus. And is he round about the palace now?
Iocasta. No, he is not. When he returned, and saw
 You ruling in the place of the dead King,
 He begged me, on his bended knees, to send him
 Into the hills as shepherd, out of sight,
 As far as could be from the city here.
 I sent him, for he was a loyal slave;
 He well deserved this favor — and much more.
Oedipus. Could he be brought back here — at once — to see me?
Iocasta. He could; but why do you desire his coming?
Oedipus. I fear I have already said, Iocasta,
 More than enough; and therefore I will see him.
Iocasta. Then he shall come. But, as your wife, I ask you,
 What is the terror that possesses you?
Oedipus. And you shall know it, since my fears have grown
 So great; for who is more to me than you,
 That I should speak to *him* at such a moment?
  My father, then, was Polybus of Corinth;
 My mother, Merope. My station there
 Was high as any man's — until a thing
 Befell me that was strange indeed, though not
 Deserving of the thought I gave to it.
 A man said at a banquet — he was full
 Of wine — that I was not my father's son.
 It angered me; but I restrained myself
 That day. The next I went and questioned both
 My parents. They were much incensed with him
 Who had let fall the insult. So, from them,
 I had assurance. Yet the slander spread
 And always chafed me. Therefore secretly,
 My mother and my father unaware,
 I went to Delphi. Phoebus would return
 No answer to my question, but declared
 A thing most horrible: he foretold that I
 Should mate with my own mother, and beget
 A brood that men would shudder to behold,
 And that I was to be the murderer
 Of my own father.
            Therefore, back to Corinth
 I never went — the stars alone have told me

Where Corinth lies — that I might never see
Cruel fulfillment of that oracle.
So journeying, I came to that same spot
Where, as you say, this King was killed. And now,
This is the truth, Iocasta: when I reached
The place where three ways meet, I met a herald,
And in a carriage drawn by colts was such
A man as you describe. By violence
The herald and the older man attempted
To push me off the road, I, in my rage,
Struck at the driver, who was hustling me.
The old man, when he saw me level with him,
Taking a double-goad, aimed at my head
A murderous blow. He paid for that, full measure.
Swiftly I hit him with my staff; he rolled
Out of his carriage, flat upon his back.
I killed them all. — But if, between this stranger
And Laius there was any bond of kinship,
Who could be in more desperate plight than I?
Who more accursèd in the eyes of Heaven?
For neither citizen nor stranger may
Receive me in his house, nor speak to me,
But he must bar the door. And it was none
But I invoked this curse on my own head!
And I pollute the bed of him I slew
With my own hands! Say, am I vile? Am I
Not all impure? Seeing I must be exiled,
And even in my exile must not go
And see my parents, nor set foot upon
My native land; or, if I do, I must
Marry my mother, and kill Polybus
My father, who engendered me and reared me.
If one should say it was a cruel god
Brought this upon me, would he not speak right?
   No, no, you holy powers above! Let me
Not see that day! but rather let me pass
Beyond the sight of men, before I see
The stain of such pollution come upon me!
Chorus-leader. My lord, this frightens me. But you must hope,
   Until we hear the tale from him that saw it.
Oedipus. That is the only hope that's left to me;
   We must await the coming of the shepherd.

Iocasta. What do you hope from him, when he is here?
Oedipus. I'll tell you: if his story shall be found
  The same as yours, then I am free of guilt.
Iocasta. But what have *I* said of especial note?
Oedipus. You said that he reported it was brigands
  Who killed the King. If he still speaks of "men,"
  It was not I; a single man, and "men,"
  Are not the same. But if he says it was
  A traveler journeying alone, why then,
  The burden of the guilt must fall on me.
Iocasta. But that *is* what he said, I do assure you!
  He cannot take it back again! Not I
  Alone, but the whole city heard him say it!
  But even if he should revoke the tale
  He told before, not even so, my lord,
  Will he establish that the King was slain
  According to the prophecy. For that was clear:
  His son, and mine, should slay him. — He, poor thing,
  Was killed himself, and never killed his father.
  Therefore, so far as divination goes,
  Or prophecy, I'll take no notice of it.
Oedipus. And that is wise. — But send a man to bring
  The shepherd; I would not have that neglected.
Iocasta. I'll send at once. — But come with me; for I
  Would not do anything that could displease you.

                              [*Exeunt Oedipus and Iocasta*]

STROPHE 1

Chorus. I pray that I may pass my life
[*in a steady rhythm*] In reverent holiness of word and deed.
  For there are laws enthroned above;
  Heaven created them,
  Olympus was their father,
  And mortal men had no part in their birth;
  Nor ever shall their power pass from sight
  In dull forgetfulness;
  A god moves in them; he grows not old.

ANTISTROPHE 1

Pride makes the tyrant — pride of wealth
And power, too great for wisdom and restraint;
For Pride will climb the topmost height;
Then is the man cast down
To uttermost destruction.
There he finds no escape, no resource.
But high contention for the city's good
May the gods preserve.
For me — may the gods be my defense!

STROPHE 2

If there is one who walks in pride
Of word or deed, and has no fear of Justice,
No reverence for holy shrines —
May utter ruin fall on him!
So may his ill-starred pride be given its reward.
Those who seek dishonorable advantage
And lay violent hands on holy things
And do not shun impiety —
Who among these will secure himself from the wrath of God?
If deeds like these are honored,
Why should I join in the sacred dance?

ANTISTROPHE 2

No longer shall Apollo's shrine,
The holy center of the Earth, receive my worship;
No, nor his seat at Abae, nor
The temple of Olympian Zeus,
If what the god foretold does not come to pass.
Mighty Zeus — if so I should address Thee —
O great Ruler of all things, look on this!
Now are thy oracles falling into contempt, and men
Deny Apollo's power.
Worship of the gods is passing away.

[*Enter Iocasta, attended by a girl carrying a wreath and incense*]

Iocasta. My lords of Thebes, I have bethought myself
    To approach the altars of the gods, and lay
    These wreaths on them, and burn this frankincense.
    For every kind of terror has laid hold
    On Oedipus; his judgment is distracted.
    He will not read the future by the past
    But yields himself to any who speaks fear.
    Since then no words of mine suffice to calm him
    I turn to Thee Apollo — Thou art nearest —
    Thy suppliant, with these votive offerings.
    Grant us deliverance and peace, for now
    Fear is on all, when we see Oedipus,
    The helmsman of the ship, so terrified.

[*A reverent silence, while Iocasta lays the wreath at the altar and sets fire to the incense. The wreath will remain and the incense smoke during the rest of the play.*]

[*Enter a shepherd from Corinth*]

Corinthian. Might I inquire of you where I may find
    The royal palace of King Oedipus?
    Or, better, where himself is to be found?
Chorus-leader. There is the palace; himself, Sir, is within,
    But here his wife and mother of his children.
Corinthian. Ever may happiness attend on her,
    And hers, the wedded wife of such a man.
Iocasta. May you enjoy the same; your gentle words
    Deserve no less. — Now, Sir, declare your purpose;
    With what request, what message have you come?
Corinthian. With good news for your husband and his house.
Iocasta. What news is this? And who has sent you here?
Corinthian. I come from Corinth, and the news I bring
    Will give you joy, though joy be crossed with grief.
Iocasta. What is this, with its two-fold influence?
Corinthian. The common talk in Corinth is that they
    Will call on Oedipus to be their king.
Iocasta. What? Does old Polybus no longer reign?
Corinthian. Not now, for Death has laid him in his grave.
Iocasta. Go quickly to your master, girl; give him
    The news. — You oracles, where are you now?

This is the man whom Oedipus so long
Has shunned, fearing to kill him; now he's dead,
And killed by Fortune, not by Oedipus.

[*Enter Oedipus, very nervous*]

Oedipus. My dear Iocasta, tell me, my dear wife,
  Why have you sent to fetch me from the palace?
Iocasta. Listen to *him*, and as you hear, reflect
  What has become of all those oracles.
Oedipus. Who is this man? — What has he to tell me?
Iocasta. He is from Corinth, and he brings you news
  About your father. Polybus is dead.
Oedipus. What say you, sir? Tell me the news yourself.
Corinthian. If you would have me first report on this,
  I tell you; death has carried him away.
Oedipus. By treachery? Or did sickness come to him?
Corinthian. A small mischance will lay an old man low.
Oedipus. Poor Polybus! He died, then, of a sickness?
Corinthian. That, and the measure of his many years.
Oedipus. Ah me! Why then, Iocasta, should a man
  Regard the Pythian house of oracles,
  Or screaming birds, on whose authority
  I was to slay my father? But he is dead;
  The earth has covered him; and here am I,
  My sword undrawn — unless perchance *my* loss
  Has killed him; so might I be called his slayer.
  But for those oracles about my father,
  Those he has taken with him to the grave
  Wherein he lies, and they are come to nothing.
Iocasta. Did I not say long since it would be so?
Oedipus. You did; but I was led astray by fear.
Iocasta. So none of this deserves another thought.
Oedipus. Yet how can I not fear my mother's bed?
Iocasta. Why should we fear, seeing that man is ruled
  By chance, and there is room for no clear forethought?
  No; live at random, live as best one can.
  So do not fear this marriage with your mother;
  Many a man has suffered this before —
  But only in his dreams. Whoever thinks
  The least of this, he lives most comfortably.
Oedipus. Your every word I do accept, if she
  That bore me did not live; but as she does —
  Despite your wisdom, how can I but tremble?

Iocasta. Yet there is comfort in your father's death.
Oedipus. Great comfort, but still fear of her who lives.
Corinthian. And who is this who makes you so afraid?
Oedipus. Meropê, my man, the wife of Polybus.
Corinthian. And what in *her* gives cause of fear in *you*?
Oedipus. There was an awful warning from the gods.
Corinthian. Can it be told, or must it be kept secret?
Oedipus. No secret. Once Apollo said that I
    Was doomed to lie with my own mother, and
    Defile my own hands with my father's blood.
    Wherefore has Corinth been, these many years,
    My home no more. My fortunes have been fair. —
    But it is good to see a parent's face.
Corinthian. It was for fear of *this* you fled the city?
Oedipus. This, and the shedding of my father's blood.
Corinthian. Why then, my lord, since I am come in friendship,
    I'll rid you here and now of that misgiving.
Oedipus. Be sure, your recompense would be in keeping.
Corinthian. It was the chief cause of my coming here
    That your return might bring me some advantage.
Oedipus. Back to my parents I will never go.
Corinthian. My son, it is clear, you know not what you do. . . .
Oedipus. Not know? What is this? Tell me what you mean.
Corinthian. If for this reason you avoid your home.
Oedipus. Fearing Apollo's oracle may come true.
Corinthian. And you incur pollution from your parents?
Oedipus. That is the thought that makes me live in terror.
Corinthian. I tell you then, this fear of yours is idle.
Oedipus. How? Am I not their child, and they my parents?
Corinthian. Because there's none of Polybus in you.
Oedipus. How can you say so? Was he not my father?
Corinthian. I am your father just as much as he!
Oedipus. A stranger equal to the father? How?
Corinthian. Neither did he beget you, nor did I.
Oedipus. Then for what reason did he call me son?
Corinthian. He had you as a gift — from my own hands.
Oedipus. And showed such love to me? Me, not his own?
Corinthian. Yes, his own childlessness so worked on him.
Oedipus. You, when you gave me: had you bought, or found me?
Corinthian. I found you in the woods upon Cithaeron.
Oedipus. Why were you traveling in that neighborhood?
Corinthian. I tended flocks of sheep upon the mountain.
Oedipus. You were a shepherd, then, wandering for hire?

Corinthian. I was, my son; but that day, your preserver.
Oedipus. How so? What ailed me when you took me up?
Corinthian. For that, your ankles might give evidence.
Oedipus. Alas! why speak of this, my life-long trouble?
Corinthian. I loosed the fetters clamped upon your feet.
Oedipus. A pretty gift to carry from the cradle!
Corinthian. It was for this they named you Oedipus.
Oedipus. Who did, my father or my mother? Tell me.
Corinthian. I cannot; he knows more, from whom I had you.
Oedipus. It was another, not yourself, that found me?
Corinthian. Yes, you were given me by another shepherd.
Oedipus. Who? Do you know him? Can you name the man?
Corinthian. They said that he belonged to Laius.
Oedipus. What — him who once was ruler here in Thebes?
Corinthian. Yes, he it was for whom this man was shepherd.
Oedipus. And is he still alive, that I can see him?
Corinthian [*turning to the Chorus*].
   You that are native here would know that best.
Oedipus. Has any man of you now present here
   Acquaintance with this shepherd, him he speaks of?
   Has any seen him, here, or in the fields?
   Speak; on this moment hangs discovery.
Chorus-leader. It is, I think, the man that you have sent for,
   The slave now in the country. But who should know
   The truth of this more than Iocasta here?
Oedipus. The man he speaks of: do you think, Iocasta,
   He is the one I have already summoned?
Iocasta. What matters who he is? Pay no regard. —
   The tale is idle; it is best forgotten.
Oedipus. It cannot be that I should have this clue
   And then not find the secret of my birth.
Iocasta. In God's name stop, if you have any thought
   For your own life! My ruin is enough.
Oedipus. Be not dismayed; nothing can prove you base.
   Not though I find my mother thrice a slave.
Iocasta. O, I beseech you, do not! Seek no more!
Oedipus. You cannot move me. I *will* know the truth.
Iocasta. I know that what I say is for the best.
Oedipus. This "best" of yours! I have no patience with it.
Iocasta. O may you never learn what man you are!
Oedipus. Go, someone, bring the herdsman here to me,
   And leave her to enjoy her pride of birth.

Iocasta. O man of doom! For by no other name
  Can I address you now or evermore.

[*Exit Iocasta*]

Chorus-leader. The Queen has fled, my lord, as if before
  Some driving storm of grief. I fear that from
  Her silence may break forth some great disaster.
Oedipus. Break forth what will! My birth, however humble,
  I am resolved to find. But she, perhaps,
  Is proud, as women will be; is ashamed
  Of my low birth. But I do rate myself
  The child of Fortune, giver of all good,
  And I shall not be put to shame, for I
  Am born of Her; the Years who are my kinsmen
  Distinguished my estate, now high, now low;
  So born, I could not make me someone else
  And not do all to find my parentage.

STROPHE 1

Chorus. If I have power of prophecy,
[*animated rhythm*] If I have judgment wise and sure, Cithaeron
  (I swear by Olympus),
  Thou shalt be honored when the moon
  Next is full, as mother and foster-nurse
  And birth-place of Oedipus, with festival and dancing,
  For thou hast given great blessings to our King.
  To Thee, Apollo, now we raise our cry:
  O grant our prayer find favor in thy sight!

ANTISTROPHE

  Who is thy mother, O my son?
  Is she an ageless nymph among the mountains,
  That bore thee to Pan?
  Or did Apollo father thee?
  For dear to him are the pastures in the hills.
  Or Hermes, who ruleth from the summit of Kyllene?

    Or Dionysus on the mountain-tops,
    Did he receive thee from thy mother's arms,
    A nymph who follows him on Helicon?
Oedipus. If I, who never yet have met the man,
    May risk conjecture, I think I see the herdsman
    Whom we have long been seeking. In his age
    He well accords; and more, I recognize
    Those who are with him as of my own household.
    But as for knowing, you will have advantage
    Of me, if you have seen the man before.
Chorus-leader. 'Tis he, for certain — one of Laius' men,
    One of the shepherds whom he trusted most.

[*Enter the Theban shepherd*]

Oedipus. You first I ask, you who have come from Corinth:
    Is that the man you mean?
Corinthian.   That very man.
Oedipus. Come here, my man; look at me; answer me
    My questions. Were you ever Laius' man?
Theban. I was; his slave — born in the house, not bought.
Oedipus. What was your charge, or what your way of life?
Theban. Tending the sheep, the most part of my life.
Oedipus. And to what regions did you most resort?
Theban. Now it was Cithaeron, now the country round.
Oedipus. And was this man of your acquaintance there?
Theban. In what employment? Which is the man you mean?
Oedipus. Him yonder. Had you any dealings with him?
Theban. Not such that I can quickly call to mind.
Corinthian. No wonder, Sir, but though he has forgotten
    I can remind him. I am very sure,
    He knows the time when, round about Cithaeron,
    He with a double flock, and I with one,
    We spent together three whole summer seasons,
    From spring until the rising of Arcturus.
    Then, with the coming on of winter, I
    Drove my flocks home, he his, to Laius' folds.
    Is this the truth? or am I telling lies?
Theban. It is true, although it happened long ago.
Corinthian. Then tell me: do you recollect a baby
    You gave me once to bring up for my own?
Theban. Why this? Why are you asking me this question?
Corinthian. My friend, *here* is the man who was that baby!

Theban. O, devil take you! Cannot you keep silent?
Oedipus. Here, Sir! This man needs no reproof from you.
  Your tongue needs chastisement much more than his.
Theban. O best of masters, how am I offending?
Oedipus. Not telling of the child of whom he speaks.
Theban. He? He knows nothing. He is wasting time.
Oedipus [*threatening*]. If you'll not speak from pleasure, speak from
    pain.
Theban. No, no, I pray! Not torture an old man!
Oedipus. Here, someone quickly! Twist this fellow's arms!
Theban. Why, wretched man? What would you know besides?
Oedipus. That child: you gave it him, the one he speaks of?
Theban. I did. Ah God, would I had died instead!
Oedipus. And die you shall, unless you speak the truth.
Theban. And if I do, then death is still more certain.
Oedipus. This man, I think, is trying to delay me.
Theban. Not I! I said I gave the child — just now.
Oedipus. And got it — where? Your own? or someone else's?
Theban. No, not my own. Someone had given it me.
Oedipus. Who? Which of these our citizens? From what house?
Theban. No, I implore you, master! Do not ask!
Oedipus. You die if I must question you again.
Theban. Then, 'twas a child of one in Laius' house.
Oedipus. You mean a slave? Or someone of his kin?
Theban. God! I am on the verge of saying it.
Oedipus. And I of hearing it, but hear I must.
Theban. His own, or so they said. But she within
  Could tell you best — your wife — the truth of it.
Oedipus. What, did she give you it?
Theban.   She did, my lord.
Oedipus. With what intention?
Theban.   That I should destroy it.
Oedipus. Her own? — How could she?
Theban.   Frightened by oracles.
Oedipus. What oracles?
Theban.   That it would kill its parents.
Oedipus. Why did you let it go to this man here?
Theban. I pitied it, my lord. I thought to send
  The child abroad, whence this man came. And he
  Saved it, for utter doom. For if you are
  The man he says, then you were born for ruin.
Oedipus. Ah God! Ah God! This is the truth, at last!

O Sun, let me behold thee this once more,
I who am proved accursed in my conception,
And in my marriage, and in him I slew.

[*Exeunt severally Oedipus, Corinthian, Theban*]

STROPHE 1

Chorus. Alas! you generations of men!
[*glyconics*] Even while you live you are next to nothing!
　　Has any man won for himself
　　More than the shadow of happiness,
　　A shadow that swiftly fades away?
　　Oedipus, now as I look on you,
　　See your ruin, how can I say that
　　Mortal man can be happy?

ANTISTROPHE 1

For who won greater prosperity?
Sovereignty and wealth beyond all desiring?
　　The crooked-clawed, riddling Sphinx,
　　Maiden and bird, you overcame;
　　You stood like a tower of strength to Thebes.
　　So you received our crown, received the
　　Highest honors that we could give —
　　King in our mighty city.

STROPHE 2

Who more wretched, more afflicted now,
With cruel misery, with fell disaster,
　　Your life in dust and ashes?
　　　O noble Oedipus!
　　　How could it be? to come again
　　A bridegroom of her who gave you birth!
　　How could such a monstrous thing
　　Endure so long, unknown?

ANTISTROPHE 2

Time sees all, and Time, in your despite,
Disclosed and punished your unnatural marriage —
A child, and then a husband.
  O son of Laius,
    Would I had never looked on you!
I mourn you as one who mourns the dead.
First you gave me back my life,
And now, that life is death.

[*Enter, from the palace, a messenger*]

Messenger. My Lords, most honored citizens of Thebes,
  What deeds am I to tell of, you to see!
  What heavy grief to bear, if still remains
  Your native loyalty to our line of kings.
  For not the Ister, no, nor Phasis' flood.
  Could purify this house, such things it hides,
  Such others will it soon display to all,
  Evils self-sought. Of all our sufferings
  Those hurt the most that we ourselves inflict.
Chorus-leader. Sorrow enough — too much — in what was known
  Already. What new sorrow do you bring?
Messenger. Quickest for me to say and you to hear:
  It is the Queen, Iocasta — she is dead.
Chorus-leader. Iocasta, dead? But how? What was the cause?
Messenger. By her own hand. Of what has passed, the worst
  Cannot be yours: that was, to see it.
  But you shall hear, so far as memory serves,
  The cruel story. — In her agony
  She ran across the courtyard, snatching at
  Her hair with both her hands. She made her way
  Straight to her chamber; she barred fast the doors
  And called on Laius, these long years dead,
  Remembering their by-gone procreation.
  "Through this did you meet death yourself, and leave
  To me, the mother, child-bearing accursed
  To my own child." She cried aloud upon
  The bed where she had borne a double brood,
  Husband from husband, children from a child.
  And thereupon she died, I know not how;
  For, groaning, Oedipus burst in, and we,

For watching him, saw not *her* agony
And how it ended. He, ranging through the palace,
Came up to each man calling for a sword,
Calling for her whom he had called his wife,
Asking where was she who had borne them all,
Himself and his own children. So he raved.
And then some deity showed him the way,
For it was none of us that stood around;
He cried aloud, as if to someone who
Was leading him; he leapt upon the doors,
Burst from their sockets the yielding bars, and fell
Into the room; and there, hanged by the neck,
We saw his wife, held in a swinging cord.
He, when he saw it, groaned in misery
And loosed her body from the rope. When now
She lay upon the ground, awful to see
Was that which followed: from her dress he tore
The golden brooches that she had been wearing,
Raised them, and with their points struck his own eyes,
Crying aloud that they should never see
What he had suffered and what he had done,
But in the dark henceforth they should behold
Those whom they ought not; nor should recognize
Those whom he longed to see. To such refrain
He smote his eyeballs with the pins, not once,
Nor twice; and as he smote them, blood ran down
His face, not dripping slowly, but there fell
Showers of black rain and blood-red hail together.

  Not on his head alone, but on them both,
Husband and wife, this common storm has broken.
Their ancient happiness of early days
Was happiness indeed; but now, today,
Death, ruin, lamentation, shame — of all
The ills there are, not one is wanting here.

Chorus-leader. Now is there intermission in his agony?

Messenger. He shouts for someone to unbar the gates,
  And to display to Thebes the parricide,
  His mother's — no, I cannot speak the words;
  For, by the doom he uttered, he will cast
  Himself beyond our borders, not remain
  To be a curse at home. But he needs strength,
  And one to guide him; for these wounds are greater
  Than he can bear — as you shall see; for look!

They draw the bolts. A sight you will behold
To move the pity even of an enemy.

[*The doors open. Oedipus slowly advances.*]

Chorus. O horrible, dreadful sight. More dreadful far [*These verses
  sung or chanted in a slow march-time.*] Than any I have yet
  seen. What cruel frenzy
Came over you? What spirit with superhuman leap
Came to assist your grim destiny?
Ah, most unhappy man!
But no! I cannot bear even to look at you,
  Though there is much that I would ask and see and hear.
But I shudder at the very sight of you.
Oedipus [*sings in the dochmiac rhythm*]. Alas! alas! and woe for my
  misery!
Where are my steps taking me?
My random voice is lost in the air.
O God! how hast thou crushed me!
Chorus-leader [*spoken*]. Too terribly for us to hear or see.
Oedipus [*sings*]. O cloud of darkness abominable,
My enemy unspeakable,
In cruel onset insuperable.
Alas! alas! Assailed at once by pain
Of pin-points and of memory of crimes.
Chorus-leader. In such tormenting pains you well may cry
A double grief and feel a double woe.
Oedipus [*sings*]. Ah, my friend!
Still at my side? Still steadfast?
Still can you endure me?
Still care for me, a blind man?
[*speaks*] For it is you, my friend; I know 'tis you;
Though all is darkness, yet I know your voice.
Chorus-leader. O, to destroy your sight! How could you bring
Yourself to do it? What god incited you?
Oedipus [*sings*]. It was Apollo, friends, Apollo.
He decreed that I should suffer what I suffer;
But the hand that struck, alas! was my own,
And not another's.
For why should I have sight.
When sight of nothing could give me pleasure?
Chorus. It was even as you say.
Oedipus. What have I left, my friends, to see,
To cherish, whom to speak with, or

To listen to, with joy?
Lead me away at once, far from Thebes;
Lead me away, my friends!
I have destroyed; I am accursed, and, what is more,
Hateful to Heaven, as no other.

Chorus-leader [speaks]. Unhappy your intention, and unhappy
Your fate. O would that I had never known you!

Oedipus [sings]. Curses on him, whoever he was,
Who took the savage fetters from my feet,
Snatched me from death, and saved me.
No thanks I owe him,
For had I died that day
Less ruin had I brought on me and mine.

Chorus. That wish is my wish too.

Oedipus. I had not then come and slain my father.
Nor then would men have called me
Husband of her that bore me.
Now am I God's enemy, child of the guilty,
And she that bore me has borne too my children;
And if there is evil surpassing evil,
That has come to Oedipus.

Chorus-leader. How can I say that you have counseled well?
Far better to be dead than to be blind.

Oedipus. That what is done was not done for the best
Seek not to teach me: counsel me no more.
I know not how I could have gone to Hades
And with these eyes have looked upon my father
Or on my mother; such things have I done
To them, death is no worthy punishment.
Or could I look for pleasure in the sight
Of my own children, born as they were born?
Never! No pleasure there, for eyes of mine,
Nor in this city, nor its battlements
Nor sacred images. From these — ah, miserable! —
I, the most nobly born of any Theban
Am banned for ever by my own decree
That the defiler should be driven forth,
The man accursed of Heaven and Laius' house.
Was I to find such taint in me, and then
With level eyes to look *them* in the face?
Nay more: if for my ears I could have built
Some dam to stay the flood of sound, that I
Might lose both sight and hearing, and seal up

My wretched body — that I would have done.
How good to dwell beyond the reach of pain!
   Cithaeron! Why did you accept me? Why
Did you not take and kill me? Never then
Should I have come to dwell among the Thebans.
   O Polybus! Corinth! and that ancient home
I thought my father's — what a thing you nurtured!
How fair, how foul beneath! For I am found
Foul in myself and in my parentage.
   O you three ways, that in a hidden glen
Do meet: you narrow branching roads within
The forest — you, through my own hands, did drink
My father's blood, that was my own. — Ah! do you
Remember what you saw me do? And what
I did again in Thebes? You marriages!
You did beget me: then, having begotten,
Bore the same crop again, and brought to light
Commingled blood of fathers, brothers, sons,
Brides, mothers, wives; all that there can be
Among the human kind most horrible!
   But that which it is foul to do, it is
Not fair to speak of. Quick as you can, I beg,
Banish me, hide me, slay me! Throw me forth
Into the sea, where I may sink from view.
I pray you, deign to touch one so afflicted,
And do not fear: there is no man alive
Can bear this load of evil but myself.
Chorus-leader. To listen to your prayers, Creon is here,
   For act or guidance opportune; for he,
   In your defection, is our champion.

   [*Enter Creon*]

Oedipus. Alas! alas! How can I speak to him?
   What word of credit find? In all my commerce
   With him aforetime I am proven false.
Creon. No exultation, Oedipus, and no reproach
   Of injuries inflicted brings me here;
   But if the face of men moves not your shame,
   Then reverence show to that all-nurturing fire,
   The holy Sun, that he be not polluted
   By such accursèd sight, which neither Earth
   Nor rain from Heaven nor sunlight can endure.
      Take him within, and quickly: it is right

His kinsmen only should behold and hear
Evils that chiefly on his kinsmen fall.

Oedipus. In Heaven's name — since you cheat my expectation,
So noble towards my baseness — grant me this:
It is for you I ask it, not myself.

Creon. What is this supplication that you make?

Oedipus. Drive me at once beyond your bounds, where I
Shall be alone, and no one speak to me.

Creon. I would have done it; but I first desired
To ask the God what he would have me do.

Oedipus. No, his command was given in full, to slay
Me, the polluter and the parricide.

Creon. Those were his words; but in our present need
It would be wise to ask what we should do.

Oedipus. You will inquire for such a wretch as I?

Creon. I will; for now *you* may believe the god.

Oedipus. Yes; and on you I lay this charge and duty:
Give burial, as you will, to her who lies
Within — for she is yours, and this is proper;
And, while I live, let not my father's city
Endure to have me as a citizen.
My home must be the mountains — on Cithaeron,
Which, while they lived, my parents chose to be
My tomb: they wished to slay me; now they shall.
For this I know: sickness can never kill me,
Nor any other evil; I was not saved
That day from death, except for some strange doom.
My fate must take the course it will. — Now, for my sons,
Be not concerned for them: they can, being men,
Fend for themselves, wherever they may be:
But my unhappy daughters, my two girls,
Whose chairs were always set beside my own
At table — they who shared in every dish
That was prepared for me — oh Creon! these
Do I commend to you. And grant me this:
To take them in my arms, and weep for them.
My lord! most noble Creon! could I now
But hold them in my arms, then I should think
I had them as I had when I could see them.
Ah! what is this?
Ah Heaven! do I not hear my dear ones, sobbing?
Has Creon, in his pity, sent to me
My darling children? Has he? Is it true?

Creon. It is; they have been always your delight;
  So, knowing this, I had them brought to you.
Oedipus. Then Heaven reward you, and for this kind service
  Protect you better than it protected me!
    Where are you, children? Where? O come to me!
  Come, let me clasp you with a brother's arms,
  These hands, which helped your father's eyes, once bright,
  To look upon you as they see you now —
  Your father who, not seeing, nor inquiring,
  Gave you for mother her who bore himself.
  See you I cannot; but I weep for you,
  For the unhappiness that must be yours,
  And for the bitter life that you must lead.
  What gathering of the citizens, what festivals,
  Will you have part in? Your high celebrations
  Will be to go back home, and sit in tears.
  And when the time for marriage comes, what man
  Will stake upon the ruin and the shame
  That *I* am to my parents and to you?
  Nothing is wanting there: your father slew
  His father, married her who gave him birth,
  And then, from that same source whence he himself
  Had sprung, got you. — With these things they will taunt you;
  And who will take you then in marriage? — Nobody;
  But you must waste, unwedded and unfruitful.
    Ah, Creon! Since they have no parent now
  But you — for both of us who gave them life
  Have perished — suffer them not to be cast out
  Homeless and beggars; for they are your kin.
  Have pity on them, for they are so young,
  So desolate, except for you alone.
  Say "Yes," good Creon! Let your hand confirm it.
    And now, my children, for my exhortation
  You are too young; but you can pray that I
  May live henceforward — where I should; and you
  More happily than the father who begot you.
Creon. Now make an end of tears, and go within.
Oedipus. Then I must go — against my will.
Creon. There is a time for everything.
Oedipus. You know what I would have you do?
Creon. If you will tell me, I shall know.
Oedipus. Send me away, away from Thebes.
Creon. The God, not I, must grant you this.

Oedipus. The gods hate no man more than me!
Creon. Then what you ask they soon will give.
Oedipus. You promise this?
Creon.   Ah no! When I
   Am ignorant, I do not speak.
Oedipus. Then lead me in; I say no more.
Creon. Release the children then, and come.
Oedipus. What? Take these children from me? No!
Creon. Seek not to have your way in all things:
   Where you had your way before,
   Your mastery broke before the end.

[*There was no doubt a short concluding utterance from the Chorus.
What stands in the mss. appears to be spurious.*]*

Classroom discussions of *Oedipus the King*, like discussions in books,
are often mostly devoted to the problem of fate and free will. Students
(who ought to be filled with youthful confidence in the freedom of the
will) generally argue that Oedipus is fated; instructors (who ought to
be old enough to know that the inexplicable and unwilled often comes
about) generally argue that Oedipus is free and of his own accord performed the actions that fulfilled the prophecy. Prophecy or prediction
or foreknowledge, instructors patiently explain, is not the same as fore-
ordination. The physician who says that the newborn babe will never
develop mentally beyond the age of six is predicting, but he is not
ordaining or willing. So, the argument usually runs, the oracle who
predicted that Oedipus would kill his father and marry his mother was
not *causing* Oedipus to do these things but was simply, in his deep
knowledge, announcing what a man like Oedipus would do. But that
may be too sophisticated a reading, and a reading that derives from the

* Editors' note: few other scholars share Professor Kitto's suspicion that the
concluding lines in the manuscript are spurious. The passage is translated thus
by J. T. Sheppard:
   Chorus. Look, ye who dwell in Thebes. This man was Oedipus.
That mighty King, who knew the riddle's mystery,
Whom all the city envied, Fortune's favorite.
Behold, in the event, the storm of his calamities,
And, being mortal, think on that last day of death,
Which all must see, and speak of no man's happiness
Till, without sorrow, he hath passed the goal of life.

much later European view of man as a creature who can shape his destiny. It is hard for us — especially if the tragedy we know best is Shakespeare's — to recognize the possibility of another sort of tragic drama which does not relate the individual's suffering to his own actions but which postulates some sort of Necessity that works within him.

Whatever the merits of these views, the spectators or readers undeniably know, when they set out to see or read the play, that Oedipus must end wretchedly. The story is known to us, fixed in Sophocles' text, and Oedipus cannot extricate himself from it. Something along these lines was suggested in the middle of the fourth century B.C. when a Greek comic dramatist complained that the comic writer's task was harder than the tragic writer's: "Tragedy has the best of it since the stories are known beforehand to the spectators even before anyone speaks; so the poet only has to remind them. For if I merely say the name Oedipus, they all know the rest — his father Laius, mother Iocasta, daughters, who his sons are, what will happen to him, what he did." In fact, it should be mentioned, the tragic writer's task was not quite so easy. First of all, we have Aristotle's statement that "even the known legends are known to only a few," and, second, we have evidence that the tragic writer could vary the details. In Homer's *Iliad* we read that Oedipus continued to rule even after his dreadful history was known, but Sophocles exiles him. And a fragment of Euripides indicates that Euripides' Oedipus was blinded by Laius' followers, but Sophocles' Oedipus blinds himself. These are details, but they are rather important ones. Probably the ancient Greeks knew the legends in a rough sort of way, as most of us know the Bible or some nuggets of Roman history. Robert Frost and Archibald MacLeish have both drawn from the Book of Job, but their works are enormously different. A writer who uses Job can scarcely omit Job's great suffering, and he can assume that his audience will know that Job had a wife and some comforters, but he is free to go on from there. Similarly, Brutus must stab Julius Caesar, but that leaves lots of room for other material in a play about Caesar. Shakespeare, by the way, could even assume that the audience that saw his *Julius Caesar* would accept a different version of the facts in his *Antony and Cleopatra*. In *Julius Caesar*, Brutus kills himself, but in *Antony and Cleopatra* Antony says (and presumably he is speaking the truth — the truth, that is, for *that* play) that Brutus died at Antony's hands.

Still, the main outline of Oedipus' life must have been fixed, and for us even the details are forever fixed in Sophocles' version. (We know that the Greeks wrote a dozen plays about Oedipus' discovery of his terrible actions, but only Sophocles' survives.) This means that as we read or watch it, each speech has for us a meaning somewhat different from the meaning it has for the speaker and the audience on the stage. Oedipus says he will hunt out the polluted man; we know, as he and the Thebans do not, that *he* is the hunted as well as the hunter. Oedipus says the killer of King Laius may well try to strike at him; we know that Oedipus will find himself out and will strike out his own eyes. A messenger from Corinth tries to allay Oedipus' fears, but he sets them going. What we are talking about, of course, is tragic irony, or Sophoclean irony, in which words and deeds have a larger meaning for the spectator than for the dramatis personae. And surely it is in part because Sophocles so persistently uses this device of giving speeches a second, awesome significance that we feel the plot is a masterpiece of construction in which Oedipus is caught. If ever a man had confidence in his will, it was Oedipus, but if ever a man moved toward a predicted point, it was Oedipus. He had solved the riddle of the sphinx (by himself, without the aid of birds, he somewhat hybristically boasts), but he did not yet know himself. That knowledge was to come later, when he commendably pursued the quest for Laius' slayer and inevitably found himself. The thing is as inevitable as the history described in the sphinx's riddle, which in J. T. Sheppard's version goes thus:

> A thing there is whose voice is one;
> Whose feet are four and two and three.
> So mutable a thing is none
> That moves in earth or sky or sea.
> When on most feet this thing doth go,
> Its strength is weakest and its pace most slow.

This is the history of man, willy-nilly. In Sophocles' time men grew from crawling infancy, through erect manhood, to bent old age supported by a stick, and so they do in our time, as the child's rhyme still claims:

> Walks on four feet,
> On two feet, on three,
> The more feet it walks on,
> The weaker it be.

There was scarcely an infant weaker than the maimed Oedipus; there was scarcely a man stronger than King Oedipus at his height; and there was scarcely a man more in need of a staff than the blind exile. However free each of his actions — and we can only feel that the man whom we see on the stage is acting freely when he abuses Teiresias and Creon — Oedipus was by fate a man, and thus the largest pattern of his life could be predicted easily enough.

The Tragedy of Othello

The Moor of Venice

WILLIAM SHAKESPEARE

William Shakespeare (1564–1616) was born in Stratford, England, of middle-class parents. Nothing of interest is known about his early years, but by 1590 he was acting and writing plays in London. He early worked in all three Elizabethan dramatic genres — tragedy, comedy, and history. Romeo and Juliet, for example, was written about 1595, the year of Richard II, and in the following year he wrote A Midsummer Night's Dream. Julius Caesar (1599) probably preceded As You Like It by one year, and Hamlet probably followed As You Like It by less than a year. Among the plays that followed Othello (1603–04) were King Lear (1605–06), Macbeth (1605–06), and several "romances" — plays that have happy endings but that seem more meditative and closer to tragedy than such comedies as A Midsummer Night's Dream, As You Like It, and Twelfth Night.

THE NAMES OF THE ACTORS

Othello, the Moor
Brabantio, father to Desdemona
Cassio, an honorable lieutenant
Iago, a villain
Roderigo, a gulled gentleman
Duke of Venice
Senators
Montano, Governor of Cyprus
Gentlemen of Cyprus
Lodovico and *Gratiano,* two noble Venetians
Sailors
Clown
Desdemona, wife to Othello
Emilia, wife to Iago
Bianca, a courtesan
Messenger, Herald, Officers, Gentlemen, Musicians,
  Attendants

SCENE

[Venice and Cyprus]

ACT I

SCENE I. [*Venice. A street.*]

(*Enter Roderigo and Iago.*)

Roderigo. Tush! Never tell me? I take it much unkindly
  That thou, Iago, who hast had my purse
  As if the strings were thine, shouldst know of this.
Iago. 'Sblood,° [1] but you'll not hear me! If ever I did dream
  Of such a matter, abhor me.
Roderigo.   Thou told'st me   5
  Thou didst hold him in thy hate.
Iago.   Despise me
  If I do not. Three great ones of the city,

Othello was first printed in 1621 in a small book of a kind called a quarto; it was printed again in 1623 in a large volume (a folio) containing 36 of Shakespeare's plays. There are numerous differences between the two texts of Othello, and scholars are divided about which text represents Shakespeare's final version of the play. The text we give is that prepared by Alvin Kernan for the Signet Shakespeare; it is based on the folio but it includes some readings from the quarto. Material added by the editor, such as indication of locale and some stage directions, is enclosed in square brackets, thus [ ].

[1] The degree sign (°) indicates a footnote, which is keyed to the text by the line number. Text references are printed in *italic* type; the annotation follows in roman type.   I.i.⁴ *'Sblood* by God's blood

In personal suit to make me his lieutenant,
Off-capped° to him; and, by the faith of man,
I know my price; I am worth no worse a place.   10
But he, as loving his own pride and purposes,
Evades them with a bombast circumstance,°
Horribly stuffed with epithets of war;
Nonsuits° my mediators. For, "Certes," says he,
"I have already chose my officer." And what was he?   15
Forsooth, a great arithmetician,°
One Michael Cassio, a Florentine,
(A fellow almost damned in a fair wife)°
That never set a squadron in the field,
Nor the division of a battle knows   20
More than a spinster; unless the bookish theoric,
Wherein the tonguèd° consuls can propose
As masterly as he. Mere prattle without practice
Is all his soldiership. But he, sir, had th' election;
And I, of whom his eyes had seen the proof   25
At Rhodes, at Cyprus, and on other grounds
Christian and heathen, must be belee'd and calmed
By debitor and creditor. This counter-caster,°
He, in good time, must his lieutenant be,
And I — God bless the mark! — his Moorship's ancient.° 30
Roderigo. By heaven, I rather would have been his hangman.
Iago. Why, there's no remedy. 'Tis the curse of service:
Preferment goes by letter and affection,°
And not by old gradation,° where each second
Stood heir to th' first. Now, sir, be judge yourself, 35
Whether I in any just term am affined°
To love the Moor.
Roderigo. 		I would not follow him then.

---

⁹ *Off-capped* doffed their caps — as a mark of respect
¹² *bombast circumstance* stuffed, roundabout speech
¹⁴ *Nonsuits* rejects	¹⁶ *arithmetician* theorist (rather than practical)
¹⁸ *A . . . wife* (a much-disputed passage, which is probably best taken as a general sneer at Cassio as a dandy and a ladies' man. But in the story from which Shakespeare took his plot the counterpart of Cassio is married, and it may be that at the beginning of the play Shakespeare had decided to keep him married but later changed his mind)
²² *tonguèd* eloquent
²⁸ *counter-caster* i.e., a bookkeeper who *casts* (reckons up) figures on a *counter* (abacus)
³⁰ *ancient* standard-bearer; an underofficer
³³ *letter and affection* recommendations (from men of power) and personal preference	³⁴ *old gradation* seniority	³⁶ *affined* bound

Iago. O, sir, content you.
    I follow him to serve my turn upon him.
    We cannot all be masters, nor all masters   40
    Cannot be truly followed. You shall mark
    Many a duteous and knee-crooking° knave
    That, doting on his own obsequious bondage,
    Wears out his time, much like his master's ass,
    For naught but provender; and when he's old, cashiered.   45
    Whip me such honest knaves! Others there are
    Who, trimmed in forms and visages of duty,
    Keep yet their hearts attending on themselves,
    And, throwing but shows of service on their lords,
    Do well thrive by them, and when they have lined their coats,   50
    Do themselves homage. These fellows have some soul;
    And such a one do I profess myself. For, sir,
    It is as sure as you are Roderigo,
    Were I the Moor, I would not be Iago.
    In following him, I follow but myself.   55
    Heaven is my judge, not I for love and duty,
    But seeming so, for my peculiar° end;
    For when my outward action doth demonstrate
    The native° act and figure of my heart
    In complement extern,° 'tis not long after   60
    But I will wear my heart upon my sleeve
    For daws to peck at; I am not what I am.
Roderigo. What a full fortune does the thick-lips owe°
    If he can carry't thus!
Iago.   Call up her father,
    Rouse him. Make after him, poison his delight,   65
    Proclaim him in the streets, incense her kinsmen,
    And though he in a fertile climate dwell,
    Plague him with flies; though that his joy be joy,
    Yet throw such chances of vexation on't
    As it may lose some color.   70
Roderigo. Here is her father's house. I'll call aloud.
Iago. Do, with like timorous° accent and dire yell
    As when, by night and negligence, the fire
    Is spied in populous cities.
Roderigo. What, ho, Brabantio! Signior Brabantio, ho!   75

---

[42] *knee-crooking* bowing   [57] *peculiar* personal   [59] *native* natural, innate
[60] *complement extern* outward appearances   [63] *owe* own
[72] *timorous* frightening

Iago. Awake! What, ho, Brabantio! Thieves! Thieves!
  Look to your house, your daughter, and your bags!
  Thieves! Thieves!

(*Brabantio above°* [*at a window*].)

Brabantio. What is the reason of this terrible summons?
  What is the matter there? 80
Roderigo. Signior, is all your family within?
Iago. Are your doors locked?
Brabantio.   Why, wherefore ask you this?
Iago. Zounds, sir, y'are robbed! For shame. Put on your gown!
  Your heart is burst, you have lost half your soul.
  Even now, now, very now, an old black ram 85
  Is tupping your white ewe. Arise, arise!
  Awake the snorting citizens with the bell,
  Or else the devil will make a grandsire of you.
  Arise, I say!
Brabantio.   What, have you lost your wits?
Roderigo. Most reverend signior, do you know my voice? 90
Brabantio. Not I. What are you?
Roderigo. My name is Roderigo.
Brabantio.   The worser welcome!
  I have charged thee not to haunt about my doors.
  In honest plainness thou hast heard me say
  My daughter is not for thee; and now, in madness, 95
  Being full of supper and distemp'ring draughts,°
  Upon malicious knavery dost thou come
  To start° my quiet.
Roderigo. Sir, sir, sir ——
Brabantio.   But thou must needs be sure
  My spirits and my place° have in their power 100
  To make this bitter to thee.
Roderigo.   Patience, good sir.
Brabantio. What tell'st thou me of robbing? This is Venice;
  My house is not a grange.°
Roderigo.   Most grave Brabantio,
  In simple and pure soul I come to you.

---

[78] s.d. *above* (i.e., on the small upper stage above and to the rear of the main platform stage, which resembled the projecting upper story of an Elizabethan house)
[96] *distemp'ring draughts* unsettling drinks   [98] *start* disrupt
[100] *place* rank, i.e., of senator   [103] *grange* isolated house

Iago. Zounds, sir, you are one of those that will not serve God if   105
   the devil bid you. Because we come to do you service and you
   think we are ruffians, you'll have your daughter covered with a
   Barbary° horse, you'll have your nephews° neigh to you, you'll
   have coursers for cousins,° and gennets for germans.°
Brabantio. What profane wretch art thou?   110
Iago. I am one, sir, that comes to tell you your daughter and the
   Moor are making the beast with two backs.
Brabantio. Thou art a villain.
Iago.   You are — a senator.
Brabantio. This thou shalt answer. I know thee, Roderigo.
Roderigo. Sir, I will answer anything. But I beseech you,   115
   If't be your pleasure and most wise consent,
   As partly I find it is, that your fair daughter,
   At this odd-even° and dull watch o' th' night,
   Transported, with no worse nor better guard
   But with a knave of common hire, a gondolier,   120
   To the gross clasps of a lascivious Moor —
   If this be known to you, and your allowance,
   We then have done you bold and saucy wrongs;
   But if you know not this, my manners tell me
   We have your wrong rebuke. Do not believe   125
   That from the sense of all civility°
   I thus would play and trifle with your reverence.
   Your daughter, if you have not given her leave,
   I say again, hath made a gross revolt,
   Tying her duty, beauty, wit, and fortunes   130
   In an extravagant° and wheeling stranger
   Of here and everywhere. Straight satisfy yourself.
   If she be in her chamber, or your house,
   Let loose on me the justice of the state
   For thus deluding you.
Brabantio.   Strike on the tinder, ho!   135
   Give me a taper! Call up all my people!
   This accident° is not unlike my dream.

---

108 *Barbary* Arabian, i.e., Moorish   108 *nephews* i.e., grandsons
109 *cousins* relations
109 *gennets for germans* Spanish horses for blood relatives
118 *odd-even* between night and morning
126 *sense of all civility* feeling of what is proper
131 *extravagant* vagrant, wandering (Othello is not Venetian and thus may be
considered a wandering soldier of fortune)   137 *accident* happening

Belief of it oppresses me already.
Light, I say! Light!   (*Exit* [*above*].)
Iago.   Farewell, for I must leave you.
It seems not meet, nor wholesome to my place,   140
To be produced — as, if I stay, I shall —
Against the Moor. For I do know the State,
However this may gall him with some check,°
Cannot with safety cast° him; for he's embarked
With such loud reason to the Cyprus wars,   145
Which even now stands in act,° that for their souls
Another of his fathom° they have none
To lead their business; in which regard,
Though I do hate him as I do hell-pains,
Yet, for necessity of present life,   150
I must show out a flag and sign of love,
Which is indeed but sign. That you shall surely find him,
Lead to the Sagittary° the raisèd search;
And there will I be with him. So farewell.   (*Exit.*)

(*Enter Brabantio* [*in his nightgown*], *with Servants and torches.*)

Brabantio. It is too true an evil. Gone she is;   155
And what's to come of my despisèd time
Is naught but bitterness. Now, Roderigo,
Where didst thou see her? — O unhappy girl! —
With the Moor, say'st thou? — Who would be a father? —
How didst thou know 'twas she? — O, she deceives me   160
Past thought! — What said she to you? Get moe° tapers!
Raise all my kindred! — Are they married, think you?
Roderigo. Truly I think they are.
Brabantio. O heaven! How got she out? O treason of the blood!
Fathers, from hence trust not your daughters' minds   165
By what you see them act.° Is there not charms
By which the property° of youth and maidhood
May be abused? Have you not read, Roderigo,
Of some such thing?
Roderigo.   Yes, sir, I have indeed.
Brabantio. Call up my brother. — O, would you had had her! —   170
Some one way, some another. — Do you know
Where we may apprehend her and the Moor?

---

¹⁴³ *check* restraint   ¹⁴⁴ *cast* dismiss   ¹⁴⁶ *stands in act* takes place
¹⁴⁷ *fathom* ability   ¹⁵³ *Sagittary* (probably the name of an inn)
¹⁶¹ *moe* more   ¹⁶⁶ *act* do   ¹⁶⁷ *property* true nature

Roderigo. I think I can discover him, if you please
  To get good guard and go along with me.
Brabantio. Pray you lead on. At every house I'll call;   175
  I may command at most. — Get weapons, ho!
  And raise some special officers of might. —
  On, good Roderigo; I will deserve your pains.°

                            (*Exeunt.*)

          SCENE II. [*A street.*]

  (*Enter Othello, Iago, Attendants with torches.*)

Iago. Though in the trade of war I have slain men,
  Yet do I hold it very stuff° o' th' conscience
  To do no contrived murder. I lack iniquity
  Sometime to do me service. Nine or ten times
  I had thought t' have yerked° him here, under the ribs.   5
Othello. 'Tis better as it is.
Iago.   Nay, but he prated,
  And spoke such scurvy and provoking terms
  Against your honor, that with the little godliness I have
  I did full hard forbear him. But I pray you, sir,
  Are you fast married? Be assured of this,   10
  That the magnifico° is much beloved,
  And hath in his effect a voice potential
  As double as the Duke's.° He will divorce you,
  Or put upon you what restraint or grievance
  The law, with all his might to enforce it on,   15
  Will give him cable.°
Othello.   Let him do his spite.
  My services which I have done the Signiory°
  Shall out-tongue his complaints. 'Tis yet to know° —
  Which when I know that boasting is an honor
  I shall promulgate — I fetch my life and being   20
  From men of royal siege;° and my demerits°
  May speak unbonneted to as proud a fortune

---

[178] *deserve your pains* be worthy of (and reward) your efforts
I.ii.[2] *stuff* essence   [5] *yerked* stabbed   [11] *magnifico* nobleman
[12–13] *hath . . . Duke's* i.e., can be as effective as the Duke
[16] *cable* range, scope   [17] *Signiory* the rulers of Venice
[18] *yet to know* unknown as yet   [21] *siege* rank   [21] *demerits* deserts

As this that I have reached.° For I know, Iago,
But that I love the gentle Desdemona,
I would not my unhousèd° free condition   25
Put into circumscription and confine
For the seas' worth. But look, what lights come yond?

(*Enter Cassio, with [Officers and] torches.*)

Iago. Those are the raisèd father and his friends.
  You were best go in.
Othello.   Not I. I must be found.
  My parts, my title, and my perfect soul°   30
  Shall manifest me rightly. Is it they?
Iago. By Janus, I think no.
Othello. The servants of the Duke? And my lieutenant?
  The goodness of the night upon you, friends.
  What is the news?
Cassio.   The Duke does greet you, general;   35
  And he requires your haste-posthaste appearance
  Even on the instant.
Othello.   What is the matter, think you?
Cassio. Something from Cyprus, as I may divine.
  It is a business of some heat. The galleys
  Have sent a dozen sequent° messengers   40
  This very night at one another's heels,
  And many of the consuls, raised and met,
  Are at the Duke's already. You have been hotly called for.
  When, being not at your lodging to be found,
  The Senate hath sent about three several° quests   45
  To search you out.
Othello.   'Tis well I am found by you.
  I will but spend a word here in the house,
  And go with you.   (*Exit.*)
Cassio.   Ancient, what makes he here?
Iago. Faith, he tonight hath boarded a land carack.°
  If it prove lawful prize, he's made forever.   50
Cassio. I do not understand.
Iago.   He's married.
Cassio.   To who?

(*Enter Othello.*)

22-23 *May ... reached,* i.e., are the equal of the family I have married into
25 *unhousèd* unconfined   30 *perfect soul* clear, unflawed conscience
40 *sequent* successive   45 *several* separate   49 *carack* treasure ship

Iago. Marry,° to — Come, captain, will you go?
Othello.   Have with you.
Cassio. Here comes another troop to seek for you.

(*Enter Brabantio, Roderigo, with Officers and torches.*)

Iago. It is Brabantio. General, be advised.
  He comes to bad intent.
Othello.   Holla! Stand there!   55
Roderigo. Signior, it is the Moor.
Brabantio.   Down with him, thief!

(*They draw swords.*)

Iago. You, Roderigo? Come, sir, I am for you.
Othello. Keep up your bright swords, for the dew will rust them.
  Good signior, you shall more command with years
  Than with your weapons.   60
Brabantio. O thou foul thief, where hast thou stowed my daughter?
  Damned as thou art, thou hast enchanted her!
  For I'll refer me to all things of sense,°
  If she in chains of magic were not bound,
  Whether a maid so tender, fair, and happy,   65
  So opposite to marriage that she shunned
  The wealthy, curlèd darlings of our nation,
  Would ever have, t' incur a general mock,°
  Run from her guardage to the sooty bosom
  Of such a thing as thou — to fear, not to delight.   70
  Judge me the world if 'tis not gross in sense°
  That thou hast practiced° on her with foul charms,
  Abused her delicate youth with drugs or minerals
  That weaken motion.° I'll have't disputed on;
  'Tis probable, and palpable to thinking.   75
  I therefore apprehend and do attach° thee
  For an abuser of the world, a practicer
  Of arts inhibited and out of warrant.°
  Lay hold upon him. If he do resist,
  Subdue him at his peril.
Othello.   Hold your hands,   80
  Both you of my inclining and the rest.

---

[52] *Marry* By Mary (an interjection)
[63] *refer . . . sense* i.e., base (my argument) on all ordinary understanding of
nature   [68] *general mock* public shame   [71] *gross in sense* obvious
[72] *practiced* used tricks   [74] *motion* thought, i.e., reason   [76] *attach* arrest
[78] *inhibited . . . warrant* prohibited and illegal (black magic)

Were it my cue to fight, I should have known it
Without a prompter. Whither will you that I go
To answer this your charge?
Brabantio.   To prison, till fit time
Of law and course of direct session   85
Call thee to answer.
Othello.   What if I do obey?
How may the Duke be therewith satisfied,
Whose messengers are here about my side
Upon some present° business of the state
To bring me to him?
Officer.   'Tis true, most worthy signior.   90
The Duke's in council, and your noble self
I am sure is sent for.
Brabantio.   How? The Duke in council?
In this time of the night? Bring him away.
Mine's not an idle cause. The Duke himself,
Or any of my brothers° of the state,   95
Cannot but feel this wrong as 'twere their own;
For if such actions may have passage free,
Bondslaves and pagans shall our statesmen be.

                                        (*Exeunt.*)

SCENE III. [*A council chamber.*]

(*Enter Duke, Senators, and Officers* [*set at a table, with lights and
    Attendants*].)

Duke. There's no composition° in this news
    That gives them credit.°
First Senator.   Indeed, they are disproportioned.
    My letters say a hundred and seven galleys.
Duke. And mine a hundred forty.
Second Senator.   And mine two hundred.
    But though they jump° not on a just accompt° —   5
    As in these cases where the aim° reports
    'Tis oft with difference — yet do they all confirm
    A Turkish fleet, and bearing up to Cyprus.

---

89 *present* immediate   95 *brothers* i.e., the other senators
I.iii.¹*composition* agreement   ² *gives them credit* makes them believable
⁵ *jump* agree   ⁵ *just accompt* exact counting   ⁶ *aim* approximation

Duke. Nay, it is possible enough to judgment.°
  I do not so secure me in the error,   10
  But the main article I do approve
  In fearful sense.°
Sailor (*Within*). What, ho! What, ho! What, ho!

  (*Enter Sailor.*)

Officer. A messenger from the galleys.
Duke.   Now? What's the business?
Sailor. The Turkish preparation makes for Rhodes.
  So was I bid report here to the State   15
  By Signior Angelo.
Duke. How say you by this change?
First Senator.   This cannot be
  By no assay of reason. 'Tis a pageant°
  To keep us in false gaze.° When we consider
  Th' importancy of Cyprus to the Turk,   20
  And let ourselves again but understand
  That, as it more concerns the Turk than Rhodes,
  So may he with more facile question° bear it,
  For that it stands not in such warlike brace,°
  But altogether lacks th' abilities   25
  That Rhodes is dressed in. If we make thought of this,
  We must not think the Turk is so unskillful
  To leave that latest which concerns him first,
  Neglecting an attempt of ease and gain
  To wake and wage a danger profitless.   30
Duke. Nay, in all confidence he's not for Rhodes.
Officer. Here is more news.

  (*Enter a Messenger.*)

Messenger. The Ottomites, reverend and gracious,
  Steering with due course toward the isle of Rhodes,
  Have there injointed them with an after° fleet.   35
First Senator. Ay, so I thought. How many, as you guess?
Messenger. Of thirty sail; and now they do restem

---

9 *to judgment* when carefully considered
10–12 *I do . . . sense* i.e., just because the numbers disagree in the reports, I do not doubt that the principal information (that the Turkish fleet is out) is fearfully true
18 *pageant* show, pretense   19 *in false gaze* looking the wrong way
23 *facile question* easy struggle   24 *warlike brace* "military posture"
35 *after* following

Their backward course, bearing with frank appearance
Their purposes toward Cyprus. Signior Montano,
Your trusty and most valiant servitor, 40
With his free duty° recommends° you thus,
And prays you to believe him.
Duke. 'Tis certain then for Cyprus.
Marcus Luccicos, is not he in town?
First Senator. He's now in Florence. 45
Duke. Write from us to him; post-posthaste dispatch.
First Senator. Here comes Brabantio and the valiant Moor.

(*Enter Brabantio, Othello, Cassio, Iago, Roderigo, and Officers.*)

Duke. Valiant Othello, we must straight° employ you
Against the general° enemy Ottoman.
[*To Brabantio*] I did not see you. Welcome, gentle signior. 50
We lacked your counsel and your help tonight.
Brabantio. So did I yours. Good your grace, pardon me.
Neither my place, nor aught I heard of business,
Hath raised me from my bed; nor doth the general care
Take hold on me; for my particular grief 55
Is of so floodgate and o'erbearing nature
That it engluts and swallows other sorrows,
And it is still itself.
Duke.   Why, what's the matter?
Brabantio. My daughter! O, my daughter!
Senators.   Dead?
Brabantio.   Aye, to me.
She is abused, stol'n from me, and corrupted 60
By spells and medicines bought of mountebanks;
For nature so prepost'rously to err,
Being not deficient, blind, or lame of sense,
Sans° witchcraft could not.
Duke. Whoe'er he be that in this foul proceeding 65
Hath thus beguiled your daughter of herself,
And you of her, the bloody book of law
You shall yourself read in the bitter letter
After your own sense; yea, though our proper° son
Stood in your action.°
Brabantio.   Humbly I thank your Grace. 70
Here is the man — this Moor, whom now, it seems,

---

⁴¹ *free duty* unlimited respect   ⁴¹ *recommends* informs
⁴⁸ *straight* at once   ⁴⁹ *general* universal   ⁶⁴ *Sans* without
⁶⁹ *proper* own   ⁷⁰ *Stood in your action* were the accused in your suit

Your special mandate for the state affairs
Hath hither brought.
All.   We are very sorry for't.
Duke [*To Othello*]. What in your own part can you say to this?
Brabantio. Nothing, but this is so.   75
Othello. Most potent, grave, and reverend signiors,
My very noble and approved° good masters,
That I have ta'en away this old man's daughter,
It is most true; true I have married her.
The very head and front° of my offending   80
Hath this extent, no more. Rude am I in my speech,
And little blessed with the soft phrase of peace,
For since these arms of mine had seven years' pith°
Till now some nine moons wasted,° they have used
Their dearest° action in the tented field;   85
And little of this great world can I speak
More than pertains to feats of broils and battle;
And therefore little shall I grace my cause
In speaking for myself. Yet, by your gracious patience,
I will a round° unvarnished tale deliver   90
Of my whole course of love — what drugs, what charms,
What conjuration, and what mighty magic,
For such proceeding I am charged withal,
I won his daughter —
Brabantio.   A maiden never bold,
Of spirit so still and quiet that her motion   95
Blushed at herself;° and she, in spite of nature,
Of years, of country, credit, everything,
To fall in love with what she feared to look on!
It is a judgment maimed and most imperfect
That will confess perfection so could err   100
Against all rules of nature, and must be driven
To find out practices of cunning hell
Why this should be. I therefore vouch again
That with some mixtures pow'rful o'er the blood,
Or with some dram, conjured to this effect,   105
He wrought upon her.

---

77 *approved* tested, proven by past performance
80 *head and front* extreme form (*front* = forehead)   83 *pith* strength
84 *wasted* past   85 *dearest* most important   90 *round* blunt
95–96 *her motion/Blushed at herself* i.e., she was so modest that she blushed at
every thought (and movement)

Duke.   To vouch this is no proof,
  Without more wider and more overt test
  Than these thin habits° and poor likelihoods
  Of modern° seeming do prefer against him.
First Senator. But, Othello, speak.   110
  Did you by indirect and forcèd courses
  Subdue and poison this young maid's affections?
  Or came it by request, and such fair question°
  As soul to soul affordeth?
Othello.   I do beseech you,
  Send for the lady to the Sagittary   115
  And let her speak of me before her father.
  If you do find me foul in her report,
  The trust, the office, I do hold of you
  Not only take away, but let your sentence
  Even fall upon my life.
Duke.   Fetch Desdemona hither.   120
Othello. Ancient, conduct them; you best know the place.

[*Exit Iago, with two or three Attendants.*]

  And till she come, as truly as to heaven
  I do confess the vices of my blood,
  So justly to your grave ears I'll present
  How I did thrive in this fair lady's love,   125
  And she in mine.
Duke.   Say it, Othello.
Othello. Her father loved me; oft invited me;
  Still° questioned me the story of my life
  From year to year, the battle, sieges, fortune
  That I have passed.   130
  I ran it through, even from my boyish days
  To th' very moment that he bade me tell it.
  Wherein I spoke of most disastrous chances,
  Of moving accidents by flood and field,
  Of hairbreadth scapes i' th' imminent° deadly breach,   135
  Of being taken by the insolent foe
  And sold to slavery, of my redemption thence
  And portance° in my travel's history,
  Wherein of anters° vast and deserts idle,°

---

¹⁰⁸ *habits* clothing   ¹⁰⁹ *modern* trivial   ¹¹³ *question* discussion
¹²⁸ *Still* regularly   ¹³⁵ *imminent* threatening
¹³⁸ *portance* manner of acting   ¹³⁹ *anters* caves   ¹³⁹ *idle* empty, sterile

Rough quarries, rocks, and hills whose heads touch heaven,   140
It was my hint to speak. Such was my process.
And of the Cannibals that each other eat,
The Anthropophagi,° and men whose heads
Grew beneath their shoulders. These things to hear
Would Desdemona seriously incline;   145
But still the house affairs would draw her thence;
Which ever as she could with haste dispatch,
She'd come again, and with a greedy ear
Devour up my discourse. Which I observing,
Took once a pliant hour, and found good means   150
To draw from her a prayer of earnest heart
That I would all my pilgrimage dilate,°
Whereof by parcels she had something heard,
But not intentively.° I did consent,
And often did beguile her of her tears   155
When I did speak of some distressful stroke
That my youth suffered. My story being done,
She gave me for my pains a world of kisses.
She swore in faith 'twas strange, 'twas passing° strange;
'Twas pitiful, 'twas wondrous pitiful.   160
She wished she had not heard it; yet she wished
That heaven had made her such a man. She thanked me,
And bade me, if I had a friend that loved her,
I should but teach him how to tell my story,
And that would woo her. Upon this hint I spake.   165
She loved me for the dangers I had passed,
And I loved her that she did pity them.
This only is the witchcraft I have used.
Here comes the lady. Let her witness it.

(*Enter Desdemona, Iago, Attendants.*)

Duke. I think this tale would win my daughter too.   170
Good Brabantio, take up this mangled matter at the best.°
Men do their broken weapons rather use
Than their bare hands.
Brabantio.   I pray you hear her speak.
If she confess that she was half the wooer,
Destruction on my head if my bad blame   175
Light on the man. Come hither, gentle mistress.

---

143 *Anthropophagi* man-eaters   152 *dilate* relate in full
154 *intentively* at length and in sequence   159 *passing* surpassing
171 *Take . . . best* i.e., make the best of this disaster

Do you perceive in all this noble company
Where most you owe obedience?
Desdemona.   My noble father,
  I do perceive here a divided duty.
  To you I am bound for life and education;   180
  My life and education both do learn me
  How to respect you. You are the lord of duty,
  I am hitherto your daughter. But here's my husband,
  And so much duty as my mother showed
  To you, preferring you before her father,   185
  So much I challenge° that I may profess
  Due to the Moor my lord.
Brabantio.   God be with you. I have done.
  Please it your Grace, on to the state affairs.
  I had rather to adopt a child than get° it.
  Come hither, Moor.   190
  I here do give thee that with all my heart
  Which, but thou hast already, with all my heart
  I would keep from thee. For your sake,° jewel,
  I am glad at soul I have no other child,
  For thy escape would teach me tyranny,   195
  To hang clogs on them. I have done, my lord.
Duke. Let me speak like yourself and lay a sentence°
  Which, as a grise° or step, may help these lovers.
  When remedies are past, the griefs are ended
  By seeing the worst, which late on hopes depended.°   200
  To mourn a mischief that is past and gone
  Is the next° way to draw new mischief on.
  What cannot be preserved when fortune takes,
  Patience her injury a mock'ry makes.
  The robbed that smiles, steals something from the thief;   205
  He robs himself that spends a bootless° grief.
Brabantio. So let the Turk of Cyprus us beguile:
  We lose it not so long as we can smile.
  He bears the sentence well that nothing bears
  But the free comfort which from thence he hears;   210
  But he bears both the sentence and the sorrow
  That to pay grief must of poor patience borrow.

---

186 *challenge* claim as right   189 *get* beget
193 *For your sake* because of you   197 *lay a sentence* provide a maxim
198 *grise* step
200 *late on hopes depended* was supported by hope (of a better outcome) until
lately   202 *next* closest, surest   206 *bootless* valueless

These sentences, to sugar, or to gall,
Being strong on both sides, are equivocal.
But words are words. I never yet did hear   215
That the bruisèd heart was piercèd° through the ear.
I humbly beseech you, proceed to th' affairs of state.

Duke. The Turk with a most mighty preparation makes for Cyprus.
  Othello, the fortitude° of the place is best known to you; and
  though we have there a substitute° of most allowed sufficiency,°   220
  yet opinion, a more sovereign mistress of effects, throws a more
  safer voice on you.° You must therefore be content to slubber°
  the gloss of your new fortunes with this more stubborn and
  boisterous° expedition.

Othello. The tyrant Custom, most grave senators,   225
Hath made the flinty and steel couch of war
My thrice-driven° bed of down. I do agnize°
A natural and prompt alacrity
I find in hardness and do undertake
This present wars against the Ottomites.   230
Most humbly, therefore, bending to your state,
I crave fit disposition for my wife,
Due reference of place, and exhibition,°
With such accommodation and besort
As levels with° her breeding.

Duke.   Why, at her father's.   235

Brabantio. I will not have it so.

Othello.   Nor I.

Desdemona.   Nor would I there reside,
To put my father in impatient thoughts
By being in his eye. Most gracious Duke,
To my unfolding° lend your prosperous° ear,
And let me find a charter° in your voice,   240
T' assist my simpleness.

---

²¹⁶ *piercèd* (some editors emend to *pieced*, i.e., "healed." But *pierced* makes
good sense: Brabantio is saying in effect that his heart cannot be further hurt
[pierced] by the indignity of the useless, conventional advice the Duke offers
him. *Pierced* can also mean, however, "lanced" in the medical sense, and would
then mean "treated")
²¹⁹ *fortitude* fortification   ²²⁰ *substitute* viceroy
²²⁰ *most allowed sufficiency* generally acknowledged capability
²²¹⁻²² *opinion . . . you* i.e., the general opinion, which finally controls affairs,
is that you would be the best man in this situation
²²² *slubber* besmear   ²²³⁻²⁴ *stubborn and boisterous* rough and violent
²²⁷ *thrice-driven* i.e., softest   ²²⁷ *agnize* know in myself
²³³ *exhibition* grant of funds   ²³⁵ *levels with* is suitable to
²³⁹ *unfolding* explanation   ²³⁹ *prosperous* favoring   ²⁴⁰ *charter* permission

Duke.   What would you, Desdemona?
Desdemona. That I love the Moor to live with him,
  My downright violence, and storm of fortunes,
  May trumpet to the world. My heart's subdued
  Even to the very quality of my lord.°   245
  I saw Othello's visage in his mind,
  And to his honors and his valiant parts
  Did I my soul and fortunes consecrate.
  So that, dear lords, if I be left behind,
  A moth of peace, and he go to the war,   250
  The rites° for why I love him are bereft me,
  And I a heavy interim shall support
  By his dear absence. Let me go with him.
Othello. Let her have your voice.°
  Vouch with me, heaven, I therefore beg it not   255
  To please the palate of my appetite.
  Nor to comply with heat° — the young affects°
  In me defunct — and proper satisfaction;°
  But to be free and bounteous to her mind;
  And heaven defend° your good souls that you think   260
  I will your serious and great business scant
  When she is with me. No, when light-winged toys
  Of feathered Cupid seel° with wanton° dullness
  My speculative and officed instrument,°
  That my disports corrupt and taint my business,   265
  Let housewives make a skillet of my helm,
  And all indign° and base adversities
  Make head° against my estimation!° —
Duke. Be it as you shall privately determine,
  Either for her stay or going. Th' affair cries haste,   270
  And speed must answer it.
First Senator.   You must away tonight.
Othello. With all my heart.
Duke. At nine i' th' morning here we'll meet again.
  Othello, leave some officer behind,

244–45 *My . . . lord* i.e., I have become one in nature and being with the man I married (therefore, I too would go to the wars like a soldier)
251 *rites* (may refer either to the marriage rites or to the rites, formalities, of war)   254 *voice* consent   257 *heat* lust   257 *affects* passions
258 *proper satisfaction* i.e., consummation of the marriage
260 *defend* forbid   263 *seel* sew up   263 *wanton* lascivious
264 *speculative . . . instrument* i.e., sight (and, by extension, the mind)
267 *indign* unworthy   268 *Make head* form an army, i.e., attack
268 *estimation* reputation

And he shall our commission bring to you,   275
And such things else of quality and respect
As doth import you.
Othello.   So please your grace, my ancient;
A man he is of honesty and trust.
To his conveyance I assign my wife,
With what else needful your good grace shall think   280
To be sent after me.
Duke.   Let it be so.
Good night to every one. [*To Brabantio*] And, noble signior,
If virtue no delighted° beauty lack,
Your son-in-law is far more fair than black.
First Senator. Adieu, brave Moor. Use Desdemona well.   285
Brabantio. Look to her, Moor, if thou hast eyes to see:
She has deceived her father, and may thee.

                    [*Exeunt Duke, Senators, Officers, etc.*]

Othello. My life upon her faith! Honest Iago,
My Desdemona must I leave to thee.
I prithee let thy wife attend on her,   290
And bring them after in the best advantage.°
Come, Desdemona. I have but an hour
Of love, of wordly matter, and direction
To spend with thee. We must obey the time.

                    (*Exit [Moor with Desdemona].*)

Roderigo. Iago?   295
Iago. What say'st thou, noble heart?
Roderigo. What will I do, think'st thou?
Iago. Why, go to bed and sleep.
Roderigo. I will incontinently° drown myself.
Iago. If thou dost, I shall never love thee after. Why, thou silly 300
gentleman?
Roderigo. It is silliness to live when to live is torment; and then
have we a prescription to die when death is our physician.
Iago. O villainous! I have looked upon the world for four times
seven years, and since I could distinguish betwixt a benefit and 305
an injury, I never found man that knew how to love himself.
Ere I would say I would drown myself for the love of a guinea
hen, I would change my humanity with a baboon.

---

[283] *delighted* delightful   [291] *advantage* opportunity
[299] *incontinently* at once

Roderigo. What should I do? I confess it is my shame to be so
fond, but it is not in my virtue° to amend it.   310

Iago. Virtue? A fig! 'Tis in ourselves that we are thus, or thus.
Our bodies are our gardens, to the which our wills are gardeners;
so that if we will plant nettles or sow lettuce, set hyssop and
weed up thyme, supply it with one gender of herbs or distract°
it with many — either to have it sterile with idleness or manured   315
with industry — why, the power and corrigible° authority of
this lies in our wills. If the balance of our lives had not one
scale of reason to poise another of sensuality, the blood and
baseness of our natures would conduct us to most prepost'rous
conclusions.° But we have reason to cool our raging motions,   320
our carnal stings or unbitted° lusts, whereof I take this that you
call love to be a sect or scion.°

Roderigo. It cannot be.

Iago. It is merely a lust of the blood and a permission of the will.
Come, be a man! Drown thyself? Drown cats and blind pup-   325
pies! I have professed me thy friend, and I confess me knit to
thy deserving with cables of perdurable toughness. I could never
better stead° thee than now. Put money in thy purse. Follow
thou the wars; defeat thy favor° with an usurped° beard. I say,
put money in thy purse. It cannot be long that Desdemona   330
should continue her love to the Moor. Put money in thy purse.
Nor he his to her. It was a violent commencement in her and
thou shalt see an answerable° sequestration — put but money
in thy purse. These Moors are changeable in their wills — fill
thy purse with money. The food that to him now is as luscious   335
as locusts° shall be to him shortly as bitter as coloquintida.°
She must change for youth; when she is sated with his body,
she will find the errors of her choice. Therefore, put money in
thy purse. If thou wilt needs damn thyself, do it a more delicate
way than drowning. Make all the money thou canst. If sancti-   340
mony° and a frail vow betwixt an erring° barbarian and super-
subtle Venetian be not too hard for my wits, and all the tribe
of hell, thou shalt enjoy her. Therefore, make money. A pox of
drowning thyself, it is clean out of the way. Seek thou rather

---

[310] *virtue* strength (Roderigo is saying that his nature controls him)
[314] *distract* vary   [316] *corrigible* corrective   [320] *conclusions* ends
[321] *unbitted* i.e., uncontrolled   [322] *sect or scion* offshoot   [328] *stead* serve
[329] *defeat they favor* disguise your face   [329] *usurped* assumed
[333] *answerable* similar   [336] *locusts* (a sweet fruit)
[336] *coloquintida* (a purgative derived from a bitter apple)
[340-41] *sanctimony* sacred bond (of marriage)   [341] *erring* wandering

to be hanged in compassing° thy joy than to be drowned and 345
go without her.

Roderigo. Wilt thou be fast to my hopes, if I depend on the
issue?

Iago. Thou art sure of me. Go, make money. I have told thee
often, and I retell thee again and again, I hate the Moor. My 350
cause is hearted;° thine hath no less reason. Let us be conjunc-
tive° in our revenge against him. If thou canst cuckold him,
thou dost thyself a pleasure, me a sport. There are many events
in the womb of time, which will be delivered. Traverse, go, provide thy money! We will have more of this tomorrow. Adieu. 355

Roderigo. Where shall we meet i' th' morning?

Iago. At my lodging.

Roderigo. I'll be with thee betimes.

Iago. Go to, farewell. Do you hear, Roderigo?

Roderigo. I'll sell all my land   (*Exit.*) 360

Iago. Thus do I ever make my fool my purse;
For I mine own gained knowledge° should profane
If I would time expend with such snipe
But for my sport and profit. I hate the Moor,
And it is thought abroad that 'twixt my sheets 365
H'as done my office. I know not if't be true,
But I, for mere suspicion in that kind,
Will do, as if for surety.° He holds me well;
The better shall my purpose work on him.
Cassio's a proper° man. Let me see now: 370
To get his place, and to plume up my will°
In double knavery. How? How? Let's see.
After some time, to abuse Othello's ears
That he is too familiar with his wife.
He hath a person and a smooth dispose° 375
To be suspected — framed° to make women false.
The Moor is of a free and open nature
That thinks men honest that but seem to be so;
And will as tenderly be led by th' nose

---

³⁴⁵ *compassing* encompassing, achieving
³⁵¹ *hearted* deep-seated in the heart   ³⁵¹⁻⁵² *conjunctive* joined
³⁶² *gained knowledge* i.e., practical, worldly wisdom
³⁶⁸ *surety* certainty   ³⁷⁰ *proper* handsome
³⁷¹ *plume up my will* (many explanations have been offered for this crucial
line, which in Q1 reads "make up my will." The general sense is something like
"to make more proud and gratify my ego")
³⁷⁵ *dispose* manner   ³⁷⁶ *framed* designed

As asses are.   380
I have it! It is engendered! Hell and night.
Must bring this monstrous birth to the world's light.

                                                          [*Exit.*]

ACT II

SCENE I. [*Cyprus.*]

(*Enter Montano and two Gentlemen* [*one above*].)°

Montano. What from the cape can you discern at sea?
First Gentleman. Nothing at all, it is a high-wrought flood.
    I cannot 'twixt the heaven and the main
    Descry a sail.
Montano. Methinks the wind hath spoke aloud at land;   5
    A fuller blast ne'er shook our battlements.
    If it hath ruffianed so upon the sea,
    What ribs of oak, when mountains melt on them,
    Can hold the mortise? What shall we hear of this?
Second Gentleman. A segregation° of the Turkish fleet.   10
    For do but stand upon the foaming shore,
    The chidden billow seems to pelt the clouds;
    The wind-shaked surge, with high and monstrous main,°
    Seems to cast water on the burning Bear
    And quench the guards on th' ever-fixèd pole.°   15
    I never did like molestation view
    On the enchafèd flood.
Montano.   If that the Turkish fleet
    Be not ensheltered and embayed, they are drowned;
    It is impossible to bear it out.

(*Enter a* [*third*] *Gentleman.*)

Third Gentleman. News, lads! Our wars are done.   20
    The desperate tempest hath so banged the Turks

II.i. s.d. (the Folio arrangement of this scene requires that the First Gentleman
stand above — on the upper stage — and act as a lookout reporting sights
which cannot be seen by Montano standing below on the main stage)
10 *segregation* separation
13 *main* (both "ocean" and "strength")
14–15 *Seems . . . pole* (the constellation Ursa Minor contains two stars which
are the *guards*, or companions, of the *pole*, or North Star)

That their designment halts. A noble ship of Venice
Hath seen a grievous wrack and sufferance°
On most part of their fleet.
Montano. How? Is this true?
Third Gentleman.   The ship is here put in,   25
A Veronesa; Michael Cassio,
Lieutenant to the warlike Moor Othello,
Is come on shore; the Moor himself at sea,
And is in full commission here for Cyprus.
Montano. I am glad on't. 'Tis a worthy governor.   30
Third Gentleman. But this same Cassio, though he speak of comfort
Touching the Turkish loss, yet he looks sadly
And prays the Moor be safe, for they were parted
With foul and violent tempest.
Montano.   Pray heavens he be;
For I have served him, and the man commands   35
Like a full soldier. Let's to the seaside, ho!
As well to see the vessel that's come in
As to throw out our eyes for brave Othello,
Even till we make the main and th' aerial blue
An indistinct regard.°
Third Gentleman.   Come, let's do so;   40
For every minute is expectancy
Of more arrivancie.°

(*Enter Cassio.*)

Cassio. Thanks, you the valiant of the warlike isle,
That so approve° the Moor. O, let the heavens
Give him defense against the elements,   45
For I have lost him on a dangerous sea.
Montano. Is he well shipped?
Cassio. His bark is stoutly timbered, and his pilot
Of very expert and approved allowance;°
Therefore my hopes, not surfeited to death,°   50
Stand in bold cure.°   (*Within*) A sail, a sail, a sail!

---

²³ *sufferance* damage
³⁹⁻⁴⁰ *the main . . . regard* i.e., the sea and sky become indistinguishable
⁴² *arrivancie* arrivals
⁴⁴ *approve* ("honor" or, perhaps, "are as warlike and valiant as your governor")
⁴⁹ *approved allowance* known and tested
⁵⁰ *not surfeited to death* i.e., not so great as to be in danger
⁵¹ *Stand in bold cure* i.e., are likely to be restored

Cassio. What noise?

First Gentleman. The town is empty; on the brow o' th' sea
  Stand ranks of people, and they cry, "A sail!"

Cassio. My hopes do shape him for the governor.   55

                                        [*A shot.*]

Second Gentleman. They do discharge their shot of courtesy:
  Our friends at least.

Cassio.   I pray you, sir, go forth
  And give us truth who 'tis that is arrived.

Second Gentleman. I shall.   (*Exit.*)

Montano. But, good lieutenant, is your general wived?   60

Cassio. Most fortunately. He hath achieved a maid
  That paragons° description and wild fame;°
  One that excels the quirks of blazoning pens,°
  And in th' essential vesture of creation°
  Does tire the ingener.°

  (*Enter [Second] Gentleman.*)

                     How now? Who has put in?   65

Second Gentleman. 'Tis one Iago, ancient to the general.

Cassio. H'as had most favorable and happy speed:
  Tempests themselves, high seas, and howling winds,
  The guttered° rocks and congregated° sands,
  Traitors ensteeped° to enclog the guiltless keel,   70
  As having sense° of beauty, do omit
  Their mortal° natures, letting go safely by
  The divine Desdemona.

Montano.   What is she?

Cassio. She that I spake of, our great captain's captain,
  Left in the conduct of the bold Iago,   75
  Whose footing° here anticipates our thoughts
  A se'nnight's° speed. Great Jove, Othello guard,
  And swell his sail with thine own pow'rful breath,
  That he may bless this bay with his tall° ship,

---

⁶² *paragons* exceeds   ⁶² *wild fame* extravagant report
⁶³ *quirks of blazoning pens* ingenuities of praising pens
⁶⁴ *essential vesture of creation* i.e., essential human nature as given by the
Creator
⁶⁵ *tire the ingener* (a difficult line which probably means something like "outdo
the human ability to imagine and picture")
⁶⁹ *guttered* jagged   ⁶⁹ *congregated* gathered
⁷⁰ *ensteeped* submerged   ⁷¹ *sense* awareness   ⁷² *mortal* deadly
⁷⁶ *footing* landing   ⁷⁷ *se'nnight's* week's   ⁷⁹ *tall* brave

Make love's quick pants in Desdemona's arms,   80
Give renewed fire to our extincted spirits.

(*Enter Desdemona, Iago, Roderigo, and Emilia.*)

O, behold! The riches of the ship is come on shore!
You men of Cyprus, let her have your knees.
                                        [*Kneeling.*]
Hail to thee, lady! and the grace of heaven,
Before, behind thee, and on every hand,   85
Enwheel thee round.
Desdemona.   I thank you, valiant Cassio.
What tidings can you tell of my lord?
Cassio. He is not yet arrived, nor know I aught
But that he's well and will be shortly here.
Desdemona. O but I fear. How lost you company?   90
Cassio. The great contention of sea and skies
Parted our fellowship.   (*Within*) A sail, a sail! [*A shot.*]
                              But hark. A sail!
Second Gentleman. They give this greeting to the citadel;
This likewise is a friend.
Cassio.   See for the news.   95

                              [*Exit Gentleman.*]

Good ancient, you are welcome. [*To Emilia*] Welcome, mistress.
Let it not gall your patience, good Iago,
That I extend° my manners. 'Tis my breeding°
That gives me this bold show of courtesy.   [*Kisses Emilia.*]
Iago. Sir, would she give you so much of her lips   100
As of her tongue she oft bestows on me,
You would have enough.
Desdemona.   Alas, she has no speech.
Iago. In faith, too much.
I find it still when I have leave to sleep.°
Marry, before your ladyship,° I grant,   105
She puts her tongue a little in her heart
And chides with thinking.
Emilia.   You have little cause to say so.

---

98 *extend* stretch
98 *breeding* careful training in manners (Cassio is considerably more the pol-
ished gentleman than Iago, and aware of it)
104 *still . . . sleep* i.e., even when she allows me to sleep she continues to scold
105 *before your ladyship* in your presence

Iago. Come on, come on! You are pictures° out of door,
    Bells in your parlors, wildcats in your kitchens,
    Saints in your injuries,° devils being offended,   110
    Players in your housewifery,° and housewives in your beds.
Desdemona. O, fie upon thee, slanderer!
Iago. Nay, it is true, or else I am a Turk:
    You rise to play, and go to bed to work.
Emilia. You shall not write my praise.
Iago.   No, let me not.   115
Desdemona. What wouldst write of me, if thou shouldst praise
    me?
Iago. O gentle lady, do not put me to't,
    For I am nothing if not critical.
Desdemona. Come on, assay. There's one gone to the harbor?
Iago. Ay, madam.
Desdemona. [*Aside*] I am not merry; but I do beguile   120
    The thing I am by seeming otherwise. —
    Come, how wouldst thou praise me?
Iago. I am about it; but indeed my invention
    Comes from my pate as birdlime° does from frieze° —
    It plucks out brains and all. But my Muse labors,   125
    And thus she is delivered:
    If she be fair° and wise: fairness and wit,
    The one's for use, the other useth it.
Desdemona. Well praised. How if she be black° and witty?
Iago. If she be black, and thereto have a wit,   130
    She'll find a white that shall her blackness fit.
Desdemona. Worse and worse!
Emilia. How if fair and foolish?
Iago. She never yet was foolish that was fair,
    For even her folly helped her to an heir.   135
Desdemona. These are old fond° paradoxes to make fools laugh
    i' th' alehouse. What miserable praise hast thou for her that's
    foul and foolish?
Iago. There's none so foul, and foolish thereunto,
    But does foul pranks which fair and wise ones do.   140

---

108 *pictures* models (of virtue)   110 *in your injuries* when you injure others
111 *housewifery* (this word can mean "careful, economical household management," and Iago would then be accusing women of only pretending to be good
housekeepers, while in bed they are either [1] economical of their favors, or
more likely [2] serious and dedicated workers)
124 *birdlime* a sticky substance put on branches to catch birds
124 *frieze* rough cloth   127 *fair* light-complexioned   129 *black* brunette
136 *fond* foolish

Desdemona. O heavy ignorance. Thou praisest the worst best. But
   what praise couldst thou bestow on a deserving woman indeed
   —one that in the authority of her merit did justly put on the
   vouch of very malice itself?°
Iago. She that was ever fair, and never proud;   145
   Had tongue at will, and yet was never loud;
   Never lacked gold, and yet went never gay;
   Fled from her wish, and yet said "Now I may";
   She that being angered, her revenge being nigh,
   Bade her wrong stay, and her displeasure fly;   150
   She that in wisdom never was so frail
   To change the cod's head for the salmon's tail;°
   She that could think, and nev'r disclose her mind;
   See suitors following, and not look behind:
   She was a wight° (if ever such wights were) —   155
Desdemona. To do what?
Iago. To suckle fools and chronicle small beer.°
Desdemona. O most lame and impotent conclusion. Do not learn
   of him, Emilia, though he be thy husband. How say you,
   Cassio? Is he not a most profane and liberal° counselor?   160
Cassio. He speaks home,° madam. You may relish him more in°
   the soldier than in the scholar.   [*Takes Desdemona's hand.*]
Iago. [*Aside*] He takes her by the palm. Ay, well said, whisper!
   With as little a web as this will I ensnare as great a fly as
   Cassio. Ay, smile upon her, do! I will gyve° thee in thine own 165
   courtship. — You say true; 'tis so, indeed! — If such tricks as
   these strip you out of your lieutenantry, it had been better you
   had not kissed your three fingers so oft — which now again you
   are most apt to play the sir° in. Very good! Well kissed! An
   excellent curtsy!° 'Tis so, indeed. Yet again your fingers to your 170
   lips? Would they were clyster pipes° for your sake! [*Trumpets
   within.*] The Moor! I know his trumpet.°
Cassio. 'Tis truly so.

143–44 *one . . . itself* i.e., a woman so honest and deserving that even malice
would be forced to approve of her
152 *To . . . tail* i.e., to exchange something valuable for something useless
155 *wight* person
157 *chronicle small beer* i.e., keep household accounts (the most trivial of occupations in Iago's opinion)
160 *liberal* licentious   161 *speaks home* thrusts deeply with his speech
161 *relish him more in* enjoy him more as   165 *gyve* bind
169 *the sir* the fashionable gentleman   170 *curtsy* courtesy, i.e., bow
171 *clyster pipes* enema tubes
172 *his trumpet* (great men had their own distinctive calls)

Desdemona. Let's meet him and receive him.
Cassio. Lo, where he comes.   175

(*Enter Othello and Attendants.*)

Othello. O my fair warrior!
Desdemona.   My dear Othello.
Othello. It gives me wonder great as my content
  To see you here before me. O my soul's joy!
  If after every tempest come such calms,
  May the winds blow till they have wakened death.   180
  And let the laboring bark climb hills of seas
  Olympus-high, and duck again as low
  As hell's from heaven. If it were now to die,
  'Twere now to be most happy; for I fear
  My soul hath her content so absolute   185
  That not another comfort like to this
  Succeeds in unknown fate.
Desdemona.   The heavens forbid
  But that our loves and comfort should increase
  Even as our days do grow.
Othello.   Amen to that, sweet powers!
  I cannot speak enough of this content;   190
  It stops me here [*touches his heart*]; it is too much of joy.
  And this, and this, the greatest discords be

                    [*They kiss.*]

  That e'er our hearts shall make!
Iago.   [*Aside*] O, you are well tuned now!
  But I'll set down the pegs° that make this music,
  As honest as I am.
Othello.   Come, let us to the castle.   195
  News, friends! Our wars are done; the Turks are drowned.
  How does my old acquaintance of this isle?
  Honey, you shall be well desired in Cyprus;
  I have found great love amongst them. O my sweet,
  I prattle out of fashion, and I dote   200
  In mine own comforts. I prithee, good Iago,
  Go to the bay and disembark my coffers.
  Bring thou the master to the citadel;
  He is a good one, and his worthiness

---

¹⁹⁴ *set down the pegs* loosen the strings (to produce discord)

Does challenge° much respect. Come, Desdemona,   205
Once more well met at Cyprus.

(*Exit Othello and Desdemona [and all but Iago and Roderigo].*)

Iago. [*To an Attendant*] Do thou meet me presently at the harbor.
[*To Roderigo*] Come hither. If thou be'st valiant (as they say
base men being in love have then a nobility in their natures
more than is native to them), list me. The lieutenant tonight   210
watches on the court of guard.° First, I must tell thee this:
Desdemona is directly in love with him.

Roderigo. With him? Why, 'tis not possible.

Iago. Lay thy finger thus [*puts his finger to his lips*], and let thy
soul be instructed. Mark me with what violence she first loved 215
the Moor but for bragging and telling her fantastical lies. To
love him still for prating? Let not thy discreet heart think it.
Her eye must be fed. And what delight shall she have to look
on the devil? When the blood is made dull with the act of
sport, there should be a game° to inflame it and to give satiety 220
a fresh appetite, loveliness in favor,° sympathy in years,° manners, and beauties; all which the Moor is defective in. Now for
want of these required conveniences,° her delicate tenderness
will find itself abused, begin to heave the gorge,° disrelish and
abhor the Moor. Very nature will instruct her in it and compel 225
her to some second choice. Now, sir, this granted — as it is a
most pregnant° and unforced position — who stands so eminent in the degree of this fortune as Cassio does? A knave very
voluble; no further conscionable° than in putting on the mere
form of civil and humane° seeming for the better compass of   230
his salt° and most hidden loose° affection. Why, none! Why,
none! A slipper° and subtle knave, a finder of occasion, that has
an eye can stamp and counterfeit advantages, though true advantage never present itself. A devilish knave. Besides, the knave
is handsome, young, and hath all those requisites in him that   235
folly and green minds look after. A pestilent complete knave,
and the woman hath found him already.

Roderigo. I cannot believe that in her; she's full of most blessed
condition.

---

205 *challenge* require, exact   211 *court of guard* guardhouse
220 *game* sport (with the added sense of "gamey," "rank")
221 *favor* countenance, appearance   221 *sympathy in years* sameness of age
223 *conveniences* advantages   224 *heave the gorge* vomit
227 *pregnant* likely   229 *no further conscionable* having no more conscience
230 *humane* polite   231 *salt* lecherous   231 *loose* immoral
232 *slipper* slippery

Iago. Blessed fig's-end! The wine she drinks is made of grapes. If   240
   she had been blessed, she would never have loved the Moor.
   Blessed pudding! Didst thou not see her paddle with the palm
   of his hand? Didst not mark that?

Roderigo. Yes, that I did; but that was but courtesy.

Iago. Lechery, by this hand! [*Extends his index finger.*] An index°   245
   and obscure prologue to the history of lust and foul thoughts.
   They met so near with their lips that their breaths embraced
   together. Villainous thoughts, Roderigo. When these mutuali-
   ties so marshal the way, hard at hand comes the master and
   main exercise, th' incorporate° conclusion: Pish! But, sir, be   250
   you ruled by me. I have brought you from Venice. Watch you
   tonight; for the command, I'll lay't upon you. Cassio knows you
   not. I'll not be far from you. Do you find some occasion to
   anger Cassio, either by speaking too loud, or tainting° his discipline, or from what other course you please which the time   255
   shall more favorably minister.

Roderigo. Well.

Iago. Sir, he's rash and very sudden in choler,° and haply may
   strike at you. Provoke him that he may; for even out of that
   will I cause these of Cyprus to mutiny, whose qualification   260
   shall come into no true taste° again but by the displanting of
   Cassio. So shall you have a shorter journey to your desires by
   the means I shall then have to prefer them; and the impedi-
   ment most profitably removed without the which there were
   no expectation of our prosperity.   265

Roderigo. I will do this if you can bring it to any opportunity.

Iago. I warrant thee. Meet me by and by at the citadel. I must
   fetch his necessaries ashore. Farewell.

Roderigo. Adieu.   (*Exit.*)

Iago. That Cassio loves her, I do well believe 't;   270
   That she loves him, 'tis apt and of great credit.
   The Moor, howbeit that I endure him not,
   Is of a constant, loving, noble nature,
   And I dare think he'll prove to Desdemona
   A most dear° husband. Now I do love her too;   275
   Not out of absolute° lust, though peradventure°

---

²⁴⁵ *index* pointer   ²⁵⁰ *incorporate* carnal
²⁵⁴ *tainting* discrediting   ²⁵⁸ *choler* anger
²⁶⁰⁻⁶¹ *qualification . . . taste* i.e., appeasement will not be brought about (wine
was "qualified" by adding water)
²⁷⁵ *dear* expensive
²⁷⁶ *out of absolute* absolutely out of   ²⁷⁶ *peradventure* perchance

I stand accountant for as great a sin,
But partly led to diet° my revenge,
For that I do suspect the lusty Moor
Hath leaped into my seat; the thought whereof   280
Doth, like a poisonous mineral, gnaw my inwards;
And nothing can or shall content my soul
Till I am evened with him, wife for wife.
Or failing so, yet that I put the Moor
At least into a jealousy so strong   285
That judgment cannot cure. Which thing to do,
If this poor trash of Venice, whom I trace°
For his quick hunting, stand the putting on,
I'll have our Michael Cassio on the hip,
Abuse him to the Moor in the right garb°   290
(For I fear Cassio with my nightcap too),
Make the Moor thank me, love me, and reward me
For making him egregiously an ass
And practicing upon° his peace and quiet,
Even to madness. 'Tis here, but yet confused: 295
Knavery's plain face is never seen till used.   (*Exit.*)

SCENE II. [*A street.*]

(*Enter Othello's Herald, with a proclamation.*)

Herald. It is Othello's pleasure, our noble and valiant general, that
upon certain tidings now arrived importing the mere perdition°
of the Turkish fleet, every man put himself into triumph.
Some to dance, some to make bonfires, each man to what sport
and revels his addition° leads him. For, besides these beneficial   5
news, it is the celebration of his nuptial. So much was his
pleasure should be proclaimed. All offices° are open, and there
is full liberty of feasting from this present hour of five till the
bell have told eleven. Bless the isle of Cyprus and our noble
general Othello!   (*Exit.*)   10

278 *diet* feed
287 *trace* (most editors emend to "trash," meaning to hang weights on a dog
to slow his hunting; but "trace" clearly means something like "put on the
trace" or "set on the track")
290 *right garb* i.e., "proper fashion"
294 *practicing upon* scheming to destroy
II.ii.2 *mere perdition* absolute destruction
5 *addition* rank   7 *offices* kitchens and storerooms of food

SCENE III. [*The citadel of Cyprus.*]

(*Enter Othello, Desdemona, Cassio, and Attendants.*)

Othello. Good Michael, look you to the guard tonight.
    Let's teach ourselves that honorable stop,
    Not to outsport discretion.
Cassio. Iago hath direction what to do;
    But notwithstanding, with my personal eye   5
    Will I look to't.
Othello.   Iago is most honest.
    Michael, good night. Tomorrow with your earliest
    Let me have speech with you.   [*To Desdemona*]
      Come, my dear love,
    The purchase made, the fruits are to ensue,
    That profit's yet to come 'tween me and you.   10
    Good night.

        (*Exit [Othello with Desdemona and Attendants].*)
(*Enter Iago.*)

Cassio. Welcome, Iago. We must to the watch.
Iago. Not this hour, lieutenant; 'tis not yet ten o' th' clock. Our
    general cast° us thus early for the love of his Desdemona; who
    let us not therefore blame. He hath not yet made wanton the   15
    night with her, and she is sport for Jove.
Cassio. She's a most exquisite lady.
Iago. And, I'll warrant her, full of game.
Cassio. Indeed, she's a most fresh and delicate creature.
Iago. What an eye she has! Methinks it sounds a parley to provo-   20
    cation.
Cassio. An inviting eye; and yet methinks right modest.
Iago. And when she speaks, is it not an alarum° to love?
Cassio. She is indeed perfection.
Iago. Well, happiness to their sheets! Come, lieutenant, I have a   25
    stoup° of wine, and here without are a brace of Cyprus gallants
    that would fain have a measure to the health of black Othello.
Cassio. Not tonight, good Iago. I have very poor and unhappy
    brains for drinking; I could well wish courtesy would invent
    some other custom of entertainment.   30
Iago. O, they are our friends. But one cup! I'll drink for you.

II.iii.[14] *cast* dismissed   [23] *alarum* the call to action, "general quarters"
[26] *stoup* two-quart tankard

Cassio. I have drunk but one cup tonight, and that was craftily
qualified° too; and behold what innovation it makes here. I am
unfortunate in the infirmity and dare not task my weakness
with any more.   35
Iago. What, man! 'Tis a night of revels, the gallants desire it.
Cassio. Where are they?
Iago. Here, at the door. I pray you call them in.
Cassio. I'll do't, but it dislikes me.   (*Exit.*)
Iago. If I can fasten but one cup upon him   40
 With that which he hath drunk tonight already,
 He'll be as full of quarrel and offense
 As my young mistress' dog. Now, my sick fool Roderigo,
 Whom love hath turned almost the wrong side out,
 To Desdemona hath tonight caroused   45
 Potations pottle-deep;° and he's to watch.
 Three else° of Cyprus, noble swelling spirits,
 That hold their honors in a wary distance,°
 The very elements of this warlike isle,
 Have I tonight flustered with flowing cups,   50
 And they watch too. Now, 'mongst this flock of drunkards
 Am I to put our Cassio in some action
 That may offend the isle. But here they come.

(*Enter Cassio, Montano, and Gentlemen.*)

 If consequence do but approve my dream,
 My boat sails freely, both with wind and stream.   55
Cassio. 'Fore God, they have given me a rouse° already.
Montano. Good faith, a little one; not past a pint, as I am a
soldier.
Iago. Some wine, ho!
 [*Sings*] And let me the canakin clink, clink;   60
   And let me the canakin clink.
   A soldier's a man;
   O man's life's but a span,
   Why then, let a soldier drink.
 Some wine, boys!   65
Cassio. 'Fore God, an excellent song!
Iago. I learned it in England, where indeed they are most potent
in potting. Your Dane, your German, and your swag-bellied°
Hollander — Drink, ho! — are nothing to your English.

---

³³ *qualified* diluted ⁴⁶ *pottle-deep* to the bottom of the cup ⁴⁷ *else* others
⁴⁸ *hold . . . distance* are scrupulous in maintaining their honor
⁵⁶ *rouse* drink ⁶⁸ *swag-bellied* hanging

Cassio. Is your Englishman so exquisite° in his drinking?   70
Iago. Why, he drinks you with facility your Dane dead drunk; he
    sweats not to overthrow your Almain; he gives your Hol-
    lander a vomit ere the next pottle can be filled.
Cassio. To the health of our general!
Montano. I am for it, lieutenant, and I'll do you justice.   75
Iago. O sweet England!
    [*Sings*] King Stephen was and a worthy peer;
            His breeches cost him but a crown;
            He held them sixpence all too dear,
            With that he called the tailor lown.°   80
            He was a wight of high renown,
            And thou art but of low degree:
            'Tis pride that pulls the country down;
            And take thine auld cloak about thee.
    Some wine, ho!   85
Cassio. 'Fore God, this is a more exquisite song than the other.
Iago. Will you hear't again?
Cassio. No, for I hold him to be unworthy of his place that does
    those things. Well, God's above all; and there be souls must
    be saved, and there be souls must not be saved.   90
Iago. It's true, good lieutenant.
Cassio. For mine own part — no offense to the general, nor any
    man of quality — I hope to be saved.
Iago. And so do I too, lieutenant.
Cassio. Ay, but, by your leave, not before me. The lieutenant is   95
    to be saved before the ancient. Let's have no more of this; let's
    to our affairs. — God forgive us our sins! — Gentlemen, let's
    look to our business. Do not think, gentlemen, I am drunk.
    This is my ancient; this is my right hand, and this is my left.
    I am not drunk now. I can stand well enough, and I speak well   100
    enough.
Gentlemen. Excellent well!
Cassio. Why, very well then. You must not think then that I am
    drunk.   (*Exit.*)
Montano. To th' platform, masters. Come, let's set the watch.   105
Iago. You see this fellow that is gone before.
    He's a soldier fit to stand by Caesar
    And give direction; and do but see his vice.
    'Tis to his virtue a just equinox,°

---

70 *exquisite* superb   80 *lown* lout
109 *just equinox* exact balance (of dark and light)

The one as long as th' other. 'Tis pity of him.   110
I fear the trust Othello puts him in,
On some odd time of his infirmity,
Will shake this island.
Montano.   But is he often thus?
Iago. 'Tis evermore his prologue to his sleep:
He'll watch the horologe a double set°   115
If drink rock not his cradle.
Montano.   It were well
The general were put in mind of it.
Perhaps he sees it not, or his good nature
Prizes the virtue that appears in Cassio
And looks not on his evils. Is not this true?   120

(*Enter Roderigo.*)

Iago. [*Aside*] How now, Roderigo?
I pray you after the lieutenant, go!   [*Exit Roderigo.*]
Montano. And 'tis great pity that the noble Moor
Should hazard such a place as his own second
With one of an ingraft° infirmity.   125
It were an honest action to say so
To the Moor.
Iago.   Not I, for this fair island!
I do love Cassio well and would do much
To cure him of this evil.   (*Help! Help! Within.*)
But hark! What noise?

(*Enter Cassio, pursuing Roderigo.*)

Cassio. Zounds, you rogue! You rascal!   130
Montano. What's the matter, lieutenant?
Cassio. A knave teach me my duty? I'll beat the knave into a
twiggen° bottle.
Roderigo. Beat me?
Cassio. Dost thou prate, rogue?   [*Strikes him.*]   135
Montano. Nay, good lieutenant! I pray you, sir, hold your hand.
                                                    [*Stays him.*]
Cassio. Let me go, sir, or I'll knock you o'er the mazzard.°
Montano. Come, come, you're drunk!
Cassio. Drunk?   [*They fight.*]
Iago. [*Aside to Roderigo*] Away, I say! Go out and cry a mutiny!   140
                                                    [*Exit Roderigo.*]

---

¹¹⁵ *watch . . . set* stay awake twice around the clock   ¹²⁵ *ingraft* ingrained
¹³³ *twiggen* wicker-covered   ¹³⁷ *mazzard* head

Nay, good lieutenant. God's will, gentlemen!
Help, ho! Lieutenant. Sir. Montano.
Help, masters! Here's a goodly watch indeed!

[*A bell rung.*]

Who's that which rings the bell? Diablo, ho!
The town will rise. God's will, lieutenant,   145
You'll be ashamed forever.

(*Enter Othello and Attendants.*)

Othello.   What is the matter here?
Montano. Zounds, I bleed still. I am hurt to the death.
   He dies.   [*He and Cassio fight again.*]
Othello. Hold for your lives!
Iago. Hold, ho! Lieutenant. Sir. Montano. Gentlemen!   150
   Have you forgot all place of sense and duty?
   Hold! The general speaks to you. Hold, for shame!
Othello. Why, how now, ho? From whence ariseth this?
   Are we turned Turks, and to ourselves do that
   Which heaven hath forbid the Ottomites?°   155
   From Christian shame put by this barbarous brawl!
   He that stirs next to carve for his own rage
   Holds his soul light;° he dies upon his motion.
   Silence that dreadful bell! It frights the isle
   From her propriety.° What is the matter, masters?   160
   Honest Iago, that looks dead with grieving,
   Speak. Who began this? On thy love, I charge thee.
Iago. I do not know. Friends all, but now, even now,
   In quarter° and in terms like bride and groom
   Devesting them for bed; and then, but now —   165
   As if some planet had unwitted men —
   Swords out, and tilting one at other's breasts
   In opposition bloody. I cannot speak
   Any beginning to this peevish odds,°
   And would in action glorious I had lost   170
   Those legs that brought me to a part of it!
Othello. How comes it, Michael, you are thus forgot?
Cassio. I pray you pardon me; I cannot speak.
Othello. Worthy Montano, you were wont to be civil;
   The gravity and stillness of your truth   175
   The world hath noted, and your name is great

---

¹⁵⁵ *heaven . . . Ottomites* i.e., by sending the storm which dispersed the Turks
¹⁵⁸ *Holds his soul light* values his soul lightly   ¹⁶⁰ *propriety* proper order
¹⁶⁴ *In quarter* on duty   ¹⁶⁹ *odds* quarrel

In mouths of wisest censure.° What's the matter
That you unlace° your reputation thus
And spend your rich opinion° for the name
Of a night-brawler? Give me answer to it.   180
Montano. Worthy Othello, I am hurt to danger.
Your officer, Iago, can inform you,
While I spare speech, which something now offends° me,
Of all that I do know; nor know I aught
By me that's said or done amiss this night,   185
Unless self-charity be sometimes a vice,
And to defend ourselves it be a sin
When violence assails us.
Othello.   Now, by heaven,
My blood begins my safer guides to rule,
And passion, having my best judgment collied,°   190
Assays to lead the way. If I once stir
Or do but lift this arm, the best of you
Shall sink in my rebuke. Give me to know
How this foul rout began, who set it on;
And he that is approved in this offense,   195
Though he had twinned with me, both at a birth,
Shall lose me. What? In a town of war
Yet wild, the people's hearts brimful of fear,
To manage° private and domestic quarrel?
In night, and on the court and guard of safety?   200
'Tis monstrous. Iago, who began't?
Montano. If partially affined, or leagued in office,°
Thou dost deliver more or less than truth,
Thou art no soldier.
Iago.   Touch me not so near.
I had rather have this tongue cut from my mouth   205
Than it should do offense to Michael Cassio.
Yet I persuade myself to speak the truth
Shall nothing wrong him. This it is, general.
Montano and myself being in speech,
There comes a fellow crying out for help,   210
And Cassio following him with determined sword

---

[177] *censure* judgment
[178] *unlace* undo (the term refers specifically to the dressing of a wild boar killed
in the hunt)   [179] *opinion* reputation   [183] *offends* harms, hurts
[190] *collied* darkened   [199] *manage* conduct
[202] *If . . . office* if you are partial because you are related ("affined") or the
brother officer (of Cassio)

To execute upon him. Sir, this gentleman
Steps in to Cassio and entreats his pause.
Myself the crying fellow did pursue,
Lest by his clamor — as it so fell out —   215
The town might fall in fright. He, swift of foot,
Outran my purpose; and I returned then rather
For that I heard the clink and fall of swords,
And Cassio high in oath; which till tonight
I ne'er might say before. When I came back —   220
For this was brief — I found them close together
At blow and thrust, even as again they were
When you yourself did part them.
More of this matter cannot I report;
But men are men; the best sometimes forget.   225
Though Cassio did some little wrong to him,
As men in rage strike those that wish them best,
Yet surely Cassio I believe received
From him that fled some strange indignity,
Which patience could not pass.°
Othello.   I know, Iago,   230
Thy honesty and love doth mince° this matter,
Making it light to Cassio. Cassio, I love thee;
But never more be officer of mine.

(*Enter Desdemona, attended.*)

Look if my gentle love be not raised up.
I'll make thee an example.
Desdemona.   What is the matter, dear.   235
Othello. All's well, sweeting; come away to bed.
[*To Montano*] Sir, for your hurts, myself will be your surgeon.
Lead him off.   [*Montano led off.*]
Iago, look with care about the town
And silence those whom this vile brawl distracted.   240
Come, Desdemona: 'tis the soldiers' life
To have their balmy slumbers waked with strife.

(*Exit [with all but Iago and Cassio].*)

Iago. What, are you hurt, lieutenant?
Cassio. Ay, past all surgery.
Iago. Marry, God forbid!   245
Cassio. Reputation, reputation, reputation! O, I have lost my repu-

---

²³⁰ *pass* allow to pass   ²³¹ *mince* cut up (i.e., tell only part of)

tation! I have lost the immortal part of myself, and what remains is bestial. My reputation, Iago, my reputation.

Iago. As I am an honest man, I had thought you had received
some bodily wound. There is more sense° in that than in repu-   250
tation. Reputation is an idle and most false imposition,° oft got
without merit and lost without deserving. You have lost no
reputation at all unless you repute yourself such a loser. What,
man, there are more ways to recover the general again. You are
but now cast in his mood° — a punishment more in policy°   255
than in malice — even so as one would beat his offenseless dog
to affright an imperious lion. Sue to him again, and he's yours.

Cassio. I will rather sue to be despised than to deceive so good a
commander with so slight, so drunken, and so indiscreet an officer. Drunk! And speak parrot!° And squabble! Swagger! Swear!   260
and discourse fustian° with one's own shadow! O thou invisible
spirit of wine, if thou hast no name to be known by, let us call
thee devil!

Iago. What was he that you followed with your sword? What had
he done to you?   265

Cassio. I know not.

Iago. Is't possible?

Cassio. I remember a mass of things, but nothing distinctly: a
quarrel, but nothing wherefore. O God, that men should put an
enemy in their mouths to steal away their brains! that we   270
should with joy, pleasance, revel, and applause transform ourselves into beasts!

Iago. Why, but you are now well enough. How came you thus
recovered?

Cassio. It hath pleased the devil drunkenness to give place to the   275
devil wrath. One unperfectness shows me another, to make me
frankly despise myself.

Iago. Come, you are too severe a moraler. As the time, the place,
and the condition of this country stands, I could heartily wish
this had not befall'n; but since it is as it is, mend it for your   280
own good.

Cassio. I will ask him for my place again: he shall tell me I am a
drunkard. Had I as many mouths as Hydra, such an answer
would stop them all. To be now a sensible man, by and by a

---

250 *sense* physical feeling   251 *imposition* external thing
255 *cast in his mood* dismissed because of his anger
255 *in policy* politically necessary   260 *speak parrot* gabble without sense
261 *discourse fustian* speak nonsense ("fustian" was a coarse cotton cloth used
for stuffing)

fool, and presently a beast! O strange! Every inordinate cup is 285
unblest, and the ingredient is a devil.

Iago. Come, come, good wine is a good familiar creature if it be
well used. Exclaim no more against it. And, good lieutenant, I
think you think I love you.

Cassio. I have well approved it, sir. I drunk? 290

Iago. You or any man living may be drunk at a time, man. I tell
you what you shall do. Our general's wife is now the general. I
may say so in this respect, for that he hath devoted and given
up himself to the contemplation, mark, and devotement of her
parts° and graces. Confess yourself freely to her; importune her 295
help to put you in your place again. She is of so free, so kind,
so apt, so blessed a disposition she holds it a vice in her goodness not to do more than she is requested. This broken joint
between you and her husband entreat her to splinter;° and my
fortunes again any lay° worth naming, this crack of your love 300
shall grow stronger than it was before.

Cassio. You advise me well.

Iago. I protest, in the sincerity of love and honest kindness.

Cassio. I think it freely; and betimes in the morning I will beseech
the virtuous Desdemona to undertake for me. I am desperate 305
of my fortunes if they check° me.

Iago. You are in the right. Good night, lieutenant; I must to the
watch.

Cassio. Good night, honest Iago. (*Exit Cassio.*)

Iago. And what's he then that says I play the villain, 310
When this advice is free° I give, and honest,
Probal to° thinking, and indeed the course
To win the Moor again? For 'tis most easy
Th' inclining° Desdemona to subdue
In an honest suit; she's framed as fruitful° 315
As the free elements.° And then for her
To win the Moor — were't to renounce his baptism,
All seals and symbols of redeemèd sin —
His soul is so enfettered to her love
That she may make, unmake, do what she list, 320
Even as her appetite° shall play the god
With his weak function.° How am I then a villain

294–95 *devotement of her parts* devotion to her qualities   299 *splinter* splint
300 *lay* wager   306 *check* repulse   311 *free* generous and open
312 *Probal to* provable by   314 *inclining* inclined (to be helpful)
315 *framed as fruitful* made as generous   316 *elements* i.e., basic nature
321 *appetite* liking   322 *function* thought

To counsel Cassio to this parallel course,
Directly to his good? Divinity of hell!
When devils will the blackest sins put on,°   325
They do suggest at first with heavenly shows,°
As I do now. For whiles this honest fool
Plies Desdemona to repair his fortune,
And she for him pleads strongly to the Moor,
I'll pour this pestilence into his ear: 330
That she repeals him° for her body's lust;
And by how much she strives to do him good,
She shall undo her credit with the Moor.
So will I turn her virtue into pitch,
And out of her own goodness make the net   335
That shall enmesh them all. How now, Roderigo?

(Enter Roderigo.)

Roderigo. I do follow here in the chase, not like a hound that
hunts, but one that fills up the cry.° My money is almost
spent; I have been tonight exceedingly well cudgeled; and I
think the issue will be, I shall have so much experience for my   340
pains; and so, with no money at all, and a little more wit, re-
turn again to Venice.
Iago. How poor are they that have not patience!
What wound did ever heal but by degrees?
Thou know'st we work by wit, and not by witchcraft;   345
And wit depends on dilatory time.
Does't not go well? Cassio hath beaten thee,
And thou by that small hurt hath cashiered Cassio.
Though other things grow fair against the sun,
Yet fruits that blossom first will first be ripe.   350
Content thyself awhile. By the mass, 'tis morning!
Pleasure and action make the hours seem short.
Retire thee; go where thou art billeted.
Away, I say! Thou shalt know more hereafter.
Nay, get thee gone!   *(Exit Roderigo.)*
          Two things are to be done: 355
My wife must move° for Cassio to her mistress;
I'll set her on;

---

³²⁵ *put on* advance, further   ³²⁶ *shows* appearances
³³¹ *repeals him* asks for (Cassio's reinstatement)
³³⁸ *fills up the cry* makes up one of the hunting pack, adding to the noise but
not actually tracking   ³⁵⁶ *move* petition

Myself awhile° to draw the Moor apart
And bring him jump° when he may Cassio find
Soliciting his wife. Ay, that's the way!   360
Dull not device by coldness and delay.   (*Exit.*)

ACT III

SCENE I. [*A street.*]

(*Enter Cassio* [*and*] *Musicians.*)

Cassio. Masters, play here. I will content your pains.°
    Something that's brief; and bid "Good morrow, general."

                                                    [*They play.*]
[*Enter Clown.*°]

Clown. Why, masters, have your instruments been in Naples°
    that they speak i' th' nose thus?
Musician. How, sir, how?   5
Clown. Are these, I pray you, wind instruments?
Musician. Ay, marry, are they, sir.
Clown. O, thereby hangs a tale.
Musician. Whereby hangs a tale, sir?
Clown. Marry, sir, by many a wind instrument that I know. But,   10
    masters, here's money for you; and the general so likes your
    music that he desires you, for love's sake, to make no more
    noise with it.
Musician. Well, sir, we will not.
Clown. If you have any music that may not be heard, to't again.   15
    But, as they say, to hear music the general does not greatly care.
Musician. We have none such, sir.
Clown. Then put up your pipes in your bag, for I'll away. Go,
    vanish into air, away!   (*Exit Musicians*).
Cassio. Dost thou hear me, mine honest friend?   20
Clown. No. I hear not your honest friend. I hear you.
Cassio. Prithee keep up thy quillets.° There's a poor piece of gold
    for thee. If the gentlewoman that attends the general's wife be
    stirring, tell her there's one Cassio entreats her a little favor of
    speech. Wilt thou do this?

---

358 *awhile* at the same time   359 *jump* at the precise moment and place
III.i.¹ *content your pains* reward your efforts   ² s.d. *Clown* fool
³ *Naples* (this may refer either to the Neapolitan nasal tone, or to syphilis —
rife in Naples — which breaks down the nose)   22 *quillets* puns

Clown. She is stirring, sir. If she will stir hither, I shall seem to   25
    notify unto her.°   (*Exit Clown.*)

    (*Enter Iago.*)

Cassio. In happy time, Iago.
Iago.   You have not been abed then?
Cassio. Why no, the day had broke before we parted.
    I have made bold, Iago, to send in your wife;
    My suit to her is that she will to virtuous Desdemona   30
    Procure me some access.
Iago.   I'll send her to you presently,
    And I'll devise a mean to draw the Moor
    Out of the way, that your converse and business
    May be more free.
Cassio. I humbly thank you for't.   (*Exit [Iago].*)
                                I never knew   35
    A Florentine° more kind and honest.

    (*Enter Emilia.*)

Emilia. Good morrow, good lieutenant. I am sorry
    For your displeasure;° but all will sure be well.
    The general and his wife are talking of it,
    And she speaks for you stoutly. The Moor replies   40
    That he you hurt is of great fame in Cyprus
    And great affinity,° and that in wholesome wisdom
    He might not but refuse you. But he protests he loves
      you,
    And needs no other suitor but his likings
    To bring you in again.
Cassio.   Yet I beseech you,   45
    If you think fit, or that it may be done,
    Give me advantage of some brief discourse
    With Desdemona alone.
Emilia.   Pray you come in.
    I will bestow you where you shall have time
    To speak your bosom° freely.   50
Cassio.   I am much bound to you.

                                            [*Exeunt.*]

25–26 *seem . . . her* (the Clown is mocking Cassio's overly elegant manner of
speaking)
36 *Florentine* i.e., Iago is as kind as if he were from Cassio's home town,
Florence
38 *displeasure* discomforting   42 *affinity* family   50 *bosom* inmost thoughts

SCENE II. [*The citadel.*]

(*Enter Othello, Iago, and Gentlemen.*)

Othello. These letters give, Iago, to the pilot
And by him do my duties to the Senate.
That done, I will be walking on the works;
Repair° there to me.
Iago.   Well, my good lord, I'll do't.
Othello. This fortification, gentlemen, shall we see't?   5
Gentlemen. We'll wait upon your lordship.   (*Exeunt.*)

SCENE III. [*The citadel.*]

(*Enter Desdemona, Cassio, and Emilia.*)

Desdemona. Be thou assured, good Cassio, I will do
All my abilities in thy behalf.
Emilia. Good madam, do. I warrant it grieves my husband
As if the cause were his.
Desdemona. O, that's an honest fellow. Do not doubt, Cassio,   5
But I will have my lord and you again
As friendly as you were.
Cassio.   Bounteous madam,
Whatever shall become of Michael Cassio,
He's never anything but your true servant.
Desdemona. I know't; I thank you. You do love my lord.   10
You have known him long, and be you well assured
He shall in strangeness stand no farther off
Than in a politic distance.°
Cassio.   Ay, but, lady,
That policy may either last so long,
Or feed upon such nice° and waterish diet,   15
Or breed itself so out of circumstances,°
That, I being absent, and my place supplied,°
My general will forget my love and service.
Desdemona. Do not doubt° that; before Emilia here
I give thee warrant of thy place. Assure thee,   20

III.ii.⁴ *Repair* go
III.iii.¹²⁻¹³ *He . . . distance* i.e., he shall act no more distant to you than is
necessary for political reasons   ¹⁵ *nice* trivial
¹⁶ *Or . . . circumstances* i.e., or grow so on the basis of accidental happenings
and political needs   ¹⁷ *supplied* filled   ¹⁹ *doubt* imagine

If I do vow a friendship, I'll perform it
To the last article. My lord shall never rest;
I'll watch him tame° and talk him out of patience;
His bed shall seem a school, his board a shrift;°
I'll intermingle everything he does   25
With Cassio's suit. Therefore be merry, Cassio,
For thy solicitor shall rather die
Than give thy cause away.

(*Enter Othello and Iago [at a distance].*)

Emilia. Madam, here comes my lord.
Cassio. Madam, I'll take my leave.   30
Desdemona. Why, stay, and hear me speak.
Cassio. Madam, not now. I am very ill at ease,
  Unfit for mine own purposes.
Desdemona. Well, do your discretion.   (*Exit Cassio.*)
Iago. Ha! I like not that.
Othello.   What dost thou say?   35
Iago. Nothing, my lord; or if — I know not what.
Othello. Was not that Cassio parted from my wife?
Iago. Cassio, my lord? No, sure, I cannot think it
  That he would steal away so guilty-like,
  Seeing your coming.
Othello.   I do believe 'twas he.   40
Desdemona. [*Coming to them*] How now, my lord?
  I have been talking with a suitor here,
  A man that languishes in your displeasure.
Othello. Who is't you mean?
Desdemona. Why, your lieutenant, Cassio. Good my lord,   45
  If I have any grace or power to move you,
  His present° reconciliation take.
  For if he be not one that truly loves you,
  That errs in ignorance, and not in cunning,
  I have no judgment in an honest face.   50
  I prithee call him back.
Othello.   Went he hence now?
Desdemona. I' sooth so humbled
  That he hath left part of his grief with me
  To suffer with him. Good love, call him back.
Othello. Not now, sweet Desdemon; some other time.   55

---

23 *watch him tame* (animals were tamed by being kept awake)
24 *board a shrift* table (seem) a confessional   47 *present* immediate

Desdemona. But shall't be shortly?
Othello.   The sooner, sweet, for you.
Desdemona. Shall't be tonight at supper?
Othello.   No, not tonight.
Desdemona. Tomorrow dinner then?
Othello.   I shall not dine at home;
  I meet the captains at the citadel.
Desdemona. Why then, tomorrow night, on Tuesday morn,   60
  On Tuesday noon, or night, on Wednesday morn.
  I prithee name the time, but let it not
  Exceed three days. In faith, he's penitent;
  And yet his trespass, in our common reason
  (Save that, they say, the wars must make example   65
  Out of her best), is not almost a fault
  T' incur a private check.° When shall he come?
  Tell me, Othello. I wonder in my soul
  What you would ask me that I should deny
  Or stand so mamm'ring° on. What? Michael Cassio,   70
  That came awooing with you, and so many a time,
  When I have spoke of you dispraisingly,
  Hath ta'en your part — to have so much to do
  To bring him in? By'r Lady, I could do much —
Othello. Prithee no more. Let him come when he will!   75
  I will deny thee nothing.
Desdemona.   Why, this is not a boon;
  'Tis as I should entreat you wear your gloves,
  Or feed on nourishing dishes, or keep you warm,
  Or sue to you to do a peculiar profit°
  To your own person. Nay, when I have a suit   80
  Wherein I mean to touch your love indeed,
  It shall be full of poise° and difficult weight,
  And fearful to be granted.
Othello.   I will deny thee nothing!
  Whereon I do beseech thee grant me this,
  To leave me but a little to myself.   85
Desdemona. Shall I deny you? No. Farewell, my lord.
Othello. Farewell, my Desdemona: I'll come to thee straight.°
Desdemona. Emilia, come. Be as your fancies teach you;
  Whate'er you be, I am obedient.   (*Exit* [*with Emilia*].)

66–67 *is . . . check* is almost not serious enough for a private rebuke (let alone
a public disgrace)
70 *mamm'ring* hesitating   79 *peculiar profit* particularly personal good
82 *poise* weight   87 *straight* at once

Othello. Excellent wretch! Perdition catch my soul   90
  But I do love thee! And when I love thee not,
  Chaos is come again.
Iago. My noble lord ——
Othello.   What dost thou say, Iago?
Iago. Did Michael Cassio, when you wooed my lady,
  Know of your love?   95
Othello. He did, from first to last. Why dost thou ask?
Iago. But for a satisfaction of my thought,
  No further harm.
Othello.   Why of thy thought, Iago?
Iago. I did not think he had been acquainted with her.
Othello. O, yes, and went between us° very oft.   100
Iago. Indeed?
Othello. Indeed? Ay, indeed! Discern'st thou aught in that?
  Is he not honest?
Iago.   Honest, my lord?
Othello.   Honest? Ay, honest.
Iago. My lord, for aught I know.
Othello. What dost thou think?
Iago.   Think, my lord?
Othello.   Think, my lord?   105
  By heaven, thou echoest me,
  As if there were some monster in thy thought
  Too hideous to be shown. Thou dost mean something.
  I heard thee say even now, thou lik'st not that,
  When Cassio left my wife. What didst not like?   110
  And when I told thee he was of my counsel°
  Of my whole course of wooing, thou cried'st "Indeed?"
  And didst contract and purse thy brow together,
  As if thou then hadst shut up in thy brain
  Some horrible conceit.° If thou dost love me,   115
  Show me thy thought.
Iago. My lord, you know I love you.
Othello.   I think thou dost;
  And, for I know thou'rt full of love and honesty
  And weigh'st thy words before thou giv'st them breath,
  Therefore these stops° of thine fright me the more;   120
  For such things in a false disloyal knave
  Are tricks of custom;° but in a man that's just

---

100 *between us* i.e., as messenger   111 *of my counsel* in my confidence
115 *conceit* thought   120 *stops* interruptions   122 *of custom* customary

They're close dilations,° working from the heart
That passion cannot rule.
Iago.   For Michael Cassio,
I dare be sworn, I think that he is honest.   125
Othello. I think so too.
Iago.   Men should be what they seem;
Or those that be not, would they might seem none!
Othello. Certain, men should be what they seem.
Iago. Why then, I think Cassio's an honest man.
Othello. Nay, yet there's more in this?   130
I prithee speak to me as to thy thinkings,
As thou dost ruminate, and give thy worst of thoughts
The worst of words.
Iago.   Good my lord, pardon me:
Though I am bound to every act of duty,
I am not bound to that all slaves are free to.   135
Utter my thoughts? Why, say they are vile and false,
As where's that palace whereinto foul things
Sometimes intrude not? Who has that breast so pure
But some uncleanly apprehensions
Keep leets and law days,° and in sessions sit   140
With meditations lawful?
Othello. Thou dost conspire against thy friend, Iago,
If thou but think'st him wronged, and mak'st his ear
A stranger to thy thoughts.
Iago.   I do beseech you —
Though I perchance am vicious in my guess   145
(As I confess it is my nature's plague
To spy into abuses, and of my jealousy
Shape faults that are not), that your wisdom
From one that so imperfectly conceits
Would take no notice, nor build yourself a trouble   150
Out of his scattering and unsure observance.
It were not for your quiet nor your good,
Nor for my manhood, honesty, and wisdom,
To let you know my thoughts.
Othello.   What dost thou mean?
Iago. Good name in man and woman, dear my lord,   155
Is the immediate jewel of their souls.
Who steals my purse steals trash; 'tis something, nothing;

---

[123] *close dilations* expressions of hidden thoughts
[140] *leets and law days* meetings of local courts

'Twas mine, 'tis his, and has been slave to thousands;
But he that filches from me my good name
Robs me of that which not enriches him   160
And makes me poor indeed.
Othello. By heaven, I'll know thy thoughts!
Iago. You cannot, if my heart were in your hand;
    Nor shall not whilst 'tis in my custody.
Othello. Ha!
Iago.   O, beware, my lord, of jealousy!   165
    It is the green-eyed monster, which doth mock
    The meat it feeds on. That cuckold lives in bliss
    Who, certain of his fate, loves not his wronger;
    But O, what damnèd minutes tells° he o'er
    Who dotes, yet doubts — suspects, yet fondly° loves!   170
Othello. O misery.
Iago. Poor and content is rich, and rich enough;
    But riches fineless° is as poor as winter
    To him that ever fears he shall be poor.
    Good God the souls of all my tribe defend   175
    From jealousy!
Othello.   Why? Why is this?
    Think'st thou I'd make a life of jealousy,
    To follow still° the changes of the moon
    With fresh suspicions? No! To be once in doubt
    Is to be resolved. Exchange me for a goat   180
    When I shall turn the business of my soul
    To such exsufflicate and blown° surmises,
    Matching thy inference. 'Tis not to make me jealous
    To say my wife is fair, feeds well, loves company,
    Is free of speech, sings, plays, and dances;   185
    Where virtue is, these are more virtuous.
    Nor from mine own weak merits will I draw
    The smallest fear or doubt of her revolt,
    For she had eyes, and chose me. No, Iago;
    I'll see before I doubt; when I doubt, prove;   190
    And on the proof there is no more but this:
    Away at once with love or jealousy!
Iago. I am glad of this; for now I shall have reason
    To show the love and duty that I bear you
    With franker spirit. Therefore, as I am bound,   195

---

[169] *tells* counts   [170] *fondly* foolishly   [173] *fineless* infinite
[178] *To* *follow still* to change always (as the phases of the moon)
[182] *exsufflicate and blown* inflated and flyblown

Receive it from me. I speak not yet of proof.
Look to your wife; observe her well with Cassio;
Wear your eyes thus: not jealous nor secure.
I would not have your free and noble nature
Out of self-bounty° be abused. Look to't.   200
I know our country disposition well:
In Venice they do let heaven see the pranks
They dare not show their husbands; their best conscience
Is not to leave't undone, but kept unknown.°
Othello. Dost thou say so?   205
Iago. She did deceive her father, marrying you;
And when she seemed to shake and fear your looks,
She loved them most.
Othello.   And so she did.
Iago.   Why, go to then!
She that so young could give out such a seeming
To seel° her father's eyes up close as oak° —   210
He thought 'twas witchcraft. But I am much to blame.
I humbly do beseech you of your pardon
For too much loving you.
Othello.   I am bound to thee forever.
Iago. I see this hath a little dashed your spirits.
Othello. Not a jot, not a jot.
Iago.   Trust me, I fear it has.   215
I hope you will consider what is spoke
Comes from my love. But I do see y' are moved.
I am to pray you not to strain° my speech
To grosser issues, nor to larger reach°
Than to suspicion.   220
Othello. I will not.
Iago.   Should you do so, my lord,
My speech should fall into such vile success
Which my thoughts aimed not. Cassio's my worthy friend —
My lord, I see y' are moved.
Othello.   No, not much moved.
I do not think but Desdemona's honest.   225
Iago. Long live she so. And long live you to think so.

---

²⁰⁰ *self-bounty* innate kindness (which attributes his own motives to others)
²⁰³⁻⁴ *their . . . unknown* i.e., their morality does not forbid adultery, but it
does forbid being found out
²¹⁰ *seel* hoodwink   ²¹⁰ *oak* (a close-grained wood)
²¹⁸ *strain* enlarge the meaning of   ²¹⁹ *reach* meaning

Othello. And yet, how nature erring from itself ———
Iago. Ay, there's the point, as (to be bold with you)
  Not to affect many proposèd matches
  Of her own clime, complexion, and degree,°   230
  Whereto we see in all things nature tends° —
  Foh! one may smell in such a will most rank,
  Foul disproportions, thoughts unnatural.
  But, pardon me, I do not in position°
  Distinctly° speak of her; though I may fear   235
  Her will, recoiling to her better judgment,
  May fall to match° you with her country forms,°
  And happily° repent.
Othello.   Farewell, farewell!
  If more thou dost perceive, let me know more.
  Set on thy wife to observe. Leave me, Iago.   240
Iago. My lord, I take my leave.   [*Going.*]
Othello. Why did I marry? This honest creature doubtless
  Sees and knows more, much more, than he unfolds.
Iago. [*Returns.*] My lord, I would I might entreat your honor
  To scan this thing no farther. Leave it to time.   245
  Although 'tis fit that Cassio have his place,
  For sure he fills it up with great ability,
  Yet, if you please to hold him off awhile,
  You shall by that perceive him and his means.
  Note if your lady strain his entertainment°   250
  With any strong or vehement importunity;
  Much will be seen in that. In the meantime
  Let me be thought too busy in my fears
  (As worthy cause I have to fear I am)
  And hold her free, I do beseech your honor.   255
Othello. Fear not my government.°
Iago.   I once more take my leave.

                        (*Exit.*)

---

230 *degree* social station
231 *in . . . tends* i.e., all things in nature seek out their own kind
234 *position* general argument
235 *Distinctly* specifically
237 *fall to match* happen to compare
237 *country forms* i.e., the familiar appearances of her countrymen
238 *happily* by chance
250 *strain his entertainment* urge strongly that he be reinstated
256 *government* self-control

Othello. This fellow's of exceeding honesty,
　　And knows all qualities,° with a learnèd spirit
　　Of human dealings. If I do prove her haggard,°
　　Though that her jesses° were my dear heartstrings,　　　　260
　　I'd whistle her off and let her down the wind°
　　To prey at fortune. Haply for° I am black
　　And have not those soft parts° of conversation
　　That chamberers° have, or for I am declined
　　Into the vale of years — yet that's not much —　　　　265
　　She's gone. I am abused, and my relief
　　Must be to loathe her. O curse of marriage,
　　That we can call these delicate creatures ours,
　　And not their appetites! I had rather be a toad
　　And live upon the vapor of a dungeon　　　　270
　　Than keep a corner in the thing I love
　　For others' uses. Yet 'tis the plague to great ones;
　　Prerogatived are they less than the base.
　　'Tis destiny unshunnable, like death.
　　Even then this forkèd° plague is fated to us　　　　275
　　When we do quicken.° Look where she comes.

(*Enter Desdemona and Emilia.*)

　　If she be false, heaven mocked itself!
　　I'll not believe't.
Desdemona.　　　　How now, my dear Othello?
　　Your dinner, and the generous islanders
　　By you invited, do attend° your presence.　　　　280
Othello. I am to blame.
Desdemona.　　　　Why do you speak so faintly?
　　Are you not well?
Othello. I have a pain upon my forehead, here.°
Desdemona. Why, that's with watching; 'twill away again.

---

²⁵⁸ *qualities* natures, types of people
²⁵⁹ *haggard* a partly trained hawk which has gone wild again
²⁶⁰ *jesses* straps which held the hawk's legs to the trainer's wrist
²⁶¹ *I'd . . . wind* I would release her (like an untamable hawk) and let her
fly free
²⁶² *Haply for* it may be because　　　²⁶³ *soft parts* gentle qualities and manners
²⁶⁴ *chamberers* courtiers — or perhaps, accomplished seducers
²⁷⁵ *forkèd* horned (the sign of the cuckold was horns)
²⁷⁶ *do quicken* are born　　　²⁸⁰ *attend* wait
²⁸³ *here* (he points to his imaginary horns)

Let me but bind it hard, within this hour   285
  It will be well.
Othello.   Your napkin° is too little;

          [*He pushes the handkerchief away, and it falls.*]

Let it° alone. Come, I'll go in with you.
Desdemona. I am very sorry that you are not well.

                              (*Exit* [*with Othello*].)

Emilia. I am glad I have found this napkin;
  This was her first remembrance from the Moor.   290
  My wayward husband hath a hundred times
  Wooed me to steal it; but she so loves the token
  (For he conjured her she should ever keep it)
  That she reserves it evermore about her
  To kiss and talk to. I'll have the work ta'en out°   295
  And give't Iago. What he will do with it,
  Heaven knows, not I; I nothing° but to please his fantasy.°

  (*Enter Iago.*)

Iago. How now? What do you here alone?
Emilia. Do not you chide; I have a thing for you.
Iago. You have a thing for me? It is a common thing ——   300
Emilia. Ha?
Iago. To have a foolish wife.
Emilia. O, is that all? What will you give me now
  For that same handkerchief?
Iago.   What handkerchief?
Emilia. What handkerchief!   305
  Why, that the Moor first gave to Desdemona,
  That which so often you did bid me steal.
Iago. Hast stol'n it from her?
Emilia. No, but she let it drop by negligence,
  And to th' advantage,° I, being here, took't up.   310
  Look, here 't is.
Iago.   A good wench. Give it me.

---

²⁸⁶ *napkin* elaborately worked handkerchief
²⁸⁷ *it* (it makes a considerable difference in the interpretation of later events
whether this "it" refers to Othello's forehead or to the handkerchief; nothing
in the text makes the reference clear)
²⁹⁵ *work ta'en out* needlework copied   ²⁹⁷ *I nothing* I wish nothing
²⁹⁷ *fantasy* fancy, whim   ³¹⁰ *to th' advantage* being lucky

Emilia. What will you do with't, that you have been so earnest
  To have me filch it?
Iago.   Why, what is that to you?

                                   [*Takes it.*]

Emilia. If it be not for some purpose of import,°
  Give't me again. Poor lady, she'll run mad   315
  When she shall lack° it.
Iago.   Be not acknown on't.°
  I have use for it. Go, leave me.   (*Exit Emilia.*)
  I will in Cassio's lodging lose this napkin
  And let him find it. Trifles light as air
  Are to the jealous confirmations strong   320
  As proofs of Holy Writ. This may do something.
  The Moor already changes with my poison:
  Dangerous conceits are in their natures poisons,
  Which at the first are scarce found to distaste,°
  But, with a little,° act upon the blood,   325
  Burn like the mines of sulfur. I did say so.

  (*Enter Othello.*)

  Look where he comes! Not poppy nor mandragora,°
  Nor all the drowsy syrups of the world,
  Shall ever medicine thee to that sweet sleep
  Which thou owedst° yesterday.
Othello.   Ha! ha! False to me?   330
Iago. Why, how now, general? No more of that.
Othello. Avaunt! be gone! Thou hast set me on the rack.
  I swear 'tis better to be much abused
  Than but to know't a little.
Iago.   How now, my lord?
Othello. What sense had I of her stol'n hours of lust? 335
  I saw't not, thought it not, it harmed not me;
  I slept the next night well, fed well, was free and merry;
  I found not Cassio's kisses on her lips.
  He that is robbed, not wanting° what is stol'n,
  Let him not know't, and he's not robbed at all.   340
Iago. I am sorry to hear this.

³¹⁴ *import* importance   ³¹⁶ *lack* miss
³¹⁶ *Be not acknown on't* forget you ever saw it
³²⁴ *are scarce found to distaste* scarcely can be tasted
³²⁵ *with a little* in a short time   ³²⁷ *poppy nor mandragora* (soporifics)
³³⁰ *owedst* possessed   ³³⁹ *wanting* missing

Othello. I had been happy if the general camp,
    Pioners° and all, had tasted her sweet body,
    So I had nothing known. O now, forever
    Farewell the tranquil mind! Farewell content!   345
    Farewell the plumèd troops, and the big wars
    That makes ambition virtue! O, farewell!
    Farewell the neighing steed and the shrill trump,
    The spirit-stirring drum, th' ear-piercing fife,
    The royal banner, and all quality,   350
    Pride, pomp, and circumstance° of glorious war!
    And O you mortal engines° whose rude throats
    Th' immortal Jove's dread clamors° counterfeit,
    Farewell! Othello's occupation's gone!
Iago. Is't possible, my lord?   355
Othello. Villain, be sure thou prove my love a whore!
    Be sure of it; give me the ocular proof;
    Or, by the worth of mine eternal soul,
    Thou hadst been better have been born a dog
    Than answer my waked wrath!
Iago.   Is't come to this?   360
Othello. Make me to see't; or at the least so prove it
    That the probation° bear no hinge nor loop
    To hang a doubt on — or woe upon thy life!
Iago. My noble lord ——
Othello. If thou dost slander her and torture me,   365
    Never pray more; abandon all remorse;
    On horror's head horrors accumulate;
    Do deeds to make heaven weep, all earth amazed;
    For nothing canst thou to damnation add
    Greater than that.
Iago.   O grace! O heaven forgive me!   370
    Are you a man? Have you a soul or sense?
    God b' wi' you! Take mine office. O wretched fool,
    That lov'st to make thine honesty a vice!
    O monstrous world! Take note, take note, O world,
    To be direct and honest is not safe.   375
    I thank you for this profit, and from hence
    I'll love no friend, sith° love breeds such offense.
Othello. Nay, stay. Thou shouldst be honest.

343 *Pioners* (the basest manual laborers in the army, who dug trenches and mines)
351 *circumstance* pageantry   352 *mortal engines* lethal weapons, i.e., cannon
353 *clamors* i.e., thunder   362 *probation* proof   377 *sith* since

Iago. I should be wise; for honesty's a fool
  And loses that it works for.
Othello.   By the world,   380
  I think my wife be honest, and think she is not;
  I think that thou art just, and think thou art not.
  I'll have some proof. My name, that was as fresh
  As Dian's° visage, is now begrimed and black
  As mine own face. If there be cords, or knives,   385
  Poison, or fire, or suffocating streams,
  I'll not endure it. Would I were satisfied!
Iago. I see you are eaten up with passion.
  I do repent me that I put it to you.
  You would be satisfied?
Othello.   Would? Nay, and I will.   390
Iago. And may; but how? How satisfied, my lord?
  Would you, the supervisor,° grossly gape on?
  Behold her topped?
Othello.   Death and damnation! O!
Iago. It were a tedious° difficulty, I think,
  To bring them to that prospect.° Damn them then, 395
  If ever mortal eyes do see them bolster°
  More than their own! What then? How then?
  What shall I say? Where's satisfaction?
  It is impossible you should see this,
  Were they as prime° as goats, as hot as monkeys, 400
  As salt° as wolves in pride,° and fools as gross
  As ignorance made drunk. But yet, I say,
  If imputation and strong circumstances
  Which lead directly to the door of truth
  Will give you satisfaction, you might have't. 405
Othello. Give me a living reason she's disloyal.
Iago. I do not like the office.°
  But sith I am entered in this cause so far,
  Pricked° to't by foolish honesty and love,
  I will go on. I lay with Cassio lately, 410
  And being troubled with a raging tooth,
  I could not sleep.

384 *Dian's* Diana's (goddess of the moon and of chastity)
392 *supervisor* onlooker   394 *tedious* hard to arrange
395 *prospect* sight (where they can be seen)   396 *bolster* go to bed
400–01 *prime, salt* lustful   401 *pride* heat   407 *office* duty
409 *Pricked* spurred

There are a kind of men so loose of soul
That in their sleeps will mutter their affairs.
One of this kind is Cassio.   415
In sleep I heard him say, "Sweet Desdemona,
Let us be wary, let us hide our loves!"
And then, sir, would he gripe° and wring my hand,
Cry "O sweet creature!" Then kiss me hard,
As if he plucked up kisses by the roots   420
That grew upon my lips; laid his leg o'er my thigh,
And sigh, and kiss, and then cry, "Cursèd fate
That gave thee to the Moor!"
Othello. O monstrous! monstrous!
Iago.   Nay, this was but his dream.
Othello. But this denoted a foregone conclusion,°   425
  'Tis a shrewd doubt,° though it be but a dream.
Iago. And this may help to thicken other proofs
  That do demonstrate° thinly.
Othello.   I'll tear her all to pieces!
Iago. Nay, yet be wise. Yet we see nothing done;
  She may be honest yet. Tell me but this: 430
Have you not sometimes seen a handkerchief
Spotted with strawberries in your wife's hand?
Othello. I gave her such a one; 'twas my first gift.
Iago. I know not that; but such a handkerchief —
  I am sure it was your wife's — did I today   435
See Cassio wipe his beard with.
Othello.   If it be that ——
Iago. If it be that, or any that was hers.
  It speaks against her with the other proofs.
Othello. O, that the slave had forty thousand lives!
  One is too poor, too weak for my revenge.   440
Now do I see 'tis true. Look here, Iago:
All my fond love thus do I blow to heaven.
'Tis gone.
Arise, black vengeance, from the hollow hell!
Yield up, O Love, thy crown and hearted° throne   445
To tyrannous hate! Swell, bosom, with thy fraught,°
For 'tis of aspics'° tongues.

---

⁴¹⁸ *gripe* seize   ⁴²⁵ *foregone conclusion* consummated fact
⁴²⁶ *shrewd doubt* penetrating guess   ⁴²⁸ *demonstrate* show, appear
⁴⁴⁵ *hearted* seated in the heart   ⁴⁴⁶ *fraught* burden   ⁴⁴⁷ *aspics'* asps'

Iago.   Yet be content.°

Othello. O, blood, blood, blood!

Iago. Patience, I say. Your mind may change.

Othello. Never, Iago. Like to the Pontic Sea,°   450
     Whose icy current and compulsive course
     Nev'r keeps retiring ebb, but keeps due on
     To the Propontic and the Hellespont,
     Even so my bloody thoughts, with violent pace,
     Shall nev'r look back, nev'r ebb to humble love,   455
     Till that a capable and wide° revenge
     Swallow them up. [*He kneels.*] Now, by yond marble heaven,
     In the due reverence of a sacred vow
     I here engage my words.

Iago.   Do not rise yet.   [*Iago kneels.*]
     Witness, you ever-burning lights above,   460
     You elements that clip° us round about,
     Witness that here Iago doth give up
     The execution° of his wit, hands, heart
     To wronged Othello's service! Let him command,
     And to obey shall be in me remorse,°   465
     What bloody business ever.°   [*They rise.*]

Othello.   I greet thy love,
     Not with vain thanks but with acceptance bounteous,°
     And will upon the instant put thee to't.°
     Within these three days let me hear thee say
     That Cassio's not alive.   470

Iago. My friend is dead. 'Tis done at your request.
     But let her live.

Othello.   Damn her, lewd minx! O, damn her! Damn her!
     Come, go with me apart. I will withdraw
     To furnish me with some swift means of death
     For the fair devil. Now art thou my lieutenant.   475

Iago. I am your own forever.   (*Exeunt.*)

---

447 *content* patient, quiet
450 *Pontic Sea* the Black Sea (famous for the strong and constant current with
which it flows through the Bosporus into the Mediterranean, where the water
level is lower)
456 *capable and wide* sufficient and far-reaching
461 *clip* enfold   463 *execution* workings, action   465 *remorse* pity
466 *ever* soever   467 *bounteous* absolute
468 *to't* i.e., to the work you have said you are prepared to do

SCENE IV. [*A street.*]

(*Enter Desdemona, Emilia, and Clown.*)

Desdemona. Do you know, sirrah, where Lieutenant Cassio lies?°
Clown. I dare not say he lies anywhere.
Desdemona. Why, man?
Clown. He's a soldier, and for me to say a soldier lies, 'tis stabbing.
Desdemona. Go to. Where lodges he?   5
Clown. To tell you where he lodges is to tell you where I lie.
Desdemona. Can anything be made of this?
Clown. I know not where he lodges, and for me to devise a lodg-
    ing, and say he lies here or he lies there, were to lie in mine
    own throat.°   10
Desdemona. Can you enquire him out, and be edified° by report?
Clown. I will catechize the world for him; that is, make ques-
    tions, and by them answer.
Desdemona. Seek him, bid him come hither. Tell him I have
    moved° my lord on his behalf and hope all will be well.   15
Clown. To do this is within the compass° of man's wit, and
    therefore I will attempt the doing it.   (*Exit Clown.*)
Desdemona. Where should° I lose the handkerchief, Emilia?
Emilia. I know not, madam.
Desdemona. Believe me, I had rather have lost my purse   20
    Full of crusadoes.° And but my noble Moor
    Is true of mind, and made of no such baseness
    As jealous creatures are, it were enough
    To put him to ill thinking.
Emilia.   Is he not jealous?
Desdemona. Who? He? I think the sun where he was born   25
    Drew all such humors° from him.
Emilia.   Look where he comes.

(*Enter Othello.*)

Desdemona. I will not leave him now till Cassio
    Be called to him. How is't with you, my lord?

III.iv.¹ *lies* lodges
9–10 *lie in mine own throat* (to lie in the throat is to lie absolutely and
completely)
¹¹ *edified* enlightened (Desdemona mocks the Clown's overly elaborate diction)
¹⁵ *moved* pleaded with   ¹⁶ *compass* reach   ¹⁸ *should* might
²¹ *crusadoes* Portuguese gold coins   ²⁶ *humors* characteristics

Othello. Well, my good lady. [*Aside*] O, hardness to dissemble!° —
　How do you, Desdemona?
Desdemona.　　　　　　　　Well, my good lord.　　　　　　　　　　30
Othello. Give me your hand. This hand is moist,° my lady.
Desdemona. It hath felt no age nor known no sorrow.
Othello. This argues° fruitfulness and liberal° heart.
　Hot, hot, and moist. This hand of yours requires
　A sequester° from liberty; fasting and prayer;　　　　　　　　35
　Much castigation; exercise devout;
　For here's a young and sweating devil here
　That commonly rebels. 'Tis a good hand,
　A frank one.
Desdemona. You may, indeed, say so;
　For 'twas that hand that gave away my heart.　　　　　　　　40
Othello. A liberal hand! The hearts of old gave hands,
　But our new heraldry° is hands, not hearts.
Desdemona. I cannot speak of this. Come now, your promise!
Othello. What promise, chuck?
Desdemona. I have sent to bid Cassio come speak with you.　　45
Othello. I have a salt and sorry rheum° offends me.
　Lend me thy handkerchief.
Desdemona.　　　　　　　　Here, my lord.
Othello. That which I gave you.
Desdemona.　　　　　　　I have it not about me.
Othello. Not?
Desdemona. No, indeed, my lord.
Othello.　　　　　　　　That's a fault.
　That handkerchief　　　　　　　　　　　　　　　　　　　50
　Did an Egyptian to my mother give.
　She was a charmer,° and could almost read
　The thoughts of people. She told her, while she kept it
　'Twould make her amiable° and subdue my father
　Entirely to her love; but if she lost it　　　　　　　　　　55

---

²⁹ *hardness to dissemble* (Othello may refer here either to the difficulty he has
in maintaining his appearance of composure, or to what he believes to be
Desdemona's hardened hypocrisy)
³¹ *moist* (a moist, hot hand was taken as a sign of a lustful nature)
³³ *argues* suggests
³³ *liberal* free, open (but also with a suggestion of "licentious"; from here on
in this scene Othello's words bear a double meaning, seeming to be normal
but accusing Desdemona of being unfaithful)
³⁵ *sequester* separation　　　⁴² *heraldry* heraldic symbolism
⁴⁶ *a salt and sorry rheum* a heavy, running head cold
⁵² *charmer* magician　　　⁵⁴ *amiable* desirable

Or made a gift of it, my father's eye
Should hold her loathèd, and his spirits should hunt
After new fancies. She, dying, gave it me,
And bid me, when my fate would have me wived,
To give it her. I did so; and take heed on't;   60
Make it a darling like your precious eye.
To lose't or give't away were such perdition
As nothing else could match.
Desdemona.   Is't possible?
Othello. 'Tis true. There's magic in the web° of it.
A sibyl that had numbered in the world   65
The sun to course two hundred compasses,
In her prophetic fury° sewed the work;
The worms were hallowed that did breed the silk,
And it was dyed in mummy° which the skillful
Conserved of maidens' hearts.
Desdemona.   Indeed? Is't true?   70
Othello. Most veritable. Therefore look to't well.
Desdemona. Then would to God that I had never seen't!
Othello. Ha! Wherefore?
Desdemona. Why do you speak so startingly and rash?
Othello. Is't lost? Is't gone? Speak, is it out o' th' way?   75
Desdemona. Heaven bless us!
Othello. Say you?
Desdemona. It is not lost. But what an if it were?
Othello. How?
Desdemona. I say it is not lost.   80
Othello. Fetch't, let me see't!
Desdemona. Why, so I can; but I will not now.
This is a trick to put me from my suit:
Pray you let Cassio be received again.
Othello. Fetch me the handkerchief! My mind misgives.   85
Desdemona. Come, come!
You'll never meet a more sufficient° man ——
Othello. The handkerchief!
Desdemona.   A man that all his time
Hath founded his good fortunes on your love,
Shared dangers with you ——   90
Othello. The handkerchief!
Desdemona. I'faith, you are to blame.

---

[64] *web* weaving   [67] *prophetic fury* seized by the spirit and able to prophesy
[69] *mummy* liquid drained from embalmed bodies
[87] *sufficient* complete, with all proper qualities

Othello. Away!   (*Exit Othello.*)
Emilia. Is not this man jealous?
Desdemona. I nev'r saw this before.   95
   Sure there's some wonder in this handkerchief;
   I am most unhappy in the loss of it.
Emilia. 'Tis not a year or two shows us a man.
   They are all but stomachs, and we all but food;
   They eat us hungerly, and when they are full,   100
   They belch us.

(*Enter Iago and Cassio.*)

                  Look you, Cassio and my husband.
Iago. There is no other way; 'tis she must do't.
   And lo the happiness! Go and importune her.
Desdemona. How now, good Cassio? What's the news with you?
Cassio. Madam, my former suit. I do beseech you   105
   That by your virtuous means I may again
   Exist, and be a member of his love
   Whom I with all the office° of my heart
   Entirely honor. I would not be delayed.
   If my offense be of such mortal kind   110
   That nor my service past, nor present sorrows,
   Nor purposed merit in futurity,
   Can ransom me into his love again,
   But to know so must be my benefit.°
   So shall I clothe me in a forced content,   115
   And shut myself up in some other course
   To fortune's alms.
Desdemona.   Alas, thrice-gentle Cassio,
   My advocation° is not now in tune.
   My lord is not my lord; nor should I know him
   Were he in favor° as in humor altered.   120
   So help me every spirit sanctified
   As I have spoken for you all my best
   And stood within the blank° of his displeasure
   For my free speech. You must awhile be patient.
   What I can do I will; and more I will   125
   Than for myself I dare. Let that suffice you.
Iago. Is my lord angry?

---

108 *office* duty   114 *benefit* good   118 *advocation* advocacy
120 *favor* countenance   123 *blank* bull's-eye of a target

Emilia.   He went hence but now,
And certainly in strange unquietness.
Iago. Can he be angry? I have seen the cannon
When it hath blown his ranks into the air   130
And, like the devil, from his very arm
Puffed his own brother. And is he angry?
Something of moment° then. I will go meet him.
There's matter in't indeed if he be angry.
Desdemona. I prithee do so.   (*Exit [Iago].*)
                    Something sure of state,°   135
Either from Venice or some unhatched practice°
Made demonstrable here in Cyprus to him,
Hath puddled° his clear spirit; and in such cases
Men's natures wrangle with inferior things,
Though great ones are their object. 'Tis even so.   140
For let our finger ache, and it endues°
Our other, healthful members even to a sense
Of pain. Nay, we must think men are not gods,
Nor of them look for such observancy
As fits the bridal. Beshrew me much, Emilia,   145
I was, unhandsome warrior as I am,
Arraigning his unkindness with my soul;
But now I find I had suborned the witness,
And he's indicted falsely.
Emilia.   Pray heaven it be
State matters, as you think, and no conception   150
Nor no jealous toy° concerning you.
Desdemona. Alas the day! I never gave him cause.
Emilia. But jealous souls will not be answered so;
They are not ever jealous for the cause,
But jealous for they're jealous. It is a monster   155
Begot upon itself, born on itself.
Desdemona. Heaven keep the monster from Othello's mind!
Emilia. Lady, amen.
Desdemona. I will go seek him. Cassio, walk here about.
If I do find him fit,° I'll move your suit   160
And seek to effect it to my uttermost.
Cassio. I humbly thank your ladyship.

                    (*Exit [Desdemona with Emilia].*)

---

¹³³ *moment* importance   ¹³⁵ *of state* state affairs
¹³⁶ *unhatched practice* undisclosed plot   ¹³⁸ *puddled* muddied
¹⁴¹ *endues* leads   ¹⁵¹ *toy* trifle   ¹⁶⁰ *fit* receptive

(*Enter Bianca.*)

Bianca. Save you, friend Cassio!
Cassio.   What make you from home?
    How is't with you, my most fair Bianca?
    I' faith, sweet love, I was coming to your house.   165
Bianca. And I was going to your lodging, Cassio.
    What, keep a week away? Seven days and nights?
    Eightscore eight hours? And lovers' absent hours
    More tedious than the dial eightscore times?
    O weary reck'ning.°
Cassio.   Pardon me, Bianca.   170
    I have this while with leaden thoughts been pressed,
    But I shall in a more continuate° time
    Strike off this score° of absence. Sweet Bianca,

            [*Gives her Desdemona's handkerchief.*]

    Take me this work out.
Bianca.   O Cassio, whence came this?
    This is some token from a newer friend.   175
    To the felt absence now I feel a cause.
    Is't come to this? Well, well.
Cassio.   Go to, woman!
    Throw your vile guesses in the devil's teeth,
    From whence you have them. You are jealous now
    That this is from some mistress, some remembrance.   180
    No, by my faith, Bianca.
Bianca.   Why, whose is it?
Cassio. I know not neither; I found it in my chamber.
    I like the work well; ere it be demanded,°
    As like enough it will, I would have it copied.
    Take it and do't, and leave me for this time.   185
Bianca. Leave you? Wherefore?
Cassio. I do attend here on the general
    And think it no addition, nor my wish,
    To have him see me womaned.
Bianca.   Why, I pray you?
Cassio. Not that I love you not.

---

170 *reck'ning* addition   172 *continuate* uninterrupted
173 *Strike off this score* i.e., pay this bill (the *score* being the account of drinks
kept in a tavern)
183 *demanded* asked for (by the person who lost it)

Bianca.   But that you do not love me!   190
  I pray you bring° me on the way a little,
  And say if I shall see you soon at night.
Cassio. 'Tis but a little way that I can bring you,
  For I attend here; but I'll see you soon.
Bianca. 'Tis very good. I must be circumstanced.°   195

                              (*Exeunt omnes.*)

ACT IV

SCENE I. [*A street.*]

(*Enter Othello and Iago.*)

Iago. Will you think so?
Othello.   Think so, Iago?
Iago.   What,
  To kiss in private?
Othello.   An unauthorized° kiss?
Iago. Or to be naked with her friend in bed
  An hour or more, not meaning any harm?
Othello. Naked in bed, Iago, and not mean harm?   5
  It is hypocrisy against the devil.
  They that mean virtuously, and yet do so,
  The devil their virtue tempts, and they tempt heaven.
Iago. If they do nothing, 'tis a venial slip.
  But if I give my wife a handkerchief ——   10
Othello. What then?
Iago. Why, then 'tis hers, my lord; and being hers,
  She may, I think, bestow't on any man.
Othello. She is protectress of her honor too.
  May she give that?   15
Iago. Her honor is an essence that's not seen;
  They have it very oft that have it not.
  But for the handkerchief ——
Othello. By heaven, I would most gladly have forgot it!
  Thou said'st — O, it comes o'er my memory   20
  As doth the raven° o'er the infected house,
  Boding to all — he had my handkerchief.

---

[191] *bring* accompany   [195] *be circumstanced* accept things as they are
IV.i.[2] *unauthorized* illicit   [21] *raven* (a harbinger of death)

Iago. Ay, what of that?

Othello.   That's not so good now.

Iago. What if I had said I had seen him do you wrong?
Or heard him say — as knaves be such abroad°   25
Who having, by their own importunate suit,
Or voluntary dotage° of some mistress,
Convincèd or supplied° them, cannot choose
But they must blab ——

Othello.   Hath he said anything?

Iago. He hath, my lord; but be you well assured,   30
No more than he'll unswear.

Othello.   What hath he said?

Iago. Why, that he did — I know not what he did.

Othello. What? what?

Iago. Lie ——

Othello. With her?

Iago.   With her, on her; what you will.   35

Othello. Lie with her? Lie on her? — We say lie on her when
they belie her. — Lie with her! Zounds, that's fulsome.° —
Handkerchief — confessions — handkerchief! — To confess,
and be hanged for his labor — first to be hanged, and then to
confess! I tremble at it. Nature would not invest herself in such   40
shadowing passion without some instruction.° It is not words
that shakes me thus. — Pish! Noses, ears, and lips? Is't possible? — Confess? — Handkerchief? — O devil!

                                        (*Falls in a trance.*)

Iago. Work on.
My med'cine works! Thus credulous fools are caught,   45
And many worthy and chaste dames even thus,
All guiltless, meet reproach.° What, ho! My lord!
My lord, I say! Othello!

(*Enter Cassio.*)

                    How now, Cassio?

Cassio. What's the matter?

---

25 *abroad* i.e., in the world   27 *voluntary dotage* weakness of the will
28 *Convincèd or supplied* persuaded or gratified (the mistress)
37 *fulsome* foul, repulsive
40–41 *Nature . . . instruction* i.e., my mind would not become so darkened
(with anger) unless there were something in this (accusation); (it should be
remembered that Othello believes in the workings of magic and supernatural
forces)   47 *reproach* shame

Iago. My lord is fall'n into an epilepsy.   50
  This is his second fit; he had one yesterday.
Cassio. Rub him about the temples.
Iago. The lethargy° must have his quiet course.
  If not, he foams at mouth, and by and by
  Breaks out to savage madness. Look, he stirs.   55
  Do you withdraw yourself a little while.
  He will recover straight. When he is gone,
  I would on great occasion° speak with you.

                                        [*Exit Cassio.*]
  How is it, general? Have you not hurt your head?
Othello. Dost thou mock° me?
Iago.   I mock you not, by heaven.   60
  Would you would bear your fortune like a man.
Othello. A hornèd man's a monster and a beast.
Iago. There's many a beast then in a populous city,
  And many a civil° monster.
Othello. Did he confess it?
Iago.   Good, sir, be a man.   65
  Think every bearded fellow that's but yoked
  May draw° with you. There's millions now alive
  That nightly lie in those unproper° beds
  Which they dare swear peculiar.° Your case is better.
  O, 'tis the spite of hell, the fiend's arch-mock,   70
  To lip a wanton in a secure couch,
  And to suppose her chaste. No, let me know;
  And knowing what I am, I know what she shall be.
Othello. O thou art wise! 'Tis certain.
Iago.   Stand you awhile apart;
  Confine yourself but in a patient list.°   75
  Whilst you were here, o'erwhelmèd with your grief —
  A passion most unsuiting such a man —
  Cassio came hither. I shifted him away°
  And laid good 'scuses upon your ecstasy;°

---

53 *lethargy* coma   58 *great occasion* very important matter
60 *mock* (Othello takes Iago's comment as a reference to his horns — which it
is)
64 *civil* city-dwelling   67 *draw* i.e., like the horned ox
68 *unproper* i.e., not exclusively the husband's   69 *peculiar* their own alone
75 *a patient list* the bounds of patience
78 *shifted him away* got rid of him by a stratagem
79 *ecstasy* trance (the literal meaning, "outside oneself," bears on the meaning
of the change Othello is undergoing)

Bade him anon return, and here speak with me;　　　　　80
The which he promised. Do but encave° yourself
And mark the fleers,° the gibes, and notable° scorns
That dwell in every region of his face.
For I will make him tell the tale anew:
Where, how, how oft, how long ago, and when　　　　　85
He hath, and is again to cope your wife.
I say, but mark his gesture. Marry patience,
Or I shall say you're all in all in spleen,°
And nothing of a man.
Othello.　　　　　　　　　Dost thou hear, Iago?
I will be found most cunning in my patience;　　　　　90
But — dost thou hear? — most bloody.
Iago.　　　　　　　　　　　　That's not amiss;
But yet keep time in all. Will you withdraw?

[*Othello moves to one side, where his remarks are not audible
to Cassio and Iago.*]

Now will I question Cassio of Bianca,
A huswife° that by selling her desires
Buys herself bread and cloth. It is a creature　　　　　95
That dotes on Cassio, as 'tis the strumpet's plague
To beguile many and be beguiled by one.
He, when he hears of her, cannot restrain
From the excess of laughter. Here he comes.

(*Enter Cassio.*)

As he shall smile, Othello shall go mad;　　　　　100
And his unbookish° jealousy must conster°
Poor Cassio's smiles, gestures, and light behaviors
Quite in the wrong. How do you, lieutenant?
Cassio. The worser that you give me the addition°
Whose want even kills me.　　　　　105
Iago. Ply Desdemona well, and you are sure on't.
Now, if this suit lay in Bianca's power,
How quickly should you speed!
Cassio.　　　　　　　　　Alas, poor caitiff!°
Othello. Look how he laughs already!

---

81 *encave* hide　　　82 *fleers* mocking looks or speeches　　　82 *notable* obvious
88 *spleen* passion, particularly anger
94 *huswife* housewife (but with the special meaning here of "prostitute")
101 *unbookish* ignorant　　　101 *conster* construe　　　104 *addition* title
108 *caitiff* wretch

Iago. I never knew woman love man so.   110
Cassio. Alas, poor rogue! I think, i' faith, she loves me.
Othello. Now he denies it faintly, and laughs it out.
Iago. Do you hear, Cassio?
Othello.   Now he importunes him
   To tell it o'er. Go to! Well said, well said!
Iago. She gives it out that you shall marry her.   115
   Do you intend it?
Cassio. Ha, ha, ha!
Othello. Do ye triumph, Roman? Do you triumph?
Cassio. I marry? What, a customer?° Prithee bear some charity to
   my wit; do not think it so unwholesome. Ha, ha, ha!   120
Othello. So, so, so, so. They laugh that win.
Iago. Why, the cry goes that you marry her.
Cassio. Prithee, say true.
Iago. I am very villain else.
Othello. Have you scored° me? Well.   125
Cassio. This is the monkey's own giving out. She is persuaded I
   will marry her out of her own love and flattery, not out of my
   promise.
Othello. Iago beckons me; now he begins the story.

                    [*Othello moves close enough to hear.*]

Cassio. She was here even now; she haunts me in every place. I   130
   was the other day talking on the sea bank with certain Vene-
   tians and thither comes the bauble,° and falls me thus about
   my neck ——
Othello. Crying "O dear Cassio!" as it were. His gesture imports it.
Cassio. So hangs, and lolls, and weeps upon me; so shakes and   135
   pulls me! Ha, ha, ha!
Othello. Now he tells how she plucked him to my chamber. O,
   I see that nose of yours, but not that dog I shall throw it to.
Cassio. Well, I must leave her company.
Iago. Before me!° Look where she comes.   140

   (*Enter Bianca.*)

Cassio. 'Tis such another fitchew!° Marry a perfumed one? What
   do you mean by this haunting of me?
Bianca. Let the devil and his dam haunt you! What did you mean

119 *customer* one who sells, a merchant (here, a prostitute)
125 *scored* marked, defaced   132 *bauble* plaything
140 *Before me!* (an exclamation of surprise)
141 *fitchew* polecat, i.e., strong-smelling creature

by that same handkerchief you gave me even now? I was a fine
fool to take it. I must take out the work? A likely piece of work 145
that you should find it in your chamber and know not who left
it there! This is some minx's token, and I must take out the
work? There! [*She throws down the handkerchief.*] Give it
your hobbyhorse.° Wheresoever you had it, I'll take out no
work on't. 150

Cassio. How now, my sweet Bianca? How now? how now?

Othello. By heaven, that should be my handkerchief!

Bianca. If you'll come to supper tonight, you may; if you will not,
come when you are next prepared for.° (*Exit.*)

Iago. After her, after her! 155

Cassio. Faith, I must; she'll rail in the streets else.

Iago. Will you sup there?

Cassio. Yes, I intend so.

Iago Well, I may chance to see you, for I would very fain speak
with you. 160

Cassio. Prithee come. Will you?

Iago. Go to, say no more. [*Exit Cassio.*]

Othello. [*Comes forward.*] How shall I murder him, Iago?

Iago. Did you perceive how he laughed at his vice?

Othello. O Iago! 165

Iago. And did you see the handkerchief?

Othello. Was that mine?

Iago. Yours, by this hand! And to see how he prizes the foolish
woman your wife! She gave it him, and he hath giv'n it his
whore. 170

Othello. I would have him nine years a-killing! — A fine woman,
a fair woman, a sweet woman?

Iago. Nay, you must forget that.

Othello. Ay, let her rot, and perish, and be damned tonight; for
she shall not live. No, my heart is turned to stone; I strike it, 175
and it hurts my hand. O, the world hath not a sweeter creature!
She might lie by an emperor's side and command him tasks.

Iago. Nay, that's not your way.°

Othello. Hang her! I do but say what she is. So delicate with her
needle. An admirable musician. O, she will sing the savageness 180
out of a bear! Of so high and plenteous wit and invention° ——

Iago. She's the worse for all this.

---

149 *hobbyhorse* prostitute   154 *next prepared for* next expected—i.e., never
178 *way* proper course   181 *invention* imagination

Othello. O, a thousand, a thousand times. And then, of so gentle
   a condition?°
Iago. Ay, too gentle.   185
Othello. Nay, that's certain. But yet the pity of it, Iago. O Iago,
   the pity of it, Iago.
Iago. If you are so fond over her iniquity, give her patent to of-
   fend; for if it touch° not you, it comes near nobody.
Othello. I will chop her into messes!° Cuckold me!   190
Iago. O, 'tis foul in her.
Othello. With mine officer!
Iago. That's fouler.
Othello. Get me some poison, Iago, this night. I'll not expostulate
   with her, lest her body and beauty unprovide my mind° again.   195
   This night, Iago!
Iago. Do it not with poison. Strangle her in her bed, even the
   bed she hath contaminated.
Othello. Good, good! The justice of it pleases. Very good!
Iago. And for Cassio, let me be his undertaker.° You shall hear   200
   more by midnight.
Othello. Excellent good!   [*A trumpet.*]
                  What trumpet is that same?
Iago. I warrant something from Venice.

   (*Enter Lodovico, Desdemona, and Attendants.*)

                                       'Tis Lodovico.
   This comes from the Duke. See, your wife's with him.
Lodovico. God save you, worthy general.
Othello.   With° all my heart, sir.   205
Lodovico. The Duke and the senators of Venice greet you.

                                       [*Gives him a letter.*]

Othello. I kiss the instrument of their pleasures.

                                       [*Opens the letter and reads.*]

Desdemona. And what's the news, good cousin Lodovico?
Iago. I am very glad to see you, signior.
   Welcome to Cyprus.   210

184 *gentle a condition* (1) well born (2) of a gentle nature
189 *touch* affects
190 *messes* bits   195 *unprovide my mind* undo my resolution
200 *undertaker* (not "burier" but "one who undertakes to do something")
205 *With* i.e., I greet you with

Lodovico. I thank you. How does Lieutenant Cassio?
Iago.   Lives, sir.
Desdemona. Cousin, there's fall'n between him and my lord
    An unkind° breach; but you shall make all well.
Othello. Are you sure of that?
Desdemona. My lord?   215
Othello. [*Reads*] "This fail you not to do, as you will ———"
Lodovico. He did not call; he's busy in the paper.
    Is there division 'twixt my lord and Cassio?
Desdemona. A most unhappy one. I would do much
    T'atone° them, for the love I bear to Cassio.   220
Othello. Fire and brimstone!
Desdemona.   My lord?
Othello.   Are you wise?
Desdemona. What, is he angry?
Lodovico.   May be th' letter moved him;
    For, as I think, they do command him home,
    Deputing Cassio in his government.°
Desdemona. Trust me, I am glad on't.
Othello.   Indeed?
Desdemona.   My lord?   225
Othello. I am glad to see you mad.
Desdemona.   Why, sweet Othello ———
Othello. Devil!   [*Strikes her.*]
Desdemona. I have not deserved this.
Lodovico. My lord, this would not be believed in Venice,
    Though I should swear I saw't. 'Tis very much.   230
    Make her amends; she weeps.
Othello.   O devil, devil!
    If that the earth could teem° with woman's tears,
    Each drop she falls° would prove a crocodile.°
    Out of my sight!
Desdemona.   I will not stay to offend you.   [*Going.*] 235
Lodovico. Truly, an obedient lady.
    I do beseech your lordship call her back.
Othello. Mistress!
Desdemona.   My lord?
Othello.   What would you with her, sir?
Lodovico. Who? I, my lord?

213 *unkind* unnatural   220 *atone* reconcile   224 *government* office
232 *teem* conceive   233 *falls* drops
233 *crocodile* (the crocodile was supposed to shed false tears to lure its victims)

Othello. Ay! You did wish that I would make her turn.   240
  Sir, she can turn, and turn, and yet go on
  And turn again; and she can weep, sir, weep;
  And she's obedient; as you say, obedient.
  Very obedient. Proceed you in your tears.
  Concerning this, sir — O well-painted passion!   245
  I am commanded home. — Get you away;
  I'll send for you anon. — Sir, I obey the mandate
  And will return to Venice. — Hence, avaunt!

                              [*Exit Desdemona.*]

  Cassio shall have my place. And, sir, tonight
  I do entreat that we may sup together.   250
  You are welcome, sir, to Cyprus. — Goats and monkeys! (*Exit.*)
Lodovico. Is this the noble Moor whom our full Senate
  Call all in all sufficient? Is this the nature
  Whom passion could not shake? whose solid virtue
  The shot of accident nor dart of chance   255
  Could neither graze nor pierce?
Iago.   He is much changed.
Lodovico. Are his wits safe? Is he not light of brain?
Iago. He's that he is; I may not breathe my censure.
  What he might be (if, what he might, he is not)
  I would to heaven he were!
Lodovico.   What, strike his wife?   260
Iago. Faith, that was not so well; yet would I knew
  That stroke would prove the worst.
Lodovico.   Is it his use?°
  Or did the letters work upon his blood°
  And new-create his fault?
Iago.   Alas, alas!
  It is not honesty in me to speak   265
  What I have seen and known. You shall observe him,
  And his own courses° will denote him so
  That I may save my speech. Do but go after
  And mark how he continues.
Lodovico. I am sorry that I am deceived in him.   270

                                        (*Exeunt.*)

262 *use* habit   263 *blood* passion   267 *courses* actions

SCENE II. [*The citadel.*]

(*Enter Othello and Emilia.*)

Othello. You have seen nothing then?
Emilia. Nor ever heard, nor ever did suspect.
Othello. Yes, you have seen Cassio and she together.
Emilia. But then I saw no harm, and then I heard
    Each syllable that breath made up° between them. 5
Othello. What, did they never whisper?
Emilia.   Never, my lord.
Othello. Nor send you out o' th' way?
Emilia. Never.
Othello. To fetch her fan, her gloves, her mask, nor nothing?
Emilia. Never, my lord. 10
Othello. That's strange.
Emilia. I durst, my lord, to wager she is honest,
    Lay down my soul at stake.° If you think other,
    Remove your thought. It doth abuse your bosom.
    If any wretch have put this in your head, 15
    Let heaven requite it with the serpent's curse,°
    For if she be not honest,° chaste, and true,
    There's no man happy. The purest of their wives
    Is foul as slander.
Othello.   Bid her come hither. Go.   (*Exit Emilia.*)
    She says enough; yet she's a simple bawd° 20
    That cannot say as much. This is a subtle whore,
    A closet lock and key of villainous secrets,
    And yet she'll kneel and pray; I have seen her do't.

(*Enter Desdemona and Emilia.*)

Desdemona. My lord, what is your will?
Othello.   Pray you, chuck, come hither.
Desdemona. What is your pleasure?
Othello.   Let me see your eyes. 25
    Look in my face.
Desdemona.   What horrible fancy's this?
Othello. [*To Emilia*] Some of your function,° mistress:

IV.ii.⁵ *that breath made up* spoken   ¹³ *at stake* as the wager
¹⁶ *serpent's curse* (God's curse on the serpent after the fall in Eden)
¹⁷ *honest* chaste   ²⁰ *bawd* procuress
²⁷ *Some of your function* do your proper work (as the operator of a brothel)

Leave procreants alone and shut the door;
Cough or cry hem if anybody come.
Your mystery,° your mystery! Nay, dispatch!   (*Exit Emilia.*)   30
Desdemona. Upon my knee, what doth your speech import?
     I understand a fury in your words.°
Othello. Why, what art thou?
Desdemona.   Your wife, my lord; your true
     And loyal wife.
Othello.   Come, swear it, damn thyself;
     Lest, being like one of heaven, the devils themselves   35
     Should fear to seize thee. Therefore be double-damned:
     Swear thou art honest.
Desdemona.   Heaven doth truly know it.
Othello. Heaven truly knows that thou art false as hell.
Desdemona. To whom, my lord? With whom? How am I false?
Othello. Ah, Desdemona! Away! Away! Away!   40
Desdemona. Alas the heavy day! Why do you weep?
     Am I the motive° of these tears, my lord?
     If haply° you my father do suspect
     An instrument of this your calling back,
     Lay not your blame on me. If you have lost him,   45
     I have lost him too.
Othello.   Had it pleased heaven
     To try me with affliction, had they rained
     All kinds of sores and shames on my bare head,
     Steeped° me in poverty to the very lips,
     Given to captivity me and my utmost hopes,   50
     I should have found in some place of my soul
     A drop of patience. But, alas, to make me
     The fixèd figure for the time of scorn°
     To point his slow and moving finger at.
     Yet could I bear that too, well, very well.   55
     But there where I have garnered up my heart,
     Where either I must live or bear no life,
     The fountain from the which my current runs
     Or else dries up — to be discarded thence,
     Or keep it as a cistern for foul toads   60
     To knot and gender° in — turn thy complexion there,

---

³⁰ *mystery* trade   ³² *words* (Q1 adds to this line, "But not the words")
⁴² *motive* cause   ⁴³ *haply* by chance   ⁴⁹ *Steeped* submerged
⁵³ *The . . . scorn* the very image of scorn in our time
⁶¹ *knot and gender* twist in bunches and procreate

Patience, thou young and rose-lipped cherubin!
I here look grim as hell!°
Desdemona. I hope my noble lord esteems me honest.
Othello. O, ay, as summer flies are in the shambles,°   65
That quicken even with blowing.° O thou weed,
Who art so lovely fair, and smell'st so sweet,
That the sense aches at thee, would thou hadst never been born!
Desdemona. Alas, what ignorant° sin have I committed?
Othello. Was this fair paper, this most goodly book,   70
Made to write "whore" upon? What committed?
Committed? O thou public commoner,°
I should make very forges of my cheeks
That would to cinders burn up modesty,
Did I but speak thy deeds. What committed?   75
Heaven stops the nose at it, and the moon winks;°
The bawdy wind that kisses all it meets
Is hushed within the hollow mine of earth
And will not hear 't. What committed?
Desdemona. By heaven, you do me wrong!   80
Othello. Are not you a strumpet?
Desdemona.   No, as I am a Christian!
If to preserve this vessel for my lord
From any other foul unlawful touch
Be not to be a strumpet, I am none.
Othello. What, not a whore?
Desdemona.   No, as I shall be saved!   85
Othello. Is't possible?
Desdemona. O, heaven forgive us!
Othello.   I cry you mercy° then.
I took you for that cunning whore of Venice
That married with Othello. [*Calling*] You, mistress,

(*Enter Emilia.*)

That have the office opposite to Saint Peter   90

---

⁶¹⁻⁶³ *turn . . . hell* (the rough sense would seem to be, "even Patience would grow pale, turn complexion, at Desdemona's perfidy, but that Othello looks grimly on")
⁶⁵ *shambles* abattoirs
⁶⁶ *quicken even with blowing* become impregnated as soon as they lay their eggs
⁶⁹ *ignorant* unknowing   ⁷² *commoner* prostitute
⁷⁶ *winks* closes its eyes (the moon was the symbol of chastity)
⁸⁷ *cry you mercy* ask your pardon

And keep the gate of hell! You, you, ay, you!
We have done our course; there's money for your pains.

[*Throws her some coins.*]

I pray you turn the key and keep our counsel.   (*Exit.*)
Emilia. Alas, what does this gentleman conceive?
    How do you, madam? How do you, my good lady?   95
Desdemona. Faith, half asleep.
Emilia. Good madam, what's the matter with my lord?
Desdemona. With who?
Emilia. Why, with my lord, madam.
Desdemona. Who is thy lord?
Emilia.   He that is yours, sweet lady.   100
Desdemona. I have none. Do not talk to me, Emilia.
    I cannot weep, nor answers have I none
    But what should go by water.° Prithee tonight
    Lay on my bed my wedding sheets, remember;
    And call thy husband hither.
Emilia.   Here's a change indeed!   (*Exit.*) 105
Desdemona. 'Tis meet I should be used so, very meet.
    How have I been behaved, that he might stick
    The small'st opinion on my least misuse?°

(*Enter Iago and Emilia.*)

Iago. What is your pleasure, madam? How is't with you?
Desdemona. I cannot tell. Those that do teach young babes   110
    Do it with gentle means and easy tasks.
    He might have chid me so; for, in good faith,
    I am a child to chiding.
Iago.   What is the matter, lady?
Emilia. Alas, Iago, my lord hath so bewhored her,
    Thrown such despite° and heavy terms upon her   115
    That true hearts cannot bear it.
Desdemona. Am I that name, Iago?
Iago.   What name, fair lady?
Desdemona. Such as she said my lord did say I was.
Emilia. He called her whore. A beggar in his drink
    Could not have laid such terms upon his callet.°   120
Iago. Why did he so?
Desdemona. I do not know; I am sure I am none such.

---

103 *water* tears   107–08 *stick . . . misuse* base any doubt on my smallest fault
115 *despite* abuse   120 *callet* slut

Iago. Do not weep, do not weep. Alas the day.
Emilia. Hath she forsook so many noble matches,
　　Her father and her country, and her friends,   125
　　To be called whore? Would it not make one weep?
Desdemona. It is my wretched fortune.
Iago.　　　　　　　　　　　Beshrew° him for 't!
　　How comes this trick upon him?
Desdemona.　　　　　　　Nay, heaven doth know.
Emilia. I will be hanged if some eternal villain,
　　Some busy and insinuating rogue,   130
　　Some cogging,° cozening slave, to get some office,
　　Have not devised this slander. I will be hanged else.
Iago. Fie, there is no such man! It is impossible.
Desdemona. If any such there be, heaven pardon him.
Emilia. A halter pardon him! And hell gnaw his bones!   135
　　Why should he call her whore? Who keeps her company?
　　What place? What time? What form? What likelihood?
　　The Moor's abused by some most villainous knave,
　　Some base notorious knave, some scurvy fellow.
　　O heavens, that such companions° thou'dst unfold,°   140
　　And put in every honest hand a whip
　　To lash the rascals naked through the world
　　Even from the east to th' west!
Iago.　　　　　　　　　　Speak within door.°
Emilia. O, fie upon them! Some such squire° he was
　　That turned your wit the seamy side without   145
　　And made you to suspect me with the Moor.
Iago. You are a fool. Go to.
Desdemona.　　　　　　Alas, Iago,
　　What shall I do to win my lord again?
　　Good friend, go to him, for, by this light of heaven,
　　I know not how I lost him. Here I kneel: 150
　　If e'er my will did trespass 'gainst his love
　　Either in discourse of thought° or actual deed,
　　Or that mine eyes, mine ears, or any sense
　　Delighted them in any other form;
　　Or that I do not yet, and ever did,   155
　　And ever will (though he do shake me off
　　To beggarly divorcement) love him dearly,
　　Comfort forswear me. Unkindness may do much,

---

127 *Beshrew* curse　　131 *cogging* cheating　　140 *companions* fellows, rogues
140 *unfold* disclose　　143 *within door* more quietly and moderately
144 *squire* (a term of contempt)　　152 *discourse of thought* thinking

And his unkindness may defeat° my life,
But never taint my love. I cannot say "whore."   160
It does abhor me now I speak the word;
To do the act that might the addition earn
Not the world's mass of vanity could make me.
Iago. I pray you be content. 'Tis but his humor.°
The business of the state does him offense.   165
Desdemona. If 'twere no other.
Iago.   It is but so, I warrant.

> [*Trumpets within.*]

Hark how these instruments summon to supper.
The messengers of Venice stay the meat.°
Go in, and weep not. All things shall be well.

> [*Exeunt Desdemona and Emilia.*]

(*Enter Roderigo.*)

How now, Roderigo?   170
Roderigo. I do not find that thou deal'st justly with me.
Iago. What in the contrary?
Roderigo. Every day thou daff'st° me with some device,° Iago,
and rather, as it seems to me now, keep'st from me all con-
veniency° than suppliest me with the least advantage of hope.   175
I will indeed no longer endure it; nor am I yet persuaded to
put up° in peace what already I have foolishly suffered.
Iago. Will you hear me, Roderigo?
Roderigo. I have heard too much, and your words and perfor-
mances are no kin together.   180
Iago. You charge me most unjustly.
Roderigo. With naught but truth. I have wasted myself out of
my means. The jewels you have had from me to deliver Desdemona would half have corrupted a votarist.° You have told
me she hath received them, and returned me expectations and   185
comforts of sudden respect° and acquaintance, but I find none.
Iago. Well, go to; very well.
Roderigo. Very well? Go to? I cannot go to, man; nor 'tis not
very well. Nay, I think it is scurvy, and begin to find myself
fopped° in it.   190
Iago. Very well.

---

159 *defeat* destroy   164 *humor* mood   168 *stay the meat* await the meal
173 *daff'st* put off   173 *device* scheme
174–175 *conveniency* what is needful   177 *put up* accept   184 *votarist* nun
186 *sudden respect* immediate consideration   190 *fopped* duped

Roderigo. I tell you 'tis not very well. I will make myself known
to Desdemona. If she will return me my jewels, I will give over
my suit and repent my unlawful solicitation. If not, assure yourself I will seek satisfaction of you.   195

Iago. You have said now?

Roderigo. Ay, and said nothing but what I protest° intendment of
doing.

Iago. Why, now I see there's mettle° in thee, and even from this
instant do build on thee a better opinion than ever before.   200
Give me thy hand, Roderigo. Thou hast taken against me a
most just exception;° but yet I protest I have dealt most
directly° in thy affair.

Roderigo. It hath not appeared.

Iago. I grant indeed it hath not appeared, and your suspicion is   205
not without wit and judgment. But, Roderigo, if thou hast that
in thee indeed which I have greater reason to believe now than
ever — I mean purpose, courage, and valor — this night show
it. If thou the next night following enjoy not Desdemona, take
me from this world with treachery and devise engines for° my   210
life.

Roderigo. Well, what is it? Is it within reason and compass?°

Iago. Sir, there is especial commission come from Venice to
depute Cassio in Othello's place.

Roderigo. Is that true? Why, then Othello and Desdemona re-   215
turn again to Venice.

Iago. O, no; he goes into Mauritania and taketh away with him
the fair Desdemona, unless his abode be lingered here by some
accident; wherein none can be so determinate° as the removing
of Cassio.   220

Roderigo. How do you mean, removing him?

Iago. Why, by making him uncapable of Othello's place — knock-
ing out his brains.

Roderigo. And that you would have me to do?

Iago. Ay, if you dare do yourself a profit and a right. He sups   225
tonight with a harlotry,° and thither will I go to him. He knows
not yet of his honorable fortune. If you will watch his going
thence, which I will fashion to fall out° between twelve and
one, you may take him at your pleasure. I will be near to sec-
ond° your attempt, and he shall fall between us. Come, stand   230

---

197 *protest* aver   199 *mettle* spirit   202 *exception* objection
203 *directly* straightforwardly   210 *engines for* schemes against
212 *compass* possibility   219 *determinate* effective   226 *harlotry* female
228 *fall out* occur   229–30 *second* support

not amazed at it, but go along with me. I will show you such
a necessity in his death that you shall think yourself bound to
put it on him. It is now high supper time, and the night grows
to waste. About it.

Roderigo. I will hear further reason for this.   235
Iago. And you shall be satisfied.   (*Exeunt.*)

SCENE III. [*The citadel.*]

(*Enter Othello, Lodovico, Desdemona, Emilia, and Attendants.*)

Lodovico. I do beseech you, sir, trouble yourself no further.
Othello. O, pardon me; 'twill do me good to walk.
Lodovico. Madam, good night. I humbly thank your ladyship.
Desdemona. Your honor is most welcome.
Othello. Will you walk, sir? O, Desdemona.   5
Desdemona. My lord?
Othello. Get you to bed on th' instant; I will be returned forth-
  with. Dismiss your attendant there. Look't be done.
Desdemona. I will, my lord.

(*Exit [Othello, with Lodovico and Attendants].*)

Emilia. How goes it now? He looks gentler than he did.   10
Desdemona. He says he will return incontinent,°
  And hath commanded me to go to bed,
  And bade me to dismiss you.
Emilia.   Dismiss me?
Desdemona. It was his bidding; therefore, good Emilia,
  Give me my nightly wearing, and adieu.   15
  We must not now displease him.
Emilia. I would you had never seen him!
Desdemona. So would not I. My love doth so approve him
  That even his stubbornness, his checks,° his frowns —
  Prithee unpin me — have grace and favor.   20
Emilia. I have laid these sheets you bade me on the bed.
Desdemona. All's one.° Good Father, how foolish are our minds!
  If I do die before, prithee shroud me
  In one of these same sheets.
Emilia.   Come, come! You talk.
Desdemona. My mother had a maid called Barbary.   25
  She was in love; and he she loved proved mad

IV.iii.[11] *incontinent* at once   [19] *checks* rebukes   [22] *All's one* no matter

And did forsake her. She had a song of "Willow";
An old thing 'twas, but it expressed her fortune,
And she died singing it. That song tonight
Will not go from my mind; I have much to do   30
But to go hang my head all at one side
And sing it like poor Barbary. Prithee dispatch.
Emilia. Shall I go fetch your nightgown?
Desdemona. No, unpin me here.
    This Lodovico is a proper man.   35
Emilia. A very handsome man.
Desdemona. He speaks well.
Emilia. I know a lady in Venice would have walked barefoot to
    Palestine for a touch of his nether lip.
Desdemona. [*Sings*]
    "The poor soul sat singing by a sycamore tree,   40
        Sing all a green willow;
    Her hand on her bosom, her head on her knee,
        Sing willow, willow, willow.
    The fresh streams ran by her and murmured her moans;
        Sing willow, willow, willow;   45
    Her salt tears fell from her, and soft'ned the stones —
        Sing willow, willow, willow —"
Lay by these.   [*Gives Emilia her clothes.*]
    "Willow, Willow" ——
Prithee hie° thee; he'll come anon.°   50
    "Sing all a green willow must be my garland.
    Let nobody blame him; his scorn I approve" ——
Nay, that's not next. Hark! Who is't that knocks?
Emilia. It is the wind.
Desdemona. [*Sings*]
    "I called my love false love; but what said he then?   55
        Sing willow, willow, willow:
    If I court moe° women, you'll couch with moe men."
So, get thee gone; good night. Mine eyes do itch.
Doth that bode weeping?
Emilia.   'Tis neither here nor there.
Desdemona. I have heard it said so. O, these men, these men.   60
    Dost thou in conscience think, tell me, Emilia,
    That there be women do abuse their husbands
    In such gross kind?
Emilia.   There be some such, no question.

---

50 *hie* hurry   50 *anon* at once   57 *moe* more

Desdemona. Wouldst thou do such a deed for all the world?

Emilia. Why, would not you?

Desdemona.   No, by this heavenly light!   65

Emilia. Nor I neither by this heavenly light.
   I might do't as well i' th' dark.

Desdemona. Wouldst thou do such a deed for all the world?

Emilia. The world's a huge thing; it is a great price for a small vice.

Desdemona. In troth, I think thou wouldst not.   70

Emilia. In troth, I think I should; and undo't when I had done.
   Marry, I would not do such a thing for a joint-ring,° nor for
   measures of lawn,° nor for gowns, petticoats, nor caps, nor any
   petty exhibition,° but for all the whole world? Why, who
   would not make her husband a cuckold to make him a mon-   75
   arch? I should venture purgatory for't.

Desdemona. Beshrew me if I would do such a wrong for the
   whole world.

Emilia. Why, the wrong is but a wrong i' th' world; and having
   the world for your labor, 'tis a wrong in your own world, and   80
   you might quickly make it right.

Desdemona. I do not think there is any such woman.

Emilia. Yes, a dozen; and as many to th' vantage as would store°
   the world they played for.
   But I do think it is their husbands' faults   85
   If wives do fall. Say that they slack their duties
   And pour our treasures into foreign° laps;
   Or else break out in peevish jealousies,
   Throwing restraint upon us; or say they strike us,
   Or scant our former having in despite° —   90
   Why, we have galls; and though we have some grace,
   Yet have we some revenge. Let husbands know
   Their wives have sense like them. They see, and smell,
   And have their palates both for sweet and sour,
   As husbands have. What is it that they do   95
   When they change° us for others? Is it sport?
   I think it is. And doth affection° breed it?
   I think it doth. Is't frailty that thus errs?
   It is so too. And have not we affections?
   Desires for sport? and frailty? as men have?   100

---

⁷² *joint-ring* (a ring with two interlocking halves)   ⁷³ *lawn* fine linen
⁷⁴ *exhibition* payment   ⁸³ *to . . . store* in addition as would fill
⁸⁷ *foreign* alien, i.e., other than the wife
⁹⁰ *scant . . . despite* reduce, in spite, our household allowance (?)
⁹⁶ *change* exchange   ⁹⁷ *affection* strong feeling, desire

Then let them use us well; else let them know,
The ills we do, their ills instruct us so.°
Desdemona. Good night, good night. Heaven me such uses° send,
Not to pick bad from bad, but by bad mend.   (*Exeunt.*)

ACT V

SCENE I. [*A street.*]

(*Enter Iago and Roderigo.*)

Iago. Here, stand behind this bulk;° straight will he come.
Wear thy good rapier bare, and put it home.
Quick, quick! Fear nothing; I'll be at thy elbow.
It makes us, or it mars us, think on that,
And fix most firm thy resolution.   5
Roderigo. Be near at hand; I may miscarry in't.
Iago. Here, at thy hand. Be bold, and take thy stand.

[*Moves to one side.*]

Roderigo. I have no great devotion to the deed,
And yet he hath given me satisfying reasons.
'Tis but a man gone. Forth my sword! He dies!   10
Iago. I have rubbed this young quat° almost to the sense,°
And he grows angry. Now, whether he kill Cassio,
Or Cassio him, or each do kill the other,
Every way makes my gain. Live Roderigo,
He calls me to a restitution large   15
Of gold and jewels that I bobbed° from him
As gifts to Desdemona.
It must not be. If Cassio do remain,
He hath a daily beauty in his life
That makes me ugly; and besides, the Moor   20
May unfold me to him; there stand I in much peril.
No, he must die. But so, I hear him coming.

(*Enter Cassio.*)

Roderigo. I know his gait. 'Tis he. Villain, thou diest!

[*Thrusts at Cassio.*]

---

102 *instruct us so* teach us to do likewise   103 *uses* practices
V.i.1 *bulk* projecting stall of a shop
11 *quat* pimple   11 *to the sense* raw   16 *bobbed* swindled

Cassio. That thrust had been mine enemy indeed
 But that my coat° is better than thou know'st.   25
 I will make proof of thine.   *[Fights with Roderigo.]*
Roderigo.   O, I am slain!°
Cassio. I am maimed forever. Help, ho! Murder! Murder!

 (*Enter Othello [to one side].*)

Othello. The voice of Cassio. Iago keeps his word.
Roderigo. O, villain that I am!
Othello.   It is even so.
Cassio. O help, ho! Light! A surgeon!   30
Othello. 'Tis he. O brave Iago, honest and just,
 That hast such noble sense of thy friend's wrong!
 Thou teachest me. Minion,° your dear lies dead,
 And your unblest° fate hies.° Strumpet, I come.
 Forth of my heart those charms, thine eyes, are blotted. 35
 Thy bed, lust-stained, shall with lust's blood be spotted.

         (*Exit Othello.*)
 (*Enter Lodovico and Gratiano.*)

Cassio. What, ho? No watch? No passage?° Murder! Murder!
Gratiano. 'Tis some mischance. The voice is very direful.
Cassio. O, help!
Lodovico. Hark!   40
Roderigo. O wretched villain!
Lodovico. Two or three groan. 'Tis heavy night.
 These may be counterfeits. Let's think't unsafe
 To come into the cry without more help.
Roderigo. Nobody come? Then shall I bleed to death. 45
Lodovico. Hark!

 (*Enter Iago [with a light].*)

Gratiano. Here's one comes in his shirt, with light and weapons.
Iago. Who's there? Whose noise is this that cries on murder?
Lodovico. We do not know.

25 *coat* i.e., a mail shirt or bulletproof vest
26 *slain* (most editors add here a stage direction which has Iago wounding
Cassio in the leg from behind, but remaining unseen. However, nothing in the
text requires this, and Cassio's wound can be given him in the fight with
Roderigo, for presumably when Cassio attacks Roderigo the latter would not
simply accept the thrust but would parry. Since Iago enters again at line 46,
he must exit at some point after line 22)
33 *Minion* hussy, i.e., Desdemona   34 *unblest* unsanctified
34 *hies* approaches swiftly 37 *passage* passers-by

Iago.   Do not you hear a cry?
Cassio. Here, here! For heaven's sake, help me!
Iago.   What's the matter?   50
Gratiano. This is Othello's ancient, as I take it.
Lodovico. The same indeed, a very valiant fellow.
Iago. What are you here that cry so grievously?
Cassio. Iago? O, I am spoiled, undone by villains.
  Give me some help.   55
Iago. O me, lieutenant! What villains have done this?
Cassio. I think that one of them is hereabout
  And cannot make away.
Iago.   O treacherous villains!
  [*To Lodovico and Gratiano*] What are you there?
    Come in, and give some help.
Roderigo. O, help me there!   60
Cassio. That's one of them.
Iago.   O murd'rous slave! O villain!

                        [*Stabs Roderigo.*]

Roderigo. O damned Iago! O inhuman dog!
Iago. Kill men i' th' dark? — Where be these bloody thieves? —
  How silent is this town! — Ho! Murder! Murder! —
  What may you be? Are you of good or evil?   65
Lodovico. As you shall prove us, praise us.
Iago. Signior Lodovico?
Lodovico. He, sir.
Iago. I cry you mercy. Here's Cassio hurt by villains.
Gratiano. Cassio?   70
Iago. How is't, brother?
Cassio. My leg is cut in two.
Iago.   Marry, heaven forbid!
  Light, gentlemen. I'll bind it with my shirt.

  (*Enter Bianca.*)

Bianca. What is the matter, ho? Who is't that cried?
Iago. Who is't that cried?   75
Bianca. O my dear Cassio! My sweet Cassio!
  O Cassio, Cassio, Cassio!
Iago. O notable strumpet! — Cassio, may you suspect
  Who they should be that have thus mangled you?
Cassio. No.   80
Gratiano. I am sorry to find you thus. I have been to seek you.

Iago. Lend me a garter. So. O for a chair
　To bear him easily hence.
Bianca. Alas, he faints! O Cassio, Cassio, Cassio!
Iago. Gentlemen all, I do suspect this trash   85
　To be a party in this injury. —
　Patience awhile, good Cassio. — Come, come.
　Lend me a light. Know we this face or no?
　Alas, my friend and my dear countryman
　Roderigo? No. — Yes, sure. — Yes, 'tis Roderigo!   90
Gratiano. What, of Venice?
Iago. Even he, sir. Did you know him?
Gratiano.   Know him? Ay.
Iago. Signior Gratiano? I cry your gentle pardon.
　These bloody accidents must excuse my manners
　That so neglected you.
Gratiano.   I am glad to see you.   95
Iago. How do you, Cassio? — O, a chair, a chair!
Gratiano. Roderigo?
Iago. He, he, 'tis he! [*A chair brought in.*] O, that's well said;°
　　the chair.
　Some good man bear him carefully from hence.
　I'll fetch the general's surgeon. [*To Bianca*] For you, mistress,   100
　Save you your labor. [*To Cassio*] He that lies slain here, Cassio,
　Was my dear friend. What malice was between you?
Cassio. None in the world; nor do I know the man.
Iago. What, look you pale? — O, bear him out o' th' air.

　　　　　　　　　　　　[*Cassio is carried off.*]

　Stay you, good gentlemen. — Look you pale, mistress?   105
　Do you perceive the gastness° of her eye?
　Nay, if you stare, we shall hear more anon.
　Behold her well; I pray you look upon her.
　Do you see, gentlemen? Nay, guiltiness will speak,
　Though tongues were out of use.°   110

　[*Enter Emilia.*]

Emilia. Alas, what is the matter? What is the matter, husband?
Iago. Cassio hath here been set on in the dark
　By Roderigo and fellows that are scaped.
　He's almost slain, and Roderigo quite dead.

---

98 *well said* well done　　106 *gastness* terror
110 *tongues were out of use* men no longer spoke

Emilia. Alas, good gentleman! Alas, good Cassio!   115
Iago. This is the fruits of whoring. Prithee, Emilia,
   Go know of Cassio where he supped tonight.
   [*To Bianca*] What, do you shake at that?
Bianca. He supped at my house; but I therefore shake not.
Iago. O, did he so? I charge° you go with me.   120
Emilia. Oh fie upon thee, strumpet!
Bianca. I am no strumpet, but of life as honest
   As you that thus abuse me.
Emilia.   As I? Fie upon thee!
Iago. Kind gentlemen, let's go see poor Cassio dressed.°
   [*To Bianca*] Come, mistress, you must tell's another tale.   125
   Emilia, run you to the citadel
   And tell my lord and lady what hath happed.

                                             [*Exit Emilia.*]

Will you go on afore?   (*Exeunt* [*all but Iago*].)
                     This is the night
That either makes me or fordoes me quite.°   [*Exit.*]

           SCENE II. [*Desdemona's chamber.*]

(*Enter Othello* [*with a light*], *and Desdemona in her bed.*)

Othello. It is the cause, it is the cause, my soul.
   Let me not name it to you, you chaste stars.
   It is the cause. Yet I'll not shed her blood,
   Nor scar that whiter skin of hers than snow,
   And smooth as monumental alabaster.   5
   Yet she must die, else she'll betray more men.
   Put out the light, and then put out the light.
   If I quench thee, thou flaming minister,°
   I can again thy former light restore,
   Should I repent me; but once put out thy light,   10
   Thou cunning'st° pattern of excelling nature,
   I know not where is that Promethean heat°

---

¹²⁰ *charge* command   ¹²⁴ *dressed* bandaged
¹²⁹ *fordoes me quite* completely ruins me   V.ii.⁸ *minister* worker, servant
¹¹ *cunning'st* most intricate and skillfully wrought (by nature excelling itself)
¹² *Promethean heat* divine fire (Prometheus is the Titan who stole fire from heaven and gave it to man)

That can thy light relume.° When I have plucked the rose,
I cannot give it vital° growth again;
It needs must wither. I'll smell thee on the tree.   15
                              [*He kisses her.*]
O balmy breath, that dost almost persuade
Justice to break her sword. One more, one more!
Be thus when thou art dead, and I will kill thee,
And love thee after. One more, and that's the last!
So sweet was ne'er so fatal. I must weep,   20
But they are cruel tears. This sorrow's heavenly;
It strikes where it doth love. She wakes.
Desdemona. Who's there? Othello?
Othello.   Ay, Desdemona.
Desdemona. Will you come to bed, my lord?
Othello. Have you prayed tonight, Desdemon?
Desdemona.   Ay, my lord.   25
Othello. If you bethink yourself of any crime
    Unreconciled as yet to heaven and grace,
    Solicit for it straight.
Desdemona. Alack, my lord, what may you mean by that?
Othello. Well, do it, and be brief; I·will walk by.°   30
    I would not kill thy unprepared spirit.
    No, heavens forfend! I would not kill thy soul.
Desdemona. Talk you of killing?
Othello.   Ay, I do.
Desdemona.   Then heaven
    Have mercy on me!
Othello.   Amen, with all my heart.
Desdemona. If you say so, I hope you will not kill me.   35
Othello. Humh.
Desdemona. And yet I fear you; for you're fatal then
    When your eyes roll so. Why I should fear I know not,
    Since guiltiness I know not; but yet I feel I fear.
Othello. Think on thy sins.
Desdemona.   They are loves I bear to you.   40
Othello. Ay, and for that thou diest.
Desdemona. That death's unnatural that kills for loving.
    Alas, why gnaw you so your nether lip?
    Some bloody passion shakes your very frame.
    These are portents; but yet I hope, I hope,   45
    They do not point on me.

13 *relume* relight   14 *vital* living   30 *by* nearby

Othello. Peace and be still.

Desdemona. I will so. What's the matter?

Othello. That handkerchief which I so loved and gave thee,
Thou gav'st to Cassio.

Desdemona. No, by my life and soul!
Send for the man and ask him.

Othello. Sweet soul, take heed, 50
Take heed of perjury; thou art on thy deathbed.

Desdemona. Ay, but not yet to die.

Othello. Presently.°
Therefore confess thee freely of thy sin,
For to deny each article° with oath
Cannot remove nor choke the strong conception 55
That I do groan withal. Thou art to die.

Desdemona. Then Lord have mercy on me.

Othello. I say, amen.

Desdemona. And have you mercy too. I never did
Offend you in my life; never loved Cassio
But with such general warranty° of heaven 60
As I might love. I never gave him token.

Othello. By heaven, I saw my handkerchief in's hand!
O perjured woman! thou dost stone° my heart,
And mak'st me call what I intend to do
A murder, which I thought a sacrifice. 65
I saw the handkerchief.

Desdemona. He found it then.
I never gave it him. Send for him hither.
Let him confess a truth.

Othello. He hath confessed.

Desdemona. What, my lord?

Othello. That he hath used thee.

Desdemona. How? Unlawfully?

Othello. Ay. 70

Desdemona. He will not say so.

Othello. No, his mouth is stopped.
Honest Iago hath ta'en order for't.°

Desdemona. O, my fear interprets. What, is he dead?

Othello. Had all his hairs been lives, my great revenge
Had stomach° for them all. 75

---

⁵² *Presently* immediately
⁵⁴ *article* item (of the charge of adultery. Othello makes heavy use of legal
terms in this scene)   ⁶⁰ *warranty* allowance   ⁶³ *stone* turn to stone
⁷² *ta'en order for't* made sure of it   ⁷⁵ *stomach* appetite

Desdemona. Alas, he is betrayed, and I undone!

Othello. Out, strumpet! Weep'st thou for him to my face?

Desdemona. O, banish me, my lord, but kill me not!

Othello. Down, strumpet!

Desdemona. Kill me tomorrow; let me live tonight!   80

Othello. Nay, if you strive ——

Desdemona. But half an hour!

Othello.   Being done, there is no pause.

Desdemona. But while I say one prayer!

Othello.   It is too late.

                       (*Smothers her.*)

(*Emilia at the door.*)

Emilia. [*Calls within.*] My lord, my lord! What, ho, my lord, my lord!

Othello. What noise is this? Not dead? Not yet quite dead?   85
   I that am cruel am yet merciful;
   I would not have thee linger in thy pain.
   So, so.

Emilia. [*Within*] What, ho! My lord, my lord!

Othello.   Who's there?

Emilia. [*Within*] O, good my lord, I would speak a word with you.

Othello. Yes, 'tis Emilia. — By and by. — She's dead. —   90
   'Tis like she comes to speak of Cassio's death.
   The noise was high.° Ha! No more moving?
   Still as the grave. — Shall she come in? Were't good? —
   I think she stirs again. No. — What's best to do?
   If she come in, she'll sure to speak to my wife.   95
   My wife! My wife! What wife? I have no wife.
   O, insupportable! O heavy hour!
   Methinks° it should be now a huge eclipse
   Of sun and moon, and that th' affrighted globe
   Should yawn° at alteration.

Emilia.   [*Within*] I do beseech you   100
   That I may speak with you, O good my lord!

Othello. I had forgot thee. O, come in, Emilia.
   Soft, by and by. — Let me the curtains draw. —

---

⁹² *high* loud (Q1 reads "here")
⁹⁸⁻¹⁰⁰ *Methinks . . . alteration* (the Elizabethans believed that great changes in human affairs were reflected by disorders in nature)
¹⁰⁰ *yawn* gape open (as in an earthquake)

[*Draws the bed hangings and then opens the door.*]

Where art thou?

(*Enter Emilia.*)

                     What's the matter with thee now?

Emilia. O my good lord, yonder's foul murders done!   105

Othello. What? Now?

Emilia. But now, my lord.

Othello. It is the very error° of the moon.

   She comes more nearer earth than she was wont

   And makes men mad.   110

Emilia. Cassio, my lord, hath killed a young Venetian

   Called Roderigo.

Othello.   Roderigo killed?

   And Cassio killed?

Emilia.   No, Cassio is not killed.

Othello. Not Cassio killed? Then murder's out of tune,

   And sweet revenge grows harsh.   115

Desdemona. O, falsely, falsely murdered!

Emilia.   O Lord! What cry is that?

Othello. That? What?

Emilia. Out and alas! that was my lady's voice.

   Help! Help, ho! Help! O lady, speak again!

   Sweet Desdemona! O sweet mistress, speak!   120

Desdemona. A guiltless death I die.

Emilia. O, who hath done this deed?

Desdemona. Nobody — I myself. Farewell.

   Commend me to my kind lord. O, farewell!

                              [*She dies.*]

Othello. Why, how should she be murd'red?

Emilia.   Alas, who knows?   125

Othello. You heard her say herself, it was not I.

Emilia. She said so. I must needs report the truth.

Othello. She's like a liar gone to burning hell!

   'Twas I that killed her.

Emilia.   O, the more angel she,

   And you the blacker devil!   130

Othello. She turned to folly, and she was a whore.

Emilia. Thou dost belie her, and thou art a devil.

---

[108] *error* wandering out of regular course (disorders in the heavens were believed by some to cause disorders on earth, as well as vice versa)

Othello. She was false as water.
Emilia.   Thou art rash as fire to say
  That she was false. O, she was heavenly true!
Othello. Cassio did top her. Ask thy husband else.   135
  O, I were damned beneath all depth in hell
  But that I did proceed upon just grounds
  To this extremity. Thy husband knew it all.
Emilia. My husband?
Othello.   Thy husband.
Emilia.   That she was false to wedlock?
Othello. Ay, with Cassio. Had she been true,   140
  If heaven would make me such another world
  Of one entire and perfect chrysolite,°
  I'd not have sold her for it.
Emilia.   My husband?
Othello. Ay, 'twas he that told me on her first.
  An honest man he is, and hates the slime   145
  That sticks on filthy deeds.
Emilia.   My husband?
Othello. What needs this iterance? Woman, I say thy husband.
Emilia. O mistress, villainy hath made mocks with love!
  My husband say she was false?
Othello.   He, woman.
  I say, thy husband. Dost understand the word?   150
  My friend, thy husband; honest, honest Iago.
Emilia. If he say so, may his pernicious soul
  Rot half a grain a day! He lies to th' heart.
  She was too fond of her most filthy bargain.
Othello. Hah?   155
Emilia. Do thy worst.
  This deed of thine is no more worthy heaven
  Than thou wast worthy her.
Othello.   Peace, you were best.°
Emilia. Thou hast not half that pow'r to do me harm
  As I have to be hurt. O gull! O dolt!   160
  As ignorant as dirt! Thou hast done a deed —

  [*Othello moves to draw his sword.*]

  I care not for thy sword; I'll make thee known.
  Though I lost twenty lives. Help! Help! Ho! Help!
  The Moor hath killed my mistress! Murder! murder!

---

¹⁴² *chrysolite* topaz   ¹⁵⁸ *Peace, you were best* i.e., you had better be silent

(*Enter Montano, Gratiano, and Iago [and Others].*)

Montano. What is the matter? How now, general?   165
Emilia. O, are you come, Iago? You have done well,
 That men must lay their murders on your neck.
Gratiano. What is the matter?
Emilia. Disprove this villain, if thou be'st a man.
 He says thou told'st him that his wife was false.   170
 I know thou didst not; thou'rt not such a villain.
 Speak, for my heart is full.
Iago. I told him what I thought, and told no more
 Than what he found himself was apt and true.
Emilia. But did you ever tell him she was false?   175
Iago. I did.
Emilia. You told a lie, an odious damnèd lie!
 Upon my soul, a lie! A wicked lie!
 She false with Cassio? Did you say with Cassio?
Iago. With Cassio, mistress. Go to, charm° your tongue.   180
Emilia. I will not charm my tongue; I am bound to speak:
 My mistress here lies murdered in her bed.
All. O heavens forfend!
Emilia. And your reports have set the murder on.
Othello. Nay, stare not, masters. It is true indeed.   185
Gratiano. 'Tis a strange truth.
Montano. O monstrous act!
Emilia.   Villainy, villainy, villainy!
 I think upon't — I think I smell't! — O villainy!
 I thought so then. — I'll kill myself for grief. —
 O villainy, villainy!   190
Iago. What, are you mad? I charge you get you home.
Emilia. Good gentlemen, let me have leave to speak.
 'Tis proper I obey him, but not now.
 Perchance, Iago, I will ne'er go home.
Othello. O! O! O!   [*Falls on the bed.*]
Emilia.   Nay, lay thee down and roar,   195
 For thou hast killed the sweetest innocent
 That e'er did lift up eye.
Othello.   O, she was foul!   [*Rises.*]
 I scarce did know you, uncle. There lies your niece,
 Whose breath, indeed, these hands have newly stopped.
 I know this act shows horrible and grim.   200

---

180 *charm* control

Gratiano. Poor Desdemon! I am glad thy father's dead.
  Thy match was mortal to him, and pure grief
  Shore his old thread in twain. Did he live now,
  This sight would make him do a desperate turn;
  Yea, curse his better angel from his side,   205
  And fall to reprobation.°
Othello. 'Tis pitiful; but yet Iago knows
  That she with Cassio hath the act of shame
  A thousand times committed. Cassio confessed it;
  And she did gratify his amorous works   210
  With that recognizance and pledge of love,
  Which I first gave her. I saw it in his hand.
  It was a handkerchief, an antique token
  My father gave my mother.
Emilia. O God! O heavenly God!   215
Iago. Zounds, hold your peace!
Emilia.   'Twill out, 'twill out! I peace?
  No, I will speak as liberal as the north.°
  Let heaven and men and devils, let them all,
  All, all, cry shame against me, yet I'll speak.
Iago. Be wise and get you home.
Emilia.   I will not.   220

                    [*Iago draws and threatens Emilia.*]

Gratiano. Fie! Your sword upon a woman?
Emilia. O thou dull Moor, that handkerchief thou speak'st of
  I found by fortune, and did give my husband;
  For often with a solemn earnestness —
  More than indeed belonged to such a trifle —   225
  He begged of me to steal't.
Iago.   Villainous whore!
Emilia. She give it Cassio? No, alas, I found it,
  And I did give't my husband.
Iago.   Filth, thou liest!
Emilia. By heaven I do not, I do not, gentlemen.
  O murd'rous coxcomb! What should such a fool   230
  Do with so good a wife?
Othello.   Are there no stones° in heaven
  But what serves for the thunder? Precious villain!

---

²⁰⁶ *reprobation* damnation
²¹⁷ *liberal as the north* freely (and bitingly) as the north wind blows
²³¹ *stones* thunderbolts

[*The Moor runs at Iago, but is disarmed by Montano. Iago stabs his wife.*]

Gratiano. The woman falls. Sure he hath killed his wife.
Emilia. Ay, ay. O, lay me by my mistress' side.

[*Exit Iago.*]

Gratiano. He's gone, but his wife's killed. 235
Montano. 'Tis a notorious° villain. Take you this weapon,
    Which I have recovered from the Moor.
    Come, guard the door without. Let him not pass,
    But kill him rather. I'll after that same villain,
    For 'tis a damnèd slave.

           (*Exit [with all but Othello and Emilia].*)

Othello.   I am not valiant neither; 240
    But every puny whipster° gets my sword.
    But why should honor outlive honesty?
    Let it go all.
Emilia.   What did thy song bode, lady?
    Hark, canst thou hear me? I will play the swan,
    And die in music. [*Sings*] "Willow, willow, willow." 245
    Moor, she was chaste. She loved thee, cruel Moor,
    So come my soul to bliss as I speak true.
    So speaking as I think, alas, I die.   [*She dies.*]
Othello. I have another weapon in this chamber;
    It was a sword of Spain, the ice-brook's temper. 250
    O, here it is. — Uncle, I must come forth.
Gratiano. [*Within*] If thou attempt it, it will cost thee dear.
    Thou hast no weapon, and perforce must suffer.
Othello. Look in upon me then and speak with me,
    Or, naked as I am, I will assault thee. 255

[*Enter Gratiano.*]

Gratiano. What is the matter?
Othello.   Behold, I have a weapon;
    A better never did itself sustain
    Upon a soldier's thigh. I have seen the day
    That with this little arm and this good sword
    I have made my way through more impediments 260
    Than twenty times your stop. But O vain boast!
    Who can control his fate? 'Tis not so now.

---

[236] *notorious* out-and-out   [241] *puny whipster* small top-whipping boy (?)

Be not afraid, though you do see me weaponed.
Here is my journey's end, here is my butt,°
And very seamark of my utmost sail.°   265
Do you go back dismayed? 'Tis a lost fear.
Man but a rush° against Othello's breast,
And he retires. Where should Othello go?
Now, how dost thou look now? O ill-starred wench!
Pale as thy smock! When we shall meet at compt,°   270
This look of thine will hurl my soul from heaven,
And fiends will snatch at it. Cold, cold, my girl?
Even like thy chastity.
O cursèd, cursèd slave! Whip me, ye devils,
From the possession of° this heavenly sight!   275
Blow me about in winds! roast me in sulfur!
Wash me in steep-down gulfs of liquid fire!
O Desdemon! Dead Desdemon; dead. O! O!

(*Enter Lodovico, Cassio, Montano, and Iago* [*as prisoner,*] *with Officers.*)

Lodovico. Where is this rash and most unfortunate man?
Othello. That's he that was Othello? Here I am.   280
Lodovico. Where is that viper? Bring the villain forth.
Othello. I look down towards his feet° — but that's a fable.
     If that thou be'st a devil, I cannot kill thee.   [*Wounds Iago.*]
Lodovico. Wrench his sword from him.   [*Othello is disarmed.*]
Iago.   I bleed, sir, but not killed.
Othello. I am not sorry neither. I'd have thee live;   285
     For in my sense, 'tis happiness to die.
Lodovico. O thou Othello that was once so good,
     Fall'n in the practice° of a cursèd slave,
     What shall be said to thee?
Othello.   Why, anything:
     An honorable murderer, if you will;   290
     For naught I did in hate, but all in honor.
Lodovico. This wretch hath part confessed his villainy.
     Did you and he consent in Cassio's death?
Othello. Ay.
Cassio. Dear general, I never gave you cause.   295

264 *butt* target, stopping place
265 *seamark of my utmost sail* marker of my farthest journey
267 *Man but a rush* attack with only a reed   270 *compt* Judgment Day
275 *the possession of* being possessed by
282 *towards his feet* i.e., for his cloven hoofs   288 *practice* plotting

Othello. I do believe it, and I ask your pardon.
 Will you, I pray, demand that demi-devil
 Why he hath thus ensnared my soul and body?
Iago. Demand me nothing. What you know, you know.
 From this time forth I never will speak word.   300
Lodovico. What, not to pray?
Gratiano.   Torments will ope your lips.
Othello. Well, thou dost best.
Lodovico. Sir, you shall understand what hath befall'n,
 Which, as I think, you know not. Here is a letter
 Found in the pocket of the slain Roderigo;   305
 And here another. The one of them imports
 The death of Cassio to be undertook
 By Roderigo.
Othello. O villain!
Cassio.   Most heathenish and most gross!
Lodovico. Now here's another discontented paper   310
 Found in his pocket too; and this, it seems,
 Roderigo meant t' have sent this damnèd villain;
 But that, belike, Iago in the interim
 Came in and satisfied him.
Othello.   O thou pernicious caitiff!
 How came you, Cassio, by that handkerchief   315
 That was my wife's?
Cassio.   I found it in my chamber;
 And he himself confessed it but even now
 That there he dropped it for a special purpose
 Which wrought to his desire.
Othello.   O fool! Fool! Fool!
Cassio. There is besides in Roderigo's letter,   320
 How he upbraids Iago that he made him
 Brave me upon the watch; whereon it came
 That I was cast; and even but now he spake,
 After long seeming dead — Iago hurt him,
 Iago set him on.   325
Lodovico. You must forsake this room and go with us.
 Your power and your command is taken off,
 And Cassio rules in Cyprus. For this slave,
 If there be any cunning cruelty
 That can torment him much and hold him long,   330
 It shall be his. You shall close prisoner rest
 Till that the nature of your fault be known
 To the Venetian state. Come, bring away.

Othello. Soft you, a word or two before you go.
  I have done the state some service, and they know't.   335
  No more of that. I pray you, in your letters,
  When you shall these unlucky deeds relate,
  Speak of me as I am. Nothing extenuate,
  Nor set down aught in malice. Then must you speak
  Of one that loved not wisely, but too well;   340
  Of one not easily jealous, but, being wrought,
  Perplexed in the extreme; of one whose hand,
  Like the base Judean,° threw a pearl away
  Richer than all his tribe; of one whose subdued eyes,
  Albeit unusèd to the melting mood,   345
  Drops tears as fast as the Arabian trees
  Their med'cinable gum. Set you down this.
  And say besides that in Aleppo once,
  Where a malignant and a turbaned Turk
  Beat a Venetian and traduced the state,   350
  I took by th' throat the circumcisèd dog
  And smote him — thus.   [*He stabs himself.*]
Lodovico. O bloody period!°
Gratiano.   All that is spoke is marred.
Othello. I kissed thee ere I killed thee. No way but this,
  Killing myself, to die upon a kiss.   355

         [*He falls over Desdemona and dies.*]

Cassio. This did I fear, but thought he had no weapon;
  For he was great of heart.
Lodovico.   [*To Iago*] O Spartan dog,
  More fell° than anguish, hunger, or the sea!
  Look on the tragic loading of this bed.
  This is thy work. The object poisons sight;   360
  Let it be hid.   [*Bed curtains drawn.*]
       Gratiano, keep° the house,
  And seize upon the fortunes of the Moor,
  For they succeed on you. To you, lord governor,
  Remains the censure of this hellish villain,
  The time, the place, the torture. O, enforce it!   365
  Myself will straight aboard, and to the state
  This heavy act with heavy heart relate.   (*Exeunt.*)

FINIS

343 *Judean* (most editors use the Q1 reading, "Indian," here, but F is clear; both readings point toward the infidel, the unbeliever)   353 *period* end   358 *fell* cruel   361 *keep* remain in

Shakespeare uses the words "tragic," "tragical," and "tragedy" some two dozen times, but in the great tragedies only *Othello* provides an instance:

> Look on the tragic loading of this bed.

"The tragic loading" is a pair of corpses, Othello's and Desdemona's. The best way to understand Shakespeare's tragic vision is, of course, to see and read the tragedies very intelligently, but some help may be gained from a brief consideration of two speeches in *Hamlet*. In the final scene, when Fortinbras and others enter the stage looking for Claudius, they find to their amazement the corpses of Claudius, Gertrude, Laertes, and Hamlet. Horatio, Hamlet's friend, endeavors to bring the visitors up to date:

> What is it you would see?
> If aught of woe or wonder, cease your search.

Fortinbras and his associates are indeed struck with woe and wonder:

> *Fortinbras.*   O proud Death,
> What feast is toward in thine eternal cell
> That thou so many princes at a shot
> So bloodily hast struck?
> *Ambassador.*   The sight is dismal.

Horatio seeks to explain: the visitors will hear

> Of carnal, bloody, and unnatural acts,
> Of accidental judgments, casual slaughters,
> Of deaths put on by cunning and forced cause,
> And, in this upshot, purposes mistook
> Fall'n on th'inventors' heads.

The spectators of the play itself have indeed seen "unnatural acts," "deaths put on by cunning," etc., and presumably these spectators have experienced the "woe" and "wonder" that the new arrivals will experience as Horatio sets forth the details.

Let us now look at a second passage from *Hamlet*. The speaker is the despicable Rosencrantz, and there is some flattery of King Claudius in his speech, but the gist of his argument about the death of a king rings true, makes sense:

> The cess of majesty
> Dies not alone, but like a gulf doth draw
> What's near it with it; or it is a massy wheel
> Fixed on the summit of the highest mount,

To whose huge spokes ten thousand lesser things
Are mortised and adjoined, which when it falls,
Each small annexment, petty consequence,
Attends the boist'rous ruin. Never alone
Did the King sigh, but with a general groan.

Surely it is understandable that the deaths of, say, Lincoln and Kennedy had a vastly greater effect upon America than the deaths of any number of men in private life.

Taken together, the speeches afford something of a justification of the Elizabethan view that tragedy is concerned with violence done to and by people of high rank. The fall of a man in high position evokes deeper woe and wonder than the snuffing out of a nonentity. The latter may evoke pity, but scarcely awe at the terrifying power of destructiveness or at the weakness that is at the heart of power.

Shakespeare does not merely slap the label of king or prince or general on a character and then assume that greatness has been established. His characters perform great deeds and speak great language. When the Venetians are threatened by the Turks, Othello is "highly called for." When Othello and Brabantio enter the duke's council chamber, the duke greets them thus:

Valiant Othello, we must straight employ you
Against the general enemy Ottoman.
[*To Brabantio*] I did not see you. Welcome, gentle signior.
We lacked your counsel and your help tonight.

Brabantio is a senator, but a great military leader is what is wanted, and the duke's brief lapse in protocol reveals Othello's importance to the community.

Such a hero has a corresponding language, of which a single example will suffice:

My services which I have·done the Signiory
Shall out-tongue his complaints. 'Tis yet to know —
Which when I know that boasting is an honor
I shall promulgate — I fetch my life and being
From men of royal siege; and my demerits
May speak unbonneted to as proud a fortune
As this that I have reached. For know, Iago,
But that I love the gentle Desdemona,
I would not my unhousèd free condition
Put into circumscription and confine
For the seas' worth.

Especially in "For the seas' worth," that vast expanse filled with pearls and other treasures, we catch the voice of the great man, though for

Iago Othello's noble diction is mere "bombast circumstance," or windy talk. (What kind of language to use for heroes is a problem that afflicts all post-Renaissance dramatists. William Butler Yeats early in the twentieth century put it thus: "When educated people are deeply moved, they look silently into the fire.") We might contrast Othello's noble voice with Iago's "Virtue? A fig!" or "Drown cats and blind puppies!" It is Othello's commanding presence, revealed in actions and words (as when he majestically stills the threatening factions with "Keep up your bright swords, for the dew will rust them") that makes him a Shakespearean hero. And it is his virtue, at least in part, his "free and open nature," that makes him vulnerable to Iago's concealed hatred. A passage from *As You Like It* is curiously relevant. Old Adam, Orlando's faithful servant, warns Orlando that his very virtues have engendered the hatred of his brother, Oliver:

> Know you not, master, to some kind of men
> Their graces serve them but as enemies?
> No more do yours. Your virtues, gentle master,
> Are sanctified and holy traitors to you.
> O, what a world is this, when what is comely
> Envenoms him that bears it!

There is, of course, much more to Othello than the previous remarks suggest. He falls not only into a fit but also into savage language ("I will chop her into messes! Cuckold me!"), and he commits a murder. And Iago, as he gains power over Othello, sometimes uses the sonorous diction we associate with Othello. In the first scene we hear Iago speak disparagingly of Othello, but when we see Othello, we understand that he has been slandered. Late in the play, after he has killed Desdemona, he is called a "gull" and a "dolt," "as ignorant as dirt," and we cannot brush off these accusations. A great man, a "noble Moor," has done a terrible deed. When he becomes aware of his paradoxical nature and regains his faith in Desdemona, he aptly characterizes himself as "an honorable murderer." Murder and honor do not easily go together, but Shakespeare contrives to unite them so that they evoke the woe and wonder we expect of tragedy.

Hedda Gabler

HENRIK IBSEN

Translated by Otto Reinert

Henrik Ibsen (1828–1906) was born in Skien, Norway, of wealthy parents who soon after his birth lost their money. Ibsen worked as a pharmacist's apprentice, but at the age of twenty-two he had written his first play, a promising melodrama entitled Cataline. *He engaged in theater work in Norway, and then in Denmark and Germany. By 1865 his plays had won him a state pension that enabled him to settle in Rome. After writing romantic, historic, and poetic plays, he turned to realistic drama with* The League of Youth *(1869). Among the major realistic "problem plays" are* A Doll's House *(1879),* Ghosts *(1881), and* An Enemy of the People *(1882). In* The Wild Duck *(1884) he moved toward a more symbolic tragic comedy, and his last plays, written in the nineties, are highly symbolic.* Hedda Gabler *(1890) looks back to the plays of the eighties rather than forward to the plays of the nineties.*

CHARACTERS

Jørgen Tesman, University Research Fellow in the
    History of Civilization
Hedda, his wife
Miss Juliane Tesman, his aunt
Mrs. Elvsted
Judge Brack
Eilert Løvborg
Berte, the Tesmans' maid

SCENE

*The Tesmans' villa in a fashionable residential sec-
tion of the town.*

A note on pronunciation

The approximate Norwegian pronunciation of names
likely to be difficult to a speaker of English is suggested below (the syllable in capitals is accented; the
unaccented *e* is close to English *e* in *quiet*).

Jørgen   YUR-gen (*g* as in *bargain*)
Julle   YOOL-le (short *oo*)
Eilert Løvborg   AY-lert LUV-borg*
Berte   BAIR-te

* *Løvborg* means, literally, "leaf-castle" — a fact of possible bearing on the play's symbolism.

150

ACT ONE

(*A spacious, handsome, tastefully furnished room. Dark décor. In the rear, a wide doorway with open portieres. Beyond is a smaller room, furnished in the same style as the front room. A door, right, leads to the front hall. Left, French doors, with portieres drawn aside, through which can be seen a part of a roofed verandah and trees with autumn foliage. Front center, an oval table covered with a cloth. Chairs around it. Front right, a wide, dark, porcelain stove, a high-backed easy chair, a footstool with a pillow, and two ottomans. In the corner far right, a sofa and a small, round table. Front left, a sofa, set out from the wall. Far left, beyond the French doors, an upright piano. On both sides of the doorway, rear center, whatnots with knickknacks. Against the rear wall of the inner room, a sofa, and in front of it a table and two chairs. Above the sofa, a portrait of a handsome, elderly man in general's uniform. Over the table hangs a lamp with milky, white glass. There are several bouquets of flowers, in vases and glasses, in various places in the front room. Others are lying on the tables. Thick carpets on the floors of both rooms. The morning sun is shining through the French doors.*)

Miss Juliane Tesman, with hat and parasol, enters right, followed by Berte, who carries a bouquet of flowers wrapped in paper. Miss Tesman is a nice-looking woman of 65, of pleasant mien, neatly but not expensively dressed in a gray suit. Berte is a middle-aged servant girl, of rather plain and countrified appearance.)

From *Hedda Gabler* by Henrik Ibsen, translated by Otto Reinert, and published by Chandler Publishing Company, San Francisco. Copyright © 1962 by Chandler Publishing Company. Reprinted by permission.

Miss Tesman (stops inside the door, listens, says in a low voice). On my word — I don't think they are even up yet!

Berte (also softly). That's what I told you, miss. When you think how late the steamer got in last night. And afterwards — ! Goodness! — all the stuff she wanted unpacked before she turned in.

Miss Tesman. Well — just let them sleep. But fresh morning air — *that* we can give them when they come in here. (*Goes and opens the French doors wide.*)

Berte (by the table, lost, still holding the flowers). Please, miss — I just don't see a bit of space anywhere! I think I'd better put these over here. (*Puts the flowers down on the piano.*)

Miss Tesman. Well, well, my dear Berte. So you've got yourself a new mistress now. The good Lord knows it was hard for me to let you go.

Berte (near tears). What about me, then, miss! What shall *I* say? I who have served you and Miss Rina all these blessed years.

Miss Tesman. We shall just have to make the best of it, Berte. That's all. Jørgen can't do without you, you know. He just can't. You've looked after him ever since he was a little boy.

Berte. Yes, but miss — I'm ever so worried about leaving Miss Rina. The poor dear lying there all helpless. With that new girl and all! She'll never learn how to make things nice and comfortable for an invalid.

Miss Tesman. Oh yes, you'll see. I'll teach her. And of course, you know, I'll do most of it myself. So don't you worry yourself about my poor sister, Berte.

Berte. Yes, but there's another thing, too, miss. I'm scared I won't be able to suit young Mrs. Tesman.

Miss Tesman. Oh, well. Good heavens. So there is a thing or two — Right at first —

Berte. For I believe she's ever so particular.

Miss Tesman. Can you wonder? General Gabler's daughter? Just think of the kind of life she was used to when the General was alive. Do you remember when she rode by with her father? That long black riding habit she wore? And the feather in her hat?

Berte. Oh, I remember, all right. But I'll be blessed if I ever thought she and the young master would make a pair of it.

Miss Tesman. Nor did I. By the way, while I think of it, Berte. Jørgen has a new title now. From now on you should call him "the Doctor."

Berte. Yes, the young mistress said something about that, too, last night. Soon as they were inside the door. Then it's really so, miss?

Miss Tesman. It certainly is. Just think, Berte — they have made him a doctor abroad. During the trip, you know. I hadn't heard a thing about it till last night on the pier.

Berte. Well, I daresay he could be anything he put his mind to, *he* could — smart as *he* is. But I must say I'd never thought he'd turn to doctoring people, too.

Miss Tesman. Oh, that's not the kind of doctor he is. (*Nods significantly.*) And as far as that is concerned, there is no telling but pretty soon you may have to call him something grander yet.

Berte. You don't say! What might that be, miss?

Miss Tesman (*smiles*). Wouldn't you like to know! (*Moved.*) Ah yes, indeed — ! If only dear Jochum could see from his grave what has become of his little boy! (*Looking around.*) But look, Berte — what's this for? Why have you taken off all the slip covers?

Berte. She told me to. Said she can't stand slip covers on chairs.

Miss Tesman. Do you think they mean to make this their everyday living room, then?

Berte. It sure sounded that way. Mrs. Tesman did, I mean. For he — the doctor — he didn't say anything.

(*Jørgen Tesman enters from the right side of the inner room. He is humming to himself. He carries an open, empty suitcase. He is of medium height, youthful-looking, thirty-three years old; somewhat stoutish. Round, open, cheerful face. Blond hair and beard. He wears glasses and is dressed in a comfortable, rather casual suit.*)

Miss Tesman. Good morning, good morning, Jørgen!

Tesman (*in the doorway*). Auntie! Dearest Aunt Julle! (*Comes forward and shakes her hand.*) All the way out here — as early as this! Hm?

Miss Tesman. Well — I just had to drop in for a moment. To see how you are getting along, you know.

Tesman. Even though you haven't had a good night's sleep.

Miss Tesman. Oh, that doesn't matter at all.

Tesman. But you did get home from the pier all right, I hope. Hm?

Miss Tesman. Oh yes, I certainly did, thank you. The Judge was kind enough to see me all the way to my door.

Tesman. We were so sorry we couldn't give you a ride in our carriage. But you saw for yourself — all the boxes Hedda had.

Miss Tesman. Yes, she certainly brought quite a collection.

Berte (*to Tesman*). Should I go and ask Mrs. Tesman if there's anything I can help her with?

Tesman. No, thank you, Berte — you'd better not. She said she'll ring if she wants you.

Berte (*going right*). Well, all right.

Tesman. But, look — you might take this suitcase with you.

Berte (*takes it*). I'll put it in the attic. (*Exits right.*)

Tesman. Just think, Auntie — that whole suitcase was brimful of copies of old documents. You wouldn't believe me if I told you all the things I have collected from libraries and archives all over. Quaint old items nobody has known anything about.

Miss Tesman. Well, no, Jørgen. I'm sure you haven't wasted your time on your honeymoon.

Tesman. No, I think I may say I have not. But take your hat off, Auntie — for goodness' sake. Here! Let me untie the ribbon for you. Hm?

Miss Tesman (while he does so). Ah, God forgive me, if this isn't just as if you were still at home with us!

Tesman (inspecting the hat). My, what a fine-looking hat you've got yourself!

Miss Tesman. I bought it for Hedda's sake.

Tesman. For Hedda's sake? Hm?

Miss Tesman. So she won't need to feel ashamed of me if we ever go out together.

Tesman (patting her cheek). If you don't think of everything, Auntie! (*Puts the hat down on a chair by the table.*) And now — over here to the sofa — we'll just sit and chat for a while till Hedda comes.

(*They seat themselves. She places her parasol in the corner by the sofa.*)

Miss Tesman (takes both his hands in hers and gazes at him). What a blessing it is to have you back again, Jørgen, big as life! You — Jochum's little boy!

Tesman. For me, too, Aunt Julle. Seeing you again. For you have been both father and mother to me.

Miss Tesman. Ah, yes — don't you think I know you'll always keep a spot in your heart for these two old aunts of yours!

Tesman. So Aunt Rina isn't any better, hm?

Miss Tesman. Oh no. We mustn't look for improvement in her case, poor dear. She is lying there just as she has been all these years. Just the same, may the good Lord keep her for me a long time yet! For else I just wouldn't know what to do with myself, Jørgen. Especially now, when I don't have you to look after any more.

Tesman (pats her back). There, there, now!

Miss Tesman (changing tone). And to think that you are a married man, Jørgen! And that you were the one to walk off with Hedda Gabler. The lovely Hedda Gabler. Just think! As many admirers as she had!

Tesman (hums a little, smiles complacently). Yes, I daresay I have quite a few good friends here in town who'd gladly be in my shoes, hm?

Miss Tesman. And such a long and lovely honeymoon you had! More than five — almost six months!

Tesman. Well, you know — for me it has been a kind of study tour as well. All the collections I had to go through. And the books I had to read!

Miss Tesman. Yes, I suppose. (*More confidentially, her voice lowered a little.*) But listen, Jørgen — haven't you got something — something special to tell me?

Tesman. About the trip?

Miss Tesman. Yes.

Tesman. No — I don't know of anything besides what I wrote in my letters. They gave me a doctor's degree down there — but I told you that last night; I'm sure I did.

Miss Tesman. Well, yes, that sort of thing — What I mean is — don't you have certain — certain — expectations?

Tesman. Expectations?

Miss Tesman. Ah for goodness' sake, Jørgen! I am your old Auntie, after all!

Tesman. Certainly I have expectations.

Miss Tesman. Well!!

Tesman. I fully expect to be made a professor one of these days.

Miss Tesman. Professor — oh yes —

Tesman. I may even say I am quite certain of it. But dear Aunt Julle — you know this just as well as I do!

Miss Tesman (*laughing a little*). Of course I do. You're quite right. (*Changing topic.*) But about the trip. It must have cost a great deal of money — hm, Jørgen?

Tesman. Well, now; you know that large stipend went quite a long way.

Miss Tesman. I just don't see how you made it do for both of you, though.

Tesman. No, I suppose that's not so easy to understand, hm?

Miss Tesman. Particularly with a lady along. For I have always heard that is ever so much more expensive.

Tesman. Well, yes, naturally. That *is* rather more expensive. But Hedda had to have this trip, Auntie! She really had to. Nothing less would do.

Miss Tesman. No, I daresay. For a wedding journey is quite the thing these days. But now tell me — have you had a chance to look around here yet?

Tesman. I certainly have. I have been up and about ever since dawn.

Miss Tesman. And what do you think of it all?

Tesman. Delightful! Perfectly delightful! The only thing is I don't see what we are going to do with the two empty rooms between the second sitting room in there and Hedda's bedroom.

Miss Tesman (with a chuckle). Oh my dear Jørgen — you may find them useful enough — when the time comes!

Tesman. Of course, you're right, Auntie! As my library expands, hm?

Miss Tesman. Quite so, my dear boy. It was your library I was thinking of.

Tesman. But I'm really most happy on Hedda's behalf. For you know, before we were engaged she used to say she wouldn't care to live anywhere but in Secretary Falk's house.

Miss Tesman. Yes, just think — wasn't that a lucky coincidence, that it was up for sale right after you had left?

Tesman. Yes, Aunt Julle. We've certainly been lucky. Hm?

Miss Tesman. But it will be expensive, my dear Jørgen. Terribly expensive — all this.

Tesman (looks at her, a bit crestfallen). Yes, I daresay it will, Auntie.

Miss Tesman. Heavens, yes!

Tesman. How much, do you think? Roughly. Hm?

Miss Tesman. No, I couldn't possibly say till all the bills arrive.

Tesman. Well, anyway, Judge Brack managed to get very reasonable terms for us. He said so himself in a letter to Hedda.

Miss Tesman. Yes, and I won't have you uneasy on that account, Jørgen. Besides, I have given security for the furniture and the carpets.

Tesman. Security? You? But dear Aunt Julle — what kind of security could you give?

Miss Tesman. The annuity.

Tesman (jumps up). What! Your and Aunt Rina's annuity?

Miss Tesman. Yes. I didn't know what else to do, you see.

Tesman (standing before her). But are you clear out of your mind, Auntie! That annuity — that's all the two of you have to live on!

Miss Tesman. Oh well, there's nothing to get so excited about, I'm sure. It's all just a matter of form, you know. That's what the Judge said, too. For he was kind enough to arrange the whole thing for me. Just a matter of form — those were his words.

Tesman. That's all very well. Still —

Miss Tesman. For now you'll have your own salary, you know. And, goodness — what if we do have a few expenses — Help out a bit right at first — ? That would only be a joy for us —

Tesman. Oh, Auntie! When will you ever stop making sacrifices for my sake!

Miss Tesman (gets up, puts her hands on his shoulders). But what other happiness do I have in this world than being able to smooth your way a little, my own dear boy? Orphan as you were, with no one to lean on but us? And now the goal is in sight, Jørgen. Things may have looked black at times. But heaven be praised; now you've arrived!

Tesman. Yes, it's really quite remarkable the way things have worked out.

Miss Tesman. Yes — and those who were against you — who tried to block your way — now they are tasting defeat. They are down, Jørgen! He, the most dangerous of them all, his fall was the greatest! He made his bed, and now he is lying in it — poor, lost wretch that he is!

Tesman. Have you had any news about Eilert? Since I went away, I mean?

Miss Tesman. Just that he is supposed to have published a new book.

Tesman. What? Eilert Løvborg? Recently? Hm?

Miss Tesman. That's what they say. But I wonder if there can be much to it. What do you think? Ah — but when *your* new book comes, that will be something quite different, Jørgen! What is it going to be about?

Tesman. It deals with the domestic industries of Brabant during the Middle Ages.

Miss Tesman. Just think — being able to write about something like that!

Tesman. But as far as that is concerned, it may be quite some time before it is ready. I have all these collections to put in order first, you see.

Miss Tesman. Yes, collecting and putting things in order — you certainly know how to do that. In that you are your father's own son.

Tesman. Well, I must say I am looking forward to getting started. Particularly now, that I've got my own delightful home to work in.

Miss Tesman. And most of all now that you have the one your heart desired, dear Jørgen.

Tesman (embracing her). Oh yes, yes, Aunt Julle! Hedda — she is the most wonderful part of it all! (*Looks toward the doorway.*) There — I think she is coming now, hm?

(*Hedda enters from the left side of the inner room. She is twenty-nine years old. Both features and figure are noble and elegant. Pale, ivory complexion. Steel-gray eyes, expressive of cold, clear calm. Beautiful brown hair, though not particularly ample. She is dressed in a tasteful, rather loose-fitting morning costume.*)

Miss Tesman (*going toward her*). Good morning, my dear Hedda! A very happy morning to you!

Hedda (*giving her hand*). Good morning, dear Miss Tesman! So early a call? That is most kind.

Miss Tesman (*seems slightly embarrassed*). And — has the little lady of the house slept well the first night in her new home?

Hedda. Passably, thank you.

Tesman (*laughs*). Passably! You are a good one, Hedda! You were sleeping like a log when I got up.

Hedda. Fortunately. And then, of course, Miss Tesman, it always takes time to get used to new surroundings. That has to come gradually. (*Looks left.*) Oh dear. The maid has left the verandah doors wide open. There's a veritable flood of sunlight in here.

Miss Tesman (*toward the doors*). Well, then, we'll just close them.

Hedda. No, no, not that. Tesman, dear, please pull the curtains. That will give a softer light.

Tesman (*over by the French doors*). Yes, dear. There, now! Now you have both shade and fresh air, Hedda.

Hedda. We certainly can use some air in here. Such loads of flowers — but, Miss Tesman, please — won't you be seated?

Miss Tesman. No thanks. I just wanted to see if everything was all right — and so it is, thank goodness. I had better get back to Rina. I know she is waiting for me, poor thing.

Tesman. Be sure to give her my love, Auntie. And tell her I'll be around to see her later today.

Miss Tesman. I'll certainly do that! — Oh my! I almost forgot! (*Searches the pocket of her dress.*) I have something for you, Jørgen. Here.

Tesman. What's that, Auntie? Hm?

Miss Tesman (*pulls out a flat parcel wrapped in newspaper and gives it to him*). Here you are, dear.

Tesman (*opens the parcel*). Well, well, well! So you took care of them for me, Aunt Julle! Hedda! Now, isn't that sweet, hm?

Hedda (*by the whatnot, right*). If you'd tell me what it is —

Tesman. My old slippers! You know!

Hedda. Oh really? I remember you often talked about them on the trip.

Tesman. Yes, for I missed them so. (*Walks over to her.*) Here — now you can see what they're like, Hedda.

Hedda (*crosses toward stove*). Thanks. I don't know that I really care.

Tesman (*following*). Just think — Aunt Rina embroidered these slippers for me. Ill as she was. You can't imagine how many memories they hold for me!

Hedda (*by the table*). Hardly for me.

Miss Tesman. That's true, you know, Jørgen.

Tesman. Yes, but — I just thought that now that she's one of the family —

Hedda (*interrupting*). I don't think we'll get on with that maid, Tesman.

Miss Tesman. Not get on with Berte?

Tesman. Whatever makes you say that, dear? Hm?

Hedda (*points*). Look — she has left her old hat on the chair over there.

Tesman (*appalled, drops the slippers*). But Hedda — !

Hedda. What if somebody were to come and see it!

Tesman. No, no, Hedda — that's Aunt Julle's hat!

Hedda. Oh?

Miss Tesman (*picking up the hat*). Yes, indeed it is. And it isn't old either, my dear young lady.

Hedda. I really didn't look that closely —

Miss Tesman (*tying the ribbons*). I want you to know that this is the first time I have had it on my head. On my word it is!

Tesman. And very handsome it is, too. Really a splendid-looking hat!

Miss Tesman. Oh, I don't know that it is anything so special, Jørgen. (*Looks around.*) My parasol — ? Ah, here it is. (*Picks it up.*) For that is mine, too. (*Mutters.*) Not Berte's.

Tesman. New hat and new parasol! What do you think of that, Hedda!

Hedda. Very nice indeed.

Tesman. Yes, don't you think so? Hm? But, Auntie, take a good look at Hedda before you leave. See how pretty and blooming she looks.

Miss Tesman. Dear me, Jørgen; that's nothing new. Hedda has been lovely all her days. (*She nods and walks right.*)

Tesman (*following*). Yes, but have you noticed how full-figured and healthy she looks after the trip? How she has filled out?

Hedda (*crossing*). Oh — stop it!

Miss Tesman (*halts, turns around*). Filled out?

Tesman. Yes, Aunt Julle. You can't see it so well now when she wears that dress. But I, who have the opportunity —

Hedda (*by the French doors, impatiently*). Oh, you haven't any opportunities at all!

Tesman. It must be the mountain air in Tyrol.

Hedda (*curtly interrupting*). I am just as I was when I left.

Tesman. Yes, so you say. I just don't think you're right. What do you think, Auntie?

Miss Tesman (has folded her hands, gazes at Hedda). Lovely — lovely — lovely; that is what Hedda is. (*Goes over to her, inclines her head forward with both her hands, and kisses her hair.*) God bless and keep Hedda Tesman. For Jørgen's sake.

Hedda (gently freeing herself). There, there. Now let me go.

Miss Tesman (in quiet emotion). Every single day I'll be over and see you two.

Tesman. Yes, please do, Auntie. Hm?

Miss Tesman. Goodbye, goodbye!

(*She leaves through door, right. Tesman sees her out. The door remains ajar. Tesman is heard repeating his greetings for Aunt Rina and his thanks for the slippers. In the meantime, Hedda paces up and down, raises her arms, clenching her fists, as in quiet rage. Opens the curtains by the French doors and stands looking out. In a few moments, Tesman re-enters and closes the door behind him.*)

Tesman (picking up the slippers). What are you looking at, Hedda?

Hedda (once again calm and controlled). Just the leaves. They are so yellow. And withered.

Tesman (wrapping the slippers in their paper, putting the parcel down on the table). Well, you know — we're in September now.

Hedda (again restless). Yes — just think. It's already — September.

Tesman. Don't you think Aunt Julle acted strange, Hedda? Almost solemn. I wonder why. Hm?

Hedda. I hardly know her, you see. Isn't she often like that?

Tesman. Not the way she was today.

Hedda (turning away from the French doors). Do you think she minded that business with the hat?

Tesman. Oh, I don't think so. Not much. Perhaps a little bit right at the moment —

Hedda. Well, I'm sorry, but I must say it strikes me as very odd — putting her hat down here in the living room. One just doesn't do that.

Tesman. Well, you may be sure Aunt Julle won't ever do it again.

Hedda. Anyway, I'll make it up to her, somehow.

Tesman. Oh yes, Hedda; if only you would!

Hedda. When you go over there today, why don't you ask her over for tonight?

Tesman. I'll certainly do that. And then there is one other thing you could do that she'd appreciate ever so much.

Hedda. What?

Tesman. If you could just bring yourself to call her Auntie. For my sake, Hedda, hm?

Hedda. No, Tesman, no. You really mustn't ask me to do that. I have already told you I can't. I'll try to call her Aunt Juliane. That will have to do.

Tesman. All right, if you say so. I just thought that now that you're in the family —

Hedda. Hmmm — I don't know about that — (*She walks toward the doorway.*)

Tesman (*after a brief pause*). Anything the matter, Hedda? Hm?

Hedda. I'm just looking at my old piano. It doesn't quite go with the other furniture in here.

Tesman. As soon as I get my first pay check we'll have it traded in.

Hedda. No — I don't want to do that. I want to keep it. But let's put it in this inner room and get another one for out here. Whenever it's convenient. I mean.

Tesman (*a little taken back*). Well — yes — we could do that —

Hedda (*picks up the bouquet from the piano*). These flowers weren't here last night.

Tesman. I suppose Aunt Julle brought them for you.

Hedda (*looking at the flowers*). There's a card here. (*Takes it out and reads.*) "Will be back later." Can you guess who it's from?

Tesman. No. Who? Hm?

Hedda. Thea Elvsted.

Tesman. No, really? Mrs. Elvsted! Miss Rysing that was.

Hedda. That's right. The one with that irritating head of hair she used to show off with. An old flame of yours, I understand.

Tesman (*laughs*). Well, now — that didn't last long! Anyway, that was before I knew you, Hedda. Just think — her being in town.

Hedda. Strange, that she'd call on us. I have hardly seen her since we went to school together.

Tesman. As far as that goes, I haven't seen her either for — God knows how long. I don't see how she can stand living in that out-of-the-way place. Hm?

Hedda (*suddenly struck by a thought*). Listen, Tesman — isn't it some place near there that he lives — what's his name — Eilert Løvborg?

Tesman. Yes, that's right. He is up there, too.

(*Berte enters right.*)

Berte. Ma'am, she's here again, that lady who brought those flowers a while back. (*Pointing.*) The flowers you're holding in your hand, ma'am.

Hedda. Ah, she is? Well, show her in, please.

(*Berte opens the door for Mrs. Elvsted and exits. Mrs. Elvsted is of slight build, with a pretty, soft face. Her eyes are light blue, large, round, rather prominent, of a timid and querying expression. Her hair is strikingly light in color, almost whitish, and unusually rich and wavy. She is a couple of years younger than Hedda. She is dressed in a dark visiting dress, tasteful, but not quite in the most recent fashion.*)

Hedda (*walks toward her. Friendly*). Good morning, my dear Mrs. Elvsted. How very nice to see you again.

Mrs. Elvsted (*nervous, trying not to show it*). Well, yes, it is quite some time since we met.

Tesman (*shaking hands*). And we, too. Hm?

Hedda. Thank you for your lovely flowers —

Mrs. Elvsted. Please, don't — I would have come here yesterday afternoon. But I was told you were still traveling —

Tesman. You've just arrived in town, hm?

Mrs. Elvsted. I got here yesterday, at noon. Oh, I was quite desperate when I learned you weren't home.

Hedda. Desperate? But why?

Tesman. But my dear Mrs. Rysing — I mean Mrs. Elvsted —

Hedda. There is nothing wrong, I hope?

Mrs. Elvsted. Yes there is. And I don't know a single soul other than you that I can turn to here.

Hedda (*putting the flowers down on the table*). Come — let's sit down here on the sofa.

Mrs. Elvsted. Oh, I'm in no mood to sit!

Hedda. Of course you are. Come on. (*She pulls Mrs. Elvsted over to the sofa and sits down next to her.*)

Tesman. Well, now, Mrs. — ? Exactly what — ?

Hedda. Has something — special happened at home?

Mrs. Elvsted. Well, yes — and no. Oh, but I am so afraid you won't understand!

Hedda. In that case, it seems to me you ought to tell us exactly what has happened, Mrs. Elvsted.

Tesman. After all, that's why you are here. Hm?

Mrs. Elvsted. Yes, yes, of course. Well, then, maybe you already know — Eilert Løvborg is in town.

Hedda. Is Løvborg — !

Tesman. No! You don't say! Just think, Hedda — Løvborg's back!

Hedda. All right. I can hear.

Mrs. Elvsted. He has been here a week already. Imagine — a whole week! In this dangerous place. Alone! With all that bad company around.

Hedda. But my dear Mrs. Elvsted — why is he a concern of yours?

Mrs. Elvsted (*with an apprehensive look at her, says quickly*). He tutored the children.

Hedda. Your children?

Mrs. Elvsted. My husband's. I don't have any.

Hedda. In other words, your stepchildren.

Mrs. Elvsted. Yes.

Tesman (*with some hesitation*). But was he — I don't quite know how to put this — was he sufficiently — regular — in his way of life to be thus employed? Hm?

Mrs. Elvsted. For the last two years, there hasn't been a thing to object to in his conduct.

Tesman. No, really? Just think, Hedda!

Hedda. I hear.

Mrs. Elvsted. Not the least little bit, I assure you! Not in any respect. And yet — knowing he's here — in the big city — And with all that money, too! I'm scared to death!

Tesman. But in that case, why didn't he remain with you and your husband? Hm?

Mrs. Elvsted. After his book came out, he was too restless to stay.

Tesman. Ah yes, that's right. Aunt Julle said he has published a new book.

Mrs. Elvsted. Yes, a big new book, about the course of civilization in general. It came out about two weeks ago. And since it has had such big sales and been discussed so much and made such a big splash —

Tesman. It has, has it? I suppose this is something he has had lying around from better days?

Mrs. Elvsted. You mean from earlier?

Tesman. Yes.

Mrs. Elvsted. No; it's all been written since he came to stay with us. During this last year.

Tesman. Well, now! That's very good news, Hedda! Just think!

Mrs. Elvsted. Yes, if it only would last!

Hedda. Have you seen him since you came to town?

Mrs. Elvsted. No, not yet. I had a great deal of trouble finding his address. But this morning I finally tracked him down.

Hedda (*looks searchingly at her*). Isn't it rather odd that your husband — hm —

Mrs. Elvsted (*with a nervous start*). My husband! What about him?

Hedda. That he sends you to town on such an errand? That he doesn't go and look after his friend himself?

Mrs. Elvsted. Oh, no, no — my husband doesn't have time for things like that. Besides, I have some — some shopping to do, anyway.

Hedda (with a slight smile). Well, in that case, of course —

Mrs. Elvsted (getting up, restlessly). And now I beg of you, Mr. Tesman — won't you please receive Eilert Løvborg nicely if he calls on you? And I am sure he will. After all — Such good friends as you two used to be. And then you both do the same kind of work — the same field of study, as far as I know.

Tesman. We used to, at any rate.

Mrs. Elvsted. Yes. And that's why I implore you to please, please, try to keep an eye on him — you too. You'll do that, Mr. Tesman, won't you? Promise?

Tesman. With the greatest pleasure, Mrs. Rysing.

Hedda. Elvsted.

Tesman. I'll gladly do as much for Eilert as I possibly can. You may certainly count on that.

Mrs. Elvsted. Oh, how good and kind you are! (*Clasps his hands.*) Thank you, thank you, thank you! (*Nervously.*) You see, my husband is so very fond of him.

Hedda (getting up). You ought to write him a note, Tesman. Maybe he won't come without an invitation.

Tesman. Yes, I suppose that would be the right thing to do, Hedda. Hm?

Hedda. The sooner the better. Right away, I think.

Mrs. Elvsted (pleadingly). If only you would!

Tesman. I'll write this minute. Do you have his address, Mrs. — Mrs. Elvsted?

Mrs. Elvsted. Yes. (*Pulls a slip of paper from her bag and gives it to him.*) Here it is.

Tesman. Very good. Well, then, if you'll excuse me — (*Looks around.*) By the way — the slippers? Ah, here we are. (*Leaving with the parcel.*)

Hedda. Be sure you write a nice, warm, friendly letter, Tesman. And a long one, too.

Tesman. Certainly, certainly.

Mrs. Elvsted. But not a word that it is I who — !

Tesman. No, that goes without saying, I should think. Hm? (*Goes out right through inner room.*)

Hedda (goes over to Mrs. Elvsted, smiles, says in a low voice). There! We just killed two birds with one stone.

Mrs. Elvsted. What do you mean?

Hedda. Didn't you see I wanted him out of the room?

Mrs. Elvsted. Yes, to write that letter —

Hedda. And to speak to you alone.

Mrs. Elvsted (flustered). About this same thing?

Hedda. Exactly.

Mrs. Elvsted (anxious). But there *is* nothing more, Mrs. Tesman! Really, there isn't!

Hedda. Oh yes, there is. There is considerably more. I can see that much. Over here — We are going to have a real, nice, confidential talk, you and I. (*She forces Mrs. Elvsted down in the easy chair and seats herself on one of the ottomans.*)

Mrs. Elvsted (worried, looks at her watch). But my dear Mrs. Tesman — I had really thought I would be on my way now.

Hedda. Oh I am sure there is no rush. Now, then. Tell me about yourself. How are things at home?

Mrs. Elvsted. That is just what I don't want to talk about.

Hedda. But to me — ! After all, we are old schoolmates.

Mrs. Elvsted. But you were a year ahead of me. And I used to be so scared of you!

Hedda. Scared of me?

Mrs. Elvsted. Terribly. For when we met on the stairs, you always ruffled my hair.

Hedda. Did I really?

Mrs. Elvsted. Yes. And once you said you were going to burn it off.

Hedda. Oh, but you know — I wasn't serious!

Mrs. Elvsted. No, but I was such a silly, then. Anyway, afterwards we drifted far apart. Our circles are so very different, you know.

Hedda. All the more reason for getting close again. Listen. In school we called each other by our first names.

Mrs. Elvsted. Oh I'm sure you're wrong —

Hedda. I'm sure I'm not! I remember it quite clearly. And now we want to be open with one another, just the way we used to. (*Moves the ottoman closer.*) There, now! (*Kisses her cheek.*) You call me Hedda.

Mrs. Elvsted (seizes her hands). Oh you are so good and kind! I'm not used to that.

Hedda. There, there! And I'll call you my dear Thora, just as in the old days.

Mrs. Elvsted. My name is Thea.

Hedda. So it is. Of course. I meant Thea. (*Looks at her with compassion*). So you're not much used to goodness and kindness, Thea? Not in your own home?

Mrs. Elvsted. If I even had a home! But I don't. I never have had one.

Hedda (*looks at her for a moment*). I thought there might be some thing like this.

Mrs. Elvsted (*helplessly, looking straight ahead*). Yes — yes — yes —

Hedda. I am not sure if I quite remember — Didn't you first come to your husband as his housekeeper?

Mrs. Elvsted. I was really hired as governess. But his wife — his first wife — was ailing already then and practically bedridden. So I had to take charge of the household as well.

Hedda. But in the end you became his wife.

Mrs. Elvsted (*dully*). So I did.

Hedda. Let's see. How long ago is that?

Mrs. Elvsted. Since my marriage?

Hedda. Yes.

Mrs. Elvsted. About five years.

Hedda. Right. It must be that long.

Mrs. Elvsted. Oh, those five years! Or mostly the last two or three! Oh, Mrs. Tesman — if you could just imagine!

Hedda (*slaps her hand lightly*). Mrs. Tesman? Shame on you!

Mrs. Elvsted. Oh yes; all right, I'll try. Yes — if you could just — conceive — understand —

Hedda (*casually*). And Eilert Løvborg has been living near you for some three years or so, hasn't he?

Mrs. Elvsted (*looks at her uncertainly*). Eilert Løvborg? Yes — he has.

Hedda. Did you know him before? Here in town?

Mrs. Elvsted. Hardly at all. That is, of course I did in a way. I mean, I knew *of* him.

Hedda. But up there — You saw a good deal of him; did you?

Mrs. Elvsted. Yes, he came over to us every day. He was supposed to tutor the children, you see. For I just couldn't do it all by myself.

Hedda. Of course not. And your husband — ? I suppose he travels quite a bit.

Mrs. Elvsted. Well, yes, Mrs. Tes — Hedda — as a public magistrate, you know, he very often has to travel all over his district.

Hedda (*leaning against the armrest on the easy chair*). Thea — poor, sweet Thea — now you have to tell me everything — just as it is.

Mrs. Elvsted. You'd better ask me, then.

Hedda. How *is* your husband, Thea? I mean — you know — *really*? To be with. What kind of person is he? Is he good to you?

Mrs. Elvsted (*evasively*). I believe he thinks he does everything for the best.

Hedda. But isn't he altogether too old for you? He is more than twenty years older, isn't he?

Mrs. Elvsted (with irritation). Yes, there is that, too. But there isn't just one thing. Every single little thing about him repels me! We don't have a thought in common, he and I. Not a thing in the world!

Hedda. But isn't he fond of you all the same? I mean in his own way?

Mrs. Elvsted. I don't know. I think I am just useful to him. And I don't use much money. I am inexpensive.

Hedda. That is foolish of you.

Mrs. Elvsted (shakes her head). Can't be changed. Not with him. I don't think he cares for anybody much except himself. Perhaps the children a little.

Hedda. And Eilert Løvborg, Thea.

Mrs. Elvsted (looks at her). Eilert Løvborg? What makes you think that?

Hedda. Well, it seems to me that when he sends you all the way to town to look after him — (*With an almost imperceptible smile.*) Besides, you said so yourself. To Tesman.

Mrs. Elvsted (with a nervous twitch). Did I? I suppose I did. (*With a muted outburst.*) No! I might as well tell you now as later. For it's bound to come out, anyway.

Hedda. But my dear Thea —?

Mrs. Elvsted. All right. My husband doesn't know I've gone!

Hedda. What! He doesn't know?

Mrs. Elvsted. He wasn't even home. He's away again. Oh, I just couldn't take it any longer, Hedda! It had become utterly impossible. All alone as I was.

Hedda. So what did you do?

Mrs. Elvsted. I packed some of my things. Just the most necessary. Without telling anybody. And left.

Hedda. Just like that?

Mrs. Elvsted. Yes. And took the next train to town.

Hedda. But dearest Thea — how did you dare to do a thing like that!

Mrs. Elvsted (rises, walks). What else could I do?

Hedda. But what do you think your husband will say when you go back?

Mrs. Elvsted (by the table; looks at her). Go back to him?

Hedda. Yes!

Mrs. Elvsted. I'll never go back.

Hedda (rises, approaches her slowly). So you have really, seriously — left everything?

Mrs. Elvsted. Yes. It seemed to me there was nothing else I could do.

Hedda. And quite openly, too.

Mrs. Elvsted. You can't keep a thing like that secret, anyway.

Hedda. But what do you think people will say, Thea?

Mrs. Elvsted. In God's name, let them say whatever they like. (*Sits down on the sofa, dully, tired.*) For I have only done what I had to do.

Hedda (*after a brief silence*). And what do you plan to do with yourself? What sort of work will you do?

Mrs. Elvsted. I don't know yet. I only know I have to live where Eilert Løvborg is. If I am to live at all.

Hedda (*moves a chair from the table closer to Mrs. Elvsted, sits down, strokes her hands*). Thea — tell me. How did this — this friendship between you and Eilert — how did it begin?

Mrs. Elvsted. Oh, it grew little by little. I got some sort of power over him.

Hedda. Oh?

Mrs. Elvsted. He dropped his old ways. Not because I asked him to. I never dared to do that. But I think he must have noticed how I felt about that kind of life. So he changed.

Hedda (*quickly suppresses a cynical smile*). So you have — rehabilitated him, as they say. Haven't you, Thea?

Mrs. Elvsted. At least, that's what *he* says. On the other hand, he has turned me into a real human being. Taught me to think — and understand — all sorts of things.

Hedda. Maybe he tutored you, too?

Mrs. Elvsted. No, not tutored exactly. But he talked to me. About so many, many things. And then came that lovely, lovely time when I could share his work with him. He let me help him!

Hedda. He did?

Mrs. Elvsted. Yes! Whatever he wrote, he wanted us to be together about it.

Hedda. Just like two good comrades.

Mrs. Elvsted (*with animation*). Comrades! — that's it! Imagine, Hedda — that's just what he called it, too. Oh, I really ought to feel so happy. But I can't. For you see, I don't know if it will last.

Hedda. You don't trust him any more than that?

Mrs. Elvsted (*heavily*). The shadow of a woman stands between Eilert Løvborg and me.

Hedda (*tensely, looks at her*). Who?

Mrs. Elvsted. I don't know. Somebody or other from — his past. I don't think he has ever really forgotten her.

Hedda. What has he told you about it?

Mrs. Elvsted. He has mentioned it only once — just casually.

Hedda. And what did he say?

Mrs. Elvsted. He said that when they parted she was going to kill him with a gun.

Hedda (cold, controlled). Oh, nonsense. People don't do that sort of thing here.

Mrs. Elvsted. No, I know. And that is why I think it must be that red-headed singer he used to —

Hedda. Yes, I suppose so.

Mrs. Elvsted. For I remember people said she carried a loaded gun.

Hedda. Well, then I'm sure it's she.

Mrs. Elvsted (wringing her hands). Yes, but just think, Hedda — now I hear that she — that singer — that she's here in town again, too! Oh, I'm just desperate — !

Hedda (with a glance toward the inner room). Shhh! Here's Tesman. (*Rises and whispers.*) Not a word about all this to anybody, Thea!

Mrs. Elvsted (jumps up). No, no. For God's sake — !

(*Tesman, carrying a letter, enters from the right side of the inner room.*)

Tesman. There now — here's the missive, all ready to go!

Hedda. Good. But I believe Mrs. Elvsted wants to be on her way. Wait a moment. I'll see you to the garden gate.

Tesman. Say, Hedda — do you think Berte could take care of this?

Hedda (takes the letter). I'll tell her.

(*Berte enters right.*)

Berte. Judge Brack is here and wants to know if you're receiving.

Hedda. Yes, ask the Judge please to come in. And — here — drop this in a mailbox, will you?

Berte (takes the letter). Yes, ma'am.

(*She opens the door for Judge Brack and exits. The Judge is forty-five years of age. Rather thickset, but well-built and with brisk athletic movements. Roundish face, aristocratic profile. His hair is short, still almost completely black, very neatly dressed. Lively, sparkling eyes. Thick eyebrows and mustache with cut-off points. He is dressed in an elegant suit, a trifle youthful for his age. He wears pince-nez glasses, attached to a string, and lets them drop from time to time.*)

Judge Brack (hat in hand, salutes). May one pay one's respects as early as this?

Hedda. One certainly may.

Tesman (*shaking his hand*). You are always welcome. (*Introducing.*)
Judge Brack — Miss Rysing —

(*Hedda groans.*)

Brack (*bowing*). Delighted!
Hedda (*looks at him, laughs*). How nice it is to see you in daylight,
Judge!
Brack. You find me changed, perhaps?
Hedda. A bit younger, I think.
Brack. Much obliged.
Tesman. But what do you think of Hedda? Hm? Did you ever see her
in such bloom? She positively —
Hedda. Will you please leave me out of this? You had better thank the
Judge for all the trouble he has taken.
Brack. Oh, nonsense. It's been a pleasure.
Hedda. Yes, you are indeed a faithful soul. But my friend here is dying
to be off. Don't leave, Judge. I'll be back in a minute.

(*Mutual goodbyes. Mrs. Elvsted and Hedda exit, right.*)

Brack. Well, now — your wife — is she tolerably satisfied?
Tesman. Yes, indeed, and we really can't thank you enough. That is,
I understand there will have to be some slight changes made here
and there. And there are still a few things — just a few trifles —
we'll have to get.
Brack. Oh? Really?
Tesman. But we certainly don't want to bother you with that. Hedda
said she's going to take care of it herself. But do sit down, hm?
Brack. Thanks. Maybe just for a moment — (*Sits down by the table.*)
There's one thing I'd like to talk to you about, my dear Tesman.
Tesman. Oh? Ah, I see! (*Sits down.*) I suppose it's the serious part
of the festivities that's beginning now. Hm?
Brack. Oh — there's no great rush as far as the money is concerned.
Though I must say I wish we could have established ourselves a trifle
more economically.
Tesman. Out of the question, my dear fellow! Remember, it's all for
Hedda! You, who know her so well — ! After all, I couldn't put her
up like any little middle-class housewife —
Brack. No, I suppose — That's just it.
Tesman. Besides — fortunately — it can't be long now before I re-
ceive my appointment.
Brack. Well, you know — things like that have a way of hanging fire.
Tesman. Perhaps you have heard something? Something definite? Hm?

Brack. No, nothing certain — (*Interrupting himself.*) But that reminds me. I have some news for you.

Tesman. Oh?

Brack. Your old friend Eilert Løvborg is back in town.

Tesman. I know that already.

Brack. So? Who told you?

Tesman. The lady who just left.

Brack. I see. What did you say her name was again? I didn't quite catch —

Tesman. Mrs. Elvsted.

Brack. Ah yes — the Commissioner's wife. Yes, it's up in her part of the country that Løvborg has been staying, too.

Tesman. And just think. I am so glad to hear it. He is quite respectable again.

Brack. Yes, so they say.

Tesman. And he has published a new book, hm?

Brack. Oh yes.

Tesman. Which is making quite a stir.

Brack. Quite an unusual stir.

Tesman. Just think! Isn't that just wonderful! He — with his remarkable gifts. And I was so sure he'd gone under for good.

Brack. That seems to have been the general opinion.

Tesman. What I don't understand, though, is what he is going to do with himself. What sort of living can he make? Hm?

(*During the last remark Hedda re-enters, right.*)

Hedda (*to Brack, with a scornful little laugh*). Tesman is forever worrying about how people are going to make a living.

Tesman. Well, you see, we are talking about poor Eilert Løvborg, Hedda.

Hedda (*with a quick look at him*). You are? (*Sits down in the easy chair by the stove and asks casually.*) What is the matter with him?

Tesman. Well, you see, I believe he's run through his inheritance a long time ago. And I don't suppose he can write a new book every year. Hm? So I really must ask how he is going to make out.

Brack. Maybe I could help you anwer that.

Tesman. Yes?

Brack. Remember, he has relatives with considerable influence.

Tesman. Ah — unfortunately, those relatives have washed their hands of him long ago.

Brack. Just the same, they used to call him the hope of the family.

Tesman. Yes, before! But he has ruined all that.

Hedda. Who knows? (*With a little smile.*) I hear the Elvsteds have rehabilitated him.

Brack. And then this book —

Tesman. Well, I certainly hope they will help him to find something or other. I just wrote him a letter. Hedda, dear, I asked him to come out here tonight.

Brack. Oh dear, I am sorry. Don't you remember — you're supposed to come to my little stag dinner tonight? You accepted last night on the pier, you know.

Hedda. Had you forgotten, Tesman?

Tesman. So I had.

Brack. Oh well. I'm sure he won't come, so it doesn't really make any difference.

Tesman. Why is that? Hm?

Brack (*gets up somewhat hesitantly, rests his hands on the back of the chair*). Dear Tesman — and you, too, Mrs. Tesman — I cannot in good conscience let you remain in ignorance of something, which — which —

Tesman. Something to do with Eilert?

Brack. With both you and him.

Tesman. But my dear Judge, do speak!

Brack. You must be prepared to find that your appointment will not come through as soon as you hope and expect.

Tesman (*jumps up, nervously*). Something's happened? Hm?

Brack. It may conceivably be made contingent upon the result of a competition.

Tesman. Competition! Just think, Hedda!

Hedda (*leaning farther back in her chair*). Ah — I see, I see — !

Tesman. But with whom? Don't tell me with — ?

Brack. Precisely. With Eilert Løvborg.

Tesman (*claps his hands together*). No, no! This can't be! It is unthinkable! Quite impossible! Hm?

Brack. All the same, that's the way it may turn out.

Tesman. No, but Judge, this would amount to the most incredible callousness toward me! (*Waving his arms.*) For just think — I'm a married man! We married on the strength of these prospects, Hedda and I. Got ourselves deep in debt. Borrowed money from Aunt Julle, too. After all, I had practically been promised the post, you know. Hm?

Brack. Well, well. I daresay you'll get it in the end. If only after a competition.

Hedda (*motionless in her chair*). Just think, Tesman. It will be like a kind of contest.

Tesman. But dearest Hedda, how can you be so unconcerned!

Hedda (*still without moving*). I'm not at all unconcerned. I'm dying to see who wins.

Brack. In any case, Mrs. Tesman, I'm glad you know the situation as it is. I mean — before you proceed to make the little additional purchases I understand you threaten us with.

Hedda. This makes no difference as far as that is concerned.

Brack. Really? Well, in that case, of course — Goodbye! (*To Tesman.*) I'll pick you up on my afternoon walk.

Tesman. What? Oh yes, yes, of course. I'm sorry; I'm just all flustered.

Hedda (*without getting up, gives her hand*). Goodbye, Judge. Come back soon.

Brack. Thanks. Goodbye, goodbye.

Tesman (*sees him to the door*). Goodbye, my dear Judge. You really must excuse me —

(*Judge Brack exits, right.*)

Tesman (*pacing the floor*). Oh, Hedda, Hedda! One should never venture into fairyland. Hm?

Hedda (*looks at him, smiles*). Do *you* do that?

Tesman. Well, yes — it can't be denied — it was most venturesome of me to rush into marriage and set up a home on the strength of mere prospects.

Hedda. Well, maybe you're right.

Tesman. Anyway — we do have our own nice, comfortable home, now. Just think, Hedda — the very home both of us dreamed about. Set our hearts on, I may almost say. Hm?

Hedda (*rises, slowly, tired*). The agreement was that we were to maintain a certain position — entertain —

Tesman. Don't I know it! Dearest Hedda — I have been so looking forward to seeing you as hostess in a select circle! Hm? Well, well, well! In the meantime, we'll just have to be content with one another. See Aunt Julle once in a while. Nothing more. And you were meant for such a different kind of life, altogether!

Hedda. I suppose a footman is completely out of the question.

Tesman. I'm afraid so. Under the circumstances, you see — we couldn't possibly —

Hedda. And as for getting my own riding horse —

Tesman (*aghast*). Riding horse!

Hedda. I suppose I mustn't even think of that.

Tesman. Good heavens, no! That goes without saying, I hope!

Hedda (*walking*). Well — at least I have one thing to amuse myself with in the meantime.

Tesman (*overjoyed*). Oh thank goodness for that! And what *is* that, Hedda, ḥm?

Hedda (*in the doorway, looks at him with suppressed scorn*). My guns — Jørgen!

Tesman (*in fear*). Your guns!

Hedda (*with cold eyes*). General Gabler's guns. (*She exits left, through the inner room.*)

Tesman (*runs up to the doorway, calls after her*). But Hedda! Good gracious! Hedda, dear! Please don't touch those dangerous things! For my sake, Hedda! Hm?

ACT TWO

(*The same room at the Tesmans'. The piano has been moved out and replaced by an elegant little writing desk. A small table has been placed near the sofa, left. Most of the flowers have been removed. Mrs. Elvsted's bouquet is on the big table front center. Afternoon.*

Hedda, dressed to receive callers, is alone. She is standing near the open French doors, loading a revolver. Its mate is lying in an open case on the desk.)

Hedda (*looking down into the garden, calls*). Hello there, Judge! Welcome back!

Judge Brack (*off stage*). Thanks, Mrs. Tesman!

Hedda (*raises the gun, sights*). I am going to shoot you, Judge Brack!

Brack (*calls off stage*). No — no — no! Don't point the gun at me like that!

Hedda. That's what you get for sneaking in the back door! (*Fires.*)

Brack (*closer*). Are you out of your mind — !

Hedda. Oh dear — did I hit you?

Brack (*still off stage*). Stop that nonsense!

Hedda. Come on in, then.

(*Judge Brack, dressed for dinner, enters, left. He carries a light overcoat over his arm.*)

Brack. Dammit! Do you still fool around with that thing? What are you shooting at, anyway?

Hedda. Oh — just firing off into blue air.

Brack (*gently but firmly taking the gun away from her*). With your permission, Mrs. Tesman. (*Looks at it.*) Ah yes, I remember this gun very well. (*Looks around.*) Where is the case? Ah, here we are. (*Puts the gun in the case and closes it.*) That's enough of that silliness for today.

Hedda. But in the name of heaven, what do you expect me to do with myself?

Brack. No callers?

Hedda (*closing the French doors*). Not a soul. All my close friends are still out of town, it seems.

Brack. And Tesman is out, too, perhaps?

Hedda (*by the desk, puts the gun case in a drawer*). Yes. He took off for the aunts' right after lunch. He didn't expect you so early.

Brack. I should have thought of that. That was stupid of me.

Hedda (*turns her head, looks at him*). Why stupid?

Brack. I would have come a little — sooner.

Hedda (*crossing*). If you had, you wouldn't have found anybody home. For I have been in my room ever since lunch, changing my clothes.

Brack. And isn't there the tiniest little opening in the door for negotiations?

Hedda. You forgot to provide one.

Brack. Another stupidity.

Hedda. So we'll have to stay in here. And wait. For I don't think Tesman will be back for some time.

Brack. By all means. I'll be very patient.

(*Hedda sits on the sofa in the corner. Brack puts his overcoat over the back of the nearest chair and sits down, keeping his hat in his hand. Brief silence. They look at one another.*)

Hedda. Well?

Brack (*in the same tone*). Well?

Hedda. I said it first.

Brack (*leans forward a little*). All right. Let's have a nice little chat, Mrs. Tesman.

Hedda (*leans back*). Don't you think it's an eternity since last time we talked! I don't count last night and this morning. That was nothing.

Brack. You mean — just the two of us?

Hedda. Mmm. If you like.

Brack. There hasn't been a day I haven't wished you were back again.

Hedda. My feelings, exactly.

Brack. Yours? Really, Mrs. Tesman? And I have been assuming you were having such a wonderful time.

Hedda. I'd say!

Brack. All Tesman's letters said so.

Hedda. Oh yes, he! He's happy just poking through old collections of books. And copying old parchments — or whatever they are.

Brack (*with a touch of malice*). Well, that's his calling, you know. Partly, anyway.

Hedda. Yes, so it is. And in that case I suppose — But I! Oh, Judge! You've no idea how bored I've been.

Brack (*with sympathy*). Really? You're serious?

Hedda. Surely you can understand that? For a whole half year never to see anyone who knows even a little bit about our circle? And talks our language?

Brack. Yes, I think I would find that trying, too.

Hedda. And then the most unbearable thing of all —

Brack. Well?

Hedda. — everlastingly to be in the company of the same person —

Brack (*nods in agreement*). Both early and late — yes. I can imagine — at all possible times —

Hedda. I said everlastingly.

Brack. All right. Still, it seems to me that with as excellent a person as our Tesman, it ought to be possible —

Hedda. My dear Judge — Tesman is a specialist.

Brack. Granted.

Hedda. And specialists are not at all entertaining travel companions. Not in the long run, at any rate.

Brack. Not even — the specialist — one happens to love?

Hedda. Bah! That nauseating word!

Brack (*puzzled*). Really, now, Mrs. Tesman — ?

Hedda (*half laughing, half annoyed*). *You* ought to try it some time! Listening to talk about the history of civilization, early and late —

Brack. Everlastingly —

Hedda. All right. And then this business about the domestic industry in the Middle Ages — ! That's the ghastliest part of it all!

Brack (*looking searchingly at her*). But in that case — tell me — how am I to explain — ?

Hedda. That Jørgen Tesman and I made a pair of it, you mean?

Brack. If you want to put it that way — yes.

Hedda. Come now. Do you really find that so strange?

Brack. Both yes and no — Mrs. Tesman.

Hedda. I had danced myself tired, my dear Judge. My season was over — (*Gives a slight start.*) No, no — I don't really mean that. Won't think it, either!

Brack. Nor do you have the slightest reason to, I am sure.

Hedda. Oh — as far as reasons are concerned — (*Looks at him as if trying to read his mind.*) And, after all, Jørgen Tesman must be said to be a most proper young man in all respects.

Brack. Both proper and substantial. Most certainly.

Hedda. And one can't say there is anything exactly comical about him. Do you think there is?

Brack. Comical? No — o. I wouldn't say that —

Hedda. All right, then. And he is a most assiduous collector. Nobody can deny that. I think it is perfectly possible he may go quite far, after all.

Brack (*looks at her rather uncertainly*). I assumed that you, like everybody else, thought he'll in time become an exceptionally eminent man?

Hedda (*with a weary expression*). Yes, I did. And then, you see — there he was, wanting so desperately to be allowed to provide for me — I don't know why I shouldn't have accepted?

Brack. No, certainly. From that point of view —

Hedda. For you know, Judge, that was considerably more than my other admirers were willing to do.

Brack (*laughs*). Well! Of course I can't answer for all the others. But as far as I am concerned, I have always had a certain degree of — respect for the bonds of matrimony. You know — as a general proposition, Mrs. Tesman.

Hedda (*lightly*). Well, I never really counted very heavily on *you* —

Brack. All I want is a nice, confidential circle, in which I can be of service, both in deed and in counsel. Be allowed to come and go like a true and trusted friend —

Hedda. You mean, of the master of the house — ?

Brack (*with a slight bow*). To be perfectly frank — rather of the mistress. But by all means — the master, too, of course. Do you know, that kind of — shall I say, triangular? — relationship can really be a great comfort to all parties involved.

Hedda. Yes, many were the times I missed a second travel companion. To be twosome in the compartment — brrr!

Brack. Fortunately, the wedding trip is over.

Hedda (*shakes her head*). There's a long journey ahead. I've just arrived at a station on the way.

Brack. Well, at the station one gets out and moves around a bit, Mrs. Tesman.

Hedda. I never get out.

Brack. Really?

Hedda. No. For there's always someone around, who —

Brack (*laughs*). — looks at one's legs; is that it?

Hedda. Exactly.

Brack. Oh well, really, now —

Hedda (*with a silencing gesture*). I won't have it! Rather stay in my seat — once I'm seated. Twosome and all.

Brack. I see. But what if a third party were to join the couple?

Hedda. Well, now — *that* would be something altogether different!

Brack. A proven, understanding friend —

Hedda. — entertaining in all sorts of lively ways —

Brack. — and not at all a specialist!

Hedda (*with audible breath*). Yes, that would indeed be a comfort.

Brack (*hearing the front door open, looking at her*). The triangle is complete.

Hedda (*half aloud*). And the train goes on.

(*Tesman, in gray walking suit and soft hat, enters, right. He carries a pile of paperbound books under his arm. Others are stuffed in his pockets.*)

Tesman (*as he walks up to the table in front of the corner sofa*). Puuhh — ! Quite some load to carry, all this — and in this heat, too. (*Puts the books down.*) I am positively perspiring, Hedda. Well, well. So you're here already, my dear Judge. Hm? And Berte didn't tell me.

Brack (*rises*). I came through the garden.

Hedda. What are all those books?

Tesman (*leafing through some of them*). Just some new publications in my special field.

Hedda. Special field, hm?

Brack. Ah yes — professional publications, Mrs. Tesman.

(*Brack and Hedda exchange knowing smiles.*)

Hedda. Do you still need more books?

Tesman. Yes, my dear. There is no such thing as having too many books in one's special field. One has to keep up with what is being written and published, you know.

Hedda. I suppose.

Tesman (*searching among the books*). And look. Here is Eilert Løvborg's new book, too. (*Offers it to her.*) Want to take a look at it, Hedda? Hm?

Hedda. No — thanks just the same. Or perhaps later.

Tesman. I glanced at it on my way home.

Brack. And what do you think of it? As a specialist yourself?

Tesman. It is remarkable for its sobriety. He never wrote like that before. (*Gathers up all the books.*) I just want to take these into my study. I am so much looking forward to cutting them open! And then I'll change. (*To Brack.*) I assume there's no rush to be off, is there?

Brack. Not at all. We have plenty of time.

Tesman. In that case, I think I'll indulge myself a little. (*On his way out with the books he halts in the doorway and turns.*) By the way, Hedda — Aunt Julle won't be out to see you tonight, after all.

Hedda. No? Is it that business with the hat, do you think?

Tesman. Oh, no — not at all. How can you believe a thing like that about Aunt Julle! Just think! No, it's Aunt Rina. She's feeling very poorly.

Hedda. Isn't she always?

Tesman. Yes, but it's especially bad today, poor thing.

Hedda. Well, in that case I suppose she ought to stay home. I shall have to put up with it; that's all.

Tesman. And you have no idea how perfectly delighted Aunt Julle was, even so. Because of how splendid you look after the trip, Hedda!

Hedda (*half aloud, rising*). Oh, these everlasting aunts!

Tesman. Hm?

Hedda (*walks over to the French doors*). Nothing.

Tesman. No? All right. Well, excuse me. (*Exits right, through inner room.*)

Brack. What is this about a hat?

Hedda. Oh, something with Miss Tesman this morning. She had put her hat down on the chair over there. (*Looks at him, smiles.*) So I pretended to think it was the maid's.

Brack (*shakes his head*). But my dear Mrs. Tesman — how could you do a thing like that! And to that excellent old lady, too!

Hedda (*nervously pacing the floor*). Well, you see — something just takes hold of me at times. And then I can't help myself — (*Throws herself down in the easy chair near the stove.*) Oh I can't explain it even to myself.

Brack (*behind her chair*). You aren't really happy — that's the trouble.

Hedda (*staring into space*). I don't know any reason why I should be. Do you?

Brack. Well, yes — partly because you've got the home you've always wanted.

Hedda (*looks up at him and laughs*). So you too believe that story about my great wish?

Brack. You mean, there is nothing to it?

Hedda. Well, yes; there is *something* to it.

Brack. Well?

Hedda. There is this much to it, that last summer I used Tesman to see me home from evening parties.

Brack. Unfortunately — my route was in quite a different direction.

Hedda. True. You walked on other roads last summer.

Brack (laughs). Shame on you, Mrs. Tesman! So, all right — you and Tesman — ?

Hedda. One evening we passed by here. And Tesman, poor thing, was practically turning himself into knots trying to find something to talk about. So I felt sorry for all that erudition —

Brack (with a doubting smile). You did? Hm —

Hedda. I really did. So, just to help him out of his misery, I happened to say that I'd like to live in this house.

Brack. Just that?

Hedda. That was all — *that* evening.

Brack. But afterwards — ?

Hedda. Yes, my frivolity had consequences, Judge.

Brack. Unfortunately — that's often the way with frivolities. It happens to all of us, Mrs. Tesman.

Hedda. Thanks! So in our common enthusiasm for Mr. Secretary Falk's villa Tesman and I found each other, you see! The result was engagement and wedding and honeymoon abroad and all the rest of it. Well, yes, my dear Judge — I've made my bed — I almost said.

Brack. But this is priceless! And you didn't really care for the house at all?

Hedda. Certainly not.

Brack. Not even now? After all, we've set up quite a comfortable home for you here, haven't we?

Hedda. Oh — it seems to me I smell lavender and rose sachets in all the rooms. But maybe that's a smell Aunt Julle brought with her.

Brack (laughs). My guess is rather the late lamented Secretary's wife.

Hedda. It smells of mortality, whoever it is. Like corsages — the next day. (*Clasps her hands behind her neck, leans back, looks at him.*) Judge, you have no idea how dreadfully bored I'll be — out here.

Brack. But don't you think life may hold some task for you, too, Mrs. Tesman?

Hedda. A task? With any kind of appeal?

Brack. Preferably that, of course.

Hedda. Heaven knows what kind of task that might be. There are times when I wonder if — (*Interrupts herself.*) No; I'm sure that wouldn't work, either.

Brack. Who knows? Tell me.

Hedda. It has occurred to me that maybe I could get Tesman to enter politics.

Brack (laughs). Tesman! No, really — I must confess that — politics doesn't strike me as being exactly Tesman's line.

Hedda. I agree. But suppose I were to prevail on him, all the same?

Brack. What satisfaction could you possibly find in that? If he can't succeed — why do you want him even to try?

Hedda. Because I am bored, I tell you! (*After a brief pause.*) So you think it's quite out of the question that Tesman could ever become prime minister?

Brack. Well, you see, Mrs. Tesman — to do that he'd first of all have to be a fairly wealthy man.

Hedda (getting up, impatiently). Yes! There we are! These shabby circumstances I've married into! (*Crosses the floor.*) That's what makes life so mean. So — so — ridiculous! For that's what it is, you know.

Brack. Personally I believe something else is to blame.

Hedda. What?

Brack. You've never been through anything that's really stirred you.

Hedda. Something serious, you mean?

Brack. If you like. But maybe it's coming now.

Hedda (with a toss of her head). You are thinking of that silly old professorship! That's Tesman's business. I refuse to give it a thought.

Brack. As you wish. But now — to put it in the grand style — now when a solemn challenge of responsibility is being posed? Demands made on you? (*Smiles.*) New demands, Mrs. Tesman.

Hedda (angry). Quiet! You'll never see anything of the kind.

Brack (cautiously). We'll talk about this a year from now — on the outside.

Hedda (curtly). I'm not made for that sort of thing, Judge! No demands for me!

Brack. But surely you, like most women, are made for a duty, which —

Hedda (over by the French doors). Oh, do be quiet! Often it seems to me there's only one thing in the world that I am made for.

Brack (coming close). And may I ask what that is?

Hedda (looking out). To be bored to death. Now you know. (*Turns, looks toward the inner room, laughs.*) Just as I thought. Here comes the professor.

Brack (warningly, in a low voice). Steady, now, Mrs. Tesman!

(*Tesman, dressed for a party, carrying his hat and gloves, enters from the right side of the inner room.*)

Tesman. Hedda, any word yet from Eilert Løvborg that he isn't coming, hm?

Hedda. No.

Tesman. In that case, I wouldn't be a bit surprised if we have him here in a few minutes.

Brack. You really think he'll come?

Tesman. I am almost certain he will. For I'm sure it's only idle gossip that you told me this morning.

Brack. Oh?

Tesman. Anyway, that's what Aunt Julle said. She doesn't for a moment believe he'll stand in my way. Just think!

Brack. I'm very glad to hear that.

Tesman (puts his hat and his gloves down on a chair, right). But you must let me wait for him as long as possible.

Brack. By all means. We have plenty of time. Nobody will arrive at my place before seven — seven-thirty, or so.

Tesman. And in the meantime we can keep Hedda company. Take our time. Hm?

Hedda (carrying Brack's hat and coat over to the sofa in the corner). And if worst comes to worst, Mr. Løvborg can stay here with me.

Brack (trying to take the things away from her). Let me, Mrs. Tesman — What do you mean — "if worst comes to worst?"

Hedda. If he doesn't want to go with you and Tesman.

Tesman (looks dubiously at her). But, dearest Hedda — do you think that will quite do? He staying here with you? Hm? Remember, Aunt Julle won't be here.

Hedda. No, but Mrs. Elvsted will. The three of us will have a cup of tea together.

Tesman. Oh yes; *that* will be perfectly all right!

Brack (with a smile). And perhaps the wiser course of action for him.

Hedda. What do you mean?

Brack. Begging your pardon, Mrs. Tesman — you've often enough looked askance at my little stag dinners. It's been your opinion that only men of the firmest principles ought to attend.

Hedda. I should think Mr. Løvborg is firm-principled enough now. A reformed sinner —

(*Berte appears in door, right.*)

Berte. Ma'am — there's a gentleman here who asks if —

Hedda. Show him in, please.

Tesman (softly). I'm sure it's he! Just think!

(*Eilert Løvborg enters, right. He is slim, gaunt. Of Tesman's age,*

*but he looks older and somewhat dissipated. Brown hair and beard.
Pale, longish face, reddish spots on the cheekbones. Dressed for
visiting in elegant, black, brand-new suit. He carries a silk hat and
dark gloves in his hand. He remains near the door, makes a quick
bow. He appears a little embarrassed.*)

Tesman (*goes over to him, shakes his hand*). My dear Eilert — at last
we meet again!

Eilert Løvborg (*subdued voice*). Thanks for your note, Jørgen!
(*Approaching Hedda.*) Am I allowed to shake your hand, too, Mrs.
Tesman?

Hedda (*accepting his proffered hand*). I am very glad to see you,
Mr. Løvborg. (*With a gesture.*) I don't know if you two gentlemen —

Løvborg (*with a slight bow*). Judge Brack, I believe.

Brack (*also bowing lightly*). Certainly. Some years ago —

Tesman (*to Løvborg, both hands on his shoulders*). And now I want
you to feel quite at home here, Eilert! Isn't that right, Hedda? For
you plan to stay here in town, I understand. Hm?

Løvborg. Yes, I do.

Tesman. Perfectly reasonable. Listen — I just got hold of your new
book, but I haven't had a chance to read it yet.

Løvborg. You may save yourself the trouble.

Tesman. Why do you say that?

Løvborg. There's not much to it.

Tesman. Just think — you saying that!

Brack. Nevertheless, people seem to have very good things to say
about it.

Løvborg. That's exactly why I wrote it — so everybody would like it.

Brack. Very wise of you.

Tesman. Yes, but Eilert — !

Løvborg. For I am trying to rebuild my position. Start all over again.

Tesman (*with some embarrassment*). Yes, I suppose you are, aren't
you? Hm?

Løvborg (*smiles, puts his hat down, pulls a parcel out of his pocket*).
When *this* appears — Jørgen Tesman — this you must read. For
this is the real thing. This is me.

Tesman. Oh really? And what is it?

Løvborg. The continuation.

Tesman. Continuation? Of what?

Løvborg. Of the book.

Tesman. Of the new book?

Løvborg. Of course.

Tesman. But Eilert — you've carried the story all the way up to the present!

Løvborg. So I have. And this is about the future.

Tesman. The future! But, heavens — we don't know a thing about the future!

Løvborg. No, we don't. But there are a couple of things to be said about it all the same. (*Unwraps the parcel.*) Here, let me show you —

Tesman. But that's not your handwriting.

Løvborg. I have dictated it. (*Leafs through portions of the manuscript.*) It's in two parts. The first is about the forces that will shape the civilization of the future. And the second (*riffling through more pages*) — about the course which that future civilization will take.

Tesman. How remarkable! It would never occur to me to write anything like that.

Hedda (*over by the French doors, her fingers drumming the pane*). Hmm — I dare say —

Løvborg (*replacing the manuscript in its wrappings and putting it down on the table*). I brought it along, for I thought maybe I'd read parts of it aloud to you this evening.

Tesman. That's very good of you, Eilert. But this evening — ? (*Looks at Brack.*) I'm not quite sure how to arrange that —

Løvborg. Some other time, then. There's no hurry.

Brack. You see, Mr. Løvborg, there's a little get-together over at my house tonight. Mainly for Tesman, you know —

Løvborg (*looking for his hat*). In that case, I certainly won't —

Brack. No, listen. Won't you do me the pleasure to join us?

Løvborg (*firmly*). No, I won't. But thanks all the same.

Brack. Oh come on! Why don't you do that? We'll be a small, select circle. And I think I can promise you a fairly lively evening, as Hed — as Mrs. Tesman would say.

Løvborg. I don't doubt that. Nevertheless — .

Brack. And you may bring your manuscript along and read aloud to Tesman over at my house. I have plenty of room.

Tesman. Just think, Eilert! Wouldn't that be nice, hm?

Hedda (*intervening*). But can't you see that Mr. Løvborg doesn't want to? I'm sure he would rather stay here and have supper with me.

Løvborg (*looks at her*). With you, Mrs. Tesman?

Hedda. And with Mrs. Elvsted.

Løvborg. Ah — ! (*Casually.*) I ran into her at noon today.

Hedda. Oh? Well, she'll be here tonight. So you see your presence is

really required, Mr. Løvborg. Otherwise she won't have anybody
to see her home.

Løvborg. True. All right, then, Mrs. Tesman — I'll stay, thank you.

Hedda. Good. I'll just tell the maid. (*She rings for Berte over by the
door, right.*)

(*Berte appears just off stage. Hedda talks with her in a low voice,
points toward the inner room. Berte nods and exits.*)

Tesman (*while Hedda and Berte are talking, to Løvborg*). Tell me,
Eilert — is it this new subject — about the future — is that what
you plan to lecture on?

Løvborg. Yes.

Tesman. For the bookseller told me you have announced a lecture
series for this fall.

Løvborg. Yes, I have. I hope you won't mind too much.

Tesman. Of course not! But —

Løvborg. For of course I realize it is rather awkward for you.

Tesman (*unhappily*). Oh well — I certainly can't expect — that just
for my sake —

Løvborg. But I will wait till you receive your appointment.

Tesman. Wait? But — but — but — you mean you aren't going to
compete with me? Hm?

Løvborg. No, Just triumph over you. In people's opinion.

Tesman. Oh, for goodness' sake! Then Aunt Julle was right, after all!
I knew it all the time. Hedda! Do you hear that! Just think —
Eilert Løvborg isn't going to stand in our way after all.

Hedda (*tersely*). Our? I have nothing to do with this.

(*Hedda walks into the inner room, where Berte is bringing in a tray
with decanters and glasses. Hedda nods her approval and comes forward again.*)

Tesman (*during the foregoing business*). How about that, Judge?
What do you say to this? Hm?

Brack. I say that moral victory and all that — hm — may be glorious
enough and beautiful enough —

Tesman. Oh, I agree. All the same —

Hedda (*looks at Tesman with a cold smile*). You look thunderstruck.

Tesman. Well, I am — pretty much — I really believe —

Brack. After all, Mrs. Tesman, that was quite a thunderstorm that
just passed over.

Hedda (*points to the inner room*). How about a glass of cold punch,
gentlemen?

Brack (*looks at his watch*). A stirrup cup. Not a bad idea.

Tesman. Splendid, Hedda. Perfectly splendid. In such a lighthearted
   mood as I am now —
Hedda. Please. You, too, Mr. Løvborg.
Løvborg (*with a gesture of refusal*). No, thanks. Really. Nothing for
   me.
Brack. Good heavens, man! Cold punch isn't poison, you know!
Løvborg. Perhaps not for everybody.
Hedda. I'll keep Mr. Løvborg company in the meantime.
Tesman. All right, Hedda. You do that.

(*He and Brack go into the inner room, sit down, drink punch,
smoke cigarettes, and engage in lively conversation during the next
scene. Eilert Løvborg remains standing near the stove. Hedda walks
over to the desk.*)

Hedda (*her voice a little louder than usual*). I'll show you some pictures, if you like. You see — Tesman and I, we took a trip through
   Tyrol on our way back.

(*She brings an album over to the table by the sofa. She sits down in
the far corner of the sofa. Løvborg approaches, stops, looks at her.
He takes a chair and sits down at her left, his back toward the inner
room.*)

Hedda (*opens the album*). Do you see these mountains, Mr. Løvborg?
   They are the Ortler group. Tesman has written their name below.
   Here it is: "The Ortler group near Meran."
Løvborg (*has looked steadily at her all this time. Says slowly*). Hedda
   — Gabler!
Hedda (*with a quick glance sideways*). Not that! Shhh!
Løvborg (*again*). Hedda Gabler!
Hedda (*looking at the album*). Yes, that used to be my name. When
   — when we two knew each other.
Løvborg. And so from now on — for the whole rest of my life — I
   must get used to never again saying Hedda Gabler.
Hedda (*still occupied with the album*). Yes, you must. And you might
   as well start right now. The sooner the better, I think.
Løvborg (*with indignation*). Hedda Gabler married? And married to
   — Jørgen Tesman!
Hedda. Yes — that's the way it goes.
Løvborg. Oh, Hedda, Hedda — how could you throw yourself away
   like that!
Hedda (*with a fierce glance at him*). What's this? I won't have any
   of that!

Løvborg. What do you mean?

(*Tesman enters from the inner room.*)

Hedda (*hears him coming and remarks casually*). And this here, Mr. Løvborg, this is from somewhere in the Ampezzo valley. Just look at those peaks over there. (*With a kindly look at Tesman.*) What did you say those peaks were called, dear?

Tesman. Let me see. Oh, they — they are the Dolomites.

Hedda. Right. Those are the Dolomites, Mr. Løvborg.

Tesman. Hedda, I thought I'd just ask you if you don't want me to bring you some punch, after all? For you, anyway? Hm?

Hedda. Well, yes; thanks. And a couple of cookies, maybe.

Tesman. No cigarettes?

Hedda. No.

Tesman. All right.

(*He returns to the inner room, then turns right. Brack is in there, keeping an eye on Hedda and Løvborg from time to time.*)

Løvborg (*still in a low voice*). Answer me, Hedda. How could you do a thing like that?

Hedda (*apparently engrossed in the album*). If you keep on using my first name I won't talk to you.

Løvborg. Not even when we're alone?

Hedda. No. You may think it, but you must not say it.

Løvborg. I see. It offends your love for — Jørgen Tesman.

Hedda (*glances at him, smiles*). Love? That's a good one!

Løvborg. Not love, then.

Hedda. But no infidelities, either! I won't have it.

Løvborg. Hedda — answer me just one thing —

Hedda. Shhh!

(*Tesman enters with a tray from the inner room.*)

Tesman. Here! Here are the goodies. (*Puts the tray down.*)

Hedda. Why don't you get Berte to do it?

Tesman (*pouring punch*). Because I think it's so much fun waiting on you, Hedda.

Hedda. But you've filled both glasses. And Mr. Løvborg didn't want any —

Tesman. I know, but Mrs. Elvsted will soon be here, won't she?

Hedda. That's right. So she will.

Tesman. Had you forgotten about her? Hm?

Hedda. We've been so busy looking at this. (*Shows him a picture.*) Remember that little village?

Tesman. That's the one just below the Brenner Pass, isn't it? We spent the night there —

Hedda. —'and ran into that lively crowd of summer guests.

Tesman. Right! Just think — if we only could have had you with us, Eilert! Oh well.

(*Returns to the inner room, sits down, and resumes his conversation with Brack.*)

Løvborg. Just tell me this, Hedda —

Hedda. What?

Løvborg. Wasn't there love in your feelings for me, either? Not a touch — not a shimmer of love? Wasn't there?

Hedda. I wonder. To me, we seemed to be simply two good comrades. Two close friends. (*Smiles.*) You, particularly, were very frank.

Løvborg. You wanted it that way.

Hedda. And yet — when I look back upon it now, there was something beautiful, something thrilling, something brave, I think, about the secret frankness — that comradeship that not a single soul so much as suspected.

Løvborg. Yes, wasn't there, Hedda? Wasn't there? When I called on your father in the afternoons — And the General sat by the window with his newspapers — his back turned —

Hedda. And we two in the sofa in the corner —

Løvborg. — always with the same illustrated magazine —

Hedda. — for want of an album, yes —

Løvborg. Yes, Hedda — and then when I confessed to you — ! Told you all about myself, things the others didn't know. Sat and told you about my orgies by day and night. Dissipation day in and day out! Oh, Hedda — what sort of power in you was it that forced me to tell you things like that?

Hedda. You think there was some power in me?

Løvborg. How else can I explain it? And all those veiled questions you asked —

Hedda. — which you understood so perfectly well —

Løvborg. That you could ask such questions! With such complete frankness!

Hedda. *Veiled*, if you please.

Løvborg. But frankly all the same. All about — that!

Hedda. And to think that you answered, Mr. Løvborg!

Løvborg. Yes, that's just what I can't understand — now, afterwards. But tell me, Hedda; wasn't love at the bottom of our whole relationship? Didn't you feel some kind of urge to — purify me — when I came to you in confession? Wasn't that it?

Hedda. No, not quite.

Løvborg. Then what made you do it?

Hedda. Do you find it so very strange that a young girl — when she can do so, without anyone knowing —

Løvborg. Yes — ?

Hedda. — that she wants to take a peek into a world which —

Løvborg. — which — ?

Hedda. — she is not supposed to know anything about?

Løvborg. So that was it!

Hedda. That, too. That, too — I think —

Løvborg. Companionship in the lust for life. But why couldn't *that* at least have continued?

Hedda. That was your own fault.

Løvborg. You were the one who broke off.

Hedda. Yes, when reality threatened to enter our relationship. Shame on you, Eilert Løvborg! How could you want to do a thing like that to your frank and trusting comrade!

Løvborg (clenching his hands). Oh, why didn't you do it! Why didn't you shoot me down, as you said you would!

Hedda. Because I'm scared of scandal.

Løvborg. Yes, Hedda. You are really a coward.

Hedda. A terrible coward. (*Changing her tone.*) But that was your good luck, wasn't it? And now the Elvsteds have healed your broken heart very nicely.

Løvborg. I know what Thea has told you.

Hedda. Perhaps you have told her about us?

Løvborg. Not a word. She is too stupid to understand.

Hedda. Stupid?

Løvborg. In things like that.

Hedda. And I'm a coward. (*Leans forward, without looking in his eyes, whispers.*) But now I am going to confess something to you.

Løvborg (tense). What?

Hedda. That I didn't dare to shoot —

Løvberg. Yes — ?

Hedda. — that was not the worst of my cowardice that night.

Løvborg (looks at her a moment, understands, whispers passionately). Oh, Hedda! Hedda Gabler! Now I begin to see what was behind the companionship! You and I! So it *was* your lust for life — !

Hedda (in a low voice, with an angry glance). Take care! Don't you believe it!

(*Darkness is falling. The door, right, is opened, and Berte enters.*)

Hedda (*closing the album, calls out, smiling*). At last! So there you are, dearest Thea! Come in!

(*Mrs. Elvsted enters. She is dressed for a party. Berte exits, closing the door behind her.*)

Hedda (*on the sofa, reaching out for Mrs. Elvsted*). Sweetest Thea, you have no idea how I've waited for you.

(*In passing, Mrs. Elvsted exchanges quick greetings with Tesman and Brack in the inner room. She walks up to the table and shakes Hedda's hand. Eilert Løvborg rises. He and Mrs. Elvsted greet one another with a silent nod.*)

Mrs. Elvsted. Shouldn't I go in and say hello to your husband?
Hedda. No, never mind that. Leave them alone. They're soon leaving, anyway.
Mrs. Elvsted. Leaving?
Hedda. They're going out to drink.
Mrs. Elvsted (*quickly, to Løvborg*). Not you?
Løvborg. No.
Hedda. Mr. Løvborg stays here with us.
Mrs. Elvsted (*pulls up a chair, is about to sit down next to Løvborg*). Oh, how wonderful it is to be here!
Hedda. Oh no, little Thea. Not that. Not there. Over here by me, please. *I* want to be in the middle.
Mrs. Elvsted. Just as you like. (*She walks in front of the table and seats herself on the sofa, on Hedda's right. Løvborg sits down again on his chair.*)
Løvborg (*after a brief pause, to Hedda*). Isn't she lovely to look at?
Hedda (*gently stroking her hair*). Just to look at?
Løvborg. Yes. For you see — she and I — we are real comrades. We have absolute faith in one another. And we can talk together in full freedom.
Hedda. Unveiled, Mr. Løvborg?
Løvborg. Well —
Mrs. Elvsted (*in a low voice, clinging to Hedda*). Oh, I am so happy, Hedda! For just think — he also says I have inspired him!
Hedda (*looks at her with a smile*). No, really! He says that?
Løvborg. And she has such courage, Mrs. Tesman! Such courage of action.
Mrs. Elvsted. Oh, my God — courage — ! I!
Løvborg. Infinite courage — when it concerns the comrade.
Hedda. Yes, courage — if one only had that.
Løvborg. What then?

Hedda. Then maybe life would be tolerable, after all. (*Changing her tone.*) But now, dearest Thea, you want a glass of nice, cold punch.

Mrs. Elvsted. No, thanks. I never drink things like that.

Hedda. Then what about you, Mr. Løvborg?

Løvborg. Thanks. Nothing for me, either.

Mrs. Elvsted. No, nothing for him, either.

Hedda (*looks firmly at him*). If I say so?

Løvborg. Makes no difference.

Hedda (*laughs*). Oh dear! So I have no power over you at all. Is that it?

Løvborg. Not in that respect.

Hedda. Seriously, though; I really think you should. For your own sake.

Mrs. Elvsted. No, but Hedda — !

Løvborg. Why so?

Hedda. Or rather for people's sake.

Løvborg. Oh?

Hedda. For else they might think you don't really trust yourself — That you lack self-confidence —

Mrs. Elvsted (*softly*). Don't, Hedda!

Løvborg. People may think whatever they like for all I care — for the time being.

Mrs. Elvsted (*happy*). Exactly!

Hedda. I could easily tell from watching Judge Brack just now.

Løvborg. Tell what?

Hedda. He smiled so contemptuously when you didn't dare to join them in there.

Løvborg. Didn't I dare to! It's just that I'd much rather stay here and talk with you!

Mrs. Elvsted. But that's only natural, Hedda.

Hedda. The Judge had no way of knowing that. And I also noticed he smiled and looked at Tesman when you didn't dare to go to his silly old party.

Løvborg. Didn't dare! Are you saying I didn't dare?

Hedda. I am not. But that's how Judge Brack understood it.

Løvborg. Let him.

Hedda. So you're not going?

Løvborg. I'm staying here with you and Thea.

Mrs. Elvsted. Of course, he is, Hedda!

Hedda (*smiles, nods approvingly*). That's what I call firm foundations. Principled forever; that's the way a man ought to be! (*Turning to Mrs. Elvsted, stroking her cheek*). What did I tell you this morning — when you came here, quite beside yourself — ?

Løvborg (*puzzled*). Beside herself?

Mrs. Elvsted (*in terror*). Hedda — Hedda — don't!

Hedda. Now do you see? There was no need at all for that mortal fear of yours — (*Interrupting herself.*) There, now! Now we can all three relax and enjoy ourselves.

Løvborg (*startled*). What's all this, Mrs. Tesman?

Mrs. Elvsted. Oh, God, Hedda — what are you saying? What are you doing?

Hedda. Please be quiet. That horrible Judge is looking at you.

Løvborg. In mortal fear? So that's it. For my sake.

Mrs. Elvsted (*softly, wailing*). Oh, Hedda — if you only knew how utterly miserable you have made me!

Løvborg (*stares at her for a moment. His face is distorted.*). So that was the comrade's happy confidence in me!

Mrs. Elvsted. Oh, my dearest friend — listen to me first — !

Løvborg (*picks up one of the glasses of punch, raises it, says hoarsely*). Here's to you, Thea! (*Empties the glass, puts it down, picks up the other one.*)

Mrs. Elvsted (*softly*). Hedda, Hedda — why did you want to do this?

Hedda. Want to! I! Are you mad?

Løvborg. And here's to you, too, Mrs. Tesman! Thanks for telling me the truth. Long live the truth! (*He drains the glass and is about to fill it again.*)

Hedda (*restrains him*). That's enough for now. Remember you are going to a party.

Mrs. Elvsted. No, no, no!

Hedda. Shhh! They are looking at you.

Løvborg (*puts his glass down*). Listen, Thea — tell me the truth —

Mrs. Elvsted. I will, I will!

Løvborg. Did your husband know you were coming after me?

Mrs. Elvsted (*wringing her hands*). Oh, Hedda — do you hear what he's asking?

Løvborg. Did the two of you agree that you were to come here and look after me? Maybe it was his idea, even? Did he send you? Ah, I know what it was — he missed me in the office, didn't he? Or was it at the card table?

Mrs. Elvsted (*softly, in agony*). Oh, Løvborg, Løvborg!

Løvborg (*grabs a glass and is about to fill it*). Here's to the old Commissioner, too!

Hedda (*stops him*). No more now. You're supposed to read aloud for Tesman tonight — remember?

Løvborg (*calm again, puts the glass down*). This was silly of me,

Thea. I'm sorry. Taking it this way. Please, don't be angry with me. You'll see — both you and all those others — that even if I have been down — ! With your help, Thea — dear comrade.

Mrs. Elvsted (*beaming*). Oh, thank God — !

(*In the meantime, Brack has looked at his watch. He and Tesman get up and come forward.*)

Brack (*picking up his coat and hat*). Well, Mrs. Tesman; our time is up.

Hedda. I suppose it is.

Løvborg (*rising*). Mine, too, Judge.

Mrs. Elvsted (*softly, pleadingly*). Oh, Løvborg — don't do it!

Hedda (*pinches her arm*). They can hear you!

Mrs. Elvsted (*with a soft exclamation*). Ouch!

Løvborg (*to Brack*). You were good enough to ask me —

Brack. So you're coming, after all?

Løvborg. If I may.

Brack. I'm delighted.

Løvborg (*picks up his manuscript and says to Tesman*). For there are a couple of things here I'd like to show you before I send it off.

Tesman. Just think! Isn't that nice! But — dearest Hedda — ? In that case, how are you going to get Mrs. Elvsted home? Hm?

Hedda. We'll manage somehow.

Løvborg (*looking at the two women*). Mrs. Elvsted? I'll be back to pick her up, of course. (*Coming closer.*) About ten o'clock, Mrs. Tesman? Is that convenient?

Hedda. Certainly. That will be fine.

Tesman. Then everything is nice and settled. But don't expect me that early, Hedda.

Hedda. You just stay as long as — as long as you want to, dear.

Mrs. Elvsted (*in secret fear*). I'll be waiting for you here, then, Mr. Løvborg.

Løvborg (*hat in hand*). Of course, Mrs. Elvsted.

Brack. All aboard the pleasure train, gentlemen! I hope we'll have a lively evening — as a certain fair lady would say.

Hedda. Ah — if only the fair lady could be present. Invisibly.

Brack. Why invisibly?

Hedda. To listen to some of your unadulterated liveliness, Judge.

Brack (*laughs*). I shouldn't advise the fair lady to do that!

Tesman (*also laughing*). You're a good one, Hedda! Just think!

Brack. Well — good night, ladies!

Løvborg (*with a bow*). Till about ten, then.

(*Brack, Løvborg, and Tesman go out, right. At the same time Berte enters from the inner room with a lighted lamp, which she places on the table, front center. She goes out the same way.*)

Mrs. Elvsted (*has risen and paces restlessly up and down*). Hedda, Hedda — how do you think all this will end?

Hedda. At ten o'clock he'll be here. I see him already. With vine leaves in his hair. Flushed and confident.

Mrs. Elvsted. I only hope you're right.

Hedda. For then, you see, he'll have mastered himself. And be a free man for all the days of his life.

Mrs. Elvsted. Dear God — how I hope you are right! That he'll come back like that.

Hedda. That is the way he will come. No other way. (*She rises and goes closer to Mrs. Elvsted.*) You may doubt as long as you like. I believe in him. And now we'll see —

Mrs. Elvsted. There is something behind all this, Hedda. Some hidden purpose.

Hedda. Yes, there is! For once in my life I want to have power over a human destiny.

Mrs. Elvsted. But don't you already?

Hedda. I don't and I never have.

Mrs. Elvsted. But your husband —?

Hedda. You think that's worth the trouble? Oh, if you knew how poor I am! And you got to be so rich! (*Embraces her passionately.*) I think I'll have to burn your hair off, after all!

Mrs. Elvsted. Let me go! Let me go! You scare me, Hedda!

Berte (*in the doorway*). Supper is served, ma'am.

Hedda. Good. We're coming.

Mrs. Elvsted. No, no, no! I'd rather go home by myself! Right now!

Hedda. Nonsense! You'll have your cup of tea first, you little silly. And then — at ten o'clock — Eilert Løvborg comes — with vine leaves in his hair! (*She almost pulls Mrs. Elvsted toward the doorway.*)

ACT THREE

(*The same room at the Tesmans'. The doorway and the French windows both have their portieres closed. The lamp, turned half down, is still on the table. The stove is open. Some dying embers can be seen. Mrs. Elvsted, wrapped in a big shawl, is in the easy chair near the stove, her feet on a footstool. Hedda, also dressed, is lying on the sofa, covered by a blanket.*)

Mrs. Elvsted (*after a while suddenly sits up, listens anxiously; then she wearily sinks back in her chair, whimpers softly*). Oh my God, my God — not yet!

(*Berte enters cautiously, right, carrying a letter.*)

Mrs. Elvsted (*turns and whispers tensely*). Well — has anybody been here?

Berte (*in a low voice*). Yes. Just now there was a girl with this letter.

Mrs. Elvsted (*quickly, reaches for it*). A letter! Give it to me.

Berte. No, ma'am. It's for the Doctor.

Mrs. Elvsted. I see.

Berte. Miss Tesman's maid brought it. I'll leave it here on the table.

Mrs. Elvsted. All right.

Berte (*puts the letter down*). I'd better put out the lamp. It just reeks.

Mrs. Elvsted. Yes, do that. It must be daylight soon, anyway.

Berte (*putting out the lamp*). It's light already, ma'am.

Mrs. Elvsted. Light already! And still not back!

Berte. No, so help us. Not that I didn't expect as much —

Mrs. Elvsted. You did?

Berte. Yes, when I saw a certain character was back in town. Taking them off with him. We sure heard enough about him in the old days!

Mrs. Elvsted. Not so loud. You are waking up Mrs. Tesman.

Berte (*looks toward the sofa, sighs*). God forbid — ! Let her sleep, poor thing. Do you want me to get the fire going again?

Mrs. Elvsted. Not on my account, thank you.

Berte. All right. (*Exits quietly, right.*)

Hedda (*awakened by the closing door*). What's that?

Mrs. Elvsted. Just the maid.

Hedda (*looks around*). Why in here — ? Oh, I remember! (*Sits up, rubs her eyes, stretches.*) What time is it, Thea?

Mrs. Elvsted (*looks at her watch*). Past Seven.

Hedda. When did Tesman get home?

Mrs. Elvsted. He didn't.

Hedda. Not home yet!

Mrs. Elvsted (*getting up*). Nobody's come.

Hedda. And we waited till four!

Mrs. Elvsted (*wringing her hands*). And *how* we waited!

Hedda (*her hand covering a yawn*). We — ll. We could have saved ourselves that trouble.

Mrs. Elvsted. Did you get any sleep at all?

Hedda. Yes, I slept pretty well, I think. Didn't you?

Mrs. Elvsted. Not a wink. I just couldn't, Hedda! It was just impossible.

Hedda (*rises, walks over to her*). Well, now! There's nothing to worry about, for heaven's sake. I know exactly what's happened.

Mrs. Elvsted. Then tell me please. Where do you think they are?

Hedda. Well, first of all, I'm sure they were terribly late leaving the Judge's —

Mrs. Elvsted. Dear, yes. I'm sure you're right. Still —

Hedda. — and so Tesman didn't want to wake us up in the middle of the night. (*Laughs.*) Maybe he didn't want us to see him, either — after a party like that.

Mrs. Elvsted. But where do you think he has gone?

Hedda. To the aunts', of course. His old room is still there, all ready for him.

Mrs. Elvsted. No, he can't be there. Just a few minutes ago there came a letter for him from Miss Tesman. It's over there.

Hedda. Oh? (*looks at the envelope.*) So it is — Auntie Julle herself. In that case, I suppose he's still at Brack's. And there's Eilert Løvborg, too — reading aloud, with vine leaves in his hair.

Mrs. Elvsted. Oh Hedda — you're only saying things you don't believe yourself.

Hedda. My, what a little imbecile you really are, Thea!

Mrs. Elvsted. Yes, I suppose I am.

Hedda. And you look dead tired, too.

Mrs. Elvsted. I *am* dead tired.

Hedda. Why don't you do as I say. Go into my room and lie down.

Mrs. Elvsted. No, no — I wouldn't be able to go to sleep, anyway.

Hedda. Of course, you would.

Mrs. Elvsted. And your husband is bound to be home any minute now. And I have to know right away.

Hedda. I'll let you know as soon as he gets here.

Mrs. Elvsted. You promise me that, Hedda?

Hedda. I do. You just go to sleep.

Mrs. Elvsted. Thanks. At least I'll try. (*Exits through inner room.*)

(*Hedda goes to the French doors, opens the portieres. The room is now in full daylight. She picks up a little hand mirror from the desk, looks at herself, smooths her hair. Walks over to door, right, rings the bell for the maid. Berte presently appears.*)

Berte. You want something, ma'am?

Hedda. Yes. You'll have to start the fire again. I'm cold.

Berte. Yes, ma'am! I'll get it warm in no time. (*Rakes the embers together and puts in another piece of wood. Then she suddenly listens.*) There's the doorbell, ma'am.

Hedda. All right. See who it is. I'll take care of the stove myself.

Berte. You'll have a nice blaze going in a minute. (*Exits right.*)

(*Hedda kneels on the footstool and puts in more pieces of wood. Presently Tesman enters, right. He looks tired and somber. He tiptoes toward the doorway and is about to disappear between the portieres.*)

Hedda (*by the stove, without looking up*). Good morning.

Tesman (*turning*). Hedda! (*Comes closer.*) For heaven's sake — you up already! Hm?

Hedda. Yes, I got up very early this morning.

Tesman. And I was sure you'd still be sound asleep! Just think!

Hedda. Not so loud. Mrs. Elvsted is asleep in my room.

Tesman. Mrs. Elvsted stayed here all night?

Hedda. Yes. Nobody came for her, you know.

Tesman. No, I suppose —

Hedda (*closes the stove, rises*). Well, did you have a good time at the Judge's?

Tesman. Were you worried about me? Hm?

Hedda. I'd never dream of worrying about you. I asked if you had a good time.

Tesman. Yes, indeed. Nice for a change anyway. But I think I liked it best early in the evening. For then Eilert read to me. Just think — we were more than an hour early! And Brack, of course, had things to see to. So Eilert read.

Hedda (*sits down at the right side of the table*). So? Tell me all about it.

Tesman (*sits down on an ottoman near the stove.*). Oh Hedda, you'll never believe what a book that will be! It must be just the most remarkable thing ever written! Just think!

Hedda. Yes, but I don't really care about that —

Tesman. I must tell you, Hedda — I have a confession to make. As he was reading — something ugly came over me —

Hedda. Ugly?

Tesman. I sat there envying Eilert for being able to write like that! Just think, Hedda!

Hedda. All right. I'm thinking!

Tesman. And yet, with all his gifts — he's incorrigible, after all.

Hedda. I suppose you mean he has more courage for life than the rest of you?

Tesman. No, no — I don't mean that. I mean that he's incapable of exercising moderation in his pleasures.

Hedda. What happened — in the end?

Tesman. Well — I would call it bacchanal, Hedda.

Hedda. Did he have vine leaves in his hair?

Tesman. Vine leaves? No, I didn't notice any vine leaves. But he gave a long, muddled speech in honor of the woman who had inspired him in his work. Those were his words.

Hedda. Did he mention her name?

Tesman. No, he didn't. But I'm sure it must be Mrs. Elvsted. You just wait and see if I'm not right!

Hedda. And where did you and he part company?

Tesman. On the way back to town. We left — the last of us did — at the same time. And Brack came along, too, to get some fresh air. Then we decided we'd better see Eilert home. You see, he had had altogether too much to drink!

Hedda. I can imagine.

Tesman. But then the strangest thing of all happened, Hedda! Or maybe I should say the saddest. I'm almost ashamed — on Eilert's behalf — even talking about it.

Hedda. Well — ?

Tesman. You see, on the way back I happened to be behind the others a little. Just for a minute or two — you know —

Hedda. All right, all right — !

Tesman. And when I hurried to catch up with them, can you guess what I found by the roadside? Hm?

Hedda. How can I possibly — ?

Tesman. You mustn't tell this to a living soul, Hedda! Do you hear! Promise me that, for Eilert's sake. (*Pulls a parcel out of his coat pocket.*) Just think — I found this!

Hedda. Isn't that what he had with him here yesterday?

Tesman. Yes! It's his whole, precious, irreplaceable manuscript! And he had dropped it — just like that! Without even noticing! Just think, Hedda! Isn't that awfully sad?

Hedda. But why didn't you give it back to him?

Tesman. In the condition he was in! Dear — I just didn't dare to.

Hedda. And you didn't tell any of the others that you had found it, either?

Tesman. Of course not. I didn't want to, for Eilert's sake — don't you see?

Hedda. So nobody knows that you have Eilert Løvborg's papers?

Tesman. Nobody. And nobody must know, either.

Hedda. And what did you and he talk about afterwards?

Tesman. I didn't have a chance to talk to him at all after that. For when we came into town, he and a couple of the others simply vanished. Just think!

Hedda. Oh? I expect they took him home.

Tesman. I suppose that must be it. And Brack took off on his own, too.

Hedda. And what have you been doing with yourself since then?

Tesman. Well, you see, I and some of the others went home with one of the younger fellows and had a cup of early morning coffee. Or night coffee maybe, rather. Hm? And now, after I've rested a bit and poor Eilert's had some sleep, I'll take this back to him.

Hedda (reaches for the parcel). No — don't do that! Not right away, I mean. Let me look at it first.

Tesman. Dearest Hedda — honestly, I just don't dare to.

Hedda. Don't you dare to?

Tesman. No, for I'm sure you realize how utterly desperate he'll be when he wakes up and finds that the manuscript is gone. For he hasn't a copy, you know. He said so himself.

Hedda (looks searchingly at him). But can't a thing like that be written over again?

Tesman. Hardly. I really don't think so. For, you see — the inspiration —

Hedda. Yes, I daresay that's the main thing. (*Casually.*) By the way, here's a letter for you.

Tesman. Imagine!

Hedda. (*gives it to him*). It came early this morning.

Tesman. It's from Aunt Julle, Hedda! I wonder what it can be. (*Puts the manuscript down on the other ottoman, opens the letter, skims the content, jumps up.*) Oh Hedda! She says here that poor Aunt Rina is dying!

Hedda. You know we had to expect that.

Tesman. And if I want to see her again I had better hurry. I'll rush over right away.

Hedda (suppressing a smile). You'll rush?

Tesman. Dearest Hedda of mine — if only you could bring yourself to come along! Hm?

Hedda (rises, weary, with an air of refusal). No, no. You mustn't ask me that. I don't want to look at death and disease. I don't want anything to do with ugliness.

Tesman. Well, all right — (*Rushing around.*) My hat? My coat? Oh — out here in the hall. I just hope I won't be too late, Hedda. Hm?

Hedda. Oh I'm sure that if you rush —

(*Berte appears in the door, right.*)

Berte. Judge Brack is here and wants to know if he may see you.
Tesman. At this hour! No, no. I can't possibly see him now!
Hedda. But I can. (*To Berte.*) Tell the Judge please to come in.

(*Berte exits.*)

Hedda (*with a quick whisper*) Tesman! The package! (*She grabs it from the ottoman.*)
Tesman. Yes! Give it to me!
Hedda. No, no. I'll hide it for you till later.

(*She walks over to the desk and sticks the parcel in among the books on the shelf. In his hurry Tesman is having difficulties getting his gloves on. Judge Brack enters, right.*)

Hedda (*nods to him*). If *you* aren't an early bird —
Brack. Yes, don't you think so? (*To Tesman.*) You're going out, too?
Tesman. Yes, I must go and see the aunts. Just think, the invalid — she's dying!
Brack. Oh, I'm terribly sorry! In that case, don't let me keep you. At such a moment —
Tesman. Yes, I really must run. Goodbye, goodbye! (*Hurries out, right.*)
Hedda (*approaching Brack*). It appears that things were quite lively last night over at your house.
Brack. Indeed, Mrs. Tesman — I didn't get to bed at all.
Hedda. You didn't either?
Brack. As you see. But tell me — what has Tesman told you about the night's adventures?
Hedda. Just some tiresome story about having coffee with somebody someplace —
Brack. I believe I know all about that coffee. Eilert Løvborg wasn't one of them, was he?
Hedda. No, they had taken him home first.
Brack. Tesman, too?
Hedda. No. Some of the others, he said.
Brack (*smiles*). Jørgen Tesman is really an ingenuous soul, you know.
Hedda. He certainly is. But why do you say that? Is there something more to all this?
Brack. Yes, there is.
Hedda. Well! In that case, why don't we make ourselves comfortable, Judge. You'll tell your story better, too.

(*She sits down at the left side of the table, Brack near her at the adjacent side.*)

Hedda. All right?

Brack. For reasons of my own I wanted to keep track of my guests' movements last night. Or, rather — some of my guests.

Hedda. Eilert Løvborg was one of them, perhaps?

Brack. As a matter of fact — he was.

Hedda. Now you are really making me curious.

Brack. Do you know where he and a couple of the others spent the rest of the night, Mrs. Tesman?

Hedda. No — tell me. If it can be told.

Brack. Oh, certainly. They turned up at an exceptionally gay early morning gathering.

Hedda. Of the lively kind?

Brack. Of the liveliest.

Hedda. A little more about this, Judge.

Brack. Løvborg had been invited beforehand. I knew about that. But he had declined. He is a reformed character, you know.

Hedda. As of his stay with the Elvsteds — yes. But he went after all?

Brack. Well, yes, you see, Mrs. Tesman — unfortunately, the spirit moved him over at my house last evening.

Hedda. Yes, I understand he became inspired.

Brack. Quite violently inspired. And that, I gather, must have changed his mind. You know, we men don't always have as much integrity as we ought to have.

Hedda. Oh, I'm sure you're an exception, Judge Brack. But about Løvborg — ?

Brack. To make a long story short — he ended up at Miss Diana's establishment.

Hedda. Miss Diana's?

Brack. She was the hostess at this gathering — a select circle of intimate friends, male and female.

Hedda. Is she a redhead, by any chance?

Brack. That's correct.

Hedda. And a singer — of sorts?

Brack. Yes — that, too. And a mighty huntress — of men, Mrs. Tesman. You seem to have heard of her. Eilert Løvborg use to be one of her most devoted protectors in his more affluent days.

Hedda. And how did it all end?

Brack. Not in a very friendly fashion, apparently. It seems that after the tenderest reception Miss Diana resorted to brute force —

Hedda. Against Løvborg?

Brack. Yes. He accused her or her women friends of having stolen something of his. Said his wallet was gone. And other things, too. In brief, he's supposed to have started a pretty wicked row.

Hedda. And — ?

Brack. Well — there was a general free-for-all — men and women both. Fortunately, the police stepped in —

Hedda. The police — !

Brack. Yes. But I'm afraid this will be an expensive escapade for Eilert Løvborg, crazy fool that he is.

Hedda. Well!

Brack. It appears that he made quite violent objection — struck an officer in the car and tore his coat. So they had to take him along.

Hedda. How do you know all this?

Brack. From the police.

Hedda (*staring straight ahead*). So that's how it was. No vine leaves in his hair.

Brack. Vine leaves, Mrs. Tesman?

Hedda (*changing her tone*). But tell me, Judge Brack — why did you keep such a close watch on Eilert Løvborg?

Brack. Well — for one thing, it is obviously of some concern to me if he testifies that he came straight from my party.

Hedda. So you think there will be an investigation?

Brack. Naturally. But I suppose that doesn't really matter too much. However, as a friend of the house I considered it my duty to give you and Tesman a full account of his night-time exploits.

Hedda. Yes, but why?

Brack. Because I very strongly suspect that he intends to use you as a kind of screen.

Hedda. Really! Why do you think that?

Brack. Oh, come now, Mrs. Tesman! We can use our eyes, can't we? This Mrs. Elvsted — she isn't leaving town right away you know.

Hedda. Well, even if there should be something going on between those two, I'd think there would be plenty of other places they could meet.

Brack. But no home. After last night, every respectable house will once again be closed to Eilert Løvborg.

Hedda. And so should mine, you mean?

Brack. Yes. I admit I would find it more than embarrassing if the gentleman were to become a daily guest here, Mrs. Tesman. If he, as an outsider — a highly dispensable outsider — if he were to intrude himself —

Hedda. — into the triangle?

Brack. Precisely. It would amount to homelessness for me.

Hedda (smiling). Sole cock-o'-the-walk — so, that's your goal, is it, Judge?

Brack (nods slowly, lowers his voice). Yes. That is my goal. And for that I will fight with every means at my disposal.

Hedda (her smile fading). You're really a dangerous person, you know — when you come right down to it.

Brack. You think so?

Hedda. Yes. I am beginning to think so now. And I must say I am exceedingly glad you don't have any kind of hold on me.

Brack (with a noncommittal laugh). Well, well, Mrs. Tesman! Maybe there is something to what you are saying, at that. Who knows what I might do if I did.

Hedda. Really, now, Judge Brack! Are you threatening me?

Brack (rising). — Nonsense! For the triangle, you see — is best maintained on a voluntary basis.

Hedda. My sentiments, exactly.

Brack. Well, I have said what I came to say. And now I should get back to town. Goodbye, Mrs. Tesman! (*Walks toward the French doors.*)

Hedda (rises). You're going through the garden?

Brack. Yes. For me that's a short cut.

Hedda. Yes, and then it's a back way.

Brack. Quite true. I have nothing against back ways. There are times when they are most intriguing.

Hedda. You mean when real ammunition is used?

Brack (in the doorway, laughs back at her). Oh good heavens! I don't suppose one shoots one's tame roosters!

Hedda (laughs also). No — not if one has only one — !

(*They nod to each other, both still laughing. He leaves. She closes the door behind him. For a few moments she remains by the door, quite serious now, looking into the garden. Then she walks over to the doorway and opens the portieres wide enough to look into the inner room. Goes to the desk, pulls Løvborg's manuscript from the bookshelf and is about to read it when Berte's voice, very loud, is heard from the hall, right. Hedda turns around, listens. She hurriedly puts the manuscript into the drawer of the desk and puts the key down on its top. Eilert Løvborg, wearing his coat and with his hat in his hand, flings open the door, right. He looks somewhat confused and excited.*)

Løvborg (turned toward the invisible Berte in the hall). — And I say I must! You can't stop me! (*He closes the door, turns, sees Hedda, immediately controls himself, greets her.*)

Hedda (by the desk). Well, well, Mr. Løvborg — aren't you a trifle late coming for Thea?

Løvborg. Or a trifle early for calling on you. I apologize.

Hedda. How do you know she is still here?

Løvborg. The people she is staying with told me she's been gone all night.

Hedda (walks over to the table). Did they seem — strange — when they said it?

Løvborg (puzzled). Strange?

Hedda. I mean, did they seem to find it a little — unusual?

Løvborg (suddenly understands). Ah, I see what you mean! Of course! I'm dragging her down with me. No, as a matter of fact, I didn't notice anything. I suppose Tesman isn't up yet?

Hedda. I — I don't think so —

Løvborg. When did he get home?

Hedda. Very late.

Løvborg. Did he tell you anything?

Hedda. Yes, he said you'd all had quite a time over at Brack's.

Løvborg. Just that?

Hedda. I think so. But I was so awfully sleepy —

(Mrs. Elvsted enters through portieres in the rear.)

Mrs. Elvsted (toward him). Oh, Løvborg! At last!

Løvborg. Yes, at last. And too late.

Mrs. Elvsted (in fear). What is too late?

Løvborg. Everything is too late now. It's all over with me.

Mrs. Elvsted. Oh no, no! Don't say things like that!

Løvborg. You'll say the same yourself when you hear —

Mrs. Elvsted. I don't want to hear — !

Hedda. Maybe you'd rather talk with her alone? I'll leave.

Løvborg. No stay — you, too. I beg you to.

Mrs. Elvsted. But I don't want to listen, do you hear?

Løvborg. It isn't last night I want to talk about.

Mrs. Elvsted. What about, then?

Løvborg. We'll have to part, Thea.

Mrs. Elvsted. Part!

Hedda (involuntarily). I knew it!

Løvborg. For I don't need you any more.

Mrs. Elvsted. And you can stand there and tell me a thing like that! Don't need me! Why can't I help you the way I did before? Aren't we going to keep on working together?

Løvborg. I don't intend to work any more.

Mrs. Elvsted (desperately). What am I going to do with my life, then?

Løvborg. You'll have to try to live your life as if you'd never known me.

Mrs. Elvsted. But I can't do that!

Løvborg. Try, Thea. Go back home.

Mrs. Elvsted (agitated). Never again! Where you are I want to be! And you can't chase me away just like that. I want to stay right here! Be with you when the book appears.

Hedda (in a tense whisper). Ah — yes — the book!

Løvborg (looks at her). My book — and Thea's. For that's what it is.

Mrs. Elvsted. That's what I feel, too. And that's why I have the right to be with you when it comes out. I want to see all the honor and all the fame you'll get. And the joy — I want to share the joy, too.

Løvborg. Thea, our book is never going to come out.

Hedda. Ah!

Mrs. Elvsted. It won't!

Løvborg. Can't ever appear.

Mrs. Elvsted (with fearful suspicion). Løvborg, what have you done with the manuscript?

Hedda (watching him tensely). Yes — what about the manuscript?

Mrs. Elvsted. Where is it?

Løvborg. Oh Thea — please, don't ask me about that!

Mrs. Elvsted. Yes, yes — I want to be told! I have the right to know — right now!

Løvborg. All right. I've torn it to pieces.

Mrs. Elvsted (screams). Oh, no! No!

Hedda (involuntarily). But that's not — !

Løvborg (looks at her). Not true, you think?

Hedda (composing herself). Well, of course, if you say so. You should know. It just sounds so — so unbelievable.

Løvborg. All the same, it's true.

Mrs. Elvsted (hands clenched). Oh God — oh God, Hedda. He has torn his own work to pieces!

Løvborg. I have torn my whole life to pieces, so why not my life's work as well?

Mrs. Elvsted. And that's what you did last night?

Løvborg. Yes, I tell you! In a thousand pieces. And scattered them in the fjord. Far out — where the water is clean and salty. Let them drift there, with wind and current. Then they'll sink. Deep, deep down. Like me, Thea.

Mrs. Elvsted. Do you know, Løvborg — this thing you've done to the
book — all the rest of my life I'll think of it as killing a little child.

Løvborg. You are right. It is like murdering a child.

Mrs. Elvsted. But then, how could you? For the child was mine, too!

Hedda (*almost soundlessly*). The child —

Mrs. Elvsted (*with a deep sigh*). So it's all over. I'll go now, Hedda.

Hedda. But you aren't leaving town?

Mrs. Elvsted. Oh, I don't know myself what I'll do. There's only darkness before me. (*Exits, right.*)

Hedda (*waits for a moment*). Aren't you going to see her home, Mr.
Løvborg?

Løvborg. I? Through the streets? Letting people see her with me?

Hedda. Of course, I don't know what else may have happened last
night. But is it really so absolutely irreparable — ?

Løvborg. Last night is not the end of it. That I know. And yet, I don't
really care for that kind of life any more. Not again. She has broken
all the courage for life and all the defiance that was in me.

Hedda (*staring ahead*). So that sweet little goose has had her hand in
a human destiny. (*Looks at him.*) But that you could be so heartless, even so!

Løvborg. Don't tell me I was heartless!

Hedda. To ruin everything that's filled her soul for a such a long time!
You don't call that heartless!

Løvborg. Hedda — to you I can tell the truth.

Hedda. The truth?

Løvborg. But first promise me — give me your word you'll never let
Thea know what I'm going to tell you now.

Hedda. You have it.

Løvborg. All right. It isn't true, what I just told her.

Hedda. About the manuscript?

Løvborg. Yes. I have not torn it up. Not thrown it in the sea, either.

Hedda. But then — where is it?

Løvborg. I've destroyed it just the same. Really, I have, Hedda!

Hedda. I don't understand.

Løvborg. Thea said that what I had done seemed to her like murdering a child.

Hedda. Yes — she did.

Løvborg. But killing a child, that's not the worst thing a father can do
to it.

Hedda. No?

Løvborg. No. And the worst is what I don't want Thea to know.

Hedda. What *is* the worst?

Løvborg. Hedda — suppose a man, say, early in the morning, after

a stupid, drunken night — suppose he comes home to his child's
mother and says: Listen, I've been in such and such a place. I've
been here — and I've been there. And I had our child with me. In
all those places. And the child is lost. Gone. Vanished. I'll be
damned if I know where it is. Who's got hold of it —

Hedda. Yes — but when all is said and done — it is only a book, you
know.

Løvborg. Thea's pure soul was in that book.

Hedda. I realize that.

Løvborg. Then you surely also realize that she and I can have no
future together.

Hedda. Where do you go from here?

Løvborg. Nowhere. Just finish everything off. The sooner the better.

Hedda (a step closer). Listen — Eilert Løvborg — Couldn't you make
sure it's done beautifully?

Løvborg. Beautifully? *(Smiles.)* With vine leaves in the hair, as you
used to say.

Hedda. Oh no. I don't believe in vine leaves any more. But still beautifully! For once. Goodbye. Go now. And don't come back.

Løvborg. Goodbye, Mrs. Tesman. Give my regards to Jørgen Tesman.
(He is about to leave.)

Hedda. Wait! I want to give you something — a remembrance. *(Goes
to the desk, opens the drawer, takes out the gun case. Returns to
Løvborg with one of the revolvers.)*

Løvborg. The gun? That's the remembrance?

Hedda (nods slowly). Do you recognize it? It was pointed at you once.

Løvborg. You should have used it then.

Hedda. Take it! *You* use it.

Løvborg (pockets the gun). Thanks!

Hedda. And beautifully, Eilert Løvborg! That's all I ask!

Løvborg. Goodbye, Hedda Gabler. *(Exits, right.)*

*(Hedda listens by the door for a moment. Then she crosses to the
desk, takes out the manuscript, glances inside the cover, pulls some
of the pages halfway out and looks at them. Carries the whole manuscript over to the chair by the stove. She sits down with the parcel in
her lap. After a moment she opens the stove and then the manuscript.)*

Hedda (throws a bundle of sheets into the fire, whispers). Now I'm
burning your child, Thea. You — curlyhead! *(Throws more sheets
in.)* Your and Eilert Løvborg's child. *(Throws all the rest of the
manuscript into the stove.)* I am burning — I am burning your
child.

ACT FOUR

(*The same rooms at the Tesmans'. Evening. The front room is dark.
The inner room is lighted by the ceiling lamp over the table. Portieres
cover the French doors.*

*Hedda, in black, is walking up and down in the dark of the front room.
She goes into the inner room, turning left in the doorway. She is
heard playing a few bars on the piano. She reappears and comes
forward again. Berte enters from the right side of the inner room.
She carries a lighted lamp, which she puts down on the table in front
of the corner sofa. Her eyes show signs of weeping; she wears black
ribbons on her uniform. She exits quietly, right. Hedda goes over to
the French windows, looks between the portieres into the dark. Presently Miss Tesman, in mourning, with hat and veil, enters, right.
Hedda walks over to meet her, gives her her hand.*)

Miss Tesman. Yes, my dearest Hedda — here you see me in my garb
of grief. For now at last my poor sister has fought her fight to the
end.
Hedda. I already know — as you see. Tesman sent word.
Miss Tesman. Yes, he promised he'd do that. But I thought that to
you, Hedda — here in the house of life — I really ought to bring
you the tidings of death myself.
Hedda. That is very kind of you.
Miss Tesman. Ah, but Rina shouldn't have died just now. There
should be no mourning in Hedda's house at this time.
Hedda (*changing the topic*). I understand she had a very quiet end.
Miss Tesman. Oh so beautiful, so peaceful! She left us so quietly! And
then the unspeakable happiness of seeing Jørgen one more time! To
say goodbye to him to her heart's content! Isn't he back yet?
Hedda. No. He wrote I mustn't expect him back very soon. But do sit
down.
Miss Tesman. No — no, thanks, my dear, blessed Hedda. Not that I
wouldn't like to. But I don't have much time. I must go back and
prepare her as best I can. I want her to look right pretty when she
goes into her grave.
Hedda. Is there anything I can help you with?
Miss Tesman. I won't have you as much as think of it! That's not for
Hedda Tesman to lend a hand to. Or lend thoughts to either. Not
now, of all times!

Hedda. Oh — thoughts! We can't always control our thoughts —

Miss Tesman (still preoccupied). Ah yes — such is life. At home we're making a shroud for Rina. And here, too, there'll be sewing to do soon, I expect. But of quite a different kind, thank God!

(*Tesman enters, right.*)

Hedda. Finally!

Tesman. You here, Aunt Julle? With Hedda? Just think!

Miss Tesman. I am just about to leave, Jørgen dear. Well — did you do all the things you promised me you'd do?

Tesman. No, I'm afraid I forgot half of them, Auntie. I'd better run in again tomorrow. I'm all confused today. I can't seem to keep my thoughts together.

Miss Tesman. But dearest Jørgen — you mustn't take it this way!

Tesman. Oh, I mustn't? How do you mean?

Miss Tesman. You ought to be joyful in the midst of your sorrow. Glad for what's happened. The way I am.

Tesman. Oh yes, of course. You're thinking of Aunt Rina.

Hedda. You're going to feel lonely now, Miss Tesman.

Miss Tesman. The first few days, yes. But I hope that won't last long. Dear Rina's little parlor won't be empty for long, if I can help it!

Tesman. Oh? And who do you want to move in there. Hm?

Miss Tesman. Ah — it's not very hard to find some poor soul who needs nursing and comfort.

Hedda. And you really want to take on such a burden all over again?

Miss Tesman. Heavens! God forgive you, child — burden? It has not been a burden to me.

Hedda. Still — a stranger, who —

Miss Tesman. Oh, it's easy to make friends with sick people. And I need somebody to live for, too. Well, the Lord be praised, maybe soon there'll be a thing or two an old aunt can turn her hand to here.

Hedda. Oh, never mind us —

Tesman. Yes, just think — how lovely it would be for the three of us, if only —

Hedda. If only — ?

Tesman (uneasy). Oh, nothing. I daresay it will all work out. Let's hope it will, hm?

Miss Tesman. Well, well. I can see that you two have something to talk about. (*With a smile.*) And perhaps Hedda has something to tell *you*, Jørgen! Goodbye! I'm going home to Rina, now. (*Turns round in the door.*) Dear, dear — how strange to think — Now Rina is both with me and with Jochum!

Tesman. Yes, just think, Aunt Julle! Hm?

(_Miss Tesman exits, right._)

Hedda (_coldly scrutinizing Tesman_). I wouldn't be at all surprised if you aren't more affected by this death than she is.

Tesman. Oh, it isn't just Aunt Rina's death, Hedda. It's Eilert I worry about.

Hedda (_quickly_). Any news about him?

Tesman. I went over to his room this afternoon to tell him the manuscript is safe.

Hedda. Well? And didn't you see him?

Tesman. No. He wasn't home. But I ran into Mrs. Elvsted and she told me he'd been here early this morning.

Hedda. Yes, right after you'd left.

Tesman. And he said he'd torn up the manuscript? Did he really say that?

Hedda. Yes. So he claimed.

Tesman. But dear God — in that case he really must have been out of his mind! So I assume you didn't give it to him either, hm, Hedda?

Hedda. No. He didn't get it.

Tesman. But you told him we had it, of course?

Hedda. No. (_Quickly._) Did you tell Mrs. Elvsted?

Tesman. No, I didn't want to. But you ought to have told him, Hedda. Just think — what if he does something rash — something to hurt himself! Give me the manuscript, Hedda! I want to rush down to him with it right this minute. Where is it?

Hedda (_cold motionless, one arm resting on the chair_). I haven't got it any more.

Tesman. You haven't got it! What do you mean by that?

Hedda. I burned it — the whole thing.

Tesman (_jumps up_). Burned it! Burned Eilert's book!

Hedda. Don't shout. The maid might hear you.

Tesman. Burned it? But good God — no, no, no — ! This can't be — !

Hedda. It is, all the same.

Tesman. But do you realize what you've done, Hedda? It's illegal! Willful destruction of lost property! You just ask Judge Brack! He'll tell you!

Hedda. You'd better not talk about this to anyone — the Judge or anybody else.

Tesman. But how could you do a thing like that! I never heard anything like it! What came over you? What can possibly have been going on in your head? Answer me! Hm?

Hedda (*suppresses an almost imperceptible smile*). I did it for your sake, Jørgen.

Tesman. For my sake!

Hedda. When you came back this morning and told me he had read aloud to you —

Tesman. Yes, yes! What then?

Hedda. You admitted you were jealous of him for having written such a book.

Tesman. But good gracious — ! I didn't mean it as seriously as all that!

Hedda. All the same. I couldn't stand the thought that somebody else was to overshadow you.

Tesman (*in an outburst of mingled doubt and joy*). Hedda — oh Hedda! Is it true what you're saying. But — but — but — I never knew you loved me like that! Just think!

Hedda. In that case, I might as well tell you — that — just at this time — (*Breaks off, vehemently.*) No, no! You can ask Aunt Julle. She'll tell you.

Tesman. I almost think I know what you mean, Hedda! (*Claps his hands.*) For goodness sake! Can that really be so! Hm?

Hedda. Don't shout so! The maid can hear you.

Tesman (*laughing with exuberant joy*). The maid! Well, if you don't take the prize, Hedda! The maid — but that's Berte! I'm going to tell Berte myself this very minute!

Hedda (*her hands clenched in despair*). Oh I'll die — I'll die, in all this!

Tesman. In what, Hedda? Hm?

Hedda (*cold and composed*). In all this — ludicrousness, Jørgen.

Tesman. Ludicrous? That I'm so happy? Still — maybe I oughtn't to tell Berte, after all.

Hedda. Oh, go ahead. What difference does it make?

Tesman. No, not yet. But on my word — Aunt Julle must be told. And that you've started to call me "Jørgen," too! Just think! She'll be ever so happy — Aunt Julle will!

Hedda. Even when you tell her that I have burned Eilert Løvborg's papers?

Tesman. No, oh no! That's true! That about the manuscript — nobody must know about that. But to think that you'd burn for me, Hedda — I certainly want to tell *that* to Aunt Julle! I wonder now — is that sort of thing usual with young wives, hm?

Hedda. Why don't you ask Aunt Julle about that, too?

Tesman. I shall — I certainly shall, when I get the chance. (*Looks uneasy and disturbed again*). But the manuscript! Good God — I don't dare to think what this is going to do to poor Eilert!

(*Mrs. Elvsted, dressed as on her first visit, wearing hat and coat, enters, right.*)

Mrs. Elvsted (*gives a hurried greeting, is obviously upset*). Oh Hedda, you must forgive me for coming here again!

Hedda. What has happened, Thea?

Tesman. Something to do with Eilert Løvborg again? Hm?

Mrs. Elvsted. Yes, yes — I'm so terribly afraid something's happened to him.

Hedda (*seizing her arm*). Ah — you think so?

Tesman. Oh dear — why do you think that, Mrs. Elvsted?

Mrs. Elvsted. I heard them talking about him in the boarding house, just as I came in. And people are saying the most incredible things about him today.

Tesman. Yes, imagine! I heard that, too! And I can testify that he went straight home to bed! Just think!

Hedda. And what did they say in the boarding house?

Mrs. Elvsted. Oh, I didn't find out anything. Either they didn't know any details or — They all became silent when they saw me. And I didn't dare to ask.

Tesman (*pacing the floor uneasily*). We'll just have to hope — to hope that you heard wrong, Mrs. Elvsted!

Mrs. Elvsted. No, no. I'm sure it was he they were talking about. And somebody said something about the hospital or —

Tesman. The hospital — !

Hedda. Surely, that can't be so!

Mrs. Elvsted. I got so terribly frightened! So I went up to his room and asked for him there.

Hedda. Could you bring yourself to do that, Thea?

Mrs. Elvsted. What else could I do? For I felt I just couldn't stand the uncertainty any longer.

Tesman. But I suppose you didn't find him in, either, did you? Hm?

Mrs. Elvsted. No. And the people there didn't know anything about him. He hadn't been home since yesterday afternoon, they said.

Tesman. Yesterday! Just think! How could they say that!

Mrs. Elvsted. I don't know what else *to* think — something bad must have happened to him!

Tesman. Hedda, dear — ? What if I were to walk downtown and ask around for him — ?

Hedda. No, no — don't you go and get mixed up in all this.

(*Judge Brack, hat in hand, enters through the door, right, which Berte opens and closes for him. He looks serious and greets the others in silence.*)

Tesman. So here you are, Judge, hm?

Brack. Yes. I had to see you this evening.

Tesman. I can see you have got Aunt Julle's message.

Brack. That, too — yes.

Tesman. Isn't it sad, though?

Brack. Well, my dear Tesman — that depends on how you look at it.

Tesman (looks at him uncertainly). Has something else happened?

Brack. Yes.

Hedda (tense). Something sad, Judge Brack?

Brack. That, too, depends on how you look at it, Mrs. Tesman.

Mrs. Elvsted (bursting out). Oh, I'm sure it has something to do with Eilert Løvborg!

Brack (looks at her for a moment). Why do you think that, Mrs. Elvsted? Maybe you already know something — ?

Mrs. Elvsted (confused). No, no; not at all. It's just —

Tesman. For heaven's sake, Brack, out with it!

Brack (shrugging his shoulders). Well — unfortunately, Eilert Løvborg's in the hospital. Dying.

Mrs. Elvsted (screams). Oh God, oh God!

Tesman. In the hospital! And dying!

Hedda (without thinking). So soon — !

Mrs. Elvsted (wailing). And we didn't even part as friends, Hedda!

Hedda (whispers). Thea, Thea — for heaven's sake — !

Mrs. Elvsted (paying no attention to her). I want to see him! I want to see him alive!

Brack. Won't do you any good, Mrs. Elvsted. Nobody can see him.

Mrs. Elvsted. Then tell me what's happened to him! What?

Tesman. For, surely, he hasn't himself — !

Hedda. I'm sure he has.

Tesman. Hedda! How can you — !

Brack (observing her all this time). I am sorry to say that your guess is absolutely correct, Mrs. Tesman.

Mrs. Elvsted. Oh, how awful!

Tesman. Did it himself! Just think!

Hedda. Shot himself!

Brack. Right again, Mrs. Tesman.

Mrs. Elvsted (trying to pull herself together). When did this happen, Judge?

Brack. This afternoon. Between three and four.

Tesman. But dear me — where can he have done a thing like that? Hm?

Brack (a little uncertain). Where? Well — I suppose in his room. I don't really know —

Mrs. Elvsted. No, it can't have been there. For I was up there some-time between six and seven.

Brack. Well, then, some other place. I really can't say. All I know is that he was found. He had shot himself — in the chest.

Mrs. Elvsted. Oh, how horrible to think! That he was to end like that!

Hedda (to Brack). In the chest?

Brack. Yes — as I just told you.

Hedda. Not the temple?

Brack. In the chest, Mrs. Tesman.

Hedda. Well, well — the chest is a good place, too.

Brack. How is that, Mrs. Tesman?

Hedda (turning him aside). Oh — nothing.

Tesman. And you say the wound is fatal? Hm?

Brack. No doubt about it — absolutely fatal. He's probably dead already.

Mrs. Elvsted. Yes, yes! I feel you're right! It's over! It's all over! Oh, Hedda!

Tesman. But tell me — how do *you* know all this?

Brack (tersely). A man on the force told me. One I had some business with.

Hedda (loudly). At last a deed!

Tesman (appalled). Oh dear — what are you saying, Hedda!

Hedda. I am saying there is beauty in this.

Brack. Well, now — Mrs. Tesman —

Tesman. Beauty — ! Just think!

Mrs. Elvsted. Oh, Hedda — how can you talk about beauty in a thing like this!

Hedda. Eilert Løvborg has settled his account with himself. He has had the courage to do — what had to be done.

Mrs. Elvsted. But you mustn't believe it happened that way! He did it when he was not himself!

Tesman. In despair! That's how!

Hedda. He did not. I am certain of that.

Mrs. Elvsted. Yes he did! He was not himself! That's the way he tore up the book, too!

Brack (puzzled). The book? You mean the manuscript? Has he torn it up?

Mrs. Elvsted. Yes, last night.

Tesman (whispers). Oh, Hedda — we'll never get clear of all this!

Brack. That is strange.

Tesman (walking the floor). To think that this was to be the end of Eilert! Not to leave behind him anything that would have preserved his name —

Mrs. Elvsted. Oh, if only it could be put together again!

Tesman. Yes, if only it could. I don't know what I wouldn't give —

Mrs. Elvsted. Maybe it can, Mr. Tesman.

Tesman. What do you mean?

Mrs. Elvsted (searching her dress pocket). Look. I have kept these little slips he dictated from.

Hedda (a step closer). Ah — !

Tesman. You've kept them, Mrs. Elvsted? Hm?

Mrs. Elvsted. Yes. Here they are. I took them with me when I left. And I've had them in my pocket ever since —

Tesman. Please, let me see —

Mrs. Elvsted (gives him a pile of small paper slips). But it's such a mess. Without any kind of system or order — !

Tesman. But just think if we could make sense out of them, all the same! Perhaps if we helped each other —

Mrs. Elvsted. Oh yes! Let's try, anyway!

Tesman. It will work! It *has* to work! I'll stake my whole life on this!

Hedda. You, Jørgen? Your life?

Tesman. Yes, or at any rate all the time I can set aside. My own collections can wait. Hedda, you understand — don't you? Hm? This is something I owe Eilert's memory.

Hedda. Maybe so.

Tesman. And now, my dear Mrs. Elvsted, we want to get to work. Good heavens, there's no point brooding over what's happened. Hm? We'll just have to acquire sufficient peace of mind to —

Mrs. Elvsted. All right, Mr. Tesman. I'll try to do my best.

Tesman. Very well, then. Come over here. Let's look at these slips right away. Where can we sit? Here? No, it's better in the other room. If you'll excuse us, Judge! Come along, Mrs. Elvsted.

Mrs. Elvsted. Oh dear God — if only it were possible — !

(Tesman and Mrs. Elvsted go into the inner room. She takes off her hat and coat. Both sit down at the table under the hanging lamp and absorb themselves in the slips. Hedda walks over toward the stove and sits down in the easy chair. After a while, Brack walks over to her.)

Hedda (in a low voice). Ah, Judge — what a liberation there is in this thing with Eilert Løvborg!

Brack. Liberation, Mrs. Tesman? Well, yes, for him perhaps one may say there was liberation of a kind —

Hedda. I mean for me. There is liberation in knowing that there is such a thing in the world as an act of free courage. Something which becomes beautiful by its very nature.

Brack (*smiles*). Well — dear Mrs. Tesman —

Hedda. Oh I know what you're going to say! For you see — you really are a kind of specialist, too!

Brack (*looks at her fixedly*). Eilert Løvborg has meant more to you than perhaps you're willing to admit, even to yourself. Or am I wrong?

Hedda. I won't answer such questions. All I know is that Eilert Løvborg had the courage to live his own life. And then now — this — magnificence! The beauty of it! Having the strength and the will to get up and leave life's feast — so early —

Brack. Believe me, Mrs. Tesman, this pains me, but I see it is necessary that I destroy a pretty illusion —

Hedda. An illusion?

Brack. Which could not have been maintained for very long, anyway.

Hedda. And what is that?

Brack. He didn't shoot himself — of his own free will.

Hedda. Not of his own — !

Brack. No. To tell the truth, the circumstances of Eilert Løvborg's death aren't exactly what I said they were.

Hedda (*tense*). You've held something back? What?

Brack. For the sake of poor Mrs. Elvsted I used a few euphemisms.

Hedda. What?

Brack. First — he is already dead.

Hedda. In the hospital.

Brack. Yes. And without regaining consciousness.

Hedda. What else haven't you told?

Brack. That fact that it didn't happen in his room.

Hedda. Well, does that really make much difference?

Brack. Some. You see — Eilert Løvborg was found shot in Miss Diana's bedroom.

Hedda (*is about to jump up, but sinks back*). That's impossible, Judge Brack! He can't have been there again today!

Brack. He was there this afternoon. He came to claim something he said they had taken from him. Spoke some gibberish about a lost child —

Hedda. So that's why — !

Brack. I thought maybe he meant his manuscript. But now I hear he has destroyed that himself. So I suppose it must have been something else.

Hedda. I suppose. So it was there — so they found him there?

Brack. Yes. With a fired gun in his pocket. Mortally wounded.

Hedda. Yes — in the chest.

Brack. No — in the guts.

Hedda (*looks at him with an expression of disgust*). That, too! What is this curse that turns everything I touch into something ludicrous and low!

Brack. There is something else, Mrs. Tesman. Something I'd call — nasty.

Hedda. And what is that.

Brack. The gun they found —

Hedda (*breathless*). What about it?

Brack. He must have stolen it.

Hedda (*jumps up*). Stolen! That's not true! He didn't!

Brack. Anything else is impossible. He *must* have stolen it. — Shhh!

(*Tesman and Mrs. Elvsted have risen from the table and come forward into the front room.*)

Tesman (*with papers in both hands*). D'you know, Hedda — you can hardly see in there with that lamp! Just think!

Hedda. I am thinking.

Tesman. I wonder if you'd let us use your desk, hm?

Hedda. Certainly, if you like. (*Adds quickly.*) Wait a minute, though! Let me clear it off a bit first.

Tesman. Ah, there's no need for that, Hedda. There's plenty of room.

Hedda. No, no. I want to straighten it up. I'll carry all this in here. I'll put it on top of the piano for the time being.

(*She has pulled an object, covered by note paper, out of the bookcase. She puts several other sheets of paper on top of it and carries the whole pile into the left part of the inner room. Tesman puts the papers down on the desk and moves the lamp from the corner table over to the desk. He and Mrs. Elvsted sit down and resume their work. Hedda returns.*)

Hedda (*behind Mrs. Elvsted's chair, softly ruffling her hair*). Well, little Thea — how is Eilert Løvborg's memorial coming along?

Mrs. Elvsted (*looks up at her, discouraged*). Oh God — I'm sure it's going to be terribly hard to make anything out of all this.

Tesman. But we have to. We just don't have a choice. And putting other people's papers in order — that's just the thing for me.

(*Hedda walks over to the stove and sits down on one of the ottomans. Brack stands over her, leaning on the easy chair.*)

Hedda (*whispers*). What were you saying about the gun?

Brack (*also softly*). That he must have stolen it.

Hedda. Why, necessarily?

Brack. Because any other explanation ought to be out of the question, Mrs. Tesman.

Hedda. Oh?

Brack (*looks at her for a moment*). Eilert Løvborg was here this morning, of course. Isn't that so?

Hedda. Yes.

Brack. Were you alone with him?

Hedda. Yes, for a while.

Brack. You didn't leave the room while he was here?

Hedda. No.

Brack. Think. Not at all? Not even for a moment?

Hedda. Well — maybe just for a moment — out in the hall.

Brack. And where was the gun case?

Hedda. In the —

Brack. Mrs. Tesman?

Hedda. On the desk.

Brack. Have you looked to see if both guns are still there?

Hedda. No.

Brack. You needn't bother. I saw the gun they found on Løvborg, and I knew it immediately. From yesterday — and from earlier occasions, too.

Hedda. Perhaps you have it?

Brack. No, the police do.

Hedda. What are the police going to do with it?

Brack. Try to find the owner.

Hedda. Do you think they will?

Brack (*leans over her, whispers*). No, Hedda Gabler — not as long as I keep quiet.

Hedda (*with a hunted look*). And if you don't?

Brack (*shrugs his shoulders*). Of course, there's always the chance that the gun was stolen.

Hedda (*firmly*). Rather die!

Brack (*smiles*). People *say* things like that. They don't *do* them.

Hedda (*without answering*). And if the gun was not stolen — and if they find the owner — then what happens?

Brack. Well, Hedda — then comes the scandal!

Hedda. The scandal!

Brack. Yes — the scandal. That you are so afraid of. You will of course be required to testify. Both you and Miss Diana. Obviously, she'll have to explain how the whole thing happened. Whether it was accidental or homicide. Did he try to pull the gun out of his pocket to threaten her? And did it fire accidentally? Or did she grab the gun away from him, shoot him, and put it back in his pocket? She might just possibly have done that. She's a pretty tough girl — Miss Diana.

Hedda. But this whole disgusting mess has nothing to do with me.

Brack. Quite so. But you'll have to answer the question: Why did you give Eilert Løvborg the gun? And what inferences will be drawn from the fact that you did?

Hedda (lowers her head). That's true. I hadn't thought of that.

Brack. Well — luckily, there's nothing to worry about as long as I don't say anything.

Hedda (looks up at him). So then I'm in your power, Judge. From now on you can do anything you like with me.

Brack (in an even softer whisper). Dearest Hedda — believe me, I'll not misuse my position.

Hedda. In your power, all the same. Dependent on your will. Servant to your demands. Not free. Not free! *(Rises suddenly.)* No — I can't stand that thought! Never!

Brack (looks at her, half mockingly). Most people submit to the inevitable.

Hedda (returning his glance). Perhaps. *(Walks over to the desk. Suppresses a smile and mimics Tesman's way of speaking.)* Well? Do you think you can do it, Jørgen? Hm?

Tesman. Lord knows, Hedda. Anyway, I can already see it will take months.

Hedda (still mimicking). Just think! *(Runs her hands lightly through Mrs. Elvsted's hair.)* Doesn't this seem strange to you, Thea? Sitting here with Tesman — just the way you used to with Eilert Løvborg?

Mrs. Elvsted. Oh dear — if only I could inspire your husband, too!

Hedda. Oh, I'm sure that will come — in time.

Tesman. Well, yes — do you know, Hedda? I really think I begin to feel something of the kind. But why don't you go and talk to the Judge again.

Hedda. Isn't there anything you two can use me for?

Tesman. No, not a thing, dear. *(Turns around.)* From now on, you must be good enough to keep Hedda company, my dear Judge!

Brack (glancing at Hedda). I'll be only too delighted.

Hedda. Thank you. But I'm tired tonight. I think I'll go and lie down for a while.

Tesman. Yes, you do that, dear; why don't you? Hm?

(Hedda goes into the inner room, closes the portieres behind her. Brief pause. Suddenly, she is heard playing a frenzied dance tune on the piano.)

Mrs. Elvsted (jumps up). Oh God! What's that!

Tesman (running to the doorway). But dearest Hedda — you mustn't play dance music tonight, for goodness' sake! Think of Aunt Rina! And Eilert, too!

Hedda (peeks in from between the portieres). And Aunt Julle. And everybody. I'll be quiet. *(She pulls the portieres shut again.)*

Tesman (back at the desk). I don't think it's good for her to see us at such a melancholy task. I'll tell you what, Mrs. Elvsted. You move in with Aunt Julle, and then I'll come over in the evenings. Then we can sit and work over there. Hm?

Mrs. Elvsted. Maybe that would be better —

Hedda (from inner room). I hear every word you're saying, Tesman. And how am I going to spend my evenings?

Tesman (busy with the papers). Oh, I'm sure Judge Brack will be good enough to come out and see you, anyway.

Brack (in the easy chair, calls out gaily). Every single night, as far as I'm concerned, Mrs. Tesman! I'm sure we're going to have a lovely time, you and I!

Hedda (loud and clear). Yes, don't you think that would be nice, Judge Brack? You — sole cock-o'-the walk —

(A shot is heard from the inner room, Tesman, Mrs. Elvsted, and Judge Brack all jump up.)

Tesman. There she is, fooling with those guns again.

(He pulls the portieres apart and runs inside. Mrs. Elvsted also. Hedda, lifeless, is lying on the sofa. Cries and confusion, Berte, flustered, enters, right.)

Tesman (shouts to Brack). She's shot herself! In the temple! Just think!

Brack (half stunned in the easy chair). But, merciful God — ! One just doesn't *do* that!

Before he was forty Ibsen had written two masterpieces of poetic drama, *Brand* (1866) and *Peer Gynt* (1867). But a few years later he came to feel, along with many others, that the future of dramatic literature was not in poetic language, but in language that closely resembled ordinary speech.* He devoted his subsequent efforts to prose

* Prose, and indeed prose clearly imitative of speech, had, of course, been occasionally used much earlier, even during the Renaissance, but prose tragedy

drama, and we find him, in his letters, occasionally prophesying that poetic drama has no future, and warning his translators to avoid all expressions that depart from "everyday speech." In the 1870's and 1880's he wrote the so-called "problem plays" (including *A Doll's House, Ghosts,* and *An Enemy of the People*) that for the next seventy-five years made his name familiar to the English-speaking world. A problem play, or "play of ideas," or *pièce à thèse,* is concerned with some troublesome social institution, its author hoping to arouse the audience to do something about the problem (for example, to modify the divorce laws, to extend the ballot, to alter the tax structure). The more successful the play, the more it insures its own demise, for when the social institutions have been altered and the problem has been solved, the play has no relevance to experience; it is merely a thing of historical importance, a museum curio. The violent reviews that *Ghosts* and some of Ibsen's other plays engendered are evidence that more was at stake than aesthetic matters; discussions of the plays inevitably became discussions of divorce, venereal disease, incest, etc. Almost a century has passed, and readers have found that Ibsen has something more to offer than thoughts on how to improve society.

In December 1890, a few weeks after he finished *Hedda Gabler,* Ibsen made the point that "it was not really my intention to deal in this play with so-called problems. What I principally wanted to do was to depict human beings, human emotions, and human destinies, upon a groundwork of certain of the social conditions and principles of the present day." We get some idea of what Ibsen meant by "the social conditions and principles of the present day" from another jotting he made while he was getting the play into shape: "Tesman represents propriety. Hedda represents *ennui.* Mrs. R. [i.e. Mrs. Elvsted] modern nervousness and hysteria. Brack the representative of bourgeois society." This early summary does not, of course, correspond exactly to the finished play, but it gives us some idea of the direction Ibsen was taking. "Propriety," "*ennui,*" "nervousness and hysteria," and even "bourgeois society" are not problems that can be solved by legislation or by any other form of tinkering. The play, after all, is not about a society that foolishly restrains energetic women from putting their energy to

---

with its middle-class figures was for a long while a poor relation of tragedy. With the increasing power of the middle class and the rise of science (which not only helped to enlarge the middle class but also helped to popularize the view that all matter is equally interesting and presumably equally fit for literature), the days of "heroic" tragedy were numbered. Probably Darwin's *Origin of Species* (1859) was the *coup de grâce;* one could hardly take a very high view of creatures that had survived because accidental variations made them more suited to their environment than other creatures.

use. The other jottings show even more clearly that Ibsen was concerned with unchanging experiences rather than with transitory problems. Here are two of them:

> They aren't all created to be mothers.
> The daemon in Hedda is that she wants to influence another human being, but once that has happened, she despises him.

Hedda wishes to influence someone, to shape a human destiny. Her own destiny, like everyone else's, has been partly shaped by the circumstances of her birth. She is the daughter of an aristocrat, General Gabler (in a letter Ibsen called attention to the fact that the play is entitled *Hedda Gabler*, and not, despite her marriage to George Tesman, *Hedda Tesman*). Her aristocratic background has given her leisure but no direction, energy but no channel for it, and we see her becoming increasingly desperate. Having married rashly, she now feels her identity is threatened. The point is obvious, but it is worth quoting Ibsen's own description, from a letter: "Jørgen Tesman, his old aunts, and the faithful servant Berte together form a picture of complete unity. They think alike, they share the same memories and have the same outlook on life. To Hedda they appear like a strange and hostile power, aimed at her very being." Tesman is a bore, scarcely worth shaping, and the aunt and the maid are no challenge. Yet this family group frightens Hedda because (she thinks) it would lessen her identity if it absorbed her. Her distress at the thought of having a child is a further indication that although she yearns to shape a human destiny, she does not want to become involved in any sort of relationship in which she herself may be shaped; that is, she evades responsibilities. Presumably when she rejected Eilert Løvborg's overtures, she did so not only because she feared scandal, but also because she feared the relationship itself. Now she seeks to fulfill herself by controlling Løvborg's life to the point that he will be a Dionysian figure who will kill himself "beautifully." Hedda apparently has in mind something of the romantic view of Greek tragedy that Ibsen himself had held twenty-five years earlier, when he rhapsodized over a statue of "the Tragic Muse," with its "laurel-crowned head with something supernaturally exuberant and bacchantic about it."

In Ibsen's world, as everywhere, people impinge upon each other and relationships are necessarily established. Miss Tesman's life, for example, is intertwined with the invalid Aunt Rina's, and when Rina dies, a replacement must be found: "Ah — it's not very hard to find some poor soul who needs nursing and comfort." To Hedda's question, "And you really want to take on such a burden all over again?" Miss Tesman replies, "Heavens! God forgive you, child — burden? It has not been a burden to me." Similarly, Mrs. Elvsted and Løvborg require each other, and are shaped by each other as they shape each other, and Tesman is at his best when he is bringing to completion someone else's work. The play is built on a groundwork of "social conditions and principles" of nineteenth-century Norwegian life, but these conditions themselves, as Ibsen presents them, are rooted in elementary facts of life and are not outmoded institutions that needlessly create problems. (In *Peer Gynt* Ibsen had earlier represented this matter of interrelationships with a brilliant image. Peer wishes "to be himself," but he finds he has no individuality when apart from others. He peels an onion, to get at the core, and finds that after all layers — or relationships — are removed, there is nothing left.) Hedda seeks power divorced from responsibility, which means that finally her power must be directed against herself. The attempt to have Løvborg do some "beautiful" deed in defiance of society fails because she cannot have full power over Løvborg unless she gives something of herself to him. When Løvborg is dead, and Tesman and Mrs. Elvsted are occupied with each other, and Hedda is at Judge Brack's mercy, Hedda releases her energy against herself, killing herself "beautifully." Judge Brack's final comment, "One just doesn't *do* that!" is the sort of scandalized remark that Hedda had feared all her life, the voice of society, a society that does not know the depths of Hedda's anguish, a society that holds itself together by dull virtues, petty vices, and all sorts of dodges. But society does help men to survive, and to reject it is to annihilate oneself.

Henry IV

A Tragedy in Three Acts

LUIGI PIRANDELLO

English version by Edward Storer

Luigi Pirandello (1867–1936) was born in Sicily, the son of the owner of a profitable sulfur mine. Pirandello studied at Rome and then at Bonn, where in 1891 he received a doctorate for a thesis on Sicilian dialect. Back in Rome he wrote poetry, fiction, and literary criticism, and taught Italian at a teachers college. Troubles came thick: his family, and his wife's, suffered financial setbacks, and his wife became intermittently insane. But from 1917 onward he had great success in the theater with many of his forty or so plays. Among the best-known plays are Right You Are (If You Think You Are) *(1917),* Six Characters in Search of an Author *(1921), and* Henry IV *(1922). In 1934 Pirandello was awarded the Nobel Prize. Curiously, this philosophic skeptic was a supporter of Italian fascism, and he gave his Nobel medal to be melted down for Mussolini's Abyssinian campaign.*

CHARACTERS

Henry IV
The Marchioness Matilda Spina
Frida, her daughter
Charles Di Nolli, the young Marquis
Baron Tito Belcredi
Doctor Dionysius Genoni
Harold [Franco]
Landolph [Lolo]
Ordulph [Momo]
Berthold [Fino]
} The four private counselors
(The names in brackets are
nicknames)
John, the old waiter
The Two Valets in Costume

A Solitary Villa in Italy in Our Own Time

ACT I

Salon in the villa, furnished and decorated so as to look exactly like the throne room of Henry IV in the royal residence at Goslar. Among the antique decorations there are two modern life-size portraits in oil painting. They are placed against the back wall, and mounted in a wooden stand that runs the whole length of the wall. (It is wide and protrudes, so that it is like a large bench.) One of the paintings is on the right; the other on the left of the throne, which is in the middle of the wall and divides the stand.

The Imperial chair and Baldachin.

The two portraits represent a lady and a gentleman, both young, dressed up in carnival costumes: one as "Henry IV," the other as the "Marchioness Matilda of Tuscany." Exits to right and left.

When the curtain goes up, the two valets jump down, as if surprised, from the stand on which they have been lying, and go and take their positions, as rigid as statues, on either side below the throne with their halberds in their hands. Soon after, from the second exit, right, enter Harold, Landolph, Ordulph and Berthold, young men employed by the Marquis Charles Di Nolli to play the part of "Secret Counsellors" at the court of "Henry IV." They are, therefore, dressed like German knights of the XIth century. Berthold, nicknamed Fino, is just entering on his duties for the first time. His companions are telling him what he has to do and amusing themselves at his expense. The scene is to be played rapidly and vivaciously.

From the book *Naked Masks: Five Plays* by Luigi Pirandello, edited by Eric Bentley. Copyright, 1922, by E. P. Dutton & Co., Inc. Renewal, 1950, by Stefano, Fausto & Lietta Pirandello. Dutton Paperback Edition. Reprinted by permission of the publishers.

Landolph (*to Berthold as if explaining*). And this is the throne room.

Harold. At Goslar.

Ordulph. Or at the castle in the Hartz, if you prefer.

Harold. Or at Wurms.

Landolph. According as to what's doing, it jumps about with us, now here, now there.

Ordulph. In Saxony.

Harold. In Lombardy.

Landolph. On the Rhine.

One of the Valets (*without moving, just opening his lips*). I say . . .

Harold (*turning round*). What is it?

First Valet (*like a statue*). Is he coming in or not? (*He alludes to Henry IV.*)

Ordulph. No, no, he's asleep. You needn't worry.

Second Valet (*releasing his pose, taking a long breath and going to lie down again on the stand*). You might have told us at once.

First Valet (*going over to Harold*). Have you got a match, please?

Landolph. What? You can't smoke a pipe here, you know.

First Valet (*while Harold offers him a light*). No; a cigarette. (*Lights his cigarette and lies down again on the stand.*)

Berthold (*who has been looking on in amazement, walking round in the room, regarding the costumes of the others*). I say . . . this room . . . these costumes . . . Which Henry IV is it? I don't quite get it. Is he Henry IV of France or not? (*At this Landolph, Harold, and Ordulph, burst out laughing.*)

Landolph (*still laughing; and pointing to Berthold as if inviting the others to make fun of him*). Henry of France he says: ha! ha!

Ordulph. He thought it was the king of France!

Harold. Henry IV of Germany, my boy: the Salian dynasty!

Ordulph. The great and tragic Emperor!

Landolph. He of Canossa. Every day we carry on here the terrible war between Church and State, by Jove.

Ordulph. The Empire against the Papacy!

Harold. Antipopes against the Pope!

Landolph. Kings against anti-kings!

Ordulph. War on the Saxons!

Harold. And all the rebels Princes!

Landolph. Against the Emperor's own sons!

Berthold (*covering his head with his hands to protect himself against this avalanche of information*). I understand! I understand! Naturally, I didn't get the idea at first. I'm right then: these aren't costumes of the XVIth century?

Harold. XVIth century be hanged!

Ordulph. We're somewhere between a thousand and eleven hundred.

Landolph. Work it out for yourself: if we are before Canossa on the 25th of January, 1071 . . .

Berthold (*more confused than ever*). Oh my God! What a mess I've made of it!

Ordulph. Well, just slightly, if you supposed you were at the French court.

Berthold. All that historical stuff I've swatted up!

Landolph. My dear boy, it's four hundred years earlier.

Berthold (*getting angry*). Good Heavens! You ought to have told me it was Germany and not France. I can't tell you how many books I've read in the last fifteen days.

Harold. But I say, surely you knew that poor Tito was Adalbert of Bremen, here?

Berthold. Not a damned bit!

Landolph. Well, don't you see how it is? When Tito died, the Marquis Di Nolli . . .

Berthold. Oh, it was he', was it? He might have told me.

Harold. Perhaps he thought you knew.

Landolph. He didn't want to engage anyone else in substitution. He thought the remaining three of us would do. But *he* began to cry out: "With Adalbert driven away . . .": because, you see, he didn't imagine poor Tito was dead; but that, as Bishop Adalbert, the rival bishops of Cologne and Mayence had driven him off . . .

Berthold (*taking his head in his hand*). But I don't know a word of what you're talking about.

Ordulph. So much the worse for you, my boy!

Harold. But the trouble is that not even we know who you are.

Berthold. What? Not even you? You don't know who I'm supposed to be?

Ordulph. Hum! "Berthold."

Berthold. But which Berthold? And why Berthold?

Landolph (*solemnly imitating Henry IV*). "They've driven Adalbert away from me. Well then, I want Berthold! I want Berthold!" That's what he said.

Harold. We three looked one another in the eyes: who's got to be Berthold?

Ordulph. And so here you are, "Berthold," my dear fellow!

Landolph. I'm afraid you will make a bit of a mess of it.

Berthold (*indignant, getting ready to go*). Ah, no! Thanks very much, but I'm off! I'm out of this!

Harold (*restraining him with the other two, amid laughter*). Steady now! Don't get excited!

Landolph. Cheer up, my dear fellow! We don't any of us know who we are really. He's Harold; he's Ordulph; I'm Landolph! That's the way he calls us. We've got used to it. But who are we? Names of the period! Yours, too, is a name of the period: Berthold! Only one of us, poor Tito, had got a really decent part, as you can read in history: that of the Bishop of Bremen. He was just like a real bishop. Tito did it awfully well, poor chap!

Harold. Look at the study he put into it!

Landolph. Why, he even ordered his Majesty about, opposed his views, guided and counselled him. We're "secret counsellors" — in a manner of speaking only; because it is written in history that Henry IV was hated by the upper aristocracy for surrounding himself at court with young men of the bourgeoise.

Ordulph. Us, that is.

Landolph. Yes, small devoted vassals, a bit dissolute and very gay . . .

Berthold. So I've got to be gay as well?

Harold. I should say so! Same as we are!

Ordulph. And it isn't too easy, you know.

Landolph. It's a pity; because the way we're got up, we could do a fine historical reconstruction. There's any amount of material in the story of Henry IV. But, as a matter of fact, we do nothing. We have the form without the content. We're worse than the real secret counsellors of Henry IV; because certainly no one had given them a part to play — at any rate, they didn't feel they had a part to play. It was their life. They looked after their own interests at the expense of others, sold investitures and — what not! We stop here in this magnificent court — for what? — Just doing nothing. We're like so many puppets hung on the wall, waiting for some one to come and move us or make us talk.

Harold. Ah, no, old sport, not quite that! We've got to give the proper answer, you know. There's trouble if he asks you something and you don't chip in with the cue.

Landolph. Yes, that's true.

Berthold. Don't rub it in too hard! How the devil am I to give him the proper answer, if I've swatted up Henry IV of France, and now he turns out to be Henry IV of Germany? (*The other three laugh.*)

Harold. You'd better start and prepare yourself at once.

Ordulph. We'll help you out.

Harold. We've got any amount of books on the subject. A brief run through the main points will do to begin with.

Ordulph. At any rate, you must have got some sort of general idea.

Harold. Look here! (*Turns him around and shows him the portrait of the Marchioness Matilda on the wall.*) Who's that?

Berthold (*looking at it*). That? Well, the thing seems to me somewhat out of place, anyway: two modern paintings in the midst of
all this respectable antiquity!

Harold. You're right! They weren't there in the beginning. There are
two niches there behind the pictures. They were going to put up
two statues in the style of the period. Then the places were covered
with those canvases there.

Landolph (*interrupting and continuing*). They would certainly be out
of place if they really were paintings!

Berthold. What are they, if they aren't paintings?

Landolph. Go and touch them! Pictures all right . . . but for him!
(*Makes a mysterious gesture to the right, alluding to Henry IV.*) . . .
who never touches them! . . .

Berthold. No? What are they for him?

Landolph. Well, I'm only supposing, you know; but I imagine I'm
about right. They're images such as . . . well — such as a mirror
might throw back. Do you understand? That one there represents
himself, as he is in this throne room, which is all in the style of the
period. What's there to marvel at? If we put you before a mirror,
won't you see yourself, alive, but dressed up in ancient costume?
Well, it's as if there were two mirrors there, which cast back living
images in the midst of a world which, as you well see, when you
have lived with us, comes to life too.

Berthold. I say, look here . . . I've no particular desire to go mad here.

Harold. Go mad, be hanged! You'll have a fine time!

Berthold. Tell me this: how have you all managed to become so
learned?

Landolph. My dear fellow, you can't go back over 800 years of history without picking up a bit of experience.

Harold. Come on! Come on! You'll see how quickly you get into it!

Ordulph. You'll learn wisdom, too, at this school.

Berthold. Well, for Heaven's sake, help me a bit! Give me the main
lines, anyway.

Harold. Leave it to us. We'll do it all between us.

Landolph. We'll put your wires on you and fix you up like a first-class
marionette. Come along! (*They take him by the arm to lead him
away.*)

Berthold (*stopping and looking at the portrait on the wall*). Wait a
minute! You haven't told me who that is. The Emperor's wife?

Harold. No! The Emperor's wife is Bertha of Susa, the sister of
Amadeus II of Savoy.

Ordulph. And the Emperor, who wants to be young with us, can't
stand her, and wants to put her away.

Landolph. That is his most ferocious enemy: Matilda, Marchioness of Tuscany.

Berthold. Ah, I've got it: the one who gave hospitality to the Pope!

Landolph. Exactly: at Canossa!

Ordulph. Pope Gregory VII!

Harold. Our *bête noir*! Come on! come on! (*All four move toward the right to go out, when, from the left, the old servant John enters in evening dress.*)

John (*quickly, anxiously*). Hss! Hss! Franco! Lolo!

Harold (*turning round*). What is it?

Berthold (*marvelling at seeing a man in modern clothes enter the throne room*). Oh! I say, this is a bit too much, this chap here!

Landolph. A man of the XXth century, here! Oh, go away! (*They run over to him, pretending to menace him and throw him out.*)

Ordulph (*heroically*). Messenger of Gregory VII, away!

Harold. Away! Away!

John (*annoyed, defending himself*). Oh, stop it! Stop it, I tell you!

Ordulph. No, you can't set foot here!

Harold. Out with him!

Landolph (*to Berthold*). Magic, you know! He's a demon conjured up by the Wizard of Rome! Out with your swords! (*Makes as if to draw a sword.*)

John (*shouting*). Stop it, will you? Don't play the fool with me! The Marquis has arrived with some friends . . .

Landolph. Good! Good! Are there ladies too?

Ordulph. Old or young?

John. There are two gentlemen.

Harold. But the ladies, the ladies, who are they?

John. The Marchioness and her daughter.

Landolph (*surprised*). What do you say?

Ordulph. The Marchioness?

John. The Marchioness! The Marchioness!

Harold. Who are the gentlemen?

John. I don't know.

Harold (*to Berthold*). They're coming to bring us a message from the Pope, do you see?

Ordulph. All messengers of Gregory VII! What fun!

John. Will you let me speak, or not?

Harold. Go on, then!

John. One of the two gentlemen is a doctor, I fancy.

Landolph. Oh, I see, one of the usual doctors.

Harold. Bravo Berthold, you'll bring us luck!

Landolph. You wait and see how we'll manage this doctor!

Berthold. It looks as if I were going to get into a nice mess right away.

John. If the gentlemen would allow me to speak . . . they want to come here into the throne room.

Landolph (*surprised*). What? She? The Marchioness here?

Harold. Then this is something quite different! No play-acting this time!

Landolph. We'll have a real tragedy: that's what!

Berthold (*curious*). Why? Why?

Ordulph (*pointing to the portrait*). She is that person there, don't you understand?

Landolph. The daughter is the fiancée of the Marquis. But what have they come for, I should like to know?

Ordulph. If he sees her, there'll be trouble.

Landolph. Perhaps he won't recognize her any more.

John. You must keep him there, if he should wake up . . .

Ordulph. Easier said than done, by Jove!

Harold. You know what he's like!

John. — even by force, if necessary! Those are my orders. Go on! Go on!

Harold. Yes, because who knows if he hasn't already wakened up?

Ordulph. Come on then!

Landolph (*going towards John with the others*). You'll tell us later what it all means.

John (*shouting after them*). Close the door there, and hide the key! That other door too. (*Pointing to the other door on right.*)

John (*to the Two Valets*). Be off, you two! There! (*Pointing to exit right.*) Close the door after you, and hide the key!

(*The Two Valets go out by the first door on right. John moves over to the left to show in: Donna Matilda Spina, the young Marchioness Frida, Dr. Dionysius Genoni, the Baron Tito Belcredi and the young Marquis Charles Di Nolli, who, as master of the house, enters last.*

Donna Matilda Spina is about 45, still handsome, although there are too patent signs of her attempts to remedy the ravages of time with make-up. Her head is thus rather like a Walkyrie. This facial make-up contrasts with her beautiful sad mouth. A widow for many years, she now has as her friend the Baron Tito Belcredi, whom neither she nor anyone else takes seriously — at least so it would appear.

What Tito Belcredi really is for her at bottom, he alone knows; and he is, therefore, entitled to laugh, if his friend feels the need of pretending not to know. He can always laugh at the jests which the beautiful Marchioness makes with the others at his expense. He is slim, prematurely gray, and younger than she is. His head is bird-like in shape. He would be a very vivacious person, if his ductile agility (which among other things makes him a redoubtable swordsman) were not enclosed in a sheath of Arab-like laziness, which is revealed in his strange, nasal drawn-out voice.

Frida, the daughter of the Marchioness is 19. She is sad; because her imperious and too beautiful mother puts her in the shade, and provokes facile gossip against her daughter as well as against herself. Fortunately for her, she is engaged to the Marquis Charles Di Nolli.

Charles Di Nolli is a stiff young man, very indulgent towards others, but sure of himself for what he amounts to in the world. He is worried about all the responsibilities which he believes weigh on him. He is dressed in deep mourning for the recent death of his mother.

Dr. Dionysius Genoni has a bold rubicund Satyr-like face, prominent eyes, a pointed beard (which is silvery and shiny) and elegant manners. He is nearly bald. All enter in a state of perturbation, almost as if afraid, and all (except Di Nolli) looking curiously about the room. At first, they speak sotto voce.)

Di Nolli (to John). Have you given the orders properly?

John. Yes, my Lord; don't be anxious about that.

Belcredi. Ah, magnificent! magnificent!

Doctor. How extremely interesting! Even in the surroundings his raving madness — is perfectly taken into account!

Donna Matilda (glancing round for her portrait, discovers it, and goes up close to it). Ah! Here it is! *(Going back to admire it, while mixed emotions stir within her.)* Yes . . . yes . . . *(Calls her daughter Frida.)*

Frida. Ah, your portrait!

Donna Matilda. No, no . . . look again; it's you, not I, there!

Di Nolli. Yes, it's quite true. I told you so, I . . .

Donna Matilda. But I would never have believed it! *(Shaking as if with a chill.)* What a strange feeling it gives one! *(Then looking at her daughter.)* Frida, what's the matter? *(She pulls her to her side, and slips an arm round her waist.)* Come: don't you see yourself in me there?

Frida. Well, I really . . .

Donna Matilda. Don't you think so? Don't you, really? *(Turning to Belcredi.)* Look at it, Tito! Speak up, man!

Belcredi (*without looking*). Ah, no! I shan't look at it. For me, *a priori*, certainly not!

Donna Matilda. Stupid! You think you are paying me a compliment! (*Turning to Doctor Genoni.*) What do you say, Doctor? Do say something, please!

Doctor (*makes a movement to go near to the picture*).

Belcredi (*with his back turned, pretending to attract his attention secretly*). — Hss! No, Doctor! For the love of Heaven, have nothing to do with it!

Doctor (*getting bewildered and smiling*). And why shouldn't I?

Donna Matilda. Don't listen to him! Come here! He's insufferable!

Frida. He acts the fool by profession, didn't you know that?

Belcredi (*to the Doctor, seeing him go over*). Look at your feet, Doctor! Mind where you're going!

Doctor. Why?

Belcredi. Be careful you don't put your foot in it!

Doctor (*laughing feebly*). No, no. After all, it seems to me there's no reason to be astonished at the fact that a daughter should resemble her mother!

Belcredi. Hullo! Hullo! He's done it now; he's said it.

Donna Matilda (*with exaggerated anger, advancing towards Belcredi*). What's the matter? What has he said? What has he done?

Doctor (*candidly*). Well, isn't it so?

Belcredi (*answering the Marchioness*). I said there was nothing to be astounded at — and you are astounded! And why so, then, if the thing is so simple and natural for you now?

Donna Matilda (*still more angry*). Fool! fool! It's just because it is so natural! Just because it isn't my daughter who is there. (*Pointing to the canvas.*) That is my portrait; and to find my daughter there instead of me fills me with astonishment, an astonishment which, I beg you to believe, is sincere. I forbid you to cast doubts on it.

Frida (*slowly and wearily*). My God! It's always like this . . . rows over nothing . . .

Belcredi (*also slowly, looking dejected, in accents of apology*). I cast no doubt on anything! I noticed from the beginning that you haven't shared your mother's astonishment; or, if something did astonish you, it was because the likeness between you and the portrait seemed so strong.

Donna Matilda. Naturally! She cannot recognize herself in me as I was at her age; while I, there, can very well recognize myself in her as she is now!

Doctor. Quite right! Because a portrait is always there fixed in the twinkling of an eye: for the young lady something far away and without memories, while, for the Marchioness, it can bring back everything: movements, gestures, looks, smiles, a whole heap of things . . .

Donna Matilda. Exactly!

Doctor (continuing, turning towards her). Naturally enough, you can live all these old sensations again in your daughter.

Donna Matilda. He always spoils every innocent pleasure for me, every touch I have of spontaneous sentiment! He does it merely to annoy me.

Doctor (frightened at the disturbance he has caused, adopts a professional tone). Likeness, dear Baron, is often the result of imponderable things. So one explains that . . .

Belcredi (interrupting the discourse). Somebody will soon be finding a likeness between you and me, my dear Professor!

Di Nolli. Oh! let's finish with this, please! *(Points to the two doors on the right, as a warning that there is someone there who may be listening.)* We've wasted too much time as it is!

Frida. As one might expect when *he's* present. *(Alludes to Belcredi.)*

Di Nolli. Enough! The Doctor is here; and we have come for a very serious purpose which you all know is important for me.

Doctor. Yes, that is so! But now, first of all, let's try to get some points down exactly. Excuse me, Marchioness, will you tell me why your portrait is here? Did you present it to him then?

Donna Matilda. No, not at all. How could I have given it to him? I was just like Frida then — and not even engaged. I gave it to him three or four years after the accident. I gave it to him because his mother wished it so much . . . *(Points to Di Nolli.)*

Doctor. She was his sister? *(Alludes to Henry IV.)*

Di Nolli. Yes, Doctor; and our coming here is a debt we pay to my mother who has been dead for more than a month. Instead of being here, she and I *(indicating Frida.)* ought to be traveling together . . .

Doctor. . . . taking a cure of quite a different kind!

Di Nolli. —Hum! Mother died in the firm conviction that her adored brother was just about to be cured.

Doctor. And can't you tell me, if you please, how she inferred this?

Di Nolli. The conviction would appear to have derived from certain strange remarks which he made, a little before mother died.

Doctor. Oh, remarks! . . . Ah! . . . It would be extremely useful for me to have those remarks, word for word, if possible.

Di Nolli. I can't remember them. I know that mother returned awfully upset from her last visit with him. On her death-bed, she made me promise that I would never neglect him, that I would have doctors see him, and examine him.

Doctor. Um! Um! Let me see! let me see! Sometimes very small reasons determine . . . and this portrait here then? . . .

Donna Matilda. For Heaven's sake, Doctor, don't attach excessive importance to this. It made an impression on me because I had not seen it for so many years!

Doctor. If you please, quietly, quietly . . .

Di Nolli. —Well, yes, it must be about fifteen years ago.

Donna Matilda. More, more: eighteen!

Doctor. Forgive me, but you don't quite know what I'm trying to get at. I attach a very great importance to these two portraits . . . They were painted, naturally, prior to the famous — and most regrettable pageant, weren't they?

Donna Matilda. Of course!

Doctor. That is . . . when he was quite in his right mind — that's what I've been trying to say. Was it his suggestion that they should be painted?

Donna Matilda. Lots of the people who took part in the pageant had theirs done as a souvenir . . .

Belcredi. I had mine done — as "Charles of Anjou!"

Donna Matilda. . . . as soon as the costumes were ready.

Belcredi. As a matter of fact, it was proposed that the whole lot of us should be hung together in a gallery of the villa where the pageant took place. But in the end, everybody wanted to keep his own portrait.

Donna Matilda. And I gave him this portrait of me without very much regret . . . since his mother . . . (*Indicates Di Nolli.*)

Doctor. You don't remember if it was he who asked for it?

Donna Matilda. Ah, that I don't remember . . . Maybe it was his sister, wanting to help out . . . .

Doctor. One other thing: was it his idea, this pageant?

Belcredi (*at once*). No, no, it was mine!

Doctor. If you please . . .

Donna Matilda. Don't listen to him! It was poor Belassi's idea.

Belcredi. Belassi! What had he got to do with it?

Donna Matilda. Count Belassi, who died, poor fellow, two or three months after . . .

Belcredi. But if Belassi wasn't there when . . .

Di Nolli. Excuse me, Doctor; but is it really necessary to establish whose the original idea was?

Doctor. It would help me, certainly!

Belcredi. I tell you the idea was mine! There's nothing to be proud of in it, seeing what the result's been. Look here, Doctor, it was like this. One evening, in the first days of November, I was looking at an illustrated German review in the club. I was merely glancing at the pictures, because I can't read German. There was a picture of the Kaiser, at some University town where he had been a student . . . I don't remember which.

Doctor. Bonn, Bonn!

Belcredi. —You are right: Bonn! He was on horseback, dressed up in one of those ancient German student guild-costumes, followed by a procession of noble students, also in costume. The picture gave me the idea. Already someone at the club had spoken of a pageant for the forthcoming carnival. So I had the notion that each of us should choose for this Tower of Babel pageant to represent some character: a king, an emperor, a prince, with his queen, empress, or lady, alongside of him — and all on horseback. The suggestion was at once accepted.

Donna Matilda. I had my invitation from Belassi.

Belcredi. Well, he wasn't speaking the truth! That's all I can say, if he told you the idea was his. He wasn't even at the club the evening I made the suggestion, just as he (*Meaning Henry IV.*) wasn't there either.

Doctor. So he chose the character of Henry IV?

Donna Matilda. Because I . . . thinking of my name, and not giving the choice any importance, said I would be the Marchioness Matilda of Tuscany.

Doctor. I . . . don't understand the relation between the two.

Donna Matilda. —Neither did I, to begin with, when he said that in that case he would be at my feet like Henry IV at Canossa. I had heard of Canossa of course; but to tell the truth, I'd forgotten most of the story; and I remember I received a curious impression when I had to get up my part, and found that I was the faithful and zealous friend of Pope Gregory VII in deadly enmity with the Emperor of Germany. Then I understood why, since I had chosen to represent his implacable enemy, he wanted to be near me in the pageant as Henry IV.

Doctor. Ah, perhaps because . . .

Belcredi. —Good Heavens, Doctor, because he was then paying furious court to her! (*Indicates the Marchioness.*) And she, naturally . . .

Donna Matilda. Naturally? Not naturally at all . . .

Belcredi (*pointing to her*). She shouldn't stand him . . .

Donna Matilda. —No, that isn't true! I didn't dislike him. Not at all!

But for me, when a man begins to want to be taken seriously, well . . .

Belcredi (*continuing for her*). He gives you the clearest proof of his stupidity.

Donna Matilda. No, dear; not in this case; because he was never a fool like you.

Belcredi. Anyway, I've never asked you to take me seriously.

Donna Matilda. Yes, I know. But with him one couldn't joke. (*Changing her tone and speaking to the Doctor.*) One of the many misfortunes which happen to us women, Doctor, is to see before us every now and again a pair of eyes glaring at us with a contained intense promise of eternal devotion. (*Bursts out laughing.*) There is nothing quite so funny. If men could only see themselves with that eternal look of fidelity in their faces! I've always thought it comic; then more even than now. But I want to make a confession — I can do so after twenty years or more. When I laughed at him then, it was partly out of fear. One might have almost believed a promise from those eyes of his. But it would have been very dangerous.

Doctor (*with lively interest*). Ah! ah! This is most interesting! Very dangerous, you say?

Donna Matilda. Yes, because he was very different from the others. And then, I am . . . well . . . what shall I say? . . . a little impatient of all that is pondered, or tedious. But I was too young then, and a woman. I had the bit between my teeth. It would have required more courage than I felt I possessed. So I laughed at him too — with remorse, to spite myself, indeed; since I saw that my own laugh mingled with those of all the others — the other fools — who made fun of him.

Belcredi. My own case, more or less!

Donna Matilda. You make people laugh at you, my dear, with your trick of always humiliating yourself. It was quite a different affair with him. There's a vast difference. And you — you know — people laugh in your face!

Belcredi. Well, that's better than behind one's back!

Doctor. Let's get to the facts. He was then already somewhat exalted, if I understand rightly.

Belcredi. Yes, but in a curious fashion, Doctor.

Doctor. How?

Belcredi. Well, cold-bloodedly so to speak.

Donna Matilda. Not at all! It was like this, Doctor! He was a bit strange, certainly; but only because he was fond of life: eccentric, there!

Belcredi. I don't say he simulated exaltation. On the contrary, he was often genuinely exalted. But I could swear, Doctor, that he saw himself at once in his own exaltation. Moreover, I'm certain it made him suffer. Sometimes he had the most comical fits of rage against himself.

Doctor. Yes?

Donna Matilda. That is true.

Belcredi (*to Donna Matilda*). And why? (*To the Doctor.*) Evidently, because that immediate lucidity that comes from acting, assuming a part, at once put him out of key with his own feelings, which seemed to him not exactly false, but like something he was obliged to give the value there and then of — what shall I say — of an act of intelligence, to make up for that sincere cordial warmth he felt lacking. So he improvised, exaggerated, let himself go, so as to distract and forget himself. He appeared inconstant, fatuous, and — yes — even ridiculous, sometimes.

Doctor. And may we say unsociable?

Belcredi. No, not at all. He was famous for getting up things: *tableaux vivants*, dances, theatrical performances for charity: all for the fun of the thing, of course. He was a jolly good actor, you know!

Di Nolli. Madness has made a superb actor of him.

Belcredi. —Why, so he was even in the old days. When the accident happened, after the horse fell . . .

Doctor. Hit the back of his head, didn't he?

Donna Matilda. Oh, it was horrible! He was beside me! I saw him between the horse's hoofs! It was rearing!

Belcredi. None of us thought it was anything serious at first. There was a stop in the pageant, a bit of disorder. People wanted to know what had happened. But they'd already taken him off to the villa.

Donna Matilda. There wasn't the least sign of a wound, not a drop of blood.

Belcredi. We thought he had merely fainted.

Donna Matilda. But two hours afterwards . . .

Belcredi. He reappeared in the drawing-room of the villa . . . that is what I wanted to say . . .

Donna Matilda. My God! What a face he had. I saw the whole thing at once!

Belcredi. No, no! that isn't true. Nobody saw it, Doctor, believe me!

Donna Matilda. Doubtless, because you were all like mad folk.

Belcredi. Everybody was pretending to act his part for a joke. It was a regular Babel.

Donna Matilda. And you can imagine, Doctor, what terror struck into us when we understood that he, on the contrary, was playing his part in deadly earnest . . .

Doctor. Oh, he was there too, was he?

Belcredi. Of course! He came straight into the midst of us. We thought he'd quite recovered, and was pretending, fooling, like all the rest of us . . . only doing it rather better; because, as I say, he knew how to act.

Donna Matilda. Some of them began to hit him with their whips and fans and sticks.

Belcredi. And then — as a king, he was armed, of course — he drew out his sword and menaced two or three of us . . . It was a terrible moment, I can assure you!

Donna Matilda. I shall never forget that scene — all our masked faces hideous and terrified gazing at him, at that terrible mask of his face, which was no longer a mask, but madness, madness personified.

Belcredi. He was Henry IV, Henry IV in person, in a moment of fury.

Donna Matilda. He'd got into it all the detail and minute preparation of a month's careful study. And it all burned and blazed there in the terrible obsession which lit his face.

Doctor. Yes, that is quite natural, of course. The momentary obsession of a dilettante became fixed, owing to the fall and the damage to the brain.

Belcredi (*to Frida and Di Nolli*). You see the kind of jokes life can play on us. (*To Di Nolli.*) You were four or five years old. (*To Frida.*) Your mother imagines you've taken her place there in that portrait; when, at the time, she had not the remotest idea that she would bring you into the world. My hair is already grey; and he — look at him — (*Points to portrait*) — ha! A smack on the head, and he never moves again: Henry IV for ever!

Doctor (*seeking to draw the attention of the others, looking learned and imposing*). —Well, well, then it comes, we may say, to this . . .

(*Suddenly the first exit to right, the one nearest footlights, opens, and Berthold enters all excited.*)

Berthold (*rushing in*). I say! I say! (*Stops for a moment, arrested by the astonishment which his appearance has cause in the others.*)

Frida (*running away terrified*). Oh dear! oh dear! it's he, it's . . .

Donna Matilda (*covering her face with her hands so as not to see*). Is it, is it he?

Di Nolli. No, no, what are you talking about? Be calm!

Doctor. Who is it then?

Belcredi. One of our masqueraders.

Di Nolli. He is one of the four youths we keep here to help him out in his madness . . .

Berthold. I beg your pardon, Marquis . . .

Di Nolli. Pardon be damned! I gave orders that the doors were to be closed, and that nobody should be allowed to enter.

Berthold. Yes, sir, but I can't stand it any longer, and I ask you to let me go away this very minute.

Di Nolli. Oh, you're the new valet, are you? You were supposed to begin this morning, weren't you?

Berthold. Yes, sir, and I can't stand it, I can't bear it.

Donna Matilda (*to Di Nolli excitedly*). What? Then he's not so calm as you said?

Berthold (*quickly*). —No, no, my lady, it isn't he; it's my companions. You say "help him out with his madness," Marquis; but they don't do anything of the kind. They're the real madmen. I come here for the first time, and instead of helping me . . .

(*Landolph and Harold come in from the same door, but hesitate on the threshold.*)

Landolph. Excuse me?

Harold. May I come in, my Lord?

Di Nolli. Come in! What's the matter? What are you all doing?

Frida. Oh God! I'm frightened! I'm going to run away. (*Makes towards exit at left.*)

Di Nolli (*restraining her at once*). No, no Frida!

Landolph. My Lord, this fool here . . . (*Indicates Berthold.*)

Berthold (*protesting*). Ah, no thanks, my friends, no thanks! I'm not stopping here! I'm off!

Landolph. What do you mean — you're not stopping here?

Harold. He's ruined everything, my Lord, running away in here!

Landolph. He's made him quite mad. We can't keep him in there any longer. He's given orders that he's to be arrested; and he wants to "judge" him at once from the throne: What is to be done?

Di Nolli. Shut the door, man! Shut the door! Go and close that door! (*Landolph goes over to close it.*)

Harold. Ordulph, alone, won't be able to keep him there.

Landolph. —My Lord, perhaps if we could announce the visitors at once, it would turn his thoughts. Have the gentlemen thought under what pretext they will present themselves to him?

Di Nolli. —It's all been arranged! (*To the Doctor.*) If you Doctor, think it well to see him at once. . . .

Frida. I'm not coming! I'm not coming! I'll keep out of this. You too, mother, for Heaven's sake, come away with me!

Doctor. —I say . . . I suppose he's not armed, is he?

Di Nolli. —Nonsense! Of course not. (*To Frida.*) Frida, you know this is childish of you. You wanted to come!

Frida. I didn't at all. It was mother's idea.

Donna Matilda. And I'm quite ready to see him. What are we going to do?

Belcredi. Must we absolutely dress up in some fashion or other?

Landolph. —Absolutely essential, indispensable, sir. Alas! as you see . . . (*Shows his costume*), there'd be awful trouble if he saw you gentlemen in modern dress.

Harold. He would think it was some diabolical masquerade.

Di Nolli. As these men seem to be in costume to you, so we appear to be in costume to him, in these modern clothes of ours.

Landolph. It wouldn't matter so much if he wouldn't suppose it to be the work of his mortal enemy.

Belcredi. Pope Gregory VII?

Landolph. Precisely. He calls him "a pagan."

Belcredi. The Pope a pagan? Not bad that!

Landolph. —Yes, sir, — and a man who calls up the dead! He accuses him of all the diabolical arts. He's terribly afraid of him.

Doctor. Persecution mania!

Harold. He'd be simply furious.

Di Nolli (*to Belcredi*). But there's no need for you to be there, you know. It's sufficient for the Doctor to see him.

Doctor. —What do you mean? . . . I? Alone?

Di Nolli. —But they are there. (*Indicates the three young men.*)

Doctor. I don't mean that . . . I mean if the Marchioness . . .

Donna Matilda. Of course. I mean to see him too, naturally. I want to see him again.

Frida. Oh, why mother, why? Do come away with me, I implore you!

Donna Matilda (*imperiously*). Let me do as I wish! I came here for this purpose! (*To Landolph.*) I shall be "Adelaide," the mother.

Landolph. Excellent! The mother of the Empress Bertha. Good! It will be enough if her Ladyship wears the ducal crown and puts on a mantle that will hide her other clothes entirely (*To Harold.*) Off you go, Harold!

Harold. Wait a moment! And this gentleman here? . . . (*Alludes to the Doctor.*)

Doctor. —Ah yes . . . we decided I was to be . . . the Bishop of Cluny, Hugh of Cluny!

Harold. The gentleman means the Abbot. Very good! Hugh of Cluny.

Landolph. —He's often been here before!

Doctor (*amazed*). —What? Been here before?

Landolph. —Don't be alarmed! I mean that it's an easily prepared disguise . . .

Harold. We've made use of it on other occasions, you see!

Doctor. But . . .

Landolph. Oh, no, there's no risk of his remembering. He pays more attention to the dress than to the person.

Donna Matilda. That's fortunate for me too then.

Di Nolli. Frida, you and I'll get along. Come on, Tito!

Belcredi. Ah no. If she (*Indicates the Marchioness.*) stops here, so do I!

Donna Matilda. But I don't need you at all.

Belcredi. You may not need me, but I should like to see him again myself. Mayn't I?

Landolph. Well, perhaps it would be better if there were three.

Harold. How is the gentleman to be dressed then?

Belcredi. Oh, try and find some easy costume for me.

Landolph (*to Harold*). Hum! Yes . . . he'd better be from Cluny too.

Belcredi. What do you mean — from Cluny?

Landolph. A Benedictine's habit of the Abbey of Cluny. He can be in attendance on Monsignor. (*To Harold*). Off you go! (*To Berthold.*) And you too get away and keep out of sight all today. No, wait a bit! (*To Berthold.*) You bring here the costumes he will give you. (*To Harold.*) You go at once and announce the visit of the "Duchess Adelaide" and "Monsignor Hugh of Cluny." Do you understand? (*Harold and Berthold go off by the first door on the right.*)

Di Nolli. We'll retire now. (*Goes off with Frida, left.*)

Doctor. Shall I be a *persona grata* to him, as Hugh of Cluny?

Landolph. Oh, rather! Don't worry about that! Monsignor has always been received here with great respect. You too, my Lady, he will be glad to see. He never forgets that it was owing to the intercession of you two that he was admitted to the Castle of Canossa and the presence of Gregory VII, who didn't want to receive him.

Belcredi. And what do I do?

Landolph. You stand a little apart, respectfully: that's all.

Donna Matilda (*irritated, nervous*). You would do well to go away, you know.

Belcredi (*slowly, spitefully*). How upset you seem! . . .

Donna Matilda (*proudly*). I am as I am. Leave me alone!

(*Berthold comes in with the costumes.*)

Landolph (*seeing him enter*). Ah, the costumes: here they are. This mantle is for the Marchioness . . .

Donna Matilda. Wait a minute! I'll take off my hat.

(*Does so and gives it to Berthold.*)

Landolph. Put it down there! (*Then to the Marchioness, while he offers to put the ducal crown on her head.*) Allow me!
Donna Matilda. Dear, dear! Isn't there a mirror here?
Landolph. Yes, there's one there (*Points to the door on the left.*) If the Marchioness would rather put it on herself . . .
Donna Matilda. Yes, yes, that will be better. Give it to me! (*Takes up her hat and goes off with Berthold, who carries the cloak and the crown.*)
Belcredi. Well, I must say, I never thought I should be a Benedictine monk! By the way, this business must cost an awful lot of money.
The Doctor. Like any other fantasy, naturally!
Belcredi. Well, there's a fortune to go upon.
Landolph. We have got there a whole wardrobe of costumes of the period, copied to perfection from old models. This is my special job. I get them from the best theatrical costumers. They cost lots of money. (*Donna Matilda re-enters, wearing mantle and crown.*)
Belcredi (*at once, in admiration*). Oh magnificent! Oh, truly regal!
Donna Matilda (*looking at Belcredi and bursting out into laughter*). Oh no, no! Take it off! You're impossible. You look like an ostrich dressed up as a monk.
Belcredi. Well, how about the Doctor?
The Doctor. I don't think I look so bad, do I?
Donna Matilda. No; the Doctor's all right . . . but you are too funny for words.
The Doctor. Do you have many receptions here then?
Landolph. It depends. He often gives orders that such and such a person appear before him. Then we have to find someone who will take the part. Women too . . .
Donna Matilda (*hurt, but trying to hide the fact*). Ah, women too?
Landolph. Oh, yes; many at first.
Belcredi (*laughing*). Oh, that's great! In costume, like the Marchioness?
Landolph. Oh well, you know, women of the kind that lend themselves to . . .
Belcredi. Ah, I see! (*Perfidiously to the Marchioness.*) Look out, you know he's becoming dangerous for you.

(*The second door on the right opens, and Harold appears making first of all a discreet sign that all conversation should cease.*)

Harold. His Majesty, the Emperor!

(*The Two Valets enter first, and go and stand on either side of the throne. Then Henry IV comes in between Ordulph and Harold, who keep a little in the rear respectfully.*

Henry IV is about 50 and very pale. The hair on the back of his head is already grey; over the temples and forehead it appears blond, owing to its having been tinted in an evident and puerile fashion. On his cheek bones he has two small, doll-like dabs of color, that stand out prominently against the rest of his tragic pallor. He is wearing a penitent's sack over his regal habit, as at Canossa. His eyes have a fixed look which is dreadful to see, and this expression is in strained contrast with the sackcloth. Ordulph carries the Imperial crown; Harold, the sceptre with eagle, and the globe with the cross.)

Henry IV (*bowing first to Donna Matilda and afterwards to the Doctor*). My lady . . . Monsignor . . . (*Then he looks at Belcredi and seems about to greet him too; when, suddenly, he turns to Landolph, who has approached him, and asks him sotto voce and with diffidence.*) Is that Peter Damiani?

Landolph. No, Sire. He is a monk from Cluny who is accompanying the Abbot.

Henry IV (*looks again at Belcredi with increasing mistrust, and then noticing that he appears embarrassed and keeps glancing at Donna Matilda and the Doctor, stands upright and cries out*). No, it's Peter Damiani! It's no use, father, your looking at the Duchess. (*Then turning quickly to Donna Matilda and the Doctor as though to ward off a danger.*) I swear it! I swear that my heart is changed towards your daughter. I confess that if he (*Indicates Belcredi.*) hadn't come to forbid it in the name of Pope Alexander, I'd have repudiated her. Yes, yes, there were people ready to favor the repudiation: the Bishop of Mayence would have done it for a matter of one hundred and twenty farms. (*Looks at Landolph a little perplexed and adds.*) But I mustn't speak ill of the bishops at this moment! (*More humbly to Belcredi.*) I am grateful to you, believe me, I am grateful to you for the hindrance you put in my way! — God knows, my life's been all made of humiliations: my mother, Adalbert, Tribur, Goslar! And now this sackcloth you see me wearing! (*Changes tone suddenly and speaks like one who goes over his part in a parenthesis of astuteness.*) It doesn't matter: clarity of ideas, perspicacity, firmness and patience under adversity that's the thing. (*Then turning to all and speaking solemnly.*) I know how to make amend for the mistakes I have made; and I can humiliate myself even before you, Peter

Damiani. (*Bows profoundly to him and remains curved. Then a suspicion is born in him which he is obliged to utter in menacing tones, almost against his will.*) Was it not perhaps you who started that obscene rumor that my holy mother had illicit relations with the Bishop of Augusta?

Belcredi (*since Henry IV has his finger pointed at him*). No, no, it wasn't I . . .

Henry IV (*straightening up*). Not true, not true? Infamy! (*Looks at him and then adds.*) I didn't think you capable of it! (*Goes to the Doctor and plucks his sleeve, while winking at him knowingly.*) Always the same, Monsignor, those bishops, always the same!

Harold (*softly, whispering as if to help out the doctor*). Yes, yes, the rapacious bishops!

The Doctor (*to Harold, trying to keep it up*). Ah, yes, those fellows . . . ah yes . . .

Henry IV. Nothing satisfies them! I was a little boy, Monsignor . . . One passes the time, playing even, when, without knowing it, one is a king. — I was six years old; and they tore me away from my mother, and made use of me against her without my knowing anything about it . . . always profaning, always stealing, stealing! . . . One greedier than the other . . . Hanno worse than Stephen! Stephen worse than Hanno!

Landolph (*sotto voce, persuasively, to call his attention*). Majesty!

Henry IV (*turning round quickly*). Ah yes . . . this isn't the moment to speak ill of the bishops. But this infamy against my mother, Monsignor, is too much. (*Looks at the Marchioness and grows tender.*) And I can't even weep for her, Lady . . . I appeal to you who have a mother's heart! She came here to see me from her convent a month ago . . . They had told me she was dead! (*Sustained pause full of feeling. Then smiling sadly.*) I can't weep for her; because if you are here now, and I am like this (*Shows the sackcloth he is wearing.*) it means I am twenty-six years old!

Harold. And that she is therefore alive, Majesty! . . .

Ordulph. Still in her convent!

Henry IV (*looking at them*). Ah yes! And I can postpone my grief to another time. (*Shows the Marchioness almost with coquetry the tint he has given to his hair.*) Look! I am still fair . . . (*Then slowly as if in confidence.*) For you . . . there's no need! But little exterior details do help! A matter of time, Monsignor, do you understand me? (*Turns to the Marchioness and notices her hair.*) Ah, but I see that you too, Duchess . . . Italian, eh? (*As much as to say "false"; but without any indignation, indeed rather with malicious admiration.*) Heaven forbid that I should show disgust or surprise! Nobody cares to recognize that obscure and fatal power which sets limits to our will. But I say, if one is born and one dies . . . Did you want to be born, Monsignor? I didn't! And in both cases, independently of our wills, so many things happen we would wish didn't happen, and to which we resign ourselves as best we can! . . .

Doctor (*merely to make a remark, while studying Henry IV carefully*). Alas! Yes, alas!

Henry IV. It's like this: When we are not resigned, out come our desires. A woman wants to be a man . . . an old man would be young again. Desires, ridiculous fixed ideas of course — But reflect! Monsignor, those other desires are not less ridiculous: I mean, those desires where the will is kept within the limits of the possible. Not one of us can lie or pretend. We're all fixed in good faith in a certain concept of ourselves. However, Monsignor, while you keep yourself in order, holding on with both your hands to your holy habit, there slips down from your sleeves, there peels off from you like . . . like a serpent . . . something you don't notice: life, Monsignor! (*Turns to the Marchioness.*) Has it never happened to you, my Lady, to find a different self in yourself? Have you always been the same? My God! One day . . . How was it, how was it you were able to commit this or that action? (*Fixes her so intently in the eyes as almost to make her blanch.*) Yes, that particular action, that very one: we understand each other! But don't be afraid: I shall reveal it to none. And you, Peter Damiani, how could you be a friend of that man? . . .

Landolph. Majesty!

Henry IV (*at once*). No, I won't name him! (*Turning to Belcredi.*) What did you think of him? But we all of us cling tight to our conceptions of ourselves, just as he who is growing old dyes his hair. What does it matter that this dyed hair of mine isn't a reality for you, if it *is*, to some extent, for me? — you, you, my Lady, certainly don't dye your hair to deceive the others, nor even yourself; but only to cheat your own image a little before the looking-glass. I do it for a joke! You do it seriously! But I assure you that you too, Madam, are in masquerade, though it be in all seriousness; and I am not speaking of the venerable crown on your brows or the ducal mantle. I am speaking only of the memory you wish to fix in yourself of your fair complexion one day when it pleased you — or of your dark complexion, if you were dark: the fading image of your youth! For you, Peter Damiani, on the contrary, the memory of what you have been, of what you have done, seems to you a recognition of past realities that remain within you like a dream. I'm in the same case too: with so many inexplicable memories — like dreams!

Ah! . . . There's nothing to marvel at in it, Peter Damiani! Tomorrow it will be the same thing with our life of today! (*Suddenly getting excited and taking hold of his sackcloth.*) This sackcloth here
. . . (*Beginning to take it off with a gesture of almost ferocious joy
while the Three Valets run over to him, frightened, as if to prevent
his doing so.*) Ah, my God! (*Draws back and throws off sackcloth.*)
Tomorrow, at Bressanone, twenty-seven German and Lombard
bishops will sign with me the act of deposition of Gregory VII! No
Pope at all! Just a false monk!

Ordulph (*with the other three*). Majesty! Majesty! In God's name! . . .

Harold (*inviting him to put on the sackcloth again*). Listen to what
he says, Majesty!

Landolph. Monsignor is here with the Duchess to intercede in your
favor. (*Makes secret signs to the Doctor to say something at once.*)

Doctor (*foolishly*). Ah yes . . . yes . . . we are here to intercede . . .

Henry IV (*repenting at once, almost terrified, allowing the three to
put on the sackcloth again, and pulling it down over him with his
own hands*) Pardon . . . yes . . . yes . . . pardon, Monsignor: forgive
me, my Lady . . I swear to you I feel the whole weight of the
anathema. (*Bends himself, takes his face between his hands, as
though waiting for something to crush him. Then changing tone,
but without moving, says softly to Landolph, Harold and Ordulph.*)
But I don't know why I cannot be humble before that man there!
(*Indicates Belcredi.*)

Landolph (*sotto voce*). But why, Majesty, do you insist on believing
he is Peter Damiani, when he isn't, at all?

Henry IV (*looking at him timorously*). He isn't Peter Damiani?

Harold. No, no, he is a poor monk, Majesty.

Henry IV (*sadly with a touch of exasperation*). Ah! None of us can
estimate what we do when we do it from instinct . . . You perhaps,
Madam, can understand me better than the others, since you are a
woman and a Duchess. This is a solemn and decisive moment. I
could, you know, accept the assistance of the Lombard bishops,
arrest the Pope, lock him up here in the castle, run to Rome and
elect an anti-Pope; offer alliance to Robert Guiscard — and Gregory
VII would be lost! I resist the temptation; and, believe me, I am
wise in doing so. I feel the atmosphere of our times and the majesty of one who knows how to be what he ought to be! a Pope!
Do you feel inclined to laugh at me, seeing me like this? You would
be foolish to do so; for you don't understand the political wisdom
which makes this penitent's sack advisable. The parts may be
changed tomorrow. What would you do then? Would you laugh to
see the Pope a prisoner? No! It would come to the same thing:

I dressed as a penitent, today; he, as prisoner tomorrow! But woe to him who doesn't know how to wear his mask, be he king or Pope! — Perhaps he is a bit too cruel! No! Yes, yes, maybe! — You remember, my Lady, how your daughter Bertha, for whom, I repeat, my feelings have changed (*Turns to Belcredi and shouts to his face as if he were being contradicted by him.*) — yes, changed on account of the affection and devotion she showed me in that terrible moment . . . (*Then once again to the Marchioness.*) . . . you remember how she came with me, my Lady, followed me like a beggar and passed two nights out in the open, in the snow? You are her mother! Doesn't this touch your mother's heart? Doesn't this urge you to pity, so that you will beg His Holiness for pardon, beg him to receive us?

Donna Matilda (*trembling, with feeble voice*). Yes, yes, at once . . .

Doctor. It shall be done!

Henry IV. And one thing more! (*Draws them in to listen to him.*) It isn't enough that he should receive me! You know he can do *everything* — *everything* I tell you! He can even call up the dead. (*Touches his chest.*) Behold me! Do you see me? There is no magic art unknown to him. Well, Monsignor, my Lady, my torment is really this: that whether here or there (*Pointing to his portrait almost in fear.*) I can't free myself from this magic. I am a penitent now, you see; and I swear to you I shall remain so until he receives me. But you two, when the excommunication is taken off, must ask the Pope to do this thing he can so easily do: to take me away from that; (*Indicating the portrait again.*) and let me live wholly and freely my miserable life. A man can't always be twenty-six, my Lady. I ask this of you for your daughter's sake too; that I may love her as she deserves to be loved, well disposed as I am now, all tender towards her for her pity. There: it's all there! I am in your hands! (*Bows.*) My Lady! Monsignor!

(*He goes off, bowing grandly, through the door by which he entered, leaving everyone stupefied, and the Marchioness so profoundly touched, that no sooner has he gone than she breaks out into sobs and sits down almost fainting.*)

ACT II

Another room of the villa, adjoining the throne room. Its furniture is antique and severe. Principal exit at rear in the background. To the left, two windows looking on the garden. To the right, a door opening into the throne room.

Late afternoon of the same day.

Donna Matilda, the Doctor and Belcredi are on the stage engaged in conversation; but Donna Matilda stands to one side, evidently annoyed at what the other two are saying; although she cannot help listening, because, in her agitated state, everything interests her in spite of herself. The talk of the other two attracts her attention, because she instinctively feels the need for calm at the moment.

Belcredi. It may be as you say, Doctor, but that was my impression.

Doctor. I won't contradict you; but, believe me, it is only . . . an impression.

Belcredi. Pardon me, but he even said so, and quite clearly (*Turning to the Marchioness.*) Didn't he, Marchioness?

Donna Matilda (turning round). What did he say? . . . (*Then not agreeing.*) Oh yes . . . but not for the reason you think!

Doctor. He was alluding to the costumes we had slipped on . . . Your cloak (*Indicating the Marchioness.*) our Benedictine habits . . . But all this is childish!

Donna Matilda (turning quickly, indignant). Childish? What do you mean, Doctor?

Doctor. From one point of view, it is — I beg you to let me say so, Marchioness! Yet, on the other hand, it is much more complicated than you can imagine.

Donna Matilda. To me, on the contrary, it is perfectly clear!

Doctor (with a smile of pity of the competent person towards those who do not understand). We must take into account the peculiar psychology of madmen; which, you must know, enables us to be certain that they observe things and can, for instance, easily detect people who are disguised; can in fact recognize the disguise and yet believe in it; just as children do, for whom disguise is both play and reality. That is why I used the word childish. But the thing is extremely complicated, inasmuch as he must be perfectly aware of being an image to himself and for himself — that image there, in fact! (*Alluding to the portrait in the throne room, and pointing to the left.*)

Belcredi. That's what he said!

Doctor. Very well then — An image before which other images, ours, have appeared: understand? Now he, in his acute and perfectly lucid delirium, was able to detect at once a difference between his image and ours: that is, he saw that ours were make-believes. So he suspected us; because all madmen are armed with a special diffidence. But that's all there is to it! Our make-believe, built up all round his, did not seem pitiful to him. While his seemed all the more tragic to us, in that he, as if in defiance — understand? — and induced by his suspicion, wanted to show us up merely as a joke. That was also partly the case with him, in coming before us with painted cheeks and hair, and saying he had done it on purpose for a jest.

Donna Matilda (*impatiently*). No, it's not that, Doctor. It's not like that! It's not like that!

Doctor. Why isn't it, may I ask?

Donna Matilda (*with decision but trembling*). I am perfectly certain he recognized me!

Doctor. It's not possible . . . it's not possible!

Belcredi (*at the same time*). Of course not!

Donna Matilda (*more than ever determined, almost convulsively*). I tell you, he recognized me! When he came close up to speak to me — looking in my eyes, right into my eyes — he recognized me!

Belcredi. But he was talking of your daughter!

Donna Matilda. That's not true! He was talking of me! Of me!

Belcredi. Yes, perhaps, when he said . . .

Donna Matilda (*letting herself go*). About my dyed hair! But didn't you notice that he added at once: "or the memory of your dark hair, if you were dark"? He remembered perfectly well that I was dark — then!

Belcredi. Nonsense! nonsense!

Donna Matilda (*not listening to him, turning to the Doctor*). My hair, Doctor, is really dark — like my daughter's! That's why he spoke of her.

Belcredi. But he doesn't even know your daughter! He's never seen her!

Donna Matilda. Exactly! Oh, you never understand anything! By my daughter, stupid, he meant me — as I was then!

Belcredi. Oh, this is catching! This is catching, this madness!

Donna Matilda (*softly, with contempt*). Fool!

Belcredi. Excuse me, were you ever his wife? Your daughter is his wife — in his delirium: Bertha of Susa.

Donna Matilda. Exactly! Because I, no longer dark — as he remembered me — but *fair*, introduced myself as "Adelaide," the mother.

My daughter doesn't exist for him: he's never seen her — you said so yourself! So how can he know whether she's fair or dark?

Belcredi. But he said dark, speaking generally, just as anyone who wants to recall, whether fair or dark, a memory of youth in the color of the hair! And you, as usual, begin to imagine things! Doctor, you said I ought not to have come! It's she who ought not to have come!

Donna Matilda (upset for a moment by Belcredi's remark, recovers herself. Then with a touch of anger, because doubtful). No, no . . . he spoke of me . . . He spoke all the time to me, with me, of me . . .

Belcredi That's not bad! He didn't leave me a moment's breathing space; and you say he was talking all the time to you? Unless you think he was alluding to you too, when he was talking to Peter Damiani!

Donna Matilda (defiantly, almost exceeding the limits of courteous discussion). Who knows? Can you tell me why, from the outset, he showed a strong dislike for you, for you alone? *(From the tone of the question, the expected answer must almost explicitly be: "because he understands you are my lover." Belcredi feels this so well that he remains silent and can say nothing.)*

Doctor. The reason may also be found in the fact that only the visit of the Duchess Adelaide and the Abbot of Cluny was announced to him. Finding a third person present, who had not been announced, at once his suspicions . . .

Belcredi. Yes, exactly! His suspicion made him see an enemy in me: Peter Damiani! But she's got it into her head, that he recognized her . . .

Donna Matilda. There's no doubt about it! I could see it from his eyes, doctor. You know, there's a way of looking that leaves no doubt whatever . . . Perhaps it was only for an instant, but I am sure!

Doctor. It is not impossible: a lucid moment . . .

Donna Matilda. Yes, perhaps . . . And then his speech seemed to me full of regret for his and my youth — for the horrible thing that happened to him, that has held him in that disguise from which he has never been able to free himself, and from which he longs to be free — he said so himself!

Belcredi. Yes, so as to be able to make love to your daughter, or you, as you believe — having been touched by your pity.

Donna Matilda. Which is very great, I would ask you to believe.

Belcredi. As one can see, Marchioness; so much so that a miracle-worker might expect a miracle from it!

Doctor. Will you let me speak? I don't work miracles, because I am a doctor and not a miracle-worker. I listened very intently to all he said; and I repeat that that certain analogical elasticity, common to all systematized delirium, is evidently with him much . . . what shall I say? — much relaxed! The elements, that is, of his delirium no longer hold together. It seems to me he has lost the equilibrium of his second personality and sudden recollections drag him — and this is very comforting — not from a state of incipient apathy, but rather from a morbid inclination to reflective melancholy, which shows a . . . a very considerable cerebral activity. Very comforting, I repeat! Now if, by this violent trick we've planned . . .

Donna Matilda (turning to the window, in the tone of a sick person complaining). But how is it that the motor has not returned? It's three hours and a half since . . .

Doctor. What do you say?

Donna Matilda. The motor, Doctor! It's more than three hours and a half . . .

Doctor (taking out his watch and looking at it). Yes, more than four hours, by this!

Donna Matilda. It could have reached here an hour ago at least! But, as usual . . .

Belcredi. Perhaps they can't find the dress . . .

Donna Matilda. But I explained exactly where it was! *(Impatiently.)* And Frida . . . where is Frida?

Belcredi (looking out of the window). Perhaps she is in the garden with Charles . . .

Doctor. He'll talk her out of her fright.

Belcredi. She's not afraid, Doctor; don't you believe it: the thing bores her rather . . .

Donna Matilda. Just don't ask anything of her! I know what she's like.

Doctor. Let's wait patiently. Anyhow, it will soon be over, and it has to be in the evening . . . It will only be the matter of a moment! If we can succeed in rousing him, as I was saying, and in breaking at one go the threads — already slack — which still bind him to this fiction of his, giving him back what he himself asks for — you remember, he said: "one cannot always be twenty-six years old, madam!" if we can give him freedom from this torment, which even *he* feels is a torment, then if he is able to recover at one bound the sensation of the distance of time . . .

Belcredi (quickly). He'll be cured! *(Then emphatically with irony.)* We'll pull him out of it all!

Doctor. Yes, we may hope to set him going again, like a watch which has stopped at a certain hour . . . just as if we had our watches in our hands and were waiting for that other watch to go again. — A shake — so — and let's hope it'll tell the time again after its long stop. (*At this point the Marquis Charles Di Nolli enters from the principal entrance.*)

Donna Matilda. Oh, Charles! . . . And Frida? Where is she?

Di Nolli. She'll be here in a moment.

Doctor. Has the motor arrived?

Di Nolli. Yes.

Donna Matilda. Yes? Has the dress come?

Di Nolli. It's been here some time.

Doctor. Good! Good!

Donna Matilda (*trembling*). Where is she? Where's Frida?

Di Nolli (*shrugging his shoulders and smiling sadly, like one lending himself unwillingly to an untimely joke*). You'll see, you'll see! . . . (*Pointing towards the hall.*) Here she is! . . . (*Berthold appears at the threshold of the hall, and announces with solemnity.*)

Berthold. Her Highness the Countess Matilda of Canossa! (*Frida enters, magnificent and beautiful, arrayed in the robes of her mother as "Countess Matilda of Tuscany," so that she is a living copy of the portrait in the throne room.*)

Frida (*passing Berthold, who is bowing, says to him with disdain*). Of Tuscany, of Tuscany! Canossa is just one of my castles!

Belcredi (*in admiration*). Look! Look! She seems another person . . .

Donna Matilda. One would say it were I! Look! — Why, Frida, look! She's exactly my portrait, alive!

Doctor. Yes, yes . . . Perfect! Perfect! The portrait, to the life.

Belcredi. Yes, there's no question about it. She *is* the portrait! Magnificent!

Frida. Don't make me laugh, or I shall burst! I say, mother, what a tiny waist you had? I had to squeeze so to get into this!

Donna Matilda (*arranging her dress a little*). Wait! . . . Keep still! . . . These pleats . . . is it really so tight?

Frida. I'm suffocating! I implore you, to be quick! . . .

Doctor. But we must wait till it's evening!

Frida. No, no, I can't hold out till evening!

Donna Matilda. Why did you put it on so soon?

Frida. The moment I saw it, the temptation was irresistible . . .

Donna Matilda. At least you could have called me, or have had someone help you! It's still all crumpled.

Frida. So I saw, mother; but they are old creases; they won't come out.

Doctor. It doesn't matter, Marchioness! The illusion is perfect. (*Then coming nearer and asking her to come in front of her daughter, without hiding her.*) If you please, stay there, there . . . at a certain distance . . . now a little more forward . . .

Belcredi. For the feeling of the distance of time . . .

Donna Matilda (*slightly turning to him*). Twenty years after! A disaster! A tragedy!

Belcredi. Now don't let's exaggerate!

Doctor (*embarrassed, trying to save the situation*). No, no! I meant the dress . . . so as to see . . . You know . . .

Belcredi (*laughing*). Oh, as for the dress, Doctor, it isn't a matter of twenty years! It's eight hundred! An abyss! Do you really want to shove him across it (*Pointing first to Frida and then to Marchioness.*) from there to here? But you'll have to pick him up in pieces with a basket! Just think now: for us it is a matter of twenty years, a couple of dresses, and a masquerade. But, if, as you say, Doctor, time has stopped for and around him: if he lives there (*Pointing to Frida.*) with her, eight hundred years ago . . . I repeat: the giddiness of the jump will be such, that finding himself suddenly among us . . . (*The Doctor shakes his head in dissent.*) You don't think so?

Doctor. No, because life, my dear baron, can take up its rhythms.' This — our life — will at once become real also to him; and will pull him up directly, wresting from him suddenly the illusion, and showing him that the eight hundred years, as you say, are only twenty! It will be like one of those tricks, such as the leap into space, for instance, of the Masonic rite, which appears to be heaven knows how far, and is only a step down the stairs.

Belcredi. Ah! An idea! Yes! Look at Frida and the Marchioness, doctor! Which is more advanced in time? We old people, Doctor! The young ones think they are more ahead; but it isn't true: we are more ahead, because time belongs to us more than to them.

Doctor. If the past didn't alienate us . . .

Belcredi. It doesn't matter at all! How does it alienate us? They (*Pointing to Frida and Di Nolli.*) have still to do what we have accomplished, Doctor: to grow old, doing the same foolish things, more or less, as we did . . . This is the illusion: that one comes forward through a door to life. It isn't so! As soon as one is born, one starts dying; therefore, he who started first is the most advanced of all. The youngest of us is father Adam! Look there: (*Pointing to Frida.*) eight hundred years younger than all of us — the Countess Matilda of Tuscany. (*He makes her a deep bow.*)

Di Nolli. I say, Tito, don't start joking.

Belcredi. Oh, you think I am joking? . . .

Di Nolli. Of course, of course . . . all the time.

Belcredi. Impossible! I've even dressed up as a Benedictine . . .

Di Nolli. Yes, but for a serious purpose.

Belcredi. Well, exactly. If it has been serious for the others . . . for

Frida, now, for instance. (*Then turning to the Doctor.*) I swear, Doctor, I don't yet understand what you want to do.

Doctor (*annoyed*). You'll see! Let me do as I wish . . . At present you see the Marchioness still dressed as . . .

Belcredi. Oh, she also . . . has to masquerade?

Doctor. Of course! of course! In another dress that's in there ready to be used when it comes into his head he sees the Countess Matilda of Canossa before him.

Frida (*while talking quietly to Di Nolli notices the doctor's mistake*). Of Tuscany, of Tuscany!

Doctor. It's all the same!

Belcredi. Oh, I see! He'll be faced by two of them . . .

Doctor. Two, precisely! And then . . .

Frida (*calling him aside*). Come here, doctor! Listen!

Doctor. Here I am! (*Goes near the two young people and pretends to give some explanations to them.*)

Belcredi (*softly to Donna Matilda*). I say, this is getting rather strong, you know!

Donna Matilda (*looking him firmly in the face*). What?

Belcredi. Does it really interest you as much as all that — to make you willing to take part in . . . ? For a woman this is simply enormous! . . .

Donna Matilda. Yes, for an ordinary woman.

Belcredi. Oh, no, my dear, for all women, — in a question like this! It's an abnegation.

Donna Matilda. I owe it to him.

Belcredi. Don't lie! You know well enough it's not hurting you!

Donna Matilda. Well, then, where does the abnegation come in?

Belcredi. Just enough to prevent you losing caste in other people's eyes — and just enough to offend me! . . .

Donna Matilda. But who is worrying about you now?

Di Nolli (*coming forward*). It's all right. It's all right. That's what we'll do! (*Turning towards Berthold.*) Here you, go and call one of those fellows!

Berthold. At once! (*Exit.*)

Donna Matilda. But first of all we've got to pretend that we are going away.

Di Nolli. Exactly! I'll see to that . . . (*To Belcredi.*) you don't mind staying here?

Belcredi (*ironically*). Oh, no, I don't mind, I don't mind! . . .

Di Nolli. We must look out not to make him suspicious again, you know.

Belcredi. Oh, Lord! *He* doesn't amount to anything!

Doctor. He must believe absolutely that we've gone away. (*Landolph followed by Berthold enters from the right.*)

Landolph. May I come in?

Di Nolli. Come in! Come in; I say — your name's Lolo, isn't it?

Landolph. Lolo, or Landolph, just as you like!

Di Nolli. Well, look here: the Doctor and the Marchioness are leaving, at once.

Landolph. Very well. All we've got to say is that they have been able to obtain the permission for the reception from His Holiness. He's in there in his own apartments repenting of all he said — and in an awful state to have the pardon! Would you mind coming a minute? . . . If you would, just for a minute . . . put on the dress again . . .

Doctor. Why, of course, with pleasure . . .

Landolph. Might I be allowed to make a suggestion? Why not add that the Marchioness of Tuscany has interceded with the Pope that he should be received?

Donna Matilda. You see, he has recognized me!

Landolph. Forgive me . . . I don't know my history very well. I am sure you gentlemen know it much better! But I thought it was believed that Henry IV had a secret passion for the Marchioness of Tuscany.

Donna Matilda (*at once*). Nothing of the kind! Nothing of the kind!

Landolph. That's what I thought! But he says he's loved her . . . he's always saying it . . . And now he fears that her indignation for this secret love of his will work him harm with the Pope.

Belcredi. We must let him understand that this aversion no longer exists.

Landolph. Exactly! Of course!

Donna Matilda (*to Belcredi*). History says — I don't know whether you know it or not — that the Pope gave way to the supplications of the Marchioness Matilda and the Abbot of Cluny. And I may say, my dear Belcredi, that I intended to take advantage of this fact — at the time of the pageant — to show him my feelings were not so hostile to him as he supposed.

Belcredi. You are most faithful to history, Marchioness . . .

Landolph. Well then, the Marchioness could spare herself a double disguise and present herself with Monsignor (*Indicating the Doctor.*) as the Marchioness of Tuscany.

Doctor (*quickly, energetically*). No, no! That won't do at all. It would ruin everything. The impression from the confrontation must be a sudden one, give a shock! No, no, Marchioness, you will appear again as the Duchess Adelaide, the mother of the Empress. And then we'll go away. This is most necessary: that he should know

we've gone away. Come on! Don't let's waste any more time!
There's a lot to prepare.

(*Exeunt the Doctor, Donna Matilda, and Landolph, right.*)

Frida. I am beginning to feel afraid again.

Di Nolli. Again, Frida?

Frida. It would have been better if I had seen him before.

Di Nolli. There's nothing to be frightened of, really.

Frida. He isn't furious, is he?

Di Nolli. Of course not! he's quite calm.

Belcredi (*with ironic sentimental affectation*). Melancholy! Didn't you
    hear that he loves you?

Frida. Thanks! That's just why I am afraid.

Belcredi. He won't do you any harm.

Di Nolli. It'll only last a minute . . .

Frida. Yes, but there in the dark with him . . .

Di Nolli. Only for a moment; and I will be near you, and all the others
    behind the door ready to run in. As soon as you see your mother,
    your part will be finished . . .

Belcredi. I'm afraid of a different thing: that we're wasting our
    time . . .

Di Nolli. Don't begin again! The remedy seems a sound one to me.

Frida. I think so too! I feel it! I'm all trembling!

Belcredi. But, mad people, my dear friends — though they don't know
    it, alas — have this felicity which we don't take into account . . .

Di Nolli (*interrupting, annoyed*). What felicity? Nonsense!

Belcredi (*forcefully*). They don't reason!

Di Nolli. What's reasoning got to do with it, anyway?

Belcredi. Don't you call it reasoning that he will have to do — accord-
    ing to us — when he sees her (*Indicates Frida.*) and her mother?
    We've reasoned it all out, surely!

Di Nolli. Nothing of the kind: no reasoning at all! We put before him
    a double image of his own fantasy, or fiction, as the doctor says.

Belcredi (*suddenly*). I say, I've never understood why they take degrees
    in medicine.

Di Nolli (*amazed*). Who?

Belcredi. The alienists!

Di Nolli. What ought they to take degrees in, then?

Frida. If they are alienists, in what else should they take degrees?

Belcredi. In law, of course! All a matter of talk! The more they talk,
    the more highly they are considered. "Analogous elasticity," "the
    sensation of distance in time!" And the first thing they tell you is
    that they don't work miracles — when a miracle's just what is

wanted! But they know that the more they say they are not miracle-workers, the more folk believe in their seriousness!

Berthold (*who has been looking through the keyhole of the door on right*). There they are! There they are! They're coming in here.

Di Nolli. Are they?

Berthold. He wants to come with them . . . Yes! . . . He's coming too!

Di Nolli. Let's get away, then! Let's get away, at once! (*To Berthold.*) You stop here!

Berthold. Must I?

(*Without answering him, Di Nolli, Frida, and Belcredi go out by the main exit, leaving Berthold surprised. The door on the right opens, and Landolph enters first, bowing. Then Donna Matilda comes in, with mantle and ducal crown as in the first act; also the Doctor as the Abbot of Cluny. Henry IV is among them in royal dress. Ordulph and Harold enter last of all.*)

Henry IV (*following up what he has been saying in the other room*). And now I will ask you a question: how can I be astute, if you think me obstinate?

Doctor. No, no, not obstinate!

Henry IV (*smiling, pleased*). Then you think me really astute?

Doctor. No, no, neither obstinate, nor astute.

Henry IV (*with benevolent irony*). Monsignor, if obstinacy is not a vice which can go with astuteness, I hoped that in denying me the former, you would at least allow me a little of the latter. I can assure you I have great need of it. But if you want to keep it all for yourself . . .

Doctor. I? I? Do I seem astute to you?

Henry IV. No. Monsignor! What do you say? Not in the least! Perhaps in this case, I may seem a little obstinate to you (*Cutting short to speak to Donna Matilda.*) With your permission: a word in confidence to the Duchess. (*Leads her aside and asks her very earnestly.*) Is your daughter really dear to you?

Donna Matilda (*dismayed*). Why, yes, certainly . . .

Henry IV. Do you wish me to compensate her with all my love, with all my devotion, for the grave wrongs I have done her — though you must not believe all the stories my enemies tell about my dissoluteness!

Donna Matilda. No, no, I don't believe them. I never have believed such stories.

Henry IV. Well, then are you willing?

Donna Matilda (*confused*). What?

Henry IV. That I return to love your daughter again? (*Looks at her and adds, in a mysterious tone of warning.*) You mustn't be a friend of the Marchioness of Tuscany!

Donna Matilda. I tell you again that she has begged and tried not less than ourselves to obtain your pardon . . .

Henry IV (softly, but excitedly). Don't tell me that! Don't say that to me! Don't you see the effect it has on me, my Lady?

Donna Matilda (looks at him; then very softly as if in confidence). You love her still?

Henry IV (puzzled). Still? Still, you say? You know, then? But nobody knows! Nobody must know!

Donna Matilda. But perhaps she knows, if she has begged so hard for you!

Henry IV (looks at her and says). And you love your daughter? (*Brief pause. He turns to the Doctor with laughing accents.*) Ah, Monsignor, it's strange how little I think of my wife! It may be a sin, but I swear to you that I hardly feel her at all in my heart. What is stranger is that her own mother scarcely feels her in her heart. Confess, my Lady, that she amounts to very little for you. (*Turning to Doctor.*) She talks to me of that other woman, insistently, insistently, I don't know why! . . .

Landolph (humbly). Maybe, Majesty, it is to disabuse you of some ideas you have had about the Marchioness of Tuscany. (*Then, dismayed at having allowed himself this observation, adds.*) I mean just now, of course . . .

Henry IV. You too maintain that she has been friendly to me?

Landolph. Yes, at the moment, Majesty.

Donna Matilda. Exactly! Exactly! . . .

Henry IV. I understand. That is to say, you don't believe I love her. I see! I see! Nobody's ever believed it, nobody's ever thought it. Better so, then! But enough, enough! (*Turns to the Doctor with changed expression.*) Monsignor, you see? The reasons the Pope has had for revoking the excommunication have got nothing at all to do with the reasons for which he excommunicated me originally. Tell Pope Gregory we shall meet again at Brixen. And you, Madame, should you chance to meet your daughter in the courtyard of the castle of your friend the Marchioness, ask her to visit me. We shall see if I succeed in keeping her close beside me as wife and Empress. Many women have presented themselves here already assuring me that they were she. And I thought to have her — yes, tried sometimes — there's no shame in it, with one's wife! — But when they said they were Bertha, and they were from Susa, all of them — I can't think why — started laughing! (*Confidentially.*) Understand? — in bed — I undressed — so did she — yes, by God, undressed — a man and a woman — it's natural after all! Like that, we don't bother much about who we are. And one's dress is like a phantom that hovers always near one. Oh, Monsignor, phantoms in general are nothing more than trifling disorders of the spirit: images we cannot contain within the bounds of sleep. They reveal themselves even when we are awake, and they frighten us. I . . . ah . . . I am always afraid when, at night time, I see disordered images before me. Sometimes I am even afraid of my own blood pulsing loudly in my arteries in the silence of night, like the sound of a distant step in a lonely corridor! . . . But, forgive me! I have kept you standing too long already. I thank you, my Lady, I thank you, Monsignor. (*Donna Matilda and the Doctor go off bowing. As soon as they have gone, Henry IV suddenly changes his tone.*) Buffoons, buffoons! One can play any tune on them! And that other fellow . . . Pietro Damiani! . . . Caught him out perfectly! He's afraid to appear before me again. (*Moves up and down excitedly while saying this; then sees Berthold, and points him out to the other three valets.*) Oh, look at this imbecile watching me with his mouth wide open! (*Shakes him.*) Don't you understand? Don't you see, idiot, how I treat them, how I play the fool with them, make them appear before me just as I wish? Miserable, frightened clowns that they are! And you (*Addressing the Valets.*) are amazed that I tear off their ridiculous masks now, just as if it wasn't I who had made them mask themselves to satisfy this taste of mine for playing the madman!

Landolph — Harold — Ordulph (*bewildered, looking at one another*). What? What does he say? What?

Henry IV (*answers them imperiously*). Enough! enough! Let's stop it. I'm tired of it. (*Then as if the thought left him no peace.*) By God! The impudence! To come here along with her lover! . . . And pretending to do it out of pity! So as not to infuriate a poor devil already out of the world, out of time, out of life! If it hadn't been supposed to be done out of pity, one can well imagine that fellow wouldn't have allowed it. Those people expect others to behave as they wish all the time. And, of course, there's nothing arrogant in that! Oh, no! Oh, no! It's merely their way of thinking, of feeling, of seeing. Everybody has his own way of thinking; you fellows, too. Yours is that of a flock of sheep — miserable, feeble, uncertain . . . But those others take advantage of this and make you accept their way of thinking; or, at least, they suppose they do; because, after all, what do they succeed in imposing on you? Words, words which anyone can interpret in his own manner! That's the way public opinion is formed! And it's a bad look out for a man who finds himself labelled one day with one of these words which everyone

repeats; for example "madman," or "imbecile." Don't you think it
is rather hard for a man to keep quiet, when he knows that there
is a fellow going about trying to persuade everybody that he is as
he sees him, trying to fix him in other people's opinion as a "madman" — according to him? Now I am talking seriously! Before I
hurt my head, falling from my horse . . . (*Stops suddenly, noticing
the dismay of the four young men.*) What's the matter with you?
(*Imitates their amazed looks.*) What? Am I, or am I not, mad?
Oh, yes! I'm mad all right! (*He becomes terrible.*) Well, then, by
God, down on your knees, down on your knees! (*Makes them go
down on their knees one by one.*) I order you to go down on your
knees before me! And touch the ground three times with your fore-
heads! Down, down! That's the way you've got to be before madmen! (*Then annoyed with their facile humiliation.*) Get up, sheep!
You obeyed me, didn't you? You might have put the strait jacket
on me! . . . Crush a man with the weight of a word — it's nothing
— a fly! all our life is crushed by the weight of words: the weight
of the dead. Look at me here: can you really suppose that Henry IV
is still alive? All the same, I speak, and order you live men about!
Do you think it's a joke that the dead continue to live? — Yes, *here*
it's a joke! But get out into the live world! — Ah, you say: what a
beautiful sunrise — for us! All time is before us! — Dawn! We will
do what we like with this day —. Ah, yes! To Hell with tradition,
the old conventions! Well, go on! You will do nothing but repeat
the old, old words, while you imagine you are living! (*Goes up to
Berthold who has now become quite stupid.*) You don't understand
a word of this, do you? What's your name?

Berthold. I? . . . What? . . . Berthold . . .

Henry IV. Poor Berthold! What's your name here?

Berthold. I . . . I . . . my name in Fino.

Henry IV (*feeling the warning and critical glances of the others, turns
to them to reduce them to silence*). Fino?

Berthold. Fino Pagliuca, sire.

Henry IV (*turning to Landolph*). I've heard you call each other by
your nick-names often enough! Your name is Lolo, isn't it?

Landolph. Yes, sire . . . (*Then with a sense of immense joy.*) Oh
Lord! Oh Lord! Then he is not mad . . .

Henry IV (*brusquely*). What?

Landolph (*hesitating*). No . . . I said . . .

Henry IV. Not mad, any more. No. Don't you see? We're having a
joke on those that think I am mad! (*To Harold.*) I say, boy, your
name's Franco . . . (*To Ordulph*) And yours . . .

Ordulph. Momo.

Henry IV. Momo, Momo . . . A nice name that!

Landolph. So he isn't . . .

Henry IV. What are you talking about? Of course not! Let's have a jolly, good laugh! . . . (*Laughs.*) Ah! . . . Ah! . . . Ah! . . .

Landolph — Harold — Ordulph (*looking at each other half happy and half dismayed*). Then he's cured! . . . he's all right! . . .

Henry IV. Silence! Silence! . . . (*To Berthold.*) Why don't you laugh? Are you offended? I didn't mean it especially for you. It's convenient for everybody to insist that certain people are mad, so they can shut up. Do you know why? Because it's impossible to hear them speak! What shall I say of these people who've just gone away? That one is a whore, another a libertine, another a swindler . . . don't you think so? You can't believe a word he says . . . don't you think so? — By the way, they all listen to me terrified. And why are they terrified, if what I say isn't true? Of course, you can't believe what madmen say — yet, at the same time, they stand there with their eyes wide open with terror! — Why? Tell me, tell me, why? — You see I'm quite calm now!

Berthold. But, perhaps, they think that . . .

Henry IV. No, no, my dear fellow! Look me well in the eyes! . . . I don't say that it's true — nothing is true, Berthold! But . . . look me in the eyes!

Berthold. Well . . .

Henry IV. You see? You see? . . . You have terror in your own eyes now because I seem mad to you! There's the proof of it. (*Laughs.*)

Landolph (*coming forward in the name of the others, exasperated*). What proof?

Henry IV. Your being so dismayed because now I seem again mad to you. You have thought me mad up to now, haven't you? You feel that this dismay of yours can become terror too — something to dash away the ground from under your feet and deprive you of the air you breathe! Do you know what it means to find yourselves face to face with a madman — with one who shakes the foundations of all you have built up in yourselves, your logic, the logic of all your constructions? Madmen, lucky folk! construct without logic, or rather with a logic that flies like a feather. Voluble! Voluble! Today like this and tomorrow — who knows? You say: "This cannot be"; but for them everything can be. You say: "This isn't true!" And why? Because it doesn't seem true to you, or you, or you . . . (*Indicates the three of them in succession.*) . . . and to a hundred thousand others! One must see what seems true to these hundred thousand others who are not supposed to be mad! What a magnificent spectacle they afford, when they reason! What flowers of logic

they scatter! I know that when I was a child, I thought the moon
in the pond was real. How many things I thought real! I believed
everything I was told — and I was happy! Because it's a terrible
thing if you don't hold on to that which seems true to you today
— to that which will seem true to you tomorrow, even if it is the
opposite of that which seemed true to you yesterday. I would never
wish you to think, as I have done, on this horrible thing which
really drives one mad: that if you were beside another and looking
into his eyes — as I one day looked into somebody's eyes — you
might as well be a beggar before a door never to be opened to you;
for he who does enter there will never be you, but someone unknown to you with his own different and impenetrable world . . .
(*Long pause. Darkness gathers in the room, increasing the sense of
strangeness and consternation in which the four young men are
involved. Henry IV remains aloof, pondering on the misery which
is not only his, but everybody's. Then he pulls himself up, and says
in an ordinary tone.*) It's getting dark here . . .
Ordulph. Shall I go for a lamp?
Henry IV (ironically). The lamp, yes the lamp! . . . Do you suppose
I don't know that as soon as I turn my back with my oil lamp to go
to bed, you turn on the electric light for yourselves, here, and even
there, in the throne room? I pretend not to see it!
Ordulph. Well, then, shall I turn it on now?
Henry IV. No, it would blind me! I want my lamp!
Ordulph. It's ready here behind the door. (*Goes to the main exit,
opens the door, goes out for a moment, and returns with an ancient
lamp which is held by a ring at the top.*)
Henry IV. Ah, a little light! Sit there around the table, no, not like
that; in an elegant, easy, manner! . . . (*To Harold.*) Yes, you, like
that! (*Poses him.*) (*Then to Berthold.*) You, so ! . . . and I, here!
(*Sits opposite them.*) We could do with a little decorative moonlight. It's very useful for us, the moonlight. I feel a real necessity
for it, and pass a lot of time looking up at the moon from my
window. Who would think, to look at her that she knows that eight
hundred years have passed, and that I, seated at the window, cannot really be Henry IV gazing at the moon like any poor devil?
But, look, look! See what a magnificent night scene we have here:
the emperor surrounded by his faithful counsellors! . . . How do
you like it?
Landolph (softly to Harold, so as not to break the enchantment).
And to think it wasn't true! . . .
Henry IV. True? What wasn't true?
Landolph (timidly as if to excuse himself). No . . . I mean . . . I was

saying this morning to him (*Indicates Berthold.*) — he has just entered on service here — I was saying: what a pity that dressed like this and with so many beautiful costumes in the wardrobe . . . and with a room like that . . . (*Indicates the throne room.*)

Henry IV. Well? what's the pity?

Landolph. Well . . . that we didn't know . . .

Henry IV. That it was all done in jest, this comedy?

Landolph. Because we thought that . . .

Harold (coming to his assistance). Yes . . . that it was done seriously!

Henry IV. What do you say? Doesn't it seem serious to you?

Landolph. But if you say that . . .

Henry IV. I say that — you are fools! You ought to have known how to create a fantasy for yourselves, not to act it for me, or anyone coming to see me; but naturally, simply, day by day, before nobody, feeling yourselves alive in the history of the eleventh century, here at the court of your emperor, Henry IV! You, Ordulph (*Taking him by the arm.*), alive in the castle of Goslar, waking up in the morning, getting out of bed, and entering straightway into the dream, clothing yourself in the dream that would be no more a dream, because you would have lived it, felt it all alive in you. You would have drunk it in with the air you breathed; yet knowing all the time that it was a dream, so you could better enjoy the privilege afforded you of having to do nothing else but live this dream, this far off and yet actual dream! And to think that at a distance of eight centuries from this remote age of ours, so colored and so sepulchral, the men of the twentieth century are torturing themselves in ceaseless anxiety to know how their fates and fortunes will work out! Whereas you are already in history with me . . .

Landolph. Yes, yes, very good!

Henry IV. . . . Everything determined, everything settled!

Ordulph. Yes, yes!

Henry IV. And sad as is my lot, hideous as some of the events are, bitter the struggles and troublous the time — still all history! All history that cannot change, understand? All fixed for ever! And you could have admired at your ease how every effect followed obediently its cause with perfect logic, how every event took place precisely and coherently in each minute particular! The pleasure, the pleasure of history, in fact, which is so great, was yours.

Landolph. Beautiful, beautiful!

Henry IV. Beautiful, but it's finished! Now that you know, I could not do it any more! (*Takes his lamp to go to bed.*) Neither could you, if up to now you haven't understood the reason of it! I am sick of it now. (*Almost to himself with violent contained rage.*) By God,

I'll make her sorry she came here! Dressed herself up as a mother-in-law for me . . . ! And he as an abbot . . . ! And they bring a doctor with them to study me . . . ! Who knows if they don't hope to cure me? . . . Clowns . . . ! I'd like to smack one of them at least in the face: yes, that one — a famous swordsman, they say! . . . He'll kill me . . . Well, we'll see, we'll see! . . . (*A knock at the door.*) Who is it?

The Voice of John. Deo Gratias!

Harold (*very pleased at the chance for another joke*). Oh, it's John, it's old John, who comes every night to play the monk.

Ordulph (*rubbing his hands*). Yes, yes! Let's make him do it!

Henry IV (*at once, severely*). Fool, why? Just to play a joke on a poor old man who does it for love of me?

Landolph (*to Ordulph*). It has to be as if it were true.

Henry IV. Exactly, as if true! Because, only so, truth is not a jest (*Opens the door and admits John dressed as a humble friar with a roll of parchment under his arm.*) Come in, come in, father! (*Then assuming a tone of tragic gravity and deep resentment.*) All the documents of my life and reign favorable to me were destroyed deliberately by my enemies. One only has escaped destruction, this, my life, written by a humble monk who is devoted to me. And you would laugh at him! (*Turns affectionately to John, and invites him to sit down at the table.*) Sit down, father, sit down! Have the lamp near you! (*Puts the lamp near him.*) Write! Write!

John (*opens the parchment and prepares to write from dictation*). I am ready, your Majesty!

Henry IV (*dictating*). "The decree of peace proclaimed at Mayence helped the poor and the good, while it damaged the powerful and the bad. (*Curtain begins to fall.*) It brought wealth to the former, hunger and misery to the latter . . ."

Curtain.

ACT III

The throne room so dark that the wall at the bottom is hardly seen. The canvases of the two portraits have been taken away; and, within their frames, Frida, dressed as the "Marchioness of Tuscany" and Charles Di Nolli, as "Henry IV," have taken the exact positions of the portraits.

For a moment, after the raising of curtain, the stage is empty. Then the door on the left opens; and Henry IV, holding the lamp by the ring on top of it, enters. He looks back to speak to the four young men, who, with John, are presumably in the adjoining hall, as at the end of the second act.

Henry IV. No, stay where you are, stay where you are. I shall manage all right by myself. Good night! (*Closes the door and walks, very sad and tired, across the hall towards the second door on the right, which leads into his apartments.*)

Frida (*as soon as she sees that he has just passed the throne, whispers from the niche like one who is on the point of fainting away with fright*). Henry . . .

Henry IV (*stopping at the voice as if someone had stabbed him traitorously in the back, turns a terror-stricken face towards the wall at the bottom of the room; raising an arm instinctively, as if to defend himself and ward off a blow*). Who is calling me? (*It is not a question, but an exclamation vibrating with terror, which does not expect a reply from the darkness and the terrible silence of the hall, which suddenly fills him with the suspicion that he is really mad.*)

Frida (*at his shudder of terror, is herself not less frightened at the part she is playing, and repeats a little more loudly*). Henry! . . . (*But, although she wishes to act the part as they have given it to her, she stretches her head a little out of the frame towards the other frame.*)

Henry IV (*gives a dreadful cry; lets the lamp fall from his hands to cover his head with his arms, and makes a movement as if to run away*).

Frida (*jumping from the frame on to the stand and shouting like a mad-woman*). Henry! . . . Henry! . . . I'm afraid! . . . I'm terrified! . . .

(*And while Di Nolli jumps in turn on to the stand and thence to the floor and runs to Frida who, on the verge of fainting, continues to cry out, the Doctor, Donna Matilda, also dressed as "Matilda of Tuscany," Tito Belcredi, Landolph, Berthold and John enter the hall from the doors on the right and on the left. One of them turns on the light: a strange light coming from lamps hidden in the ceiling so that only the upper part of the stage is well lighted. The others without taking notice of Henry IV, who looks on astonished by the unexpected inrush, after the moment of terror which still causes him to tremble, run anxiously to support and comfort the still shaking Frida, who is moaning in the arms of her fiancé. All are speaking at the same time.*)

Di Nolli. No, no, Frida . . . Here I am . . . I am beside you!

Doctor (coming with the others). Enough! Enough! There's nothing more to be done! . . .

Donna Matilda. He is cured, Frida. Look! He is cured! Don't you see?

Di Nolli (astonished). Cured?

Belcredi. It was only for fun! Be calm!

Frida. No! I am afraid! I am afraid!

Donna Matilda. Afraid of what? Look at him! He was never mad at all! . . .

Di Nolli. That isn't true! What are you saying? Cured?

Doctor. It appears so. I should say so . . .

Belcredi. Yes, yes! They have told us so. (*Pointing to the four young men.*)

Donna Matilda. Yes, for a long time! He has confided in them, told them the truth!

Di Nolli (now more indignant than astonished). But what does it mean? If, up to a short time ago . . . ?

Belcredi. Hum! He was acting, to take you in and also us, who in good faith . . .

Di Nolli. Is it possible? To deceive his sister, also, right up to the time of her death?

Henry IV (remains apart, peering at one and now at the other under the accusation and the mockery of what all believe to be a cruel joke of his, which is now revealed. He has shown by the flashing of his eyes that he is meditating a revenge, which his violent contempt prevents him from defining clearly, as yet. Stung to the quick and with a clear idea of accepting the fiction they have insidiously worked up as true, he bursts forth at this point). Go on, I say! Go on!

Di Nolli (astonished at the cry). Go on! What do you mean?

Henry IV. It isn't *your* sister only that is dead!

Di Nolli. My sister? Yours, I say, whom you compelled up to the last moment, to present herself here as your mother Agnes!

Henry IV. And was she not *your* mother?

Di Nolli. My mother? Certainly my mother!

Henry IV. But your mother is dead for me, *old and far away!* You have just got down now from there. (*Pointing to the frame from which he jumped down.*) And how do you know whether I have not wept her long in secret, dressed even as I am?

Donna Matilda (dismayed, looking at the others). What does he say? (*Much impressed, observing him.*) Quietly! quietly, for Heaven's sake!

Henry IV. What do I say? I ask all of you if Agnes was not the mother of Henry IV? (*Turns to Frida as if she were really the "Marchioness of Tuscany."*) You, Marchioness, it seems to me, ought to know.

Frida (*still frightened, draws closer to Di Nolli*). No, no, I don't know. Not I!

Doctor. It's the madness returning. . . . Quiet now, everybody!

Belcredi (*indignant*). Madness indeed, Doctor! He's acting again! . . .

Henry IV (*suddenly*). I? You have emptied those two frames over there, and he stands before my eyes as Henry IV . . .

Belcredi. We've had enough of this joke now.

Henry IV. Who said joke?

Doctor (*loudly to Belcredi*). Don't excite him, for the love of God!

Belcredi (*without lending an ear to him, but speaking louder*). But they have said so (*Pointing again to the four young men.*), they, they!

Henry IV (*turning round and looking at them*). You? Did you say it was all a joke?

Landolph (*timid and embarrassed*). No . . . really we said that you were cured.

Belcredi. Look here! Enough of this! (*To Donna Matilda.*) Doesn't it seem to you that the sight of him, (*Pointing to Di Nolli.*) Marchioness, and that of your daughter dressed so, is becoming an intolerable puerility?

Donna Matilda. Oh, be quiet! What does the dress matter, if he is cured?

Henry IV. Cured, yes! I am cured! (*To Belcredi.*) ah, but not to let it end this way all at once, as you suppose! (*Attacks him.*) Do you know that for twenty years nobody has ever dared to appear before me here like you and that gentleman? (*Pointing to the Doctor.*)

Belcredi. Of course I know it. As a matter of fact, I too appeared before you this morning dressed . . .

Henry IV. As a monk, yes!

Belcredi. And you took me for Peter Damiani! And I didn't even laugh, believing, in fact, that . . .

Henry IV. That I was mad! Does it make you laugh seeing her like that, now that I am cured? And yet you might have remembered that in my eyes her appearance now . . . (*Interrupts himself with a gesture of contempt.*) Ah (*Suddenly turns to the Doctor.*) You are a doctor, aren't you?

Doctor. Yes.

Henry IV. And you also took part in dressing her up as the Marchioness of Tuscany? To prepare a counter-joke for me here, eh?

Donna Matilda (*impetuously*). No, no! What do you say? It was done for you! I did it for your sake.

Doctor (*quickly*). To attempt, to try, not knowing . . .

Henry IV (*cutting him short*). I understand. I say counter-joke, in his case (*Indicates Belcredi.*) because he believes that I have been carrying on a jest . . .

Belcredi. But excuse me, what do you mean? You say yourself you are cured.

Henry IV. Let me speak! (*To the Doctor.*) Do you know, Doctor, that for a moment you ran the risk of making me mad again? By God, to make the portraits speak; to make them jump alive out of their frames . . .

Doctor. But you saw that all of us ran in at once, as soon as they told us . . .

Henry IV. Certainly! (*Contemplates Frida and Di Nolli, and then looks at the Marchioness, and finally at his own costume.*) The combination is very beautiful . . . Two couples . . . Very good, very good, Doctor! For a madman, not bad! . . . (*With a slight wave of his hand to Belcredi.*) It seems to him now to be a carnival out of season, eh? (*Turns to look at him.*) We'll get rid now of this masquerade costume of mine, so that I may come away with you. What do you say?

Belcredi. With me? With us?

Henry IV. Where shall we go? To the Club? In dress coats and with white ties? Or shall both of us go to the Marchioness' house?

Belcredi. Wherever you like! Do you want to remain here still, to continue — alone — what was nothing but the unfortunate joke of a day of carnival? It is really incredible, incredible how you have been able to do all this, freed from the disaster that befell you!

Henry IV. Yes, you see how it was! The fact is that falling from my horse and striking my head as I did, I was really mad for I know not how long . . .

Doctor. Ah! Did it last long?

Henry IV (*very quickly to the Doctor*). Yes, Doctor, a long time! I think it must have been about twelve years. (*Then suddenly turning to speak to Belcredi.*) Thus I saw nothing, my dear fellow, of all that, after that day of carnival, happened for you but not for me: how things changed, how my friends deceived me, how my place was taken by another, and all the rest of it! And suppose my place had been taken in the heart of the woman I loved? . . . And how should I know who was dead or who had disappeared? . . . All this, you know, wasn't exactly a jest for me, as it seems to you . . .

Belcredi. No, no! I don't mean that if you please. I mean after . . .

Henry IV. Ah, yes? After? One day (*Stops and addresses the Doctor.*) — A most interesting case, Doctor! Study me well! Study me carefully! (*Trembles while speaking.*) All by itself, who knows how, one day the trouble here (*Touches his forehead.*) mended. Little by little, I open my eyes, and at first I don't know whether I am asleep or awake. Then I know I am awake. I touch this thing and that; I see clearly again . . . Ah! — then, as *he* says (*Alludes to Belcredi.*) away, away with this masquerade, this incubus! Let's open the windows, breathe life once again! Away! Away! Let's run out! (*Suddenly pulling himself up.*) But where? And to do what? To show myself to all, secretly, as Henry IV, not like this, but arm in arm with you, among my dear friends?

Belcredi. What are you saying?

Donna Matilda. Who could think it? It's not to be imagined. It was an accident.

Henry IV. They all said I was mad before. (*To Belcredi.*) And you know it! You were more ferocious than any one against those who tried to defend me.

Belcredi. Oh, that was only a joke!

Henry IV. Look at my hair. (*Shows him the hair on the nape of his neck.*)

Belcredi. But mine is grey too!

Henry IV. Yes, with this difference: that mine went grey here, as Henry IV, do you understand? And I never knew it! I perceived it all of a sudden, one day, when I opened my eyes; and I was terrified because I understood at once that not only had my hair gone grey, but that I was all grey, inside; that everything had fallen to pieces, that everything was finished; and I was going to arrive, hungry as a wolf, at a banquet which had already been cleared away . . .

Belcredi. Yes, but, what about the others? . . .

Henry IV (*quickly*). Ah, yes, I know! They couldn't wait until I was cured, not even those, who, behind my back, pricked my saddled horse till it bled. . . .

Di Nolli (*agitated*). What, what?

Henry IV. Yes, treacherously, to make it rear and cause me to fall.

Donna Matilda (*quickly, in horror*). This is the first time I knew that.

Henry IV. That was also a joke, probably!

Donna Matilda. But who did it? Who was behind us then?

Henry IV. It doesn't matter who it was. All those that went on feasting and were ready to leave me their scrapings, Marchioness, of miserable pity, or some dirty remnant of remorse in the filthy plate! Thanks! (*Turning quickly to the Doctor.*) Now, Doctor, the case must be absolutely new in the history of madness; I preferred to remain mad — since I found everything ready and at my disposal for this new exquisite fantasy. I would live it — this madness of mine — with the most lucid consciousness; and thus revenge myself on the brutality of a stone which had dinted my head. The solitude — this solitude — squalid and empty as it appeared to me when I opened my eyes again — I determined to deck it out with all the colors and splendors of that far off day of carnival, when you (*Looks at Donna Matilda and points Frida out to her.*) — when you, Marchioness, triumphed. So I would oblige all those who were around me to follow, by God, at my orders that famous pageant which had been — for you and not for me — the jest of a day. I would make it become — for ever — no more a joke but a reality, the reality of a real madness: here, all in masquerade, with throne room, and these my four secret counsellors: secret and, of course, traitors. (*He turns quickly towards them.*) I should like to know what you have gained by revealing the fact that I was cured! If I am cured, there's no longer any need of you, and you will be discharged! To give anyone one's confidence . . . that is really the act of a madman. But now I accuse you in my turn. (*Turning to the others.*) Do you know? They thought (*Alludes to the Valets.*) they could make fun of me too with you. (*Bursts out laughing. The others laugh, but shamefacedly, except Donna Matilda.*)

Belcredi (*to Di Nolli*). Well, imagine that . . . That's not bad . . .

Di Nolli (*to the Four Young Men*). You?

Henry IV. We must pardon them. This dress (*Plucking his dress.*) which is for me the evident, involuntary caricature of that other continuous, everlasting masquerade, of which we are the involuntary puppets (*Indicates Belcredi.*), when, without knowing it, we mask ourselves with that which we appear to be . . . ah, that dress of theirs, this masquerade of theirs, of course, we must forgive it them, since they do not yet see it is identical with themselves . . . (*Turning again to Belcredi.*) You know, it is quite easy to get accustomed to it. One walks about as a tragic character, just as if it were nothing . . . (*Imitates the tragic manner.*) in a room like this . . . Look here, doctor! I remember a priest, certainly Irish, a nice-looking priest, who was sleeping in the sun one November day, with his arm on the corner of the bench of a public garden. He was lost in the golden delight of the mild sunny air which must have seemed for him almost summery. One may be sure that in that moment he did not know any more that he was a priest, or even where he was. He was dreaming . . . A little boy passed with a flower in his hand. He touched the priest with it here on the neck. I saw him open his laughing eyes, while all his mouth smiled with the beauty of his dream. He was forgetful of everything . . . But all at once, he pulled himself together, and stretched out his priest's cassock; and there came back to his eyes the same seriousness which you have seen in mine; because the Irish priests defend the seriousness of their Catholic faith with the same zeal with which I defend the sacred rights of hereditary monarchy! I am cured, gentlemen: because I can act the madman to perfection, here; and I do it very quietly. I'm only sorry for you that have to live your madness so agitatedly, without knowing it or seeing it.

Belcredi. It comes to this, then, that it is we who are mad. That's what it is!

Henry IV (containing his irritation). But if you weren't mad, both you and she (*Indicating the Marchioness.*) would you have come here to see me?

Belcredi. To tell the truth, I came here believing that you were the madman.

Henry IV (suddenly indicating the Marchioness). And she?

Belcredi. Ah, as for her . . . I can't say. I see she is all fascinated by your words, by this *conscious* madness of yours. (*Turns to her.*) Dressed as you are (*Speaking to her.*), you could even remain here to live it out, Marchioness.

Donna Matilda. You are insolent!

Henry IV (conciliatingly). No, Marchioness, what he means to say is that the miracle would be complete, according to him, with you here, who — as the Marchioness of Tuscany, you well know, — could not be my friend, save, as at Canossa, to give me a little pity . . .

Belcredi. Or even more than a little! She said so herself!

Henry IV (to the Marchioness, continuing). And even, shall we say, a little remorse! . . .

Belcredi. Yes, that too she has admitted.

Donna Matilda (angry). Now look here . . .

Henry IV (quickly, to placate her). Don't bother about him! Don't mind him! Let him go on infuriating me — though the Doctor's told him not to. (*Turns to Belcredi.*) But do you suppose I am going to trouble myself any more about what happened between us — the share you had in my misfortune with her (*Indicates the Marchioness to him and pointing Belcredi out to her.*) the part he has now in your life? This is my life! Quite a different thing from your life! Your life, the life in which you have grown old — I have not lived that life. (*To Donna Matilda.*) Was this what you wanted to show me with this sacrifice of yours, dressing yourself up like this, according to the Doctor's idea? Excellently done, Doctor! Oh, an excellent idea: — "As we were then, eh? and as we are now?" But I am not a madman according to your way of thinking, Doctor. I know very well that that man there (*Indicates Di Nolli.*) cannot be me; because I am Henry IV, and have been, these twenty years, cast in this eternal masquerade. She has lived these years! (*Indicates the Marchioness.*) She has enjoyed them and has become — look at her! — a woman I can no longer recognize. It is so that I knew her! (*Points to Frida and draws near her.*) This is the Marchioness I know, always this one! . . . You seem a lot of children to be so easily frightened by me . . . (*To Frida.*) And you're frightened too, little girl, aren't you, by the jest that they made you take part in — though they didn't understand it wouldn't be the jest they meant it to be, for me? Oh miracle of miracles! Prodigy of prodigies! The dream alive in you! More than alive in you! It was an image that wavered there and they've made you come to life! Oh, mine! You're mine, mine, mine, in my own right! (*He holds her in his arms, laughing like a madman, while all stand still terrified. Then as they advance to tear Frida from his arms, he becomes furious, terrible and cries imperiously to his Valets.*) Hold them! Hold them! I order you to hold them!

(*The Four Young Men amazed, yet fascinated, move to execute his orders, automatically, and seize Di Nolli, the Doctor, and Belcredi.*)

Belcredi (*freeing himself*). Leave her alone! Leave her alone! You're no madman!

Henry IV (*in a flash draws the sword from the side of Landolph, who is close to him*). I'm not mad, eh! Take that, you! . . . (*Drives sword into him. A cry of horror goes up. All rush over to assist Belcredi, crying out together.*)

Di Nolli. Has he wounded you?

Berthold. Yes, yes, seriously!

Doctor. I told you so!

Frida. Oh God, oh God!

Di Nolli. Frida, come here!

Donna Matilda. He's mad, mad!

Di Nolli. Hold him!

Belcredi (*while They take him away by the left exit, He protests as he is borne out*). No, no, you're not mad! You're not mad. He's not mad!

(*They go out by the left amid cries and excitement. After a moment, one hears a still sharper, more piercing cry from Donna Matilda, and then, silence.*)

*Henry IV (who has remained on the stage between Landolph, Harold
and Ordulph, with his eyes almost starting out of his head, terrified
by the life of his own masquerade which has driven him to crime.)
Now, yes . . . we'll have to (Calls his Valets around him as if to
protect him.) here we are . . . together . . . for ever!*

Curtain.

It would be hard to find another tragedy in which there is so much
talk about laughing, joking, and jests as there is in *Henry IV*. (There
are, of course, comic scenes in Shakespeare's tragedies, but there is no
talk *about* comedy in them.) Roughly speaking, until the middle of
the nineteenth century most theories of laughter were of two sorts.
One held that we laugh good-naturedly, in genial fellow-feeling, out of
a spirit of play. An adult sees an infant, smiles affectionately, and the
infant returns the smile and adds a giggle, stimulating the adult to
even more genial feelings. This spirit of play allegedly can be seen
also in persons splashing each other in the water, in the host smiling
as he heaps food on a guest's plate, etc. The other theory holds that
laughter is derisive, proceeding from a sense of superiority. We laugh
at the child trying to walk because he does badly with effort what we
do well and easily; we laugh at the pompous man slipping on a banana
peel because his pretensions are knocked down as he suddenly assumes
an ungainly posture, while we remain squarely on our feet in full control of ourselves. Similarly, we laugh at the lover who is blind to the
faults that we clearly see in his beloved, and we laugh at the hen-
pecked husband who is less than the man we are. The distinction
between the two theories is easily seen in the distinction we make
between laughing *with* someone and laughing *at* someone, though it
should be added that the theories are often combined in various ways
that blur the distinction.

From the middle of the nineteenth-century to the present, another
theory — not unknown earlier, but not often held — gains prominence, a theory holding that we laugh in order to escape from the sorrows of existence. Ancient literature and ancient history attest to man's
perennial unhappiness, but the usual response was to lament it; in the
last hundred years there has developed a sort of tragic comedy, a literature that laughs or jokes to fend off pain. Something more will be
said in the afterword to Tennessee Williams' *A Streetcar Named
Desire* about the triple blows delivered by Darwin, Marx, and Freud
to man's heroic image of himself; here it need only be mentioned that

Darwinism saw man not as a special creation but as a soulless animal that had evolved by means of "accidental variations"; Marxism saw him as the creature of economic forces; and Freudianism as the victim of infantile experiences. Still, despite his ignoble origin and his help-lessness, man has reason and has aspirations unknown to the other animals. As the joke puts it, astronomically speaking man is nothing — but man is the astronomer. Of all the created things, man alone sees the ludicrousness and loathesomeness of life. His superiority to the rest of creation is his curse, for it painfully informs him that he is different from the rest and that despite his noble dreams, he is sentenced to the same ignoble end.

To make the point, one could quote the heavyweights at length, Dostoevsky and Kierkegaard, but fortunately it can also be made briefly:

> And if I laugh at any mortal thing,
> Tis that I may not weep.
> Byron, *Don Juan*

> I own any form of humor shows fear and inferiority. . . . At bottom the world isn't a joke. We only joke about it to avoid an issue. . . . Humor is the most engaging cowardice. With it myself I have been able to hold some of my enemy in play far out of gunshot.
> Robert Frost, *Selected Letters*

> The laugh of laughs, the *risus purus*, the laugh laughing at the laugh, the beholding, the saluting of the highest joke, in a word the laugh that laughs — silence please — [is] at that which is unhappy.
> Samuel Beckett, *Watt*

Pirandello had much to be unhappy about: his parents lost their wealth in a flood that destroyed the family's profitable sulfur mine, his wife lost her dowry, and, worst, his wife became insanely suspicious of her husband, who was forced to lock himself in his room to assure her of his fidelity. But it would be unjust to Pirandello to suggest that his deep unhappiness was due simply to personal misfortunes; his un-happiness was that of a thinking man, not that of a mismatched hus-band. Something must be said of his thinking, which can be found not only in the plays and in his preface to *Six Characters in Search of an Author*, but also in an essay of 1908 entitled "Umorismo" ("Humor"). Reality is fluid, and beyond the grasp of reason. But man *has* reason, and he cannot tolerate a fluid, irrational world, so he sets up reason-able — but false — categories. He establishes laws, codes of ethics, religions, and other "communal lies," but in certain dreadful moments he may become aware that these creations are distortions of the unknowable reality. So great is the dread, however, that he clings to his illusory conceptions. Such is (in the words of the preface to *Six Characters*) "the inherent tragic conflict between life (which is always moving and changing) and form (which fixes it, immutable)." The "form" is, in Pirandello's terminology, a "mask," and we all have our masks. We think we have made ourselves into loyal citizens or rebels, virtuous husbands or libertines, etc., but whatever the mask, the face beneath it is a bundle of indeterminate instincts. A man wears the mask of an elderly Supreme Court judge, but the face, the real man, wishes to marry a girl of twenty-one. Instantly there is an outcry from respectable masks, demanding that the judge be subjected to a mental examination, so inconceivable is it, to these others, that an aged jurist should harbor such feelings. (The example is not from Pirandello but from contemporary American life, but Pirandello does have a play, *When One Is Somebody*, about a poet in late middle age who finds that he must choose between being the respected poet who has gained official recognition or the lyric poet whom the new generation applauds. So powerful is the pressure of society that he accepts the official honor and becomes an automaton.) Sometimes in a passionate moment the suffering face bursts through the mask, but usually the mask succeeds in confining the face, so great is the individual's dread of confessing that he has a face different from his mask. Most often man finds it best to play the game, to cherish the illusion that masks are faces. Men therefore greet each other politely, feign interest in one another's problems, and so forth. Moreover, the mask is adopted not merely to conceal the truth from one's fellows but even from oneself; a man lies to himself to protect himself from the horrifying truth of a meaningless or unknowable reality. To reject the illusions is to confront a reality that is maddening. It is also tragically comic: the gap between illusions or masks and reality or faces is so great that when seen it evokes not only lamentation but bitter laughter.

In "Umorismo" Pirandello quotes Machiavelli with approval: "If I sometimes laugh or sing, it is to have an outlet for tears." The mere comic writer, Pirandello says, will laugh at man's deception and self-deception, but the "humorist will see its serious and painful side." He will take the construction apart, but not merely to laugh at it; and even though he laughs, he will sympathize. Among the instances Pirandello cites is Copernicus' invention of the telescope. The telescope does not reveal the real nature of the universe, but it did demolish the cherished illusion that man's earth was the center of the universe. The loss of this illusion is, for some, dreadful, but the "humorist," with his interest in contradictions replies that if man can conceive of infinite distances, he can conceive of infinite grandeur too, and that is no small thing.

In *Henry IV* the masquerade that has been a trivial joke for the participants became a bitter joke, a reality, for the man whose head struck a stone and who was left with the insane belief that he was Henry IV. During his insanity, the illusions of the rest of the world meant nothing to him, and he succeeded in arresting time. Life outside went on, but his moment as Henry remained. Twenty years later, the woman he loved was no longer young and beautiful, but her daughter now resembled the mother of that earlier period, and for Henry the daughter is the beloved. Ordinarily, Pirandello says, the lover is comic: in the words of this play, men look at a woman "with that eternal look of fidelity in their faces! I've always thought it comic; then more than now." For Henry, twenty years later, the lover and beloved are unchanged. The parts that were initially played as a joke have given the madman a reality, a release from the world of flux. "The jest of the day" became "no more a joke but a reality, the reality of a real madness."

A meddling pretentious physician has a plan — which he calls a "trick" akin to a practical joke — to cure Henry of his madness and to bring him into the "real" world of the present. The man of science does not, of course, understand that the real world cannot be catalogued, and that what he thinks is the real world is a world of illusory constructions. Henry explains what the doctor's "real" world is. (The doctor is disguised as a clergyman.)

> We are all fixed in good faith in a certain concept of ourselves. However, Monsignor, while you keep yourself in order, holding on with both your hands to your holy habit, there slips down from your sleeves, there peels off from you . . . like a serpent . . . something you don't notice: life, Monsignor! (*Turns to the Marchioness*) Has it never happened to you, my Lady, to find a different self in yourself? Have you always been the same? My god! One day . . . how was it, how was it you were able to commit this or that action?

Nor does the doctor understand — so attached is he to his mask of know-it-all — that real life is a horror. But Henry knows:

> It's a terrible thing if you don't hold on to that which seems true to you. . . . I would never wish you to think, as I have done, on this horrible thing which really drives one mad: that if you were beside another and looking into his eyes — as I one day looked into somebody's eyes — you might as well be a beggar before a door never to be opened to you; for he who does enter there will never be you, but someone unknown to you with his own different and impenetrable world.

We may try to dismiss such skepticism with the same shrug we give to the ancient paradox that a man cannot twice cross the same river:

the man is different, and so is the river. But the ancient paradox was not embodied in an imaginative plot with such arresting characters. When at the end of the play Henry IV, having killed a man because of the doctor's "trick" to bring Henry back to "reality," gathers his servants about him with "Here we are . . . together . . . forever!" we do not feel that we are listening to ingenious paradoxes; we feel that we are looking at an image of life. At the end of *Oedipus the King* the chorus tells the audience to count no man happy until his life is over; similarly, Henry's years of madness, real and feigned, culminate in an action that forever deprives him of happiness.

A Streetcar Named Desire

TENNESSEE WILLIAMS

*Tennessee Williams (1911–   ), born Thomas Lanier
Williams in Columbus, Mississippi, was the son of an
extrovert shoe salesman and a genteel daughter of an
Episcopalian clergyman. Williams was born in his grandfather's rectory, where his mother was living while his
father was on the road. In 1919 the family moved to bleak
quarters in St. Louis. Williams spent two years at the
University of Missouri, then worked two years in a shoe
warehouse, and then had a nervous breakdown. He resumed college studies, first at Washington University in
St. Louis, later at the University of Iowa where he studied
theater arts and received a bachelor's degree in 1938. He
did odd jobs for a while, wrote stories and screenplays in
Hollywood, and turned one of his rejected scripts into
The Glass Menagerie, a highly autobiographical play which
opened in 1944 and brought him fame. A Streetcar Named
Desire was produced in 1947. Williams continues to be
productive, and is widely regarded as America's most talented dramatist.*

THE CHARACTERS

Blanche
Stella
Stanley
Mitch
Eunice
Steve
Pablo
A Negro Woman
A Doctor
A Nurse
A Young Collector
A Mexican Woman

SCENE ONE

The exterior of a two-story corner building on a street in New Orleans which is named Elysian Fields and runs between the L & N tracks and the river. The section is poor but, unlike corresponding sections in other American cities, it has a raffish charm. The houses are mostly white frame, weathered grey, with rickety outside stairs and galleries and quaintly ornamented gables. This building contains two flats, upstairs and down. Faded white stairs ascend to the entrances of both.

It is first dark of an evening early in May. The sky that shows around the dim white building is a peculiarly tender blue, almost a turquoise, which invests the scene with a kind of lyricism and gracefully attenuates the atmosphere of decay. You can almost feel the warm breath of the brown river beyond the river warehouses with their faint redolences of bananas and coffee. A corresponding air is evoked by the music of Negro entertainers at a barroom around the corner. In this part of New Orleans you are practically always just around the corner, or a few doors down the street, from a tinny piano being played with the infatuated fluency of brown fingers. This "blue piano" expresses the spirit of the life which goes on here.

Two women, one white and one colored, are taking the air on the steps of the building. The white woman is Eunice, who occupies the upstairs flat; the colored woman a neighbor, for New Orleans is a cosmopolitan city where there is a relatively warm and easy intermingling of races in the old part of town.

283

Above the music of the "blue piano" the voices of people on the street can be heard overlapping.

> (*Two men come around the corner, Stanley Kowalski and Mitch. They are about twenty-eight or thirty years old, roughly dressed in blue denim work clothes. Stanley carries his bowling jacket and a red-stained package from a butcher's. They stop at the foot of the steps.*)

Stanley (*bellowing*). Hey, there! Stella, Baby!

> (*Stella comes out on the first floor landing, a gentle young woman, about twenty-five, and of a background obviously quite different from her husband's.*)

Stella (*mildly*). Don't holler at me like that. Hi, Mitch.
Stanley. Catch!
Stella. What?
Stanley. Meat!

> (*He heaves the package at her. She cries out in protest but manages to catch it; then she laughs breathlessly. Her husband and his companion have already started back around the corner.*)

Stella (*calling after him*). Stanley! Where are you going?
Stanley. Bowling!
Stella. Can I come watch?
Stanley. Come on. (*He goes out.*)
Stella. Be over soon. (*To the white woman*) Hello, Eunice. How are you?
Eunice. I'm all right. Tell Steve to get him a poor boy's sandwich 'cause nothing's left here.

> (*They all laugh; the colored woman does not stop. Stella goes out.*)

Colored Woman. What was that package he th'ew at 'er? (*She rises from steps, laughing louder.*)
Eunice. You hush, now!
Negro Woman. Catch what!

> (*She continues to laugh. Blanche comes around the corner, carrying a valise. She looks at a slip of paper, then at the building, then again at the slip and again at the building. Her expression is one of shocked disbelief. Her appearance is incongruous to this setting. She is daintily dressed in a white suit with a fluffy bodice, necklace and earrings of pearl, white gloves and hat, looking as if she were arriving at a summer tea or cocktail party in the garden district. She is about*)

five years older than Stella. Her delicate beauty must avoid a strong light. There is something about her uncertain manner, as well as her white clothes, that suggests a moth.)

Eunice (*finally*). What's the matter, honey? Are you lost?

Blanche (*with faintly hysterical humor*). They told me to take a streetcar named Desire, and then transfer to one called Cemeteries and ride six blocks and get off at — Elysian Fields!

Eunice. That's where you are now.

Blanche. At Elysian Fields?

Eunice. This here is Elysian Fields.

Blanche. They mustn't have — understood — what number I wanted.

Eunice. What number you lookin' for?

(*Blanche wearily refers to the slip of paper.*)

Blanche. Six thirty-two.

Eunice. You don't have to look no further.

Blanche (*uncomprehendingly*). I'm looking for my sister, Stella DuBois. I mean — Mrs. Stanley Kowalski.

Eunice. That's the party. — You just did miss her, though.

Blanche. This — can this be — her home?

Eunice. She's got the downstairs here and I got the up.

Blanche. Oh. She's — out?

Eunice. You noticed that bowling alley around the corner?

Blanche. I'm — not sure I did.

Eunice. Well, that's where she's at, watchin' her husband bowl. (*There is a pause*) You want to leave your suitcase here an' go find her?

Blanche. No.

Negro Woman. I'll go tell her you come.

Blanche. Thanks.

Negro Woman. You welcome. (*She goes out.*)

Eunice. She wasn't expecting you?

Blanche. No. No, not tonight.

Eunice. Well, why don't you just go in and make yourself at home till they get back.

Blanche. How could I — do that?

Eunice. We own this place so I can let you in.

(*She gets up and opens the downstairs door. A light goes on behind the blind, turning it light blue. Blanche slowly follows her into the downstairs flat. The surrounding areas dim out as the interior is lighted.*)

(*Two rooms can be seen, not too clearly defined. The one first entered is primarily a kitchen but contains a folding bed to be used by Blanche. The room beyond this is a bedroom. Off this room is a narrow door to a bathroom.*)

Eunice (*defensively, noticing Blanche's look*). It's sort of messed up right now but when it's clean it's real sweet.

Blanche. Is it?

Eunice. Uh-huh, I think so. So you're Stella's sister?

Blanche. Yes. (*Wanting to get rid of her*) Thanks for letting me in.

Eunice. Por nada, as the Mexicans say, *por nada!* Stella spoke of you.

Blanche. Yes?

Eunice. I think she said you taught school.

Blanche. Yes.

Eunice. And you're from Mississippi, huh?

Blanche. Yes.

Eunice. She showed me a picture of your home-place, the plantation.

Blanche. Belle Reve?

Eunice. A great big place with white columns.

Blanche. Yes . . .

Eunice. A place like that must be awful hard to keep up.

Blanche. If you will excuse me. I'm just about to drop.

Eunice. Sure, honey. Why don't you set down?

Blanche. What I meant was I'd like to be left alone.

Eunice. Aw. I'll make myself scarce, in that case.

Blanche. I didn't mean to be rude, but —

Eunice. I'll drop by the bowling alley an' hustle her up. (*She goes out the door.*)

(*Blanche sits in a chair very stiffly with her shoulders slightly hunched and her legs pressed close together and her hands tightly clutching her purse as if she were cold. After a while the blind look goes out of her eyes and she begins to look slowly around. A cat screeches. She catches her breath with a startled gesture. Suddenly she notices something in a half opened closet. She springs up and crosses to it, and removes a whiskey bottle. She pours a half tumbler of whiskey and tosses it down. She carefully replaces the bottle and washes out the tumbler at the sink. Then she resumes her seat in front of the table.*)

Blanche (*faintly to herself*). I've got to keep hold of myself!

(*Stella comes quickly around the corner of the building and runs to the door of the downstairs flat.*)

Stella (*calling out joyfully*). *Blanche!*

(*For a moment they stare at each other. Then Blanche springs up and runs to her with a wild cry.*)

Blanche. Stella, oh, Stella, Stella! Stella for Star!

(*She begins to speak with feverish vivacity as if she feared for either of them to stop and think. They catch each other in a spasmodic embrace.*)

Blanche. Now, then, let me look at you. But don't you look at me, Stella, no, no, no, not till later, not till I've bathed and rested! And turn that over-light off! Turn that off! I won't be looked at in this merciless glare! (*Stella laughs and complies*) Come back here now! Oh, my baby! Stella! Stella for Star! (*She embraces her again*) I thought you would never come back to this horrible place! What am I saying? I didn't mean to say that. I meant to be nice about it and say — Oh, what a convenient location and such — Ha-a-ha! Precious lamb! You haven't said a *word* to me.

Stella. You haven't given me a chance to, honey! (*She laughs, but her glance at Blanche is a little anxious.*)

Blanche. Well, now you talk. Open your pretty mouth and talk while I look around for some liquor! I know you must have some liquor on the place! Where could it be, I wonder? Oh, I spy, I spy!

(*She rushes to the closet and removes the bottle; she is shaking all over and panting for breath as she tries to laugh. The bottle nearly slips from her grasp.*)

Stella (*noticing*). Blanche, you sit down and let me pour the drinks. I don't know what we've got to mix with. Maybe a coke's in the icebox. Look'n see, honey, while I'm —

Blanche. No coke, honey, not with my nerves tonight! Where — where — where is — ?

Stella. Stanley? Bowling! He loves it. They're having a — found some soda! — tournament . . .

Blanche. Just water, baby, to chase it! Now don't get worried, your sister hasn't turned into a drunkard, she's just all shaken up and hot and tired and dirty! You sit down, now, and explain this place to me! What are you doing in a place like this?

Stella. Now Blanche —

Blanche. Oh, I'm not going to be hypocritical, I'm going to be honestly critical about it! Never, never, never in my worst dreams could I picture — Only Poe! Only Mr. Edgar Allan Poe! — could do it justice! Out there I suppose is the ghoul-haunted woodland of Weir! (*She laughs.*)

Stella. No, honey, those are the L & N tracks.

Blanche. No, now seriously, putting joking aside. Why didn't you tell me, why didn't you write me, honey, why didn't you let me know?

Stella (*carefully, pouring herself a drink*). Tell you what, Blanche?

Blanche. Why, that you had to live in these conditions!

Stella. Aren't you being a little intense about it? It's not that bad at all! New Orleans isn't like other cities.

Blanche. This has got nothing to do with New Orleans. You might as well say — forgive me, blessed baby! (*She suddenly stops short*) The subject is closed!

Stella (*a little drily*). Thanks.

(*During the pause, Blanche stares at her. She smiles at Blanche.*)

Blanche (*looking down at her glass, which shakes in her hand*). You're all I've got in the world, and you're not glad to see me!

Stella (*sincerely*). Why, Blanche, you know that's not true.

Blanche. No? — I'd forgotten how quiet you were.

Stella. You never did give me a chance to say much, Blanche. So I just got in the habit of being quiet around you.

Blanche (*vaguely*). A good habit to get into . . . (*then, abruptly*) You haven't asked me how I happened to get away from the school before the spring term ended.

Stella. Well, I thought you'd volunteer that information — if you wanted to tell me.

Blanche. You thought I'd been fired?

Stella. No, I — thought you might have — resigned . . .

Blanche. I was so exhausted by all I'd been through my — nerves broke. (*Nervously tamping cigarette*) I was on the verge of — lunacy, almost! So Mr. Graves — Mr. Graves is the high school superintendent — he suggested I take a leave of absence. I couldn't put all of those details into the wire . . . (*She drinks quickly*) Oh, this buzzes right through me and feels so *good!*

Stella. Won't you have another?

Blanche. No, one's my limit.

Stella. Sure?

Blanche. You haven't said a word about my appearance.

Stella. You look just fine.

Blanche. God love you for a liar! Daylight never exposed so total a ruin! But you — you've put on some weight, yes, you're just as plump as a little partridge! And it's so becoming to you!

Stella. Now, Blanche —

Blanche. Yes, it is, it is or I wouldn't say it! You just have to watch around the hips a little. Stand up.

Stella. Not now.

Blanche. You hear me? I said stand up! (*Stella complies reluctantly*) Yes messy child, you, you've spilt something on the pretty white lace collar! About your hair — you ought to have it cut in a feather bob with your dainty features. Stella, you have a maid, don't you?

Stella. No. With only two rooms it's —

Blanche. What? *Two* rooms, did you say?

Stella. This one and — (*She is embarrassed.*)

Blanche. The other one? (*She laughs sharply. There is an embarrassed silence.*)

Blanche. I am going to take just one little tiny nip more, sort of to put the stopper on, so to speak. . . . Then put the bottle away so I won't be tempted. (*She rises*) I want you to look at *my* figure! (*She turns around*) You know I haven't put on one ounce in ten years, Stella? I weigh what I weighed the summer you left Belle Reve. The summer Dad died and you left us . . .

Stella (*a little wearily*). It's just incredible, Blanche, how well you're looking.

Blanche. (*They both laugh uncomfortably*) But, Stella, there's only two rooms, I don't see where you're going to put me!

Stella. We're going to put you in here.

Blanche. What kind of bed's this — one of those collapsible things?

(*She sits on it.*)

Stella. Does it feel all right?

Blanche (*dubiously*). Wonderful, honey. I don't like a bed that gives much. But there's no door between the two rooms, and Stanley — will it be decent?

Stella. Stanley is Polish, you know.

Blanche. Oh, yes. They're something like Irish, aren't they?

Stella. Well —

Blanche. Only not so — highbrow? (*They both laugh again in the same way*) I brought some nice clothes to meet all your lovely friends in.

Stella. I'm afraid you won't think they are lovely.

Blanche. What are they like?

Stella. They're Stanley's friends.

Blanche. Polacks?

Stella. They're a mixed lot, Blanche.

Blanche. Heterogeneous — types?

Stella. Oh, yes. Yes, types is right!

Blanche. Well — anyhow — I brought nice clothes and I'll wear them. I guess you're hoping I'll say I'll put up at a hotel, but I'm not going to put up at a hotel. I want to be *near* you, got to be *with* somebody, I *can't* be *alone!* Because — as you must have noticed — I'm — *not* very *well* . . . (*Her voice drops and her look is frightened.*)

Stella. You seem a little bit nervous or overwrought or something.

Blanche. Will Stanley like me, or will I be just a visiting in-law, Stella? I couldn't stand that.

Stella. You'll get along fine together, if you'll just try not to — well — compare him with men that we went out with at home.

Blanche. Is he so — different?

Stella. Yes. A different species.

Blanche. In what way; what's he like?

Stella. Oh, you can't describe someone you're in love with! Here's a picture of him! (*She hands a photograph to Blanche.*)

Blanche. An officer?

Stella. A Master Sergeant in the Engineers' Corps. Those are decorations!

Blanche. He had those on when you met him?

Stella. I assure you I wasn't just blinded by all the brass.

Blanche. That's not what I —

Stella. But of course there were things to adjust myself to later on.

Blanche. Such as his civilian background! (*Stella laughs uncertainly*) How did he take it when you said I was coming?

Stella. Oh, Stanley doesn't know yet.

Blanche (*frightened*). You — haven't told him?

Stella. He's on the road a good deal.

Blanche. Oh. Travels?

Stella. Yes.

Blanche. Good. I mean — isn't it?

Stella (*half to herself*). I can hardly stand it when he is away for a night . . .

Blanche. Why, Stella!

Stella. When he's away for a week I nearly go wild!

Blanche. Gracious!

Stella. And when he comes back I cry on his lap like a baby . . .

(*She smiles to herself.*)

Blanche. I guess that is what is meant by being in love . . . (*Stella looks up with a radiant smile.*) Stella —

Stella. What?

Blanche (*in an uneasy rush*). I haven't asked you the things you probably thought I was going to ask. And so I'll expect you to be understanding about what *I* have to tell *you.*

Stella. What, Blanche? (*Her face turns anxious.*)

Blanche. Well, Stella — you're going to reproach me, I know that you're bound to reproach me — but before you do — take into consideration — you left! I stayed and struggled! You came to New Orleans and looked out for yourself! *I* stayed at *Belle Reve* and tried to hold it together! I'm not meaning this in any reproachful way, but *all* the burden descended on *my* shoulders.

Stella. The best I could do was make my own living, Blanche.

(*Blanche begins to shake again with intensity.*)

Blanche. I know, I know. But you are the one that abandoned Belle Reve, not I! I stayed and fought for it, bled for it, almost died for it!

Stella. Stop this hysterical outburst and tell me what's happened? What do you mean fought and bled? What kind of —

Blanche. I knew you would, Stella. I knew you would take this attitude about it!

Stella. About — what? — please!

Blanche (*slowly*). The loss — the loss . . .

Stella. Belle Reve? Lost, is it? No!

Blanche. Yes, Stella.

(*They stare at each other across the yellow-checked linoleum of the table. Blanche slowly nods her head and Stella looks slowly down at her hands folded on the table. The music of the "blue piano" grows louder. Blanche touches her handkerchief to her forehead.*)

Stella. But how did it go? What happened?

Blanche (*springing up*). You're a fine one to ask me how it went!

Stella. Blanche!

Blanche. You're a fine one to sit there *accusing me* of it!

Stella. Blanche!

Blanche. I, I, I took the blows in my face and my body! All of those deaths! The long parade to the graveyard! Father, mother! Margaret, that dreadful way! So big with it, it couldn't be put in a coffin! But had to be burned like rubbish! You just came home in time for the funerals, Stella. And funerals are pretty compared to deaths. Funerals are quiet, but deaths — not always. Sometimes their breathing is hoarse, and sometimes it rattles, and sometimes they even cry out to you, "Don't let me go!" Even the old, sometimes, say, "Don't let me go." As if you were able to stop them! But funerals are quiet, with pretty flowers. And, oh, what gorgeous boxes they pack them away in! Unless you were there at the bed when they cried out, "Hold me!" you'd never suspect there was the struggle for breath and bleeding. You didn't dream, but I saw! *Saw! Saw!* And now you sit there telling me with your eyes that I let the place go! How in hell do you think all that sickness and dying was paid for? Death is expensive, Miss Stella! And old Cousin Jessie's right after Margaret's, hers! Why, the Grim Reaper had put up his tent on our doorstep! . . . Stella. Belle Reve was his headquarters! Honey — that's how it slipped through my fingers! Which of them left us a fortune? Which of them left a cent of insurance even? Only poor Jessie —, one hundred to pay for her coffin. That was all, Stella! And I with my pitiful salary at the school. Yes, accuse me! Sit there and stare at me, thinking I let the place go! *I* let the place go? Where were *you!* In bed with your — Polack!

Stella (springing). Blanche! You be still! That's enough! (*She starts out.*)

Blanche. Where are you going?

Stella. I'm going into the bathroom to wash my face.

Blanche. Oh, Stella, Stella, you're crying!

Stella. Does that surprise you?

Blanche. Forgive me — I didn't mean to —

(*The sound of men's voices is heard. Stella goes into the bathroom, closing the door behind her. When the men appear, and Blanche realizes it must be Stanley returning, she moves uncertainly from the bathroom door to the dressing table, looking apprehensively towards the front door. Stanley enters, followed by Steve and Mitch. Stanley pauses near his door, Steve by the foot of the spiral stair, and Mitch is slightly above and to the right of them, about to go out. As the men enter, we hear some of the following dialogue.*)

Stanley. Is that how he got it?

Steve. Sure that's how he got it. He hit the old weather-bird for 300 bucks on a six-number-ticket.

Mitch. Don't tell him those things; he'll believe it.

(*Mitch starts out.*)

Stanley (restraining Mitch). Hey, Mitch — come back here.

(*Blanche, at the sound of voices, retires in the bedroom. She picks up Stanley's photo from dressing table, looks at it, puts it down. When Stanley enters the apartment, she darts and hides behind the screen at the head of bed.*)

Steve (to Stanley and Mitch). Hey, are we playing poker tomorrow?

Stanley. Sure — at Mitch's.

Mitch (hearing this, returns quickly to the stair rail). No — not at my place. My mother's still sick!

Stanley. Okay, at my place . . . (*Mitch starts out again*) But you bring the beer!

(*Mitch pretends not to hear, — calls out "Goodnight all," and goes out, singing. Eunice's voice is heard, above*).

Break it up down there! I made the spaghetti dish and ate it myself.

Steve (going upstairs). I told you and phoned you we was playing. (*To the men*) Jax beer!

Eunice. You never phoned me once.

Steve. I told you at breakfast — and phoned you at lunch . . .

Eunice. Well, never mind about that. You just get yourself home here once in a while.

Steve. You want it in the papers?

(*More laughter and shouts of parting come from the men. Stanley throws the screen door of the kitchen open and comes in. He is of medium height, about five feet eight or nine, and strongly, compactly built. Animal joy in his being is implicit in all his movements and attitudes. Since earliest manhood the center of his life has been pleasure with women, the giving and taking of it, not with weak indulgence, dependently, but with the power and pride of a richly feathered male bird among hens. Branching out from this complete and satisfying center are all the auxiliary channels of his life, such as his heartiness with men, his appreciation of rough humor, his love of good drink and food and games, his car, his radio, everything that is his, that bears his emblem of the gaudy seed-bearer. He sizes women up at a glance, with sexual classifications, crude images flashing into his mind and determining the way he smiles at them.*)

Blanche (drawing involuntarily back from his stare). You must be Stanley. I'm Blanche.

Stanley. Stella's sister?

Blanche. Yes.

Stanley. H'lo. Where's the little woman?

Blanche. In the bathroom.

Stanley. Oh. Didn't know you were coming in town.

Blanche. I — uh —

Stanley. Where you from, Blanche?

Blanche. Why, I — live in Laurel.

(*He has crossed to the closet and removed the whiskey bottle.*)

Stanley. In Laurel, huh? Oh, yeah. Yeah, in Laurel, that's right. Not in my territory. Liquor goes fast in hot weather. (*He holds the bottle to the light to observe its depletion.*) Have a shot?

Blanche. No, I — rarely touch it.

Stanley. Some people rarely touch it, but it touches them often.

Blanche (*faintly*). Ha-ha.

Stanley. My clothes're stickin' to me. Do you mind if I make myself comfortable? (*He starts to remove his shirt.*)

Blanche. Please, please do.

Stanley. Be comfortable is my motto.

Blanche. It's mine, too. It's hard to stay looking fresh. I haven't washed or even powdered my face and — here you are!

Stanley. You know you can catch cold sitting around in damp things, especially when you been exercising hard like bowling is. You're a teacher, aren't you?

Blanche. Yes.

Stanley. What do you teach, Blanche?

Blanche. English.

Stanley. I never was a very good English student. How long you here for, Blanche?

Blanche. I — don't know yet.

Stanley. You going to shack up here?

Blanche. I thought I would if it's not inconvenient for you all.

Stanley. Good.

Blanche. Traveling wears me out.

Stanley. Well, take it easy.

(*A cat screeches near the window. Blanche springs up.*)

Blanche. What's that?

Stanley. Cats . . . Hey, Stella!

Stella (*faintly, from the bathroom*). Yes, Stanley.

Stanley. Haven't fallen in, have you? (*He grins at Blanche. She tries unsuccessfully to smile back. There is a silence.*) I'm afraid I'll strike you as being the unrefined type. Stella's spoke of you a good deal. You were married once, weren't you?

(*The music of the polka rises up, faint in the distance.*)

Blanche. Yes. When I was quite young.

Stanley. What happened?

Blanche. The boy — the boy died. (*She sinks back down.*) I'm afraid I'm — going to be sick!

(*Her head falls on her arms.*)

SCENE TWO

It is six o'clock the following evening. Blanche is bathing. Stella is completing her toilette. Blanche's dress, a flowered print, is laid out on Stella's bed.

Stanley enters the kitchen from outside, leaving the door open on the perpetual "blue piano" around the corner.

Stanley. What's all this monkey doings?

Stella. Oh, Stan! (*She jumps up and kisses him which he accepts with lordly composure*) I'm taking Blanche to Galatoire's for supper and then to a show, because it's your poker night.

Stanley. How about my supper, huh? I'm not going to no Galatoire's for supper!

Stella. I put you a cold plate on ice.

Stanley. Well, isn't that just dandy!

Stella. I'm going to try to keep Blanche out till the party breaks up because I don't know how she would take it. So we'll go to one of the little places in the Quarter afterwards and you'd better give me some money.

Stanley. Where is she?

Stella. She's soaking in a hot hub to quiet her nerves. She's terribly upset.

Stanley. Over what?

Stella. She's been through such an ordeal.

Stanley. Yeah?

Stella. Stan, we've — lost Belle Reve!

Stanley. The place in the country?

Stella. Yes.

Stanley. How?

Stella (*vaguely*). Oh, it had to be — sacrificed or something. (*There is a pause while Stanley considers. Stella is changing into her dress.*) When she comes in be sure to say something nice about her appearance. And, oh! Don't mention the baby. I haven't said anything yet, I'm waiting until she gets in a quieter condition.

Stanley (*ominously*). So?

Stella. And try to understand her and be nice to her, Stan.

Blanche (*singing in the bathroom*).

"From the land of the sky blue water,
They brought a captive maid!"

Stella. She wasn't expecting to find us in such a small place. You see I'd tried to gloss things over a little in my letters.

Stanley. So?

Stella. And admire her dress and tell her she's looking wonderful. That's important with Blanche. Her little weakness!

Stanley. Yeah. I get the idea. Now let's skip back a little to where you said the country place was disposed of.

Stella. Oh! — yes . . .

Stanley. How about that? Let's have a few more details on that subjeck.

Stella. It's best not to talk much about it until she's calmed down.

Stanley. So that's the deal, huh? Sister Blanche cannot be annoyed with business details right now!

Stella. You saw how she was last night.

Stanley. Uh-hum, I saw how she was. Now let's have a gander at the bill of sale.

Stella. I haven't seen any.

Stanley. She didn't show you no papers, no deed of sale or nothing like that, huh?

Stella. It seems like it wasn't sold.

Stanley. Well what in hell was it then, give away? To charity?

Stella. Shhh! She'll hear you.

Stanley. I don't care if she hears me. Let's see the papers!

Stella. There weren't any papers, she didn't show any papers, I don't care about papers.

Stanley. Have you ever heard of the Napoleonic code?

Stella. No, Stanley, I haven't heard of the Napoleonic code and if I have, I don't see what it —

Stanley. Let me enlighten you on a point or two, baby.

Stella. Yes?

Stanley. In the state of Louisiana we have the Napoleonic code according to which what belongs to the wife belongs to the husband and vice versa. For instance if I had a piece of property, or you had a piece of property —

Stella. My head is swimming!

Stanley. All right. I'll wait till she gets through soaking in a hot tub and then I'll inquire if *she* is acquainted with the Napoleonic code. It looks to me like you have been swindled, baby, and when you're swindled under the Napoleonic code I'm swindled *too*. And I don't like to be *swindled*.

Stella. There's plenty of time to ask her questions later but if you do now she'll go to pieces again. I don't understand what happened to Belle Reve but you don't know how ridiculous you are being when you suggest that my sister or I or anyone of our family could have perpetrated a swindle on anyone else.

Stanley. Then where's the money if the place was sold?

Stella. Not sold — *lost, lost!* (*He stalks into bedroom, and she follows him.*) Stanley!

(*He pulls open the wardrobe trunk standing in middle of room and jerks out an armful of dresses.*)

Stanley. Open your eyes to this stuff! You think she got them out of a teacher's pay?

Stella. Hush!

Stanley. Look at these feathers and furs that she come here to preen herself in! What's this here? A solid-gold dress, I believe! And this one! What is these here? Fox-pieces! (*He blows on them*) Genuine fox fur-pieces, a half a mile long! Where are your fox-pieces, Stella? Bushy snow-white ones, no less! Where are your white fox-pieces?

Stella. Those are inexpensive summer furs that Blanche has had a long time.

Stanley. I got an acquaintance who deals in this sort of merchandise. I'll have him in here to appraise it. I'm willing to bet you there's thousands of dollars invested in this stuff here!

Stella. Don't be such an idiot, Stanley!

(*He hurls the furs to the daybed. Then he jerks open small drawer in the trunk and pulls up a fist-full of costume jewelry.*)

Stanley. And what have we here? The treasure chest of a pirate!

Stella. Oh, Stanley!

Stanley. Pearls! Ropes of them! What is this sister of yours, a deep-sea diver? Bracelets of solid gold, too! Where are your pearls and gold bracelets?

Stella. Shhh! Be still, Stanley!

Stanley. And diamonds! A crown for an empress!

Stella. A rhinestone tiara she wore to a costume ball.

Stanley. What's rhinestone?

Stella. Next door to glass.

Stanley. Are you kidding? I have an acquaintance that works in a jewelry store. I'll have him in here to make an appraisal of this. Here's your plantation, or what was left of it, here!

Stella. You have no idea how stupid and horrid you're being! Now close that trunk before she comes out of the bathroom!

(*He kicks the trunk partly closed and sits on the kitchen table.*)

Stanley. The Kowalskis and the DuBois have different notions.

Stella (*angrily*). Indeed they have, thank heavens! — *I'm* going out-side. (*She snatches up her white hat and gloves and crosses to the outside door*) You come out with me while Blanche is getting dressed.

Stanley. Since when do you give me orders?

Stella. Are you going to stay here and insult her?

Stanley. You're damn tootin' I'm going to stay here.

(*Stella goes out to the porch. Blanche comes out of the bathroom in a red satin robe.*)

Blanche (*airily*). Hello, Stanley! Here I am, all freshly bathed and scented, and feeling like a brand new human being!

(*He lights a cigarette.*)

Stanley. That's good.

Blanche (*drawing the curtains at the windows*). Excuse me while I slip on my pretty new dress!

Stanley. Go right ahead, Blanche.

(*She closes the drapes between the rooms.*)

Blanche. I understand there's to be a little card party to which we ladies are cordially *not* invited!

Stanley (*ominously*). Yeah?

(*Blanche throws off her robe and slips into a flowered print dress.*)

Blanche. Where's Stella?

Stanley. Out on the porch.

Blanche. I'm going to ask a favor of you in a moment.

Stanley. What could that be, I wonder?

Blanche. Some buttons in back! You may enter! (*He crosses through drapes with a smoldering look.*) How do I look?

Stanley. You look all right.

Blanche. Many thanks! Now the buttons!

Stanley. I can't do nothing with them.

Blanche. You men with your big clumsy fingers. May I have a drag on your cig?

Stanley. Have one for yourself.

Blanche. Why, thanks! . . . It looks like my trunk has exploded.

Stanley. Me an' Stella were helping you unpack.

Blanche. Well, you certainly did a fast and thorough job of it!

Stanley. It looks like you raided some stylish shops in Paris.

Blanche. Ha-ha! Yes — clothes are my passion!

Stanley. What does it cost for a string of fur-pieces like that?

Blanche. Why, those were a tribute from an admirer of mine!

Stanley. He must have had a lot of — admiration!

Blanche. Oh, in my youth I excited some admiration. But look at me now! (*She smiles at him radiantly*) Would you think it possible that I was once considered to be — attractive?

Stanley. Your looks are okay.

Blanche. I was fishing for a compliment, Stanley.

Stanley. I don't go in for that stuff.

Blanche. What — stuff?

Stanley. Compliments to women about their looks. I never met a woman that didn't know if she was good-looking or not without being told, and some of them give themselves credit for more than they've got. I once went out with a doll who said to me, "I am the glamorous type, I am the glamorous type!" I said, "So what?"

Blanche. And what did she say then?

Stanley. She didn't say nothing. That shut her up like a clam.

Blanche. Did it end the romance?

Stanley. It ended the conversation — that was all. Some men are took in by this Hollywood glamor stuff and some men are not.

Blanche. I'm sure you belong in the second category.

Stanley. That's right.

Blanche. I cannot imagine any witch of a woman casting a spell over you.

Stanley. That's — right.

Blanche. You're simple, straightforward and honest, a little bit on the primitive side I should think. To interest you a woman would have to — (*She pauses with an indefinite gesture.*)

Stanley (*slowly*). Lay . . . her cards on the table.

Blanche (*smiling*). Well, I never cared for wishy-washy people. That was why, when you walked in here last night, I said to myself — "My sister has married a man!" — Of course that was all that I could tell about you.

Stanley (*booming*). Now let's cut the re-bop!

Blanche (*pressing hands to her ears*). Ouuuuu!

Stella (*calling from the steps*). Stanley! You come out here and let Blanche finish dressing!

Blanche. I'm through dressing, honey.

Stella. Well, you come out, then.

Stanley. Your sister and I are having a little talk.

Blanche (*lightly*). Honey, do me a favor. Run to the drug-store and get me a lemon-coke with plenty of chipped ice in it! — Will you do that for me, Sweetie?

Stella (*uncertainly*). Yes. (*She goes around the corner of the building.*)

Blanche. The poor little thing was out there listening to us, and I have an idea she doesn't understand you as well as I do. . . . All right; now, Mr. Kowalski, let us proceed without any more double-talk. I'm ready to answer all questions. I've nothing to hide. What is it?

Stanley. There is such a thing in this State of Louisiana as the Napoleonic code, according to which whatever belongs to my wife is also mine — and vice versa.

Blanche. My, but you have an impressive judicial air!

(*She sprays herself with her atomizer; then playfully sprays him with it. He seizes the atomizer and slams it down on the dresser. She throws back her head and laughs.*)

Stanley. If I didn't know that you was my wife's sister I'd get ideas about you!

Blanche. Such as what!

Stanley. Don't play so dumb. You know what!

Blanche (*she puts the atomizer on the table*). All right. Cards on the table. That suits me. (*She turns to Stanley.*) I know I fib a good deal. After all, a woman's charm is fifty per cent illusion, but when a thing is important I tell the truth, and this is the truth: I haven't cheated my sister or you or anyone else as long as I have lived.

Stanley. Where's the papers? In the trunk?

Blanche. Everything that I own is in that trunk.

(*Stanley crosses to the trunk, shoves it roughly open and begins to open compartments.*)

Blanche. What in the name of heaven are you thinking of! What's in the back of that little boy's mind of yours? That I am absconding with something, attempting some kind of treachery on my sister? — let me do that! It will be faster and simpler . . . (*She crosses to the trunk and takes out a box.*) I keep my papers mostly in this tin box.

(*She opens it.*)

Stanley. What's them underneath? (*He indicates another sheaf of papers.*)

Blanche. These are love-letters, yellowing with antiquity, all from one boy. (*He snatches them up. She speaks fiercely.*) Give those back to me!

Stanley. I'll have a look at them first!

Blanche. The touch of your hands insults them!

Stanley. Don't pull that stuff!

(He rips off the ribbon and starts to examine them. Blanche snatches them from him, and they cascade to the floor.)

Blanche. Now that you've touched them I'll burn them!

Stanley (staring, baffled). What in hell are they?

Blanche (on the floor gathering them up). Poems a dead boy wrote. I hurt him the way that you would like to hurt me, but you can't! I'm not young and vulnerable any more. But my young husband was and I — never mind about that! Just give them back to me!

Stanley. What do you mean by saying you'll have to burn them?

Blanche. I'm sorry, I must have lost my head for a moment. Everyone has something he won't let others touch because of their — intimate nature . . .

(She now seems faint with exhaustion and she sits down with the strong box and puts on a pair of glasses and goes methodically through a large stack of papers.)

Ambler & Ambler. Hmmmmm. . . . Crabtree. . . . More Ambler & Ambler.

Stanley. What is Ambler & Ambler?

Blanche. A firm that made loans on the place.

Stanley. Then it *was* lost on a mortgage?

Blanche (touching her forehead). That must've been what happened.

Stanley. I don't want no ifs, ands or buts! What's all the rest of them papers?

(She hands him the entire box. He carries it to the table and starts to examine the papers.)

Blanche (picking up a large envelope containing more papers). There are thousands of papers, stretching back over hundreds of years, affecting Belle Reve as, piece by piece, our improvident grandfathers and father and uncles and brothers exchanged the land for their epic fornications — to put it plainly! *(She removes her glasses with an exhausted laugh)* The four-letter word deprived us of our plantation, till finally all that was left — and Stella can verify that! — was the house itself and about twenty acres of ground, including a graveyard, to which now all but Stella and I have retreated. *(She pours the contents of the envelope on the table)* Here all of them are, all papers! I hereby endow you with them! Take them, peruse them — commit them to memory, even! I think it's wonderfully fitting that Belle Reve should finally be this bunch of old papers in your big, capable hands! . . . I wonder if Stella's come back with my lemon-coke . . . *(She leans back and closes her eyes.)*

Stanley. I have a lawyer acquaintance who will study these out.

Blanche. Present them to him with a box of aspirin tablets.

Stanley (becoming somewhat sheepish). You see, under the Napoleonic code — a man has to take an interest in his wife's affairs — especially now that she's going to have a baby.

(Blanche opens her eyes. The "blue piano" sounds louder.)

Blanche. Stella? Stella going to have a baby? *(dreamily)* I didn't know she was going to have a baby!

(She gets up and crosses to the outside door. Stella appears around the corner with a carton from the drugstore.)

(Stanley goes into the bedroom with the envelope and the box.)

(The inner rooms fade to darkness and the outside wall of the house is visible. Blanche meets Stella at the foot of the steps to the sidewalk.)

Blanche. Stella, Stella for star! How lovely to have a baby! It's all right. Everything's all right.

Stella. I'm sorry he did that to you.

Blanche. Oh, I guess he's just not the type that goes for jasmine perfume, but maybe he's what we need to mix with our blood now that we've lost Belle Reve. We thrashed it out. I feel a bit shaky, but I think I handled it nicely, I laughed and treated it all as a joke. *(Steve and Pablo appear, carrying a case of beer.)* I called him a little boy and laughed and flirted. Yes, I was flirting with your husband! *(as the men approach)* The guests are gathering for the poker party. *(The two men pass between them, and enter the house.)* Which way do we go now, Stella — this way?

Stella. No, this way. *(She leads Blanche away.)*

Blanche (laughing). The blind are leading the blind!

(A tamale Vendor is heard calling.)

Vendor's Voice. Red-hot!

SCENE THREE

THE POKER NIGHT

There is a picture of Van Gogh's of a billiard-parlor at night. The kitchen now suggests that sort of a lurid nocturnal brilliance, the raw colors of childhood's spectrum. Over the yellow linoleum of the kitchen

*table hangs an electric bulb with a vivid green glass shade. The poker
players — Stanley, Steve, Mitch and Pablo — wear colored shirts, solid
blues, a purple, a red-and-white check, a light green, and they are men
at the peak of their physical manhood, as coarse and direct and powerful as the primary colors. There are vivid slices of watermelon on the
table, whiskey bottles and glasses. The bedroom is relatively dim with
only the light that spills between the portieres and through the wide
window on the street.*

For a moment, there is absorbed silence as a hand is dealt.

Steve. Anything wild this deal?

Pablo. One-eyed jacks are wild.

Steve. Give me two cards.

Pablo. You, Mitch?

Mitch. I'm out.

Pablo. One.

Mitch. Anyone want a shot?

Stanley. Yeah. Me.

Pablo. Why don't somebody go to the Chinaman's and bring back
a load of chop suey?

Stanley. When I'm losing you want to eat! Ante up! Openers? Openers!
Get y'r ass off the table, Mitch. Nothing belongs on a poker table
but cards, chips and whiskey.

(*He lurches up and tosses some watermelon rinds to the floor.*)

Mitch. Kind of on your high horse, ain't you?

Stanley. How many?

Steve. Give me three.

Stanley. One.

Mitch. I'm out again. I oughta go home pretty soon.

Stanley. Shut up.

Mitch. I gotta sick mother. She don't go to sleep until I come in at
night.

Stanley. Then why don't you stay home with her?

Mitch. She says to go out, so I go, but I don't enjoy it. All the while
I keep wondering how she is.

Stanley. Aw, for the sake of Jesus, go home, then!

Pablo. What've you got?

Steve. Spade flush.

Mitch. You all are married. But I'll be alone when she goes. — I'm
going to the bathroom.

Stanley. Hurry back and we'll fix you a sugar-tit.

Mitch. Aw, go rut. (*He crosses through the bedroom into the bath-room.*)

Steve (*dealing a hand*). Seven card stud. (*Telling his joke as he deals*) This ole farmer is out in back of his house sittin' down th'owing corn to the chickens when all at once he hears a loud cackle and this young hen comes lickety split around the side of the house with the rooster right behind her and gaining on her fast.

Stanley (*impatient with the story*). Deal!

Steve. But when the rooster catches sight of the farmer th'owing the corn he puts on the brakes and lets the hen get away and starts pecking corn. And the old farmer says, "Lord God, I hopes I never gits *that* hongry!"

(*Steve and Pablo laugh. The sisters appear around the corner of the building.*)

Stella. The game is still going on.

Blanche. How do I look?

Stella. Lovely, Blanche.

Blanche. I feel so hot and frazzled. Wait till I powder before you open the door. Do I look done in?

Stella. Why no. You are as fresh as a daisy.

Blanche. One that's been picked a few days.

(*Stella opens the door and they enter.*)

Stella. Well, well, well. I see you boys are still at it!

Stanley. Where you been?

Stella. Blanche and I took in a show. Blanche, this is Mr. Gonzales and Mr. Hubbell.

Blanche. Please don't get up.

Stanley. Nobody's going to get up, so don't be worried.

Stella. How much longer is this game going to continue?

Stanley. Till we get ready to quit.

Blanche. Poker is so fascinating. Could I kibitz?

Stanley. You could not. Why don't you women go up and sit with Eunice?

Stella. Because it is nearly two-thirty. (*Blanche crosses into the bed-room and partially closes the portieres*) Couldn't you call it quits after one more hand?

(*A chair scrapes. Stanley gives a loud whack of his hand on her thigh.*)

Stella (*sharply*). That's not fun, Stanley.

(*The men laugh. Stella goes into the bedroom.*)

Stella. It makes me so mad when he does that in front of people.
Blanche. I think I will bathe.
Stella. Again?
Blanche. My nerves are in knots. Is the bathroom occupied?
Stella. I don't know.

(*Blanche knocks. Mitch opens the door and comes out, still wiping his hands on a towel.*)

Blanche. Oh! — good evening.
Mitch. Hello. (*He stares at her.*)
Stella. Blanche, this is Harold Mitchell. My sister, Blanche DuBois.
Mitch (*with awkward courtesy*). How do you do, Miss DuBois.
Stella. How is your mother now, Mitch?
Mitch. About the same, thanks. She appreciated your sending over that custard. — Excuse me, please.

(*He crosses slowly back into the kitchen, glancing back at Blanche and coughing a little shyly. He realizes he still has the towel in his hands and with an embarrassed laugh hands it to Stella. Blanche looks after him with a certain interest.*)

Blanche. That one seems — superior to the others.
Stella. Yes, he is.
Blanche. I thought he had a sort of sensitive look.
Stella. His mother is sick.
Blanche. Is he married?
Stella. No.
Blanche. Is he a wolf?
Stella. Why Blanche! (*Blanche laughs.*) I don't think he would be.
Blanche. What does — what does he do?

(*She is unbuttoning her blouse.*)

Stella. He's on the precision bench in the spare parts department. At the plant Stanley travels for.
Blanche. Is that something much?
Stella. No. Stanley's the only one of his crowd that's likely to get anywhere.
Blanche. What makes you think Stanley will?
Stella. Look at him.
Blanche. I've looked at him.
Stella. Then you should know.
Blanche. I'm sorry, but I haven't noticed the stamp of genius even on Stanley's forehead.

(*She takes off the blouse and stands in her pink silk brassiere and white skirt in the light through the portieres. The game has continued in undertones.*)

Stella. It isn't on his forehead and it isn't genius.
Blanche. Oh. Well, what is it, and where? I would like to know.
Stella. It's drive that he has. You're standing in the light, Blanche!
Blanche. Oh, am I!

(*She moves out of the yellow streak of light. Stella has removed her dress and put on a light blue satin kimono.*)

Stella (*with girlish laughter*).You ought to see their wives.
Blanche (*laughingly*). I can imagine. Big, beefy things, I suppose.
Stella. You know that one upstairs? (*More laughter*) One time (*laughing*) the plaster — (*laughing*) cracked —
Stanley. You hens cut out that conversation in there!
Stella. You can't hear us.
Stanley. Well, you can hear me and I said to hush up!
Stella. This is my house and I'll talk as much as I want to!
Blanche. Stella, don't start a row.
Stella. He's half drunk! —- I'll be out in a minute.

(*She goes into the bathroom. Blanche rises and crosses leisurely to a small white radio and turns it on.*)

Stanley. Awright, Mitch you in?
Mitch. What? Oh! — No, I'm out!

(*Blanche moves back into the streak of light. She raises her arms and stretches, as she moves indolently back to the chair.*)

(*Rhumba music comes over the radio. Mitch rises at the table.*)

Stanley. Who turned that on in there?
Blanche. I did. Do you mind?
Stanley. Turn it off!
Steve. Aw, let the girls have their music.
Pablo. Sure, that's good, leave it on!
Steve. Sounds like Xavier Cugat!

(*Stanley jumps up and, crossing to the radio, turns it off. He stops short at the sight of Blanche in the chair. She returns his look without flinching. Then he sits again at the poker table.*)

(*Two of the men have started arguing hotly.*)

Steve. I didn't hear you name it.
Pablo. Didn't I name it, Mitch?

Mitch. I wasn't listenin'.

Pablo. What were you doing, then?

Stanley. He was looking through them drapes. (_He jumps up and jerks roughly at curtains to close them_) Now deal the hand over again and let's play cards or quit. Some people get ants when they win.

(_Mitch rises as Stanley returns to his seat._)

Stanley (_yelling_). Sit down!

Mitch. I'm going to the "head." Deal me out.

Pablo. Sure he's got ants now. Seven five-dollar bills in his pants pocket folded up tight as spitballs.

Steve. Tomorrow you'll see him at the cashier's window getting them changed into quarters.

Stanley. And when he goes home he'll deposit them one by one in a piggy bank his mother give him for Christmas. (_Dealing_) This game is Spit in the Ocean.

(_Mitch laughs uncomfortably and continues through the portieres. He stops just inside._)

Blanche (_softly_). Hello! The Little Boys' Room is busy right now.

Mitch. We've — been drinking beer.

Blanche. I hate beer.

Mitch. It's — a hot weather drink.

Blanche. Oh, I don't think so; it always makes me warmer. Have you got any cigs? (_She has slipped on the dark red satin wrapper._)

Mitch. Sure.

Blanche. What kind are they?

Mitch. Luckies.

Blanche. Oh, good. What a pretty case. Silver?

Mitch. Yes. Yes; read the inscription.

Blanche. Oh, is there an inscription? I can't make it out. (_He strikes a match and moves closer_) Oh! (_reading with feigned difficulty_).

> "And if God choose,
> I shall but love thee better — after — death!"

Why, that's from my favorite sonnet by Mrs. Browning!

Mitch. You know it?

Blanche. Certainly I do!

Mitch. There's a story connected with that inscription.

Blanche. It sounds like a romance.

Mitch. A pretty sad one.

Blanche. Oh?

Mitch. The girl's dead now.

Blanche (*in a tone of deep sympathy*). Oh!

Mitch. She knew she was dying when she give me this. A very strange girl, very sweet — very!

Blanche. She must have been fond of you. Sick people have such deep, sincere attachments.

Mitch. That's right, they certainly do.

Blanche. Sorrow makes for sincerity, I think.

Mitch. It sure brings it out in people.

Blanche. The little there is belongs to people who have experienced some sorrow.

Mitch. I believe you are right about that.

Blanche. I'm positive that I am. Show me a person who hasn't known any sorrow and I'll show you a shuperficial — Listen to me! My tongue is a little — thick! You boys are responsible for it. The show let out at eleven and we couldn't come home on account of the poker game so we had to go somewhere and drink. I'm not accustomed to having more than one drink. Two is the limit — and *three!* (*She laughs*) Tonight I had three.

Stanley. Mitch!

Mitch. Deal me out. I'm talking to Miss —

Blanche. DuBois.

Mitch. Miss DuBois?

Blanche. It's a French name. It means woods and Blanche means white, so the two together mean white woods. Like an orchard in spring! You can remember it by that.

Mitch. You're French?

Blanche. We are French by extraction. Our first American ancestors were French Huguenots.

Mitch. You are Stella's sister, are you not?

Blanche. Yes, Stella is my precious little sister. I call her little in spite of the fact she's somewhat older than I. Just slightly. Less than a year. Will you do something for me?

Mitch. Sure. What?

Blanche. I bought this adorable little colored paper lantern at a Chinese shop on Bourbon. Put it over the light bulb! Will you, please?

Mitch. Be glad to.

Blanche. I can't stand a naked light bulb, any more than I can a rude remark or a vulgar action.

Mitch (*adjusting the lantern*). I guess we strike you as being a pretty rough bunch.

Blanche. I'm very adaptable — to circumstances.

Mitch. Well, that's a good thing to be. You are visiting Stanley and Stella?

Blanche. Stella hasn't been so well lately, and I came down to help her for a while. She's very run down.

Mitch. You're not — ?

Blanche. Married? No, no. I'm an old maid schoolteacher!

Mitch. You may teach school but you're certainly not an old maid.

Blanche. Thank you, sir! I appreciate your gallantry!

Mitch. So you are in the teaching profession?

Blanche. Yes, Ah, yes . . .

Mitch. Grade school or high school or —

Stanley (bellowing). Mitch!

Mitch. Coming!

Blanche. Gracious, what lung-power! . . . I teach high school. In Laurel.

Mitch. What do you teach? What subject?

Blanche. Guess!

Mitch. I bet you teach art or music? (*Blanche laughs delicately*) Of course I could be wrong. You might teach arithmetic.

Blanche. Never arithmetic, sir, never arithmetic! (*with a laugh*) I don't even know my multiplication tables! No, I have the misfortune of being an English instructor. I attempt to instill a bunch of bobby-soxers and drug-store Romeos with reverence for Hawthorne and Whitman and Poe!

Mitch. I guess that some of them are more interested in other things.

Blanche. How very right you are! Their literary heritage is not what most of them treasure above all else! But they're sweet things! And in the spring, it's touching to notice them making their first discovery of love! As if nobody had ever known it before!

(*The bathroom door opens and Stella comes out. Blanche continues talking to Mitch.*)

Oh! Have you finished? Wait — I'll turn on the radio.

(*She turns the knobs on the radio and it begins to play "Wien, Wien, nur du allein." Blanche waltzes to the music with romantic gestures. Mitch is delighted and moves in awkward imitation like a dancing bear.*)

(*Stanley stalks fiercely through the portieres into the bedroom. He crosses to the small white radio and snatches it off the table. With a shouted oath, he tosses the instrument out the window.*)

Stella. Drunk — drunk — animal thing, you! (*She rushes through to the poker table*) All of you — please go home! If any of you have one spark of decency in you —
Blanche (*wildly*). Stella, watch out, he's —

(*Stanley charges after Stella.*)

Men (*feebly*). Take it easy, Stanley. Easy, fellow. — Let's all —
Stella. You lay your hands on me and I'll —

(*She backs out of sight. He advances and disappears. There is the sound of a blow. Stella cries out. Blanche screams and runs into the kitchen. The men rush forward and there is grappling and cursing. Something is overturned with a crash.*)

Blanche (*shrilly*). My sister is going to have a baby!
Mitch. This is terrible.
Blanche. Lunacy, absolute lunacy!
Mitch. Get him in here, men.

(*Stanley is forced, pinioned by the two men, into the bedroom. He nearly throws them off. Then all at once he subsides and is limp in their grasp.*)

(*They speak quietly and lovingly to him and he leans his face on one of their shoulders.*)

Stella (*in a high, unnatural voice, out of sight*). I want to go away, I want to go away!
Mitch. Poker shouldn't be played in a house with women.

(*Blanche rushes into the bedroom.*)

Blanche. I want my sister's clothes! We'll go to that woman's upstairs!
Mitch. Where is the clothes?
Blanche (*opening the closet*). I've got them! (*She rushes through to Stella*) Stella, Stella, precious! Dear, dear little sister, don't be afraid!

(*With her arms around Stella, Blanche guides her to the outside door and upstairs.*)

Stanley (*dully*). What's the matter; what's happened?
Mitch. You just blew your top, Stan.
Pablo. He's okay, now.
Steve. Sure, my boy's okay!
Mitch. Put him on the bed and get a wet towel.

Pablo. I think coffee would do him a world of good, now.
Stanley (*thickly*). I want water.
Mitch. Put him under the shower!

(*The men talk quietly as they lead him to the bathroom.*)

Stanley. Let the rut go of me, you sons of bitches!

(*Sounds of blows are heard. The water goes on full tilt.*)

Steve. Let's get quick out of here!

(*They rush to the poker table and sweep up their winnings on their way out.*)

Mitch (*sadly but firmly*). Poker should not be played in a house with women.

(*The door closes on them and the place is still. The Negro entertainers in the bar around the corner play "Paper Doll" slow and blue. After a moment Stanley comes out of the bathroom dripping water and still in his clinging wet polka dot drawers.*)

Stanley. Stella! (*There is a pause*) My baby doll's left me! (*He breaks into sobs. Then he goes to the phone and dials, still shuddering with sobs.*) Eunice? I want my baby! (*He waits a moment; then he hangs up and dials again*) Eunice! I'll keep on ringin' until I talk with my baby!

(*An indistinguishable shrill voice is heard. He hurls phone to floor. Dissonant brass and piano sounds as the rooms dim out to darkness and the outer walls appear in the night light. The "blue piano" plays for a brief interval.*)

(*Finally, Stanley stumbles half-dressed out to the porch and down the wooden steps to the pavement before the building. There he throws back his head like a baying hound and bellows his wife's name: "Stella! Stella, sweetheart! Stella!"*)

Stanley. Stell-*lahhhhh!*
Eunice (*calling down from the door of her upper apartment*). Quit that howling out there an' go back to bed!
Stanley. I want my baby down here. Stella, Stella!
Eunice. She ain't comin' down so you quit! Or you'll git th' law on you!
Stanley. Stella!

Eunice. You can't beat on a woman an' then call 'er back! She won't come! And her goin' t' have a baby! . . . You stinker! You whelp of a Polack, you! I hope they do haul you in and turn the fire hose on you, same as the last time!

Stanley (*humbly*). Eunice, I want my girl to come down with me!

Eunice. Hah! (*She slams her door.*)

Stanley (*with heaven-splitting violence*). STELL-LAHHHHH!

(*The low-tone clarinet moans. The door upstairs opens again. Stella slips down the rickety stairs in her robe. Her eyes are glistening with tears and her hair loose about her throat and shoulders. They stare at each other. Then they come together with low, animal moans. He falls to his knees on the steps and presses his face to her belly, curving a little with maternity. Her eyes go blind with tenderness as she catches his head and raises him level with her. He snatches the screen door open and lifts her off her feet and bears her into the dark flat.*)

(*Blanche comes out on the upper landing in her robe and slips fearfully down the steps.*)

Blanche. Where is my little sister? Stella? Stella?

(*She stops before the dark entrance of her sister's flat. Then catches her breath as if struck. She rushes down to the walk before the house. She looks right and left as if for a sanctuary.*)

(*The music fades away. Mitch appears from around the corner.*)

Mitch. Miss DuBois?

Blanche. Oh!

Mitch. All quiet on the Potomac now?

Blanche. She ran downstairs and went back in there with him.

Mitch. Sure she did.

Blanche. I'm terrified.

Mitch. Ho-ho! There's nothing to be scared of. They're crazy about each other.

Blanche. I'm not used to such —

Mitch. Naw, it's a shame this had to happen when you just got here. But don't take it serious.

Blanche. Violence! Is so —

Mitch. Set down on the steps and have a cigarette with me.

Blanche. I'm not properly dressed.

Mitch. That doesn't make no difference in the Quarter.

Blanche. Such a pretty silver case.

Mitch. I showed you the inscription, didn't I?

Blanche. Yes. (*During the pause, she looks up at the sky*) There's so much — so much confusion in the world . . . (*He coughs diffidently*) Thank you for being so kind! I need kindness now.

SCENE FOUR

It is early the following morning. There is a confusion of street cries like a choral chant.

Stella is lying down in the bedroom. Her face is serene in the early morning sunlight. One hand rests on her belly, rounding slightly with new maternity. From the other dangles a book of colored comics. Her eyes and lips have that almost narcotized tranquility that is in the faces of Eastern idols.

The table is sloppy with remains of breakfast and the debris of the preceding night, and Stanley's gaudy pyjamas lie across the threshold of the bathroom. The outside door is slightly ajar on a sky of summer brilliance.

Blanche appears at this door. She has spent a sleepless night and her appearance entirely contrasts with Stella's. She presses her knuckles nervously to her lips as she looks through the door, before entering.

Blanche. Stella?
Stella (*stirring lazily*). Hmmh?

(*Blanche utters a moaning cry and runs into the bedroom, throwing herself down beside Stella in a rush of hysterical tenderness.*)

Blanche. Baby, my baby sister!
Stella (*drawing away from her*). Blanche, what is the matter with you?

(*Blanche straightens up slowly and stands beside the bed looking down at her sister with knuckles pressed to her lips.*)

Blanche. He's left?
Stella. Stan? Yes.
Blanche. Will he be back?
Stella. He's gone to get the car greased. Why?
Blanche. Why! I've been half crazy, Stella! When I found out you'd been insane enough to come back in here after what happened — I started to rush in after you!
Stella. I'm glad you didn't.

Blanche. What were you thinking of? (*Stella makes an indefinite gesture*) Answer me! What? What?

Stella. Please, Blanche! Sit down and stop yelling.

Blanche. All right, Stella. I will repeat the question quietly now. How could you come back in this place last night? Why, you must have slept with him!

(*Stella gets up in a calm and leisurely way.*)

Stella. Blanche, I'd forgotten how excitable you are. You're making much too much fuss about this.

Blanche. Am I?

Stella. Yes, you are, Blanche. I know how it must have seemed to you and I'm awful sorry it had to happen, but it wasn't anything as serious as you seem to take it. In the first place, when men are drinking and playing poker, anything can happen. It's always a powder-keg. He didn't know what he was doing. . . . He was as good as a lamb when I came back and he's really very, very ashamed of himself.

Blanche. And that — that makes it all right?

Stella. No, it isn't all right for anybody to make such a terrible row, but — people do sometimes. Stanley's always smashed things. Why, on our wedding night — soon as we came in here — he snatched off one of my slippers and rushed about the place smashing the light-bulbs with it.

Blanche. He did — *what?*

Stella. He smashed all the light-bulbs with the heel of my slipper!

(*She laughs.*)

Blanche. And you — you *let* him? Didn't *run*, didn't *scream?*

Stella. I was — sort of — thrilled by it. (*She waits for a moment*) Eunice and you had breakfast?

Blanche. Do you suppose I wanted any breakfast?

Stella. There's some coffee left on the stove.

Blanche. You're so — matter of fact about it. Stella.

Stella. What other can I be? He's taken the radio to get it fixed. It didn't land on the pavement so only one tube was smashed.

Blanche. And you are standing there smiling!

Stella. What do you want me to do?

Blanche. Pull yourself together and face the facts.

Stella. What are they, in your opinion?

Blanche. In my opinion? You're married to a madman!

Stella. No!

Blanche. Yes, you are, your fix is worse than mine is! Only you're not being sensible about it. I'm going to *do* something. Get hold of myself and make myself a new life!

Stella. Yes?

Blanche. But you've given in. And that isn't right, you're not old! You can get out.

Stella (*slowly and emphatically*). I'm not in anything I want to get out of.

Blanche (*incredulously*). What — Stella?

Stella. I said I am not in anything that I have a desire to get out of. Look at the mess in this room! And those empty bottles! They went through two cases last night! He promised this morning that he was going to quit having these poker parties, but you know how long such a promise is going to keep. Oh, well, it's his pleasure, like mine is movies and bridge. People have got to tolerate each other's habits, I guess.

Blanche. I don't understand you. (*Stella turns toward her*) I don't understand your indifference. Is this a Chinese philosophy you've — cultivated?

Stella. Is what — what?

Blanche. This — shuffling about and mumbling — "One tube smashed — beer-bottles — mess in the kitchen" — as if nothing out of the ordinary has happened! (*Stella laughs uncertainly and picking up the broom, twirls it in her hands.*)

Blanche. Are you deliberately shaking that thing in my face?

Stella. No.

Blanche. Stop it. Let go of that broom. I won't have you cleaning up for him!

Stella. Then who's going to do it? Are you?

Blanche. I? I!

Stella. No, I didn't think so.

Blanche. Oh, let me think, if only my mind would function! We've got to get hold of some money, that's the way out!

Stella. I guess that money is always nice to get hold of.

Blanche. Listen to me. I have an idea of some kind. (*Shakily she twists a cigarette into her holder*) Do you remember Shep Huntleigh? (*Stella shakes her head*) Of course you remember Shep Huntleigh. I went out with him at college and wore his pin for a while. Well —

Stella. Well?

Blanche. I ran into him last winter. You know I went to Miami during the Christmas holidays?

Stella. No.

Blanche. Well, I did. I took the trip as an investment, thinking I'd meet someone with a million dollars.

Stella. Did you?

Blanche. Yes. I ran into Shep Huntleigh — I ran into him on Biscayne Boulevard, on Christmas Eve, about dusk . . . getting into his car — Cadillac convertible; must have been a block long!

Stella. I should think it would have been — inconvenient in traffic!

Blanche. You've heard of oil-wells?

Stella. Yes — remotely.

Blanche. He has them, all over Texas. Texas is literally spouting gold in his pockets.

Stella. My, my.

Blanche. Y'know how indifferent I am to money. I think of money in terms of what it does for you. But he could do it, he could certainly do it!

Stella. Do what, Blanche?

Blanche. Why — set us up in a — shop!

Stella. What kind of a shop?

Blanche. Oh, a — shop of some kind! He could do it with half what his wife throws away at the races.

Stella. He's married?

Blanche. Honey, would I be here if the man weren't married? (*Stella laughs a little. Blanche suddenly springs up and crosses to phone. She speaks shrilly.*) How do I get Western Union? — Operator! Western Union!

Stella. That's a dial phone, honey.

Blanche. I can't dial, I'm too —

Stella. Just dial O.

Blanche. O?

Stella. Yes, "O" for Operator! (*Blanche considers a moment; then she puts the phone down.*)

Blanche. Give me a pencil. Where is a slip of paper? I've got to write it down first — the message, I mean . . .

(*She goes to the dressing table, and grabs up a sheet of Kleenex and an eyebrow pencil for writing equipment.*)

Let me see now . . . (*She bites the pencil*) "Darling Shep. Sister and I in desperate situation."

Stella. I beg your pardon!

Blanche. "Sister and I in desperate situation. Will explain details later. Would you be interested in — ?" (*She bites the pencil again*) "Would you be — interested — in . . ." (*She smashes the pencil on the table and springs up*) You never get anywhere with direct appeals!

Stella (*with a laugh*). Don't be so ridiculous, darling!

Blanche. But I'll think of something, I've *got* to think of — *something!* Don't, don't laugh at me, Stella! Please, please don't — I — I want you to look at the contents of my purse! Here's what's in it! (*She snatches her purse open*) Sixty-five measly cents in coin of the realm!

Stella (*crossing to bureau*). Stanley doesn't give me a regular allowance, he likes to pay bills himself, but — this morning he gave me ten dollars to smooth things over. You take five of it, Blanche, and I'll keep the rest.

Blanche. Oh, no. No, Stella.

Stella (*insisting*). I know how it helps your morale just having a little pocket-money on you.

Blanche. No, thank you — I'll take to the streets!

Stella. Talk sense! How did you happen to get so low on funds?

Blanche. Money just goes — it goes places. (*She rubs her forehead*) Sometime today I've got to get hold of a bromo!

Stella. I'll fix you one now.

Blanche. Not yet — I've got to keep thinking!

Stella. I wish you'd just let things go, at least for a — while . . .

Blanche. Stella, I can't live with him! You can, he's your husband. But how could I stay here with him, after last night, with just those curtains between us?

Stella. Blanche, you saw him at his worst last night.

Blanche. On the contrary, I saw him at his best! What such a man has to offer is animal force and he gave a wonderful exhibition of that! But the only way to live with such a man is to — go to bed with him! And that's your job — not mine!

Stella. After you've rested a little, you'll see it's going to work out. You don't have to worry about anything while you're here. I mean — expenses . . .

Blanche. I have to plan for us both, to get us both — out!

Stella. You take it for granted that I am in something that I want to get out of.

Blanche. I take it for granted that you still have sufficient memory of Belle Reve to find this place and these poker players impossible to live with.

Stella. Well, you're taking entirely too much for granted.

Blanche. I can't believe you're in earnest.

Stella. No?

Blanche. I understand how it happened — a little. You saw him in uniform, an officer, not here but —

Stella. I'm not sure it would have made any difference where I saw him.

Blanche. Now don't say it was one of those mysterious electric things between people! If you do I'll laugh in your face.

Stella. I am not going to say anything more at all about it!

Blanche. All right, then, don't!

Stella. But there are things that happen between a man and a woman in the dark — that sort of make everything else seem — unimportant. (*Pause.*)

Blanche. What you are talking about is brutal desire — just — Desire! — the name of that rattle-trap streetcar that bangs through the Quarter, up one old narrow street and down another . . .

Stella. Haven't you ever ridden on that streetcar?

Blanche. It brought me here. — Where I'm not wanted and where I'm ashamed to be . . .

Stella. Then don't you think your superior attitude is a bit out of place?

Blanche. I am not being or feeling at all superior, Stella. Believe me I'm not! It's just this. This is how I look at it. A man like that is someone to go out with — once — twice — three times when the devil is in you. But live with? Have a child by?

Stella. I have told you I love him.

Blanche. Then I *tremble* for you! I just — tremble for you. . . .

Stella. I can't help your trembling if you insist on trembling!

(*There is a pause.*)

Blanche. May I — speak — *plainly?*

Stella. Yes, do. Go ahead. As plainly as you want to.

(*Outside, a train approaches. They are silent till the noise subsides. They are both in the bedroom.*)

(*Under cover of the train's noise Stanley enters from outside. He stands unseen by the women, holding some packages in his arms, and overhears their following conversation. He wears an undershirt and grease-stained seersucker pants.*)

Blanche. Well — if you'll forgive me — he's *common!*

Stella. Why, yes, I suppose he is.

Blanche. Suppose! You can't have forgotten that much of our bringing up, Stella, that you just *suppose* that any part of a gentleman's in his nature! *Not one particle, no!* Oh, if he was just — *ordinary!* Just *plain* — but good and wholesome, but — *no.* There's something downright — *bestial* — about him! You're hating me saying this, aren't you?

Stella (*coldly*). Go on and say it all, Blanche.

Blanche. He acts like an animal, has an animal's habits! Eats like one, moves like one, talks like one! There's even something — sub-human — something not quite to the stage of humanity yet! Yes, something ape-like about him, like one of those picture I've seen in — anthropological studies! Thousands and thousands of years have passed him right by, and there he is — Stanley Kowalski — survivor of the stone age! Bearing the raw meat home from the kill in the jungle! And you — *you* here — *waiting* for him! Maybe he'll strike you or maybe grunt and kiss you! That is, if kisses have been discovered yet! Night falls and the other apes gather! There in the front of the cave, all grunting like him, and swilling and gnawing and hulking! His poker night! — you call it — this party of apes! Somebody growls — Some creature snatches at something — the fight is on! *God!* Maybe we are a long way from being made in God's image, but Stella — my sister — there has been *some* progress since then! Such things as art — as poetry and music — such kinds of new light have come into the world since then! In some kinds of people some tenderer feelings have had some little beginning! That we have got to make *grow!* And *cling* to, and hold as our flag! In this dark march toward whatever it is we're approaching. . . . *Don't — don't hang back with the brutes!*

(*Another train passes outside. Stanley hesitates, licking his lips. Then suddenly he turns stealthily about and withdraws through front door. The women are still unaware of his presence. When the train has passed he calls through the closed front door.*)

Stanley. Hey! Hey, Stella!

Stella (*who has listened gravely to Blanche*). Stanley!

Blanche. Stell, I —

(*But Stella has gone to the front door. Stanley enters casually with his packages.*)

Stanley. Hiyuh, Stella. Blanche back?

Stella. Yes, she's back.

Stanley. Hiyuh, Blanche. (*He grins at her.*)

Stella. You must've got under the car.

Stanley. Them darn mechanics at Fritz's don't know their ass fr'm — Hey!

(*Stella has embraced him with both arms, fiercely, and full in the view of Blanche. He laughs and clasps her head to him. Over her head he grins through the curtains at Blanche.*)

(*As the lights fade away, with a lingering brightness on their embrace, the music of the "blue piano" and trumpet and drums is heard.*)

SCENE FIVE

Blanche is seated in the bedroom fanning herself with a palm leaf as she reads over a just completed letter. Suddenly she bursts into a peal of laughter. Stella is dressing in the bedroom.

Stella. What are you laughing at, honey?

Blanche. Myself, myself, for being such a liar! I'm writing a letter to Shep. (*She picks up the letter*) "Darling Shep. I am spending the summer on the wing, making flying visits here and there. And who knows, perhaps I shall take a sudden notion to *swoop* down on *Dallas!* How would you feel about that? Ha-ha! (*She laughs nervously and brightly, touching her throat as if actually talking to Shep*) Forewarned is forearmed, as they say!" — How does that sound?

Stella. Uh-huh . . .

Blanche (*going on nervously*). "Most of my sister's friends go north in the summer but some have homes on the Gulf and there has been a continued round of entertainments, teas, cocktails, and luncheons —"

(*A disturbance is heard upstairs at the Hubbell's apartment.*)

Stella. Eunice seems to be having some trouble with Steve.

(*Eunice's voice shouts in terrible wrath.*)

Eunice. I heard about you and that blonde!

Steve. That's a damn lie!

Eunice. You ain't pulling the wool over my eyes! I wouldn't mind if you'd stay down at the Four Deuces, but you always going up.

Steve. Who ever seen me up?

Eunice. I seen you chasing her 'round the balcony — I'm gonna call the vice squad!

Steve. Don't you throw that at me!

Eunice (*shrieking*). You hit me! I'm gonna call the police!

(*A clatter of aluminum striking a wall is heard, followed by a man's angry roar, shouts and overturned furniture. There is a crash; then a relative hush.*)

Blanche (*brightly*). Did he *kill* her?

(*Eunice appears on the steps in daemonic disorder.*)

Stella. No! She's coming downstairs.

Eunice. Call the police. I'm going to call the police! (*She rushes around the corner.*)

(*They laugh lightly. Stanley comes around the corner in his green and scarlet silk bowling shirt. He trots up the steps and bangs into the kitchen. Blanche registers his entrance with nervous gestures.*)

Stanley. What's a mattter with Eun-uss?

Stella. She and Steve had a row. Has she got the police?

Stanley. Naw. She's gettin' a drink.

Stella. That's much more practical!

(*Steve comes down nursing a bruise on his forehead and looks in the door.*)

Steve. She here?

Stanley. Naw, naw. At the Four Deuces.

Steve. That rutting hunk! (*He looks around the corner a bit timidly, then turns with affected boldness and runs after her.*)

Blanche. I must jot that down in my notebook. Ha-ha! I'm compiling a notebook of quaint little words and phrases I've picked up here.

Stanley. You won't pick up nothing here you ain't heard before.

Blanche. Can I count on that?

Stanley. You can count on it up to five hundred.

Blanche. That's a mighty high number. (*He jerks open the bureau drawer, slams it shut and throws shoes in a corner. At each noise Blanche winces slightly. Finally she speaks*). What sign were you born under?

Stanley (*while he is dressing*). Sign?

Blanche. Astrological sign. I bet you were born under Aries. Aries people are forceful and dynamic. They dote on noise! They love to bang things around! You must have had lots of banging around in the army and now that you're out, you make up for it by treating inanimate objects with such a fury!

(*Stella has been going in and out of closet during this scene. Now she pops her head out of the closet.*)

Stella. Stanley was born just five minutes after Christmas.

Blanche. Capricorn — the Goat!

Stanley. What sign were *you* born under?

Blanche. Oh, my birthday's next month, the fifteenth of September; that's under Virgo.

Stanley. What's Virgo?

Blanche. Virgo is the Virgin.

Stanley (*contemptuously*). Hah! (*He advances a little as he knots his tie*) Say, do you happen to know somebody named Shaw?

(*Her face expresses a faint shock. She reaches for the cologne bottle and dampens her handkerchief as she answers carefully.*)

Blanche. Why, everybdy knows somebody named Shaw!

Stanley. Well, this somebody named Shaw is under the impression he met you in Laurel, but I figure he must have got you mixed up with some other party because this other party is someone he met at a hotel called the Flamingo.

(*Blanche laughs breathlessly as she touches the cologne-dampened handkerchief to her temples.*)

Blanche. I'm afraid he does have me mixed up with this "other party." The Hotel Flamingo is not the sort of establishment I would dare to be seen in!

Stanley. You know of it?

Blanche. Yes, I've seen it and smelled it.

Stanley. You must've got pretty close if you could smell it.

Blanche. The odor of cheap perfume is penetrating.

Stanley. That stuff you use is expensive?

Blanche. Twenty-five dollars an ounce! I'm nearly out. That's just a hint if you want to remember my birthday! (*She speaks lightly but her voice has a note of fear.*)

Stanley. Shaw must've got you mixed up. He goes in and out of Laurel all the time so he can check on it and clear up any mistake.

(*He turns away and crosses to the portieres. Blanche closes her eyes as if faint. Her hand trembles as she lifts the handkerchief again to her forehead.*)

(*Steve and Eunice come around corner. Steve's arm is around Eunice's shoulder and she is sobbing luxuriously and he is cooing love-words. There is a murmur of thunder as they go slowly upstairs in a tight embrace.*)

Stanley (*to Stella*). I'll wait for you at the Four Deuces!

Stella. Hey! Don't I rate one kiss?

Stanley. Not in front of your sister.

(*He goes out. Blanche rises from her chair. She seems faint; looks about her with an expression of almost panic.*)

Blanche. Stella! What have you heard about me?

Stella. Huh?

Blanche. What have people been telling you about me?

Stella. Telling?

Blanche. You haven't heard any — unkind — gossip about me?

Stella. Why, no, Blanche, of course not!

Blanche. Honey, there was — a good deal of talk in Laurel.

Stella. About *you*, Blanche?

Blanche. I wasn't so good the last two years or so, after Belle Reve had started to slip through my fingers.

Stella. All of us do things we —

Blanche. I never was hard or self-sufficient enough. When people are soft — soft people have got to shimmer and glow — they've got to put on soft colors, the colors of butterfly wings, and put a — paper lantern over the light. . . . It isn't enough to be soft. You've got to be soft *and attractive*. And I — I'm fading now! I don't know how much longer I can turn the trick.

(*The afternoon has faded to dusk. Stella goes into the bedroom and turns on the light under the paper lantern. She holds a bottled soft drink in her hand.*)

Blanche. Have you been listening to me?

Stella. I don't listen to you when you are being morbid! (*She advances with the bottled coke.*)

Blanche (*with abrupt change to gaiety*). Is that coke for me?

Stella. Not for anyone else! ˙

Blanche. Why, you precious thing, you! Is it just coke?

Stella (*turning*). You mean you want a shot in it!

Blanche. Well, honey, a shot never does a coke any harm! Let me! you mustn't wait on me!

Stella. I like to wait on you, Blanche. It makes it seem more like home. (*She goes into the kitchen, finds a glass and pours a shot of whiskey into it.*)

Blanche. I have to admit I love to be waited on . . .

(*She rushes into the bedroom. Stella goes to her with the glass. Blanche suddenly clutches Stella's free hand with a moaning sound*) *and presses the hand to her lips. Stella is embarrassed by her show of emotion. Blanche speaks in a choked voice.*)

You're — you're — so *good* to me! And I —
Stella. Blanche.
Blanche. I know, I won't! You hate me to talk sentimental! But honey, *believe* I feel things more than I *tell* you! I *won't* stay long! I won't, I *promise* I —
Stella. Blanche!
Blanche (*hysterically*). I won't, I promise, *I'll* go; Go *soon!* I will *really!* I won't hang around until he — throws me out . . .
Stella. Now will you stop talking foolish?
Blanche. Yes, honey. Watch how you pour — that fizzy stuff foams over!

(*Blanche laughs shrilly and grabs the glass, but her hand shakes so it almost slips from her grasp. Stella pours the coke into the glass. It foams over and spills. Blanche gives a piercing cry.*)

Stella (*shocked by the cry*). Heavens!
Blanche. Right on my pretty white skirt!
Stella. Oh . . . Use my hanky. Blot gently.
Blanche (*slowly recovering*). I know — gently — gently . . .
Stella. Did it stain?
Blanche. Not a bit. Ha-ha! Isn't that lucky? (*She sits down shaking, taking a grateful drink. She holds the glass in both hands and continues to laugh a little.*)
Stella. Why did you scream like that?
Blanche. I don't know why I screamed! (*continuing nervously*) Mitch — Mitch is coming at seven. I guess I am just feeling nervous about our relations. (*She begins to talk rapidly and breathlessly*) He hasn't gotten a thing but a goodnight kiss, that's all I have given him, Stella. I want his respect. And men don't want anything they get too easy. But on the other hand men lose interest quickly. Especially when the girl is over — thirty. They think a girl over thirty ought to — the vulgar term is — "put out." . . . And I — I'm not "putting out." Of course he — he doesn't know — I mean I haven't informed him — of my real age!
Stella. Why are you sensitive about your age?
Blanche. Because of hard knocks my vanity's been given. What I mean is — he thinks I'm sort of — prim and proper, you know! (*She laughs out sharply*) I want to *deceive* him enough to make him — want me . . .
Stella. Blanche, do you want *him?*

Blanche. I want to *rest!* I want to breathe quietly again! Yes — I *want* Mitch . . . *very badly!* Just think! If it happens! I can leave here and not be anyone's problem . . .

(*Stanley comes around the corner with a drink under his belt.*)

Stanley (*bawling*). Hey, Steve! Hey, Eunice! Hey, Stella!

(*There are joyous calls from above. Trumpet and drums are heard from around the corner.*)

Stella (*kissing Blanche impulsively*). It *will* happen!
Blanche (*doubtfully*). It will?
Stella. It *will!* (*She goes across into the kitchen, looking back at Blanche.*) It will, honey, *it will.* . . . But don't take another drink! (*Her voice catches as she goes out the door to meet her husband.*)

(*Blanche sinks faintly back in her chair with her drink. Eunice shrieks with laughter and runs down the steps. Steve bounds after her with goat-like screeches and chases her around corner. Stanley and Stella twine arms as they follow, laughing.*)

(*Dusk settles deeper. The music from the Four Deuces is slow and blue.*)

Blanche. Ah, me, ah, me, ah, me . . .

(*Her eyes fall shut and the palm leaf fan drops from her fingers. She slaps her hand on the chair arm a couple of times. There is a little glimmer of lightning about the building.*)

(*A Young Man comes along the street and rings the bell.*)

Blanche. Come in.

(*The Young Man appears through the portieres. She regards him with interest.*)

Blanche. Well, well! What can I do for *you?*
Young Man. I'm collecting for *The Evening Star.*
Blanche. I didn't know that stars took up collections.
Young Man. It's the paper.
Blanche. I know. I was joking — feebly! Will you — have a drink?
Young Man. No, ma'am. No, thank you. I can't drink on the job.
Blanche. Oh, well, now, let's see. . . . No, I don't have a dime! I'm not the lady of the house. I'm her sister from Mississippi. I'm one of those poor relations you've heard about.
Young Man. That's all right. I'll drop by later. (*He starts to go out. She approaches a little.*)

Blanche. Hey! (*He turns back shyly. She puts a cigarette in a long holder*) Could you give me a light? (*She crosses toward him. They meet at the door between the two rooms.*)

Young Man. Sure. (*He takes out a lighter*) This doesn't always work.

Blanche. It's temperamental? (*It flares*) Ah! — thank you. (*He starts away again*) Hey! (*He turns again, still more uncertainly. She goes close to him.*) Uh — what time is it?

Young Man. Fifteen of seven, ma'am.

Blanche. So late? Don't you just love these long rainy afternoons in New Orleans when an hour isn't just an hour — but a little piece of eternity dropped into your hands — and who knows what to do with it? (*She touches his shoulders.*) You — uh — didn't get wet in the rain?

Young Man. No, ma'am. I stepped inside.

Blanche. In a drug store? And had a soda?

Young Man. Uh-huh.

Blanche. Chocolate?

Young Man. No, ma'am. Cherry.

Blanche (*laughing*). Cherry!

Young Man. A cherry soda.

Blanche. You make my mouth water. (*She touches his cheek lightly, and smiles. Then she goes to the trunk.*)

Young Man. Well, I'd better be going —

Blanche (*stopping him*). Young man!

(*He turns. She takes a large, gossamer scarf from the trunk and drapes it about her shoulders.*)

(*In the ensuing pause, the "blue piano" is heard. It continues through the rest of this scene and the opening of the next. The young man clears his throat and looks yearningly at the door.*)

Young man! Young, young, young man! Has anyone ever told you that you look like a young Prince out of the Arabian Nights?

(*The Young Man laughs uncomfortably and stands like a bashful kid. Blanche speaks softly to him.*)

Well, you do, honey lamb! Come here. I want to kiss you, just once, softly and sweetly on your mouth!

(*Without waiting for him to accept, she crosses quickly to him and presses her lips to his.*)

Now run along, now, quickly! It would be nice to keep you, but I've got to be good — and keep my hands off children.

(*He stares at her a moment. She opens the door for him and blows a kiss at him as he goes down the steps with a dazed look. She stands there a little dreamily after he has disappeared. Then Mitch appears around the corner with a bunch of roses.*)

Blanche (*gaily*). Look who's coming! My Rosenkavalier! Bow to me first . . . now present them! *Ahhh — Merciiii!*

(*She looks at him over them, coquettishly pressing them to her lips. He beams at her selfconsciously.*)

SCENE SIX

It is about two A.M. *on the same evening. The outer wall of the building is visible. Blanche and Mitch come in. The utter exhaustion which only a neurasthenic personality can know is evident in Blanche's voice and manner. Mitch is stolid but depressed. They have probably been out to the amusement park on Lake Pontchartrain, for Mitch is bearing, upside down, a plaster statuette of Mae West, the sort of prize won at shooting-galleries and carnival games of chance.*

Blanche (*stopping lifelessly at the steps*). Well — (*Mitch laughs uneasily.*) Well . . .
Mitch. I guess it must be pretty late — and you're tired.
Blanche. Even the hot tamale man has deserted the street, and he hangs on till the end. (*Mitch laughs uneasily again*) How will you get home?
Mitch. I'll walk over to Bourbon and catch an owl-car.
Blanche (*laughing grimly*). Is that streetcar named Desire still grinding along the tracks at this hour?
Mitch (*heavily*). I'm afraid you haven't gotten much fun out of this evening, Blanche.
Blanche. I spoiled it for *you.*
Mitch. No, you didn't, but I felt all the time that I wasn't giving you much — entertainment.
Blanche. I simply couldn't rise to the occasion. That was all. I don't think I've ever tried so hard to be gay and made such a dismal mess of it. I get ten points for trying! — I *did* try.
Mitch. Why did you try if you didn't feel like it, Blanche?
Blanche. I was obeying the law of nature.
Mitch. Which law is that?

Blanche. The one that says the lady must entertain the gentleman —
or no dice! See if you can locate my door-key in this purse. When
I'm so tired my fingers are all thumbs!

Mitch (*rooting in her purse*). This it?

Blanche. No, honey, that's the key to my trunk which I must soon be
packing.

Mitch. You mean you are leaving here soon?

Blanche. I've outstayed my welcome.

Mitch. This it?

(*The music fades away.*)

Blanche. Eureka! Honey, you open the door while I take a last look
at the sky. (*She leans on the porch rail. He opens the door and
stands awkwardly behind her.*) I'm looking for the Pleiades, the
Seven Sisters, but these girls are not out tonight. Oh, yes they are,
there they are! God bless them! All in a bunch going home from
their little bridge party. . . . Y'get the door open? Good boy! I guess
you — want to go now . . .

(*He shuffles and coughs a little.*)

Mitch. Can I — uh — kiss you — goodnight?

Blanche. Why do you always ask me if you may?

Mitch. I don't know whether you want me to or not.

Blanche. Why should you be so doubtful?

Mitch. That night when we parked by the lake and I kissed you,
you —

Blanche. Honey, it wasn't the kiss I objected to. I liked the kiss very
much. It was the other little — familiarity — that I — felt obliged
to — discourage. . . . I didn't resent it! Not a bit in the world! In
fact, I was somewhat flattered that you — desired me! But, honey,
you know as well as I do that a single girl, a girl alone in the world,
has got to keep a firm hold on her emotions or she'll be lost!

Mitch (*solemnly*). Lost?

Blanche. I guess you are used to girls that like to be lost. The kind that
get lost immediately, on the first date!

Mitch. I like you to be exactly the way that you are, because in all
my — experience — I have never known anyone like you.

(*Blanche looks at him gravely; then she bursts into laughter and
then claps a hand to her mouth.*)

Mitch. Are you laughing at me?

Blanche. No, honey. The lord and lady of the house have not yet

returned, so come in. We'll have a night-cap. Let's leave the lights
off. Shall we?

Mitch. You just — do what you want to.

(*Blanche precedes him into the kitchen. The outer wall of the building disappears and the interiors of the two rooms can be dimly
seen.*)

Blanche (*remaining in the first room*). The other room's more comfortable — go on in. This crashing around in the dark is my search
for some liquor.

Mitch. You want a drink?

Blanche. I want *you* to have a drink! You have been so anxious and
solemn all evening, and so have I; we have both been anxious and
solemn and now for these few last remaining moments of our lives
together — I want to create — *joie de vivre!* I'm lighting a candle.

Mitch. That's good.

Blanche. We are going to be very Bohemian. We are going to pretend
that we are sitting in a little artists' cafe on the Left Bank in Paris!
(*She lights a candle stub and puts it in a bottle.*) *Je suis la Dame
aux Camélias! Vous êtes* — Armand! Understand French?

Mitch (*heavily*). Naw. Naw, I —

*Blanche. Voulez-vous coucher avec moi ce soir? Vous ne comprenez
pas? Ah, quel dommage!* — I mean it's a damned good thing. . . .
I've found some liquor! Just enough for two shots without any dividends, honey . . .

Mitch (*heavily*). That's — good.

(*She enters the bedroom with the drinks and the candle.*)

Blanche. Sit down! Why don't you take off your coat and loosen your
collar?

Mitch. I better leave it on.

Blanche. No. I want you to be comfortable.

Mitch. I am ashamed of the way I perspire. My shirt is sticking to me.

Blanche. Perspiration is healthy. If people didn't perspire they would
die in five minutes. (*She takes his coat from him*) This is a nice
coat. What kind of material is it?

Mitch. They call that stuff alpaca.

Blanche. Oh. Alpaca.

Mitch. It's very light weight alpaca.

Blanche. Oh. Light weight alpaca.

Mitch. I don't like to wear a wash-coat even in summer because I
sweat through it.

Blanche. Oh.

Mitch. And it don't look neat on me. A man with a heavy build has got to be careful of what he puts on him so he don't look too clumsy.

Blanche. You are not too heavy.

Mitch. You don't think I am?

Blanche. You are not the delicate type. You have a massive bone-structure and a very imposing physique.

Mitch. Thank you. Last Christmas I was given a membership to the New Orleans Athletic Club.

Blanche. Oh, good.

Mitch. It was the finest present I ever was given. I work out there with the weights and I swim and I keep myself fit. When I started there, I was getting soft in the belly but now my belly is hard. It is so hard now that a man can punch me in the belly and it don't hurt me. Punch me! Go on! See?

(*She pokes lightly at him.*)

Blanche. Gracious. (*Her hand touches her chest.*)

Mitch. Guess how much I weigh, Blanche?

Blanche. Oh, I'd say in the vicinity of — one hundred and eighty?

Mitch. Guess again.

Blanche. Not that much?

Mitch. No. More.

Blanche. Well, you're a tall man and you can carry a good deal of weight without looking awkward.

Mitch. I weigh two hundred and seven pounds and I'm six feet one and one half inches tall in my bare feet — without shoes on. And that is what I weigh stripped.

Blanche. Oh, my goodness, me! It's awe-inspiring.

Mitch (*embarrassed*). My weight is not a very interesting subject to talk about. (*He hesitates for a moment*) What's yours?

Blanche. My weight?

Mitch. Yes.

Blanche. Guess!

Mitch. Let me lift you.

Blanche. Samson! Go on, lift me. (*He comes behind her and puts his hands on her waist and raises her lightly off the ground*) Well?

Mitch. You are light as a feather.

Blanche. Ha-ha! (*He lowers her but keeps his hands on her waist. Blanche speaks with an affectation of demureness.*) You may release me now.

Mitch. Huh?

Blanche (*gaily*). I said unhand me, sir. (*He fumblingly embraces her.*

Her voice sounds gently reproving.) Now, Mitch. Just because Stanley and Stella aren't at home is no reason why you shouldn't behave like a gentleman.

Mitch. Just give me a slap whenever I step out of bounds.

Blanche. That won't be necessary. You're a natural gentleman, one of the very few that are left in the world. I don't want you to think that I am severe and old maid schoolteacherish or anything like that. It's just — well —

Mitch. Huh?

Blanche. I guess it is just that I have — old-fashioned ideals! (*She rolls her eyes, knowing he cannot see her face. Mitch goes to the front door. There is a considerable silence between them. Blanche sighs and Mitch coughs selfconsciously.*)

Mitch (*finally*). Where's Stanley and Stella tonight?

Blanche. They have gone out. With Mr. and Mrs. Hubbell upstairs.

Mitch. Where did they go?

Blanche. I think they were planning to go to a midnight prevue at Loew's State.

Mitch. We should all go out together some night.

Blanche. No. That wouldn't be a good plan.

Mitch. Why not?

Blanche. You are an old friend of Stanley's?

Mitch. We was together in the Two-forty-first.

Blanche. I guess he talks to you frankly?

Mitch. Sure.

Blanche. Has he talked to you about me?

Mitch. Oh — not very much.

Blanche. The way you say that, I suspect that he has.

Mitch. No, he hasn't said much.

Blanche. But what he *has* said. What would you say his attitude toward me was?

Mitch. Why do you want to ask that?

Blanche. Well —

Mitch. Don't you get along with him?

Blanche. What do you think?

Mitch. I don't think he understands you.

Blanche. That is putting it mildly. If it weren't for Stella about to have a baby, I wouldn't be able to endure things here.

Mitch. He isn't — nice to you?

Blanche. He is insufferably rude. Goes out of his way to offend me.

Mitch. In what way, Blanche?

Blanche. Why, in every conceivable way.

Mitch. I'm surprised to hear that.

Blanche. Are you?

Mitch. Well, I — don't see how anybody could be rude to you.

Blanche. It's really a pretty frightful situation. You see, there's no privacy here. There's just these portieres between the two rooms at night. He stalks through the rooms in his underwear at night. And I have to ask him to close the bathroom door. That sort of commonness isn't necessary. You probably wonder why I don't move out. Well, I'll tell you frankly. A teacher's salary is barely sufficient for her living-expenses. I didn't save a penny last year and so I had to come here for the summer. That's why I have to put up with my sister's husband. And he has to put up with me, apparently so much against his wishes. . . . Surely he must have told you how much he hates me!

Mitch. I don't think he hates you.

Blanche. He hates me. Or why would he insult me? The first time I laid eyes on him I thought to myself, that man is my executioner! That man will destroy me, unless —

Mitch. Blanche —

Blanche. Yes, honey?

Mitch. Can I ask you a question?

Blanche. Yes. What?

Mitch. How old are you?

(*She makes a nervous gesture.*)

Blanche. Why do you want to know?

Mitch. I talked to my mother about you and she said, "How old is Blanche?" And I wasn't able to tell her. (*There is another pause.*)

Blanche. You talked to your mother about me?

Mitch. Yes.

Blanche. Why?

Mitch. I told my mother how nice you were, and I liked you.

Blanche. Were you sincere about that?

Mitch. You know I was.

Blanche. Why did your mother want to know my age?

Mitch. Mother is sick.

Blanche. I'm sorry to hear it. Badly?

Mitch. She won't live long. Maybe just a few months.

Blanche. Oh.

Mitch. She worries because I'm not settled.

Blanche. Oh.

Mitch. She wants me to be settled down before she — (*His voice is hoarse and he clears his throat twice, shuffling nervously around with his hands in and out of his pockets.*)

Blanche. You love her very much, don't you?

Mitch. Yes.

Blanche. I think you have a great capacity for devotion. You will be lonely when she passes on, won't you? (*Mitch clears his throat and nods.*) I understand what that is.

Mitch. To be lonely?

Blanche. I loved someone, too, and the person I loved I lost.

Mitch. Dead? (*She crosses to the window and sits on the sill, looking out. She pours herself another drink.*) A man?

Blanche. He was a boy, just a boy, when I was a very young girl. When I was sixteen, I made the discovery — love. All at once and much, much too completely. It was like you suddenly turned a blinding light on something that had always been half in shadow, that's how it struck the world for me. But I was unlucky. Deluded. There was something different about the boy, a nervousness, a softness and tenderness which wasn't like a man's, although he wasn't the least bit effeminate looking — still — that thing was there. . . . He came to me for help. I didn't know that. I didn't find out anything till after our marriage when we'd run away and come back and all I knew was I'd failed him in some mysterious way and wasn't able to give the help he needed but couldn't speak of! He was in the quicksands and clutching at me — but I wasn't holding him out, I was slipping in with him! I didn't know that. I didn't know any-thing except I loved him unendurably but without being able to help him or help myself. Then I found out. In the worst of all possible ways. By coming suddenly into a room that I thought was empty — which wasn't empty, but had two people in it . . . the boy I had married and an older man who had been his friend for years. . . .

(*A locomotive is heard approaching outside. She claps her hands to her ears and crouches over. The headlight of the locomotive glares into the room as it thunders past. As the noise recedes she straightens slowly and continues speaking.*)

Afterwards we pretended that nothing had been discovered. Yes, the three of us drove out to Moon Lake Casino, very drunk and laughing all the way.

(*Polka music sounds, in a minor key faint with distance.*)

We danced the Varsouviana! Suddenly in the middle of the dance the boy I had married broke away from me and ran out of the casino. A few moments later — a shot!

(*The Polka stops abruptly.*)

(*Blanche rises stiffly. Then, the Polka resumes in a major key.*)

I ran out — all did! — all ran and gathered about the terrible thing at the edge of the lake! I couldn't get near for the crowding. Then somebody caught my arm. "Don't go any closer! Come back! You don't want to see!" See? See what! Then I heard voices say — Allan! Allan! The Grey boy! He'd stuck the revolver into his mouth, and fired — so that the back of his head had been — blown away!

(*She sways and covers her face.*)

It was because — on the dance-floor — unable to stop myself — I'd said — "I saw! I know! You disgust me . . ." And then the searchlight which had been turned on the world was turned off again and never for one moment since has there been any light that's stronger than this — kitchen — candle . . .

(*Mitch gets up awkwardly and moves toward her a little. The Polka music increases. Mitch stands beside her.*)

Mitch (*drawing her slowly into his arms*). You need somebody. And I need somebody, too. Could it be — you and me, Blanche?

(*She stares at him vacantly for a moment. Then with a soft cry huddles in his embrace. She makes a sobbing effort to speak but the words won't come. He kisses her forehead and her eyes and finally her lips. The Polka tune fades out. Her breath is drawn and released in long, grateful sobs.*)

Blanche. Sometimes — there's God — so quickly!

SCENE SEVEN

It is late afternoon in mid-September.

The portieres are open and a table is set for a birthday supper, with cake and flowers.

Stella is completing the decorations as Stanley comes in.

Stanley. What's all this stuff for?
Stella. Honey, it's Blanche's birthday.
Stanley. She here?
Stella. In the bathroom.
Stanley (*mimicking*). "Washing out some things"?
Stella. I reckon so.
Stanley. How long she been in there?

Stella. All afternoon.

Stanley (*mimicking*). "Soaking in a hot tub"?

Stella. Yes.

Stanley. Temperature 100 on the nose, and she soaks herself in a hot tub.

Stella. She says it cools her off for the evening.

Stanley. And you run out an' get her cokes, I suppose? And serve 'em to Her Majesty in the tub? (*Stella shrugs*) Set down here a minute.

Stella. Stanley, I've got things to do.

Stanley. Set down! I've got th' dope on your big sister, Stella.

Stella. Stanley, stop picking on Blanche.

Stanley. That girl calls *me* common!

Stella. Lately you been doing all you can think of to rub her the wrong way, Stanley, and Blanche is sensitive and you've got to realize that Blanche and I grew up under very different circumstances than you did.

Stanley. So I been told. And told and told and told! You know she's been feeding us a pack of lies here?

Stella. No, I don't, and —

Stanley. Well, she has, however. But now the cat's out of the bag! I found out some things!

Stella. What — things?

Stanley. Things I already suspected. But now I got proof from the most reliable sources — which I have checked on!

(*Blanche is singing in the bathroom a saccharine popular ballad which is used contrapuntally with Stanley's speech.*)

Stella (*to Stanley*). Lower your voice!

Stanley. Some canary-bird, huh!

Stella. Now please tell me quietly what you think you've found out about my sister.

Stanley. Lie Number One: All this squeamishness she puts on! You should just know the line she's been feeding to Mitch. He thought she had never been more than kissed by a fellow! But Sister Blanche is no lily! Ha-ha! Some lily she is!

Stella. What have you heard and who from?

Stanley. Our supply-man down at the plant has been going through Laurel for years and he knows all about her and everybody else in the town of Laurel knows all about her. She is as famous in Laurel as if she was the President of the United States, only she is not respected by any party! This supply-man stops at a hotel called the Flamingo.

Blanche (*singing blithely*). "Say, it's only a paper moon, Sailing over a cardboard sea — But it wouldn't be make-believe If you believed in me!"

Stella. What about the — Flamingo?

Stanley. She stayed there, too.

Stella. My sister lived at Belle Reve.

Stanley. This is after the home-place had slipped through her lily-white fingers! She moved to the Flamingo! A second-class hotel which has the advantage of not interfering in the private social life of the personalities there! The Flamingo is used to all kinds of goings-on. But even the management of the Flamingo was impressed by Dame Blanche! In fact they was so impressed by Dame Blanche that they requested her to turn in her room-key — for permanently! This happened a couple of weeks before she showed here.

Blanche (*singing*). "It's a Barnum and Bailey world, Just as phony as it can be — But it wouldn't be make-believe If you believed in me!"

Stella. What — contemptible — lies!

Stanley. Sure, I can see how you would be upset by this. She pulled the wool over your eyes as much as Mitch's!

Stella. It's pure invention! There's not a word of truth in it and if I were a man and this creature had dared to invent such things in my presence —

Blanche (*singing*). "Without your love, It's a honky-tonk parade! Without your love, It's a melody played In a penny arcade . . ."

Stanley. Honey, I told you I thoroughly checked on these stories! Now wait till I finished. The trouble with Dame Blanche was that she couldn't put on her act any more in Laurel! They got wised up after two or three dates with her and then they quit, and she goes on to another, the same old line, same old act, same old hooey! But the town was too small for this to go on forever! And as time went by she became a town character. Regarded as not just different but downright loco — nuts. (*Stella draws back.*) And for the last year or two she has been washed up like poison. That's why she's here this summer, visiting royalty, putting on all this act — because she's practically told by the mayor to get out of town! Yes, did you know there was an army camp near Laurel and your sister's was one of the places called "Out-of-Bounds"?

Blanche. "It's only a paper moon, Just as phony as it can be — But it wouldn't be make-believe If you believed in me!"

Stanley. Well, so much for her being such a refined and particular type of girl. Which brings us to Lie Number Two.

Stella. I don't want to hear any more!

Stanley. She's not going back to teach school! In fact I am willing to bet you that she never had no idea of returning to Laurel! She didn't resign temporarily from the high school because of her nerves! No, siree, Bob! She didn't. They kicked her out of that high school before the spring term ended — and I hate to tell you the reason that step was taken! A seventeen-year-old boy — she'd gotten mixed up with!

Blanche. "It's a Barnum and Bailey world, Just as phony as it can be —"

(*In the bathroom the water goes on loud; little breathless cries and peals of laughter are heard as if a child were frolicking in the tub.*)

Stella. This is making me — sick!

Stanley. The boy's dad learned about it and got in touch with the high school superintendent. Boy, oh, boy, I'd like to have been in that office when Dame Blanche was called on the carpet! I'd like to have seen her trying to squirm out of that one! But they had her on the hook good and proper that time and she knew that the jig was all up! They told her she better move on to some fresh territory. Yep, it was practickly a town ordinance passed against her!

(*The bathroom door is opened and Blanche thrusts her head out, holding a towel about her hair.*)

Blanche. Stella!

Stella (*faintly*). Yes, Blanche?

Blanche. Give me another bath-towel to dry my hair with. I've just washed it.

Stella. Yes, Blanche. (*She crosses in a dazed way from the kitchen to the bathroom door with a towel.*)

Blanche. What's the matter, honey?

Stella. Matter? Why?

Blanche. You have such a strange expression on your face!

Stella. Oh — (*She tries to laugh*) I guess I'm a little tired!

Blanche. Why don't you bathe, too, soon as I get out?

Stanley (*calling from the kitchen*). How soon is that going to be?

Blanche. Not so terribly long! Possess your soul in patience!

Stanley. It's not my soul, it's my kidneys I'm worried about!

(*Blanche slams the door. Stanley laughs harshly. Stella comes slowly back into the kitchen.*)

Stanley. Well, what do you think of it?

Stella. I don't believe all of those stories and I think your supply-man was mean and rotten to tell them. It's possible that some of the things he said are partly true. There are things about my sister I don't approve of — things that caused sorrow at home. She was always — flighty!

Stanley. Flighty!

Stella. But when she was young, very young, she married a boy who wrote poetry. . . . He was extremely good-looking. I think Blanche didn't just love him but worshipped the ground he walked on! Adored him and thought him almost too fine to be human! But then she found out —

Stanley. What?

Stella. This beautiful and talented young man was a degenerate. Didn't your supply-man give you that information?

Stanley. All we discussed was recent history. That must have been a pretty long time ago.

Stella. Yes, it was — a pretty long time ago . . .

(*Stanley comes up and takes her by the shoulders rather gently. She gently withdraws from him. Automatically she starts sticking little pink candles in the birthday cake.*)

Stanley. How many candles you putting in that cake?

Stella. I'll stop at twenty-five.

Stanley. Is company expected?

Stella. We asked Mitch to come over for cake and ice-cream.

(*Stanley looks a little uncomfortable. He lights a cigarette from the one he has just finished.*)

Stanley. I wouldn't be expecting Mitch over tonight.

(*Stella pauses in her occupation with candles and looks slowly around at Stanley.*)

Stella. Why?

Stanley. Mitch is a buddy of mine. We were in the same outfit together — Two-forty-first Engineers. We work in the same plant and now on the same bowling team. You think I could face him if —

Stella. Stanley Kowalski, did you — did you repeat what that — ?

Stanley. You're goddam right I told him! I'd have that on my conscience the rest of my life if I know all that stuff and let my best friend get caught!

Stella. Is Mitch through with her?

Stanley. Wouldn't you be if — ?

Stella. I said, *Is Mitch through with her?*

(*Blanche's voice is lifted again, serenely as a bell. She sings, "But it wouldn't be make-believe if you believed in me."*)

Stanley. No, I don't think he's necessarily through with her — just wised up!

Stella. Stanley, she thought Mitch was — going to — going to marry her. I was hoping so, too.

Stanley. Well, he's not going to marry her. Maybe he *was*, but he's not going to jump in a tank with a school of sharks — now! (*He rises*) Blanche! Oh, Blanche! Can I please get in my bathroom?

(*There is a pause.*)

Blanche. Yes, indeed, sir! Can you wait one second while I dry?

Stanley. Having waited one hour I guess one second ought to pass in a hurry.

Stella. And she hasn't got her job? Well, what will she do!

Stanley. She's not stayin' here after Tuesday. You know that, don't you? Just to make sure I bought her ticket myself. A bus-ticket!

Stella. In the first place, Blanche wouldn't go on a bus.

Stanley. She'll go on a bus and like it.

Stella. No, she won't, no, she won't, Stanley!

Stanley. *She'll go!* Period. P.S. She'll go *Tuesday!*

Stella (*slowly*). What'll — she — do? What on earth will she — *do!*

Stanley. Her future is mapped out for her.

Stella. What do you mean?

(*Blanche sings.*)

Stanley. Hey, canary bird! Toots! Get OUT of the BATHROOM!

(*The bathroom door flies open and Blanche emerges with a gay peal of laughter, but as Stanley crosses past her, a frightened look appears on her face, almost a look of panic. He doesn't look at her but slams the bathroom door shut as he goes in.*)

Blanche (*snatching up a hair-brush*). Oh, I feel so good after my long, hot bath, I feel so good and cool and — rested!

Stella (*sadly and doubtfully from the kitchen*). Do you, Blanche?

Blanche (*brushing her hair vigorously*). Yes, I do, so refreshed! (*She tinkles her highball glass.*) A hot bath and a long, cold drink always give me a brand new outlook on life! (*She looks through the portieres at Stella, standing between them, and slowly stops brushing*) Something has happened! — What is it?

Stella (*turning away quickly*). Why, nothing has happened, Blanche.

Blanche. You're lying! Something has!

(*She stares fearfully at Stella, who pretends to be busy at the table. The distant piano goes into a hectic breakdown.*)

SCENE EIGHT

Three-quarters of an hour later.

The view through the big windows is fading gradually into a still-golden dusk. A torch of sunlight blazes on the side of a big water-tank or oil-drum across the empty lot toward the business district which is now pierced by pin-points of lighted windows or windows reflecting the sunset.

The three people are completing a dismal birthday supper. Stanley looks sullen. Stella is embarrassed and sad.

Blanche has a tight, artificial smile on her drawn face. There is a fourth place at the table which is left vacant.

Blanche (suddenly). Stanley, tell us a joke, tell us a funny story to make us all laugh. I don't know what's the matter, we're all so solemn. Is it because I've been stood up by my beau?

(Stella laughs feebly.)

It's the first time in my entire experience with men, and I've had a good deal of all sorts, that I've actually been stood up by anybody! Ha-ha! I don't know how to take it. . . . Tell us a funny little story, Stanley! Something to help us out.

Stanley. I didn't think you liked my stories, Blanche.

Blanche. I like them when they're amusing but not indecent.

Stanley. I don't know any refined enough for your taste.

Blanche. Then let me tell one.

Stella. Yes, you tell one, Blanche. You used to know lots of good stories.

(The music fades.)

Blanche. Let me see, now. . . . I must run through my repertoire! Oh, yes — I love parrot stories! Do you all like parrot stories? Well, this one's about the old maid and the parrot. This old maid, she had a parrot that cursed a blue streak and knew more vulgar expressions than Mr. Kowalski!

Stanley. Huh.

Blanche. And the only way to hush the parrot up was to put the cover back on its cage so it would think it was night and go back to sleep. Well, one morning the old maid had just uncovered the parrot for the day — when who should she see coming up the front walk but the preacher! Well, she rushed back to the parrot and slipped the cover back on the cage and then she let in the preacher. And the parrot was perfectly still, just as quiet as a mouse, but just as she was asking the preacher how much sugar he wanted in his coffee — the parrot broke the silence with a loud — (*She whistles*) — and said — "God *damn*, but that was a short day!"

(*She throws back her head and laughs, Stella also makes an ineffectual effort to seem amused. Stanley pays no attention to the story but reaches way over the table to spear his fork into the remaining chop which he eats with his fingers.*)

Blanche. Apparently Mr. Kowalski was not amused.
Stella. Mr. Kowalski is too busy making a pig of himself to think of anything else!
Stanley. That's right, baby.
Stella. Your face and your fingers are disgustingly greasy. Go and wash up and then help me clear the table.

(*He hurls a plate to the floor.*)

Stanley. That's how I'll clear the table! (*He seizes her arm*) Don't ever talk that way to me! "Pig — Polack — disgusting — vulgar — greasy!" — them kind of words have been on your tongue and your sister's too much around here! What do you two think you are? A pair of queens? Remember what Huey Long said — "Every Man is a King!" And I am the king around here, so don't forget it! (*He hurls a cup and saucer to the floor*) My place is cleared! You want me to clear your places?

(*Stella begins to cry weakly. Stanley stalks out on the porch and lights a cigarette.*)

(*The Negro entertainers around the corner are heard.*)

Blanche. What happened while I was bathing? What did he tell you, Stella?
Stella. Nothing, nothing, nothing!
Blanche. I think he told you something about Mitch and me! You know why Mitch didn't come but you won't tell me! (*Stella shakes her head helplessly*) I'm going to call him!
Stella. I wouldn't call him, Blanche.
Blanche. I am, I'm going to call him on the phone.
Stella (*miserably*). I wish you wouldn't.
Blanche. I intend to be given some explanation from someone!

(*She rushes to the phone in the bedroom. Stella goes out on the porch and stares reproachfully at her husband. He grunts and turns away from her.*)

Stella. I hope you're pleased with your doings. I never had so much trouble swallowing food in my life, looking at that girl's face and the empty chair! (*She cries quietly.*)

Blanche (*at the phone*). Hello. Mr. Mitchell, please. . . . Oh. . . . I would like to leave a number if I may. Magnolia 9047. And say it's important to call. . . . Yes, very important. . . . Thank you.

(*She remains by the phone with a lost, frightened look.*)

(*Stanley turns slowly back toward his wife and takes her clumsily in his arms.*)

Stanley. Stell, it's gonna be all right after she goes and after you've had the baby. It's gonna be all right again between you and me the way that it was. You remember that way that it was? Them nights we had together? God, honey, it's gonna be sweet when we can make noise in the night the way that we used to and get the colored lights going with nobody's sister behind the curtains to hear us!

(*Their upstairs neighbors are heard in bellowing laughter at something. Stanley chuckles.*)

Steve an' Eunice . . .

Stella. Come on back in. (*She returns to the kitchen and starts lighting the candles on the white cake.*) Blanche?

Blanche. Yes. (*She returns from the bedroom to the table in the kitchen.*) Oh, those pretty, pretty little candles! Oh, don't burn them, Stella.

Stella. I certainly will.

(*Stanley comes back in.*)

Blanche. You ought to save them for baby's birthdays. Oh, I hope candles are going to glow in his life and I hope that his eyes are going to be like candles, like two blue candles lighted in a white cake!

Stanley (*sitting down*). What poetry!

Blanche (*she pauses reflectively for a moment*). I shouldn't have called him.

Stella. There's lots of things could have happened.

Blanche. There's no excuse for it, Stella. I don't have to put up with insults. I won't be taken for granted.

Stanley. Goddamn, it's hot in here with the steam from the bathroom.

Blanche. I've said I was sorry three times. (*The piano fades out.*) I take hot baths for my nerves. Hydro-therapy, they call it. You healthy Polack, without a nerve in your body, of course you don't know what anxiety feels like!

Stanley. I am not a Polack. People from Poland are Poles, not Polacks. But what I am is a one hundred percent American, born and raised in the greatest country on earth and proud as hell of it, so don't ever call me a Polack.

(*The phone rings. Blanche rises expectantly.*)

Blanche. Oh, that's for me, I'm sure.

Stanley. I'm not sure. Keep your seat. (*He crosses leisurely to phone.*) H'lo. Aw, yeh, hello, Mac.

(*He leans against wall, staring insultingly in at Blanche. She sinks back in her chair with a frightened look. Stella leans over and touches her shoulder.*)

Blanche. Oh, keep your hands off me, Stella. What is the matter with you? Why do you look at me with that pitying look?

Stanley (*bawling*). QUIET IN THERE! — We've got a noisy woman on the place. — Go on, Mac. At Riley's? No, I don't wanta bowl at Riley's. I had a little trouble with Riley last week. I'm the team-captain, ain't I? All right, then, we're not gonna bowl at Riley's, we're gonna bowl at the West Side or the Gala! All right, Mac. See you!

(*He hangs up and returns to the table. Blanche fiercely controls herself, drinking quickly from her tumbler of water. He doesn't look at her but reaches in a pocket. Then he speaks slowly and with false amiability.*)

Sister Blanche, I've got a little birthday remembrance for you.

Blanche. Oh, have you, Stanley? I wasn't expecting any, I — I don't know why Stella wants to observe my birthday! I'd much rather forget it — when you — reach twenty-seven! Well — age is a subject that you'd prefer to — ignore!

Stanley. Twenty-seven?

Blanche (*quickly*). What is it? Is it for *me*?

(*He is holding a little envelope toward her.*)

Stanley. Yes, I hope you like it!

Blanche. Why, why — Why, it's a —

Stanley. Ticket! Back to Laurel! On the Greyhound! Tuesday!

(*The Varsouviana music steals in softly and continues playing. Stella rises abruptly and turns her back. Blanche tries to smile. Then she tries to laugh. Then she gives both up and springs from the table and runs into the next room. She clutches her throat and then runs into the bathroom. Coughing, gagging sounds are heard.*)

Well!

Stella. You didn't need to do that.

Stanley. Don't forget all that I took off her.

Stella. You needn't have been so cruel to someone alone as she is.

Stanley. Delicate piece she is.

Stella. She is. She was. You didn't know Blanche as a girl. Nobody, nobody, was tender and trusting as she was. But people like you abused her, and forced her to change.

(*He crosses into the bedroom, ripping off his shirt, and changes into a brilliant silk bowling shirt. She follows him.*)

Do you think you're going bowling now?

Stanley. Sure.

Stella. You're not going bowling. (*She catches hold of his shirt*) Why did you do this to her?

Stanley. I done nothing to no one. Let go of my shirt. You've torn it.

Stella. I want to know why. Tell me why.

Stanley. When we first met, me and you, you thought I was common. How right you was, baby. I was common as dirt. You showed me the snapshot of the place with the columns. I pulled you down off them columns and how you loved it, having them colored lights going! And wasn't we happy together, wasn't it all okay till she showed here?

(*Stella makes a slight movement. Her look goes suddenly inward as if some interior voice had called her name. She begins a slow, shuffling progress from the bedroom to the kitchen, leaning and resting on the back of the chair and then on the edge of a table with a blind look and listening expression. Stanley, finishing with his shirt, is unaware of her reaction.*)

And wasn't we happy together? Wasn't it all okay? Till she showed here. Hoity-toity, describing me as an ape. (*He suddenly notices the change in Stella*) Hey, what is it, Stel?

(*He crosses to her.*)

Stella (*quietly*). Take me to the hospital.

(*He is with her now, supporting her with his arm, murmuring indistinguishably as they go outside.*)

SCENE NINE

A while later that evening. Blanche is seated in a tense hunched posi-
tion in a bedroom chair that she has re-covered with diagonal green
and white stripes. She has on her scarlet satin robe. On the table
beside chair is a bottle of liquor and a glass. The rapid, feverish polka
tune, the "Varsouviana," is heard. The music is in her mind; she is
drinking to escape it and the sense of disaster closing in on her, and
she seems to whisper the words of the song. An electric fan is turning
back and forth across her.

Mitch comes around the corner in work clothes: blue denim shirt and
pants. He is unshaven. He climbs the steps to the door and rings.
Blanche is startled.

Blanche. Who it is, please?
Mitch (*hoarsely*). Me. Mitch.

   (*The polka tune stops.*)

Blanche. Mitch! — Just a minute.

   (*She rushes about frantically, hiding the bottle in a closet, crouch-*
   ing at the mirror and dabbing her face with cologne and powder.
   She is so excited that her breath is audible as she dashes about. At
   last she rushes to the door in the kitchen and lets him in.)

Mitch! — Y'know, I really shouldn't let you in after the treatment
I have received from you this evening! So utterly uncavalier! But
hello, beautiful!

   (*She offers him her lips. He ignores it and pushes past her into the*
   flat. She looks fearfully after him as he stalks into the bedroom.)

My, my, what a cold shoulder! And such uncouth apparel! Why,
you haven't even shaved! The unforgivable insult to a lady! But I
forgive you. I forgive you because it's such a relief to see you.
You've stopped that polka tune that I had caught in my head.
Have you ever had anything caught in your head? No, of course
you haven't, you dumb angel-puss, you'd never get anything awful
caught in your head!

   (*He stares at her while she follows him while she talks. It is obvious*
   that he has had a few drinks on the way over.)

Mitch. Do we have to have that fan on?

Blanche. No!

Mitch. I don't like fans.

Blanche. Then let's turn it off honey. I'm not partial to them!

(*She presses the switch and the fan nods slowly off. She clears her throat uneasily as Mitch plumps himself down on the bed in the bedroom and lights a cigarette.*)

I don't know what there is to drink. I — haven't investigated.

Mitch. I don't want Stan's liquor.

Blanche. It isn't Stan's. Everything here isn't Stan's. Some things on the premises are actually mine! How is your mother? Isn't your mother well?

Mitch. Why?

Blanche. Something's the matter tonight, but never mind. I won't cross-examine the witness. I'll just — (*She touches her forehead vaguely. The polka tune starts up again.*) — pretend I don't notice anything different about you! That — music again . . .

Mitch. What music?

Blanche. The "Varsouviana"! The polka tune they were playing when Allan — Wait!

(*A distant revolver shot is heard. Blanche seems relieved.*)

There now, the shot! It always stops after that.

(*The polka music dies out again.*)

Yes, now it's stopped.

Mitch. Are you boxed out of your mind?

Blanche. I'll go and see what I can find in the way of — (*She crosses into the closet, pretending to search for the bottle.*) Oh, by the way, excuse me for not being dressed. But I'd practically given you up! Had you forgotten your invitation to supper?

Mitch. I wasn't going to see you any more.

Blanche. Wait a minute. I can't hear what you're saying and you talk so little that when you do say something, I don't want to miss a single syllable of it. . . . What am I looking around here for? Oh, yes — liquor! We've had so much excitement around here this evening that I *am* boxed out of my mind! (*She pretends suddenly to find the bottle. He draws his foot up on the bed and stares at her contemptuously.*) Here's something. Southern Comfort! What is that, I wonder?

Mitch. If you don't know, it must belong to Stan.

Blanche. Take your foot off the bed. It has a light cover on it. Of course you boys don't notice things like that. I've done so much with this place since I've been here.

Mitch. I bet you have.

Blanche. You saw it before I came. Well, look at it now! This room is almost — dainty! I want to keep it that way. I wonder if this stuff ought to be mixed with something? Ummm, it's sweet, so sweet! It's terribly, terribly sweet! Why, it's a *liqueur*, I believe! Yes, that's what it *is*, a liqueur! (*Mitch grunts.*) I'm afraid you won't like it, but try it, and maybe you will.

Mitch. I told you already I don't want none of his liquor and I mean it. You ought to lay off his liquor. He says you been lapping it up all summer like a wild-cat!

Blanche. What a fantastic statement! Fantastic of him to say it, fantastic of you to repeat it! I won't descend to the level of such cheap accusations to answer them, even!

Mitch. Huh.

Blanche. What's in your mind? I see something in your eyes!

Mitch (*getting up*). It's dark in here.

Blanche. I like it dark. The dark is comforting to me.

Mitch. I don't think I ever seen you in the light. (*Blanche laughs breathlessly*) That's a fact!

Blanche. Is it?

Mitch. I've never seen you in the afternoon.

Blanche. Whose fault is that?

Mitch. You never want to go out in the afternoon.

Blanche. Why Mitch, you're at the plant in the afternoon!

Mitch. Not Sunday afternoon. I've asked you to go out with me sometimes on Sundays but you always make an excuse. You never want to go out till after six and then it's always some place that's not lighted much.

Blanche. There is some obscure meaning in this but I fail to catch it.

Mitch. What it means is I've never had a real good look at you, Blanche. Let's turn the light on here.

Blanche (*fearfully*) Light? Which light? What for?

Mitch. This one with the paper thing on it. (*He tears the paper lantern off the light bulb. She utters a frightened gasp.*)

Blanche. What did you do that for?

Mitch. So I can take a look at you good and plain!

Blanche. Of course you don't really mean to be insulting!

Mitch. No, just realistic.

Blanche. I don't want realism. I want magic! (*Mitch laughs*) Yes, yes,

magic! I try to give that to people. I misrepresent things to them.
I don't tell truth, I tell what *ought* to be truth. And if that is
sinful, then let me be damned for it! — *Don't turn the light on!*

(*Mitch crosses to the switch. He turns the light on and stares at
her. She cries out and covers her face. He turns the light off again.*)

Mitch (*slowly and bitterly*). I don't mind you being older than what
  I thought. But all the rest of it — Christ! That pitch about your
  ideals being so old-fashioned and all the malarkey that you've dished
  out all summer. Oh, I knew you weren't sixteen any more. But I
  was a fool enough to believe you was straight.
Blanche. Who told you I wasn't — "straight"? My loving brother-in-
  law. And you believed him.
Mitch. I called him a liar at first. And then I checked on the story.
  First I asked our supply-man who travels through Laurel. And then
  I talked directly over long-distance to this merchant.
Blanche. Who is this merchant?
Mitch. Kiefaber.
Blanche. The merchant Kiefaber of Laurel! I know the man. He
  whistled at me. I put him in his place. So now for revenge he
  makes up stories about me.
Mitch. Three people, Kiefaber, Stanley and Shaw, swore to them!
Blanche. Rub-a-dub-dub, three men in a tub! And such a filthy tub!
Mitch. Didn't you stay at a hotel called The Flamingo?
Blanche. Flamingo? No! Tarantula was the name of it! I stayed at a
  hotel called The Tarantula Arms!
Mitch (*stupidly*). Tarantula?
Blanche. Yes, a big spider! That's where I brought my victims. (*She
  pours herself another drink*) Yes, I had many intimacies with
  strangers. After the death of Allan — intimacies with strangers was
  all I seemed able to fill my empty heart with. . . . I think it was
  panic, just panic, that drove me from one to another, hunting for
  some protection — here and there, in the most — unlikely places
  — even, at last in a seventeen-year-old boy but — somebody wrote
  the superintendent about it — "This woman is morally unfit for
  her position!"

(*She throws back her head with convulsive, sobbing laughter. Then
she repeats the statement, gasps, and drinks.*)

True? Yes, I suppose — unfit somehow — anyway. . . . So I came
here. There was nowhere else I could go. I was played out. You
know what played out is? My youth was suddenly gone up the
water-spout, and — I met you. You said you needed somebody.

Well, I needed somebody, too. I thanked God for you, because you seemed to be gentle — a cleft in the rock of the world that I could hide in! But I guess I was asking, hoping — too much! Kiefaber, Stanley and Shaw have tied an old tin can to the tail of the kite.

(*There is a pause. Mitch stares at her dumbly.*)

Mitch. You lied to me, Blanche.
Blanche. Don't say I lied to you.
Mitch. Lies, lies, inside and out, all lies.
Blanche. Never inside, I didn't lie in my heart . . .

(*A Vendor comes around the corner. She is a blind Mexican woman in a dark shawl, carrying bunches of those gaudy tin flowers that lower class Mexicans display at funerals and other festive occasions. She is calling barely audibly. Her figure is only faintly visible outside the building.*)

Mexican Woman. Flores. Flores. Flores para los muertos. Flores. Flores.
Blanche. What? Oh! Somebody outside . . . (*She goes to the door, opens it and stares at the Mexican Woman.*)
Mexican Woman (*she is at the door and offers Blanche some of her flowers*). Flores? Flores para los muertos?
Blanche (*frightened*). No, no! Not now! Not now!

(*She darts back into the apartment, slamming the door.*)

Mexican Woman (*she turns away and starts to move down the street*). Flores para los muertos.

(*The polka tune fades in.*)

Blanche (*as if to herself*). Crumble and fade and — regrets — recriminations . . . "If you'd done this, it wouldn't've cost me that!"
Mexican Woman. Corones para los muertos. Corones . . .
Blanche. Legacies! Huh . . . And other things such as bloodstained pillowslips — "Her linen needs changing" — "Yes Mother. But couldn't we get a colored girl to do it?" No, we couldn't of course. Everything gone but the —
Mexican Woman. Flores.
Blanche. Death — I used to sit here and she used to sit over there and death was as close as you are. . . . We didn't dare even admit we had ever heard of it!
Mexican Woman. Flores para los muertos, flores — flores . . .
Blanche. The opposite is desire. So do you wonder? How could you possibly wonder! Not far from Belle Reve, before we had lost Belle

Reve, was a camp where they trained young soldiers. On Saturday nights they would go in town to get drunk —

Mexican Woman (softly). Corones . . .

Blanche. — and on the way back they would stagger onto my lawn and call — "Blanche! Blanche!" — The deaf old lady remaining suspected nothing. But sometimes I slipped outside to answer their calls. . . . Later the paddy-wagon would gather them up like daisies . . . the long way home . . .

(*The Mexican Woman turns slowly and drifts back off with her soft mournful cries. Blanche goes to the dresser and leans forward on it. After a moment, Mitch rises and follows her purposefully. The polka music fades away. He places his hands on her waist and tries to turn her about.*)

Blanche. What do you want?

Mitch (fumbling to embrace her). What I been missing all summer.

Blanche. Then marry me, Mitch!

Mitch. I don't think I want to marry you any more.

Blanche. No?

Mitch (dropping his hands from her waist). You're not clean enough to bring in the house with my mother.

Blanche. Go away, then. (*He stares at her*) Get out of here quick before I start screaming fire! (*Her throat is tightening with hysteria*) Get out of here quick before I start screaming fire. (*He still remains staring. She suddenly rushes to the big window with its pale blue square of the soft summer light and cries wildly.*) Fire! Fire! Fire!

(*With a startled gasp, Mitch turns and goes out the outer door, clatters awkwardly down the steps and around the corner of the building. Blanche staggers back from the window and falls to her knees. The distant piano is slow and blue.*)

SCENE TEN

It is a few hours later that night.

Blanche has been drinking fairly steadily since Mitch left.

She has dragged her wardrobe trunk into the center of the bedroom. It hangs open with flowery dresses thrown across it. As the drinking and packing went on a mood of hysterical exhilaration came into her and she has decked herself out in a somewhat soiled and crumpled white satin evening gown and a pair of scuffed silver slippers with brilliants set in their heels.

Now she is placing the rhinestone tiara on her head before the mirror of the dressing-table and murmuring excitedly as if to a group of spectral admirers.

Blanche. How about taking a swim, a moonlight swim at the old rock-quarry? If anyone's sober enough to drive a car! Ha-ha! Best way in the world to stop your head buzzing! Only you've got to be careful to dive where the deep pool is — if you hit a rock you don't come up till tomorrow . . .

(Tremblingly she lifts the hand mirror for a closer inspection. She catches her breath and slams the mirror face down with such violence that the glass cracks. She moans a little and attempts to rise.)

(Stanley appears around the corner of the building. He still has on the vivid green silk bowling shirt. As he rounds the corner the honky-tonk music is heard. It continues softly throughout the scene.)

(He enters the kitchen, slamming the door. As he peers in at Blanche, he gives a low whistle. He has had a few drinks on the way and has brought some quart beer bottles home with him.)

Blanche. How is my sister?
Stanley. She is doing okay.
Blanche. And how is the baby?
Stanley *(grinning amiably)*. The baby won't come before morning so they told me to go home and get a little shut-eye.
Blanche. Does that mean we are to be alone in here?
Stanley. Yep. Just me and you, Blanche. Unless you got somebody hid under the bed. What've you got on those fine feathers for?
Blanche. Oh, that's right. You left before my wire came.
Stanley. You got a wire?
Blanche. I received a telegram from an old admirer of mine.
Stanley. Anything good?
Blanche. I think so. An invitation.
Stanley. What to? A fireman's ball?
Blanche. *(throwing back her head)*. A cruise of the Caribbean on a yacht!
Stanley. Well, well. What do you know?
Blanche. I have never been so surprised in my life.
Stanley. I guess not.

Blanche. It came like a bolt from the blue!

Stanley. Who did you say it was from?

Blanche. An old beau of mine.

Stanley. The one that give you the white fox-pieces?

Blanche. Mr. Shep Huntleigh. I wore his ATO pin my last year at college. I hadn't seen him again until last Christmas. I ran into him on Biscayne Boulevard. Then — just now — this wire — inviting me on a cruise of the Caribbean! The problem is clothes. I tore into my trunk to see what I have that's suitable for the tropics!

Stanley. And come up with that — gorgeous — diamond — tiara?

Blanche. This old relic? Ha-ha! It's only rhinestones.

Stanley. Gosh. I thought it was Tiffany diamonds. (*He unbuttons his shirt.*)

Blanche. Well, anyhow, I shall be entertained in style.

Stanley. Uh-huh. It goes to show, you never know what is coming.

Blanche. Just when I thought my luck had begun to fail me —

Stanley. Into the picture pops this Miami millionaire.

Blanche. This man is not from Miami. This man is from Dallas.

Stanley. This man is from Dallas?

Blanche. Yes, this man is from Dallas where gold spouts out of the ground!

Stanley. Well, just so he's from somewhere! (*He starts removing his shirt.*)

Blanche. Close the curtains before you undress any further.

Stanley (*amiably*). This is all I'm going to undress right now. (*He rips the sack off a quart beer-bottle*) Seen a bottle-opener?

(*She moves slowly toward the dresser, where she stands with her hands knotted together.*)

I used to have a cousin who could open a beer-bottle with his teeth. (*Pounding the bottle cap on the corner of table*) That was his only accomplishment, all he could do — he was just a human bottle-opener. And then one time, at a wedding party he broke his front teeth off! After that he was so ashamed of himself he used t' sneak out of the house when company came . . .

(*The bottle cap pops off and a geyser of foam shoots up. Stanley laughs happily, holding up the bottle over his head.*) Ha-ha! Rain from heaven! (*He extends the bottle toward her*) Shall we bury the hatchet and make it a loving-cup? Huh?

Blanche. No, thank you.

Stanley. Well, it's a red letter night for us both. You having an oil-millionaire and me having a baby.

(*He goes to the bureau in the bedroom and crouches to remove something from the bottom drawer.*)

Blanche (*drawing back*). What are you doing in here?

Stanley. Here's something I always break out on special occasions like this. The silk pyjamas I wore on my wedding night!

Blanche. Oh.

Stanley. When the telephone rings and they say, "You've got a son!" I'll tear this off and wave it like a flag! (*He shakes out a brilliant pyjama coat*) I guess we are both entitled to put on the dog. (*He goes back to the kitchen with the coat over his arm.*)

Blanche. When I think of how divine it is going to be to have such a thing as privacy once more — I could weep with joy!

Stanley. This millionaire from Dallas is not going to interfere with your privacy any?

Blanche. It won't be the sort of thing you have in mind. This man is a gentleman and he respects me. (*Improvising feverishly*) What he wants is my companionship. Having great wealth sometimes makes people lonely! A cultivated woman, a woman of intelligence and breeding, can enrich a man's life — immeasurably! I have those things to offer, and this doesn't take them away. Physical beauty is passing. A transitory possession. But beauty of the mind and richness of the spirit and tenderness of the heart — and I have all of those things — aren't taken away, but grow! Increase with the years! How strange that I should be called a destitute woman! When I have all of these treasures locked in my heart. (*A choked sob comes from her*) I think of myself as a very, very rich woman! But I have been foolish — casting my pearls before swine!

Stanley. Swine, huh?

Blanche. Yes, swine! Swine! And I'm thinking not only of you but of your friend, Mr. Mitchell. He came to see me tonight. He dared to come here in his work-clothes! And to repeat slander to me, vicious stories that he had gotten from you! I gave him his walking papers . . .

Stanley. You did, huh?

Blanche. But then he came back. He returned with a box of roses to beg my forgiveness! He implored my forgiveness. But some things are not forgivable. Deliberate cruelty is not forgivable. It is the one unforgivable thing in my opinion and it is the one thing of which I have never, never been guilty. And so I told him, I said to him, "Thank you," but it was foolish of me to think that we could ever adapt ourselves to each other. Our ways of life are too different. Our attitudes and our backgrounds are incompatible. We have to

be realistic about such things. So farewell, my friend! And let there
be no hard feelings . . .

Stanley. Was this before or after the telegram came from the Texas
oil millionaire?

Blanche. What telegram? No! No, after! As a matter of fact, the wire
came just as —

Stanley. As a matter of fact there wasn't no wire at all!

Blanche. Oh, oh!

Stanley. There isn't no millionaire! And Mitch didn't come back with
roses 'cause I know where he is —

Blanche. Oh!

Stanley. There isn't a goddam thing but imagination!

Blanche. Oh!

Stanley. And lies and conceit and tricks!

Blanche. Oh!

Stanley. And look at yourself! Take a look at yourself in that worn-
out Mardi Gras outfit, rented for fifty cents from some ragpicker!
And with the crazy crown on! What queen do you think you are?

Blanche. Oh — God . . .

Stanley. I've been on to you from the start! Not once did you pull
any wool over this boy's eyes! You come in here and sprinkle the
place with powder and spray perfume and cover the light-bulb with
a paper lantern, and lo and behold the place has turned into Egypt
and you are the Queen of the Nile! Sitting on your throne and
swilling down my liquor! I say — Ha! — Ha! Do you hear me? Ha
— ha — ha! (*He walks into the bedroom.*)

Blanche. Don't come in here!

(*Lurid reflections appear on the walls around Blanche. The shadows
are of a grotesque and menacing form. She catches her breath,
crosses to the phone and jiggles the hook. Stanley goes into the
bathroom and closes the door.*)

Operator, operator! Give me long-distance, please. . . . I want to get
in touch with Mr. Shep Huntleigh of Dallas. He's so well-known
he doesn't require any address. Just ask anybody who — Wait!! —
— No, I couldn't find it right now. . . . Please understand, I — No!
No, wait! . . . One moment! Someone is — Nothing! Hold on,
please!

(*She sets the phone down and crosses warily into the kitchen. The
night is filled with inhuman voices like cries in a jungle.*)

(*The shadows and lurid reflections move sinuously as flames along
the wall spaces.*)

(*Through the back wall of the rooms, which have become transparent, can be seen the sidewalk. A prostitute has rolled a drunkard. He pursues her along the walk, overtakes her and there is a struggle. A policeman's whistle breaks it up. The figures disappear.*)

(*Some moments later the Nego Woman appears around the corner with a sequined bag which the prostitute had dropped on the walk. She is rooting excitedly through it.*)

(*Blanche presses her knuckles to her lips and returns slowly to the phone. She speaks in a hoarse whisper.*)

Blanche. Operator! Operator! Never mind long-distance. Get Western Union. There isn't time to be — Western — Western Union!

(*She waits anxiously.*)

Western Union? Yes! I — want to — Take down this message! "In desperate, desperate circumstances! Help me! Caught in a trap. Caught in — " *Oh!*

(*The bathroom door is thrown open and Stanley comes out in the brilliant silk pyjamas. He grins at her as he knots the tasseled sash about his waist. She gasps and backs away from the phone. He stares at her for a count of ten. Then a clicking becomes audible from the telephone, steady and rasping.*)

Stanley. You left th' phone off th' hook.

(*He crosses to it deliberately and sets it back on the hook. After he has replaced it, he stares at her again, his mouth slowly curving into a grin, as he weaves between Blanche and the outer door.*)

(*The barely audible "blue piano" begins to drum up louder. The sound of it turns into the roar of an approaching locomotive. Blanche crouches, pressing her fists to her ears until it has gone by.*)

Blanche (*finally straightening*). Let me — let me get by you!
Stanley. Get by me? Sure. Go ahead. (*He moves back a pace in the doorway.*)
Blanche. You — you stand over there! (*She indicates a further position.*)
Stanley (*grinning*). You got plenty of room to walk by me now.
Blanche. Not with you there! But I've got to get out somehow!
Stanley. You think I'll interfere with you? Ha-ha!

(*The 'blue piano" goes softly. She turns confusedly and makes a faint gesture. The inhuman jungle voices rise up. He takes a step toward her, biting his tongue which protrudes between his lips.*)

Stanley (*softly*). Come to think of it — maybe you wouldn't be bad to — interfere with . . .

(*Blanche moves backward through the door into the bedroom.*)

Blanche. Stay back! Don't you come toward me another step or I'll —
Stanley. What?
Blanche. Some awful thing will happen! It will!
Stanley. What are you putting on now?

(*They are now both inside the bedroom.*)

Blanche. I warn you, don't, I'm in danger!

(*He takes another step. She smashes a bottle on the table and faces him, clutching the broken top.*)

Stanley. What did you do that for?
Blanche. So I could twist the broken end in your face!
Stanley. I bet you would do that!
Blanche. I would! I will if you —
Stanley. Oh! So you want some rough-house! All right, let's have some rough-house!

(*He springs toward her, overturning the table. She cries out and strikes at him with the bottle top but he catches her wrist.*)

Tiger — tiger! Drop the bottle-top! Drop it! We've had this date with each other from the beginning!

(*She moans. The bottle-top falls. She sinks to her knees. He picks up her inert figure and carries her to the bed. The hot trumpet and drums from the Four Deuces sound loudly.*)

SCENE ELEVEN

It is some weeks later. Stella is packing Blanche's things. Sound of water can be heard running in the bathroom.

The portieres are partly open on the poker players — Stanley, Steve, Mitch and Pablo — who sit around the table in the kitchen. The atmosphere of the kitchen is now the same raw, lurid one of the disastrous poker night.

The building is framed by the sky of turquoise. Stella has been crying as she arranges the flowery dresses in the open trunk.

Eunice comes down the steps from her flat above and enters the kitchen. There is an outburst from the poker table.

Stanley. Drew to an inside straight and made it, by God.

Pablo. *Maldita sea tu suerte!*

Stanley. Put it in English, greaseball.

Pablo. I am cursing your rutting luck.

Stanley (*prodigiously elated*). You know what luck is? Luck is believing you're lucky. Take at Salerno. I believed I was lucky. I figured that 4 out of 5 would not come through but I would . . . and I did. I put that down as a rule. To hold front position in this rat-race you've got to believe you are lucky.

Mitch. You . . . you . . . you. . . . Brag. . . . brag . . . bull . . . bull.

(*Stella goes into the bedroom and starts folding a dress.*)

Stanley. What's the matter with him?

Eunice (*walking past the table*). I always say that men are callous things with no feelings, but this does beat anything. Making pigs of yourselves. (*She comes through the portieres into the bedroom.*)

Stanley. What's the matter with her?

Stella. How is my baby?

Eunice. Sleeping like a little angel. Brought you some grapes. (*She puts them on a stool and lowers her voice.*) Blanche?

Stella. Bathing.

Eunice. How is she?

Stella. She wouldn't eat anything but asked for a drink.

Eunice. What did you tell her?

Stella. I — just told her that — we'd made arrangements for her to rest in the country. She's got it mixed in her mind with Shep Huntleigh.

(*Blanche opens the bathroom door slightly.*)

Blanche. Stella.

Stella. Yes, Blanche?

Blanche. If anyone calls while I'm bathing take the number and tell them I'll call right back.

Stella. Yes.

Blanche. That cool yellow silk — the bouclé. See if it's crushed. If it's not too crushed I'll wear it and on the lapel that silver and turquoise pin in the shape of a seahorse. You will find them in the heart-shaped box I keep my accessories in. And Stella . . . Try and locate a bunch of artificial violets in that box, too, to pin with the seahorse on the lapel of the jacket.

(*She closes the door. Stella turns to Eunice.*)

Stella. I don't know if I did the right thing.

Eunice. What else could you do?

Stella. I couldn't believe her story and go on living with Stanley.

Eunice. Don't ever believe it. Life has got to go on. No matter what happens, you've got to keep on going.

(*The bathroom door opens a little.*)

Blanche (*looking out*). Is the coast clear?

Stella. Yes, Blanche. (*To Eunice*) Tell her how well she's looking.

Blanche. Please close the curtains before I come out.

Stella. They're closed.

Stanley. —How many for you?

Pablo. —Two.

Steve. —Three.

(*Blanche appears in the amber light of the door. She has a tragic radiance in her red satin robe following the sculptural lines of her body. The "Varsouviana" rises audibly as Blanche enters the bedroom.*)

Blanche (*with faintly hysterical vivacity*). I have just washed my hair.

Stella. Did you?

Blanche. I'm not sure I got the soap out.

Eunice. Such fine hair!

Blanche (*accepting the compliment*). It's a problem. Didn't I get a call?

Stella. Who from Blanche?

Blanche. Shep Huntleigh . . .

Stella. Why, not yet, honey!

Blanche. How strange! I —

(*At the sound of Blanche's voice Mitch's arm supporting his cards has sagged and his gaze is dissolved into space. Stanley slaps him on the shoulder.*)

Stanley. Hey, Mitch, come to!

(*The sound of this new voice shocks Blanche. She makes a shocked gesture, forming his name with her lips. Stella nods and looks quickly away. Blanche stands quite still for some moments — the silverbacked mirror in her hand and a look of sorrowful perplexity as though all human experience shows on her face. Blanche finally speaks but with sudden hysteria.*)

Blanche. What's going on here?

(*She turns from Stella to Eunice and back to Stella. Her rising voice penetrates the concentration of the game. Mitch ducks his head lower but Stanley shoves back his chair as if about to rise. Steve places a restraining hand on his arm.*)

Blanche (*continuing*). What's happened here? I want an explanation of what's happened here.

Stella (*agonizingly*). Hush! Hush!

Eunice. Hush! Hush! Honey.

Stella. Please, Blanche.

Blanche. Why are you looking at me like that? Is something wrong with me?

Eunice. You look wonderful, Blanche. Don't she look wonderful?

Stella. Yes.

Eunice. I understand you are going on a trip.

Stella. Yes, Blanche *is*. She's going on a vacation.

Eunice. I'm green with envy.

Blanche. Help me, help me get dressed!

Stella (*handing her dress*). Is this what you —

Blanche. Yes, it will do! I'm anxious to get out of here — this place is a trap!

Eunice. What a pretty blue jacket.

Stella. It's lilac colored.

Blanche. You're both mistaken. It's Della Robbia blue. The blue of the robe in the old Madonna pictures. Are these grapes washed?

(*She fingers the bunch of grapes which Eunice had brought in.*)

Eunice. Huh?

Blanche. Washed, I said. Are they washed?

Eunice. They're from the French Market.

Blanche. That doesn't mean they've been washed. (*The cathedral bells chime*). Those cathedral bells — they're the only clean thing in the Quarter. Well, I'm going now. I'm ready to go.

Eunice (*whispering*) She's going to walk out before they get here.

Stella. Wait, Blanche.

Blanche. I don't want to pass in front of those men.

Eunice. Then wait'll the game breaks up.

Stella. Sit down and . . .

(*Blanche turns weakly, hesitantly about. She lets them push her into a chair.*)

Blanche. I can smell the sea air. The rest of my time I'm going to spend on the sea. And when I die, I'm going to die on the sea. You know what I shall die of? (*She plucks a grape*) I shall die of eating an unwashed grape one day out on the ocean. I will die — with my hand in the hand of some nice-looking ship's doctor, a very young one with a small blond mustache and a big silver watch. "Poor lady," they'll say, "the quinine did her no good. That unwashed grape has transported her soul to heaven." (*The cathedral chimes are heard*) And I'll be buried at sea sewn up in a clean white sack and dropped overboard — at noon — in the blaze of summer — and into an ocean as blue as (*Chimes again*) my first lover's eyes!

(*A Doctor and a Matron have appeared around the corner of the building and climbed the steps to the porch. The gravity of their profession is exaggerated — the unmistakable aura of the state institution with its cynical detachment. The Doctor rings the doorbell. The murmur of the game is interrupted.*)

Eunice (*whispering to Stella*). That must be them.

(*Stella presses her fists to her lips.*)

Blanche (*rising slowly*). What is it?
Eunice (*affectedly casual*). Excuse me while I see who's at the door.
Stella. Yes.

(*Eunice goes into the kitchen.*)

Blanche (*tensely*). I wonder if it's for me.

(*A whispered colloquy takes place at the door.*)

Eunice (*returning, brightly*). Someone is calling for Blanche.
Blanche. It is for me, then! (*She looks fearfully from one to the other and then to the portieres. The "Varsouviana" faintly plays.*) Is it the gentleman I was expecting from Dallas?
Eunice. I think it is, Blanche.
Blanche. I'm not quite ready.
Stella. Ask him to wait outside.
Blanche. I . . .

(*Eunice goes back to the portieres. Drums sound very softly.*)

Stella. Everything packed?
Blanche. My silver toilet articles are still out.
Stella. Ah!
Eunice (*returning*). They're waiting in front of the house.

Blanche. They! Who's "they"?

Eunice. There's a lady with him.

Blanche. I cannot imagine who this "lady" could be! How is she dressed?

Eunice. Just — just a sort of a — plain-tailored outfit.

Blanche. Possibly she's — (*Her voice dies out nervously.*)

Stella. Shall we go Blanche?

Blanche. Must we go through that room?

Stella. I will go with you.

Blanche. How do I look?

Stella. Lovely.

Eunice (*echoing*). Lovely.

(*Blanche moves fearfully to the portieres. Eunice draws them open for her. Blanche goes into the kitchen.*)

Blanche (*to the men*). Please don't get up. I'm only passing through.

(*She crosses quickly to outside door. Stella and Eunice follow. The poker players stand awkwardly at the table — all except Mitch, who remains seated, looking down at the table. Blanche steps out on a small porch at the side of the door. She stops short and catches her breath.*)

Doctor. How do you do?

Blanche. You are not the gentleman I was expecting. (*She suddenly gasps and starts back up the steps. She stops by Stella, who stands just outside the door, and speaks in a frightening whisper.*) That man isn't Shep Huntleigh.

Matron. That's all right.

Stanley. What did you forget, Blanche?

Blanche. I — I —

Matron. It don't matter. We can pick it up later.

Stanley. Sure. We can send it along with the trunk.

Blanche (*retreating in panic*). I don't know you — I don't know you. I want to be — left alone — please!

Matron. Now, Blanche!

Echoes (*rising and falling*). Now, Blanche — now, Blanche — now, Blanche!

Stanley. You left nothing here but spilt talcum and old empty perfume bottles — unless it's the paper lantern you want to take with you. You want the lantern?

(*He crosses to dressing table and seizes the paper lantern, tearing it off the light bulb, and extends it toward her. She cries out as if*) *the lantern was herself. The Matron steps boldly toward her. She screams and tries to break past the Matron. All the men spring to their feet. Stella runs out to the porch, with Eunice following to comfort her, simultaneously with the confused voices of the men in the kitchen. Stella rushes into Eunice's embrace on the porch.)*

Stella. Oh, my God, Eunice help me! Don't let them do that to her, don't let them hurt her! Oh, God, oh, please God, don't hurt her! What are they doing to her? What are they doing?

(She tries to break from Eunice's arms.)

Eunice. No, honey, no, no, honey. Stay here. Don't go back in there. Stay with me and don't look.

(The "Varsouviana" is playing distantly.)

(Stella stares back at Blanche. Eunice is holding Stella's arm. There is a moment of silence — no sound but that of Stanley steadily shuffling the cards.)

(Blanche catches her breath again and slips back into the flat with a peculiar smile, her eyes wide and brilliant. As soon as her sister goes past her, Stella closes her eyes and clenches her hands. Eunice throws her arms comfortingly about her. Then she starts up to her flat. Blanche stops just inside the door. Mitch keeps staring down at his hands on the table, but the other men look at her curiously. At last she starts around the table toward the bedroom. As she does, Stanley suddenly pushes back his chair and rises as if to block her way. The Matron follows her into the flat.)

Stanley. Did you forget something?
Blanche *(shrilly)*. Yes! Yes, I forgot something!

(She rushes past him into the bedroom. Lurid reflections appear on the walls in odd, sinuous shapes. The "Varsouviana" is filtered into a weird distortion, accompanied by the cries and noises of the jungle. Blanche seizes the back of a chair as if to defend herself.)

Stanley *(sotto voce)*. Doc, you better go in.
Doctor *(sotto voce, motioning to the Matron)*. Nurse, bring her out.

(The Matron advances on one side, Stanley on the other. Divested of all the softer properties of womanhood, the Matron is a peculiarly sinister figure in her severe dress. Her voice is bold and toneless as a firebell.)

Matron. Hello Blanche.

(*The greeting is echoed and re-echoed by other mysterious voices behind the walls, as if reverberated through a canyon of rock.*)

Stanley. She says that she forgot something.

(*The echo sounds in threatening whispers.*)

Stella. What have I done to my sister? Oh, God, what have I done to my sister?

Eunice. You done the right thing, the only thing you could do. She couldn't stay here; there wasn't no other place for her to go.

(*While Stella and Eunice are speaking on the porch the voices of the men in the kitchen overlap them. Mitch has started toward the bedroom. Stanley crosses to block him. Stanley pushes him aside. Mitch lunges and strikes at Stanley. Stanley pushes Mitch back. Mitch collapses at the table, sobbing.*)

(*During the preceding scenes, the Matron catches hold of Blanche's arm and prevents her flight. Blanche turns wildly and scratches at the Matron. The heavy woman pinions her arms. Blanche cries out hoarsely and slips to her knees.*)

Matron. These fingernails have to be trimmed. (*The Doctor comes into the room and she looks at him.*) Jacket, Doctor?

Doctor. Not unless necessary.

(*He takes off his hat and now he becomes personalized. The unhuman quality goes. His voice is gentle and reassuring as he crosses to Blanche and crouches in front of her. As he speaks her name, her terror subsides a little. The lurid reflections fade from the walls, the inhuman cries and noises die out and her own hoarse crying is calmed.*)

Doctor. Miss DuBois.

(*She turns her face to him and stares at him with desperate pleading. He smiles; then he speaks to the Matron.*)

It won't be necessary.

Blanche (*faintly*). Ask her to let go of me.

Doctor (*to the Matron*). Let go.

(*The Matron releases her. Blanche extends her hands toward the Doctor. He draws her up gently and supports her with his arm and leads her through the portieres.*)

Blanche (*holding tight to his arm*). Whoever you are — I have always depended on the kindness of strangers.

(*The poker players stand back as Blanche and the Doctor cross the kitchen to the front door. She allows him to lead her as if she were blind. As they go out on the porch, Stella cries out her sister's name from where she is crouched a few steps up on the stairs.*)

Stella. Blanche! Blanche! Blanche!

(*Blanche walks on without turning, followed by the Doctor and the Matron. They go around the corner of the building.*)

(*Eunice descends to Stella and places the child in her arms.*)

(*It is wrapped in a pale blue blanket. Stella accepts the child, sobbingly. Eunice continues downstairs and enters the kitchen where the men, except for Stanley, are returning silently to their places about the table. Stanley has gone out on the porch and stands at the foot of the steps looking at Stella.*)

Stanley (*a bit uncertainly*). Stella.

(*She sobs with inhuman abandon. There is something luxurious in her complete surrender to crying now that her sister is gone.*)

Stanley (*voluptuously, soothingly*). Now, honey. Now, love. Now, now, love. (*He kneels beside her and his fingers find the opening of her blouse*) Now, now, love. Now, love. . . .

(*The luxurious sobbing, the sensual murmur fade away under the swelling music of the "blue piano" and the muted trumpet.*)

Steve. This game is seven-card stud.

Curtain

For the ancient Greeks, at least for Aristotle, *pathos* was the destructive or painful act common in tragedy; but in English "pathos" refers to an element in art or life that evokes tenderness or sympathetic pity. Modern English usage distinguishes between tragic figures and pathetic figures by recognizing some element either of strength or of regeneration in the former that is not in the latter. The tragic protagonist perhaps acts so that he brings his destruction upon himself, or if his destruction comes from outside, he resists it. The pathetic figure, however, is largely passive, an unknowing and unresisting innocent.

In such a view Macbeth is tragic, Duncan pathetic; Lear is tragic, Cordelia pathetic; Othello is tragic, Desdemona pathetic; Hamlet is tragic (the situation is not of his making, but he does what he can to alter it), Ophelia pathetic. (Note, by the way, that of the four pathetic figures named, the first is old and the remaining three are women. Pathos is more likely to be evoked by the relatively defenseless than by an able-bodied man.)

Most of the best-known Greek tragedies show the protagonist either *doing* some terrible deed, or resisting mightily. But Greek drama has its pathetic figures too, especially in the choruses, groups of rather commonplace persons who do not perform a tragic deed but who suffer in sympathy with the tragic hero, who lament the hardness of the times, and who draw the spectators into the range of the hero's suffering.

That the spectators were not themselves heroic figures seems to have been assumed by the Greeks and by the Elizabethans; at least there are usually these lesser choral figures, nameless citizens, who interpret the action and call attention to the fact that even highly-placed great heroes are not exempt from pain; indeed, high place and strenuous activity invite pain: the lofty pine tree, or the mariner who ventures far from the coast, are more likely to meet destruction than the lowly shrub or the fair-weather sailor. For Greeks of the fifth century B.C., and for Elizabethans, high place was not a mere matter of rank, but of worth. In both ages, it was of course known that a king may be unkingly, but it was assumed that kingship required a special nature — though that nature was not always forthcoming. Put it this way: tragedy deals with kings not because they are men with a certain title (though of course the title does give them special power), but because they are men with a certain nature. This nature is an extraordinary capacity for action and for feeling; when they make an error its consequences are enormous, and they themselves feel it as lesser people would not. Infidelity means one thing to Othello, quite another to Emilia.

Inevitably the rise of the bourgeoisie brought about the rise of bourgeois drama, and in the eighteenth century we get a fair number of tragedies with prologues that insist that characters like ourselves deserve our *pity:*

> No fustian hero rages here tonight,
> No armies fall, to fix a tyrant's right.
> From lower life we draw our scene's distress:
> — Let not your equals move your pity less.
>   George Lillo, *Fatal Curiosity* (1733)

Note the deflation of older tragedy, the implication that its heroes were "fustian" (bombastic, pretentious) rather than genuinely heroic persons of deep feelings and high aspirations. Or, to put it differently, older tragedy in the bourgeois view dealt with persons of high rank, but rank (in this view) is not signficant; therefore one may as well show persons of middle rank with whom the middle-class audience may readily identify. At the same time, the dismissal of heroic activities ("no fustian hero *rages*," "no armies *fall*") and the substitution of "distress" indicates that we are well on the road to The Hero As Victim.

And we have kept on that road. (A few remarks in the afterword to Pirandello's *Henry IV* must now be amplified.) As early as the sixteenth century Copernicus had shown that man and his planet were not the center of the universe, but the thought did not distress the bulk of men until much later. In 1859 Darwin published *The Origin of Species*, arguing that man was not a special creation but a creature that had evolved because "accidental variations" had aided him in the struggle for survival. At about the same time, Marx (who wished to dedicate *Capital* to Darwin) argued that economic forces guided men's lives. Early in the twentieth century Freud seemed to argue that men are conditioned by infantile experiences and are enslaved by the dark forces of the id. All in all, by the time of the Depression of the 1930's, it was difficult to have much confidence in man's ability to shape his destiny. The human condition was a sorry one; man was an insignificant lust-ridden, soulless creature in a terrifying materialistic universe. He was no Oedipus whose moral pollution infected a great city, no Brutus whose deed might bring civil war to Rome. He was really not much of anything, except perhaps to a few who immediately depended upon him. In Tennessee Williams' *Suddenly Last Summer* (1958) we get something of this vision. Sebastian Venable and his mother visited the Galapagos Islands, extinct volcanoes (i.e. our burned out once-glorious planet) on which sea-turtles annually lay their eggs. Returning when the eggs hatch, the pair sees the sky black with "flesh-eating birds" who attack the infant turtles that struggle toward the sea. Mrs. Venable says:

> They were diving down on the hatched sea-turtles, turning them over to expose their soft undersides, tearing the undersides open and rending and eating their flesh. Sebastian guessed that possibly only a hundredth of one per cent of their number would escape to the sea. . . . My son *was* looking for God, I mean for a clear image of him. He spent that whole blazing equatorial day in the crow's-nest of the schooner watching this thing on the beach till it was too dark to see it, and when he came down

the rigging he said "Well, now I've seen Him!" and he meant God. —
And for several weeks after that he had a fever, he was delirious with it.

A Streetcar Named Desire gives us something of this world of
carnivores and victims. Stanley Kowalski, who feels "animal joy" and
has a "love of good drink and food and games," is concerned with
satisfying himself. It happens that this life of self-satisfaction also
brings pleasure to his wife, Stella: "There are things that happen
between a man and a woman in the dark — that sort of make everything else seem — unimportant." Stanley's delight in exhibiting his
masculinity sometimes manifests itself in destructive actions: he
smashes plates, throws a radio out the window, and rapes his neurotic
sister-in-law. He is the carnivorous bird, whom we first see "roughly
dressed in blue denim work clothes," carrying "a red-stained package
from the butcher's" which he "heaves" at his wife. Into this setting
comes Blanche, whose very name suggests her unfitness to survive in
this jungle. Blanche is a loser: her responsibility for her husband's
death, her sense of guilt, her need of love, her dying relatives, the
dying southern tradition to which she is attached, her precarious
economic situation, have all conspired to drive her into Stanley's
house, then into his arms, and finally into a mental institution. It is
pretty clear that our sympathies are with Blanche, despite her pretensions, her lies, her dodges, her promiscuity, and even despite the
laughs Stanley scores. All of her faults, it seems, are more or less
excused by the onslaughts reality has made upon her, and by her
goal. In the real world, sex (Desire) drives people, and the strong
and attractive are the conquerors. But Blanche explains to Mitch: "I
don't want realism. I want magic! . . . Yes, yes magic! I try to give
that to people. I misrepresent things to them. I don't tell truth,
I tell what *ought* to be truth. And if that is sinful, then let me be
damned for it." Blanche's fantasy is that she can "make myself a new
life," but Stanley destroys her one chance when he tells Mitch that
Blanche has deceived him.

To get back to the first point, Blanche is a Hero-as-Victim, a suf-
ferer whose suffering is largely due to a passion that she cannot control
and to a world that exploits her weakness. Blanche is vulnerable, as
Stanley is not, and so Stanley triumphs. One might argue that King
Oedipus was vulnerable too, and was struck down mercilessly, but in
Oedipus the King, even if one holds that Oedipus was fated, there
is always the sense of heroic deeds and of a universe that is concerned
about man. The fact that Oedipus is struck down is pitiable and
terrifying, but it is also proof that there *is* an established order that

is concerned with human beings. In *A Streetcar* there is no greatness (Blanche is an hysteric, Stanley a sometimes amusing, a sometimes appalling clod), only suffering, and suffering that brings no wisdom or redemption. Zeus decreed, Aeschylus had said, that men learn through suffering, but in *A Streetcar* Williams gives no sign of assenting. Blanche tells Mitch that "sorrow makes for sincerity," and we can believe she has had sorrow, but at the moment she says it she is deceiving Mitch about her age and her background.

It would be wrong, however, to end with reference to Blanche's deceptions: in the context, if they are vices, they are petty vices, far overshadowed by the suffering that afflicts anyone who must "depend on the kindness of strangers."

The Birds

ARISTOPHANES

English Version by Dudley Fitts

Nothing of much interest is known about Aristophanes (c. 450 B.C.–c. 385 B.C.). An Athenian, he competed for about forty years in the annual festivals of comic drama to which three playwrights each contributed one play. His first play was produced in 427 B.C., his last extant play in 388 B.C., but he is known to have written two comedies after this date. Of the forty or so plays he wrote, eleven survive. The Birds, widely regarded as his masterpiece, won second prize in 414 B.C.

PERSONS REPRESENTED[1]

Euelpides
Pisthetairos
A Bird Servant
Epops
Chorus of Birds
A Priest
A Poet
A Travelling Prophet
Meton
An Inspector
A Decree-Vendor

Three Messengers
Iris
A Herald
A Parricide
Kinesias
An Informer
Prometheus
Poseidon
A Triballian God
Herakles

The supernumeraries include various servants and liturgical attendants, Prokne the Nightingale wife of Epops, Manes a slave, and Basileia the bride of Pisthetairos.

Σ = Scholiast

[1] Persons Represented: The Protagonist's name is in doubt. "Peisthetairos," attested by most of the MSS., is unsatisfactory; of various other forms, "Pisthetairos" — "trusty friend" — seems to be the best.

PROLOGUE

(*A waste region. Rocks, low bushes, a few thin trees. In the background, a steep rock face surmounted by a single tree.*[2] *Enter two old men, Pisthetairos and Euelpides, followed by slaves carrying baggage. Pisthetairos has a raven perched upon his wrist; Euelpides has a jackdaw. Weariness and frustration.*)

Euelpides (*to the jackdaw*). Straight ahead? Over by that tree?
Pisthetairos (*to the raven*).   Oh,
    damn your feathers!
    — Euelpidês, this fool fowl keeps cawing
    a retreat.

---

[2] The scene is deliberately vague. Although Pisthetairos and Euelpidês have come on foot from Athens, the site of the future Cloudcuckooland seems neither terrestrial nor aerial: a dream region, suitable for a dream city. If the transformed King Tereus has chosen to remain in the country that he ruled as a man, the location is Thrace — northward, at any rate, in the direction of witchcraft and delusion.

Aristophanes: The Birds: A New English Version by Dudley Fitts, © 1957 by Harcourt, Brace & World, Inc.

Euelpides. I know. What's the use?
  All this humping up and down hills,
  we'll be wrecks before we find the right road.
Pisthetairos. Miles and miles, walking around in circles,
  all because of a brainless bird.
Euelpides.   Yes,
  tramping my toenails off for a damned jackdaw.
Pisthetairos. I wonder where we are.
Euelpides.   Do you think we could find our way back?
Pisthetairos. Exekestidês himself couldn't find his way back.
Euelpides. Hell!
Pisthetairos.   That's a road you'll have to go on your own.
Euelpides. No, damn it, but I was thinking of that birdseller.
  Nice service that was,
  swearing that these two specimens would lead us straight
  to Tereus,[3] the king who turned into a Hoopoe;
  selling us a jackdaw for a penny, the damned jackass,
  and three pennies for that raven. What a pair!
  All they can do is peck.

  (*To the jackdaw*)

                              — What's the matter now?
  Forgotten how to shut your beak? Or a brilliant thought
  like leading us bang up against that rock?
  I don't see any road.
Pisthetairos.   Not so much as a path.
Euelpides. Do you think that raven of yours is still conscious?
Pisthetairos. I don't know. He sort of grunts, every once in a while.
Euelpides. I mean, do you think he knows what he's up to?
Pisthetairos. He seems to know enough to chew on my finger.
Euelpides. Silly, isn't it?
  Here we are, two of us for the birds,
  and we can't even find the road.

---

[3] Tereus was a king of Thrace who violated Philomelê, the sister of his wife
Proknê, and tore out her tongue so that she should not tell. The sisters
avenged themselves by cooking Itys, Tereus' infant son, and serving him up to
his father at dinner. The gods' criticism of this Faulknerian episode took the
form of changing all three agonists into birds: Tereus became a Hoopoe,
Proknê a Swallow, and Philomelê a Nightingale. It is worth noting that A.
follows the variant that transforms Proknê, not Philomelê, into the Nightingale. Moreover, she seems to have forgiven Tereus for his affair with her
sister, and Tereus has forgotten the dreadful business about Itys. The Nightingale and the Hoopoe are on exemplary domestic terms with each other.

(*Addresses the audience.*)

                              — Gentlemen:
Our trouble's just the reverse of Sakas's.
He isn't a citizen, and he's dying to become one;
but we,
native born, pure strain, citizens all our lives,
we can't get away from Athens fast enough.
Not that we don't like Athens:
it's a fine city, progressive, full of opportunities
to appear in court, citizens
happy as locusts droning in the shade —
only I must say they seem to do most of their droning
before a judge.[4]
                    To come right down to it,
that's why the two of us are taking this walk,
fitted out with baskets and braziers and myrtle boughs.
We're looking for a less strenuous residence,
a City where we can pass our lives in peace;
and we thought of Tereus:
what with all the flying he's done, maybe
he'll know a nice restricted —
Pisthetairos.   Look! Look!
Euelpides. What's the matter?
Pisthetairos.   The rock! Look at my raven!
Euelpides. Yes, and my jackdaw sees something: his beak's
    open again. I'll give you odds
    there's birds around that rock. Let's do something.
Pisthetairos. Why don't you go bang your foot against that rock?
Euelpides. You go bang your head. It'll make twice the noise.
Pisthetairos. Pick up a stone and knock.
Euelpides.   Anything you say.
    — Porter! Porter!
Pisthetairos.   Idiot, that's no way
    to call a Hoopoe. You should say "Hoop! Hoop!"

---

[4] A losing war is hard on the nation's nerves, but A.'s grievance against
Athens is that of any intelligent citizen whose government has yielded to
fanaticism and public hysteria. Certainly there were traitors and dangerous
malcontents in Athens, working for Sparta or for their own interests, but it is
also true that the inevitable Informer was providing harmless citizens and
defenceless aliens with all too many "opportunities / to appear in court" on
"loyalty" charges. After the scandals that attended the sailing of the Sicilian
Expedition (415 B.C.) professional patriotism had become a golden racket.

Euelpides. Hoop! Hoop!
  Have I got to knock again?
  Hoop! Hoop! Hoop!

(A door in the rock face opens; enter Servant, wearing an enormous bird mask.)

Servant.   Whoop are youp? What do you want?
Pisthetairos. Holy Apollo, what a beak! It's a canyon!
Servant. That's all we needed: a couple of bird-watchers!
Euelpides. Not so bad as all that.
                — Come, let's think this thing through.
Servant. You'd better make it good.
Euelpides.   Well, first of all,
  we're not really men, you see.
Servant.   Then what are you?
Euelpides. I am a Yellowyammer, a Libyan bird.
Servant. Never heard of you.
Euelpides.   Just look at the mess on my feet.
Servant. I see. — And your friend: what kind of bird is he?
Pisthetairos. A Crapulet, from Phartia.
Euelpides.   For that matter,
  what animal are *you*, for all the gods' sake?
Servant. A slave bird.
Euelpides.   You mean you were beaten by some cock?
Servant. Not that, no. But when the Chief became a Hoopoe,
  he made me turn into a bird, too, to keep him company
  and do little jobs for him.
              Say he wants a mess
  of sardines from Phaleron: off I run with my jug
  to buy some. Or maybe it's pea soup,
  and we need a tureen and a ladle: well, off I go
  and arrange everything. See?
Euelpides.   I'd call this bird a Kitchern.
  Well, Kitch, you can do a little job for us.
  Bring out Tereus.
Servant.   I wouldn't think of it!
  He's just had a lunch of ant and myrtle salad,
  and now it's time for his nap.
Euelpides.   Bother his nap!
Servant. He won't like this a bit. But if you say so,
  I'll do it. It's no skin off my beak.

Pisthetairos.   Get going!

(*Exit Servant*)

To hell with him and that chasm he calls a beak!
Euelpides. He scared away my jackdaw.
Pisthetairos.   You got scared,
you mean, and let it loose.
Euelpides.   How about you?
When you were falling flat on your face over there,
didn't you let your raven fly away?
Pisthetairos. I certainly did not.
Euelpides.   Then where is it?
Pisthetairos.   Absent.
Euelpides. You can wash your hands of it now, old lion-heart.
Epops (*within*). Open the door. I'm going out to meet them.

(*Enter Epops, the Hoopoe. He is inadequately covered by thin
drooping feathers, and wears a mask with a very long pointed beak
and a tall radiant crest.*)

Euelpides. What in the name of High Heraklês is that?
Those feathers! That tiara!
Epops.   Gentlemen,
your names, if you please? The purpose of your visit?
Euelpides. The Twelve Gods[5] seem to have visited something, friend,
on you.
Epops.   You find my feathers laughable?
Remember: once I was a man.
Euelpides.   We are not laughing at you.
Epops. At what, then?
Euelpides.   That damned funny beak of yours.
Epops. I can't help it. It's Sophoklês fault,[6]
the way he misrepresented me in his plays.
Euelpides. You are really Tereus? A bird, or a parody?
Epops. Every inch a bird.
Euelpides.   What's the matter with your wings?
Epops. Feathers missing.
Euelpides.   Some bird disease, or what?

[5] *The Twelve Gods*: Zeus, Hêra, Poseidon, Demêter, Hephaistos, Arês, Athêna,
Artemis, Aphroditê, Hestia, Apollo, Hermês.
[6] *It's Sophoklês' fault*: The reference is to the *Tereus* of Sophoklês, a play no
longer extant.

Epops. Every bird moults in the wintertime.
  We get new feathers in the spring.
                                — But tell me:
  who are you two?
Euelpides.   Mortal men.
Epops.   Nationality?
Euelpides. Land of the Free. Home of the Brave.
Epops.   I suppose
  you're jurymen?
Euelpides.   No; you might call us *de
  jure* men.
Epops.   Isn't that a new crop down there?
Euelpides. If you work hard enough you can grow it in some fields.
Epops. Well, well. — But what brings you to this place?
Euelpides. We want to integrate ourselves with you.
Epops. Why?
Euelpides. Because you were a man once, like us;
  because you owed money, like us, and because,
  like us, you hated to pay it. Now you are a bird,
  with a bird's-eye view of things and a man's knowledge
  of all lands under the sun, of every sea.
  So we have come to you
  as to an authority, meaning no disrespect,
  to ask if you can tell us where to find
  a soft snug woolly city
  where a man can loaf and stretch and lie down in peace.
Epops. A nobler city than Kranaos' town?
Euelpides. Not nobler, no; but something more to our taste.
Epops. More aristocratic?
Euelpides.   The Social Register
  pains me in a spot I needn't describe.
Epops. What sort of city?
Euelpides.   What I have in mind
  is a place where the worst of your troubles would be
  friends crowding in early in the morning
  with invitations: "Look, Euelpidês,
  "I'm giving a dinner today. For God's sake,
  "get a bath somewhere, pick up your wife and kids,
  "come early and stay late. If you forget,
  "I'll never turn to you when I need a friend."
Epops. I can see that you're fond of troubles.
                                — How about you?

Pisthetairos. I feel the same way he does.
Epops.   For example?
Pisthetairos. I'd like to live in a town
  where a friend of mine, father of a goodlooking boy,
  would meet me and, "You old bastard," he'd say,
  "what's this I hear about you from that son of mine?
  "He tells me he ran into you outside the gymnasium,
  "and though he was fresh from his bath
  "you didn't say anything nice to him, or kiss him,
  "or feel his balls or his biceps —
  "Why, I thought you were a friend of the family!"
Epops. It's clear that both of you want to live the hard life.
  Well, this city of yours
  does exist, after all. You'll find it on the Red Sea.[7]
Euelpides. And have the *Salaminia* turn up some morning
  with a constable on board? Thanks, no sea for us!
  Haven't you a Greek city you can recommend?
Epops. How about Lepreon?
Euelpides.   No. I've never been there,
  but the name reminds me of Melanthios.
Epops. Then there's Opûs, over in Lokris.
Euelpides.   No.
  You couldn't pay me enough to be Opuntios.
  But tell me,
  what is life like up here among you Birds?
Epops. Not bad, take it by and large. No money, of course.
Euelpides. There go most of your problems right away.
Epops. As for food, we have poppy seed and myrtle,
  white sesame, mint —
Euelpides.   It's a non-stop honeymoon![8]
Pisthetairos. I have it! I have it!
  I've just dreamed the most powerful dream in the world
  for you Birds, if you only do what I tell you to.
Epops. What's that?
Pisthetairos.   Well, first of all
  I advise you to stop flying around aimlessly
  with your beaks open. It isn't dignified.

---

[7] *the Red Sea*: "He means Arabia Felix," says Σ. Actually he means Cockaigne
or Arcady, Bali or Boston, or whatever your personal Eldorado may be.
[8] *It's a non-stop honeymoon!*: Bridal wreaths were made of mint leaves and
myrtle-berries. Poppy seeds dipped in honey were esteemed as an aphrodisiac
and eaten at weddings. The sesame plant was associated with Aphroditê.

Back in Athens when we see a man running around,
somebody asks "Who's that?", and Teleas
or someone else says, "Him? He's a hot bird, *he* is!
"Jittery, ants up his tail, all over the place, un-
"dependable type."
Epops.   You're right, by Dionysos!
What else do you advise?
Pisthetairos.   I advise you to found a city.
Epops. We birds? Found a city?
Pisthetairos.   O ye of little faith!
Look down there.
Epops.   I'm looking.
Pisthetairos.   Now up there.
Epops.   I'm
looking.
Pisthetairos. Look all around you.
Epops.   Whatever you say.
I hope you're not trying to make me sprain my neck.
Pisthetairos. Do you see anything?
Epops.   Clouds, and a lot of sky.
Pisthetairos. That's the birds' sphere.
Epops.   Sphere? What do you mean?
Pisthetairos. It's a space, really; but it revolves,
and everything passes through it, so we scientists
call it a sphere.
                    Very well. You settle this sphere,
build walls around it, and you'll have a city.
And what's more,
you can lord it over the human race as though
they were so many grasshoppers. And the gods —
why, you can starve them out like the Mêlians.
Epops. How?
Pisthetairos. Just as we manage these things on earth.
Suppose a man wants to consult the Oracle
at Delphoi: well, he has to get a pass
from the Boiotians, because Boiotia's on the way
to the Shrine. And so it will be with the gods:
there's all that air between earth and the top of Olympos,
so if they won't pay tribute to the Birds
you can make it illegal
for the smoke of offering to pass up to them.
Epops. Oh by Earth, by Nets, by Traps, by Springes,

I never heard a cleverer idea in my life!
With you to help me, I will build that city —
that is, if we can get the other Birds to agree.
Pisthetairos. Who will explain it to them?
Epops.   You.
I've lived with them so long that they have learned
to speak Man now instead of twittering.
Pisthetairos. Can you call an Assembly?
Epops.   Nothing easier.
I'll just step back into the coppice here
and wake my darling wife, my Nightingale.
We'll summon them, she and I,
and they'll come racing when they hear our voices.
Pisthetairos. Oh do, do! Dear Tereus, be quick!
Into the woods, wake the Nightingale!

(*Exit Epops; presently his voice is heard singing within.*)

Epops. Awake, Love, lazy sleeper,
                    Awake, and pour
        The lilting glory of your golden throat
        For Itys, ours no more.
                    Ah, the liquid trill
                    Of the holy monody rising
        To God's house from the stillness of the woods!
                    Phoibos himself, that high
        Singer, struck by your music, would sweep
        The lutestrings with his delicate fingers
            Antiphonal, and all the air along
                Lead the quiring
        Of the tireless gods responsive to your song.
Euelpides. Heavenly God, what a voice that little bird has!
        He is drowning the forest with honey.
Pisthetairos. You!
Euelpides.   What?
Pisthetairos.   Be quiet, can't you?
Euelpides.   Why?
Pisthetairos. The Hoopoe is going to sing for us again.

(*During the following monody, birdcalls are heard from various points behind the scene, distant and uncertain at first, but increasing in volume and in urgency until the Chorus of Birds enters for the* Párodos.)

Epops (within). Epopoí
                    popoì epopopoí
          popoì
                    iô
          iô
                    iô
                    To me,
               to
me here, here, here, O
     friends, O feathery
myriads!
                    Leave your
fields now, furrows
               deep
     in seed, beak-
wielders,
                    swift
     spiralers,
                    melodists
of delight
     tíotiotíotì
          All you
divers for stingvoiced gnats
     in dusky wet ravines,
               you
curlew, curlew crying,
          you,
     spume-guests of the halcyon
on the enchanted water:
          Come to me, come,
hear this remarkable old man
     whose brain
brims for our common gain:
          Hear him,
     come
here, here, here,
     hear him!

Chorus (within). Tórotorotórotíx
                    tototíx
               whit tuwhít tuwhít
          Tórotorotórotorolílilíx

Pisthetairos. Do you see any birds?

Euelpides.   Not a single bird.
There's not so much as a feather in the sky.
Pisthetairos. It seems to have done no good
for the Hoopoe to go gargling in the glade.[9]

PÁRODOS[1]

(*The Chorus is composed of twenty-six persons dressed in stylized
representation of various birds, each with a large beak-mask. These
enter separately from every direction, gathering about their leader,
the Flamingo, in the* orchêstra. *The entrance should be complete by
the end of the Hoopoe's catalogue.*)

A Bird. Torotìx torotíx.
Pisthetairos.   Look, there's one coming now!
Euelpides. What do you suppose it is? A peacock, maybe?
Pisthetairos. The Hoopoe can tell us.

                — What kind of bird is that?
Epops. That, Sir, is a water bird; you don't see
that sort every day.
Euelpides.   Nice color; flame-y.
Epops. Naturally. He's a Flamingo.
Euelpides.   Oh look!
Pisthetairos. Now what?
Euelpides.   Another bird.
Pisthetairos.   I should say so!
He's a weird sister, all right, as the poet puts it.
See how he struts! I wonder what he is.
Epops. We call him the Bird of Araby.[2]
Pisthetairos.   Araby?
Did he come on a flying camel?

---

[9] *gargling in the glade*: The word (ἐπῴζε) is unexpectedly harsh. Pisthetairos
is disappointed by the Hoopoe's apparent failure to attract an audience.

[1] The *Párodos* is the formal entrance of the Chorus into the *orchêstra*, and in
Aves it is almost entirely spectacle. There is relatively little singing for the
Chorus, and the chief interest lies in the costumes of the individual Birds and
in the commenting dialogue. Here, as throughout the play, the Koryphaios is
spokesman for the Chorus as a whole.

[2] *Bird of Araby*: This is the Cock, the Persian Bird, here called *Médos*, "the
Median." (The phallic pun is the same in Greek as in English.) My "Araby"
is a licence, intended to make the "camel" more assimilable.

Euelpides.   There's another one!
By Poseidon, he looks as if he had been dyed!
Pisthetairos. This is astonishing. Do you mean to say
there's more than one Hoopoe in the world?
Epops. He's the son of Philoklês and a lady Hoopoe,
and I am his grandfather. It's like the formula
"Kallias : Hipponikos :: Hipponikos : Kallias II."[3]
Euelpides. So that's Kallias II. I see he's losing his feathers.
Epops. A man about town, you know, always getting plucked
by parasites and party girls feathering their own nests.
Pisthetairos. Here comes one with a crest. What's he called?
Epops. That one? Gobbler.
Euelpides.   I thought Kleonymos was the Gobbler.
Pisthetairos. This can't be Kleonymos: he hasn't thrown away
                    his crest.
Euelpides.   Speaking of that, why do birds
wear crests? To compete in the Armed Men's Race?
Epops. It's like the Karians: crests make fighting safer.
Pisthetairos. I never saw so many birds! They make me nervous.
Euelpides. You said it.
When they lift their wings you can't see where you're going.
Epops. That's the Partridge; and that's — let's see — that one's
the Francolin; the Egyptian Mallard; and that female's
a Hen Kingfisher.
Pisthetairos.   What's that in back of her?
Epops. A Shavetail, of course.
Pisthetairos.   Do birds shave tails?
Epops. Doesn't Sporgilos?
                    — And that's a female
Owl.
Euelpides. That's an idea! Bringing Owls to Athens.
Epops. Magpie. Turtledove. Lark. Warbler. Spryneck.
Pigeon. Snirt. Falcon. Ringdove. Cuckoo.

---

[3] *"Kallias : Hipponikos :: Hipponikos : Kallias II"*: The names are *ad hoc,* for
illustrative purposes. In ordinary circumstances the grandson takes his grandfather's name. The Hoopoe is explaining the presence on stage of a younger
Hoopoe, whom we may call Hoopoe II. Philoklês was a tragic poet of un-
savoury reputation [Σ] who plagiarized the *Tereus* of Sophoklês: that is to say,
the monstrous cohabitation of Philoklês with Sophoklês' "Lady" Hoopoe produced Hoopoe II. Kallias, grandson of Kallias I, was a real enough person:
dissolute and wasteful ("always getting plucked"), he is best remembered for
Plato's making his house the scene of the *Protágoras.*

Redleg. Firepate. Purple Hatch. Kestrel.
Grebe. Bunting. Lämmergeier. Woodpecker.[4]
Pisthetairos. Birds and more birds!
Euelpides.   Even white Blackbirds!
Pisthetairos. The way they chatter and screech at each other!
Euelpides. Do you think they're dangerous?
Pisthetairos.   Their beaks are wide open,
    and they're certainly looking hard at both of us.
Euelpides. I think so, too.
Koryphaios.   Who-oo-oo called this Assembly?
    Where is he?
Epops.   Here I am, your tried
    and trusted old friend.
Koryphaios.   Spea-pea-pea-peak:
    What clever new message have you to give us?
Epops. A profitable one, safe, correct, ingenious.
    These two gentlemen, both of them keen thinkers,
    came here looking for me.
Koryphaios.   Looking for you? Why?
Epops. I am telling you.
               — These elegant old men
    have detached themselves temporarily from
    the human race and brought us what I am sure
    is a plan of promising proportions.
Koryphaios.   I think
    you have made the greatest blunder in history.
    What are you talking about?
Epops.   Be not afraid.
Koryphaios.   Why not?
    What have you done to us?
Epops.   I have lent an ear
    to two respectable bird-struck Senators.
Koryphaios. You have?
Epops.   I have. And I am proud of it.
Koryphaios. What, in our house?
Epops.   As sure as I'm standing here.

Chorus.   Oh misery!   (*Strophe*)
              Duplicity!
              Oh horror without end!

[4] *Magpie*, &c. Some of A.'s birds, in this list and later, are no longer identifiable — "a bird of some sort," says Σ —; and the translation reflects this uncertainty.

Who lays the snare
And leaves us there?
Our old familiar friend!
Is this the Hoopoe of our heart,
Copartner of our fields and skies,
Who bids our ancient laws depart
And sells us to our enemies?

Koryphaios. We can take care of him later. Just now
it's a matter of these two old fools. Look at them!
The usual penalty is clearly in order:
death by dissection.
Pisthetairos.   Done for, by God Almighty!
Euelpides. Your fault, your fault entirely. Why did you ever
lead me here?
Pisthetairos.   So that you could follow me.
Euelpides. It's blood and tears for us!
Pisthetairos.   Hardly tears for you,
once the Birds have pecked out both your eyes.

Chorus.   The cock-trump sings.   (*Antistrophe*)
Advance both wings,
O army of the air!
The hour has struck
That ends the luck
Of this repulsive pair.
No clouds that cluster in the sky,
No raindark mountain peaks,
Shall save them from the battery
Of our insulted beaks.

Koryphaios. Forward! Peck them apart! Flay them!
                                                    — Where's
that Wing Commander? Tell him to get moving
on the right!

(*Immense confusion of movement among the Birds in the* orchêstra.
Euelpides and Pisthetairos confer apart.)

Euelpides.   That settles that.
How do we get out of this mess?
Pisthetairos.   Why not
stick around?
Euelpides.   Of course. And get pulled apart?

Pisthetairos. I suppose you have figured out some way of escape?
Euelpides. You know I haven't.
Pisthetairos.   Then listen to me.
   Let them come on. We'll stand here and fight them
   with these kitchen pots.
Euelpides.   Pots? What good are pots?
Pisthetairos. They'll keep the Owl from attacking us.[5]
Euelpides. How about those fellows with the horrible claws?
Pisthetairos. Stick that spit up in front of you like a spear.
Euelpides. But our eyes?
Pisthetairos.   Use a couple of saucers.
Euelpides.   What a mind!
   You remind me of Nikias. You ought to be
   on the General Staff, in charge of secret weapons.
Koryphaios. Eleleú!
   Ready, beaks at the charge! Let 'em have it!
   Grab! Claw! Tear! Gouge! Break the pots first!

   (*Much noise on both sides, but no other activity; the Hoopoe intervenes.*)

Epops. Permit me. Just a minute, please.
                               — With the best intentions,
   you are behaving like besotted beasts.
   What is the good of killing two harmless men,
   both of them perfect strangers and, what's more,
   related to my wife?[6]
Koryphaios.   Are you promoting
   a Be Kind to Wolves week?
Epops.   Oh, come. I'll admit,
   men are our natural enemies; but these men
   are different, they really mean us well.
   More than that,
   they have a practical plan for the good of us all.
Koryphaios. A practical plan? Nonsense. Our enemies,
   our fathers' enemies — what can they teach us?
Epops. Why, people before this have learned from their enemies
   An open mind's a weapon in itself.
   It's not our friends teach us resourcefulness,
   but our wise enemies. Cities and princes

[5] *They'll keep the Owl from attacking us*: Athêna invented pottery; hence the Owl, sacred to her, will not attack pots.
[6] *related to my wife*: Proknê was the daughter of King Pandión of Athens, hence of the same "tribe" as Pisthetairos and Euelpidês.

have learned the use of warships and fortresses
from necessity, not from friends. Enmity saves
our homes, our children, everything that we love.
Koryphaios. You may be right.

                      At least it can do no harm
to hear what they have to say.

                     It may be
we shall take some profit even from what we hate.

(*The Birds cluster in doubtful conference about the Koryphaios.*)

Pisthetairos (*apart to Euelpides*). They're coming to their senses.
    Easy, now!
Epops (*to the Birds*). Think over what I've said. You'll thank me
    for it.
Koryphaios. We have always admired the Hoopoe's intellect.
Pisthetairos. Now we can breathe again.

    Leave your pot there on the ground. Pick up your
      spear —
your spit, I mean — and let's walk around
and see what the place is like.

                    Keep this side
of the pots, and keep your eye on those Birds. Above all,
don't act as though you were nervous.
Euelpides.   I'd like to know:
if they kill us, where'll we get buried?
Pisthetairos.   I should hope,
in the National Cemetery.[7] For a first-rate funeral
at the public expense, we'd say we fell gloriously
in combat with the common enemy
at Gettysbird.[8]

                  (*The Birds decide upon a truce.*)
Koryphaios.   At ease! Stack arms!
Now we must find out who these strangers are
and what they want.

               Listen, Epops!
Epops.   I am listening.   *
Koryphaios. Who are these men? Do you know where they are from?
Epops. Travelers from Greece, where education is general.

---

[7] *National Cemetery*: Here were buried those Athenians who died in battle
for their country. The reservation was called Kerameikos, which is "Potters-
ville" rather than "Potter's Field."

[8] *Gettysbird*: The bloodless one-day siege of Orneai (416 B.C.); hence, no one
died in that battle. The Greek name makes the pun inevitable.

Koryphaios. What brings them to the Birds?
Epops.   Ornithophily.
  They have heard of your laws and customs and they long
  to live with you for ever.
Koryphaios.   Is it possible?
  What else do they say?
Epops.   Incredible things, transcending
  utterance.
Koryphaios. What do they ask from us?
  Does "living with us" mean living as honest friends,
  or serving their own interests at our cost?
Epops. This savant speaks of benefits to you
  that fairly rob me of words to describe them.
  It's all for you. He will tell you so himself.
Koryphaios. Is the man crazy?
Epops.   His sanity defies
  definition.
Koryphaios. Really?
Epops.   Pure fox, subtle, deep.
Koryphaios. Then let him speak, let him speak!
  These hints of yours have got me all a-twitter.

AGON

(*Order is now restored. As Epops takes command of the situation,
the Chorus forms itself at opposite sides of the* orchêstra *to listen to
the ensuing debate.*)

Epops. You there, and you,
  carry these weapons in and hang them up
  in the kitchen again, next to the tripod.
  Fair fortune befall them!

(*Exeunt two Bird Servants with the pots, spits, and other utensils.*)

                              — And you, friend,
  inform the Birds why I have summoned them
  to this Assembly. Expound.
Pisthetairos.   No, by Apollo!
  Not unless they promise me first

what Monk the Knifeman[1] made that wife of his
promise *him*: no biting, no tickling, no unseemly
prodding in the —
Euelpides.   The arse, you would say?
Pisthetairos.   No;
I mean my eyes.
Koryphaios.   Sir, you have our promise.
Pisthetairos. Swear it.
Koryphaios.   I swear it; but on condition that
this Comedy of ours win First Prize
by unanimous vote of the judges and audience.
Epops. NOW HEAR THIS:
Break ranks! Every private will pick up his arms
and go back to barracks. See your bulletin boards
for further announcements.

Chorus.   Men were deceivers ever; and it may be,   (*Strophe*)
              Friend, that the quality of our guilelessness
                    Tempts you to gull us. Nevertheless,
                         Nothing risked may be gain rejected when

              Truth as a Stranger comes. If you have discerned
              New forces in us, talents earthed over, dis-
                    used instruments of old artifice:
                         Speak out. Let age edify unfledged youth.

Koryphaios. You are at liberty to say whatever you like.
You have our promise:
We shall not be the first to break the truce.
Pisthetairos. I thank you.
                         — Gentlemen, you will find
much to chew on in the following message.
But first, with your permission —

(*To a Servant*)
                                   Boy, bring me
a garland and a bowl of water to wash my hands.
Euelpides (*apart*). Do you see dinner coming?[2]

[1] *Monk the Knifeman*: From the disorderly gossip of Σ we gather that this was
one Panaitios, a grumpy ugly cutler who had an actively amorous wife. The
general purport sems to be: "You lay off me, and I'll lay off you." Panaitios'
nickname was Pithêkos, "Monkey."
[2] *Do you see dinner coming?*: Pisthetairos, in accordance with correct procedure at the beginning of an address, has asked for the ceremonial wreath and
the lustral water. Euelpidès affects to mistake this for preparation for a formal
dinner.

Pisthetairos (apart).   No; I am trying to think
of something to tell them, some enormous concept
that will knock them silly.
                                    — Gentlemen: My heart
bleeds — bleeds, I say — when I reflect that you
who once were kings —
Koryphaios.   Kings? Kings of what?
Pisthetairos. Why, kings of everything! Kings of myself, of this
poor friend of mine, yes, kings of Zeus the King!
Before Time was, you were: you antedate
Kronos, the Titans, Earth —
Koryphaios.   Earth?
Pisthetairos.   Yes, by Heaven!
Koryphaios. That's something that I never knew before.
Pisthetairos. Ignorance, acedia. There are authorities
for what I say: Aisôpos, to go no farther.
He tells us — don't you remember? — that the Lark
was the first Bird born in those chaotic times
before even Earth was thought of; and the Lark's
father died — have you forgotten? —, and because
there was no earth on Earth to bury him in,
the Lark finally laid him away in her head.
Euelipides. Exactly. That's how Hyde Lark[3] got its name.
Pisthetairos. You see my point, I hope? If birds existed
before the Creation, before the gods themselves,
then you Birds must be heirs apparent: the royal power
belongs to you.
Euelpides.   Of course. At the same time,
they'd better keep their beaks in fighting trim:
Zeus won't give in to the first woodpecker.
Pisthetairos. In those glorious days it was not the gods who ruled
over men, but the Birds. Let me cite you a few proofs.
Consider the Cock.
Long before any Dareioses or Megabazoses
the Cock was King of the Persians, and such a king
that ever since he's been called the Persian Bird.
Euelpides. That's why, even now,
Cocks strut like the Shah; and of all birds living
only they have a right to the tiara.

---

[3] *Hyde Lark*: The Greek says that when the Lark's father died he was en-
cephalated, or hidden in the Lark's head — an absurd allusion to the gestation
of Athêna. Euelpidês sees a chance for a joke about the place-name Kephalai,
which means "heads."

Pisthetairos. What power he had! Why, to this very day
  when the Cock sings at dawn
  everyone jumps out of bed and goes to work:
  blacksmiths, potters, tanners, shoemakers,
  grocers, masseurs, lyre-&-shield-manufacturers —
  Some of them are hard at it before it's light.
Euelpides. Some of them certainly are! That's how I lost
  a perfectly good new Phrygian all-wool coat.
  I'd been asked to a party to celebrate
  naming somebody's baby. Well, when I got there
  I had a couple of short ones, so I felt sleepy
  and lay down for a minute; and — would you believe it? —
  some damned cock began to crow, and I woke up
  and thought it was morning, before the other guests
  had even sat down to dinner! Well, I started out
  on the Halimos road, but I'd hardly poked my nose
  past the drive when, baff! somebody boffed me
  with something blunt, and I went down for the count.
  When I came to, my coat was somewhere else.
Pisthetairos. At that same time the Kite reigned over the Greeks.
Koryphaios. The Greeks?
Pisthetairos.   The Greeks. That's when they learned
  to prostrate themselves[4] when the kites come back in the spring.
Euelpides. I remember I prostrated myself one day
  when I saw a Kite, or I tried to, but somehow
  I fell on my back by mistake and my market money
  went down my throat. That day I ate no more.
Pisthetairos. Then there's the Cuckoo.
  Once upon a time
  in Egypt and in Phoinikia the Cuckoo
  was king. As a matter of fact, when the Cuckoo
  said "Cuckoo!",
  all the Phoinikians went out and mowed their fields.
Euelpides. "Cuckoo! Back to the furrows, you foreskinless!"[5]
  as the proverb has it.
Pisthetairos.   Another thing: You will find

---

[4] *to prostrate themselves*: Probably a genuflection [Σ]. At any rate it is to be
taken literally: the Kite was so greeted as the harbinger of spring. Euelpidès,
carrying his market money in his mouth, seems to have genuflected too vigorously.
[5] *"Cuckoo! Back to the furrows . . .":* The meaning of the proverb is obscure;
sed latet, as the Commentators happily remark, *spurci aliquid*.

    that whenever a man managed to become a king,
    an Agamemnon, say, or a Menelaos,
    he would always carry a bird on the end of his sceptre
    to share the royal gifts.
Euelpides.   That explains something.
    I used to go to the theatre; and whenever Priam
    came on in the tragedies, he'd have a bird
    on his sceptre, just as you say. I used to think
    the bird was there to keep an eye on our friend
    Lysikratês when the bribes were passed around.
Pisthetairos. But the best proof is that Zeus, the current King,
    wears an Eagle on his head as a sign of power.
    His Daughter has an Owl; his son Apollo,
    as a medical man, has a Hawk.
Euelpides.   That's perfectly true.
    Why do you suppose those gods have those birds?
Pisthetairos. Why? So that when the sacrificial roasts
    are offered to the gods, the birds may taste them first.
    And here's something else:
    In the old days men never swore by the gods,
    but always by birds.
Euelpides.   Lampôn still does today.
    He always says "Holy Kites!"[6] when he makes a mistake.
Pisthetairos. You understand, then, that years and years ago
    you were great, even holy, in the minds of men.

              But now? Now you are rejects, fools,
              worse than slaves, stoned
              in the streets by arrogant men, hunted
              down even in your sanctuaries
              by trappers with nets, springes, limed
              twigs, cages, decoy-
              boxes;

                    caught, sold
              wholesale, goosed, prodded
              by fat fingers, denied
              even the grace of wholesome frying,
              but served up sleazily, choked

---

[6] *"Holy Kites!"*: Lampôn, possibly because he didn't want to be bound by his oracles, used to confirm them with this diluted oath; or maybe he was one of those mistaken persons who think that "My Cow!", or something of the sort, avoids the profanity of "My God!"

with cheese, smeared with oil,
sprayed with vinegar, doused
as though you were dead meat, too gamy,
in rivers of sweet slab sauce.

Chorus. Tears, and no idle tears, Stranger, distress us   (*Antistrophe*)
Hearing your plain account of calamity.
    Clearly our primeval dignity
      Has lapsed in the long sliding of the years.

You, by a happy chance or some divine influence sent to guide us, have indicated
Future recovery, joy ahead.
      Ourselves, our wives, our chicks depend on you.

Koryphaios. What can we do? Instruct us, since you say
you have a plan. Life's no life for us
till we win back the power that we have lost.
Pisthetairos. My plan is a great City for All Birds,
a single City, with the surrounding air
and all the space between encircled by
massive brick walls like those at Babylon.
Euelpides. Bring on your Giants! What a mighty fortress!
Pisthetairos. Once the wall's built, you must send an embassy
to Zeus and lay your grievances before him.
If he denies them, if he temporizes,
then you should declare a Holy War
against the whole of Olympos: no more free passage
for divinities in an obvious state of erection
on their way through your land to flirt with their Alopês,
their Sémelês, their Alkmenês! No; once across the border,
each strutting member must be stamped and sealed.
That should give them something to think about!
                         As for Mankind,
you must send another bird to them, a herald
to announce that from now on, since the Birds are kings,
the first sacrifices must be made to them,
and then (if convenient) to the Olympian gods.
But even in sacrifices to the gods
an appropriate Bird must be adored as well:
thus, Aphroditê and a Phalarope; Poseidon
and a Duck; Heraklês and a Cormorant;
or, if the victim is offered up to King Zeus,

let the Wren, the Wren, the king of all birds,[7] receive
the flesh of the Balled Gnat.
Euelpides.   What price gnat-flesh?
Let the Good Gosh[8] bounce thunderballs in the sky!
Koryphaios. What if men refuse to treat us as gods?
What if they say, "Them? Jackdaws, that's all,
"flying around up there with their silly wings"?
Pisthetairos. I can't believe you are serious. Why, good Lord!
Hermês has wings, and he flies; yes, and Nikê,
she has wings; and Erôs — all sorts of gods
fly, don't they? Why, even Iris,
the one that Homer refers to as "Trembling Dove" —
Iris has wings, Iris flies.
Euelpides.   Speaking of wings,
what if Zeus drops one of his wingèd bolts on us?
Koryphaios. But what if Mankind is so unregenerate
that only the regulars of the Olympos clique
are recognized?
Pisthetairos.   We'll draft a regiment
of Sparrows and march them off to steal the seeds
in the new-planted fields. Demêter can set up
a Farm Program to fend off starvation.
Euelpides. Demêter will also find a thousand ways
to get around any program that she sets up.
Pisthetairos. If the Sparrows fail, we'll send some Elite Crows
to the grazing lands and have them bite out the eyes
of herdsmen and herds. Let Apollo cure them:
he's a doctor, he gets paid.
Euelpides.   Let me know in advance:
I'll want to sell my yoke of oxen first.
Pisthetairos. But if they sense the indwelling divinity
of the Birds, as they should, knowing that you are God,
and Life and Earth, and Kronos, and Poseidon —
then everything will end as they would have it.
Koryphaios. Everything? What do you mean?
Pisthetairos.   For example,
locusts will not touch their budding vines:

[7] The attendant or surrogate birds are appropriate. Aphroditê's phalarope is
suggested by *phallos*; as a sea god, Poseidon should have a water bird; cor-
morants, like Heraklês, are greedy; and it has always been the wren, not the
eagle, who is King of the Birds.
[8] *the Good Gosh*: Not a softening, like Lampôn's oath noted above, but a
whimsical variation: *Zan* for *Zeus*.

the Hawks and Owls will see to that. Then, too,
a single platoon of indoctrinated Redwings
will be assigned to keep the gall-flies and emmets
from chewing up fig-shoots.
Koryphaios.   But how shall we manage
money? Men seem to set great store by money.
Pisthetairos. The Auspice birds will show them where rich mines
lie in the earth. The Augurs, too, will learn
the secret of quick returns. Shipwrecks will end —
Koryphaios. How so?
Pisthetairos.   They'll consult the Birds before each voyage:
"Is it safe to sail?" "Not today; a storm's blowing up."
Euelpides. I'll invest in a boat. Yo-ho for the briny deep!
Pisthetairos. Then, of course, there are those buried pots
of treasure. The Birds know. Haven't you heard
"A little bird told me where to look for it"?
Euelpides. I'll sell my boat. Me for the buried pots!
Koryphaios. But what about health? That's the gift of the gods.
Pisthetairos. When business is good, health takes care of itself.
Euelpides. I never heard of a bankrupt whose health was good.
Koryphaios. How will they ever live to reach old age?
Surely that's an Olympian dispensation.
Or must they die in the cradle?
Pisthetairos.   Not at all.
The Birds will add three centuries to their lives.
Koryphaios. Where will they get three centuries?
Pisthetairos.   From themselves.
The poet says:
"One crow caws down five generations of man."[9]
Euelpides. Almost thou persuadest me to be a bird.
Pisthetairos. Why not be birds? They demand no marble temples
intricate with golden doors; their shrines
are the ilex, the sparkling shrubs. Their highest gods
live in the sanctuary of olive trees.
We need no Delphoi or Ammon for this worship,
but at home, on our own ground,
in peace among our own familiar flowers,
we can raise hands full of grain to them in prayer,
invoking their dear aid:

---

[9] "*One crow caws down . . .*": A parody of a line of Hesiod (Frag. 50): "Nine generations lives the cawing crow." [Σ]

and when our words fly up, they will be answered
in blessings that fall upon the scattered grain.
Koryphaios. Dearest of old men, you have won me utterly
to your cause. From this hour your words are my words.

Chorus.   My mind applauds.
                  Swear faith to me,
                  And I will swear
                  Death to the gods.
                  The fight is fair:
                  Sing Victory.

Koryphaios. We are ready to do whatever must be done.
The plans and stratagems we leave to you.
Epops. Action, quick action. By God, this is no time
for taking naps or dawdling like Nikias!
But first, gentlemen,
this is my nest, a poor thing of twigs and straw,[10]
but my own. Will you permit me to entertain you
inside? And will you tell me who you are?
Pisthetairos. Of course. Pisthetairos is the name. That one's
Euelpidês; comes from Kriôa.
Epops.   Very happy
to meet you both.
Pisthetairos.   Not at all.
Epops.   Will you please step in?
Pisthetairos. After you.
Epops.   Right this way.
Pisthetairos.   There, I almost forgot!
Tell me, how can a couple of men like us
live with birds? You can fly. We don't know how.
Epops. I see.
Pisthetairos. And speaking of Aisôpos again,
he has a fable about a fox and an eagle.
The fox lost.
Epops.   Really, it's no problem at all.
There's a useful little herb. You nibble it
and, presto! — you sprout wings.
Pisthetairos.   That's fair enough.
— Here, Xanthias, Manodôros: pick up the baggage.

---

[10] *A poor thing of twigs and straw*: The Hoopoe's nest is proverbially filthy,
Proknê being a career musician rather than a housewife.

Koryphaios. Hi! Epops! Before you go —
Epops.   What's the matter?
Koryphaios. You'll invite our venerable guests to dine, of course;
   but the Nightingale,
   the Muses' love, sweet cataract of song —
   will you send her out and let us play with her?
Pisthetairos. A sound idea, by God, and I second it.
   Ask the delightful bird to step this way.
Euelpides. Yes, just for a minute. You can't imagine how long
   we've longed, my friend and I, for a nightingale.
Epops. You are too kind.
                — Proknê, Proknê,
   come here and show yourself to our noble guests.

(*Enter the Nightingale: a flute-girl, nude except for her mask and wings.*)

Pisthetairos. God of our fathers, what a heavenly little bird!
   So soft, so white —
   How I should like to get between those thighs!
Euelpides. The gold, all the gold, like a bride on her wedding day!
   I can't help it; I am obliged to kiss this young woman.
Pisthetairos. Stupid, don't you see the little spikes on her beak?
   You'll get hurt.
Euelpides.   No, I shan't. It's like opening an egg.
   Tap her on the head, the shell falls away,
   and there's my kiss.
Epops (*indicating the door*). Gentlemen.
Pisthetairos.   Let's go in.

                                       (*Exeunt*)

PARÁBASIS I[1]

(*In the* orchêstra *the Chorus turns to face the audience; the Nightingale accompanies the lyric passages on her flute.*)

Chorus (*a solo voice*). Tawnythroat, Partner   (*Kommation*)
                       In song, dark
                       Muse, dearest of Birds:

---

[1] *Parábasis*: At this point the action of the play is suspended while the author, speaking through the Koryphaios, addresses the audience. The Parábasis proper begins as a parody of the Theogonies, the philosophical accounts of the origin of the gods and the creation of the world; but this tone, which is precariously balanced between the solemn and the bantering, passes into mild topical satire.

Come, let the curving long
Line of your fluting
Fall, sparkling
Undersong to our words.

Koryphaios. Come now, let us consider the generations   (*Parábasis*)
    of Man,
Compound of dust and clay, strengthless,
Tentative, passing away as leaves in autumn
Pass, shadows wingless, forlorn
Phantoms deathbound, a dream. Let Men turn
To the Birds, aerial philosophers of
Forever, safe from age, from change, from death.
Let them be humble and learn from us
The truth of Being, the essential germ,
The Bird, first Cause of Gods and Rivers,
Of Erebos, and of the great Void of Chaos.

Here is the absolute Theogony:
Professor Pródikos can lecture somewhere else.

CHAOS and NIGHT: that was the start of it,
And black Erebos, and the long nothing of Tártaros;
No Earth as yet, no Air, no Heaven. There,
In the untried lap of Erebos, sombre Night
Laid a wind-egg,[2] whence, with the circling year,
Erôs was hatched, golden Erôs, wind-swift
Love, the world's longing. His was the sleight
Joined Night and wingèd Chaos in that first
Tartarean marriage and brought the race of Birds
To the shores of light. It was Erôs
Created the line of Gods also, mixing
The urgent elements in adorable ways
To make the Sky and Sea and Earth and all
The Blessèd Ones.
                        So it appears that we
Are móre ancient than these same Blessèd Ones,
Older in the line of Love. What I say is clear
In a thousand proofs:
                        We are wing'd, and so is Love.
Love is our art: how many a handsome boy

[2] *Laid a wind-egg:* This is an unfertilized egg, appropriate for the genesis of
Love. Σ obscurely alludes to the Ledaian egg from which the Heavenly Twins,
Kastor and Polydeukês, were hatched.

Has armed his heart with scorn, only to yield
His proud thighs to the persuasion of the Birds,
Won by a gift of quail, or geese, or cocks!
And birds are good to men in numberless ways.
We lead in the seasons. The clanging Crane
Flies towards Libya, and the sowing begins;
She it is who tells the mariner
When it is time to take his winter sleep,
The unshipped rudder hanging against the wall.
This same Crane
Inspires our friend Orestês of the Alleys[3]
To knit himself a shirt against the cold,
Thus winning the gratitude of citizens waylaid
Who otherwise would shiver in nudity.
Later, the Kite brings back the brilliant Spring
And you barber your sheep; and then the summer Swallow
Suggests bargains of thin dress at the shops.

We are Ammon, Delphoi, Dodôna, Phoibos Apollo.
Are you not always taking the advice of birds
In matters of business, of marriage, of daily life?
You see Bird in everything:[4] your rumours are what
A small Bird told you; your sneeze is a Bird, your chance
Hello in the street's a Bird; a stranger encountered;
An ass on the road: all Birds, all signs of Birds.
Are we not right to call ourselves your Apollos?

Therefore confess us gods, for so   (*Makron*)
We are, to you; and you shall have
Feathery Muses to foretell
The winter wind, the summer breeze.
We will not perch like Zeus, at ease
In some remote cloud-citadel,
But live with you and with your sons,
Your sons' sons, and their sons as well,
Bringing you gifts of youth and peace,
Love, laughter, wealth, new dances, brave
Festivals, more than the human tongue

[3] *Orestês of the Alleys*: This hoodlum with the glorious nickname, who is mentioned again on p. 425, seems to have impressed A. rather deeply. He must
also have had a sense of humour, for there is something comic, to the non-
participant, in his habit of stripping his victims of all their clothes after robbing them.
[4] *You see Bird in everything*: Birds as omens, a fashionable fad.

Can tell, more than the heart can know.
This is our pledge, this is our song.

Chorus.   Woodland Muse   (*Ode*)
                tiotiotínx tiotínx
                   Lucency
           Darting voice
                  Valley
           Wanderer, circling flight
                tíotinx tíotiotínx
                      on the bright hills:
                  My singing
          Spills
                     duskiness into the light
          For Pan
                   and thou hearest
                            For
          The Great Mother, Mountaindweller,
                tótototótotototínx
                   and thou
                     hearest
          In air
                  on the heights
                         fields
              where Phrynichos
          Tastes the ambrosial finality
                tiotínx
                       of song.

Koryphaios. If any gentleman in the audience is   (*Epirrhema*)
    interested
In a pleasant life, he should get in touch with us.
We practise what your laws forbid: You would like to beat
Your father? Good. According to your code
It's an off-colour pastime and, moreover, illegal.
All right; but if you were one of us Birds,
You'd just walk up to the old man, tap him
On the snout, and say: "Put 'em up, if you want to fight!"
Or say you're on the lam, branded and all that: here,
We'd refer to you as a Mottled Francolin, and forget you.
You're a sub-asiatic type like Spíntharos?
Here you'd be a Migrant Finch, Philêmon species.
Even a creeping calamity like Exekestidês

Can hatch ancestors up here and become respectable.
Why, if Peisias' son himself
Should take after the old man and cohabit
With subversives by the dozens, we'd only say
"What a clever bird he is, always drumming up trade!"

Chorus.   So the wild Swans   (*Antode*)
                           tíotiotínx tíotínx
                                  calling
                           Above the roar
                           Of their great wings,
                                              cry
                           tíotínx tíotiotínx
                                 "Apollo!"
                              on the Hebros
                     Shore:
                                The company
                     Of spotted wood-beasts fly
                                    for dread,
                     The sea
                                 hearing
                           tótotototótotototínx
                                   falls
                                 hearing
                              and is still:
                     Olympos
                              is hushed
                                       The Graces
                                 shriek back against
                     The liquid instancy
                              tíotínx
                                     of song.

Koryphaios. There is nothing more practical or   (*Antepirrhema*)
           more enjoyable
     Than a pair of wings. Suppose you go to the theater
     And find it's some Tragedy or other: well, of course
     You're bored, and hungry, so off you fly home,
     Take care of your belly, and get back for the last act.
     Or say you develop a sudden case of the runs.
     Do you sit there and spoil your suit? No. You simply
     Zoom up into the air, do your job, fart twice,
     Catch your breath, and coast back to your seat again.

Or maybe you're an Adulterer, of all things, and there's
Your girl's husband in the front row gawking at the Chorus.
A flap of the wings, and you're off you know where; and when
You've laid the lady — a flap of the wings, and you're back.
Wings? There's nothing like them!
Look at Dieitrephês, if you want a good example:
Those wicker wing baskets he manufactures got him
A captaincy, then a colonelcy, and now, rags to riches,
He's a full-fledged Horsecock[5] in a yellow uniform!

SCENE

(*Re-enter Pisthetairos and Euelpides. Both are now absurdly feathered, winged, and beaked.*)

Pisthetairos. So far, so good.
Euelpides.   By God, it's the funniest thing
   I ever saw in my life!
Pisthetairos.   What is?
Euelpides.   You,
   with those pinfeathers. Know what you look like?
Pisthetairos. You look like a cut-rate reproduction
   of an unsuccessful sketch of a goose.
Euelpides. Do I?
   You look like a blackbird tonsured in the dark.
Pisthetairos. These similes are futile. Remember the poem:
   "I shot an arrow into the air . . ."[1]
Koryphaios.   Next business?
Pisthetairos. First we must find
   a name for our City, a glorious name;
   and then we must sacrifice to the gods.
Euelpides.   You said it.
Koryphaios. Let's get busy. What shall we call this City of ours?
Pisthetairos. Shall we go in for a touch of Lakonian *je ne sais quoi*
   and name it New Sparta?

[5] *a full-fledged Horsecock*: An unhappy Aischylean compound, which A. ridicules again in *Frogs*. Aischylos intended it as a kind of heraldic beast, half fowl, half horse, a figurehead for a ship.
[1] "*I shot an arrow . . .*": Pisthetairos quotes a verse from the lost *Myrmidones* of Aischylos, where a wounded eagle recognizes his own feathers on the shaft of the arrow that struck him.

Euelpides.   I want no part of Sparta.
  Gosh, I wouldn't tie a name like that
  to a flop-house bunk!
Pisthetairos.   Well, have you any ideas?
Euelpides. Somewhere, what with all these clouds and all this air,
  there must be a rare name, somewhere . . .
Pisthetairos.   How do you like
  "Cloudcuckooland"?
Koryphaios.   That's it! That's it!
  What a name, what a jewel of a name you've thought of!
Euelpides. Cloudcuckooland. Isn't that the place
  where Aischinês and Theogenês rent castles?
Pisthetairos. Yes; and it's where the Giants met the Gods
  and got themselves bluffed off the battlefield.
Koryphaios. Cloudcuckooland's a city with a future!
  What god or goddess shall we choose for Patron?
Euelpides. Why not Athêna?
Pisthetairos.   In a City with a Future,
  "what boots a mailèd warrior goddess in arms,"[2]
  since Kleisthenês tends to the weaving?
Koryphaios.   But the Akropolis?
  Who will guard the Pelargic Wall?[3]
Pisthetairos.   A bird.
Koryphaios. One of us? What kind?
Pisthetairos.   Something Persian, I should say,
  something with a reputation for ferocity.
  An Arês-chicken, maybe?
Euelpides.   Hail, Arês, Master Cluck!
  He's used to uncomfortable roosts, at any rate.
Pisthetairos. But now,   (*To Euelpides*)
  off you go into the air! See what the builders
  are up to. Make sure they have enough stones.
  Get plenty of tubs. Make the mortar yourself. (Better
  strip first.) Carry the hods up —
Euelpides.   And fall off the ladder.[4]

---

[2] *"what boots a mailèd warrior goddess"*: The whole speech parodies a passage
from the lost *Meleagros* of Euripidês.
[3] *the Pelargic Wall*: This was a part of the fortifications of the Akropolis. The
more common name was "Pelasgic"; "Pelargic," however, has the advantage
of meaning "Stork [Wall]."
[4] *And fall off the ladder*: There is no authority for assigning this interpolation
and the next one to Euelpidês, but surely the conjecture is allowable. In-
corporated in Pisthetairos' speech they have no comic force at all.

Pisthetairos. Bank the fires. Post sentries in the right places.
   Make the round of the guards at night —
Euelpides.   And take a snooze.
Pisthetairos. Send out two heralds, one to the gods above,
   one to mankind below.
   When you have done this, report back here to me.
Euelpides. And here you'll be on your back! I wish to God
   you'd do some of the work.
Pisthetairos.   Friend, that's not like you.
   We all depend on you to get things done.
   I shall be busy too:

                                    (*Exit Euelpides*)

   I must arrange for the dedication service
   and collar a priest to recite the liturgy.
   Boy! — You, boy! — Bring me the basket and the lavabo.

Chorus.   Inevitably right! My mind   (*Strophe*)
           Melts in your mind's embrace.
        High rituals of any kind
           Are proper in this place.
        Here let our piety devote
        To the blest gods one skinny goat.

        So may they look down from above
           Upon our sacred feast,
        Accept our sparsely offered love,
           And overlook the rest.
        Sing one, sing all! Sing deaf, sing mute!
        Chairis, assist us with your flute.

Pisthetairos (*to the Fluteplayer*). You, there, stop that futile tooting!
   What a man! I swear by my God, I've seen
   strange sights in my life, but this is the first
   crow I ever saw with a leather beak-rest.[5]

(*Enter a Priest*)

   Holiness, get busy. Sacrifice to the gods.
Priest. I would fain do so.
                — Where is my acolyte?
LET US PRAY:
TO HESTIA NESTIARCH, TO THE HIGH HAWK OF THE
   HALL, TO ALL OLYMPIAN BIRDS AND BIRDETTES —

[5] *a leather beak-rest*: The Crow, as *auletès*, or flute accompanist for the singing, would be wearing a leather lip-guard.

Pisthetairos. Hail Storkissimo! Hail, Super of Sûnion!

Priest. — TO THE PYTHODELIAN SWAN, TO LETO CORN-CRAKE, TO ARTEMIS SISKIN —[6]

Pisthetairos. That's a pretty association of ideas!

Priest. — TO SABAZIOS THE PHRYGILLATOR, TO THE GREAT OSTRICH MOTHER OF GODS AND MEN —

Pisthetairos. Lady Kybelê, Ostrichess, Mother of Kleokritos!

Priest. THAT THEY MAY VOUCHSAFE HEALTH AND LENGTH OF DAYS TO ALL CLOUDCUCKOOLANDERS, and also to the Chians —

Pisthetairos. My heart leaps up when someone mentions the Chians!

Priest. AND TO ALL HERO BIRDS AND BIRDSONS OF HEROES: MORE ESPECIALLY TO THE PORPHYRION, THE WRY PECKER, THE PELICAN, THE PYROPHLEX, THE RUDDY GUINEA, THE PEACOCK, THE MAJOR OUSEL, THE TEAL, THE BANDED BITTERN, THE HERON, THE DISTELFINK, THE BALMY PETREL, THE PIPIT, THE GOATGREEN TITMOUSE, THE —

Pisthetairos. Birds, birds, birds! Enough! Why, what a man
you are, to summon all those vultures and sea-eagles
to our Eucharist! Can't you see that a single hawk
could take our entire victim at one gulp?
Go away, and take your portable altar with you.

(*Exit Priest*)

I'll finish the service myself.

Chorus.	If that is so, it seems that I	(*Antistrophe*)

        If that is so, it seems that I
           Must tune my voice again
        In sacramental hymnody
           Of even deeper strain:
        O Gods, and thou our Patron's God,
        Exact no more from us than laud.

        Behold our sacrificial beast,
           Sick bones and stringy hair:
        If you partake of the thin feast,
           How shall we laymen fare?
        Reject our poor oblation, then,
        And feed your worshippers. Amen.

---

[6] *Artemis Siskin*: One of the mystical names of Artemis was Kolainis [Σ]. The *Akalanthis* is a bird, the siskin. This is straining for a pun; but a pun of sorts emerges.

Pisthetairos. Let us propitiate the Feathery Gods.

(*Enter a Poet, singing*)

Poet. Cloudcuckooland, my happy home,
    Sung by the Muses Nine —
Pisthetairos. How did this one get in?
                        — Who are you?
Poet. Who am I? A honeythroated bard,
  a "willing slave of the Muse," as Homer puts it.
Pisthetairos. A slave? With that haircut?
Poet.   You misunderstand.
  I am a poet. All we poets are
  "willing slaves of the Muse," as Homer puts it.
Pisthetairos. That cloak of yours has seen service, willing or not.
  Speak, O Bard: What catastrophe brings you here?
  I have composed the following lyric items:
Poet. In honour of Cloudcuckooland, that great City,
    a] a batch of cyclic verses
    b] a few simple virginations
    c] some odes in the manner of Simonidês.
Pisthetairos. God forbid. When did you start writing them?
Poet. Long have I meditated on this City, long.
Pisthetairos. Impossible. Why, only a minute ago
  I was dedicating the place, giving it a name!
Poet. Ah, swift is the speech of the Muses,
    Yea, swifter than swivelling steeds!
  Mark me, man:
      Thou Author of Aitna,[7] Father,
      At whose dire doom do foregather
        All the high hierarchs —
      Och! wad
      Thy nod
        Some giftie gi'e me:
  I don't care what, just a token of your regard.
Pisthetairos. He'll be around all day if we don't pay him off.
  Here, you in the new overcoat:
  take it off and give it to this lyric has-been.

  — Put it on. You look as though you were catching cold.

---

[7] *Author of Aitna:* The Poet's lyrics are a farrago of imperfectly remembered fragments from the standard poets. Here he is mutilating a Pindaric ode on Hiero, Tyrant of Syracuse and founder of the town of Aitna.

Poet. Thy, Sir, high gratuity
      Compels gratitudinity.
   Brace yourself. I will now address you
   in the vein of Pindar.
Pisthetairos.   It's a vein I can do without.
Poet. Ill fares the man amid the Skythian spears,
      Beset by Nomads, who no 'pparel wears.
      Nil is his number, nameless is his name,
      Who hath no garment to refúge his shame.
   Do you get me?
Pisthetairos. I get the idea that you want some underwear.
   — Take that off too, man, and let him have it.
   He's a poet, after all.
                  — There you are. Get out!
Poet. Out, out, poor poet!

         Sing, O Muse in gold enthroned,
            This chilly City!
         Naked in many a snowbank have I moaned,
            Which seems a pity.
               But still I'll chant, where'er I roam,
               Cloudcuckooland my happy home.
      Alalaí!

                                          (*Exit Poet*)

Pisthetairos. God, what a nuisance! I hope I never meet
   another one like that. How did he hear so soon
   about our City? Well . . .
                  — You, there:
   Go around again with the holy water.

   (*Enter a Travelling Prophet*)

   DEARLY BELOVED: WE GATHER TOGETHER IN —
Prophet. Silence!
   Begin not the sacrifice of the goat!
Pisthetairos. Who says so?
Prophet.   I; an Expounder of Oracles.
Pisthetairos. Expounders be damned!
Prophet.   Tut. We mustn't blaspheme.
   I come to reveal an oracle of Bakis
   That bears directly on Cloudcuckooland.
Pisthetairos. In God's name, why did you wait to reveal it
   until I'd gone and founded Cloudcuckooland?

Prophet. God moves in a mysterious way.

Pisthetairos. He does.

Well, since you're here, let's have your revelation.

Prophet. WHAT TIME WOLVES AND WHITE CROWS CON-
FECT BUNGALOWS
'TWIXT SIKYON AND KORINTH —

Pisthetairos. It's a lie! I never had any dealings with Korinth.

Prophet. That is Bakis' way of referring to the Air.

Now listen:

TO PANDORA THIS DAY
A WHITE RAM THOU MUST SLAY,
AND TO WHOSO DIVINES ME THOU SHALT NOT
REFUSE
A WARM WINTER SUIT AND A PAIR OF NEW SHOES.

Pisthetairos. Does it say shoes?

Prophet. Look in the book.

PLUS A GENEROUS CUP,
PLUS A SLICE OFF THE TOP —

Pisthetairos. A slice off the top, hey?

Prophet. Look in the book.

AND IF, GODLY INFANT, THOU DOST AS I SAY,
A HEAV'N-KISSING EAGLE SHALT THOU BE TODAY,
NOT SO MUCH AS A TITTYMOUSE IF THOU SAY'ST
NAY.

Pisthetairos. Is that there too?

Prophet. Look in the book.

Pisthetairos. Strange. It's so unlike the oracle
I took down from Apollo's dictation.

Prophet. What was that one?

Pisthetairos. BUT IF BY ILL HAP A CHEAP ORACLE-MONGER
DISTURBETH THE SERVICE WITH LIES BORN OF
HUNGER,
THOU SHALT BASH IN HIS RIBS —

Prophet. I don't believe it says
that.

Pisthetairos. Look in the book.

AS FOR HEAV'N-KISSING EAGLES AND ARSE-KISSING
SEERS,
TO HELL WITH THEM ALL. END OF MESSAGE. (LOUD
CHEERS)

Prophet. Is that there too?

Pisthetairos.   Look in the book.

                                        (*Suddenly losing patience*)

   Damn you, get out of here!

                                        (*Strikes him with his staff*)

Prophet.   Ouch! I'll go! Ouch!

                                              (*Exit Prophet*)

Pisthetairos (*calling after him*). Peddle your damned oracles somewhere else!

   (*Enter Meton, wearing a saffron gown embroidered with geometri-
   cal figures.*)

Meton. My aim in coming here —
Pisthetairos.   Another headache!
   What's your project? And above all,
   why that absurd costume?
Meton.   I have come
   to subdivide the air into square acres.
Pisthetairos. May I ask who you are?
Meton.   You may. My name is Metôn.
   The word's a commonplace in Greece and Kolonos.
Pisthetairos. What's that you've got with you?
Meton.   An aerial straight-edge.
   Observe:
   The conformation of the air, considered as
   a total entity, is that of a conical damper.
   Very well. At the apex of this cone we apply
   the ruler, bracketing in the dividers to allow
   for the congruent curve. Q.E.D.
Pisthetairos.   Q.E.D.?
Meton. We calculate the declination by cathexis
   according to the sine. Thus we square the circle.
   In the centre we postulate a forum, the focus
   of convergent streets that, stelliform,
   subtend the radii extended from this point.
   Q.E.D.
Pisthetairos. Q.E.D.! The man's a Thalês!
   Metôn.
Meton.   Yes?
Pisthetairos.   I admire you. I really do.
   Take my advice and subdivide somewhere else.
Meton. Why? Is it dangerous here?

Pisthetairos. Yes, here and in Sparta.
You know how they're treating aliens these days:
nasty demonstrations in the streets.
Meton. You apprehend
seditious manifestations in Cloudcuckooland?
Pisthetairos. God forbid.
Meton. Then what?
Pisthetairos. Well, we've passed a law
that charlatans shall be whipped in the public square.
Meton. Oh. Then I'd better be going.
Pisthetairos. You're almost too late.
Here' a sample, God help you!

(*Knocks him down*)

Meton. My head! My head!
Pisthetairos. I warned you. On your way, and be quick about it!

(*Exit Meton; enter an Inspector, elegant in full uniform, carrying two urns for balloting.*)

Inspector. Summon the Consuls.
Pisthetairos. Who's this Sardanápalos?
Inspector. My good man, I am a legally designated
Inspector, empowered to investigate
the civic status of Cloudcuckooland.
Pisthetairos. Your warrant?
Inspector. This illegible document
endorsed by Teleas.
Pisthetairos. My dear Inspector,
it seems a pity to waste your valuable time.
Suppose you collect your pay and go right home?
Inspector. A first-rate idea! As a matter of fact,
I ought not to have left Athens at all.
There are certain sensitive foreign affairs — you know? —
that Pharnakês leaves to me.
Pisthetairos. Is that so?
Here's your pay.

(*Slaps his face*)

Inspector. Sir, I demand the meaning of this.
Pisthetairos. It's a sensitive foreign affair.
Inspector. I make formal protest
that you have assaulted and battered an Inspector.

Pisthetairos. Take your voting-jugs and get out of my sight!
It's an outrage:
Inspectors before there's a City to inspect!

(*The Inspector withdraws, but hides behind one of the Acolytes; enter a Decree-Vendor, who begins to read from a scroll.*)

Decree-Vendor. "AND IF ANY CLOUDCUCKOOLANDER WHATSOEVER SHALL CAUSE INJURY OR DISTRESS TO ANY ATHENIAN CITIZEN WHATSOEVER —"

Pisthetairos. Another one! A walking law-book this time.

Decree-Vendor. Your Honor, I am a dealer in the latest decrees.
Satisfaction guaranteed.

Pisthetairos.   As for example?

Decree-Vendor. "VOTED: THAT FROM THE DATE HEREIN-UNDER SUBSCRIBED ALL WEIGHTS MEASURES AND STATUTES WHATSOEVER OF CLOUDCUCKOOLAND SHALL BE IDENTICAL WITH THE SAME OBTAINING IN OLOPHYXOS."

Pisthetairos. That ought to fix us.
                          — Look here, you!

Decree-Vendor. What's the matter with you? Something you ate?

Pisthetairos. Go back where you came from with your silly laws,
or you'll get some rough and ready legislation.

(*Strikes him; exit Decree-Vendor hurriedly; the Inspector reappears.*)

Inspector. I charge Pisthetairos with felonious assault,
returnable April Session.

Pisthetairos.   How did *you* get back?

(*The Decree-Vendor re-enters.*)

Decree-Vendor. "AND IF ANY MAN SHALL SCUTTLE A MAGIS-TRATE AFTER THE NAME OF SAME HAS BEEN POSTED ON THE PILLAR IN ACCORDANCE WITH THE LAW —"

Pisthetairos. Holy God! You too?

(*Drives him away with blows*)

Inspector. I'll have your license! This will cost a cool thousand!

Pisthetairos. I'll smash those jugs of yours in a thousand pieces!

Inspector. Do you remember the evening you polluted the pillar?

Pisthetairos. Go pollute yourself!
                          — Grab him! That's it!

(*Inspector escapes.*)

Let's hope that's the end of him.
                              — Gentlemen:
If we're going to sacrifice our goat at all,
I'm afraid we'll have to do the job inside.

                              (*Exeunt; manet Chorus*)

PARÁBASIS II

(*The Chorus again addresses itself to the audience.*)

Chorus. We are Lords of Earth and of all upon it,   (*Ode*)
        Marking all, all-knowing, in tireless session
        Guiding, weighing, judging the varied drama.
            Come and adore us!

        Guardians of young fruit in the open orchards,
        Our swift beaks transfix the insect marauder,
        And he falls, struck down by the feath'ry ictus
            Whirring from heaven.

Koryphaios. You see CRIMINAL WANTED notices   (*Epirrhema*)
        everywhere:
    "Whoever kills Diágoras the Mêlian,"
    So much reward; "Whoever kills
    "A dead tyrant or so," still more
    Reward. Well, then, I proclaim:
    "Whoever kills Philókratês the Birdseller,
    "One talent, cash; whoever brings him in
    "Alive, four talents" — twice as much
    As for poor old Diágoras. This Philókratês
    Hangs bullfinches on hooks in his shop
    And sells them at cut rates; he inflates thrushes
    With air pumps and exposes their abused puffy
    Bodies for sale; he mutilates blackbirds; he
    Stuffs live pigeons into nets and makes them
    Act as decoys. That's Philókratês for you!
                              — And
    If any members of this audience
    Maintain a bird in a gilded cage at home,
    We beg you let it go. Refuse, and you'll see
    How quickly the Birds will make decoys of you!

Chorus. Joy of birds! In summer the long thick sunlight   (*Antode*)
  When the locust drones in the trance of noontime:
  Mad with sun we shout, and the forest dances
    Heavy with music.

  Wintertime is sun on the tropic headlands
  Where the Nymphs play counterpoint to our singing;
  Spring is myrtle, pang of the pink sweet prickling
    Buds of the Graces.

Koryphaios. Now for a word or two, Judges, about   (*Antepirrhema*)
  This Competition. If you give us the Prize,
  We'll pay you better for it than Prince Paris
  Was paid by the Goddess. First of all,
  The Owls of Laureion[1] will never desert you:
  They'll be everywhere in your houses, nesting
  In your purses, maniacally producing
  Miniature Owls. Judges are fond of Owls.
  More than that, we'll add new wings
  To your houses: you'll dream that you dwell
  In marble halls, and you'll be right.
                      If your jobs
  Are slow pay, if your fingers begin to itch,
  We'll send you a little confidential Hawk
  To perch on your wrist. For state dinners you can have
  The loan of a bird-crop to solve capacity problems.
  But if we lose the Prize,
  Take portable canopies with you on your strolls,
  Or your new white robes will suffer
  Avine criticism dropping from the skies.

SCENE

(*Re-enter Pisthetairos with his attendants.*)

Pisthetairos. The omens are favourable, I'm glad to say.
  Strange that we've had no news
  about the wall.
          — But here comes a messenger now,
  puffing like an Olympic sprinter.

(*Enter First Messenger, wildly.*)

[1] *Owls of Laureion*: Coins begetting smaller coins.

Messenger. Where is he? Where is he? Where is he?

Pisthetairos.   Where is who?

Messenger. The Chief. Pisthetairos.

Pisthetairos.   Here.

Messenger.   Great news! Great news!
  Your Wall is finished!

Pisthetairos.   That *is* great news.

Messenger.   Oh how
  shall I describe the splendour of that Wall,
  the apocalyptic hugeness? Take two chariots,
  hitch four fat Wooden Horses to each one,
  let Theogenês and old Proxenidês
  of Belchertown meet head-on — , they'd pass each other
  without a scratch. It's that big.

Pisthetairos.   Holy Heraklês!

Messenger. And tall? Look, I measured it myself:
  it stands six hundred feet!

Pisthetairos.   Merciful Poseidon!
  What workmen could build a wall as high as that?

Messenger. Birds, only birds. Not a single Egyptian
  hodcarrier[1] or stonemason or carpenter
  in the gang; birds did it all, and my eyes
  are popping yet.
                      Imagine thirty thousand Cranes
  from Libya,[2] each one with a belly full of stones
  for the Rails to shape up with their beaks; ten
  thousand Storks, at least,
  all of them making bricks with clay and water
  flown up by Curlews from the earth below.

Pisthetairos. Mortar?

Messenger.   Herons with hods.

Pisthetairos.   How did they manage it?

Messenger. That was a triumph of technology!
  The Geese shovelled it up with their big feet.

Pisthetairos. Ah feet, to what use can ye not be put![3]

Messenger. Why, good Lord! There were Ducks to set the bricks,

---

[1] *Egyptian hodcarrier*: A. is thinking of the accounts — Herodotos, for example — of the building of the Pyramids by the slave workmen of Cheops.

[2] *Cranes from Libya*: Because of their improbable shape, cranes were supposed to need a ballast of stones in order to fly.

[3] *Ah feet . . . .*: A proverb; but Pisthetairos substitutes "feet" for the "hands" of the original.

and flights of little apprentice Swallows
with trowel tails for the mortar in their bills.
Pisthetairos. Who wants hired labour after this?
— But the joists and beams?
Messenger.   All handled by birds.
When the Woodpeckers went to work on those portals
it sounded like a shipyard!
                    — So there's your Wall,
complete with gates and locks, watchfires burning,
patrols circling, the guard changed every hour.
But I must wash off this long trek of mine.
You'll know what to do next.

(*Exit First Messenger*)

Koryphaios. Surprises you, hey? That quick job on your Wall?
Pisthetairos. Surprises me? Why, it's a lie come true!
But here's another non-stop messenger,
and this one looks like trouble.

(*Enter Second Messenger: tragic manner.*)

Messenger. Alas! Alas! Alas!
Pisthetairos.   What's the matter with *you?*
Messenger. Confusion now hath made his masterpiece!
One of the gods, I do not know his name,
has invaded our air and slipped through the gate
right under the beaks of the Jackdaws on day duty.
Pisthetairos. Murther and treason!
                    — What god did you say?
Messenger. Identity not established. But he has wings,
we know that.
Pisthetairos.   Alert the Air Cadets!
Messenger. Cadets! We've alerted everything we have.
Ten thousand mounted Arrowhawks,
to say nothing of claw-to-claw raiders
of every calibre: Kestrels, Buzzards,
Kites, Vultures, Nighthawks, Eagles —
every mortal inch of air
they've ploughed up with their wings, looking for that god.
He won't get away,
he's somewhere around here; I feel it in my feathers.
Pisthetairos. Slings and arrows, slings and arrows! All of you,
here: get shooting, quick! Give me my bow!

Chorus.	War to the end,	(*Strophe*)
	Inexpressible war,	
	God against Bird!	
	Arm to defend	
	Our fathers' Air!	
	Olympos' host	
	Must not get past	
	Our border guard!	

Koryphaios. Each one of you keep watch on every side.
   I hear, or seem to hear, an ominous clack
   of wings, as though some Deity were descending.

(*The goddess Iris appears from above, suspended in the machina; she has broad static wings and wears a large rainbow around her head and shoulders.*)

Pisthetairos. Heave to! Let go halyards! Lower the flaps! Easy all!

(*The machina stops with a violent jerk.*)

   Who are you? Where are you bound? What's your home port?
Iris (*tragic tone*). I come to you from the Olympian gods.
Pisthetairos. Your name? Are you sea-going, or a flying
   hat-rack?
Iris.   Fleet Iris am I.
Pisthetairos.   Deep sea or
   inland waters?
Iris.   What *are* you talking about?
Pisthetairos. Some of you birds had better get on the ball
   and board this crate.
Iris.   Board me? I never
   heard such a thing!
Pisthetairos.   Well, you heard it now.
   We'll give you something to squawk about.
Iris.   Well, really!
Pisthetairos. All right, all right. What gate did you come through?
Iris. How should I know? Gates mean nothing to me.
Pisthetairos. Oh. So that's the way it is.
                          — Well, then,
   did you report to the Chief Jackdaw? Say something!
   Did you get your passport countersigned by the Storks?
   You did not?
Iris.   Are you in your right mind?

Pisthetairos.   Not a single
  bird there punched your card for you?
Iris.   No, or punched
  anything else for me, you poor idiot.
Pisthetairos.   So
  you're flying over foreign territory
  without any papers.
Iris.   How else should gods fly?
Pisthetairos. Good God, how should I know?

                                 But they can't do it here!
  I don't care if you're a whole fleet of Irises:
  you've committed a violation, and the penalty
  for that is death.
Iris.   Mortal, I am immortal.
Pisthetairos. Death just the same!

                                 Things have come to a pretty pass
  if we set up a system of border controls, only to have
  you gods flying back and forth whenever you feel like it.
  But tell me:
  What was the destination you had in mind?
Iris. Destination? I am about my Father's business.
  He has commanded me to remind mankind
  that they must sacrifice to the eternal gods,
  smiting the hornèd beasts upon their altars
  and filling their streets with the smoke of immolation.
Pisthetairos. What do you mean? Sacrifice to what gods?
Iris. Why, to us gods in Heaven.
Pisthetairos.   So you are gods too?
Iris. Can you think of others?
Pisthetairos.   I am thinking of the Birds.
  So far as mankind is concerned, Birds are now gods.
  It's they must have sacrifices — not God, by God!
Iris. Alas, deluded worm, think not to stir
  the guts of wrath eterne: else heavenly Justice,
  with Zeus's pitchfork arm'd, drops from on high
  to man's undoing and leaves not a rack
  behind. Fried and consumèd shalt thou be,
  as i' th' Euripidean Tragedy![4]
Pisthetairos. Madam, wipe the foam from your mouth,
  and do stop quivering so. Am I a slave,

---

[4] *Euripidean Tragedy:* "In the [lost] *Likymnios* of Euripides, somebody or
something gets struck by lightning." [Σ]

some Lydian or Phrygian slave,[5] that you imagine
you scare me with talk of this kind?

                              As for Zeus:
you can inform your Zeus
that if he gets in my way I'll burn him out,
yea, I will blast him in Amphíon's hall
with eagles lightningbeak'd that heed my call.
Notify him furthermore
that I command a squadron of six hundred
sky-scaling porphyrion birds in panther skin.
That will hold him, I think: a single Porphyrion once
kept him busy enough.

                      — And if *you* get in my way,
Iris or no Iris, messenger or whatever you are,
I'll just hoist up your legs and get in between:
then, by God, you can tell your wondering friends
how you met an old battleship with a triple prow!
Iris. No gentleman would address a lady so.
Pisthetairos. On your way! Scat!
Iris.   I shall certainly tell my Father.
Pisthetairos. Next time, consume someone your own age!

                              (*Exit Iris in the machina*)

Chorus.   My word is sure: (*Antistrophe*)
                             Children of Zeus,
                             No entrance here!
                             And it shall stand.
                             Let no man dare
                             Cajole the skies
                             With ritual brand
                             Or sacrifice.

Pisthetairos. Speaking of mankind, I am worried about our herald.
   It's strange that his commission should keep him so long.

   (*Enter a Herald, in haste*)

Herald. O Pisthetairos! O Blessedest! O Sagaciousest!
   O Superlativest! O Sagaciousest! O Perspicaciousest!
   O Thrice Blessedest! O And-so-forth!

[5] *some Lydian or Phrygian slave*: A parody of Euripides: *Alkestis* 675, Pherês
to Admêtos.

Pisthetairos.   Did you speak?
Herald. I crown you with this golden crown, the gift
    of your admiring public.
Pisthetairos.   I thank you.
    Tell me. Why does mankind admire me?
Herald. O Pisthetairos, mighty father of
    Cloudcuckooland the Beautiful, how slight
    your skill in understanding human thought
    if you must ask that question!
                              What is man?
    Or, rather, what was man before your triumph?
    An abject Spartomaniac[6] — long hair,
    infrequent baths, bad honest food, knobbly
    accessories, the Sokratês pose.[7]
                              What is man now?
    Mad about birds! Birds, birds, from the moment
    they get out of nest in the morning: eggs and birdseed
    for breakfast, and then bird business,
    reeding and piping till clucking-off time.
    They even affect bird names:
    "Partridge" is any man gone in one leg;
    Menippos is "Swallow"; Opûntios,
    "Monocle de Mon Oncle"; Philoklês
    is "Lark"; Theogenês, "Gypsy Goose"; Lykûrgos,
    "Ibis"; Chairephôn, "Bats"; Syrakosios, "Jaybird";
    and Meidias, of course, is called "Goon Quail" —
    one look at that bashed-in face of his
    will tell you why.
                    As for song-writing,
    you can't so much as buy a hearing unless
    you stuff your lyrics with assorted wild ducks
    and swallows, or doves, or geese, or maybe
    a few last feathers from a cast-off wing.

    That's what it's like down there. And mark my words:
    you'll soon be getting visitors by the thousands,
    all sorts of men begging to be fitted out

[6] *An abject Spartomaniac*: It is curious that in a long war it should become
fashionable among certain people to ape the manners of the enemy.
[7] *the Sokratês pose*: Here, as in the *chorikon* on p. 425, A. reveals his inability
to admire the Great Martyr. The full-dress attack takes place in *Clouds*, but
even in these minor skirmishes the animus is apparent, and only by shutting
our minds to the plain sense of words can we conclude that this is a friendly
raillery.

with wings and beaks and claws. Take my advice
and lay in a pile of pinions.
Pisthetairos.   Heavens, yes!
I can see we'll be busy.
                    — Quick, you:

                                        (*To a Servant*)

fill every last basket you can find with wings
and tell Manês to bring them out to me here.
I want to be prepared for these gentlemen.

Chorus.   My City is Cloudcuckooland,   (*Strophe*)
            And men of every nation
         Confer on us, I understand,
            Ecstatic approbation.

Pisthetairos. And surplus population.

Chorus.   What wonder though it should be so?
            Here Love and Wisdom dwell,
         And through the streets the Graces go,
            And Peace contrives her spell.

Pisthetairos. The servant problem's hell!

Chorus.   Manês, awake! New wings, new beaks!   (*Antistrophe*)
            Surely there never was
         A slower slave. Your master speaks!
            The precious moments pass!

(*Enter Manes emptyhanded.*)

Pisthetairos. This Manês is an ass.

                                        (*Exit Manes*)

Chorus.   Wings make the man; let each man wear
            The crest that suits his bent:
         Musician, merchant, privateer,
            Cleric, or laic gent,

(*Re-enter Manes as before.*)

Pisthetairos. Or slave of snail descent.
         Manês, I swear by All Hawks, I'll haul you
         hairless if you don't get busy! Come on; service!

(*General confusion. Manes and other servants appear and reappear
carrying wings of all shapes and sizes. These are arranged on a
bench.*)

Parricide (*within, singing*). "Ah that the eagle's eager wings were mine,
   To gyre above the waste of bloomless brine!"[8]
Pisthetairos. That messenger seems to have been right.
   Here comes somebody singing about eagles.

   (*Enter a young Parricide*)

Parricide. Here we are!
   I vow, there's nothing like flying.
                                             — Sir,
   I'm mad about birds, I'm
   always up in the air. More than that,
   I apply for citizenship under your laws.
Pisthetairos. What laws? We Birds have many laws.
Parricide. All of them; especially that glorious statute
   that gives Birds the right to strangle their own fathers.
Pisthetairos. We *do* consider it a sign of manliness
   when a chick stands up to his father and faces him down.
Parricide. Exactly my own motive in emigrating:
   I propose to throttle the old man for his property.
Pisthetairos. At the same time we have an ancient decree
   (you'll find it in the Book of Storks) that says:
   STORKLINGS CARED FOR BY THE STORK THEIR SIRE
   AND BY HIM TAUGHT TO FLY SHALL IN THEIR TURN
   CARE FOR THE STORK THEIR SIRE IN HIS OLD AGE.
Parricide. What was the use of my coming all this distance
   if I've got to support my father after all?
Pisthetairos. Come, it's not so bad.
   You obviously mean well, and we'll make
   a decent orphan bird[9] of you yet, young man.
   But first
   permit me to recite a useful thought
       "that was given me
       at my mother's knee.":
   Sons, don't beat your fathers. It's unkind.

   (*During the following speech Pisthetairos arms the Parricide with a
   toy sword, shield, and helmet.*)

   Stick out your hand: receive this bright cock-spur.
   Your other hand: receive this shining wing.

[8] "*Ah that the eagle's . . .*": Σ notes that these verses are quoted [in parody?]
from the lost *Oinomaos* of Sophoklês.
[9] *a decent orphan bird*: A male war-orphan would be educated by the State.
There are vestiges of a dim ornithological pun.

Stick out your neck: receive this crested helm.
Now you're in the Army, cock.
Keep awake on guard duty, live on your pay, and let
    your father alone. If you feel like fighting,
    take a trip to Thrace: there's always a war on there.
Parricide. You're right. I'll do it, by God!

                                                    (*Exit*)

Pisthetairos.   By God, you'd better!

(*Enter the dithyrambic poet Kinesias.*)

Kinesias (*singing*). "Lifted aloft on wings of song,
    Towards high Olympos winging — "[10]
Pisthetairos. This man needs wings if ever a poet did!
Kinesias (*singing*). "Pure in mind, in body strong,
    Ever of thee, love, singing — "
Pisthetairos. Kinêsias, as I live. Old limpety-lop,
    why did your limping feet bring you up here?
Kinesias (*singing*). "I aim, nor shall my purpose fail,
    To be a Neo-Nightingale."
Pisthetairos. Damn your aim. I suppose you can talk sense?
Kinesias. Oh, ay. Enwingèd, man, by thee I'd be,
    that from the gravid clouds I may charm down
    a meed of music for my sacred soul,
        "Batter'd by ev'ry wind that blows,
        And snow'd upon by snowing snows."[11]
Pisthetairos. This meed of music: you find it in the clouds?
Kinesias. Yea, i' the clouds my Muse doth perch and preen.
    Wottest thou not that th' dithyrambic gene
    burns in the air, most dark, and bright with gloom?
    Plastic with pinions, too.
                        I'll give you an example.
Pisthetairos. Never mind.
Kinesias.   No trouble at all. For instance,
    here's a description of the upper air:
        Pteroid shapes
        Thro' th' aether traipse,
        Longneck'd wrynecks —
Pisthetairos. Hard alee!

---

[10] "*Lifted aloft . . .*": Kinêsias enters singing a love-poem by Anakreôn.
[11] *Oh, ay. Enwingèd . . .*: The absurd diction parodies the manner of the dithyrambic poets, but there is a serious criticism implied: the poetry of Kinêsias is "wingèd" not because of its exaltation, but because of its vain triviality (πρὸς τὸ κοῦφον, says Σ).

Kinesias. Zigging upon the zagging blast,
　　Free in the vast anemoplast —
Pisthetairos. By God, I'll free your blast!
Kinesias. Free to fly at the wind's behest,
　　Now north, now south, now east, now west:
　　Furrowing with my feather'd feet
　　Those fields where eagles eagles meet,
　　Praying a blessing on thy name,
　　Old Architect, for this high game.
Pisthetairos. Stop and put on your wings, damn it, your wings!

　　(*A brief scuffle about the stage*)

Kinesias. And is it thus thoudst serve a modern poet?
　　A poet to whom so many tribes[12] lay claim?
Pisthetairos. Let Leotrophidès claim you to train his squabs!
Kinesias. Thou mockest me, proud Patriarch. Farewell.
　　These wings I'll flap, high water come or hell.

　　(*Exit Kinesias. Enter an informer, singing, unnoticed at first in the
　　confusion of the poet's departure.*)

Informer. "What birds are these whose patchwork dress
　　Reveals that they are penniless?
　　O Swallow, Swallow, tell me."[13]
Pisthetairos (*aside*). That Kinêsias was a rough customer.
　　　　　　　　　　　　　　　　　　— And, by God,
here comes another one!
Informer. "O Swallow, Swallow, tell me."
　　I repeat.
Pisthetairos. He seems to be singing about his coat.
　　Can't blame him: it would take more than one swallow
　　to make that bearable.
Informer. 　　　　　　　A little service, please!
　　Who's distributing wings here?
Pisthetairos. 　　　　　　　Just step this way.
　　Now then: what do you want?

---

[12] *so many tribes:* Although there may be a comic allusion here to the many
cities that claimed Homer as a native son, the central irony is more topical.
The office of Choragos, or Trainer of the Chorus for the dramatic festivals,
was important and much sought after. A. suggests that Kinêsias, a vapid poet,
would be much in demand among the various tribes competing at the festivals, but that no one could have a better claim to his services as Choragos
than Leotrophidès, himself a silly unsubstantial dramatist.
[13] "*What birds are these . . .*": Parody of a song by Alkaios of Mytilenê.

Informer.   Wings, man, wings.
  You deaf?
Pisthetairos. I suppose you're in a hurry
  to get to a clothier's.
Informer.   Wrong. Plumb wrong.
  I am process-server for the Islands.[14]
  Also an Informer.
Pisthetairos.   Thanks for the information.
Informer. Also a professional accuser. So I need some wings.
  Great thing for this Island Circuit. Big business.
Pisthetairos. A pair of wings will make your business bigger?
Informer. Couldn't. But the pirates, you know: always hanging around.
  With wings I could fly right over them like a crane,
  belly full of lawsuits[15] for ballast.
Pisthetairos.   Of course you could.
  Tell me: are you good at spying on aliens?
Informer. Well, a man's got to live. I never learned how to work.[16]
Pisthetairos. Aren't there enough honest jobs in the world,
  that a healthy man like you
  must pick up money selling false information?
Informer. Wings I came for, not sermons.
Pisthetairos.   I just gave you wings.
Informer. The devil you did. All you've done is talk.
Pisthetairos. Haven't you ever heard of "wingèd words"?
Informer. Wingèd words?
Pisthetairos.   Yes, or wingèd actions?
  Say you go into a barber's. Well, they're all
  sitting around there, swapping lies
  about their sons and grandsons. "I swear to God,"
  one of them says,
  "I don't know what to make of that boy of mine.
  "The horses have got him. Can't keep his feet on the ground."
  Another one says, "That's nothing.
  "Mine wants to take a flier at writing plays.
  "The tragic bug's bitten him."
Informer.   So you think
  words can make wings?

---

[14] *the Islands*: The Greek Islanders, not being Athenians, would be easy prey for the Informer.
[15] *belly full of lawsuits*: For the cranes' ballast, see note on p. 413.
[16] *I never learned how to work*: See Luke 16:3: *Ait autem vilicus intra se: Quid faciam quia dominus meus aufert a me vilicationem? fodere no valeo, mendicare erubesco.*

Pisthetairos.   That's it exactly.
  Words heighten concepts; words raise a man
  out of himself. You came to me for wings:
  all right, you can have them; and, what's more,
  I'll throw in a word or two of good advice
  about getting a job that you won't have to blush for.
Informer. No good. No good at all.
Pisthetairos.   Why not?
Informer. Family pride. Can't let the old name down.
  There's been Informers in our family
  since I don't know when.
                                 — But come:
  give me a couple of good swift wings, I don't care
  what model, and I'll get back,
  denounce a few aliens, get them indicted here,
  and then I'm off.
Pisthetairos. You mean you'll have these men
  indicted before they get a chance to appear?
Informer. You said it.
Pisthetairos. And while they're on their way to court
  you'll swoop down on the Islands and grab their goods?
Informer. You get the idea. I'm busy as a top.
Pisthetairos. (*Takes a long whiplash from the bench.*)
  Top? Here's something to make tops spin:
  first-class goods from Korkyra.
Informer.   Put it away!
Pisthetairos. Call it a pair of wings. By God, it'll send *you*
  into a nose-dive!

  (*Lashes him*)

Informer.   Stop it! Police! Stop it!

                                 (*Exit Informer*)

Pisthetairos. All of a flap, hey? Can't wait around? Too bad!
  You sneaking patriot,
  this time you pay the court costs!

                                 (*To his attendants*)
                     Come,
  let's gather up these wings and go inside.

  (*Exit, followed by attendants carrying the bench, wings, and the rest of the paraphernalia*)

CHORIKON:
CHORAL INTERLUDE[1]

Chorus. Numberless are the world's wonders, and we   (*Strophe*)
Have roosted on most of them. In wicked Thrace
There grows the remarkable Kleonymos tree,
Immense, heart-rotted, that in summer yields
Informative fruit; but in winter time its grace
Forsakes it, and its boughs shed unused shields.

And we have seen a region of the dead   (*Antistrophe*)
Where men with Heroes dine before nightfall,
But where the reveller walks home in dread
Lest from the shades a new Orestês come,
Accost him at the turning of the wall,
Strip him, beat him, and leave him bare and numb.

SCENE

(*Enter Prometheus, muffled from head to foot in a red and yellow
cloak and carrying a large black open umbrella.*)

Prometheus. I hope to God Zeus can't see me!
                                                    — Pisthetairos!
    Where's Pisthetairos?

(*Re-enter Pisthetairos*)

Pisthetairos.   What's going on here?
    Who are you in the blankets?
Prometheus.   Look:
    is any god following me?

---

[1] *Chorikon*: In this short ode the Birds begin to describe the strange places
that they have seen in their migrations. The Thracian tree stands for the
recreant bully Kleonymos, the shed "unused shields" representing his own
shield, disgracefully thrown away in battle. Kleonymos made part of his living
as a paid informer: the money would come in during the summer sessions,
slack off during the winter. The Antistrophe, which at first sight seems to
change the subject, actually pursues it. Kleonymos is being equated with the
notorious bandit Orestês (see note on p. 398), while, at the level of myth,
he becomes a kind of burlesque Aigisthos accosted by Agamemnon's avenging
son: the double allusion enforces a shift in the point of view. Σ explains
"numb" by recalling that a chance encounter with a Hero (the bandit had
an heroic nickname) was supposed to paralyze one's side.

Pisthetairos.   God? No.
  Who are you?
Prometheus.   Can you give me the correct time?
Pisthetairos. Noon. Maybe a little later. But who
  are you?
Prometheus. Noon, you said?
Pisthetairos.   Oh, for God's sake!
Prometheus. What's the weather like?
Pisthetairos.   Hey?
Prometheus.   I said, "What's
  the weather like?"
Pisthetairos.   Go to hell!
Prometheus.   Splendid. I'll just
  take off these cerements.

(*Throws off the cloak and stands revealed in scarlet tights.*)

Pisthetairos.   Well, I'll be damned! Prometheus!
Prometheus. Sh, sh, keep your voice down!
Pisthetairos.   What's the matter?
Prometheus. Just don't mention my name. If Zeus finds me here
  he'll scalp me. You don't know the half of it.
  I'll tell you; only,
  please hold this umbrella over my head
  so the gods can't look down and see me from up there.
Pisthetairos. The same old Prometheus! All right; get under,
  and begin to talk.
Prometheus. Listen.
Pisthetairos.   I am.
Prometheus.   Zeus is through.
Pisthetairos.   Since when?
Prometheus. Since you organized Cloudcukooland.
  There's not been so much as a sniff of sacred smoke
  coming up to us from a single human altar.
  I swear, we're hungrier
  than a Thesmophoria fast-day; and, what's worse,
  the damnedest lot of starving yowling gods
  from the back country are talking about revolt
  if Zeus doesn't manage to get a decent consignment
  of sacrificial cuts to keep us going.
Pisthetairos. Do you mean to tell me the Barbarians
  have gods of their own?
Prometheus.   What about Exekestidês?
  Doesn't he have to pray to something?

Pisthetairos.   I see.
But these godforsaken gods: what are they called?

Prometheus. Triballians.

Pisthetairos.   Tribal totems.

Prometheus.   I suppose so.
— But this is what I have come down to tell you:
Zeus and these Triballians
are sending a delegation to look into
what's going on here. Take my advice:
laugh at every offer they make to you
until they swear to restore the Birds to power
and give you Basileia[1] for a wife.

Pisthetairos. Basileia? Who is this Basileia?

Prometheus. She's the prettiest girl you ever saw:
manages Zeus, takes care of his thunderbolts
and all the rest of his weapons — sagacity,
legislation, rearmament, ideology, ultimatums,
revenue officers, jurymen —

Pisthetairos.   She does all that?

Prometheus. That's only an outline. When you get Basileia,
you've got everything.

                        I thought I ought to tell you:
I have a certain stake in humanity.

Pisthetairos. A well-broiled one[2] thanks to your foresightedness.

Prometheus. And I hate the gods.

Pisthetairos.   And the gods hate you.

Prometheus. Yes. I'm a regular Timôn.
                                — But it's late.
I must be getting back.
                        Give me my umbrella:
Zeus will think I'm a Virgin of the Escort.

Pisthetairos. Take this footstool[3] with you; it will make a better effect.

                                        (Exeunt)

---

[1] *Basileia:* Her name means Sovereignty, Imperium. She has no place in the official Pantheon, but is an *ad hoc* creation to provide Pisthetairos with a mate equivalent to Zeus' Hêra. The final mockery of this drama, of course, is the apotheosis of the bungling Hero.

[2] *A well-broiled one:* Prometheus first taught men the use of fire.

[3] *Take this footstool:* At the Panathenaia Festival the daughters of Athenian aristocrats were attended by wealthy girls of foreign ancestry who carried ceremonial footstools and parasols. Prometheus hopes that Zeus, looking down from Olympos, will mistake him for one of these attendants.

CHORIKON:
CHORAL INTERLUDE[1]

Chorus.   There is a mystic river   (*Strophe*)
              In the land of the Shadowfeet
              Where Sokratês the Bathless calls
              The souls of men to meet.

              There Chickenheart Peisandros
              Made sacrifice one day
              To conjure up his own dim soul
              And hear what it would say.

              Odysseus-like he cut the throat
              Of a kind of camel-cat;
              But all he raised was the squeaking ghost
              Of Chairephôn the Bat.

SCENE

(*Enter the Ambassadors from Olympos:*[1] *Poseidon, Herakles, and a Triballian God. The first wears a sea-weed crown, a cloak embroidered with large horse-heads, and carries a trident and a rigid stuffed fish; the second wears a lion skin and carries a club; the third, blackface, wears a stovepipe hat and is desperately entangled in a multicoloured cloak.*)

Poseidon. So this is Cloudcuckooland. Very well,
       let us proceed to act like a Delegation.

                                        (*To the Triballian*)
       You there,
       what are you up to now? Don't you know better

[1] *Chorikon:* The Birds' travel lecture proceeds. The Shadowfeet were a remarkable tribe, said to live in Libya, who enjoyed feet so large that they could be used as parasols during siesta time. This is a fit setting for the deplorable Sokratês, who is represented as "leading the souls of men" — leading them, that is to say, as Odysseus did the souls in Hadês, but also misleading them by perverse teaching, a charge that A. constantly makes against this philosopher. The Strophê is a comic *Nekuia*, parodying the eleventh book of the *Odyssey*. The fainthearted Peisandros, having lost his own soul, goes to the land of the Shadowfeet to conjure it back.
[1] *the Ambassadors from Olympos:* This theophany seems outrageous to us, but our ideas of what constitutes blasphemy are different from the Greeks', who would find A. brilliantly but conventionally comic.

than to drape your cloak on the left side? Look,
you celestial rustic, it ought to hang on the right,
gracefully, like this. Do you want these people
to take you for Laispodias? Hold still,
can't you? There!
Democracy, what sins are committed in thy name![2]
Damn it, of all the barbarous gods I've met
you're the barbarousest.
                    — What's your plan, Heraklês?
Herakles. You heard what I said. Just cream the guy
what shut the gods out with this here Stone Curtain.
Poseidon. Yes, my good fellow; but we're supposed to discuss peace.
Herakles. All the more reason for creaming him, I say.

(*Enter Pisthetairos attended by various birds in kitchen costume,
he elaborately disregards the Ambassadors.*)

Pisthetairos.   Quick, now,
let's have the cheesegrater. Where's the horseradish?[3]
Grate that cheese, somebody. Keep the fire hot.
Poseidon. In the name of the Divine Authority,
three gods greet thee, O Man.
Pisthetairos.   The horseradish.
Herakles. Say Mac, what kind of a roast is that?
Pisthetairos. Bird roast. Subjects condemned for subversion
of the Authority of the Birds.
Herakles.   And you use
horseradish?
Pisthetairos.   Why, it's Heraklês! Good
afternoon, Heraklês.
Poseidon.   The Divine Authority
empowers three gods to consider conciliation.
A Cook. Oil's out. What do I do now?
Herakles.   No oil?
Damn bad. You can't barbecue without oil.
Poseidon. Regarded disinterestedly, this war
subserves no aim of the Divine Authority.
Similarly, your Delegates should reflect
how much you have to gain from a friendly Olympos:
I instance only

---

[2] *Democracy, what sins . . .*: Zeus, to be fair, has decided that even the Barbarians should be represented in this embassage.
[3] *The horseradish*: Literally, *silphion*.

fresh rain water for your swamps, and halcyon days.
Shall we initiate talks?
Pisthetairos.   I don't see why.
In the first place, we were not the ones
who started hostilities. But let that pass.
As for peace, we are perfectly willing to agree
if the gods will meet our terms. We demand
restoration of our ancient sovereignty
and the return of the sceptre to the Birds.
Let Zeus accept that much, and I'll invite
all three of you to dinner.
Herakles.   I vote Yes.
Poseidon. You gastric monomaniac, would you vote away
your own Father's crown?
Pisthetairos.   That's a silly question.
Do you gods imagine that you will be losing power
by delegating the imperium of the skies?
Surely you know that all over the earth
men are hiding under clouds and breaking your laws
with impunity. Suppose you had the Birds
on your side: then if a man swore
by Zeus and the Crow, say, and broke his oath,
we'd simply have a Crow swoop down upon him
and peck out his right eye.
Poseidon.   Good, by Myself![4]
Herakles. I think so too.
Pisthetairos (*to Triballian*). What do *you* say?
Triballian.   Wockle.[5]
Herakles. The poor fish says Yes.
Pisthetairos.   And here's something else.
Suppose a man promises an offering
to some god or other, and maybe greed
gets the better of him, and he thinks: *Well,*
the gods are used to waiting:
                              we birds
will know how to handle him.
Poseidon.   How? Instruct me.
Pisthetairos. Well, say that man's
sitting in his office some day, counting his money,

[4] *by Myself!*: Poseidon swears "By Poseidon!"
[5] *Wockle*: The Triballian speaks a murky language rather like that of Muta
and Juva in *Finnegans Wake*. Much needless ingenuity has been expended by
Professors attempting to reduce it to sense.

or say he's in the tub enjoying a nice hot bath:
down comes one of the Kites when he isn't looking
and zooms off to Olympos with a couple of his sheep.

Herakles. I say it again: give the Birds what they ask for.

Poseidon. What do *you* think?

Pisthetairos. Speak, you divine Mistake.

Triballian. Treeballs beetee gnaw ouch, Glapp.

Herakles. He says Yes.

Poseidon. If you say so. I suppose I must say so too.
Very well. Divine Authority cedes the Scepter.

Pisthetairos. Hold on! I nearly forgot.
The Birds are prepared to confirm Zeus' right to Hêra,
but in return
they insist upon my having Basileia.

Poseidon. I can see that you are not interested in peace.
Good-bye.

Pisthetairos. It makes no difference to me.
— Now this gravy, cook: see that it's thick enough.

Herakles. Hey, damn it, Admiral, hold on, what the hell?
Who wants to fight a war for a damn woman?[6]

Poseidon. What else can we do?

Herakles. Damn it, make peace!

Poseidon. Idiot, can't you see he's trying to ruin you?
And you walk right into the trap.
Think a moment: if Zeus
gives the Birds what they ask for, and then dies —
Where are you then? Where's your inheritance?

Pisthetairos. Heraklês, don't listen to the man.
Every word he speaks is a delusion.

(*Beckons him aside*)

Step over here a minute.
— My poor fellow,
that Ancient Mariner is just leading you on.
You inherit from Zeus? You couldn't, not a penny.
You, being a bastard —

Herakles. Me, a bastard?
Say, listen, you —

Pisthetairos. Well, your mother
was an alien, wasn't she? Besides, Athêna

---

[6] *Who wants to fight a war for a damn woman?*: As the Trojan War was
fought for Helen.

is heir apparent, and how could she be that
if she had legitimate brothers?
Herakles.   What if the Boss
says I'm his heir, bastard or no bastard?
Pisthetairos. Illegal. And suppose he does:
Poseidon will be the first to contest the will,
as the decedent's brother.
                          Here is the law,
straight from Solôn:
A BASTARD SHALL NOT INHERIT IF THERE BE LEGIT-
    IMATE ISSUE. IF THERE BE NO LEGITIMATE ISSUE,
    THE PROPERTY SHALL PASS TO THE NEXT OF KIN.
Herakles. So I can't get nothing out of the Old Man's estate?
Pisthetairos. Nothing at all.
                          — For that matter,
has your Father enrolled you yet?[7]
Herakles.   No. I guess I know why.
Pisthetairos. Come, what's the use of snapping at empty wind?
Join the Birds:
you'll live like a king and feed on pie in the sky.[8]

(*They return to the others.*)

Herakles. About that dame we were beating our gums about:
I said, and I say it again: Give him what he wants.
Pisthetairos. You, Poseidon?
Poseidon.   No.
Pisthetairos.   Then the Triballian
must break the tie. Vote, heavenly Hayseed!
Triballian. Quiffing gamsel cockitty, gotta tweet tweet.
Herakles. He says Yes.
Poseidon.   I doubt very much if he says Yes
or anything else that matters. But let it pass.
Herakles. He's ready to pass her over, anyhow.
Poseidon. Have it your way, you two. Make your peace,
and I'll hold mine.
Herakles.   These here top-level talks
are all over, and we say he gets the green light.
Come on, man, you got a date up in the sky
with Basileia and any other damn thing you want.

[7] *has your Father enrolled you yet?*: In the register of citizens; as the illegiti-
mate son of a foreign woman, Heraklês would be ineligible.
[8] *pie in the sky*: The Greek phrase was "birds' milk," but this seems too
esoteric.

Pisthetairos. It's a lucky thing that I had these roasts ready.
   They'll do for the wedding.
Herakles.   You birds run along:
   I'll stick around here and keep an eye on the cook.
Poseidon. Can't you rise superior to food? You come with us.
Pisthetairos. And somebody bring along my wedding clothes.

(*Exeunt omnes; manet Chorus*)

CHORIKON:
CHORAL INTERLUDE[1]

Chorus.   Phonéya is that far country   (*Antistrophe*)
             Where the Englottogasters dwell:
           They plough the fields there with their tongues
             And sow and reap as well.

           Oh blest Englottogasters!
             And yet we need not roam
           In search of tongues as versatile —
             They twitch for us at home:

           The tongue that tells for ready cash,
             The slimy tongue that smiles,
           The paid, applauded, patriot tongue
             That guards us, and defiles.

EXODOS[1]

(*Enter Third Messenger*.)

Messenger. Thrice happy generation of Birds, O winged
   with joy beyond words' contriving: receive

[1] *Chorikon*: The travelogue resumed. The Englottogasters, "men who live by
their tongues," are nearer home than the Shadowfeet: they are to be found
wherever men make money by informing on their fellows, and are particularly
flagrant in times of political uncertainty.
[1] *Exodos*: The conclusion of the play is dictated not only by dramatic appro-
priateness — the marriage and deification of the Hero —, but by ritual inheritance. Comedy culminates in marriage, and the final scene (*cf*. the *Peace*
and, though slightly different in vein, the *Lysistrata*) has overtones of an
ancestral fertility rite. The Chorus sings of the wedding of Zeus and Hêra,
thus equating Pisthetairos and Basileia with the King and Queen of Heaven.
The ordinary man has found Cloudcuckooland, his Utopia, and now becomes
God. Like God, he insists upon the recital of his own meritorious exploits.

your great Prince in his palace of delight!
His glory burns: no star
flames brighter in the wheeling vault, no sun
has ever blazed so pure. He comes,
and beauty walks beside him crowned
with lightning from God's hand, his divine
Bride, veiled i' th' smoke of incense rising.
Your King, your Queen!
Sing them a song of the Nine Sisters' devising.

(*Re-enter Pisthetairos, splendidly gowned, with newly gilded wings;
he is accompanied by Basileia, in cloth of gold, crowned, her face
hidden by a veil.*)

Chorus. Back!
                    Make way there!
                                        Circle them!
                                                            Dance!
                    Beat on the bright ground with quick feet
                    For the Prince of Luck, for His Bride —
                            Oh sweet! Oh fair! —
                    Dance, dance the marriage in the air.

Koryphaios. Dance in the sky,
                            joy in the sky!
                    Dance in the reign of the Birds,
                                                dance in
                    The augury of his polity:
                    Dance Hymen
                                the wedding chorus
                                                        dance

Chorus.   When heavenly Hêra was the bride   (*Strophe*)
                            Of Zeus in his high hall,
                    The Fatal Ladies danced and sang
                            This for their festival:
                                *Round the royal pair we go:
                                Hymen O! The wedding O!*

                    Erôs flicked his golden wings   (*Antistrophe*)
                            To be their charioteer,
                    And through the swaying skies their car
                            Darted in sweet career.
                                *Round the royal pair we go:
                                Hymen O! The wedding O!*

Pisthetairos. For your songs, for your good wishes, thanks:
I am gratified, and I am sure
that I speak for my wife as well. I should be
even more gratified to hear you perform
two or three odes in honor of my triumph
over the dangerous thunderbolts of Zeus,
the difficult lightning.

Chorus.   O fire lancing the black night,   (*Epode*)
         O rage of voices under ground,
      Thunder, hurly of rain, bright
         Tempest of sound:
      Sing, sing his audacity
         Who draws down from God's throne
      God's Basileia, Sovereignty,
         And crowns her his own.
            Round the royal pair we go:
            Hymen O! The wedding O!

Pisthetairos. Follow the bridal, follow, fortunate friends,
to the high lands of God, to the happy bed.
And oh my darling, take
my wings in your shining hands, and I
will lift you, lift you above the sky
in the Birds' dance, the whirring dance.

Chorus.   *Iô! Iô!*
            Iê Paián![2] *Alalaí!*
         See the conquering hero go!
         Hymen O! The wedding O!

Of the hundreds of ancient Greek comedies that were written, only
eleven by Aristophanes and four by Menander (c. 342 B.C.–299 B.C.)
are extant, and three of Menander's four survive only in long fragments. Aristophanes seems to have written about 40 plays, Menander
more than twice as many. Hundreds of other men wrote comedies in
ancient Greece, but they are mere names, or names attached to brief
fragments. This means that when we talk about Greek comedy we are

---

[2] *Iê Paián!*: The play ends with a volley of ritual phrases, among which rings
the Athenian battle-cry *Alalai!*, which had been *Eleleú!* among the Birds.

really talking about a fraction of Aristophanes' work, and an even smaller fraction of Menander's.

Greek comedy is customarily divided into three kinds: Old Comedy (486 B.C., when comedy was first given official recognition at the festival called the City Dionysia, to 404 B.C., the end of the Peloponnesian War, when Athens was humbled and freedom of speech was curtailed); Middle Comedy (404 B.C., to 336 B.C., the accession of Alexander, when Athens was no longer free); and New Comedy (336 B.C., to c. 250 B.C., the approximate date of the last fragments). Of Old Comedy, there are Aristophanes' plays; of Middle Comedy, there is *Plutus*, one of Aristophanes' last plays; of New Comedy, there are Menander's fragments and his recently discovered *Dyskolos* (*The Disagreeable Man*).

Old Comedy is a curious combination of obscenity, farce, political allegory, satire, and lyricism. Puns, literary allusions, phallic jokes, political jibes, etc. periodically give way to joyful song; Aristophanes seems to have been something of a combination of Joyce, Swift, and Shelley. Normally his plays have the following structure:

1) *prologos*, prologue or exposition. Someone has a bright idea, and sets it forth either in monologue or dialogue. In *The Birds* the prologue consists of pages 371–380, in which Pisthetairos suggests that the birds unite to regain their sovereignty over the universe by intercepting sacrificial smoke and thus starving the gods into submission.

2) *parodos*, entrance of the fantastically dressed chorus. The twenty-four or so members of the chorus express their opinion of the idea. (The *koryphaios* or leader of the chorus perhaps sang some lines by himself.) *The Birds* is unusual in devoting part of the *parodos* (pages 380–387) to the lyrics of Epops instead of entirely to choral songs.

3) *agon*, or debate. In pages 387–396 Pisthetairos persuades the chorus of birds to accept his idea. Aristophanes now adds a short scene (page 396) introducing the nightingale, which gets the actors (as distinguished from the chorus) off the stage.

4) *parabasis* (pages 396–401), an elaborate composition in which the leader of the chorus ordinarily sheds his dramatic character and addresses the audience on the poet's behalf, the other actors having briefly retired. (Its parts are the *kommation*, or introductory song; the *parabasis* itself, or "coming forward"; the *makron* or *pnigos*, lines to be recited at one breath; the *strophe* or *ode*; the *epirrhema*; the *antistrophe* or *antode*; and the *antepirrhema*.) In *The Birds*, atypically, the chorus retains its identity

during the *parabasis*. Also atypical is the second *parabasis*, pages 411–412, full of warnings to men who maltreat birds.

5) *epeisodia*, scenes or episodes (pages 412–424, 425–427, 428–433), briefly separated by choral songs. These episodes have to do with putting the original idea into practice. In *The Birds*, they are devoted to talk of building the new city, and to fending off various intruders. After the second *parabasis* the episodes set forth further problems having to do with Cloudcuckooland.

6) *exodos* or final scene (pages 433–435), customarily of rejoicing. There is often talk of a wedding and a feast. In this play the chorus sings in honor of the marriage of Pisthetairos and Basileia ("Sovereignty"), and then marches out joyfully.

Perhaps all Old Comedy was rather like this, but it should be remembered that even Aristophanes' eleven plays do not all follow the pattern exactly. *The Birds*, for example, is unusual in having the chorus retain its identity during the parabasis, in having a second parabasis, and in the sparseness of its obscenity. But *The Birds* is typical in its fantasy, in its variety, in its political concern, and in its revelry. It is joyous and extravagant, it touches on serious themes (What ought a city to be?), and it follows the usual comic formula of ending with a newly unified society. It begins with Pisthetairos and Euelpides complaining of the frustrating life in Athens, and it ends with talk of a *gamos* (sexual union) in a new city where men live among birds. Pisthetairos is wed to Zeus' daughter, Basileia, in the city of his whim. The *polos* (pole, sky, heaven) has paradoxically become a *polis* (city), a city of wind, a city of nothingness, and yet a city that is rather like an Athens ruled by Pisthetairos — who had left Athens because it was troublesome. It should be noted that this new society is not conspicuously more moral than the Athens abandoned by Pisthetairos. If Aristophanes was voicing a criticism of Athens at the outset, he did not follow it with a depiction of an ideal city. Pisthetairos is as much rascal as reformer, and scholarly attempts to see in his city some sort of allegory furnishing a blueprint for reforming Athens are unconvincing. Utopia as well as Athens is satirized. What is celebrated is not so much a vision of a new Athens as a vision of the powers of fantasy. Aristophanes toys with ideas, turns them around and around, holds them up and laughs at them; they are soap bubbles or smoke rings, clever and attractive things that the creator delights in and yet demolishes with no less delight. Something of this double vision, this playing seriously with an idea that one doesn't believe, and treating playfully something one does believe, can be neatly seen in Matthew Arnold's, "Poor Mathias," a poem on the death of a pet canary. Arnold, recalling Aristophanes'

celebration of birds as superior to men, in his elegy for the canary
included a passage that (although devoid of bawdry and exuberance) is
Aristophanic in its lyricism and in the play of mind it reveals:

> Was it, as the Grecian sings,
> Birds were born the first of things,
> Before the sun, before the wind,
> Before the gods, before mankind,
> Airy, ante-mundane throng —
> Witness their unworldly song!
> Proof they give, too, primal powers,
> Of a prescience more than ours —
> Teach us, while they come and go,
> When to sail, and when to sow.
> Cuckoo calling from the hill,
> Swallow skimming by the mill,
> Swallows trooping in the sedge,
> Starlings swirling from the hedge,
> Mark the seasons, map our year,
> As they show and disappear.
> But, with all this travail sage
> Brought from that anterior age,
> Goes an unreversed decree
> Whereby strange are they and we,
> Making want of theirs, and plan,
> Indiscernible by man.

A few words should be said about Middle Comedy and New Comedy. Middle Comedy is a convenient label to apply to the lost plays
that must have marked the transition from Old Comedy to New
Comedy. In New Comedy, written when Athens' political greatness
was gone, and when political invective was impossible, the chorus has
dwindled to musicians and dancers who perform intermittently, characters tend to be types (the young lover, the crabby old father, etc.),
and the plot is regularly a young man's wooing of a maid. The personal
satire and obscenity of Old Comedy are gone, and in their place is a
respectably conducted tale showing how, after humorous difficulties,
the young man achieves his goal. The happy ending is the thing toward
which the plot steadily moves, and it is far more integral than the
more or less elusive allegoric (or metaphoric) union at the end of
The Birds. It was New Comedy that influenced Rome (which could
scarcely have imitated the political satire of Old Comedy), and
through Rome modern Europe. Shakespeare, for example, whose
comedies have been described as obstacle races to the altar, was a
descendant of Menander though he knew nothing of Menander's work
first-hand.

As You Like It

WILLIAM SHAKESPEARE

Edited by Albert Gilman

William Shakespeare (1564–1616) was born in Stratford, England, of middle-class parents. Nothing of interest is known about his early years, but by 1590 he was acting and writing plays in London. He early worked in all three Elizabethan dramatic genres — tragedy, comedy, and history. Romeo and Juliet, for example, was written about 1595, the year of Richard II, and in the following year he wrote A Midsummer Night's Dream. Julius Caesar (1599) probably preceded As You Like It by one year, and Hamlet probably followed As You Like It by less than a year. Among the plays that followed Othello (1603–1604) were King Lear (1605–06), Macbeth (1605–06), and several "romances" — plays that have happy endings but that seem more meditative and closer to tragedy than such comedies as A Midsummer Night's Dream, As You Like It, and Twelfth Night.

[DRAMATIS PERSONAE

Duke Senior, in banishment in the Forest of Arden
Duke Frederick, his brother, usurper of the Dukedom
Amiens
Jaques } lords attending on Duke Senior
Le Beau, a courtier
Charles, a wrestler
Oliver
Jaques } sons of Sir Rowland de Boys
Orlando
Adam
Dennis } servants to Oliver
Touchstone, a clown
Sir Oliver Mar-text, a vicar
Corin
Silvius } shepherds
William, a country fellow
Hymen
Rosalind, daughter to Duke Senior
Celia, daughter to Duke Frederick
Phebe, a shepherdess
Audrey, a country girl
Lords, *Pages*, *Foresters*, and *Attendants*

SCENE

(*Oliver's house; the court; the Forest of Arden*)]

440

ACT I

SCENE 1. [*Orchard of Oliver's house.*]

(*Enter Orlando and Adam.*)

Orlando. As I remember, Adam, it was upon this fashion be-
queathed me by will but poor a°¹ thousand crowns, and, as
thou say'st, charged my brother on his blessing to breed me
well; and there begins my sadness. My brother Jaques he keeps
at school, and report speaks goldenly of his profit.° For my part,   5
he keeps me rustically° at home or, to speak more properly,
stays me here at home unkept;° for call you that keeping for a
gentleman of my birth that differs not from the stalling of an
ox? His horses are bred better, for, besides that they are fair°
with their feeding, they are taught their manage,° and to that   10
end riders dearly hired; but I, his brother, gain nothing under
him but growth, for the which his animals on his dunghills are
as much bound to him as I. Besides this nothing that he so
plentifully gives me, the something that nature gave me his

---

¹ The degree sign (°) indicates a footnote, which is keyed to the text by
line number. Text references are printed in *italic* type; the annotation follows
in roman type.
I.i.² *poor a* a mere   ⁵ *goldenly of his profit* glowingly of his progress
⁶ *keeps me rustically* supports me like a peasant
⁷ *unkept* uncared for   ⁹ *fair* handsome   ¹⁰ *manage* paces

441

countenance° seems to take from me. He lets me feed with his   15
hinds,° bars me the place of a brother, and, as much as in him
lies, mines my gentility° with my education. This is it, Adam,
that grieves me; and the spirit of my father, which I think is
within me, begins to mutiny against this servitude. I will no
longer endure it, though yet I know no wise remedy how to   20
avoid it.

(*Enter Oliver.*)

Adam. Yonder comes my master, your brother.
Orlando. Go apart, Adam, and thou shalt hear how he will shake
   me up.°
Oliver. Now, sir, what make you° here?   25
Orlando. Nothing. I am not taught to make anything.
Oliver. What mar you then, sir?
Orlando. Marry,° sir, I am helping you to mar that which God
   made, a poor unworthy brother of yours, with idleness.
Oliver. Marry, sir, be better employed, and be naught awhile.°   30
Orlando. Shall I keep your hogs and eat husks with them? What
   prodigal portion have I spent° that I should come to such
   penury?
Oliver. Know you where° you are, sir?
Orlando. O, sir, very well. Here in your orchard.   35
Oliver. Know you before whom, sir?
Orlando. Ay, better than him I am before knows me. I know you
   are my eldest brother, and in the gentle condition of blood° you
   should so know me. The courtesy of nations° allows you my
   better in that you are the first born, but the same tradition   40
   takes not away my blood were there twenty brothers betwixt
   us. I have as much of my father in me as you, albeit I confess
   your coming before me is nearer to his reverence.°

---

¹⁵ *countenance* behavior   ¹⁶ *hinds* farm hands
¹⁷ *mines my gentility* undermines my good birth
²³⁻²⁴ *shake me up* berate me
²⁵ *make you* are you doing (in the next line Orlando pretends to take the
phrase to mean "accomplish")
²⁸ *Marry* (an expletive, from "By the Virgin Mary")
³⁰ *be naught awhile* i.e., don't bother me
³¹⁻³² *Shall I . . . spent* (an allusion to the story of the Prodigal Son. See Luke
15:11–32)
³⁴ *where* i.e., in whose presence (Orlando pretends to take it literally)
³⁸ *in the gentle condition of blood* i.e., of the same good blood
³⁹ *courtesy of nations* i.e., sanctioned custom of primogeniture
⁴³ *your coming . . . reverence* i.e., as the eldest son you are head of the family
and therefore entitled to respect

Oliver. What, boy!   [*Strikes him.*]

Orlando. Come, come, elder brother, you are too young in this.   45
                                    [*Seizes him.*]

Oliver. Wilt thou lay hands on me, villain?°

Orlando. I am no villain. I am the youngest son of Sir Rowland de Boys; he was my father, and he is thrice a villain that says such a father begot villains. Wert thou not my brother, I would not take this hand from thy throat till this other had pulled   50 out thy tongue for saying so. Thou hast railed on thyself.

Adam. Sweet masters, be patient. For your father's remembrance, be at accord.

Oliver. Let me go, I say.

Orlando. I will not till I please. You shall hear me. My father   55 charged you in his will to give me good education. You have trained me like a peasant, obscuring and hiding from me all gentlemanlike qualities.° The spirit of my father grows strong in me, and I will no longer endure it. Therefore allow me such exercises° as may become a gentleman, or give me the poor   60 allottery° my father left me by testament; with that I will go buy my fortunes.

Oliver. And what wilt thou do? Beg when that is spent? Well, sir, get you in. I will not long be troubled with you. You shall have some part of your will. I pray you leave me.   65

Orlando. I will no further offend you than becomes me for my good.

Oliver. Get you with him, you old dog.

Adam. Is "old dog" my reward? Most true, I have lost my teeth in your service. God be with my old master; he would not have   70 spoke such a word.

(*Exeunt Orlando, Adam.*)

Oliver. Is it even so? Begin you to grow upon me?° I will physic your rankness° and yet give no thousand crowns neither. Holla, Dennis!

(*Enter Dennis.*)

Dennis. Calls your worship?   75

---

⁴⁶ *villain* (Oliver uses it in the sense of "wicked person," but Orlando plays on its other meaning, "low-born person")
⁵⁸ *qualities* accomplishments   ⁶⁰ *exercises* occupations   ⁶¹ *allottery* share
⁷² *grow upon me* i.e., usurp my place
⁷²⁻⁷³ *physic your rankness* purge your overgrowth

Oliver. Was not Charles, the Duke's wrestler, here to speak with me?

Dennis. So please you, he is here at the door and importunes access to you.

Oliver. Call him in. [*Exit Dennis.*] 'Twill be a good way; and   80
tomorrow the wrestling is.

(*Enter Charles.*)

Charles. Good morrow to your worship.

Oliver. Good Monsieur Charles, what's the new news at the new court?

Charles. There's no news at the court, sir, but the old news. That   85
is, the old Duke° is banished by his younger brother the new
Duke, and three or four loving lords have put themselves into
voluntary exile with him, whose lands and revenues enrich the
new Duke; therefore he gives them good leave to wander.

Oliver. Can you tell if Rosalind, the Duke's daughter, be ban-   90
ished with her father?

Charles. O, no; for the Duke's daughter, her cousin, so loves her,
being ever from their cradles bred together, that she would have
followed her exile, or have died to stay behind her. She is at
the court, and no less beloved of her uncle than his own   95
daughter, and never two ladies loved as they do.

Oliver. Where will the old Duke live?

Charles. They say he is already in the Forest of Arden,° and a
many merry men with him; and there they live like the old
Robin Hood of England. They say many young gentlemen flock   100
to him every day, and fleet the time carelessly° as they did in
the golden world.°

Oliver. What, you wrestle tomorrow before the new Duke?

Charles. Marry, do I, sir; and I came to acquaint you with a matter. I am given, sir, secretly to understand that your younger   105
brother, Orlando, hath a disposition to come in disguised
against me to try a fall.° Tomorrow, sir, I wrestle for my credit,
and he that escapes me without some broken limb shall acquit
him well. Your brother is but young and tender, and for your
love I would be loath to foil° him, as I must for my own honor   110

---

⁸⁶ *old Duke* i.e., Duke Senior
⁹⁸ *Forest of Arden* Ardennes (in France; though Shakespeare may also have
had in mind the Forest of Arden near his birthplace)
¹⁰¹ *fleet the time carelessly* pass the time at ease
¹⁰² *golden world* (the Golden Age of classical mythology, when men were free
of sin, want, and care)   ¹⁰⁷ *fall* bout   ¹¹⁰ *foil* throw, defeat

if he come in. Therefore, out of my love to you, I came hither
to acquaint you withal, that either you might stay him from his
intendment, or brook° such disgrace well as he shall run into,
in that it is a thing of his own search and altogether against
my will.   115

Oliver. Charles, I thank thee for thy love to me, which thou shalt
find I will most kindly requite. I had myself notice of my
brother's purpose herein and have by underhand means° la-
bored to dissuade him from it; but he is resolute. I'll tell thee,
Charles, it is the stubbornest young fellow of France; full of   120
ambition, an envious emulator° of every man's good parts,° a
secret and villainous contriver against me his natural° brother.
Therefore use thy discretion. I had as lief° thou didst break his
neck as his finger. And thou wert best look to't; for if thou
dost him any slight disgrace, or if he do not mightily grace   125
himself on thee,° he will practice° against thee by poison, en-
trap thee by some treacherous device, and never leave thee till
he hath ta'en thy life by some indirect means or other; for, I
assure thee, and almost with tears I speak it, there is not one
so young and so villainous this day living. I speak but brotherly   130
of him, but should I anatomize° him to thee as he is, I must
blush and weep, and thou must look pale and wonder.

Charles. I am heartily glad I came hither to you. If he come
tomorrow, I'll give him his payment. If ever he go alone° again,
I'll never wrestle for prize more. And so God keep your worship.   135

                                                                                    (*Exit.*)

Oliver. Farewell, good Charles. Now will I stir this gamester.°
I hope I shall see an end of him; for my soul, yet I know not
why, hates nothing more than he. Yet he's gentle,° never
schooled and yet learned, full of noble device,° of all sorts°   140
enchantingly beloved; and indeed so much in the heart of the
world, and especially of my own people, who best know him,
that I am altogether misprized.° But it shall not be so long;
this wrestler shall clear all.° Nothing remains but that I kindle
the boy thither, which now I'll go about.   (*Exit.*)   145

---

113 *brook* endure   118 *by underhand means* indirectly
121 *envious emulator* malicious rival   121 *parts* abilities   122 *natural* blood
123 *lief* soon   125–126 *grace himself on thee* gain credit at your expense
126 *practice* plot   131 *anatomize* fully describe
134 *go alone* i.e., walk without crutches   136 *gamester* athlete, sportsman
139 *gentle* endowed with the qualities of a gentleman
140 *noble device* gentleman-like purposes   140 *all sorts* all kinds of people
143 *misprized* scorned   144 *clear all* settle matters

SCENE 2. [*The Duke's palace.*]

(*Enter Rosalind and Celia.*)

Celia. I pray thee, Rosalind, sweet my coz,° be merry.

Rosalind. Dear Celia, I show more mirth than I am mistress of,
and would you yet I were merrier? Unless you could teach me
to forget a banished father, you must not learn° me how to remember any extraordinary pleasure.   5

Celia. Herein I see thou lov'st me not with the full weight that I
love thee. If my uncle, thy banished father, had banished thy
uncle, the Duke my father, so° thou hadst been still with me,
I could have taught my love to take thy father for mine. So
wouldst thou, if the truth of thy love to me were so righteously   10
tempered° as mine is to thee.

Rosalind. Well, I will forget the condition of my estate° to rejoice
in yours.

Celia. You know my father hath no child but I, nor none is like
to have; and truly, when he dies, thou shalt be his heir; for what   15
he hath taken away from thy father perforce,° I will render thee
again in affection. By mine honor, I will, and when I break that
oath, let me turn monster. Therefore, my sweet Rose, my dear
Rose, be merry.

Rosalind. From henceforth I will, coz, and devise sports. Let me   20
see, what think you of falling in love?

Celia. Marry, I prithee, do, to make sport withal; but love no man
in good earnest, nor no further in sport neither than with safety
of a pure° blush thou mayst in honor come off° again.

Rosalind. What shall be our sport then?   25

Celia. Let us sit and mock the good housewife° Fortune from her
wheel,° that her gifts may henceforth be bestowed equally.

Rosalind. I would we could do so, for her benefits are mightily
misplaced, and the bountiful blind woman doth most mistake
in her gifts to women.   30

Celia. 'Tis true, for those that she makes fair,° she scarce makes

---

I.ii.¹ *sweet my coz* my sweet cousin   ⁴ *learn* teach   ⁸ *so* provided that
¹⁰⁻¹¹ *righteously tempered* perfectly composed   ¹² *estate* fortune
¹⁶ *perforce* forcibly   ²⁴ *pure* mere   ²⁴ *come off* get away
²⁶ *housewife* (1) woman of the house (with a spinning wheel) (2) inconstant
hussy
²⁷ *wheel* (the wheel turned by Fortune, blind goddess who distributed her
favors at random, elevated some men and hurled others down)
³¹ *fair* beautiful

honest,° and those that she makes honest, she makes very ill-favoredly.°

Rosalind. Nay, now thou goest from Fortune's office° to Nature's. Fortune reigns in gifts of the world,° not in the lineaments of Nature.° 35

(*Enter* [*Touchstone, the*] *Clown.*)

Celia. No; when Nature hath made a fair creature, may she not by Fortune fall into the fire? Though Nature hath given us wit to flout at Fortune, hath not Fortune sent in this fool to cut off the argument? 40

Rosalind. Indeed, there is Fortune too hard for Nature when Fortune makes Nature's natural° the cutter-off of Nature's wit.

Celia. Peradventure° this is not Fortune's work neither, but Nature's, who perceiveth our natural wits too dull to reason of such goddesses and hath sent this natural for our whetstone. 45 For always the dullness of the fool is the whetstone of the wits. How now, wit; whither wander you?

Touchstone. Mistress, you must come away to your father.

Celia. Were you made the messenger?

Touchstone. No, by mine honor, but I was bid to come for you. 50

Rosalind. Where learned you that oath, fool?

Touchstone. Of a certain knight that swore by his honor they were good pancakes, and swore by his honor the mustard was naught.° Now I'll stand to it,° the pancakes were naught, and the mustard was good, and yet was not the knight forsworn.° 55

Celia. How prove you that in the great heap of your knowledge?

Rosalind. Ay, marry, now unmuzzle your wisdom.

Touchstone. Stand you both forth now. Stroke your chins, and swear by your beards that I am a knave.

Celia. By our beards, if we had them, thou art. 60

Touchstone. By my knavery, if I had it, then I were; but if you swear by that that is not, you are not forsworn; no more was this knight, swearing by his honor, for he never had any; or if he had, he had sworn it away before ever he saw those pancakes or that mustard. 65

Celia. Prithee, who is't that thou mean'st?

Touchstone. One that old Frederick, your father, loves.

---

³² *honest* chaste   ³³ *ill-favoredly* ugly   ³⁴ *office* function
³⁵ *gifts of the world* e.g., wealth, power
³⁵⁻³⁶ *lineaments of Nature* e.g., virtue, intelligence
⁴² *natural* born fool, halfwit   ⁴³ *Peradventure* perhaps
⁵⁴ *naught* worthless   ⁵⁴ *stand to it* swear   ⁵⁵ *forsworn* perjured

Celia. My father's love is enough to honor him enough. Speak no
  more of him; you'll be whipped for taxation° one of these days.
Touchstone. The more pity that fools may not speak wisely what   70
  wise men do foolishly.
Celia. By my troth,° thou sayest true, for since the little wit that
  fools have was silenced, the little foolery that wise men have
  makes a great show. Here comes Monsieur Le Beau.

(*Enter Le Beau.*)

Rosalind. With his mouth full of news.   75
Celia. Which he will put° on us as pigeons feed their young.
Rosalind. Then shall we be news-crammed.
Celia. All the better; we shall be the more marketable. Bon jour,
  Monsieur Le Beau, what's the news?
Le Beau. Fair princess, you have lost much good sport.   80
Celia. Sport? Of what color?°
Le Beau. What color, madam? How shall I answer you?
Rosalind. As wit and fortune° will.
Touchstone. Or as the Destinies decrees.°
Celia. Well said; that was laid on with a trowel.   85
Touchstone. Nay, if I keep not my rank —
Rosalind. Thou losest thy old smell.
Le Beau. You amaze° me, ladies. I would have told you of good
  wrestling, which you have lost the sight of.°
Rosalind. Yet tell us the manner of the wrestling.   90
Le Beau. I will tell you the beginning; and if it please your lady-
  ships, you may see the end, for the best is yet to do,° and here,
  where you are, they are coming to perform it.
Celia. Well, the beginning that is dead and buried.
Le Beau. There comes an old man and his three sons —   95
Celia. I could match this beginning with an old tale.°
Le Beau. Three proper° young men, of excellent growth and
  presence.
Rosalind. With bills° on their necks, "Be it known unto all men
  by these presents."°   100

---

⁶⁹ *taxation* slander   ⁷² *troth* faith   ⁷⁶ *put* force
⁸¹ *color* sort   ⁸³ *fortune* good luck
⁸⁴ *decrees* (the ending *s* was a common variant in the third person plural)
⁸⁸ *amaze* confuse   ⁸⁹ *lost the sight of* missed   ⁹² *do* be done
⁹⁶ *old tale* (Le Beau's story has a "Once upon a time" beginning)
⁹⁷ *proper* fine   ⁹⁹ *bills* notices
¹⁰⁰ *by these presents* (part of the opening formula of many legal documents.
Rosalind puns on Le Beau's use of "presence," meaning "bearing")

Le Beau. The eldest of the three wrestled with Charles, the Duke's wrestler; which Charles in a moment threw him and broke three of his ribs, that there is little hope of life in him. So he served the second, and so the third. Yonder they lie, the poor old man, their father, making such pitiful dole° over them that all the beholders take his part with weeping. 105

Rosalind. Alas!

Touchstone. But what is the sport, monsieur, that the ladies have lost?

Le Beau. Why, this that I speak of. 110

Touchstone. Thus men may grow wiser every day. It is the first time that ever I heard breaking of ribs was sport for ladies.

Celia. Or I, I promise thee.

Rosalind. But is there any° else longs to see this broken music° in his sides? Is there yet another dotes upon rib-breaking? Shall we see this wrestling, cousin? 115

Le Beau. You must, if you stay here, for here is the place appointed for the wrestling, and they are ready to perform it.

Celia. Yonder sure they are coming. Let us now stay and see it.

(*Flourish.° Enter Duke [Frederick], Lords, Orlando, Charles, and Attendants.*)

Duke Frederick. Come on. Since the youth will not be entreated, his own peril on his forwardness. 120

Rosalind. Is yonder the man?

Le Beau. Even he, madam.

Celia. Alas, he is too young; yet he looks successfully.°

Duke Frederick. How now, daughter and cousin; are you crept hither to see the wrestling? 125

Rosalind. Ay, my liege, so please you give us leave.

Duke Frederick. You will take little delight in it, I can tell you, there is such odds in the man.° In pity of the challenger's youth I would fain° dissuade him, but he will not be entreated. Speak to him, ladies; see if you can move him. 130

Celia. Call him hither, good Monsieur Le Beau.

Duke Frederick. Do so. I'll not be by.

Le Beau. Monsieur the challenger, the princess calls for you.

Orlando. I attend them with all respect and duty. 135

---

105 *dole* lamentation   114 *any* anyone
114 *broken music* music arranged in parts for different instruments
119 *s.d. Flourish* trumpet fanfare   124 *successfully* able to succeed
129 *such odds in the man* i.e., the odds are all in Charles' favor
130 *fain* like to

Rosalind. Young man, have you challenged Charles the wrestler?

Orlando. No, fair princess. He is the general challenger; I come
but in as others do, to try with him the strength of my youth.

Celia. Young gentleman, your spirits are too bold for your years.
You have seen cruel proof of this man's strength; if you saw   140
yourself with your eyes or knew yourself with your judgment,
the fear of your adventure would counsel you to a more equal
enterprise. We pray you for your own sake to embrace your
own safety and give over this attempt.

Rosalind. Do, young sir. Your reputation shall not therefore be   145
misprized;° we will make it our suit to the Duke that the wrestling might not go forward.

Orlando. I beseech you, punish me not with your hard thoughts,
wherein I confess me much guilty to deny so fair and excellent
ladies anything. But let your fair eyes and gentle wishes go with   150
me to my trial; wherein if I be foiled,° there is but one shamed
that was never gracious;° if killed, but one dead that is willing
to be so. I shall do my friends no wrong, for I have none to
lament me; the world no injury, for in it I have nothing. Only
in the world I° fill up a place, which may be better supplied   155
when I have made it empty.

Rosalind. The little strength that I have, I would it were with you.

Celia. And mine to eke° out hers.

Rosalind. Fare you well. Pray heaven I be deceived in you!°

Celia. Your heart's desires be with you!   160

Charles. Come, where is this young gallant that is so desirous to
lie with his mother earth?

Orlando. Ready, sir; but his will hath in it a more modest working.°

Duke Frederick. You shall try but one fall.   165

Charles. No, I warrant your Grace you shall not entreat him to a
second that have so mightily persuaded him from a first.

Orlando. You mean to mock me after. You should not have
mocked me before. But come your ways.°

Rosalind. Now Hercules be thy speed,° young man!   170

Celia. I would I were invisible, to catch the strong fellow by the
leg.   (*Wrestle.*)

---

146 *misprized* despised   151 *foiled* thrown   152 *gracious* graced by Fortune
154–155 *Only in the world I* in the world I only   158 *eke* stretch
159 *deceived in you* i.e., wrong in my estimation of your strength
163–164 *modest working* humble aim
169 *come your ways* i.e., let's get started
170 *Hercules be thy speed* may Hercules help you

Rosalind. O excellent young man!
Celia. If I had a thunderbolt in mine eye, I can tell who should
    down.   [*Charles is thrown.*] (*Shout.*)   175
Duke Frederick. No more, no more.
Orlando. Yes, I beseech your Grace; I am not yet well breathed.°
Duke Frederick. How dost thou, Charles?
Le Beau. He cannot speak, my lord.
Duke Frederick. Bear him away. What is thy name, young man?   180
Orlando. Orlando, my liege, the youngest son of Sir Rowland de
    Boys.
Duke Frederick. I would thou hadst been son to some man else.
    The world esteemed thy father honorable,
    But I did find him still° mine enemy.   185
    Thou shouldst have better pleased me with this deed
    Hadst thou descended from another house.
    But fare thee well; thou art a gallant youth;
    I would thou hadst told me of another father.

                      (*Exit Duke,* [*with Train*].)

Celia. Were I my father, coz, would I do this?   190
Orlando. I am more proud to be Sir Rowland's son,
    His youngest son, and would not change that calling°
    To be adopted heir to Frederick.
Rosalind. My father loved Sir Rowland as his soul,
    And all the world was of my father's mind.   195
    Had I before known this young man his son,
    I should have given him tears unto° entreaties
    Ere he should thus have ventured.
Celia.   Gentle cousin,
    Let us go thank him and encourage him.
    My father's rough and envious disposition   200
    Sticks° me at heart. Sir, you have well deserved;
    If you do keep your promises in love
    But justly° as you have exceeded all promise,
    Your mistress shall be happy.
Rosalind.   Gentleman,   [*gives chain*]
    Wear this for me, one out of suits° with fortune,   205
    That could° give more but that her hand lacks means.
    Shall we go, coz?
Celia.   Ay. Fare you well, fair gentleman.

---

¹⁷⁷ *well breathed* fully warmed up   ¹⁸⁵ *still* always   ¹⁹² *calling* name
¹⁹⁷ *unto* as well as   ²⁰¹ *Sticks* pains   ²⁰³ *justly* exactly
²⁰⁵ *out of suits* in disfavor   ²⁰⁶ *could* would

Orlando. Can I not say "I thank you"? My better parts°
   Are all thrown down, and that which here stands up
   Is but a quintain,° a mere lifeless block.   210
Rosalind. He calls us back. My pride fell with my fortunes;
   I'll ask him what he would. Did you call, sir?
   Sir, you have wrestled well, and overthrown
   More than your enemies.
Celia.   Will you go, coz?
Rosalind. Have with you.° Fare you well.   215

                           (*Exit [with Celia]*.)

Orlando. What passion° hangs these weights upon my tongue?
   I cannot speak to her, yet she urged conference.°

   (*Enter Le Beau*.)

   O poor Orlando, thou art overthrown!
   Or Charles or something weaker masters thee.
Le Beau. Good sir, I do in friendship counsel you   220
   To leave this place. Albeit you have deserved
   High commendation, true applause, and love,
   Yet such is now the Duke's condition
   That he misconsters° all that you have done.
   The Duke is humorous.° What he is, indeed,   225
   More suits you to conceive° than I to speak of.
Orlando. I thank you, sir; and pray you, tell me this:
   Which of the two was daughter of the Duke,
   That here was at the wrestling?
Le Beau. Neither his daughter, if we judge by manners,   230
   But yet indeed the taller° is his daughter,
   The other is daughter to the banished Duke,
   And here detained by her usurping uncle
   To keep his daughter company, whose loves
   Are dearer than the natural bond of sisters.   235
   But I can tell you that of late this Duke
   Hath ta'en displeasure 'gainst his gentle niece,
   Grounded upon no other argument°
   But that the people praise her for her virtues

---

208 *parts* qualities   210 *quintain* wooden post (used for tilting practice)
215 *Have with you* I'm coming   216 *passion* strong feeling
217 *conference* conversation   224 *misconsters* misinterprets
225 *humorous* moody   226 *conceive* understand
231 *taller* (unless "taller" is a printer's slip for "smaller," Shakespeare here
erred. Rosalind is later said to be taller)   238 *argument* basis

And pity her for her good father's sake; 240
And, on my life, his malice 'gainst the lady
Will suddenly break forth. Sir, fare you well.
Hereafter, in a better world° than this,
I shall desire more love and knowledge of you.
Orlando. I rest much bounden° to you. Fare you well. 245

[*Exit Le Beau.*]

Thus must I from the smoke into the smother,°
From tyrant Duke unto a tyrant brother.
But heavenly Rosalind!   (*Exit.*)

SCENE 3. [*The palace.*]

(*Enter Celia and Rosalind.*)

Celia. Why cousin, why, Rosalind! Cupid have mercy, not a
word?
Rosalind. Not one to throw at a dog.
Celia. No, thy words are too precious to be cast away upon curs;
throw some of them at me; come, lame me with reasons. 5
Rosalind. Then there were two cousins laid up, when the one
should be lamed with reasons and the other mad° without any.
Celia. But is all this for your father?
Rosalind. No, some of it is for my child's father.° O, how full of
briers is this working-day world! 10
Celia. They are but burrs, cousin, thrown upon thee in holiday
foolery; if we walk not in the trodden paths, our very petticoats
will catch them.
Rosalind. I could shake them off my coat; these burrs are in my
heart. 15
Celia. Hem° them away.
Rosalind. I would try, if I could cry "hem,"° and have him.
Celia. Come, come, wrestle with thy affections.°
Rosalind. O, they take the part of a better wrestler than myself!
Celia. O, a good wish upon you! You will try° in time, in despite 20

²⁴³ *a better world* better times   ²⁴⁵ *bounden* indebted
²⁴⁶ *smother* smothering smoke (the idea is: "Out of the frying pan into the
fire")
I.iii.⁷ *mad* melancholy   ⁹ *child's father* i.e., future husband, Orlando
¹⁶ *Hem* (1) cough (2) tuck
¹⁷ *cry "hem"* clear my throat (with a pun on "him")   ¹⁸ *affections* feelings
²⁰ *try* i.e., chance a bout

of a fall. But turning these jests out of service,° let us talk in
good earnest. Is it possible on such a sudden you should fall
into so strong a liking with old Sir Rowland's youngest son?

Rosalind. The Duke my father loved his father dearly.

Celia. Doth it therefore ensue that you should love his son dearly?   25
By this kind of chase,° I should hate him, for my father hated
his father dearly; yet I hate not Orlando.

Rosalind. No, faith, hate him not, for my sake.

Celia. Why should I not? Doth he not deserve well?°

(*Enter Duke [Frederick], with Lords.*)

Rosalind. Let me love him for that,° and do you love him be-   30
cause I do. Look, here comes the Duke.

Celia. With his eyes full of anger.

Duke Frederick. Mistress, dispatch you with your safest haste
And get you from our court.

Rosalind.   Me, uncle?

Duke Frederick.   You, cousin.°
Within these ten days if that thou beest found   35
So near our public court as twenty miles,
Thou diest for it.

Rosalind.   I do beseech your Grace
Let me the knowledge of my fault bear with me.
If with myself I hold intelligence°
Or have acquaintance with mine own desires,   40
If that I do not dream or be not frantic,°
As I do trust I am not; then, dear uncle,
Never so much as in a thought unborn
Did I offend your Highness.

Duke Frederick.   Thus do all traitors.
If their purgation° did consist in words,   45
They are as innocent as grace° itself.
Let it suffice thee that I trust thee not.

Rosalind. Yet your mistrust cannot make me a traitor.
Tell me whereon the likelihoods° depends.

Duke Frederick. Thou art thy father's daughter, there's enough.   50

Rosalind. So was I when your Highness took his dukedom;

---

²¹ *turning . . . service* to stop joking   ²⁶ *chase* pursuit (of the argument)
²⁹ *deserve well* i.e., deserve to be hated (if Rosalind's reasoning is valid, it
follows that Celia should hate Orlando)
³⁰ *for that* i.e., for his virtues (Rosalind takes "deserve well" in its usual sense)
³⁴ *cousin* kinsman   ³⁹ *hold intelligence* communicate   ⁴¹ *frantic* insane
⁴⁵ *purgation* clearance   ⁴⁶ *grace* virtue   ⁴⁹ *likelihoods* possibilities

So was I when your Highness banished him.
Treason is not inherited, my lord,
Or if we did derive it from our friends,°
What's that to me? My father was no traitor.   55
Then, good my liege, mistake me not so much
To think my poverty is treacherous.
Celia. Dear sovereign, hear me speak.
Duke Frederick. Ay, Celia. We stayed° her for your sake,
Else had she with her father ranged° along.   60
Celia. I did not then entreat to have her stay;
It was your pleasure and your own remorse.°
I was too young that time to value her,
But now I know her. If she be a traitor,
Why, so am I. We still° have slept together,   65
Rose at an instant, learned, played, eat° together;
And wheresoe'er we went, like Juno's swans,
Still we went coupled and inseparable.
Duke Frederick. She is too subtile° for thee; and her smoothness,
Her very silence and her patience,   70
Speak to the people, and they pity her.
Thou art a fool. She robs thee of thy name,
And thou wilt show more bright and seem more virtuous°
When she is gone. Then open not thy lips.
Firm and irrevocable is my doom°   75
Which I have passed upon her; she is banished.
Celia. Pronounce that sentence then on me, my liege;
I cannot live out of her company.
Duke Frederick. You are a fool. You, niece, provide yourself;
If you outstay the time, upon mine honor,   80
And in the greatness° of my word, you die.

                       (Exit Duke, &c.)

Celia. O my poor Rosalind, whither wilt thou go?
Wilt thou change fathers? I will give thee mine.
I charge thee be not thou more grieved than I am.
Rosalind. I have more cause.
Celia.   Thou hast not, cousin.   85
Prithee be cheerful. Know'st thou not the Duke
Hath banished me, his daughter?
Rosalind.   That he hath not.

---

⁵⁴ *friends* relatives   ⁵⁹ *stayed* kept   ⁶⁰ *ranged* wandered
⁶² *remorse* pity   ⁶⁵ *still* always   ⁶⁶ *eat* eaten   ⁶⁹ *subtile* crafty
⁷³ *virtuous* full of good qualities   ⁷⁵ *doom* sentence   ⁸¹ *greatness* power

Celia. No? Hath not? Rosalind lacks then the love
Which teacheth thee that thou and I am one.
Shall we be sund'red, shall we part, sweet girl?   90
No, let my father seek another heir.
Therefore devise with me how we may fly,
Whither to go, and what to bear with us;
And do not seek to take your change° upon you,
To bear your griefs yourself and leave me out;   95
For, by this heaven, now at our sorrows pale,°
Say what thou canst, I'll go along with thee.
Rosalind. Why, whither shall we go?
Celia. To seek my uncle in the Forest of Arden.
Rosalind. Alas, what danger will it be to us,   100
Maids as we are, to travel forth so far!
Beauty provoketh thieves sooner than gold.
Celia. I'll put myself in poor and mean° attire
And with a kind of umber° smirch my face;
The like do you; so shall we pass along   105
And never stir assailants.
Rosalind.   Were it not better,
Because that I am more than common° tall,
That I did suit me all points° like a man?
A gallant curtle-ax° upon my thigh,
A boar-spear in my hand; and, in my heart   110
Lie there what hidden woman's fear there will,
We'll have a swashing° and a martial outside,
As many other mannish cowards have
That do outface° it with their semblances.°
Celia. What shall I call thee when thou art a man?   115
Rosalind. I'll have no worse a name than Jove's own page,
And therefore look you call me Ganymede.
But what will you be called?
Celia. Something that hath a reference to my state:
No longer Celia, but Aliena.°   120
Rosalind. But, cousin, what if we assayed° to steal

---

94 *change* i.e., change of fortune
96 *now at our sorrows pale* now pale at our sorrows   103 *mean* lowly
104 *umber* reddish-brown color   107 *common* usually
108 *suit me at all points* dress myself entirely   109 *curtle-ax* cutlass
112 *swashing* blustering   114 *outface* bluff
114 *semblances* appearances (of bravery)
120 *Aliena* (Latin: the estranged one)   121 *assayed* attempted

The clownish fool out of your father's court;
Would he not be a comfort to our travel?
Celia. He'll go along o'er the wide world with me;
    Leave me alone to woo° him. Let's away   125
    And get our jewels and our wealth together,
    Devise the fittest time and safest way
    To hide us from pursuit that will be made
    After my flight. Now go in we content
    To liberty, and not to banishment.   (*Exeunt.*)   130

ACT II

SCENE 1. [*The Forest of Arden.*]

(*Enter Duke Senior, Amiens, and two or three Lords, like Foresters.*)

Duke Senior. Now, my co-mates and brothers in exile,°
    Hath not old custom made this life more sweet
    Than that of painted pomp? Are not these woods
    More free from peril than the envious court?
    Here feel we not° the penalty of Adam;°   5
    The seasons' difference, as° the icy fang
    And churlish° chiding of the winter's wind,
    Which, when it bites and blows upon my body
    Even till I shrink with cold, I smile and say
    "This is no flattery; these are counselors   10
    That feelingly° persuade me what I am."
    Sweet are the uses of adversity,
    Which, like the toad, ugly and venomous,
    Wears yet a precious jewel° in his head;
    And this our life, exempt from public haunt,°   15
    Finds tongues in trees, books in the running brooks,
    Sermons in stones, and good in everything.

---

125 *woo* coax
II.i.¹ *exile* (accent on second syllable)
⁵ *feel we not* we do not feel (some editors emend "not" to "but")
⁵ *penalty of Adam* loss of Eden   ⁶ *as* for example   ⁷ *churlish* harsh
¹¹ *feelingly* (1) through the senses (2) with intensity
¹⁴ *a precious jewel* (the fabled toadstone)   ¹⁵ *public haunt* society

Amiens. I would not change it; happy is your Grace
    That can translate the stubbornness° of fortune
    Into so quiet and so sweet a style.   20
Duke Senior. Come, shall we go and kill us venison?
    And yet it irks me the poor dappled fools,°
    Being native burghers° of this desert° city,
    Should, in their own confines, with forkèd heads°
    Have their round haunches gored.
First Lord.   Indeed, my lord,   25
    The melancholy Jaques° grieves at that,
    And in that kind° swears you do more usurp
    Than doth your brother that hath banished you.
    Today my Lord of Amiens and myself
    Did steal behind him as he lay along°   30
    Under an oak, whose antique root peeps out
    Upon the brook that brawls° along this wood;
    To the which place a poor sequest'red° stag
    That from the hunter's aim had ta'en a hurt
    Did come to languish; and indeed, my lord,   35
    The wretched animal heaved forth such groans
    That their discharge did stretch his leathern coat
    Almost to bursting, and the big round tears
    Coursed one another down his innocent nose
    In piteous chase; and thus the hairy fool,   40
    Much markèd of° the melancholy Jaques,
    Stood on th' extremest verge of the swift brook,
    Augmenting it with tears.
Duke Senior.   But what said Jaques?
    Did he not moralize° this spectacle?
First Lord. O, yes, into a thousand similes.   45
    First, for his weeping into the needless° stream:
    "Poor deer," quoth he, "thou mak'st a testament
    As worldlings do, giving thy sum of more
    To that which had too much." Then, being there alone,
    Left and abandoned of his velvet° friend: 50

---

¹⁹ *stubbornness* hardness   ²² *fools* simple creatures   ²³ *burghers* citizens
²³ *desert* deserted   ²⁴ *forkèd heads* arrows
²⁶ *Jaques* (dissylabic, pronounced "Jā' kis")   ²⁷ *kind* way
³⁰ *along* stretched out   ³² *brawls* makes noise   ³³ *sequest'red* separated
⁴¹ *markèd of* noted by   ⁴⁴ *moralize* sermonize
⁴⁶ *needless* i.e., needing no more water
⁵⁰ *velvet* i.e., courtierlike (the furry skin on the antlers, or the sleek hide, makes the deer resemble a velvet-clad courtier)

"'Tis right," quoth he, "thus misery doth part
The flux° of company." Anon a careless° herd,
Full of the pasture, jumps along by him
And never stays to greet him; "Ay," quoth Jaques,
"Sweep on, you fat and greasy citizens,   55
'Tis just the fashion; wherefore do you look°
Upon that poor and broken bankrupt there?"
Thus most invectively he pierceth through
The body of the country, city, court,
Yea, and of this our life, swearing that we   60
Are mere usurpers, tyrants, and what's worse,
To fright the animals and to kill them up
In their assigned° and native dwelling place.
Duke Senior. And did you leave him in this contemplation?
Second Lord. We did, my lord, weeping and commenting   65
Upon the sobbing deer.
Duke Senior.   Show me the place.
I love to cope° him in these sullen fits,
For then he's full of matter.
First Lord. I'll bring you to him straight.°   (*Exeunt.*)

SCENE 2. [*The palace.*]

(*Enter Duke [Frederick], with Lords.*)

Duke Frederick. Can it be possible that no man saw them?
It cannot be; some villains of my court
Are of consent and sufferance° in this.
First Lord. I cannot hear of any that did see her.
The ladies, her attendants of her chamber,   5
Saw her abed, and in the morning early
They found the bed untreasured of their mistress.
Second Lord. My lord, the roynish° clown at whom so oft
Your Grace was wont to laugh is also missing.
Hisperia, the princess' gentlewoman,   10
Confesses that she secretly o'erheard
Your daughter and her cousin much commend
The parts and graces° of the wrestler

---

⁵² *flux* stream   ⁵² *Anon a careless* soon an untroubled
⁵⁶ *wherefore do you look* why should you bother looking
⁶³ *assigned* allotted (by nature)   ⁶⁷ *cope* encounter   ⁶⁹ *straight* at once
II.ii.³ *Are of consent and sufferance* approved and helped   ⁸ *roynish* scurvy
¹³ *parts and graces* good qualities and manner

That did but lately foil the sinewy Charles,
And she believes, wherever they are gone,   15
That youth is surely in their company.
Duke Frederick. Send to his brother, fetch that gallant hither;
  If he be absent, bring his brother to me;
  I'll make him find him. Do this suddenly,°
  And let not search and inquisition quail°   20
  To bring again these foolish runaways.   (*Exeunt.*)

SCENE 3. [*Oliver's house.*]

(*Enter Orlando and Adam.*)

Orlando. Who's there?
Adam. What, my young master, O my gentle master,
  O my sweet master, O you memory
  Of old Sir Rowland, why, what make you° here?
  Why are you virtuous? Why do people love you?   5
  And wherefore are you gentle, strong, and valiant?
  Why would you be so fond° to overcome
  The bonny prizer° of the humorous° Duke?
  Your praise is come too swiftly home before you.
  Know you not, master, to some kind of men   10
  Their graces serve them but as enemies?
  No more° do yours. Your virtues, gentle master,
  Are sanctified and holy traitors to you°
  O, what a world is this, when what is comely
  Envenoms him that bears it!   15
Orlando. Why, what's the matter?
Adam.   O unhappy youth,
  Come not within these doors; within this roof
  The enemy of all your graces lives.
  Your brother — no, no brother, yet the son —
  Yet not the son, I will not call him son,   20
  Of him I was about to call his father —
  Hath heard your praises, and this night he means
  To burn the lodging where you use° to lie

And you within it. If he fail of that,
He will have other means to cut you off.   25
I overheard him, and his practices;°
This is no place, this house is but a butchery;°
Abhor it, fear it, do not enter it!
Orlando. Why, whither, Adam, wouldst thou have me go?
Adam. No matter whither, so you come not here.   30
Orlando. What, wouldst thou have me go and beg my food,
  Or with a base and boist'rous° sword enforce
  A thievish living on the common road?°
  This I must do, or know not what to do;
  Yet this I will not do, do how I can.   35
  I rather will subject me to the malice
  Of a diverted° blood and bloody brother.
Adam. But do not so. I have five hundred crowns,
  The thrifty hire I saved° under your father,
  Which I did store to be my foster nurse   40
  When service should in my old limbs lie lame
  And unregarded age in corners thrown.
  Take that, and he that doth the ravens feed,
  Yea, providently caters for the sparrow,°
  Be comfort to my age. Here is the gold;   45
  All this I give you. Let me be your servant;
  Though I look old, yet I am strong and lusty,
  For in my youth I never did apply
  Hot and rebellious° liquors in my blood,
  Nor did not with unbashful forehead° woo   50
  The means of weakness and debility;
  Therefore my age is as a lusty winter,
  Frosty, but kindly. Let me go with you;
  I'll do the service of a younger man
  In all your business and necessities.   55
Orlando. O good old man, how well in thee appears
  The constant° service of the antique world,°
  When service sweat for duty, not for meed!°
  Thou art not for the fashion of these times,
  Where none will sweat but for promotion,   60

---

[26] *practices* plots   [27] *butchery* slaughterhouse
[32] *base and boist'rous* low and swaggering   [33] *common road* highway
[37] *diverted* estranged   [39] *thrifty hire I saved* wages I carefully saved
[43–44] *he that . . . the sparrow* (see Psalms 147:9, Luke 12:6)
[49] *rebellious* i.e., causing the flesh to rebel   [50] *unbashful forehead* bold face
[57] *constant* faithful   [57] *the antique world* the past   [58] *meed* reward

And having that, do choke their service up
Even with the having; it is not so with thee.
But, poor old man, thou prun'st a rotten tree
That cannot so much as a blossom yield
In lieu of° all thy pains and husbandry.   65
But come thy ways, we'll go along together,
And ere we have thy youthful wages spent,
We'll light upon some settled low content.°
Adam. Master, go on, and I will follow thee
To the last gasp with truth and loyalty.   70
From seventeen years till now almost fourscore
Here livèd I, but now live here no more;
At seventeen years many their fortunes seek,
But at fourscore it is too late a week;°
Yet fortune cannot recompense me better.   75
Than to die well and not my master's debtor.   (*Exeunt.*)

SCENE 4. [*The Forest of Arden.*]

(*Enter Rosalind for Ganymede, Celia for Aliena, and Clown,
alias Touchstone.*)

Rosalind. O Jupiter, how weary are my spirits!
Touchstone. I care not for my spirits if my legs were not weary.
Rosalind. I could find in my heart to disgrace my man's apparel
and to cry like a woman; but I must comfort the weaker vessel,
as doublet and hose° ought to show itself courageous to petti-   5
coat. Therefore, courage, good Aliena!
Celia. I pray you bear with me; I cannot go no further.
Touchstone. For my part, I had rather bear with you than bear
you; yet I should bear no cross° if I did bear you, for I think
you have no money in your purse.   10
Rosalind. Well, this is the Forest of Arden.
Touchstone. Ay, now am I in Arden, the more fool I. When I
was at home, I was in a better place, but travelers must be
content.

(*Enter Corin and Silvius.*)

Rosalind. Ay, be so, good Touchstone. Look you, who comes   15
here, a young man and an old in solemn talk.

---

⁶⁵ *In lieu of* in return for   ⁶⁸ *low content* humble way of life   ⁷⁴ *week* time
II.iv.⁵ *doublet and hose* jacket and breeches
⁹ *cross* (1) trouble (2) coin stamped with a cross

Corin. That is the way to make her scorn you still.

Silvius. O Corin, that thou knew'st how I do love her!

Corin. I partly guess, for I have loved ere now.

Silvius. No, Corin, being old, thou canst not guess,   20
     Though in thy youth thou wast as true a lover
     As ever sighed upon a midnight pillow.
     But if thy love were ever like to mine,
     As sure I think did never man love so,
     How many actions most ridiculous   25
     Hast thou been drawn to by thy fantasy?°

Corin. Into a thousand that I have forgotten.

Silvius. O, thou didst then never love so heartily!
     If thou rememb'rest not the slightest folly
     That ever love did make thee run into,   30
     Thou hast not loved.
     Or if thou hast not sat as I do now,
     Wearing° thy hearer in thy mistress' praise,
     Thou hast not loved.
     Or if thou hast not broke from company   35
     Abruptly, as my passion now makes me,
     Thou has not loved.
     O Phebe, Phebe, Phebe!   *(Exit.)*

Rosalind. Alas, poor shepherd! Searching of° thy wound, I have
     by hard adventure° found mine own.   40

Touchstone. And I mine. I remember, when I was in love I broke
     my sword upon a stone and bid him take that for coming
     a-night to Jane Smile; and I remember the kissing of her batler,°
     and the cow's dugs that her pretty chopt° hands had milked;
     and I remember the wooing of a peascod° instead of her, from   45
     whom I took two cods, and giving her them again, said with
     weeping tears, "Wear these for my sake." We that are true
     lovers run into strange capers; but as all is mortal in nature,
     so is all nature in love mortal in folly.°

Rosalind. Thou speak'st wiser than thou art ware° of.   50

Touchstone. Nay, I shall ne'er be ware of mine own wit° till I
     break my shins against it.

---

²⁶ *fantasy* love (and all its fancies)   ³³ *Wearing* exhausting
³⁹ *Searching of* probing   ⁴⁰ *hard adventure* bad luck
⁴³ *batler* wooden paddle (used in washing clothes)
⁴⁴ *chopt* chapped   ⁴⁵ *peascod* peapod
⁴⁸⁻⁴⁹ *as all is mortal . . . folly* just as everything that lives must die, so all
who love inevitably do foolish things
⁵⁰ *art ware* know   ⁵¹ *wit* wisdom

Rosalind. Jove, Jove! This shepherd's passion
  Is much upon my fashion.
Touchstone. And mine, but it grows something stale with me.   55
Celia. I pray you, one of you question yond man
  If he for gold will give us any food.
  I faint almost to death.
Touchstone. Holla, you clown!°
Rosalind. Peace, fool! He's not thy kinsman.   60
Corin. Who calls?
Touchstone. Your betters, sir.
Corin.   Else are they very wretched.
Rosalind. Peace, I say! Good even to you, friend.
Corin. And to you, gentle sir, and to you all.
Rosalind. I prithee, shepherd, if that love or gold   65
  Can in this desert place buy entertainment,°
  Bring us where we may rest ourselves and feed.
  Here's a young maid with travel much oppressed,
  And faints for succor.
Corin.   Fair sir, I pity her
  And wish, for her sake more than for mine own,   70
  My fortunes were more able to relieve her;
  But I am shepherd to another man
  And do not shear the fleeces that I graze.
  My master is of churlish° disposition
  And little recks° to find the way to heaven   75
  By doing deeds of hospitality.
  Besides, his cote,° his flocks, and bounds of feed°
  Are now on sale, and at our sheepcote now,
  By reason of his absence, there is nothing
  That you will feed on; but what is, come see,   80
  And in my voice° most welcome shall you be.
Rosalind. What is he that shall buy his flock and pasture?
Corin. That young swain that you saw here but erewhile,°
  That little cares for buying anything.
Rosalind. I pray thee, if it stand° with honesty,   85
  Buy thou the cottage, pasture, and the flock,
  And thou shalt have° to pay for it of us.

---

⁵⁹ *clown* (1) rustic (2) fool   ⁶⁶ *entertainment* food and shelter
⁷⁴ *churlish* miserly   ⁷⁵ *recks* thinks   ⁷⁷ *cote* cottage
⁷⁷ *bounds of feed* pastures   ⁸¹ *in my voice* as far as my position allows
⁸³ *erewhile* a short while ago   ⁸⁵ *stand* be consistent
⁸⁷ *have* i.e., have the money

Celia. And we will mend° thy wages. I like this place
  And willingly could waste° my time in it.
Corin. Assuredly the thing is to be sold.   90
  Go with me; if you like upon report
  The soil, the profit, and this kind of life,
  I will your very faithful feeder° be
  And buy it with your gold right suddenly.   (*Exeunt.*)

SCENE 5. [*The forest.*]

(*Enter Amiens, Jaques, and others.*)

Song.

Amiens. Under the greenwood tree
      Who loves to lie with me,
    And turn° his merry note
      Unto the sweet bird's throat,
    Come hither, come hither, come hither.   5
      Here shall he see no enemy
    But winter and rough weather.
Jaques. More, more, I prithee more!
Amiens. It will make you melancholy, Monsieur Jaques.
Jaques. I thank it. More, I prithee more! I can suck melancholy   10
  out of a song as a weasel sucks eggs. More, I prithee more!
Amiens. My voice is ragged. I know I cannot please you.
Jaques. I do desire you to please me; I do desire you to sing.
  Come, more, another stanzo! Call you 'em stanzos?
Amiens. What you will, Monsieur Jaques.   15
Jaques. Nay, I care not for their names; they owe me nothing.°
  Will you sing?
Amiens. More at your request than to please myself.
Jaques. Well then, if ever I thank any man, I'll thank you. But
  that they call compliment° is like th' encounter of two dog-   20
  apes,° and when a man thanks me heartily, methinks I have
  given him a penny and he renders me the beggarly thanks.°
  Come, sing; and you that will not, hold your tongues.

88 *mend* improve   89 *waste* spend   93 *feeder* servant
II.v.3 *turn* attune, adapt
16 *names . . . nothing* (Jaques plays on the word "name," a term for the bor-
rower's signature on a loan)
20 *compliment* politeness   21 *dog-apes* baboons
21–22 *and when . . . beggarly thanks* i.e., the hearty thanks of polite society
are no more sincere than the extravagant gratitude of a beggar given a small
coin

Amiens. Well, I'll end the song. Sirs, cover the while;° the Duke
will drink under this tree. He hath been all this day to look you.   25
Jaques. And I have been all this day to avoid him. He is too dis-
putable for my company. I think of as many matters as he, but
I give heaven thanks and make no boast of them. Come,
warble, come.

Song.

(*All together here.*)

> Who doth ambition shun   30
>   And loves to live i' th' sun,
> Seeking the food he eats,
>   And pleased with what he gets,
> Come hither, come hither, come hither.
>   Here shall he see no enemy   35
> But winter and rough weather.

Jaques. I'll give you a verse to this note° that I made yesterday
in despite of my invention.°
Amiens. And I'll sing it.
Jaques. Thus it goes.   40

>   If it do come to pass
>   That any man turn ass,
>   Leaving his wealth and ease
>   A stubborn will to please,
>   Ducdame,° ducdame, ducdame,   45
>   Here shall he see gross fools as he,
>   An if° he will come to me.

Amiens. What's that "ducdame"?
Jaques. 'Tis a Greek° invocation to call fools into a circle. I'll go
sleep, if I can; if I cannot, I'll rail against all the first-born of   50
Egypt.°
Amiens. And I'll go seek the Duke. His banquet° is prepared.

(*Exeunt.*)

---

²⁴ *cover the while* lay the table in the meantime   ³⁷ *note* tune
³⁸ *in despite of my invention* without using my imagination
⁴⁵ *Ducdame* (various derivations have been suggested: Romany *dukrā mē* ["I
tell fortunes"]; Welsh *dewch 'da mi* ["come with me"]; Latin *duc ad me*
["bring (him) to me"]; Italian *Duc' da mè* ["duke by myself" or "duke without a dukedom"]. Probably the word is nonsense)
⁴⁷ *An if* if only   ⁴⁷ *Greek* unintelligible
⁵⁰⁻⁵¹ *first-born of Egypt* (perhaps "persons of high rank," but perhaps an
allusion to life in the Forest of Arden. Exodus 11, 12 reports that when the
first-born of Egypt died, the Israelites were sent into the wilderness)
⁵² *banquet* light meal

SCENE 6. [*The forest.*]

(*Enter Orlando and Adam.*)

Adam. Dear master, I can go no further. O, I die for food. Here
lie I down and measure out my grave. Farewell, kind master.

Orlando. Why, how now, Adam? No greater heart in thee? Live a
little, comfort° a little, cheer thyself a little. If this uncouth°
forest yield anything savage, I will either be food for it or bring   5
it for food to thee. Thy conceit° is nearer death than thy
powers. For my sake be comfortable; hold death awhile at the
arm's end. I will here be with thee presently,° and if I bring
thee not something to eat, I will give thee leave to die; but if
thou diest before I come, thou art a mocker of my labor. Well   10
said; thou look'st cheerly, and I'll be with thee quickly. Yet
thou liest in the bleak air. Come, I will bear thee to some shelter, and thou shalt not die for lack of a dinner if there live
anything in this desert. Cheerly, good Adam.   (*Exeunt.*)

SCENE 7. [*The forest.*]

(*Enter Duke Senior, and Lords, like Outlaws.*)

Duke Senior. I think he be transformed into a beast,
For I can nowhere find him like a man.

First Lord. My lord, he is but even now gone hence;
Here was he merry, hearing of a song.

Duke Senior. If he, compact of jars,° grow musical,   5
We shall have shortly discord in the spheres.°
Go seek him; tell him I would speak with him.

(*Enter Jaques.*)

First Lord. He saves my labor by his own approach.

Duke Senior. Why, how now, monsieur, what life is this,
That your poor friends must woo your company?   10
What, you look merrily.

Jaques. A fool, a fool! I met a fool i' th' forest,

II.vi.⁴ *comfort* take comfort   ⁴ *uncouth* wild
⁶ *conceit* thought   ⁸ *presently* at once
II.vii.⁵ *compact of jars* made up of discord
⁶ *discord in the spheres* (Ptolemaic astronomy taught that the planetary spheres
produced a ravishing harmony as they revolved)

A motley° fool! A miserable world!
As I do live by food, I met a fool
Who laid him down and basked him in the sun   15
And railed on Lady Fortune in good terms,
In good set terms,° and yet a motley fool.
"Good morrow, fool," quoth I. "No, sir," quoth he,
"Call me not fool till heaven hath sent me fortune."°
And then he drew a dial from his poke,°   20
And looking on it with lack-luster eye,
Says very wisely, "It is ten o'clock.
Thus we may see," quoth he, "how the world wags.°
'Tis but an hour ago since it was nine,
And after one hour more 'twill be eleven;   25
And so, from hour to hour,° we ripe and ripe,
And then, from hour to hour, we rot and rot;
And thereby hangs a tale." When I did hear
The motley fool thus moral° on the time,
My lungs began to crow like chanticleer°   30
That fools should be so deep contemplative;
And I did laugh sans intermission°
An hour by his dial. O noble fool,
A worthy fool! Motley's the only wear.
Duke Senior. What fool is this?   35
Jaques. O worthy fool! One that hath been a courtier,
And says, if ladies be but young and fair,
They have the gift to know it. And in his brain,
Which is as dry as the remainder biscuit°
After a voyage, he hath strange places crammed   40
With observation, the which he vents°
In mangled forms. O that I were a fool!
I am ambitious for a motley coat.
Duke Senior. Thou shalt have one.
Jaques.   It is my only suit,°
Provided that you weed your better judgments   45

---

¹³ *motley* garbed in the multicolored costume of the court fool (a motley costume is commonly thought to be checkered or patched; Leslie Hotson, in *Shakespeare's Motley*, argues it was of varicolored threads but drab, like a tweed)   ¹⁷ *set terms* precise phrases
¹⁹ *Call me . . . fortune* (fortune proverbially favors fools)
²⁰ *dial from his poke* sundial from his pocket   ²³ *wags* goes
²⁶ *hour to hour* (perhaps with a pun on "whore")   ²⁹ *moral* moralize
³⁰ *chanticleer* (traditional name for a rooster)
³² *sans intermission* without stop   ³⁹ *remainder biscuit* leftover hardtack
⁴¹ *vents* gives forth   ⁴⁴ *suit* (1) garment (2) petition

Of all opinion that grows rank° in them
That I am wise. I must have liberty
Withal, as large a charter° as the wind,
To blow on whom I please, for so fools have.
And they that are most gallèd° with my folly,　　　　50
They most must laugh. And why, sir, must they so?
The why is plain as way to parish church:
He that a fool doth very wisely hit
Doth very foolishly, although he smart,
Not to seem senseless of the bob.° If not,　　　　55
The wise man's folly is anatomized°
Even by the squand'ring glances° of the fool.
Invest° me in my motley, give me leave
To speak my mind, and I will through and through
Cleanse the foul body of th' infected world,　　　　60
If they will patiently receive my medicine.
Duke Senior. Fie on thee! I can tell what thou wouldst do.
Jaques. What, for a counter,° would I do but good?
Duke Senior. Most mischievous foul sin, in chiding sin.
For thou thyself hast been a libertine,　　　　65
As sensual as the brutish sting° itself;
And all th' embossèd° sores and headed evils
That thou with license of free foot° hast caught,
Wouldst thou disgorge into the general world.
Jaques. Why, who cries out on pride　　　　70
That can therein tax any private party?°
Doth it not flow as hugely as the sea
Till that the weary very means do ebb?°
What woman in the city do I name
When that I say the city woman bears　　　　75
The cost° of princes on unworthy shoulders?
Who can come in and say that I mean her,
When such a one as she, such is her neighbor?
Or what is he of basest function°

---

46 *rank* luxuriant　　　48 *large a charter* liberal license　　　50 *gallèd* chafed
55 *senseless of the bob* unaware of the hit　　　56 *anatomized* revealed
57 *squand'ring glances* chance hits　　　58 *Invest* clothe
63 *counter* worthless coin　　　66 *the brutish sting* lust　　　67 *embossèd* swollen
68 *license of free foot* complete freedom
71 *tax any private party* criticize any particular person
73 *weary very means do ebb* (perhaps: "ostentation eventually exhausts the wealth that makes it possible." Some editors emend "weary" to "wearer's")
76 *cost* wealth　　　79 *function* position

That says his bravery is not on my cost,°   80
Thinking that I mean him, but therein suits
His folly to the mettle of my speech?°
There then, how then, what then? Let me see wherein
My tongue hath wronged him. If it do him right,
Then he hath wronged himself. If he be free,°   85
Why, then my taxing like a wild goose flies
Unclaimed of any man. But who comes here?

(*Enter Orlando [with his sword drawn].*)

Orlando. Forbear, and eat no more!
Jaques.   Why, I have eat none yet.
Orlando. Nor shalt not, till necessity be served.
Jaques. Of what kind° should this cock come of?   90
Duke Senior. Art thou thus boldened, man, by thy distress,
    Or else a rude despiser of good manners,
    That in civility thou seem'st so empty?
Orlando. You touched my vein at first.° The thorny point
    Of bare distress hath ta'en from me the show   95
    Of smooth civility; yet am I inland bred°
    And know some nurture.° But forbear, I say!
    He dies that touches any of this fruit
    Till I and my affairs are answerèd.°
Jaques. An° you will not be answered with reason,° I must die.   100
Duke Senior. What would you have? Your gentleness shall force
    More than your force move us to gentleness.
Orlando. I almost die for food, and let me have it!
Duke Senior. Sit down and feed, and welcome to our table.
Orlando. Speak you so gently? Pardon me, I pray you.   105
    I thought that all things had been savage here,
    And therefore put I on the countenance
    Of stern commandment. But whate'er you are
    That in this desert inaccessible,
    Under the shade of melancholy boughs,   110
    Lose and neglect the creeping hours of time;

---

80 *his bravery . . . cost* his fine dress is not paid for by me (and therefore is
not my business)
81–82 *suits . . . my speech* matches his folly to the substance of my words
85 *free* innocent   90 *kind* breed
94 *You touched . . . first* i.e., the Duke's first supposition is correct
96 *inland bred* brought up in civilized society   97 *nurture* good breeding
99 *answerèd* provided for   100 *An* if
100 *reason* (perhaps Jaques puns, eating a raisin [grape])

If ever you have looked on better days,
If ever been where bells have knolled° to church,
If ever sat at any good man's feast,
If ever from your eyelids wiped a tear   115
And know what 'tis to pity and be pitied,
Let gentleness my strong enforcement° be;
In the which hope I blush, and hide my sword.
Duke Senior. True is it that we have seen better days,
And have with holy bell been knolled to church,   120
And sat at good men's feasts, and wiped our eyes
Of drops that sacred pity hath engend'red;
And therefore sit you down in gentleness,
And take upon command° what help we have
That to your wanting° may be minist'red.   125
Orlando. Then but forbear your food a little while,
Whiles, like a doe, I go to find my fawn
And give it food. There is an old poor man
Who after me hath many a weary step
Limped in pure love. Till he be first sufficed,   130
Oppressed with two weak evils,° age and hunger,
I will not touch a bit.
Duke Senior.   Go find him out,
And we will nothing waste° till you return.
Orlando. I thank ye, and be blest for your good comfort!   [*Exit.*]
Duke Senior. Thou seest we are not all alone unhappy: 135
This wide and universal theater
Presents more woeful pageants° than the scene
Wherein we play in.
Jaques.   All the world's a stage,
And all the men and women merely players;
They have their exits and their entrances,   140
And one man in his time plays many parts,
His acts being seven ages.° At first, the infant,
Mewling° and puking in the nurse's arms.
Then the whining schoolboy, with his satchel
And shining morning face, creeping like snail   145

---

113 *knolled* rung   117 *enforcement* support   124 *upon command* as you wish
125 *wanting* need   131 *weak evils* evils causing weakness
133 *waste* consume   137 *pageants* scenes
142 *seven ages* (for a survey in art and literature of the image of man's life
divided into ages, see Samuel C. Chew, " 'This Strange Eventful History,' " in
John Quincy Adams Memorial Studies, ed. James G. McManaway *et al.*)
143 *Mewling* bawling

Unwillingly to school. And then the lover,
Sighing like furnace, with a woeful ballad
Made to his mistress' eyebrow. Then a soldier,
Full of strange oaths and bearded like the pard,°
Jealous° in honor, sudden° and quick in quarrel,   150
Seeking the bubble reputation
Even in the cannon's mouth. And then the justice,
In fair round belly with good capon lined,°
With eyes severe and beard of formal cut,
Full of wise saws° and modern instances;°   155
And so he plays his part. The sixth age shifts
Into the lean and slippered pantaloon,°
With spectacles on nose and pouch on side;
His youthful hose,° well saved, a world too wide
For his shrunk shank, and his big manly voice,   160
Turning again toward childish treble, pipes
And whistles in his° sound. Last scene of all,
That ends this strange eventful history,
Is second childishness and mere° oblivion,
Sans teeth, sans eyes, sans taste, sans everything.   165

(Enter Orlando, with Adam.)

Duke Senior. Welcome. Set down your venerable burden
    And let him feed.
Orlando. I thank you most for him.
Adam.   So had you need.
    I scarce can speak to thank you for myself.
Duke Senior. Welcome, fall to. I will not trouble you   170
    As yet to question you about your fortunes.
    Give us some music; and, good cousin, sing.

Song.

Amiens. Blow, blow, thou winter wind,
        Thou art not so unkind°
            As man's ingratitude: 175
        Thy tooth is not so keen,

---

¹⁴⁹ *pard* leopard   ¹⁵⁰ *Jealous* touchy   ¹⁵⁰ *sudden* rash
¹⁵³ *capon lined* (perhaps an allusion to the practice of bribing a judge with a
capon)   ¹⁵⁵ *saws* sayings   ¹⁵⁵ *modern instances* commonplace examples
¹⁵⁷ *pantaloon* ridiculous old man (from Pantalone, a stock figure in Italian
comedy)
¹⁵⁹ *hose* breeches   ¹⁶² *his* its   ¹⁶⁴ *mere* utter   ¹⁷⁴ *unkind* unnatural

Because thou art not seen,
  Although thy breath be rude.
Heigh-ho, sing heigh-ho, unto the green holly.
Most friendship is faining,° most loving mere folly: 180
  Then, heigh-ho, the holly.
  This life is most jolly.

Freeze, freeze, thou bitter sky
That dost not bite so nigh
  As benefits forgot: 185
Though thou the waters warp,°
Thy sting is not so sharp
  As friend rememb'red not.
Heigh-ho, sing, &c.

Duke Senior. If that you were the good Sir Rowland's son,   190
As you have whispered faithfully you were,
And as mine eye doth his effigies° witness
Most truly limned° and living in your face,
Be truly welcome hither. I am the Duke
That loved your father. The residue of your fortune   195
Go to my cave and tell me. Good old man,
Thou art right welcome, as thy master is.
Support him by the arm. Give me your hand,
And let me all your fortunes understand.   (*Exeunt.*)

ACT III

SCENE 1. [*The palace.*]

(*Enter Duke* [*Frederick*], *Lords, and Oliver.*)

Duke Frederick. Not see him since? Sir, sir, that cannot be.
But were I not the better part made mercy,°
I should not seek an absent argument°
Of my revenge, thou present. But look to it:
Find out thy brother, wheresoe'er he is;   5
Seek him with candle; bring him dead or living

---

180 *faining* longing (perhaps with a pun on "feigning" [pretending])
186 *warp* turn (into ice)   192 *effigies* likeness (accent on second syllable)
193 *limned* depicted
III.i.2 *the better part made mercy* so merciful
3 *argument* object (i.e., Orlando)

Within this twelvemonth, or turn° thou no more
To seek a living in our territory.
Thy lands, and all things that thou dost call thine
Worth seizure, do we seize into our hands   10
Till thou canst quit° thee by thy brother's mouth°
Of what we think against thee.

Oliver. O that your Highness knew my heart in this!
I never loved my brother in my life.

Duke Frederick. More villain thou. Well, push him out of doors,   15
And let my officers of such a nature°
Make an extent upon° his house and lands.
Do this expediently° and turn him going.   (*Exeunt.*)

SCENE 2. [*The forest.*]

(*Enter Orlando [with a paper].*)

Orlando. Hang there, my verse, in witness of my love;
    And thou, thrice-crownèd Queen of Night,° survey
With thy chaste eye, from thy pale sphere above,
    Thy huntress' name° that my full life doth sway.
O Rosalind! These trees shall be my books,   5
    And in their barks my thoughts I'll character,°
That every eye which in this forest looks
    Shall see thy virtue witnessed° everywhere.
Run, run, Orlando, carve on every tree
The fair, the chaste, and unexpressive she.°   (*Exit.*)   10

(*Enter Corin and [Touchstone, the] Clown.*)

Corin. And how like you this shepherd's life, Master Touchstone?

Touchstone. Truly, shepherd, in respect of itself, it is a good life;
but in respect that it is a shepherd's life, it is naught.° In respect that it is solitary, I like it very well; but in respect that it
is private,° it is a very vile life. Now in respect it is in the fields,   15
it pleaseth me well; but in respect it is not in the court, it is

---

7 *turn* return   11 *quit* acquit   11 *mouth* testimony
16 *of such a nature* i.e., appropriate   17 *Make an extent upon* seize by writ
18 *expediently* speedily
III.ii.2 *thrice-crownèd Queen of Night* Diana (goddess of the moon, the hunt, and of chastity)
4 *Thy huntress' name* i.e., Rosalind, who, because she is chaste, serves Diana
6 *character* write   8 *virtue witnessed* power attested to
10 *unexpressive she* i.e., woman beyond description
13 *naught* worthless   15 *private* lonely

tedious. As it is a spare° life, look you, it fits my humor° well;
but as there is no more plenty in it, it goes much against my
stomach. Hast any philosophy° in thee, shepherd?

Corin. No more, but that I know the more one sickens, the worse   20
at ease he is; and that he that wants° money, means, and content is without three good friends; that the property of rain is
to wet and fire to burn; that good pasture makes fat sheep, and
that a great cause of the night is lack of the sun; that he that
hath learned no wit by nature nor art° may complain° of good   25
breeding, or comes of a very dull kindred.

Touchstone. Such a one is a natural philosopher.° Wast ever in
court, shepherd?

Corin. No, truly.

Touchstone. Then thou art damned.   30

Corin. Nay, I hope.

Touchstone. Truly thou art damned, like an ill-roasted egg, all on
one side.

Corin. For not being at court? Your reason.

Touchstone. Why, if thou never wast at court, thou never saw'st   35
good manners;° if thou never saw'st good manners, then thy
manners must be wicked; and wickedness is sin, and sin is damnation. Thou art in a parlous° state, shepherd.

Corin. Not a whit, Touchstone. Those that are good manners at
the court are as ridiculous in the country as the behavior of the   40
country is most mockable at the court. You told me you salute
not at the court but you kiss° your hands. That courtesy would
be uncleanly if courtiers were shepherds.

Touchstone. Instance,° briefly. Come, instance.

Corin. Why, we are still° handling our ewes, and their fells° you   45
know are greasy.

Touchstone. Why, do not your courtier's hands sweat? And is not
the grease of a mutton as wholesome as the sweat of a man?
Shallow, shallow. A better instance, I say. Come.

Corin. Besides, our hands are hard.   50

Touchstone. Your lips will feel them the sooner. Shallow again.
A more sounder instance, come.

---

[17] *spare* frugal   [17] *humor* disposition
[19] *philosophy* learning   [21] *wants* lacks
[25] *by nature nor art* by birth or education   [25] *complain* cry the lack
[27] *a natural philosopher* (1) wise by nature (2) a wise idiot
[36] *manners* (1) behavior (2) morals   [38] *parlous* dangerous
[42] *but you kiss* without kissing   [44] *Instance* proof
[45] *still* always   [45] *fells* fleeces

Corin. And they are often tarred over with the surgery° of our sheep, and would you have us kiss tar? The courtier's hands are perfumed with civet.° 55

Touchstone. Most shallow man! Thou worms' meat° in respect of° a good piece of flesh indeed! Learn of the wise, and perpend.° Civet is of a baser birth than tar, the very uncleanly flux° of a cat. Mend the instance,° shepherd.

Corin. You have too courtly a wit for me; I'll rest. 60

Touchstone. Wilt thou rest damned? God help thee, shallow man! God make incision in thee!° Thou art raw.°

Corin. Sir, I am a true laborer; I earn that° I eat, get that I wear, owe no man hate, envy no man's happiness, glad of other men's good, content with my harm;° and the greatest of my 65 pride is to see my ewes graze and my lambs suck.

Touchstone. That is another simple sin in you: to bring the ewes and the rams together and to offer to get your living by the copulation of cattle, to be bawd to a bell-wether° and to betray a she-lamb of a twelve-month to a crookèd-pated° old cuck- 70 oldly° ram, out of all reasonable match. If thou beest not damned for this, the devil himself will have no shepherds; I cannot see else how thou shouldst 'scape.

Corin. Here comes young Master Ganymede, my new mistress' brother. 75

(*Enter Rosalind* [*reading a paper*].)

Rosalind.   "From the east to western Ind,
                 No jewel is like Rosalind.
                 Her worth, being mounted on the wind,
                 Through all the world bears Rosalind.
                 All the pictures fairest lined° 80
                 Are but black to Rosalind.
                 Let no face be kept in mind
                 But the fair° of Rosalind."

---

53 *tarred . . . surgery* (shepherds used tar as an ointment)
55 *civet* perfume obtained from the civet cat
56 *worms' meat* food for worms   56–57 *respect of* comparison with
57–58 *perpend* consider   59 *flux* secretion
59 *Mend the instance* give a better example
62 *make incision in thee* let your blood (a common cure, here for folly)
62 *raw* (1) inexperienced (2) sore   63 *that* what
65 *content with my harm* bear with my troubles
69 *bell-wether* (the leading sheep of a flock carries a bell)
70 *crookèd-pated* i.e., with crooked horns   70–71 *cuckoldy* (because horned)
80 *lined* drawn   83 *fair* lovely face

Touchstone. I'll rhyme you so eight years together, dinners and
suppers and sleeping hours excepted. It is the right butter- 85
women's rank to market.°
Rosalind. Out, fool!
Touchstone. For a taste:

        If a hart do lack a hind,
        Let him seek out Rosalind. 90
        If the cat will after kind,°
        So be sure will Rosalind.
        Wintred° garments must be lined,°
        So must slender Rosalind.
        They that reap must sheaf and bind, 95
        Then to cart° with Rosalind.
        Sweetest nut hath sourest rind,
        Such a nut is Rosalind.
        He that sweetest rose will find
        Must find love's prick, and Rosalind. 100
This is the very false gallop of verses. Why do you infect yourself with them?
Rosalind. Peace, you dull fool! I found them on a tree.
Touchstone. Truly the tree yields bad fruit.
Rosalind. I'll graff° it with you and then I shall graff it with a 105
medlar.° Then it will be the earliest fruit i' th' country; for
you'll be rotten ere you be half ripe, and that's the right virtue°
of the medlar.
Touchstone. You have said; but whether wisely or no, let the
forest judge. 110

(*Enter Celia, with a writing.*)

Rosalind. Peace! Here comes my sister reading; stand aside.
Celia. "Why should this a desert be?
      For° it is unpeopled? No.
    Tongues I'll hang on every tree
    That shall civil sayings° show: 115
Some, how brief the life of man
Runs his erring pilgrimage,

85–86 *right butterwomen's rank to market* i.e., the verses jog along exactly like
a procession of women riding to market   91 *kind* its own kind
93 *Wintred* i.e., prepared for winter   93 *lined* stuffed
96 *to cart* (perhaps an allusion not only to the harvest but to the custom of
transporting prostitutes to jail in a cart)   105 *graff* graft
106 *medlar* (1) an applelike fruit, not ready to eat until it is almost rotten
(2) interferer   107 *right virtue* true quality
113 *For* because   115 *civil sayings* civilized maxims

That the stretching of a span°
  Buckles in° his sum of age;
Some, of violated vows   120
  'Twixt the souls of friend and friend;
But upon the fairest boughs,
  Or at every sentence end,
Will I 'Rosalinda' write,
  Teaching all that read to know   125
The quintessence of every sprite°
  Heaven would in little° show.
Therefore heaven Nature charged
  That one body should be filled
With all graces wide-enlarged.   130
  Nature presently° distilled
Helen's cheek, but not her heart,°
  Cleopatra's majesty,
Atalanta's better part,°
  Sad° Lucretia's° modesty.   135
Thus Rosalind of many parts
  By heavenly synod° was devised,
Of many faces, eyes, and hearts,
  To have the touches° dearest prized.
Heaven would that she these gifts should have,   140
And I to live and die her slave."

Rosalind. O most gentle pulpiter, what tedious homily of love
  have you wearied your parishioners withal, and never cried,
  "Have patience, good people"!

Celia. How now? Back, friends. Shepherd, go off a little. Go with   145
  him, sirrah.

Touchstone. Come, shepherd, let us make an honorable retreat;
  though not with bag and baggage, yet with scrip and scrippage.°

                                 (Exit [with Corin].)

---

[118] *stretching of a span* span of an open hand   [119] *Buckles in* limits
[126] *sprite* soul   [127] *in little* in miniature (i.e., the microcosm)
[131] *presently* thereupon
[132] *cheek . . . heart* i.e., Helen's beauty but not her false heart
[134] *Atalanta's better part* i.e., Rosalind has the gracefulness but not the cruelty
of Atalanta, a huntress famed in Greek mythology for her fleetness
[135] *Sad* dignified
[135] *Lucretia* (a Roman matron who killed herself rather than live dishonored)
[137] *synod* council   [139] *touches* features
[148–149] *scrip and scrippage* shepherd's pouch and its contents

Celia. Didst thou hear these verses? 150

Rosalind. O, yes, I heard them all, and more too; for some of
them, had in them more feet° than the verses would bear.

Celia. That's no matter. The feet might bear the verses.

Rosalind. Ay, but the feet were lame, and could not bear themselves without the verse, and therefore stood lamely in the 155
verse.

Celia. But didst thou hear without wondering how thy name
should be hanged and carved upon these trees?

Rosalind. I was seven of the nine days° out of the wonder before
you came; for look here what I found on a palm tree. I was 160
never so berhymed since Pythagoras'° time that° I was an Irish
rat,° which I can hardly remember.

Celia. Trow° you who hath done this?

Rosalind. Is it a man?

Celia. And a chain that you once wore, about his neck. Change 165
your color?

Rosalind. I prithee who?

Celia. O Lord, Lord, it is a hard matter for friends to meet; but
mountains may be removed with earthquakes, and so encounter.

Rosalind. Nay, but who is it? 170

Celia. Is it possible?

Rosalind. Nay, I prithee now with most petitionary vehemence,°
tell me who it is.

Celia. O wonderful, wonderful, and most wonderful wonderful,
and yet again wonderful, and after that, out of all hooping!° 175

Rosalind. Good my complexion!° Dost thou think, though I am
caparisoned° like a man, I have a doublet and hose in my disposition! One inch of delay more is a South Sea of discovery.°
I prithee tell me who is it quickly, and speak apace.° I would
thou couldst stammer, that thou mightst pour this concealed 180
man out of thy mouth as wine comes out of a narrow-mouthed

---

152 *feet* metrical units
159 *seven of the nine days* (cf. the phrase "nine days' wonder")
161 *Pythagoras* (Greek philosopher who taught the doctrine of the transmigra-
tion of souls)
161 *that* when
161–162 *Irish rat* (it was believed that Irish sorcerers could kill rats with rhymed
spells)
163 *Trow* know   172 *with most petitionary vehemence* i.e., I beg you
175 *out of all hooping* beyond all measure
176 *Good my complexion* (a mild expletive)   177 *caparisoned* dressed
178 *One inch . . . discovery* i.e., another minute more will seem as long as it
takes to voyage to the South Seas   179 *apace* quickly

bottle; either too much at once, or none at all. I prithee take
the cork out of thy mouth, that I may drink thy tidings.

Celia. So you may put a man in your belly.

Rosalind. Is he of God's making? What manner of man? Is his   185
head worth a hat? Or his chin worth a beard?

Celia. Nay, he hath but a little beard.

Rosalind. Why, God will send more, if the man will be thankful.
Let me stay° the growth of his beard, if thou delay me not the
knowledge of his chin.   190

Celia. It is young Orlando, that tripped up the wrestler's heels and
your heart both in an instant.

Rosalind. Nay, but the devil take mocking! Speak sad brow and
true maid.°

Celia. I' faith, coz, 'tis he.   195

Rosalind. Orlando?

Celia. Orlando.

Rosalind. Alas the day! What shall I do with my doublet and
hose? What did he when thou saw'st him? What said he? How
looked he? Wherein went he?° What makes he here? Did he   200
ask for me? Where remains he? How parted he with thee?
And when shalt thou see him again? Answer me in one word.

Celia. You must borrow me Gargantua's° mouth first; 'tis a word
too great for any mouth of this age's size. To say "ay" and "no"
to these particulars is more than to answer in a catechism.   205

Rosalind. But doth he know that I am in this forest, and in man's
apparel? Looks he as freshly° as he did the day he wrestled?

Celia. It is as easy to count atomies° as to resolve the propositions°
of a lover; but take a taste of my finding him, and relish it with
good observance.° I found him under a tree, like a dropped   210
acorn.

Rosalind. It may well be called Jove's tree° when it drops forth
fruit.

Celia. Give me audience,° good madam.

Rosalind. Proceed.   215

Celia. There lay he stretched along like a wounded knight.

---

189 *stay* wait for
193–194 *sad brow and true maid* i.e., seriously and truthfully
200 *Wherein went he* how was he dressed
203 *Gargantua* (a giant in Rabelais and other writers)
207 *freshly* handsome   208 *atomies* motes
208 *resolve the propositions* answer the questions
210 *good observance* close attention
212 *Jove's tree* (the oak, sacred to Jove)   214 *Give me audience* listen

Rosalind. Though it be pity to see such a sight, it well becomes the ground.

Celia. Cry "holla"° to the tongue, I prithee; it curvets° unseasonably. He was furnished° like a hunter. 220

Rosalind. O, ominous! He comes to kill my heart.°

Celia. I would sing my song without a burden.° Thou bring'st me out of tune.

Rosalind. Do you not know I am a woman? When I think, I must speak. Sweet, say on. 225

(Enter Orlando and Jaques.)

Celia. You bring me out. Soft. Comes he not here?

Rosalind. 'Tis he! Slink by, and note him.

Jaques. I thank you for your company; but, good faith, I had as lief have been myself alone. 230

Orlando. And so had I; but yet for fashion sake I thank you too for your society.

Jaques. God b' wi' you; let's meet as little as we can.

Orlando. I do desire we may be better strangers.

Jaques. I pray you mar no more trees with writing love songs in 235 their barks.

Orlando. I pray you mar no moe° of my verses with reading them ill-favoredly.°

Jaques. Rosalind is your love's name?

Orlando. Yes, just. 240

Jaques. I do not like her name.

Orlando. There was no thought of pleasing you when she was christened.

Jaques. What stature is she of?

Orlando. Just as high as my heart. 245

Jaques. You are full of pretty answers. Have you not been acquainted with goldsmiths' wives, and conned them out of rings?°

Orlando. Not so; but I answer you right painted cloth,° from whence you have studied your questions. 250

---

²¹⁹ *holla* whoa   ²¹⁹ *curvets* frolics   ²²⁰ *furnished* dressed
²²¹ *heart* (pun on "hart")   ²²² *burden* refrain
²³⁷ *moe* more   ²³⁸ *ill-favoredly* badly
²⁴⁷⁻²⁴⁸ *conned them out of rings* i.e., memorized the sentimental sayings inscribed in rings
²⁴⁹ *painted cloth* (cheap substitute for tapestry, on which were painted pictures with trite sayings)

Jaques. You have a nimble wit; I think 'twas made of Atalanta's heels.° Will you sit down with me, and we two will rail against our mistress the world and all our misery.

Orlando. I will chide no breather° in the world but myself, against whom I know most faults. 255

Jaques. The worst fault you have is to be in love.

Orlando. 'Tis a fault I will not change for your best virtue. I am weary of you.

Jaques. By my troth, I was seeking for a fool when I found you.

Orlando. He is drowned in the brook. Look but in and you shall 260 see him.

Jaques. There I shall see mine own figure.

Orlando. Which I take to be either a fool or a cipher.°

Jaques. I'll tarry no longer with you. Farewell, good Signior Love.

Orlando. I am glad of your departure. Adieu, good Monsieur 265 Melancholy. [*Exit Jaques.*]

Rosalind. I will speak to him like a saucy lackey, and under that habit° play the knave with him. Do you hear, forester?

Orlando. Very well. What would you?

Rosalind. I pray you, what is't o'clock? 270

Orlando. You should ask me, what time o' day. There's no clock in the forest.

Rosalind. Then there is no true lover in the forest, else sighing every minute and groaning every hour would detect° the lazy foot of Time as well as a clock. 275

Orlando. And why not the swift foot of Time? Had not that been as proper?

Rosalind. By no means, sir. Time travels in divers paces with divers persons. I'll tell you who Time ambles withal, who Time trots withal, who Time gallops withal, and who he stands still 280 withal.

Orlando. I prithee, who doth he trot withal?

Rosalind. Marry, he trots hard with a young maid between the contract of her marriage° and the day it is solemnized. If the interim be but a se'nnight,° Time's pace is so hard that it 285 seems the length of seven year.

Orlando. Who ambles Time withal?

Rosalind. With a priest that lacks Latin and a rich man that hath not the gout; for the one sleeps easily because he cannot study, and the other lives merrily because he feels no pain; the one 290

251–252 *Atalanta's heels* (Atalanta was a symbol of speed)
254 *breather* creature   263 *cipher* zero   268 *habit* guise   274 *detect* show
284 *contract of her marriage* betrothal   285 *a se'nnight* seven days, a week

lacking the burden of lean and wasteful° learning, the other
knowing no burden of heavy tedious penury. These Time
ambles withal.

Orlando. Who doth he gallop withal?

Rosalind. With a thief to the gallows; for though he go as softly°   295
as foot can fall, he thinks himself too soon there.

Orlando. Who stays it still withal?

Rosalind. With lawyers in the vacation; for they sleep between
term° and term, and then they perceive not how time moves.

Orlando. Where dwell you, pretty youth?   300

Rosalind. With this shepherdess, my sister; here in the skirts of
the forest, like fringe upon a petticoat.

Orlando. Are you native of this place?

Rosalind. As the cony° that you see dwell where she is kindled.°

Orlando. Your accent is something finer than you could purchase°   305
in so removed° a dwelling.

Rosalind. I have been told so of many. But indeed an old reli-
gious° uncle of mine taught me to speak, who was in his youth
an inland° man; one that knew courtship° too well, for there
he fell in love. I have heard him read many lectures against it;   310
and I thank God I am not a woman, to be touched° with so
many giddy° offenses as he hath generally taxed their whole
sex withal.

Orlando. Can you remember any of the principal evils that he laid
to the charge of women?   315

Rosalind. There were none principal. They were all like one another as halfpence are, every one fault seeming monstrous till
his fellow fault came to match it.

Orlando. I prithee recount some of them.

Rosalind. No, I will not cast away my physic but on those that are   320
sick. There is a man haunts the forest that abuses our young
plants with carving "Rosalind" on their barks, hangs odes upon
hawthorns, and elegies on brambles; all, forsooth, deifying the
name of Rosalind. If I could meet that fancy-monger,° I would
give him some good counsel, for he seems to have the quotid-   325
ian° of love upon him.

---

291 *wasteful* i.e., causing one to waste away   295 *softly* slowly
299 *term* court session   304 *cony* rabbit   304 *kindled* born
305 *purchase* acquire   306 *removed* remote
307–308 *religious* i.e., a member of a religious order   309 *inland* city
309 *courtship* (1) court manners (2) wooing   311 *touched* tainted
312 *giddy* frivolous   324 *fancy-monger* dealer in love
325–326 *quotidian* daily fever

Orlando. I am he that is so love-shaked. I pray tell me your
remedy.

Rosalind. There is none of my uncle's marks upon you. He taught
me how to know a man in love; in which cage of rushes° I am   330
sure you are not prisoner.

Orlando. What were his marks?

Rosalind. A lean cheek, which you have not; a blue eye° and
sunken, which you have not; an unquestionable° spirit, which
you have not; a beard neglected, which you have not — but I   335
pardon you for that, for simply your having° in beard is a
younger brother's revenue.° Then your hose should be ungar-
tered, your bonnet unbanded, your sleeve unbuttoned, your
shoe untied, and everything about you demonstrating a careless
desolation.° But you are no such man: you are rather point-   340
device in your accouterments,° as loving yourself than seeming
the lover of any other.

Orlando. Fair youth, I would I could make thee believe I love.

Rosalind. Me believe it? You may as soon make her that you love
believe it, which I warrant she is apter to do than to confess   345
she does; that is one of the points in the which women still give
the lie to their consciences. But in good sooth, are you he that
hangs the verses on the trees wherein Rosalind is so admired?

Orlando. I swear to thee, youth, by the white hand of Rosalind,
I am that he, that unfortunate he.   350

Rosalind. But are you so much in love as your rhymes speak?

Orlando. Neither rhyme nor reason can express how much.

Rosalind. Love is merely° a madness, and, I tell you, deserves as
well a dark house and a whip° as madmen do; and the reason
why they are not so punished and cured is that the lunacy   355
is so ordinary that the whippers are in love too. Yet I profess
curing it by counsel.

Orlando. Did you ever cure any so?

Rosalind. Yes, one, and in this manner. He was to imagine me
his love, his mistress; and I set him every day to woo me. At   360

---

³³⁰ *cage of rushes* i.e., prison easy to escape from
³³³ *a blue eye* i.e., dark circles under the eyes
³³⁴ *unquestionable* averse to conversation
³³⁶ *simply your having* truthfully what you have
³³⁷ *a younger brother's revenue* i.e., a small portion
³³⁹⁻³⁴⁰ *a careless desolation* indifferent despondency
³⁴¹⁻³⁴² *point-device in your accouterments* precise in your dress
³⁵⁵ *merely* completely
³⁵⁴ *a dark house and a whip* (the usual treatment of the insane in Shakespeare's
day)

which time would I, being but a moonish° youth, grieve, be
effeminate, changeable, longing and liking, proud, fantastical,°
apish, shallow, inconstant, full of tears, full of smiles; for every
passion something and for no passion truly anything, as boys
and women are for the most part cattle of this color; would   365
now like him, now loathe him; then entertain him, then forswear him; now weep for him, then spit at him; that I drave my
suitor from his made humor° of love to a living° humor of madness, which was, to forswear the full stream of the world and
to live in a nook merely monastic. And thus I cured him; and   370
this way will I take upon me to wash your liver° as clean as a
sound sheep's heart, that there shall not be one spot of love in't.
Orlando. I would not be cured, youth.
Rosalind. I would cure you, if you would but call me Rosalind
and come every day to my cote and woo me.   375
Orlando. Now, by the faith of my love, I will. Tell me where it is.
Rosalind. Go with me to it, and I'll show it you; and by° the way
you shall tell me where in the forest you live. Will you go?
Orlando. With all my heart, good youth.
Rosalind. Nay, you must call me Rosalind. Come sister, will you   380
go?   (*Exeunt.*)

SCENE 3. [*The forest.*]

(*Enter* [*Touchstone, the*] *Clown, Audrey; and Jaques* [*apart*].)

Touchstone. Come apace,° good Audrey. I will fetch up your
goats, Audrey. And how, Audrey, am I the man yet? Doth my
simple feature° content you?
Audrey. Your features, Lord warrant° us! What features?
Touchstone. I am here with thee and thy goats, as the most   5
capricious poet, honest Ovid, was among the Goths.°
Jaques. [*Aside*] O knowledge ill-inhabited,° worse than Jove in a
thatched house!
Touchstone. When a man's verses cannot be understood, nor a
man's good wit seconded with° the forward child, understand-   10

³⁶¹ *moonish* changeable   ³⁶² *fantastical* capricious   ³⁶⁸ *humor* condition
³⁶⁸ *living* real   ³⁷¹ *liver* (thought to be the seat of love)   ³⁷⁷ *by* along
III.iii.¹ *apace* swiftly   ³ *feature* appearance   ⁴ *warrant* save
⁶ *capricious . . . Goths* (the Roman poet Ovid was exiled among the Goths —
pronounced in Elizabethan England the same as "goats" — for the immorality
of his verses. Touchstone plays on the words "honest" [chaste] and "capricious" [derived from Latin *caper*, male goat])
⁷ *ill-inhabited* ill-housed   ¹⁰ *with* by

ing, it strikes a man more dead than a great reckoning in a little room.° Truly, I would the gods had made thee poetical.

Audrey. I do not know what poetical is. Is it honest in deed and word? Is it a true thing?

Touchstone. No, truly; for the truest poetry is the most feigning, 15 and lovers are given to poetry, and what they swear in poetry may be said as lovers they do feign.°

Audrey. Do you wish then that the gods had made me poetical?

Touchstone. I do truly; for thou swear'st to me thou art honest. Now, if thou wert a poet, I might have some hope thou didst 20 feign.

Audrey. Would you not have me honest?

Touchstone. No, truly, unless thou wert hard-favored;° for honesty coupled to beauty is to have honey a sauce to sugar.

Jaques. [*Aside*] A material° fool. 25

Audrey. Well, I am not fair, and therefore I pray the gods make me honest.

Touchstone. Truly, and to cast away honesty upon a foul slut were to put good meat into an unclean dish.

Audrey. I am not a slut, though I thank the gods I am foul. 30

Touchstone. Well, praised be the gods for thy foulness! Sluttishness may come hereafter. But be it as it may be, I will marry thee; and to that end I have been with Sir° Oliver Mar-text, the vicar of the next village, who hath promised to meet me in this place of the forest and to couple us. 35

Jaques. [*Aside*] I would fain see this meeting.

Audrey. Well, the gods give us joy!

Touchstone. Amen. A man may, if he were of a fearful heart, stagger° in this attempt; for here we have no temple but the wood, no assembly but horn-beasts.° But what though? Cour- 40 age! As horns are odious, they are necessary.° It is said, "Many a man knows no end of his goods." Right! Many a man has good horns and knows no end of them. Well, that is the dowry of his wife; 'tis none of his own getting. Horns! Even so, poor men alone. No, no; the noblest deer hath them as huge as 45 the rascal.° Is the single man therefore blessed? No; as a walled

---

¹¹⁻¹² *great reckoning . . . room* large bill for poor accommodations
¹⁷ *feign* (1) pretend (2) desire (a pun on "fain")
²³ *hard-favored* ugly   ²⁵ *material* full of good matter
³³ *Sir* (an old form of address for a priest)   ³⁹ *stagger* tremble
⁴⁰ *hornbeasts* (1) horned animals (2) cuckolds
⁴¹ *necessary* inevitable   ⁴⁶ *rascal* inferior deer

town is more worthier than a village, so is the forehead of a
married man more honorable than the bare brow of a bachelor;
and by how much defense° is better than no skill, by so much
is a horn more precious than to want.°   50

(*Enter Sir Oliver Mar-text.*)

Here comes Sir Oliver. Sir Oliver Mar-text, you are well met.
Will you dispatch us° here under this tree, or shall we go with
you to your chapel?
Oliver Mar-text. Is there none here to give the woman?
Touchstone. I will not take her on gift of any man.   55
Oliver Mar-text. Truly, she must be given, or the marriage is not
lawful.
Jaques. [*Comes forward*] Proceed, proceed; I'll give her.
Touchstone. Good even, good Master What-ye-call't.° How do
you, sir? You are very well met. God 'ield you for your last   60
company;° I am very glad to see you. Even a toy° in hand here,
sir. Nay, pray be covered.°
Jaques. Will you be married, motley?
Touchstone. As the ox hath his bow,° sir, the horse his curb, and
the falcon her bells, so man hath his desires; and as pigeons   65
bill, so wedlock would be nibbling.
Jaques. And will you, being a man of your breeding, be married
under a bush like a beggar? Get you to church, and have a good
priest that can tell you what marriage is. This fellow will but
join you together as they join wainscot;° then one of you will   70
prove a shrunk panel, and like green timber warp, warp.
Touchstone. [*Aside*] I am not in the mind but° I were better to
be married of him than of another; for he is not like to marry
me well; and not being well married,° it will be a good excuse
for me hereafter to leave my wife.   75
Jaques. Go thou with me and let me counsel thee.

---

⁴⁹ *defense* the art of defense   ⁵⁰ *want* i.e., lack horns
⁵² *dispatch us* finish our business
⁵⁹ *Master What-ye-call't* (Touchstone delicately avoids the name "Jaques,"
which could be pronounced "jakes," a privy)
⁶⁰⁻⁶¹ *God 'ield . . . company* God reward you for the last time we met
⁶¹ *toy* trifle   ⁶² *pray be covered* (Jaques has removed his hat)
⁶⁴ *bow* yoke   ⁷⁰ *wainscot* wood paneling
⁷² *I am not in the mind but* I am not sure but that
⁷⁴ *well married* (1) legally married (2) happily married (3) married into
wealth

Touchstone. Come, sweet Audrey.
We must be married, or we must live in bawdry.
Farewell, good Master Oliver: not

O sweet Oliver,   80
O brave Oliver,
Leave me not behind thee;

but

Wind° away,
Be gone, I say;   85
I will not to wedding with thee.

Oliver Mar-text. 'Tis no matter. Ne'er a fantastical° knave of
them all shall flout me out of my calling.   (*Exeunt.*)

SCENE 4. [*The forest.*]

(*Enter Rosalind and Celia.*)

Rosalind. Never talk to me; I will weep.
Celia. Do, I prithee; but yet have the grace to consider that tears
do not become a man.
Rosalind. But have I not cause to weep?
Celia. As good cause as one would desire; therefore weep.   5
Rosalind. His very hair is of the dissembling color.°
Celia. Something browner than Judas'. Marry, his kisses are Judas'
own children.
Rosalind. I' faith, his hair is of a good color.
Celia. An excellent color. Your chestnut was ever the only color.   10
Rosalind. And his kissing is as full of sanctity as the touch of
holy bread.°
Celia. He hath bought a pair of cast° lips of Diana.° A nun of
winter's sisterhood° kisses not more religiously; the very ice of
chastity is in them.   15
Rosalind. But why did he swear he would come this morning, and
comes not?
Celia. Nay, certainly there is no truth in him.

<hr>

[84] *Wind* turn   [87] *fantastical* odd
III.iv.[6] *dissembling color* i.e., red, like the hair of Judas
[12] *holy bread* (not the sacramental wafer, but bread brought to church to be
blessed and then distributed to the poor)
[13] *cast* (1) molded (2) castoff   [13] *Diana* goddess of chastity
[14] *winter's sisterhood* i.e., the most rigorous chastity

Rosalind. Do you think so?

Celia. Yes; I think he is not a pickpurse nor a horse-stealer, but 20
for his verity in love, I do think him as concave° as a covered
goblet or a worm-eaten nut.

Rosalind. Not true in love?

Celia. Yes, when he is in, but I think he is not in.

Rosalind. You have heard him swear downright he was. 25

Celia. "Was" is not "is." Besides, the oath of a lover is no
stronger than the word of a tapster;° they are both the con-
firmer of false reckonings. He attends here in the forest on the
Duke your father.

Rosalind. I met the Duke yesterday and had much question° 30
with him. He asked me of what parentage I was. I told him,
of as good as he; so he laughed and let me go. But what talk
we of fathers when there is such a man as Orlando?

Celia. O, that's a brave° man; he writes brave verses, speaks brave
words, swears brave oaths, and breaks them bravely, quite 35
traverse,° athwart the heart of his lover, as a puisny° tilter, that
spurs his horse but on one side, breaks his staff like a noble
goose. But all's brave that youth mounts and folly guides. Who
comes here?

(*Enter Corin.*)

Corin. Mistress and master, you have oft enquired 40
After the shepherd that complained° of love,
Who you saw sitting by me on the turf,
Praising the proud disdainful shepherdess
That was his mistress.

Celia.   Well, and what of him?

Corin. If you will see a pageant° truly played 45
Between the pale complexion of true love
And the red glow of scorn and proud disdain,
Go hence a little, and I shall conduct you,
If you will mark it.

Rosalind.   O, come, let us remove:
The sight of lovers feedeth those in love. 50
Bring us to this sight, and you shall say
I'll prove a busy actor in their play.   (*Exeunt.*)

---

²¹ *concave* hollow   ²⁷ *tapster* waiter in a tavern   ³⁰ *question* talk
³⁴ *brave* fine   ³⁶ *traverse* at an angle (instead of head-on)
³⁶ *puisny* inexperienced   ⁴¹ *complained* lamented
⁴⁵ *pageant* scene, show

SCENE 5. [*The forest.*]

(*Enter Silvius and Phebe.*)

Silvius. Sweet Phebe, do not scorn me; do not, Phebe!
　　Say that you love me not, but say not so
　　In bitterness. The common executioner
　　Whose heart th' accustomed sight of death makes hard,
　　Falls° not the ax upon the humbled neck   5
　　But first begs pardon. Will you sterner be
　　Than he that dies and lives° by bloody drops?

(*Enter [apart] Rosalind, Celia, and Corin.*)

Phebe. I would not be thy executioner.
　　I fly thee, for I would not injure thee.
　　Thou tell'st me there is murder in mine eye: 10
　　'Tis pretty, sure, and very probable
　　That eyes, that are the frail'st and softest things,
　　Who shut their coward gates on atomies,°
　　Should be called tyrants, butchers, murderers.
　　No I do frown on thee with all my heart,   15
　　And if mine eyes can wound, now let them kill thee.
　　Now counterfeit to swound,° why, now fall down;
　　Or if thou canst not, O, for shame, for shame,
　　Lie not, to say mine eyes are murderers.
　　Now show the wound mine eye hath made in thee;   20
　　Scratch thee but with a pin, and there remains
　　Some scar of it; lean upon a rush,
　　The cicatrice and capable impressure°
　　Thy palm some moment keep; but now mine eyes,
　　Which I have darted at thee, hurt thee not,   25
　　Nor I am sure there is no force in eyes
　　That can do hurt.
Silvius.　　　　　　O dear Phebe,
　　If ever, as that ever may be near,°
　　You meet in some fresh cheek the power of fancy,°
　　Then shall you know the wounds invisible   30
　　That love's keen arrows make.

III.v.⁵ *Falls* lets fall　　　⁷ *dies and lives* earns his living　　　¹³ *atomies* motes
¹⁷ *counterfeit to swound* pretend to swoon
²³ *cicatrice and capable impressure* mark and visible impression
²⁸ *as that ever may be near* and may the time be soon　　　²⁹ *fancy* love

Phebe.   But till that time
  Come thou not near me; and when that time comes,
  Afflict me with thy mocks, pity me not,
  As till that time I shall not pity thee.
Rosalind. And why, I pray you? Who might be your mother,   35
  That you insult, exult, and all at once,
  Over the wretched? What though you have no beauty
  (As, by my faith, I see no more in you
  Than without candle may go dark to bed°)
  Must you be therefore proud and pitiless?   40
  Why, what means this? Why do you look on me?
  I see no more in you than in the ordinary
  Of nature's sale-work.° 'Od's° my little life,
  I think she means to tangle my eyes too!
  No, faith, proud mistress, hope not after it;   45
  'Tis not your inky brows, your black silk hair,
  Your bugle° eyeballs, nor your cheek of cream
  That can entame my spirits to your worship.
  You foolish shepherd, wherefore do you follow her,
  Like foggy south,° puffing with wind and rain?   50
  You are a thousand times a properer° man
  Than she a woman. 'Tis such fools as you
  That makes the world full of ill-favored children.
  'Tis not her glass,° but you, that flatters her,
  And out of you she sees herself more proper   55
  Than any of her lineaments can show her.
  But mistress, know yourself. Down on your knees,
  And thank heaven, fasting, for a good man's love;
  For I must tell you friendly in your ear,
  Sell when you can, you are not for all markets.   60
  Cry the man mercy,° love him, take his offer;
  Foul° is most foul, being foul to be a scoffer;
  So take her to thee, shepherd. Fare you well.
Phebe. Sweet youth, I pray you chide a year together;
  I had rather hear you chide than this man woo.   65
Rosalind. [*Aside*] He's fall'n in love with your foulness, and she'll
  fall in love with my anger. If it be so, as fast as she answers

---

³⁹ *Than . . . to bed* i.e., your beauty is not so dazzling as to light up the room
⁴²⁻⁴³ *ordinary/Of nature's sale-work* usual product of nature's manufacture
⁴³ *'Od's* God save   ⁴⁷ *bugle* black and glassy   ⁵⁰ *south* south wind
⁵¹ *properer* more handsome   ⁵⁴ *glass* mirror
⁶¹ *Cry the man mercy* ask the man's forgiveness
⁶² *Foul* (1) ugliness (2) wickedness

thee with frowning looks, I'll sauce her with bitter words. [*To
Phebe*] Why look you so upon me?

Phebe. For no ill will I bear you.   70

Rosalind. I pray you do not fall in love with me,
For I am falser than vows made in wine.
Besides, I like you not. If you will know my house,
'Tis at the tuft of olives, here hard° by.
Will you go, sister? Shepherd, ply her hard.   75
Come, sister. Shepherdess, look on him better
And be not proud. Though all the world could see,
None could be so abused° in sight as he.
Come, to our flock.   (*Exit* [*with Celia and Corin*].)

Phebe. Dead shepherd, now I find thy saw° of might,   80
"Who ever loved that loved not at first sight?"°

Silvius. Sweet Phebe.

Phebe.   Ha! What say'st thou, Silvius?

Silvius. Sweet Phebe, pity me.

Phebe. Why, I am sorry for thee, gentle Silvius.

Silvius. Wherever sorry is, relief would be.   85
If you do sorrow at my grief in love,
By giving love your sorrow and my grief
Were both extermined.°

Phebe. Thou hast my love. Is not that neighborly?°

Silvius. I would have you.

Phebe.   Why, that were covetousness.   90
Silvius, the time was that I hated thee;
And yet it is not that I bear thee love,
But since that thou canst talk of love so well,
Thy company, which erst° was irksome to me,
I will endure; and I'll employ thee too;   95
But do not look for further recompense
Than thine own gladness that thou art employed.

Silvius. So holy and so perfect is my love,
And in such a poverty of grace,°
That I shall think it a most plenteous crop   100
To glean the broken ears after the man

---

⁷⁴ *hard* near   ⁷⁸ *abused* deceived   ⁸⁰ *saw* saying
⁸¹ *Who ever . . . sight* (a line from Christopher Marlowe's poem *Hero and
Leander*, published in 1598. The "Dead shepherd" is Marlowe, who died in
1593)   ⁸⁸ *extermined* ended
⁸⁹ *neighborly* friendly (perhaps alluding to the commandment to love one's
neighbor)   ⁹⁴ *erst* formerly   ⁹⁹ *a poverty of grace* small favor

That the main harvest reaps. Loose now and then
A scatt'red° smile, and that I'll live upon.
Phebe. Know'st thou the youth that spoke to me erewhile?°
Silvius. Not very well, but I have met him oft,   105
And he hath bought the cottage and the bounds
That the old carlot° once was master of.
Phebe. Think not I love him, though I ask for him;
'Tis but a peevish boy; yet he talks well.
But what care I for words? Yet words do well   110
When he that speaks them pleases those that hear.
It is a pretty youth. Not very pretty.
But sure he's proud. And yet his pride become him.
He'll make a proper man. The best thing in him
Is his complexion. And faster than his tongue   115
Did make offense, his eye did heal it up.
He is not very tall. Yet for his years he's tall.
His leg is but so so. And yet 'tis well.
There was a pretty redness in his lip,
A little riper and more lusty red   120
Than that mixed in his cheek. 'Twas just the difference
Betwixt the constant° red and mingled damask.°
There be some women, Silvius, had they marked him
In parcels° as I did, would have gone near
To fall in love with him; but, for my part,   125
I love him not nor hate him not. And yet
I have more cause to hate him than to love him;
For what had he to do to chide at me?
He said mine eyes were black and my hair black;
And, now I am rememb'red,° scorned at me.   130
I marvel why I answered not again.
But that's all one: omittance is no quittance.°
I'll write to him a very taunting letter,
And thou shalt bear it. Wilt thou, Silvius?
Silvius. Phebe, with all my heart.
Phebe.   I'll write it straight;°   135
The matter's in my head and in my heart;
I will be bitter with him and passing short.°
Go with me, Silvius.   (*Exeunt.*)

---

[103] *scatt'red* stray   [104] *erewhile* a short time ago   [107] *carlot* countryman
[122] *constant* uniform   [122] *mingled damask* pink and white
[124] *In parcels* piece by piece   [130] *rememb'red* reminded
[132] *omittance is no quittance* i.e., the fact that I did not reply does not mean
I will not do so later   [135] *straight* at once   [137] *passing short* very curt

ACT IV

SCENE 1. *[The forest.]*

(*Enter Rosalind and Celia and Jaques.*)

Jaques. I prithee, pretty youth, let me be better acquainted with thee.

Rosalind. They say you are a melancholy fellow.

Jaques. I am so; I do love it better than laughing.

Rosalind. Those that are in extremity of° either are abominable   5
fellows, and betray themselves to every modern censure° worse than drunkards.

Jaques. Why, 'tis good to be sad and say nothing.

Rosalind. Why then, 'tis good to be a post.

Jaques. I have neither the scholar's melancholy, which is emula-   10
tion;° nor the musician's, which is fantastical; nor the cour-tier's, which is proud; nor the soldier's, which is ambitious; nor the lawyer's, which is politic;° nor the lady's, which is nice;° nor the lover's, which is all these: but it is a melancholy of mine own, compounded of many simples,° extracted from   15
many objects, and indeed the sundry contemplation of my travels, in which my often rumination° wraps me in a most humorous sadness.

Rosalind. A traveler! By my faith, you have great reason to be sad. I fear you have sold your own lands to see other men's. Then   20
to have seen much and to have nothing is to have rich eyes and poor hands.

Jaques. Yes, I have gained my experience.

(*Enter Orlando.*)

Rosalind. And your experience makes you sad. I had rather have a fool to make me merry than experience to make me sad —   25
and to travel° for it too.

Orlando. Good day and happiness, dear Rosalind.

Jaques. Nay then, God b'wi'you, an° you talk in blank verse.

[*Exit.*]

IV.i.⁵ *are in extremity of* go to extremes in
⁶ *every modern censure* i.e., the average man's disapproval
¹⁰⁻¹¹ *emulation* envy   ¹³ *politic* i.e., put on to seem grave
¹³ *nice* fastidious   ¹⁵ *simples* ingredients
¹⁷ *often rumination* constant reflection
²⁶ *travel* (pun on "travail")   ²⁸ *an* if

Rosalind. Farewell, Monsieur Traveler. Look you lisp° and wear
strange suits, disable° all the benefits of your own country, be   30
out of love with your nativity,° and almost chide God for
making you that countenance you are; or I will scarce think
you have swam in a gundello.° Why, how now, Orlando, where
have you been all this while? You a lover? An you serve me
such another trick, never come in my sight more.   35

Orlando. My fair Rosalind, I come within an hour of my promise.

Rosalind. Break an hour's promise in love? He that will divide a
minute into a thousand parts and break but a part of the
thousand part of a minute in the affairs of love, it may be
said of him that Cupid hath clapped° him o' th' shoulder, but   40
I'll warrant him heart-whole.

Orlando. Pardon me, dear Rosalind.

Rosalind. Nay, an you be so tardy, come no more in my sight. I
had as lief be wooed of a snail.

Orlando. Of a snail?   45

Rosalind. Ay, of a snail; for though he comes slowly, he carries
his house on his head; a better jointure,° I think, than you
make a woman. Besides, he brings his destiny with him.

Orlando. What's that?

Rosalind. Why, horns; which such as you are fain to be beholding   50
to your wives for; but he comes armed° in his fortune and
prevents° the slander of his wife.

Orlando. Virtue is no horn-maker, and my Rosalind is virtuous.

Rosalind. And I am your Rosalind.

Celia. It pleases him to call you so; but he hath a Rosalind of a   55
better leer° than you.

Rosalind. Come, woo me, woo me; for now I am in a holiday
humor and like enough to consent. What would you say to me
now, an I were your very very Rosalind?

Orlando. I would kiss before I spoke.   60

Rosalind. Nay, you were better speak first, and when you were
graveled for lack of matter,° you might take occasion to kiss.
Very good orators, when they are out,° they will spit; and for
lovers, lacking — God warn° us! — matter, the cleanliest shift
is to kiss.   65

Orlando. How if the kiss be denied?

---

²⁹ *lisp* speak affectedly   ³⁰ *disable* disparage   ³¹ *nativity* birthplace
³³ *gundello* gondola   ⁴⁰ *clapped* touched   ⁴⁷ *jointure* marriage settlement
⁵¹ *armed* i.e., with horns   ⁵² *prevents* (1) forestalls (2) anticipates (?)
⁵⁶ *leer* face   ⁶² *graveled for lack of matter* hard put for something to say
⁶³ *out* i.e., out of material   ⁶⁴ *warn* protect (warrant)

Rosalind. Then she puts you to entreaty, and there begins new matter.

Orlando. Who could be out, being before his beloved mistress?

Rosalind. Marry, that should you, if I were your mistress, or I   70
should think my honesty ranker° than my wit.

Orlando. What, of my suit?

Rosalind. Not out of your apparel, and yet out of your suit.° Am not I your Rosalind?

Orlando. I take some joy to say you are, because I would be   75
talking of her.

Rosalind. Well, in her person, I say I will not have you.

Orlando. Then, in mine own person, I die.

Rosalind. No faith, die by attorney.° The poor world is almost six thousand years old, and in all this time there was not any man   80
died in his own person,° videlicet,° in a love cause. Troilus°
had his brains dashed out with a Grecian club; yet he did what he could to die before, and he is one of the patterns of love.
Leander,° he would have lived many a fair year though Hero had turned nun, if it had not been for a hot midsummer night;   85
for, good youth, he went but forth to wash him in the Helles-
pont, and being taken with the cramp, was drowned; and the foolish chroniclers of that age found° it was "Hero of Sestos."
But these are all lies. Men have died from time to time, and worms have eaten them, but not for love.   90

Orlando. I would not have my right Rosalind of this mind, for I protest her frown might kill me.

Rosalind. By this hand, it will not kill a fly. But come, now I will be your Rosalind in a more coming-on disposition; and ask me what you will, I will grant it.   95

Orlando. Then love me, Rosalind.

Rosalind. Yes, faith, will I, Fridays and Saturdays and all.

Orlando. And wilt thou have me?

Rosalind. Ay, and twenty such.

Orlando. What sayest thou?   100

Rosalind. Are you not good?

Orlando. I hope so.

---

71 *honesty ranker* virtue fouler   73 *suit* (1) apparel (2) entreaty
79 *attorney* proxy   81 *in his own person* in real life (as opposed to fiction)
81 *videlicet* that is to say
81 *Troilus* (Priam's son, betrayed in love by Cressida and killed by the spear of Achilles. "As true as Troilus" became a proverbial expression)
84 *Leander* (a prototype of dedicated love, who swam the Hellespont nightly to see his mistress, Hero of Sestos)   88 *found* gave the verdict

Rosalind. Why then, can one desire too much of a good thing? Come, sister, you shall be the priest and marry us. Give me your hand, Orlando. What do you say, sister? 105

Orlando. Pray thee marry us.

Celia. I cannot say the words.

Rosalind. You must begin, "Will you, Orlando — "

Celia. Go to.° Will you, Orlando, have to wife this Rosalind?

Orlando. I will. 110

Rosalind. Ay, but when?

Orlando. Why now, as fast as she can marry us.

Rosalind. Then you must say, "I take thee, Rosalind, for wife."

Orlando. I take thee, Rosalind, for wife.

Rosalind. I might ask you for your commission;° but I do take 115 thee, Orlando, for my husband. There's a girl goes before° the priest, and certainly a woman's thought runs before her actions.

Orlando. So do all thoughts; they are winged.

Rosalind. Now tell me how long you would have her after you have possessed her. 120

Orlando. For ever and a day.

Rosalind. Say "a day," without the "ever." No, no, Orlando. Men are April when they woo, December when they wed. Maids are May when they are maids, but the sky changes when they are wives. I will be more jealous of thee than a Barbary 125 cock-pigeon° over his hen, more clamorous than a parrot against° rain, more newfangled° than an ape, more giddy° in my desires than a monkey. I will weep for nothing, like Diana in the fountain,° and I will do that when you are disposed to be merry; I will laugh like a hyen, and that when thou art 130 inclined to sleep.

Orlando. But will my Rosalind do so?

Rosalind. By my life, she will do as I do.

Orlando. O, but she is wise.

Rosalind. Or else she could not have the wit to do this; the wiser, 135 the waywarder. Make° the doors upon a woman's wit, and it will out at the casement; shut that, and 'twill out at the keyhole; stop that, 'twill fly with the smoke out at the chimney.

---

[109] *Go to* that's enough   [115] *commission* license
[116] *goes before* runs ahead (Rosalind has not waited for Celia to say, "Will you, Rosalind, have to husband")
[125–126] *Barbary cock-pigeon* Barb pigeon ("Barbary" suggests jealousy)
[127] *against* before   [127] *newfangled* given to novelty   [127] *giddy* changeable
[128–129] *like Diana in the fountain* i.e., steadily (Diana was a popular subject for fountain statuary)   [136] *Make* shut

Orlando. A man that had a wife with such a wit, he might say, "Wit, whither wilt?"° 140

Rosalind. Nay, you might keep that check° for it till you met your wife's wit going to your neighbor's bed.

Orlando. And what wit could wit have to excuse that?

Rosalind. Marry, to say she came to seek you there. You shall never take her without her answer unless you take her without 145 her tongue. O, that woman that cannot make her fault her husband's occasion,° let her never nurse her child herself, for she will breed it like a fool.

Orlando. For these two hours, Rosalind, I will leave thee.

Rosalind. Alas, dear love, I cannot lack thee two hours! 150

Orlando. I must attend the Duke at dinner. By two o'clock I will be with thee again.

Rosalind. Ay, go your ways, go your ways; I knew what you would prove. My friends told me as much, and I thought no less. That flattering tongue of yours won me. 'Tis but one cast away,° and 155 so, come death! Two o'clock is your hour?

Orlando. Ay, sweet Rosalind.

Rosalind. By my troth, and in good earnest, and so God mend me, and by all pretty oaths that are not dangerous, if you break one jot of your promise or come one minute behind your hour, I 160 will think you the most pathetical° break-promise, and the most hollow lover, and the most unworthy of her you call Rosalind, that may be chosen out of the gross° band of the unfaithful. Therefore beware my censure and keep your promise.

Orlando. With no less religion° than if thou wert indeed my 165 Rosalind. So adieu.

Rosalind. Well, Time is the old justice that examines all such offenders, and let Time try. Adieu. (*Exit* [*Orlando*].)

Celia. You have simply misused° our sex in your loveprate. We must have your doublet and hose plucked over your head, and 170 show the world what the bird hath done to her own nest.

Rosalind. O coz, coz, coz, my pretty little coz, that thou didst know how many fathom deep I am in love! But it cannot be sounded. My affection hath an unknown bottom, like the Bay of Portugal. 175

---

[140] Wit, *whither wilt* i.e., where are your senses   [141] *check* rebuke
[146–147] *make . . . occasion* i.e., turn defense of her own actions into an accusation of her husband's   [155] *one cast away* i.e., one girl deserted
[161] *pathetical* (1) pitiful (2) passionate (?)   [163] *gross* large
[165] *religion* faith   [169] *simply misused* completely abused

Celia. Or rather, bottomless, that as fast as you pour affection in, it runs out.

Rosalind. No, that same wicked bastard of Venus° that was begot of thought,° conceived of spleen,° and born of madness, that blind rascally boy that abuses every one's eyes because his own 180 are out, let him be judge how deep I am in love. I'll tell thee, Aliena, I cannot be out of the sight of Orlando. I'll go find a shadow, and sigh till he come.

Celia. And I'll sleep. (*Exeunt.*)

SCENE 2. [*The forest.*]

(*Enter Jaques; and Lords,* [*like*] *Foresters.*)

Jaques. Which is he that killed the deer?

Lord. Sir, it was I.

Jaques. Let's present him to the Duke like a Roman conqueror; and it would do well to set the deer's horns upon his head for a branch of victory. Have you no song, forester, for this 5 purpose?

Another Lord. Yes, sir.

Jaques. Sing it. 'Tis no matter how it be in tune, so it make noise enough. (*Music.*)

Song.

What shall he have that killed the deer? 10
His leather skin and horns to wear:
    Then sing him home. The rest shall bear
    This burden.°

Take thou no scorn° to wear the horn,
It was a crest ere thou wast born, 15
    Thy father's father wore it,
    And thy father bore it.
The horn, the horn, the lusty horn,
Is not a thing to laugh to scorn.° (*Exeunt.*)

178 *bastard of Venus* Cupid
179 *thought* despondency   179 *spleen* sheer impulse
IV.ii.12–13 *The rest shall bear This burden* i.e., not only the forester who killed the deer but all men will wear the horns of cuckoldry (many editors read the line as a stage direction: the other foresters ["the rest"] are to join in the refrain ["burden"] after one forester has sung the first three lines of the song. If the Folio version — here followed — is correct, it is likely that all sing the song from the beginning)
14 *Take thou no scorn* do not be ashamed   19 *laugh to scorn* ridicule

SCENE 3. [*The forest.*]

(*Enter Rosalind and Celia.*)

Rosalind. How say you now, is it not past two o'clock? And here
much° Orlando!
Celia. I warrant you, with pure love and troubled brain, he hath
ta'en his bow and arrows and is gone forth to sleep.

(*Enter Silvius.*)

Look who comes here.   5
Silvius. My errand is to you, fair youth.
My gentle Phebe bid me give you this.
I know not the contents, but, as I guess
By the stern brow and waspish action
Which she did use as she was writing of it,   10
It bears an angry tenor. Pardon me;
I am but as a guiltless messenger.
Rosalind. Patience herself would startle at this letter
And play the swaggerer. Bear this, bear all!
She says I am not fair, that I lack manners;   15
She calls me proud, and that she could not love me,
Were man as rare as phoenix.° 'Od's my will!
Her love is not the hare that I do hunt.
Why writes she so to me? Well, shepherd, well,
This is a letter of your own device.   20
Silvius. No, I protest, I know not the contents.
Phebe did write it.
Rosalind.   Come, come, you are a fool,
And turned into the extremity° of love.
I saw her hand. She has a leathern hand.
A freestone-colored° hand. I verily did think   25
That her old gloves were on, but 'twas her hands.
She has a housewife's hand; but that's no matter:
I say she never did invent° this letter;
This is a man's invention and his hand.
Silvius. Sure it is hers.   30

IV.iii.² *much* i.e., not much
¹⁷ *phoenix* (a legendary bird, of which there was only one in the world at any
time)
²³ *turned into the extremity* became the very essence
²⁵ *freestone-colored* i.e., yellowish-brown   ²⁸ *invent* compose

Rosalind. Why, 'tis a boisterous and a cruel style,
   A style for challengers. Why, she defies me
   Like Turk to Christian. Women's gentle brain
   Could not drop forth such giant-rude° invention,
   Such Ethiop words, blacker in their effect   35
   Than in their countenance. Will you hear the letter?
Silvius. So please you, for I never heard it yet;
   Yet heard too much of Phebe's cruelty.
Rosalind. She Phebes me.° Mark how the tyrant writes.
   (*Read.*) "Art thou god, to shepherd turned,   40
         That a maiden's heart hath burned?"
   Can a woman rail thus?
Silvius. Call you this railing?
Rosalind.
   (*Read.*) "Why, thy godhead laid apart,°
         Warr'st thou with a woman's heart?"   45
   Did you ever hear such railing?
         "Whiles the eye of man did woo me,
         That could do no vengeance° to me."
   Meaning me a beast.
         "If the scorn of your bright eyne°   50
         Have power to raise such love in mine,
         Alack, in me what strange effect
         Would they work in mild aspect!°
         Whiles you chid me, I did love;
         How then might your prayers move!   55
         He that brings this love to thee
         Little knows this love in me;
         And by him seal up thy mind,°
         Whether that thy youth and kind°
         Will the faithful offer take   60
         Of me and all that I can make,°
         Or else by him my love deny,
         And then I'll study how to die."
Silvius. Call you this chiding?

---

³⁴ *giant-rude* incredibly rude
³⁹ *She Phebes me* i.e., she writes with her customary disdain
⁴⁴ *thy godhead laid apart* i.e., having assumed human form
⁴⁸ *vengeance* harm   ⁵⁰ *eyne* eyes
⁵³ *aspect* (1) look (2) planetary influence
⁵⁸ *seal up thy mind* i.e., tell your feelings in a letter
⁵⁹ *youth and kind* youthful nature   ⁶¹ *make* give

Celia. Alas poor shepherd!   65
Rosalind. Do you pity him? No, he deserves no pity. Wilt thou
  love such a woman? What, to make thee an instrument,° and
  play false strains upon thee? Not to be endured! Well, go your
  way to her, for I see love hath made thee a tame snake,° and
  say this to her: that if she love me, I charge her to love thee;   70
  if she will not, I will never have her unless thou entreat for
  her. If you be a true lover, hence, and not a word; for here
  comes more company.   (*Exit Silvius.*)

(*Enter Oliver.*)

Oliver. Good morrow, fair ones. Pray you, if you know,
  Where in the purlieus° of this forest stands   75
  A sheepcote, fenced about with olive trees?
Celia. West of this place, down in the neighbor bottom.°
  The rank of osiers° by the murmuring stream
  Left on your right hand brings you to the place.
  But at this hour the house doth keep itself;   80
  There's none within.
Oliver. If that an eye may profit by a tongue,
  Then should I know you by description,
  Such garments and such years: "The boy is fair,
  Of female favor,° and bestows° himself   85
  Like a ripe sister;° the woman low,°
  And browner than her brother." Are not you
  The owner of the house I did enquire for?
Celia. It is no boast, being asked, to say we are.
Oliver. Orlando doth commend him to you both,   90
  And to that youth he calls his Rosalind
  He sends this bloody napkin.° Are you he?
Rosalind. I am. What must we understand by this?
Oliver. Some of my shame, if you will know of me
  What man I am, and how and why and where   95
  This handkercher was stained.
Celia.   I pray you tell it.
Oliver. When last the young Orlando parted from you,
  He left a promise to return again
  Within an hour; and pacing through the forest,

---

⁶⁷ *make thee an instrument* use you   ⁶⁹ *tame snake* poor worm
⁷⁵ *purlieus* borders   ⁷⁷ *neighbor bottom* nearby valley
⁷⁸ *rank of osiers* row of willows   ⁸⁵ *favor* features   ⁸⁵ *bestows* carries
⁸⁶ *ripe sister* grown-up woman (some editors emend "sister" to "forester")
⁸⁶ *low* short   ⁹² *napkin* handkerchief

Chewing the food of sweet and bitter fancy,°   100
Lo, what befell. He threw his eye aside,
And mark what object did present itself:
Under an old oak, whose boughs were mossed with age
And high top bald with dry antiquity,
A wretched ragged man, o'ergrown with hair,   105
Lay sleeping on his back; about his neck
A green and gilded snake had wreathed itself,
Who with her head, nimble in threats, approached
The opening of his mouth; but suddenly,
Seeing Orlando, it unlinked itself   110
And with indented° glides did slip away
Into a bush, under which bush's shade
A lioness, with udders all drawn dry,
Lay couching,° head on ground, with catlike watch
When that the sleeping man should stir; for 'tis   115
The royal disposition of that beast
To prey on nothing that doth seem as dead.
This seen, Orlando did approach the man
And found it was his brother, his elder brother.

Celia. O, I have heard him speak of that same brother,   120
And he did render° him the most unnatural
That lived amongst men.

Oliver.   And well he might so do,
For well I know he was unnatural.

Rosalind. But, to Orlando: did he leave him there,
Food to the sucked and hungry lioness?   125

Oliver. Twice did he turn his back and purposed so;
But kindness,° nobler ever than revenge,
And nature, stronger than his just occasion,°
Made him give battle to the lioness,
Who quickly fell before him; in which hurtling   130
From miserable slumber I awaked.

Celia. Are you his brother?

Rosalind.   Was't you he rescued?

Celia. Was't you that did so oft contrive° to kill him?

Oliver. 'Twas I. But 'tis not I. I do not shame
To tell you what I was, since my conversion   135
So sweetly tastes, being the thing I am.

Rosalind. But, for the bloody napkin?

---

100 *fancy* love   111 *indented* serpentine   114 *couching* crouching
121 *render* describe   127 *kindness* familial affection
128 *occasion* opportunity   133 *contrive* plot

Oliver.   By and by.°
  When from the first to last, betwixt us two,
  Tears our recountments° had most kindly bathed,
  As how I came into that desert place: 140
  In brief, he led me to the gentle Duke,
  Who gave me fresh array and entertainment,°
  Committing me unto my brother's love,
  Who led me instantly unto his cave,
  There stripped himself, and here upon his arm   145
  The lioness had torn some flesh away,
  Which all this while had bled; and now he fainted,
  And cried, in fainting, upon Rosalind.
  Brief, I recovered° him, bound up his wound;
  And after some small space, being strong at heart,   150
  He sent me hither, stranger as I am,
  To tell this story, that you might excuse
  His broken promise, and to give this napkin,
  Dyed in his blood, unto the shepherd youth
  That he in sport doth call his Rosalind.   [*Rosalind swoons.*] 155
Celia. Why, how now, Ganymede, sweet Ganymede!
Oliver. Many will swoon when they do look on blood.
Celia. There is more in it. Cousin Ganymede!
Oliver. Look, he recovers.
Rosalind. I would I were at home.
Celia.   We'll lead you thither.   160
  I pray you, will you take him by the arm?
Oliver. Be of good cheer, youth. You a man! You lack a man's
  heart.
Rosalind. I do so, I confess it. Ah, sirrah, a body would think this
  was well counterfeited.° I pray you tell your brother how well   165
  I counterfeited. Heigh-ho!
Oliver. This was not counterfeit. There is too great testimony in
  your complexion that it was a passion of earnest.°
Rosalind. Counterfeit, I assure you.
Oliver. Well then, take a good heart and counterfeit to be a man.   170
Rosalind. So I do; but, i' faith, I should have been a woman by
  right.

---

[137] *By and by* soon
[139] *recountments* recital (of our adventures since we last met)
[142] *entertainment* hospitality   [149] *recovered* revived
[165] *counterfeited* pretended   [168] *passion of earnest* real emotion

Celia. Come, you look paler and paler. Pray you draw homewards.
   Good sir, go with us.
Oliver. That will I, for I must bear answer back   **175**
   How you excuse my brother, Rosalind.
Rosalind. I shall devise something. But I pray you commend my
   counterfeiting to him. Will you go?   (*Exeunt.*)

ACT V

SCENE 1. [*The Forest.*]

(*Enter* [*Touchstone, the*] *Clown and Audrey.*)

Touchstone. We shall find a time, Audrey. Patience, gentle
   Audrey.
Audrey. Faith, the priest was good enough, for all the old gentleman's saying.
Touchstone. A most wicked Sir Oliver, Audrey, a most vile Mar-   **5**
   text. But, Audrey, there is a youth here in the forests lays claim
   to you.
Audrey. Ay, I know who 'tis. He hath no interest in me in the
   world. Here comes the man you mean.

(*Enter William.*)

Touchstone. It is meat and drink to me to see a clown;° by my   **10**
   troth, we that have good wits have much to answer for. We
   shall be flouting;° we cannot hold.°
William. Good ev'n, Audrey.
Audrey. God ye° good ev'n, William.
William. And good ev'n to you, sir.   **15**
Touchstone. Good ev'n, gentle friend. Cover thy head,° cover thy
   head. Nay, prithee be covered. How old are you, friend?
William. Five-and-twenty, sir.
Touchstone. A ripe° age. Is thy name William?
William. William, sir.   **20**
Touchstone. A fair name. Wast born i' th' forest here?
William. Ay, sir, I thank God.

V.i.¹⁰ *clown* yokel   ¹² *flouting* mocking
¹² *hold* i.e., keep from mocking   ¹⁴ *God ye* God give you
¹⁶ *Cover thy head* (William has removed his hat)   ¹⁹ *ripe* fine

Touchstone. "Thank God." A good answer. Art rich?

William. Faith, sir, so so.

Touchstone. "So so" is good, very good, very excellent good; and   25
yet it is not, it is but so so. Art thou wise?

William. Ay, sir, I have a pretty wit.

Touchstone. Why, thou say'st well. I do now remember a saying,
"The fool doth think he is wise, but the wise man knows himself to be a fool." The heathen philosopher, when he had a   30
desire to eat a grape, would open his lips when he put it into
his mouth, meaning thereby that grapes were made to eat and
lips to open. You do love this maid?

William. I do, sir.

Touchstone. Give me your hand. Art thou learned?   35

William. No, sir.

Touchstone. Then learn this of me: to have is to have; for it is a
figure° in rhetoric that drink, being poured out of a cup into a
glass, by filling the one doth empty the other; for all your
writers do consent that *ipse*° is he. Now, you are not *ipse*, for   40
I am he.

William. Which he, sir?

Touchstone. He, sir, that must marry this woman. Therefore, you
clown, abandon — which is in the vulgar, leave — the society
— which in the boorish is, company — of this female — which   45
in the common is, woman. Which together is, abandon the
society of this female, or, clown, thou perishest; or, to thy
better understanding, diest; or, to wit, I kill thee, make thee
away, translate thy life into death, thy liberty into bondage.
I will deal in poison with thee, or in bastinado,° or in steel; I   50
will bandy with thee in faction;° I will o'errun thee with policy;° I will kill thee a hundred and fifty ways. Therefore tremble and depart.

Audrey Do, good William.

Wililam. God rest you merry, sir.   (*Exit.*)   55

(*Enter Corin.*)

Corin. Our master and mistress seeks you. Come away, away!

Touchstone. Trip, Audrey, trip, Audrey. I attend,° I attend.

(*Exeunt.*)

---

³⁸ *figure* figure of speech   ⁴⁰ *ipse* he himself (Latin)
⁵⁰ *bastinado* cudgeling
⁵¹ *bandy with thee in faction* i.e., argue with you as do politicians
⁵¹⁻⁵² *o'errun thee with policy* overwhelm you with craft   ⁵⁷ *attend* come

SCENE 2. [*The forest.*]

(*Enter Orlando and Oliver.*)

Orlando. Is't possible that on so little acquaintance you should
like her? That but seeing, you should love her? And loving,
woo? And wooing, she should grant? And will you persever to
enjoy her?

Oliver. Neither call the giddiness° of it in question, the poverty   5
of her, the small acquaintance, my sudden wooing, nor her sudden consenting; but say with me, I love Aliena; say with her
that she loves me; consent with both that we may enjoy each
other. It shall be to your good; for my father's house, and all
the revenue that was old Sir Rowland's, will I estate° upon you,   10
and here live and die a shepherd.

(*Enter Rosalind.*)

Orlando. You have my consent. Let your wedding be tomorrow:
thither will I invite the Duke and all's contented followers. Go
and prepare Aliena; for look you, here comes my Rosalind.

Rosalind. God save you, brother.   15

Oliver. And you, fair sister.   [*Exit.*]

Rosalind. O my dear Orlando, how it grieves me to see thee wear
thy heart in a scarf!°

Orlando. It is my arm.

Rosalind. I thought thy heart had been wounded with the claws   20
of a lion.

Orlando. Wounded it is, but with the eyes of a lady.

Rosalind. Did your brother tell you how I counterfeited to sound°
when he showed me your handkercher?

Orlando. Ay, and greater wonders than that.   25

Rosalind. O, I know where you are! Nay, 'tis true. There was
never anything so sudden but the fight of two rams and Caesar's
thrasonical° brag of "I came, saw, and overcame"; for your
brother and my sister no sooner met but they looked; no sooner
looked but they loved; no sooner loved but they sighed; no   30
sooner sighed but they asked one another the reason; no sooner
knew the reason but they sought the remedy: and in these
degrees° have they made a pair of stairs to marriage, which they
will climb incontinent, or else be incontinent° before marriage:

V.ii.⁵ *giddiness* suddenness   ¹⁰ *estate* settle   ¹⁸ *scarf* sling   ²³ *sound* swoon
²⁸ *thrasonical* boastful (after the braggart soldier Thraso in Terence's comedy
Eunuchus)   ³³ *degrees* (a pun on the literal meaning, "steps")
³⁴ *incontinent . . . incontinent* with all haste . . . unchaste

they are in the very wrath of love, and they will together; clubs   35
cannot part them.

Orlando. They shall be married tomorrow, and I will bid the Duke
to the nuptial. But, O, how bitter a thing it is to look into
happiness through another man's eyes! By so much the more
shall I tomorrow be at the height of heart-heaviness, by how   40
much I shall think my brother happy in having what he wishes
for.

Rosalind. Why then, tomorrow I cannot serve your turn for
Rosalind?

Orlando. I can live no longer by thinking.   45

Rosalind. I will weary you then no longer with idle talking. Know
of me then, for now I speak to some purpose, that I know you
are a gentleman of good conceit.° I speak not this that you
should bear a good opinion of my knowledge, insomuch I say I
know you are; neither do I labor for a greater esteem than may   50
in some little measure draw a belief from you, to do yourself
good, and not to grace me.° Believe then, if you please, that
I can do strange things. I have, since I was three year old, con-
versed° with a magician, most profound in his art and yet not
damnable.° If you do love Rosalind so near the heart as your   55
gesture° cries it out, when your brother marries Aliena shall
you marry her. I know into what straits of fortune she is driven;
and it is not impossible to me, if it appear not inconvenient°
to you, to set her before your eyes tomorow, human as she is,°
and without any danger.   60

Orlando. Speak'st thou in sober meanings?

Rosalind. By my life, I do, which I tender dearly,° though I say
I am a magician.° Therefore put you in your best array, bid
your friends; for if you will be married tomorrow, you shall; and
to Rosalind, if you will.   65

(*Enter Silvius and Phebe.*)

Look, here comes a lover of mine and a lover of hers.

Phebe. Youth, you have done me much ungentleness
To show the letter that I writ to you.

---

48 *conceit* understanding   52 *to grace me* to do credit to myself
53–54 *conversed* spent time
54–55 *and yet not damnable* (because he practices white, not black, magic)
56 *gesture* conduct   58 *inconvenient* unfitting
59 *human as she is* i.e., Rosalind herself, not a spirit
62 *tender dearly* hold precious
62–63 *though . . . magician* (a magician could be punished with death)

Rosalind. I care not if I have. It is my study°
    To seem despiteful° and ungentle to you. 70
    You are there followed by a faithful shepherd:
    Look upon him, love him; he worships you.
Phebe. Good shepherd, tell this youth what 'tis to love.
Silvius. It is to be all made of sighs and tears;
    And so am I for Phebe. 75
Phebe. And I for Ganymede.
Orlando. And I for Rosalind.
Rosalind. And I for no woman.
Silvius. It is to be all made of faith and service;
    And so am I for Phebe. 80
Phebe. And I for Ganymede.
Orlando. And I for Rosalind.
Rosalind. And I for no woman.
Silvius. It is to be all made of fantasy,°
    All made of passion, and all made of wishes, 85
    All adoration, duty, and observance,°
    All humbleness, all patience, and impatience,
    All purity, all trial, all observance;°
    And so am I for Phebe.
Phebe. And so am I for Ganymede. 90
Orlando. And so am I for Rosalind.
Rosalind. And so am I for no woman.
Phebe. If this be so, why blame you me to love you?
Silvius. If this be so, why blame you me to love you?
Orlando. If this be so, why blame you me to love you? 95
Rosalind. Why do you speak too,° "Why blame you me to love
    you?"
Orlando. To her that is not here, nor doth not hear.
Rosalind. Pray you, no more of this; 'tis like the howling of Irish
    wolves against the moon. [*To Silvius*] I will help you if I can. 100
    [*To Phebe*] I would love you if I could. Tomorrow meet me
    all together. [*To Phebe*] I will marry you if ever I marry woman,
    and I'll be married tomorrow. [*To Orlando*] I will satisfy you if
    ever I satisfied man, and you shall be married tomorrow. [*To
    Silvius*] I will content you if what pleases you contents you, and 105
    you shall be married tomorrow. [*To Orlando*] As you love Rosa-
    lind, meet. [*To Silvius*] As you love Phebe, meet. And as I love

---

⁶⁹ *study* intention   ⁷⁰ *despiteful* scornful   ⁸⁴ *fantasy* fancy
⁸⁶ *observance* devoted attention
⁸⁸ *observance* (some editors emend to "obedience")
⁹⁶ *Why do you speak too* (some editors emend to "Who do you speak to")

no woman, I'll meet. So fare you well. I have left you com-
mands.
Silvius. I'll not fail if I live.   110
Phebe. Nor I.
Orlando. Nor I.   (*Exeunt.*)

SCENE 3. [*The forest.*]

(*Enter [Touchstone, the] Clown and Audrey.*)

Touchstone. Tomorrow is the joyful day, Audrey; tomorrow will
  we be married.
Audrey. I do desire it with all my heart; and I hope it is no dishonest desire to desire to be a woman of the world.° Here come
  two of the banished Duke's pages.   5

(*Enter two Pages.*)

First Page. Well met, honest° gentleman.
Touchstone. By my troth, well met. Come, sit, sit, and a song!
Second Page. We are for you. Sit i'th'middle.
First Page. Shall we clap into't roundly,° without hawking or spit-
  ting or saying we are hoarse, which are the only° prologues to   10
  a bad voice?
Second Page. I'faith, i'faith! and both in a tune,° like two gypsies
  on a horse.

                           Song.

        It was a lover and his lass,
            With a hey, and a ho, and a hey nonino,   15
        That o'er the green cornfield° did pass
            In springtime, the only pretty ringtime,°
        When birds do sing, hey ding a ding, ding.
        Sweet lovers love the spring.

        Betwen the acres° of the rye,   20
            With a hey, and a ho, and a hey nonino,
        These pretty country folks would lie
            In springtime, &c.

V.iii.⁴ *a woman of the world* i.e., (1) married (2) fashionable
⁶ *honest* honorable   ⁹ *clap into't roundly* begin directly
¹⁰ *the only* merely the   ¹² *in a tune* in unison   ¹⁶ *cornfield* wheatfield
¹⁷ *ring-time* i.e., the time for giving marriage rings
²⁰ *Between the acres* i.e., in the strips of unploughed land

> This carol they began that hour,
>   With a hey, and a ho, and a hey nonino,   25
> How that a life was but a flower
>   In springtime, &c.
>
> And therefore take° the present time,
>   With a hey, and a ho, and a hey nonino,
> For love is crowned with the prime°   30
>   In springtime, &c.

Touchstone. Truly, young gentlemen, though there was no great
matter in the ditty,° yet the note° was very untuneable.
First Page. You are deceived, sir. We kept time, we lost not our
    time.   35
Touchstone. By my troth, yes; I count it but time lost to hear
such a foolish song. God b' wi' you, and God mend your voices.
Come, Audrey.   (*Exeunt.*)

SCENE 4. [*The forest.*]

(*Enter Duke Senior, Amiens, Jaques, Orlando, Oliver, Celia.*)

Duke Senior. Dost thou believe, Orlando, that the boy
  Can do all this that he hath promisèd?
Orlando. I sometimes do believe, and sometimes do not,
  As those that fear they hope,° and know they fear.

(*Enter Rosalind, Silvius, and Phebe.*)

Rosalind. Patience once more, whiles our compact is urged.°   5
  You say, if I bring in your Rosalind.
  You will bestow her on Orlando here?
Duke Senior. That would I, had I kingdoms to give with her.
Rosalind. And you say you will have her when I bring her?
Orlando. That would I, were I of all kingdoms king.   10
Rosalind. You say you'll marry me, if I be willing?
Phebe. That will I, should I die the hour after.
Rosalind. But if you do refuse to marry me,
  You'll give yourself to this most faithful shepherd?
Phebe. So is the bargain.   15
Rosalind. You that you'll have Phebe, if she will?
Silvius. Though to have her and death were both one thing.

---

²⁸ *take* seize   ³⁰ *prime* spring   ³³ *ditty* words of the song   ³³ *note* melody
V.iv.⁴ *hope* i.e., hope in vain   ⁵ *compact is urged* agreement is restated

Rosalind. I have promised to make all this matter even.°
  Keep you your word, O Duke, to give your daughter;
  You yours, Orlando, to receive his daughter;   20
  Keep you your word, Phebe, that you'll marry me,
  Or else, refusing me, to wed this shepherd;
  Keep your word, Silvius, that you'll marry her
  If she refuse me; and from hence I go,
  To make these doubts all even.   25

                              (*Exit Rosalind and Celia.*)

Duke Senior. I do remember in this shepherd boy
  Some lively° touches of my daughter's favor.°
Orlando. My lord, the first time that I ever saw him
  Methought he was a brother to your daughter.
  But, my good lord, this boy is forest-born,   30
  And hath been tutored in the rudiments
  Of many desperate° studies by his uncle,
  Whom he reports to be a great magician,
  Obscurèd° in the circle of this forest.

  (*Enter [Touchstone, the] Clown and Audrey.*)

Jaques. There is, sure, another flood toward,° and these couples   35
  are coming to the ark.° Here comes a pair of very strange beasts,
  which in all tongues are called fools.
Touchstone. Salutation and greeting to you all!
Jaques. Good my lord, bid him welcome. This is the motley-
  minded gentleman that I have so often met in the forest. He   40
  hath been a courtier, he swears.
Touchstone. If any man doubt that, let him put me to my purgation.° I have trod a measure;° I have flattered a lady; I have
  been politic° with my friend, smooth with mine enemy; I have
  undone° three tailors; I have had four quarrels, and like to have   45
  fought one.°
Jaques. And how was that ta'en up?°

---

¹⁸ *make all this matter even* straighten out everything   ²⁷ *lively* living
²⁷ *favor* features   ³² *desperate* dangerous
³⁴ *Obscurèd* hidden   ³⁵ *toward* approaching
³⁵⁻³⁶ *couples are coming to the ark* (cf. Genesis 7:2, "and of beasts that are
not clean by two, the male and his female")
⁴²⁻⁴³ *put me to my purgation* test me   ⁴³ *measure* stately dance
⁴⁴ *politic* crafty   ⁴⁵ *undone* ruined (by not paying his bills)
⁴⁵⁻⁴⁶ *like to have fought one* almost fought over one   ⁴⁷ *ta'en up* settled

Touchstone. Faith, we met, and found the quarrel was upon the seventh cause.

Jaques. How seventh cause? Good my lord, like this fellow. 50

Duke Senior. I like him very well.

Touchstone. God 'ield° you sir; I desire you of the like.° I press in here, sir, amongst the rest of the country copulatives,° to swear and to forswear, according as marriage binds and blood breaks.° A poor virgin, sir, an ill-favored thing, sir, but mine 55 own; a poor humor° of mine, sir, to take that that no man else will. Rich honesty° dwells like a miser, sir, in a poor house, as your pearl in your foul oyster.

Duke Senior. By my faith, he is very swift and sententious.°

Touchstone. According to the fool's bolt,° sir, and such dulcet 60 diseases.°

Jaques. But, for the seventh cause. How did you find the quarrel on the seventh cause?

Touchstone. Upon a lie seven times removed — bear your body more seeming,° Audrey — as thus, sir. I did dislike the cut of a 65 certain courtier's beard. He sent me word, if I said his beard was not cut well, he was in the mind it was: this is called the Retort Courteous. If I sent him word again it was not well cut, he would send me word he cut it to please himself: this is called the Quip Modest.° If again, it was not well cut, he dis- 70 abled° my judgment: this is called the Reply Churlish. If again, it was not well cut, he would answer I spake not true: this is called the Reproof Valiant. If again, it was not well cut, he would say I lie: this is called the Countercheck° Quarrelsome: and so to the Lie Circumstantial° and the Lie Direct. 75

Jaques. And how oft did you say his beard was not well cut?

Touchstone. I durst go no further than the Lie Circumstantial, nor he durst not give me the Lie Direct; and so we measured swords° and parted.

---

⁵² *God 'ield* God reward
⁵² *I desire you of the like* may I return the compliment
⁵³ *copulatives* couples soon to be wed
⁵⁴⁻⁵⁵ *blood breaks* sexual interest wanes
⁵⁶ *humor* whim   ⁵⁷ *honesty* virtue
⁵⁹ *swift and sententious* quick-witted and pithy
⁶⁰ *According to the fool's bolt* (cf. the proverb "A fool's bolt [arrow] is soon shot")   ⁶⁰⁻⁶¹ *dulcet diseases* pleasing weaknesses
⁶⁵ *seeming* becomingly   ⁷⁰ *Modest* moderate   ⁷⁰⁻⁷¹ *disabled* did not value
⁷⁴ *Countercheck* contradiction   ⁷⁵ *Circumstantial* indirect
⁷⁸⁻⁷⁹ *measured swords* (swords were measured before a duel)

Jaques. Can you nominate° in order now the degrees of the lie?　　80
Touchstone. O sir, we quarrel in print, by the book,° as you have
　books for good manners. I will name you the degrees. The first,
　the Retort Courteous; the second, the Quip Modest; the third,
　the Reply Churlish; the fourth, the Reproof Valiant; the fifth,
　the Countercheck Quarrelsome; the sixth, the Lie with Circum-　　85
　stance; the seventh, the Lie Direct. All these you may avoid but
　the Lie Direct, and you may avoid that too, with an If. I knew
　when seven justices could not take up° a quarrel, but when the
　parties were met themselves, one of them thought but of an
　If: as, "If you said so, then I said so"; and they shook hands　　90
　and swore brothers. Your If is the only peace-maker. Much
　virtue in If.
Jaques. Is not this a rare fellow, my lord? He's as good at any-
　thing, and yet a fool.
Duke Senior. He uses his folly like a stalking horse,° and under　　95
　the presentation° of that he shoots his wit.

　　(*Enter Hymen,° Rosalind, and Celia. Still° music.*)

Hymen. Then is there mirth in heaven
　　　When earthly things made even°
　　　　Atone together.°
　　　Good Duke, receive thy daughter;　　　　　　　　　　　100
　　　Hymen from heaven brought her,
　　　　Yea, brought her hither,
　　　That thou mightst join her hand with his
　　　Whose heart within his bosom is.
Rosalind. [*To Duke*] To you I give myself, for I am yours.　　105
　[*To Orlando*] To you I give myself, for I am yours.
Duke Senior. If there be truth in sight, you are my daughter.
Orlando. If there be truth in sight, you are my Rosalind.
Phebe. If sight and shape be true,
　　Why then, my love adieu!　　　　　　　　　　　　　　110
Rosalind. [*To Duke*] I'll have no father, if you be not he.
　[*To Orlando*] I'll have no husband, if you be not he.
　[*To Phebe*] Nor ne'er wed woman, if you be not she.
Hymen. Peace ho! I bar confusion:
　　'Tis I must make conclusion　　　　　　　　　　　　115
　　　Of these most strange events.

80 *nominate* name　　81 *by the book* according to the rules　　88 *take up* settle
95 *stalking horse* (any object under cover of which a hunter pursues his game)
96 *presentation* protection　　96 s.d. *Hymen* god of marriage　　96 s.d. *Still* soft
98 *made even* i.e., reconciled　　99 *Atone together* are set at one

Here's eight that must take hands
To join in Hymen's bands,
   If truth holds true contents.°
[*To Orlando and Rosalind*]
You and you no cross° shall part.   120
[*To Oliver and Celia*]
You and you are heart in heart.
[*To Phebe*]
You to his love must accord,°
Or have a woman to your lord.
[*To Touchstone and Audrey*]
You and you are sure together°
As the winter to foul weather.   125
[*To all*]
Whiles a wedlock hymn we sing,
Feed yourselves with questioning,
That reason wonder may diminish
How thus we met, and these things finish.

            Song.

Wedding is great Juno's crown,   130
   O blessèd bond of board and bed!
'Tis Hymen peoples every town;
   High° wedlock then be honorèd.
Honor, high honor, and renown
To Hymen, god of every town!   135
Duke Senior. O my dear niece, welcome thou art to me,
Even daughter,° welcome, in no less degree!
Phebe. [*To Silvius*] I will not eat my word, now thou art mine;
Thy faith my fancy to thee doth combine.°

(*Enter Second Brother [Jaques de Boys].*)

Second Brother. Let me have audience for a word or two.   140
I am the second son of old Sir Rowland
That bring these tidings to this fair assembly.
Duke Frederick, hearing how that every day
Men of great worth resorted to this forest,
Addressed a mighty power,° which were on foot   145

---

[119] *If truth . . . contents* if the truth is true   [120] *cross* quarrel
[122] *accord* agree   [124] *sure together* securely bound   [133] *High* solemn
[137] *Even daughter* i.e., even as a daughter   [139] *combine* unite
[145] *Addressed a mighty power* prepared a mighty army

In his own conduct,° purposely to take
His brother here and put him to the sword;
And to the skirts of this wild wood he came,
Where, meeting with an old religious man,°
After some question° with him, was converted   150
Both from his enterprise and from the world,
His crown bequeathing to his banished brother,
And all their lands restored to them again
That were with him exiled. This to be true
I do engage° my life.
Duke Senior.   Welcome, young man.   155
Thou offer'st fairly° to thy brothers' wedding:
To one, his lands withheld; and to the other,
A land itself at large, a potent° dukedom.
First, in this forest let us do those ends°
That here were well begun and well begot;   160
And after, every° of this happy number
That have endured shrewd° days and nights with us
Shall share the good of our returnèd fortune,
According to the measure° of their states.
Meantime forget this new-fall'n° dignity   165
And fall into our rustic revelry.
Play, music, and you brides and bridegrooms all,
With measure heaped in joy, to th' measures° fall.
Jaques. Sir, by your patience. If I heard you rightly,
The Duke hath put on a religious life   170
And thrown into neglect the pompous court.°
Second Brother. He hath.
Jaques. To him will I. Out of these convertites°
There is much matter to be heard and learned.
[*To Duke*] You to your former honor I bequeath;   175
Your patience and your virtue well deserves it.
[*To Orlando*] You to a love that your true faith doth merit;
[*To Oliver*] You to your land and love and great allies;
[*To Silvius*] You to a long and well-deservèd bed;

---

¹⁴⁶ *conduct* leadership   ¹⁴⁹ *old religious man* (a hermit?)
¹⁵⁰ *question* talk   ¹⁵⁵ *engage* pledge
¹⁵⁶ *offer'st fairly* bring a good gift   ¹⁵⁸ *potent* powerful
¹⁵⁹ *do those ends* complete those purposes   ¹⁶¹ *every* each one
¹⁶² *shrewd* hard   ¹⁶⁴ *measure* rank
¹⁶⁵ *new-fall'n* newly acquired   ¹⁶⁸ *measures* dance steps
¹⁷¹ *thrown into . . . court* given up the ceremonious life of the court
¹⁷³ *convertites* converts

[*To Touchstone*] And you to wrangling, for thy loving voyage   180
Is but for two months victualled. So, to your pleasures:
I am for other than for dancing measures.
Duke Senior. Stay, Jaques, stay.
Jaques. To see no pastime I. What you would have
I'll stay to know at your abandoned cave.   (*Exit.*)   185
Duke Senior. Proceed, proceed. We will begin these rites.
As we do trust they'll end, in true delights.

(*Exit [after the dance].*)

[EPILOGUE]

Rosalind. It is not the fashion to see the lady the epilogue, but it
is no more unhandsome° than to see the lord the prologue. If
it be true that good wine needs no bush,° 'tis true that a good
play needs no epilogue; yet to good wine they do use good
bushes, and good plays prove the better by the help of good   5
epilogues. What a case am I in then, that am neither a good
epilogue, nor cannot insinuate with you° in the behalf of a
good play! I am not furnished° like a beggar; therefore to beg
will not become me. My way is to conjure° you, and I'll begin
with the women. I charge you, O women, for the love you bear   10
to men, to like as much of this play as please you; and I charge
you, O men, for the love you bear to women — as I perceive by
your simpering none of you hates them — that between you
and the women the play may please. If I were a woman,° I
would kiss as many of you as had beards that pleased me, com-   15
plexions that liked° me, and breaths that I defied° not; and I
am sure, as many as have good beards, or good faces, or sweet
breaths, will, for my kind offer, when I make curtsy, bid me
farewell.°   (*Exit.*)

FINIS

Epilogue ² *unhandsome* unbecoming
³ *no bush* no advertisement (in Shakespeare's time vintners used an ivy bush
as a sign)
⁷ *insinuate with you* slyly get your approval   ⁸ *furnished* dressed
⁹ *conjure* (1) solemnly entreat (2) charm (by magic)
¹⁴ *If I were a woman* (Rosalind, of course, was played by a boy)
¹⁶ *liked* pleased   ¹⁶ *defied* disliked   ¹⁹ *bid me farewell* i.e., applaud

Shakespeare is today perhaps most highly valued for his tragedies, but this is because somehow we glumly rank tragedy above comedy; other generations have realized that his comedies represent no less an achievement. Shakespeare is the only playwright who wrote great works in both genres, and he seems to have written them more or less simultaneously. The romantic view that Shakespeare suffered a depression and wrote tragedies, and then pulled out of it to write comedies is refuted by the facts: *As You Like It* (1599–1600), for example, intervened between *Julius Caesar* (1599) and *Hamlet* (1600).

Following his usual practice, Shakespeare borrowed the gist of his story, this time from Thomas Lodge's prose romance, *Rosalynde* (1590). Like Shakespeare's other great comedies, *As You Like It* is a play about love, dominated by a heroine who is no less witty and charming because she is in love. She spoofs love ("Men have died from time to time, and worms have eaten them, but not for love") and she spoofs lovers ("I must tell you friendly in your ear,/Sell when you can, you are not for all markets"), but she herself is "many fathom deep . . . in love," which makes her spoofing the more engaging. And sometimes Shakespeare spoofs her, as when he contrives a plot that by chance brings her, disguised in male attire, into the forest that contains her beloved Orlando:

> What shall I do with my doublet and hose? What did he when thou saw'st him? What said he? How looked he? Wherein went he? What makes he here? Did he ask for me? Where remains he? How parted he with thee? And when shalt thou see him again? Answer me in one word.

Though in love, Rosalind never loses her wits more than momentarily, and she pulls the strings of the plot, but even she, "out of suits with fortune," is subject to Fortune and is at times helpless and absurd. Her father was banished by a usurper before the play began; in I.iii Rosalind is banished too. Fortune's gifts "are mightily misplaced." But in Shakespeare's comic world, despite appearances, a benevolent deity (which we may call Nature) reigns, and banishment to the Forest of Arden is scarcely a hard fate; it is in Arden, rather than in "the envious court," that the benevolent powers (sometimes seen in rather pagan terms, sometimes seen in more biblical terms, such as "He that doth the ravens feed") can most effectively operate. The Forest of Arden is a place where "merry men . . . fleet the time carelessly [i.e. without care] as they did in the golden world," but it should be noted that Arden is not a utopia. It has its icy winter (though an icy winter about which one sings so exquisitely can not be very bad), and even its detractors, Touchstone ("When I was at home, I was in a better place") and Jaques ("Here shall he see gross fools as he"). Still, in the fifth act spring comes to Arden:

> It was a lover and his lass,
>   With a hey, and a ho, and a hey nonino,
> That o'er the green cornfield did pass
>   In springtime, the only pretty ringtime,
> When birds do sing, hey ding a ding, ding,
> Sweet lovers love the spring.

It is in the Forest of Arden that lovers meet, tyrants reform, good Fortune returns to the outcasts, the corrupt return to their better selves, and those who wish can return to their proper place in the city to constitute a happy and renewed society. Nature and Fortune, that is, are joined in bounty. Joy and forgiveness triumph in this as in most of Shakespeare's comedies; if men are fools and sinners and no one is wholly exempt from comic exposure, still, no one is denied redemption. All are offered the possibility of a new life of "true delights," and the last speech of the play, Rosalind's epilogue, assumes a delighted audience and explicitly asks the audience to extend its goodwill to the performers.

Speaking broadly, there are in the Renaissance two comic traditions, which may be called "critical comedy" (or "bitter comedy") and "romantic comedy" (or "sweet comedy"). The former claims, in Hamlet's words, that the "purpose of playing . . . is to hold, as 'twere, the mirror up to nature; to show virtue her own feature, scorn her own image, and the very age and body of the time his form and pressure." Because it aims to hold a mirror up to the audience, its dramatis personae are usually urban citizens — jealous husbands, foolish merchants, and the like. These are ultimately punished, at times merely by exposure, at times by imprisonment or fines or some such thing. The second kind of comedy, romantic comedy, seeks less to correct than to delight with scenes of pleasant behavior. It does not hold a mirror to the audience; rather, it leads the audience into an elegant dream world where charming gentlefolk live a timeless existence. Thomas Heywood, who claimed to have collaborated often with Shakespeare, briefly set forth the characteristics of both traditions in *An Apology for Actors* (1612). A comedy, he said,

> is pleasantly contrived with merry accidents, and intermixed with apt and witty jests. . . . And what then is the subject of this harmless mirth? Either in the shape of a clown to show others their slovenly behavior, that they may reform that simplicity in themselves, which others make

their sport, . . . or to refresh such weary spirits as are tired with labors or study, to moderate the cares and heaviness of the mind, that they may return to their trades and faculties with more zeal and earnestness, after some small soft and pleasant retirement.

When we think of *As You Like It*, we think of "harmless mirth," "sport," and the refreshing of weary spirits. But even *As You Like It* has its touches of critical comedy, its elements that, in Heywood's words, "may reform" by holding up a mirror to unsocial behavior. There is some satire — not spoken only by Jaques, but *of* Jaques — but mostly the play is pervaded by genial spirits and a humane vision that make it moral without moralizing. Not every reader will agree with Dr. Johnson that "by hastening to the end of his work Shakespeare suppressed the dialogue between the usurper and the hermit, and lost an opportunity of exhibiting a moral lesson in which he might have found matter worthy of his highest powers." It is enough that the usurper met "an old religious man" who dwells in the forest. We do not need the hermit's speech, because we have already found "sermons in stones, and good in everything."

The Misanthrope

MOLIERE

English version by Richard Wilbur

Jean Baptiste Poquelin (1622–1673), who took the name Molière, was born into a prosperous middle-class family. For a while he studied law and philosophy, but by 1643 he was acting. He became the head of a theatrical company which had its initial difficulties and later, thanks largely to Molière's comedies, its great successes. In 1662 he married Armande Béjart. The marriage apparently was unhappy, but the capricious and flirtatious Armande proved to be an accomplished actress. Molière continued to act, with great success in comedy, until his death. In one of those improbable things that happen in real life but that are too strange for art, Molière died of a hemorrhage that he suffered while playing the title role in his comedy The Hypochondriac. *The early plays are highly farcical; among the later and greater plays are* The Highbrow Ladies *(1659),* Tartuffe *(1664),* Don Juan *(1665),* The Misanthrope *(1666), and* The Miser *(1668).*

CHARACTERS

Alceste, in love with Célimène
Philinte, Alceste's friend
Oronte, in love with Célimène
Célimène, Alceste's beloved
Éliante, Célimène's cousin
Arsinoé, a friend of Célimène's
Acaste
Clitandre } Marquesses
Basque, Célimène's servant
A *Guard* of the Marshalsea
DuBois, Alceste's valet

The Scene throughout is in Célimène's house at Paris.

522

ACT I

SCENE 1. [*Philinte, Alceste*]

Philinte. Now, what's got into you?
Alceste (*seated*).   Kindly leave me alone.
Philinte. Come, come, what is it? This lugubrious tone . . .
Alceste. Leave me, I said; you spoil my solitude.
Philinte. Oh, listen to me, now, and don't be rude.
Alceste. I choose to be rude, Sir, and to be hard of hearing.
Philinte. These ugly moods of yours are not endearing;
    Friends though we are, I really must insist . . .

Alceste (*abruptly rising*). Friends? Friends, you say? Well, cross me
    off your list.
    I've been your friend till now, as you well know;
    But after what I saw a moment ago
    I tell you flatly that our ways must part.
    I wish no place in a dishonest heart.
Philinte. Why, what have I done, Alceste? Is this quite just?
Alceste. My God, you ought to die of self-disgust.
    I call your conduct inexcusable, Sir,
    And every man of honor will concur.
    I see you almost hug a man to death,
    Exclaim for joy until you're out of breath,
    And supplement these loving demonstrations
    With endless offers, vows, and protestations;
    Then when I ask you "Who was that?" I find
    That you can barely bring his name to mind!
    Once the man's back is turned, you cease to love him,
    And speak with absolute indifference of him!
    By God, I say it's base and scandalous
    To falsify the heart's affections thus;
    If I caught myself behaving in such a way,
    I'd hang myself for shame, without delay.
Philinte. It hardly seems a hanging matter to me;
    I hope that you will take it graciously
    If I extend myself a slight reprieve,
    And live a little longer, by your leave.
Alceste. How dare you joke about a crime so grave?
Philinte. What crime? How else are people to behave?
Alceste. I'd have them be sincere, and never part
    With any word that isn't from the heart.
Philinte. When someone greets us with a show of pleasure,
    It's but polite to give him equal measure,
    Return his love the best that we know how,
    And trade him offer for offer, vow for vow.
Alceste. No, no, this formula you'd have me follow,
    However fashionable, is false and hollow,
    And I despise the frenzied operations
    Of all these barterers of protestations,
    These lavishers of meaningless embraces,
    These utterers of obliging commonplaces,
    Who court and flatter everyone on earth
    And praise the fool no less than the man of worth.
    Should you rejoice that someone fondles you,

Offers his love and service, swears to be true,
And fills your ears with praises of your name,
When to the first damned fop he'll say the same?
No, no: no self-respecting heart would dream
Of prizing so promiscuous an esteem;
However high the praise, there's nothing worse
Than sharing honors with the universe.
Esteem is founded on comparison:
To honor all men is to honor none.
Since you embrace this indiscriminate vice,
Your friendship comes at far too cheap a price;
I spurn the easy tribute of a heart
Which will not set the worthy man apart:
I choose, Sir, to be chosen; and in fine,
The friend of mankind is no friend of mine.

Philinte. But in polite society, custom decrees
That we show certain outward courtesies. . . .

Alceste. Ah, no! we should condemn with all our force
Such false and artificial intercourse.
Let men behave like men; let them display
Their inmost hearts in everything they say;
Let the heart speak, and let our sentiments
Not mask themselves in silly compliments.

Philinte. In certain cases it would be uncouth
And most absurd to speak the naked truth;
With all respect for your exalted notions,
It's often best to veil one's true emotions.
Wouldn't the social fabric come undone
If we were wholly frank with everyone?
Suppose you met with someone you couldn't bear;
Would you inform him of it then and there?

Alceste. Yes.

Philinte.   Then you'd tell old Emilie it's pathetic
The way she daubs her features with cosmetic
And plays the gay coquette at sixty-four?

Alceste. I would.

Philinte.   And you'd call Dorilas a bore,
And tell him every ear at court is lame
From hearing him brag about his noble name?

Alceste. Precisely.

Philinte.   Ah, you're joking.

Alceste.   *Au contraire:*
In this regard there's none I'd choose to spare.

All are corrupt; there's nothing to be seen
In court or town but aggravates my spleen.
I fall into deep gloom and melancholy
When I survey the scene of human folly,
Finding on every hand base flattery,
Injustice, fraud, self-interest, treachery. . . .
Ah, it's too much; mankind has grown so base,
I mean to break with the whole human race.

Philinte. This philosophic rage is a bit extreme;
You've no idea how comical you seem;
Indeed, we're like those brothers in the play
Called *School for Husbands*, one of whom was prey . . .

Alceste. Enough, now! None of your stupid similes.

Philinte. Then let's have no more tirades, if you please.
The world won't change, whatever you say or do;
And since plain speaking means so much to you,
I'll tell you plainly that by being frank
You've earned the reputation of a crank,
And that you're thought ridiculous when you rage
And rant against the manners of the age.

Alceste. So much the better; just what I wish to hear.
No news could be more grateful to my ear.
All men are so destestable in my eyes,
I should be sorry if they thought me wise.

Philinte. Your hatred's very sweeping, is it not?

Alceste. Quite right: I hate the whole degraded lot.

Philinte. Must all poor human creatures be embraced,
Without distinction, by your vast distaste?
Even in these bad times, there are surely a few . . .

Alceste. No, I include all men in one dim view:
Some men I hate for being rogues: the others
I hate because they treat the rogues like brothers,
And, lacking a virtuous scorn for what is vile,
Receive the villain with a complaisant smile.
Notice how tolerant people choose to be
Toward that bold rascal who's at law with me.
His social polish can't conceal his nature;
One sees at once that he's a treacherous creature;
No one could possibly be taken in
By those soft speeches and that sugary grin.
The whole world knows the shady means by which
The low-brow's grown so powerful and rich,
And risen to a rank so bright and high

That virtue can but blush, and merit sigh.
Whenever his name comes up in conversation,
None will defend his wretched reputation;
Call him knave, liar, scoundrel, and all the rest,
Each head will nod, and no one will protest.
And yet his smirk is seen in every house,
He's greeted everywhere with smiles and bows,
And when there's any honor that can be got
By pulling strings, he'll get it, like as not.
My God! It chills my heart to see the ways
Men come to terms with evil nowadays;
Sometimes, I swear, I'm moved to flee and find
Some desert land unfouled by humankind.

Philinte. Come, let's forget the follies of the times
And pardon mankind for its petty crimes;
Let's have an end of rantings and of railings,
And show some leniency toward human failings.
This world requires a pliant rectitude;
Too stern a virtue makes one stiff and rude;
Good sense views all extremes with detestation,
And bids us to be noble in moderation.
The rigid virtues of the ancient days
Are not for us; they jar with all our ways
And ask of us too lofty a perfection.
Wise men accept their times without objection,
And there's no greater folly, if you ask me,
Than trying to reform society.
Like you, I see each day a hundred and one
Unhandsome deeds that might be better done,
But still, for all the faults that meet my view,
I'm never known to storm and rave like you.
I take men as they are, or let them be,
And teach my soul to bear their frailty;
And whether in court or town, whatever the scene,
My phlegm's as philosophic as your spleen.

Alceste. This phlegm which you so eloquently commend,
Does nothing ever rile it up, my friend?
Suppose some man you trust should treacherously
Conspire to rob you of your property,
And do his best to wreck your reputation?
Wouldn't you feel a certain indignation?

Philinte. Why, no. These faults of which you so complain
Are part of human nature, I maintain,

And it's no more a matter for disgust
That men are knavish, selfish and unjust,
Than that the vulture dines upon the dead,
And wolves are furious, and apes ill-bred.

Alceste. Shall I see myself betrayed, robbed, torn to bits,
And not . . . Oh, let's be still and rest our wits.
Enough of reasoning, now. I've had my fill.

Philinte. Indeed, you would do well, Sir, to be still.
Rage less at your opponent, and give some thought
To how you'll win this lawsuit that he's brought.

Alceste. I assure you I'll do nothing of the sort.

Philinte. Then who will plead your case before the court?

Alceste. Reason and right and justice will plead for me.

Philinte. Oh, Lord. What judges do you plan to see?

Alceste. Why, none. The justice of my cause is clear.

Philinte. Of course, man; but there's politics to fear. . . .

Alceste. No, I refuse to lift a hand. That's flat.
I'm either right, or wrong.

Philinte.   Don't count on that.

Alceste. No, I'll do nothing.

Philinte.   Your enemy's influence
Is great, you know . . .

Alceste.   That makes no difference.

Philinte. It will; you'll see.

Alceste.   Must honor bow to guile?
If so, I shall be proud to lose the trial.

Philinte. Oh, really . . .

Alceste.   I'll discover by this case
Whether or not men are sufficiently base
And impudent and villainous and perverse
To do me wrong before the universe.

Philinte. What a man!

Alceste.   Oh, I could wish, whatever the cost,
Just for the beauty of it, that my trial were lost.

Philinte. If people heard you talking so, Alceste,
They'd split their sides. Your name would be a jest.

Alceste. So much the worse for jesters.

Philinte.   May I enquire
Whether this rectitude you so admire,
And these hard virtues you're enamored of
Are qualities of the lady whom you love?
It much surprises me that you, who seem

To view mankind with furious disesteem,
Have yet found something to enchant your eyes
Amidst a species which you so despise.
And what is more amazing, I'm afraid,
Is the most curious choice your heart has made.
The honest Eliante is fond of you,
Arsinoé, the prude, admires you too;
And yet your spirit's been perversely led
To choose the flighty Célimène instead,
Whose brittle malice and coquettish ways
So typify the manners of our days.
How is it that the traits you most abhor
Are bearable in this lady you adore?
Are you so blind with love that you can't find them?
Or do you contrive, in her case, not to mind them?

Alceste. My love for that young widow's not the kind
    That can't perceive defects; no, I'm not blind.
    I see her faults, despite my ardent love,
    And all I see I fervently reprove.
    And yet I'm weak; for all her falsity,
    That woman knows the art of pleasing me,
    And though I never cease complaining of her,
    I swear I cannot manage not to love her.
    Her charm outweighs her faults; I can but aim
    To cleanse her spirit in my love's pure flame.

Philinte. That's no small task; I wish you all success.
    You think then that she loves you?

Alceste.   Heavens, yes!
    I wouldn't love her did she not love me.

Philinte. Well, if her taste for you is plain to see,
    Why do these rivals cause you such despair?

Alceste. True love, Sir, is possessive, and cannot bear
    To share with all the world. I'm here today
    To tell her she must send that mob away.

Philinte. If I were you, and had your choice to make,
    Éliante, her cousin, would be the one I'd take;
    That honest heart, which cares for you alone,
    Would harmonize far better with your own.

Alceste. True, true: each day my reason tells me so;
    But reason doesn't rule in love, you know.

Philinte. I fear some bitter sorrow is in store;
    This love . . .

SCENE 2. [*Oronte, Alceste, Philinte*]

Oronte (*to Alceste*). The servants told me at the door
    That Eliante and Célimène were out,
    But when I heard, dear Sir, that you were about,
    I came to say, without exaggeration,
    That I hold you in the vastest admiration,
    And that it's always been my dearest desire
    To be the friend of one I so admire.
    I hope to see my love of merit requited,
    And you and I in friendship's bond united.
    I'm sure you won't refuse — if I may be frank —
    A friend of my devotedness — and rank.

(*During this speech of Oronte's, Alceste is abstracted, and seems unaware that he is being spoken to. He only breaks off his reverie when Oronte says:*)

    It was for you, if you please, that my words were intended.
Alceste. For me, Sir?
Oronte.   Yes, for you. You're not offended?
Alceste. By no means. But this much surprises me. . . .
    The honor comes most unexpectedly. . . .
Oronte. My high regard should not astonish you;
    The whole world feels the same. It is your due.
Alceste. Sir . . .
Oronte.   Why, in all the State there isn't one
    Can match your merits; they shine, Sir, like the sun.
Alceste. Sir . . .
Oronte.   You are higher in my estimation
    Than all that's most illustrious in the nation.
Alceste. Sir . . .
Oronte.   If I lie, may heaven strike me dead!
    To show you that I mean what I have said,
    Permit me, Sir, to embrace you most sincerely,
    And swear that I will prize our friendship dearly.
    Give me your hand. And now, Sir, if you choose,
    We'll make our vows.
Alceste.   Sir . . .
Oronte.   What! You refuse?
Alceste. Sir, it's a very great honor you extend:
    But friendship is a sacred thing, my friend;
    It would be profanation to bestow
    The name of friend on one you hardly know.

All parts are better played when well-rehearsed;
Let's put off friendship, and get acquainted first.
We may discover it would be unwise
To try to make our natures harmonize.
Oronte. By heaven! You're sagacious to the core;
This speech has made me admire you even more.
Let time, then, bring us closer day by day;
Meanwhile, I shall be yours in every way.
If, for example, there should be anything
You wish at court, I'll mention it to the King.
I have his ear, of course; it's quite well known
That I am much in favor with the throne.
In short, I am your servant. And now, dear friend,
Since you have such fine judgment, I intend
To please you, if I can, with a small sonnet
I wrote not long ago. Please comment on it,
And tell me whether I ought to publish it.
Alceste. You must excuse me, Sir; I'm hardly fit
To judge such matters.
Oronte.   Why not?
Alceste.   I am, I fear,
Inclined to be unfashionably sincere.
Oronte. Just what I ask; I'd take no satisfaction
In anything but your sincere reaction.
I beg you not to dream of being kind.
Alceste. Since you desire it, Sir, I'll speak my mind.
Oronte. Sonnet. It's a sonnet. . . . *Hope* . . . The poem's addressed
To a lady who wakened hopes within my breast.
Hope . . . this is not the pompous sort of thing,
Just modest little verses, with a tender ring.
Alceste. Well, we shall see.
Oronte.   *Hope* . . . I'm anxious to hear
Whether the style seems properly smooth and clear,
And whether the choice of words is good or bad.
Alceste. We'll see, we'll see.
Oronte.   Perhaps I ought to add
That it took me only a quarter-hour to write it.
Alceste. The time's irrelevant, Sir: kindly recite it.
Oronte (reading). Hope comforts us awhile, 'tis true,
             Lulling our cares with careless laughter,
             And yet such joy is full of rue,
             My Phyllis, if nothing follows after.
Philinte. I'm charmed by this already; the style's delightful.

Alceste (*sotto voce, to Philinte*). How can you say that? Why, the
thing is frightful.

Oronte.   *Your fair face smiled on me awhile,*
            But was it kindness so to enchant me?
            'Twould have been fairer not to smile,
            If hope was all you meant to grant me.

Philinte. What a clever thought! How handsomely you phrase it!

Alceste (*sotto voce, to Philinte*). You know the thing is trash.
   How dare you praise it?

Oronte.   *If it's to be my passion's fate*
            Thus everlastingly to wait,
            Then death will come to set me free:
            For death is fairer than the fair;
            Phyllis, to hope is to despair
            When one must hope eternally.

Philinte. The close is exquisite — full of feeling and grace.

Alceste (*sotto voce, aside*). Oh, blast the close; you'd better close your
   face
Before you send your lying soul to hell.

Philinte. I can't remember a poem I've liked so well.

Alceste (*sotto voce, aside*). Good Lord!

Oronte (*to Philinte*).   I fear you're flattering me a bit.

Philinte. Oh, no!

Alceste (*sotto voce, aside*). What else d'you call it, you hypocrite?

Oronte (*to Alceste*). But you, Sir, keep your promise now: don't shrink
From telling me sincerely what you think.

Alceste. Sir, these are delicate matters; we all desire
To be told that we've the true poetic fire.
But once, to one whose name I shall not mention,
I said, regarding some verse of his invention,
That gentlemen should rigorously control
That itch to write which often afflicts the soul;
That one should curb the heady inclination
To publicize one's little avocation;
And that in showing off one's works of art
One often plays a very clownish part.

Oronte. Are you suggesting in a devious way
That I ought not . . .

Alceste.   Oh, that I do not say.
Further, I told him that no fault is worse
Than that of writing frigid, lifeless verse,
And that the merest whisper of such a shame

Suffices to destroy a man's good name.

Oronte. D'you mean to say my sonnet's dull and trite?

Alceste. I don't say that. But I went on to cite
　　Numerous cases of once-respected men
　　Who came to grief by taking up the pen.

Oronte. And am I like them? Do I write so poorly?

Alceste. I don't say that. But I told this person, "Surely
　　You're under no necessity to compose;
　　Why you should wish to publish, heaven knows.
　　There's no excuse for printing tedious rot
　　Unless one writes for bread, as you do not.
　　Resist temptation, then, I beg of you;
　　Conceal your pastimes from the public view;
　　And don't give up, on any provocation,
　　Your present high and courtly reputation,
　　To purchase at a greedy printer's shop
　　The name of silly author and scribbling fop."
　　These were the points I tried to make him see.

Oronte. I sense that they are also aimed at me;
　　But now — about my sonnet — I'd like to be told . . .

Alceste. Frankly, that sonnet should be pigeonholed.
　　You've chosen the worst models to imitate.
　　The style's unnatural. Let me illustrate:
　　　　For example, *Your fair face smiled on me awhile,*
　　　　Followed by, *'Twould have been fairer not to smile!*
　　　　Or this: *such joy is full of rue;*
　　　　Or this: *For death is fairer than the fair;*
　　　　Or, *Phyllis, to hope is to despair*
　　　　　　When one must hope eternally!
　　This artificial style, that's all the fashion,
　　Has neither taste, nor honesty, nor passion;
　　It's nothing but a sort of wordy play,
　　And nature never spoke in such a way.
　　What, in this shallow age, is not debased?
　　Our fathers, though less refined, had better taste;
　　I'd barter all that men admire today
　　For one old love song I shall try to say:
　　　　If the King had given me for my own
　　　　Paris, his citadel,
　　　　And I for that must leave alone
　　　　Her whom I love so well,
　　　　I'd say then to the Crown,

> *Take back your glittering town;*
> *My darling is more fair, I swear,*
> *My darling is more fair.*

The rhyme's not rich, the style is rough and old,
But don't you see that it's the purest gold
Beside the tinsel nonsense now preferred,
And that there's passion in its every word?

> *If the King had given me for my own*
> *Paris, his citadel,*
> *And I for that must leave alone*
> *Her whom I love so well,*
> *I'd say then to the Crown,*
> *Take back your glittering town;*
> *My darling is more fair, I swear,*
> *My darling is more fair.*

There speaks a loving heart. (*To Philinte.*) You're laughing, eh?
Laugh on, my precious wit. Whatever you say,
I hold that song's worth all the bibelots
That people hail today with ah's and oh's.

Oronte. And I maintain my sonnet's very good.

Alceste. It's not at all surprising that you should.
You have your reasons; permit me to have mine
For thinking that you cannot write a line.

Oronte. Others have praised my sonnet to the skies.

Alceste. I lack their art of telling pleasant lies.

Oronte. You seem to think you've got no end of wit.

Alceste. To praise your verse, I'd need still more of it.

Oronte. I'm not in need of your approval, Sir.

Alceste. That's good; you couldn't have it if you were.

Oronte. Come now, I'll lend you the subject of my sonnet;
I'd like to see you try to improve upon it.

Alceste. I might, by chance, write something just as shoddy;
But then I wouldn't show it to everybody.

Oronte. You're most opinionated and conceited.

Alceste. Go find your flatterers, and be better treated.

Oronte. Look here, my little fellow, pray watch your tone.

Alceste. My great big fellow, you'd better watch your own.

Philinte (*stepping between them*). Oh, please, please, gentlemen!
This will never do.

Oronte. The fault is mine, and I leave the field to you.
I am your servant, Sir, in every way.

Alceste. And I, Sir, am your most abject valet.

SCENE 3. [*Philinte, Alceste*]

Philinte. Well, as you see, sincerity in excess
    Can get you into a very pretty mess;
    Oronte was hungry for appreciation. . . .
Alceste. Don't speak to me.
Philinte.   What?
Alceste.   No more conversation.
Philinte. Really, now . . .
Alceste.   Leave me alone.
Philinte.   If I . . .
Alceste.   Out of my sight!
Philinte. But what . . .
Alceste.   I won't listen.
Philinte.   But . . .
Alceste.   Silence!
Philinte.   Now, is it polite . . .
Alceste. By heaven, I've had enough. Don't follow me.
Philinte. Ah, you're just joking. I'll keep you company.

ACT II

SCENE 1. [*Alceste, Célimène*]

Alceste. Shall I speak plainly, Madam? I confess
    Your conduct gives me infinite distress,
    And my resentment's grown too hot to smother.
    Soon, I foresee, we'll break with one another.
    If I said otherwise, I should deceive you;
    Sooner or later, I shall be forced to leave you,
    And if I swore that we shall never part,
    I should misread the omens of my heart.
Célimène. You kindly saw me home, it would appear,
    So as to pour invectives in my ear.
Alceste. I've no desire to quarrel. But I deplore
    Your inability to shut the door
    On all these suitors who beset you so.
    There's what annoys me, if you care to know.
Célimène. Is it my fault that all these men pursue me?
    Am I to blame if they're attracted to me?

And when they gently beg an audience,
Ought I to take a stick and drive them hence?
Alceste. Madam, there's no necessity for a stick;
A less responsive heart would do the trick.
Of your attractiveness I don't complain;
But those your charms attract, you then detain
By a most melting and receptive manner,
And so enlist their hearts beneath your banner.
It's the agreeable hopes which you excite
That keep these lovers round you day and night;
Were they less liberally smiled upon,
That sighing troop would very soon be gone.
But tell me, Madam, why it is that lately
This man Clitandre interests you so greatly?
Because of what high merits do you deem
Him worthy of the honor of your esteem?
Is it that your admiring glances linger
On the splendidly long nail of his little finger?
Or do you share the general deep respect
For the blond wig he chooses to affect?
Are you in love with his embroidered hose?
Do you adore his ribbons and his bows?
Or is it that this paragon bewitches
Your tasteful eye with his vast German breeches?
Perhaps his giggle, or his falsetto voice,
Makes him the latest gallant of your choice?
Célimène. You're much mistaken to resent him so.
Why I put up with him you surely know:
My lawsuit's very shortly to be tried,
And I must have his influence on my side.
Alceste. Then lose your lawsuit, Madam, or let it drop;
Don't torture me by humoring such a fop.
Célimène. You're jealous of the whole world, Sir.
Alceste.   That's true,
Since the whole world is well-received by you.
Célimène. That my good nature is so unconfined
Should serve to pacify your jealous mind;
Were I to smile on one, and scorn the rest,
Then you might have some cause to be distressed.
Alceste. Well, if I musn't be jealous, tell me, then,
Just how I'm better treated than other men.
Célimène. You know you have my love. Will that not do?
Alceste. What proof have I that what you say is true?

Célimène. I would expect, Sir, that my having said it
 Might give the statement a sufficient credit.
Alceste. But how can I be sure that you don't tell
 The selfsame thing to other men as well?
Célimène. What a gallant speech! How flattering to me!
 What a sweet creature you make me out to be!
 Well then, to save you from the pangs of doubt,
 All that I've said I hereby cancel out;
 Now, none but yourself shall make a monkey of you:
 Are you content?
Alceste.   Why, why am I doomed to love you?
 I swear that I shall bless the blissful hour
 When this poor heart's no longer in your power!
 I make no secret of it: I've done my best
 To exorcise this passion from my breast;
 But thus far all in vain; it will not go;
 It's for my sins that I must love you so.
Célimène. Your love for me is matchless, Sir; that's clear.
Alceste. Indeed, in all the world it has no peer;
 Words can't describe the nature of my passion,
 And no man ever loved in such a fashion.
Célimène. Yes, it's a brand-new fashion, I agree:
 You show your love by castigating me,
 And all your speeches are enraged and rude.
 I've never been so furiously wooed.
Alceste. Yet you could calm that fury, if you chose.
 Come, shall we bring our quarrels to a close?
 Let's speak with open hearts, then, and begin . . .

SCENE 2. [*Célimène, Alceste, Basque*]

Célimène. What is it?
Basque.   Acaste is here.
Célimène.   Well, send him in.

SCENE 3. [*Célimène, Alceste*]

Alceste. What! Shall we never be alone at all?
 You're always ready to receive a call,
 And you can't bear, for ten ticks of the clock,
 Not to keep open house for all who knock.
Célimène. I couldn't refuse him: he'd be most put out.

Alceste. Surely that's not worth worrying about.

Célimène. Acaste would never forgive me if he guessed
  That I consider him a dreadful pest.

Alceste. If he's a pest, why bother with him then?

Célimène. Heavens! One can't antagonize such men;
  Why, they're the chartered gossips of the court,
  And have a say in things of every sort.
  One must receive them, and be full of charm;
  They're no great help, but they can do you harm,
  And though your influence be ever so great,
  They're hardly the best people to alienate.

Alceste. I see, dear lady, that you could make a case
  For putting up with the whole human race;
  These friendships that you calculate so nicely . . .

SCENE 4. [*Alceste, Célimène, Basque*]

Basque. Madam, Clitandre is here as well.

Alceste.   Precisely.

Célimène. Where are you going?

Alceste.   Elsewhere.

Célimène.   Stay.

Alceste.   No, no.

Célimène. Stay, Sir.

Alceste.   I can't.

Célimène.   I wish it.

Alceste.   No, I must go.
  I beg you, Madam, not to press the matter;
  You know I have no taste for idle chatter.

Célimène. Stay. I command you.

Alceste.   No, I cannot stay.

Célimène. Very well; you have my leave to go away.

SCENE 5. [*Éliante, Philinte, Acaste, Clitandre,
              Alceste, Célimène, Basque*]

Éliante (*to Célimène*). The Marquesses have kindly come to call.
  Were they announced?

Célimène.   Yes. Basque, bring chairs for all.

  (*Basque provides the chairs, and exits.*)

  (*To Alceste.*) You haven't gone?

Alceste. No; and I shan't depart
Till you decide who's foremost in your heart.
Célimène. Oh, hush.
Alceste. It's time to choose; take them, or me.
Célimène. You're mad.
Alceste. I'm not, as you shall shortly see.
Célimène. Oh?
Alceste. You'll decide.
Célimène. You're joking now, dear friend.
Alceste. No, no; you'll choose; my patience is at an end.
Clitandre. Madam, I come from court, where poor Cléonte
Behaved like a perfect fool, as is his wont.
Has he no friend to counsel him, I wonder,
And teach him less unerringly to blunder?
Célimène. It's true, the man's a most accomplished dunce;
His gauche behavior charms the eye at once;
And every time one sees him, on my word,
His manner's grown a trifle more absurd.
Acaste. Speaking of dunces, I've just now conversed
With old Damon, who's one of the very worst;
I stood a lifetime in the broiling sun
Before his dreary monologue was done.
Célimène. Oh, he's a wondrous talker, and has the power
To tell you nothing hour after hour:
If, by mistake, he ever came to the point,
The shock would put his jawbone out of joint.
Éliante (to Philinte). The conversation takes its usual turn,
And all our dear friends' ears will shortly burn.
Clitandre. Timante's a character, Madam.
Célimène. Isn't he, though?
A man of mystery from top to toe,
Who moves about in a romantic mist
On secret missions which do not exist.
His talk is full of eyebrows and grimaces;
How tired one gets of his momentous faces;
He's always whispering something confidential
Which turns out to be quite inconsequential;
Nothing's too slight for him to mystify;
He even whispers when he says "good-by."
Acaste. Tell us about Géralde.
Célimène. That tiresome ass.
He mixes only with the titled class,

And fawns on dukes and princes, and is bored
With anyone who's not at least a lord.
The man's obsessed with rank, and his discourses
Are all of hounds and carriages and horses;
He uses Christian names with all the great,
And the word Milord, with him, is out of date.
Clitandre. He's very taken with Bélise, I hear.
Célimène. She is the dreariest company, poor dear.
Whenever she comes to call, I grope about
To find some topic which will draw her out,
But, owing to her dry and faint replies,
The conversation wilts, and droops, and dies.
In vain one hopes to animate her face
By mentioning the ultimate commonplace;
But sun or shower, even hail or frost
Are matters she can instantly exhaust.
Meanwhile her visit, painful though it is,
Drags on and on through mute eternities,
And though you ask the time, and yawn, and yawn,
She sits there like a stone and won't be gone.
Acaste. Now for Adraste.
Célimène.   Oh, that conceited elf
Has a gigantic passion for himself;
He rails against the court, and cannot bear it
That none will recognize his hidden merit;
All honors given to others give offense
To his imaginary excellence.
Clitandre. What about young Cléon? His house, they say,
Is full of the best society, night and day.
Célimène. His cook has made him popular, not he:
It's Cléon's table that people come to see.
Éliante. He gives a splendid dinner, you must admit.
Célimène. But must he serve himself along with it?
For my taste, he's a most insipid dish
Whose presence sours the wine and spoils the fish.
Philinte. Damis, his uncle, is admired no end.
What's your opinion, Madam?
Célimène.   Why, he's my friend.
Philinte. He seems a decent fellow, and rather clever.
Célimène. He works too hard at cleverness, however.
I hate to see him sweat and struggle so
To fill his conversation with bons mots.
Since he's decided to become a wit

His taste's so pure that nothing pleases it;
He scolds at all the latest books and plays,
Thinking that wit must never stoop to praise,
That finding fault's a sign of intellect,
That all appreciation is abject,
And that by damning everything in sight
One shows oneself in a distinguished light.
He's scornful even of our conversations:
Their trivial nature sorely tries his patience;
He folds his arms, and stands above the battle,
And listens sadly to our childish prattle.

Acaste. Wonderful, Madam! You've hit him off precisely.

Clitandre. No one can sketch a character so nicely.

Alceste. How bravely, Sirs, you cut and thrust at all
These absent fools, till one by one they fall:
But let one come in sight, and you'll at once
Embrace the man you lately called a dunce,
Telling him in a tone sincere and fervent
How proud you are to be his humble servant.

Clitandre. Why pick on us? *Madame's* been speaking, Sir.
And you should quarrel, if you must, with her.

Alceste. No, no, by God, the fault is yours, because
You lead her on with laughter and applause,
And make her think that she's the more delightful
The more her talk is scandalous and spiteful.
Oh, she would stoop to malice far, far less
If no such claque approved her cleverness.
It's flatterers like you whose foolish praise
Nourishes all the vices of these days.

Philinte. But why protest when someone ridicules
Those you'd condemn, yourself, as knaves or fools?

Célimène. Why, Sir? Because he loves to make a fuss.
You don't expect him to agree with us,
When there's an opportunity to express
His heaven-sent spirit of contrariness?
What other people think, he can't abide;
Whatever they say, he's on the other side;
He lives in deadly terror of agreeing;
'Twould make him seem an ordinary being.
Indeed, he's so in love with contradiction,
He'll turn against his most profound conviction
And with a furious eloquence deplore it,
If only someone else is speaking for it.

Alceste. Go on, dear lady, mock me as you please;
   You have your audience in ecstasies.
Philinte. But what she says is true: you have a way
   Of bridling at whatever people say;
   Whether they praise or blame, your angry spirit
   Is equally unsatisfied to hear it.
Alceste. Men, Sir, are always wrong, and that's the reason
   That righteous anger's never out of season;
   All that I hear in all their conversation
   Is flattering praise or reckless condemnation.
Célimène. But . . .
Alceste.   No, no, Madam, I am forced to state
   That you have pleasures which I deprecate,
   And that these others, here, are much to blame
   For nourishing the faults which are your shame.
Clitandre. I shan't defend myself, Sir; but I vow
   I'd thought this lady faultless until now.
Acaste. I see her charms and graces, which are many;
   But as for faults, I've never noticed any.
Alceste. I see them, Sir; and rather than ignore them,
   I strenuously criticize her for them.
   The more one loves, the more one should object
   To every blemish, every least defect.
   Were I this lady, I would soon get rid
   Of lovers who approved of all I did,
   And by their slack indulgence and applause
   Endorsed my follies and excused my flaws.
Célimène. If all heart beat according to your measure,
   The dawn of love would be the end of pleasure;
   And love would find its perfect consummation
   In ecstasies of rage and reprobation.
Éliante. Love, as a rule, affects men otherwise,
   And lovers rarely love to criticize.
   They see their lady as a charming blur,
   And find all things commendable in her.
   If she has any blemish, fault, or shame,
   They will redeem it by a pleasing name.
   The pale-faced lady's lily-white, perforce;
   The swarthy one's a sweet brunette, of course;
   The spindly lady has a slender grace;
   The fat one has a most majestic pace;
   The plain one, with her dress in disarray,
   They classify as *beauté négligée*;

The hulking one's a goddess in their eyes,
The dwarf, a concentrate of Paradise;
The haughty lady has a noble mind;
The mean one's witty, and the dull one's kind;
The chatterbox has liveliness and verve,
The mute one has a virtuous reserve.
So lovers manage, in their passion's cause,
To love their ladies even for their flaws.

Alceste. But I still say . . .

Célimène.   I think it would be nice
To stroll around the gallery once or twice.
What! You're not going, Sirs?

Clitandre and Acaste.   No, Madam, no.

Alceste. You seem to be in terror lest they go.
Do what you will, Sirs; leave, or linger on,
But I shan't go till after you are gone.

Acaste. I'm free to to linger, unless I should perceive
Madame is tired, and wishes me to leave.

Clitandre. And as for me, I needn't go today
Until the hour of the King's *coucher.*

Célimène (to Alceste). You're joking, surely?

Alceste.   Not in the least; we'll see
Whether you'd rather part with them, or me.

SCENE 6. [*Alceste, Célimène, Éliante, Acaste,*
Philinte, Clitandre, Basque]

Basque (to Alceste). Sir, there's a fellow here who bids me state
That he must see you, and that it can't wait.

Alceste. Tell him that I have no such pressing affairs.

Basque. It's a long tailcoat that this fellow wears,
With gold all over.

Célimène (to Alceste). You'd best go down and see.
Or — have him enter.

SCENE 7. [*Alceste, Célimène, Éliante, Acaste,*
Philinte, Clitandre, Guard]

Alceste (confronting the Guard). Well, what do you want with me?
Come in, Sir.

Guard.   I've a word, Sir, for your ear.

Alceste. Speak it aloud, Sir; I shall strive to hear.
Guard. The Marshals have instructed me to say
   You must report to them without delay.
Alceste. Who? Me, Sir?
Guard.   Yes, Sir; you.
Alceste.   But what do they want?
Philinte (*to Alceste*). To scotch your silly quarrel with Oronte.
Célimène (*to Philinte*). What quarrel?
Philinte.   Oronte and he have fallen out
   Over some verse he spoke his mind about;
   The Marshals wish to arbitrate the matter.
Alceste. Never shall I equivocate or flatter!
Philinte. You'd best obey their summons; come, let's go.
Alceste. How can they mend our quarrel, I'd like to know?
   Am I to make a cowardly retraction,
   And praise those jingles to his satisfaction?
   I'll not recant; I've judged that sonnet rightly.
   It's bad.
Philinte. But you might say so more politely. . . .
Alceste. I'll not back down; his verses make me sick.
Philinte. If only you could be more politic!
   But come, let's go.
Alceste.   I'll go, but I won't unsay
   A single word.
Philinte.   Well, let's be on our way.
Alceste. Till I am ordered by my lord the King
   To praise that poem, I shall say the thing
   Is scandalous, by God, and that the poet
   Ought to be hanged for having the nerve to show it.

(*To Clitandre and Acaste, who are laughing.*)

   By heaven, Sirs, I really didn't know
   That I was being humorous.
Célimène.   Go, Sir, go;
   Settle your business.
Alceste.   I shall, and when I'm through,
   I shall return to settle things with you.

ACT III

SCENE 1. [*Clitandre, Acaste*]

Clitandre. Dear Marquess, how contented you appear;
    All things delight you, nothing mars your cheer.
    Can you, in perfect honesty, declare
    That you've a right to be so debonair?
Acaste. By Jove, when I survey myself, I find
    No cause whatever for distress of mind.
    I'm young and rich; I can in modesty
    Lay claim to an exalted pedigree;
    And owing to my name and my condition
    I shall not want for honors and position.
    Then as to courage, that most precious trait,
    I seem to have it, as was proved of late
    Upon the field of honor, where my bearing,
    They say, was very cool and rather daring.
    I've wit, of course; and taste in such perfection
    That I can judge without the least reflection,
    And at the theater, which is my delight,
    Can make or break a play on opening night,
    And lead the crowd in hisses or bravos,
    And generally be known as one who knows.
    I'm clever, handsome, gracefully polite;
    My waist is small, my teeth are strong and white;
    As for my dress, the world's astonished eyes
    Assure me that I bear away the prize.
    I find myself in favor everywhere,
    Honored by men, and worshiped by the fair;
    And since these things are so, it seems to me
    I'm justified in my complacency.
Clitandre. Well, if so many ladies hold you dear,
    Why do you press a hopeless courtship here?
Acaste. Hopeless, you say? I'm not the sort of fool
    That likes his ladies difficult and cool.
    Men who are awkward, shy, and peasantish
    May pine for heartless beauties, if they wish,
    Grovel before them, bear their cruelties,
    Woo them with tears and sighs and bended knees,
    And hope by dogged faithfulness to gain

What their poor merits never could obtain.
For men like me, however, it makes no sense
To love on trust, and foot the whole expense.
Whatever any lady's merits be,
I think, thank God, that I'm as choice as she;
That if my heart is kind enough to burn
For her, she owes me something in return;
And that in any proper love affair
The partners must invest an equal share.

Clitandre. You think, then, that our hostess favors you?
Acaste. I've reason to believe that that is true.
Clitandre. How did you come to such a mad conclusion?
    You're blind, dear fellow. This is sheer delusion.
Acaste. All right, then: I'm deluded and I'm blind.
Clitandre. Whatever put the notion in your mind?
Acaste. Delusion.
Clitandre.   What persuades you that you're right?
Acaste. I'm blind.
Clitandre.   But have you any proofs to cite?
Acaste. I tell you I'm deluded.
Clitandre.   Have you, then,
    Received some secret pledge from Célimène?
Acaste. Oh, no: she scorns me.
Clitandre.   Tell me the truth, I beg.
Acaste. She just can't bear me.
Clitandre.   Ah, don't pull my leg.
    Tell me what hope she's given you, I pray.
Acaste. I'm hopeless, and it's you who win the day.
    She hates me thoroughly, and I'm so vexed
    I mean to hang myself on Tuesday next.
Clitandre. Dear Marquess, let us have an armistice
    And make a treaty. What do you say to this?
    If ever one of us can plainly prove
    That Célimène encourages his love,
    The other must abandon hope, and yield,
    And leave him in possession of the field.
Acaste. Now, there's a bargain that appeals to me;
    With all my heart, dear Marquess, I agree.
    But hush.

SCENE 2. [*Célimène, Acaste, Clitandre*]

Célimène. Still here?
Clitandre. 'Twas love that stayed our feet.
Célimène. I think I heard a carriage in the street.
 Whose is it? D'you know?

SCENE 3. [*Célimène, Acaste, Clitandre, Basque*]

Basque. Arsinoé is here,
 Madame.
Célimène. Arsinoé, you say? Oh, dear.
Basque. Éliante is entertaining her below.
Célimène. What brings the creature here, I'd like to know?
Acaste. They say she's dreadfully prudish, but in fact
 I think her piety . . .
Célimène. It's all an act.
 At heart she's worldly, and her poor success
 In snaring men explains her prudishness.
 It breaks her heart to see the beaux and gallants
 Engrossed by other women's charms and talents,
 And so she's always in a jealous rage
 Against the faulty standards of the age.
 She lets the world believe that she's a prude
 To justify her loveless solitude,
 And strives to put a brand of moral shame
 On all the graces that she cannot claim.
 But still she'd love a lover; and Alceste
 Appears to be the one she'd love the best.
 His visits here are poison to her pride;
 She seems to think I've lured him from her side;
 And everywhere, at court or in the town,
 The spiteful, envious woman runs me down.
 In short, she's just as stupid as can be,
 Vicious and arrogant in the last degree,
 And . . .

SCENE 4. [*Arsinoé, Célimène, Clitandre, Acaste*]

Célimène. Ah! What happy chance has brought you here?
 I've thought about you ever so much, my dear.
Arsinoé. I've come to tell you something you should know.
Célimène. How good of you to think of doing so!

(*Clitandre and Acaste go out, laughing.*)

SCENE 5. [*Arsinoé, Célimène*]

Arsinoé. It's just as well those gentlemen didn't tarry.
Célimène. Shall we sit down?
Arsinoé.   That won't be necessary.
   Madam, the flame of friendship ought to burn
   Brightest in matters of the most concern,
   And as there's nothing which concerns us more
   Than honor, I have hastened to your door
   To bring you, as your friend, some information
   About the status of your reputation.
   I visited, last night, some virtuous folk,
   And, quite by chance, it was of you they spoke;
   There was, I fear, no tendency to praise
   Your light behavior and your dashing ways.
   The quantity of gentlemen you see
   And your by now notorious coquetry
   Were both so vehemently criticized
   By everyone, that I was much surprised.
   Of course, I needn't tell you where I stood;
   I came to your defense as best I could,
   Assured them you were harmless, and declared
   Your soul was absolutely unimpaired.
   But there are some things, you must realize,
   One can't excuse, however hard one tries,
   And I was forced at last into conceding
   That your behavior, Madam, is misleading,
   That it makes a bad impression, giving rise
   To ugly gossip and obscene surmise,
   And that if you were more *overtly* good,
   You wouldn't be so much misunderstood.
   Not that I think you've been unchaste — no! no!
   The saints preserve me from a thought so low!
   But mere good conscience never did suffice:
   One must avoid the outward show of vice.
   Madam, you're too intelligent, I'm sure,
   To think my motives anything but pure
   In offering you this counsel — which I do
   Out of a zealous interest in you.
Célimène. Madam, I haven't taken you amiss;
   I'm very much obliged to you for this;
   And I'll at once discharge the obligation
   By telling you about *your* reputation.

You've been so friendly as to let me know
What certain people say of me, and so
I mean to follow your benign example
By offering you a somewhat similar sample.
The other day, I went to an affair
And found some most distinguised people there
Discussing piety, both false and true.
The conversation soon came round to you.
Alas! Your prudery and bustling zeal
Appeared to have a very slight appeal.
Your affectation of a grave demeanor,
Your endless talk of virtue and of honor,
The aptitude of your suspicious mind
For finding sin where there is none to find,
Your towering self-esteem, that pitying face
With which you contemplate the human race,
Your sermonizings and your sharp aspersions
On people's pure and innocent diversions —
All these were mentioned, Madam, and, in fact,
Were roundly and concertedly attacked.
"What good," they said, "are all these outward shows,
When everything belies her pious pose?
She prays incessantly; but then, they say,
She beats her maids and cheats them of their pay;
She shows her zeal in every holy place,
But still she's vain enough to paint her face;
She holds that naked statues are immoral,
But with a naked *man* she'd have no quarrel."
Of course, I said to everybody there
That they were being viciously unfair;
But still they were disposed to criticize you,
And all agreed that someone should advise you
To leave the morals of the world alone,
And worry rather more about your own.
They felt that one's self-knowledge should be great
Before one thinks of setting others straight;
That one should learn the art of living well
Before one threatens other men with hell,
And that the Church is best equipped, no doubt,
To guide our souls and root our vices out.
Madam, you're too intelligent, I'm sure,
To think my motives anything but pure
In offering you this counsel — which I do

Out of a zealous interest in you.

Arsinoé. I dared not hope for gratitude, but I
    Did not expect so acid a reply;
    I judge, since you've been so extremely tart,
    That my good counsel pierced you to the heart.

Célimène. Far from it, Madam. Indeed, it seems to me
    We ought to trade advice more frequently.
    One's vision of oneself is so defective
    That it would be an excellent corrective.
    If you are willing, Madam, let's arrange
    Shortly to have another frank exchange
    In which we'll tell each other, *entre nous*,
    What you've heard tell of me, and I of you.

Arsinoé. Oh, people never censure you, my dear;
    It's me they criticize. Or so I hear.

Célimène. Madam, I think we either blame or praise
    According to our taste and length of days.
    There is a time of life for coquetry,
    And there's a season, too, for prudery.
    When all one's charms are gone, it is, I'm sure,
    Good strategy to be devout and pure:
    It makes one seem a little less forsaken.
    Some day, perhaps, I'll take the road you've taken:
    Time brings all things. But I have time aplenty,
    And see no cause to be a prude at twenty.

Arsinoé. You give your age in such a gloating tone
    That one would think I was an ancient crone;
    We're not so far apart, in sober truth,
    That you can mock me with a boast of youth!
    Madam, you baffle me. I wish I knew
    What moves you to provoke me as you do.

Célimène. For my part, Madam, I should like to know
    Why you abuse me everywhere you go.
    Is it my fault, dear lady, that your hand
    Is not, alas, in very great demand?
    If men admire me, if they pay me court
    And daily make me offers of the sort
    You'd dearly love to have them make to you,
    How can I help it? What would you have me do?
    If what you want is lovers, please feel free
    To take as many as you can from me.

Arsinoé. Oh, come. D'you think the world is losing sleep
    Over the flock of lovers which you keep,

Or that we find it difficult to guess
What price you pay for their devotedness?
Surely you don't expect us to suppose
Mere merit could attract so many beaux?
It's not your virtue that they're dazzled by;
Nor is it virtuous love for which they sigh.
You're fooling no one, Madam; the world's not blind;
There's many a lady heaven has designed
To call men's noblest, tenderest feelings out,
Who has no lovers dogging her about;
From which it's plain that lovers nowadays
Must be acquired in bold and shameless ways,
And only pay one court for such reward
As modesty and virtue can't afford.
Then don't be quite so puffed up, if you please,
About your tawdry little victories;
Try, if you can, to be a shade less vain,
And treat the world with somewhat less disdain.
If one were envious of your amours,
One soon could have a following like yours;
Lovers are no great trouble to collect
If one prefers them to one's self-respect.
Célimène. Collect them then, my dear; I'd love to see
You demonstrate that charming theory;
Who knows, you might . . .
Arsinoé.   Now, Madam, that will do;
It's time to end this trying interview.
My coach is late in coming to your door,
Or I'd have taken leave of you before.
Célimène. Oh, please don't feel that you must rush away;
I'd be delighted, Madam, if you'd stay.
However, lest my conversation bore you,
Let me provide some better company for you;
This gentleman, who comes most apropos,
Will please you more than I could do, I know.

SCENE 6. [*Alceste, Célimène, Arsinoé*]

Célimène. Alceste, I have a little note to write
Which simply must go out before tonight;
Please entertain *Madame*; I'm sure that she
Will overlook my incivility.

SCENE 7. [*Alceste, Arsinoé*]

Arsinoé. Well, Sir, our hostess graciously contrives
    For us to chat until my coach arrives;
    And I shall be forever in her debt
    For granting me this little tête-à-tête.
    We women very rightly give our hearts
    To men of noble character and parts,
    And your especial merits, dear Alceste,
    Have roused the deepest sympathy in my breast.
    Oh, how I wish they had sufficient sense
    At court, to recognize your excellence!
    They wrong you greatly, Sir. How it must hurt you
    Never to be rewarded for your virtue!
Alceste. Why, Madam, what cause have I to feel aggrieved?
    What great and brilliant thing have I achieved?
    What service have I rendered to the King
    That I should look to him for anything?
Arsinoé. Not everyone who's honored by the State
    Has done great services. A man must wait
    Till time and fortune offer him the chance.
    Your merit, Sir, is obvious at a glance,
    And . . .
Alceste. Ah, forget my merit; I am not neglected.
    The court, I think, can hardly be expected
    To mine men's souls for merit, and unearth
    Our hidden virtues and our secret worth.
Arsinoé. *Some* virtues, though, are far too bright to hide;
    Yours are acknowledged, Sir, on every side.
    Indeed, I've heard you warmly praised of late
    By persons of considerable weight.
Alceste. This fawning age has praise for everyone,
    And all distinctions, Madam, are undone.
    All things have equal honor nowadays,
    And no one should be gratified by praise.
    To be admired, one only need exist,
    And every lackey's on the honors list.
Arsinoé. I only wish, Sir, that you had your eye
    On some position at court, however high;
    You'd only have to hint at such a notion
    For me to set the proper wheels in motion;

I've certain friendships I'd be glad to use
To get you any office you might choose.
Alceste. Madam, I fear that any such ambition
Is wholly foreign to my disposition.
The soul God gave me isn't of the sort
That prospers in the weather of a court.
It's all too obvious that I don't possess
The virtues necessary for success.
My one great talent is for speaking plain;
I've never learned to flatter or to feign;
And anyone so stupidly sincere
Had best not seek a courtier's career.
Outside the court, I know, one must dispense
With honors, privilege, and influence;
But still one gains the right, foregoing these,
Not to be tortured by the wish to please.
One needn't live in dread of snubs and slights,
Nor praise the verse that every idiot writes,
Nor humor silly Marquesses, nor bestow
Politic sighs on Madam So-and-So.
Arsinoé. Forget the court, then; let the matter rest.
But I've another cause to be distressed
About your present situation, Sir.
It's to your love affair that I refer.
She whom you love, and who pretends to love you,
Is, I regret to say, unworthy of you.
Alceste. Why, Madam? Can you seriously intend
To make so grave a charge against your friend?
Arsinoé. Alas, I must. I've stood aside too long
And let that lady do you grievous wrong;
But now my debt to conscience shall be paid:
I tell you that your love has been betrayed.
Alceste. I thank you, Madam; you're extremely kind.
Such words are soothing to a lover's mind.
Arsinoé. Yes, though she *is* my friend, I say again
You're very much too good for Célimène.
She's wantonly misled you from the start.
Alceste. You may be right; who knows another's heart?
But ask yourself if it's the part of charity
To shake my soul with doubts of her sincerity.
Arsinoé. Well, if you'd rather be a dupe than doubt her,
That's your affair. I'll say no more about her.

Alceste. Madam, you know that doubt and vague suspicion
　　Are painful to a man in my position;
　　It's most unkind to worry me this way
　　Unless you've some real proof of what you say.
Arsinoé. Sir, say no more: all doubts shall be removed,
　　And all that I've been saying shall be proved.
　　You've only to escort me home, and there
　　We'll look into the heart of this affair.
　　I've ocular evidence which will persuade you
　　Beyond a doubt, that Célimène's betrayed you.
　　Then, if you're saddened by that revelation,
　　Perhaps I can provide some consolation.

ACT IV

SCENE 1. [*Éliante, Philinte*]

Philinte. Madam, he acted like a stubborn child;
　　I thought they never would be reconciled;
　　In vain we reasoned, threatened, and appealed;
　　He stood his ground and simply would not yield.
　　The Marshals, I feel sure, have never heard
　　An argument so splendidly absurd.
　　"No, gentlemen," said he, "I'll not retract.
　　His verse is bad: extremely bad, in fact.
　　Surely it does the man no harm to know it.
　　Does it disgrace him, not to be a poet?
　　A gentleman may be respected still,
　　Whether he writes a sonnet well or ill.
　　That I dislike his verse should not offend him;
　　In all that touches honor, I commend him;
　　He's noble, brave, and virtuous — but I fear
　　He can't in truth be called a sonneteer.
　　I'll gladly praise his wardrobe; I'll endorse
　　His dancing, or the way he sits a horse;
　　But, gentlemen, I cannot praise his rhyme.
　　In fact, it ought to be a capital crime
　　For anyone so sadly unendowed
　　To write a sonnet, and read the thing aloud."
　　At length he fell into a gentler mood
　　And, striking a concessive attitude,

He paid Oronte the following courtesies:
"Sir, I regret that I'm so hard to please,
And I'm profoundly sorry that your lyric
Failed to provoke me to a panegyric."
After these curious words, the two embraced,
And then the hearing was adjourned — in haste.
Éliante. His conduct has been very singular lately;
  Still, I confess that I respect him greatly.
  The honesty in which he takes such pride
  Has — to my mind — it's noble, heroic side.
  In this false age, such candor seems outrageous;
  But I could wish that it were more contagious.
Philinte. What most intrigues me in our friend Alceste
  Is the grand passion that rages in his breast.
  The sullen humors he's compounded of
  Should not, I think, dispose his heart to love;
  But since they do, it puzzles me still more
  That he should choose your cousin to adore.
Éliante. It does, indeed, belie the theory
  That love is born of gentle sympathy,
  And that the tender passion must be based
  On sweet accords of temper and of taste.
Philinte. Does she return his love, do you suppose?
Éliante. Ah, that's a difficult question, Sir. Who knows?
  How can we judge the truth of her devotion?
  Her heart's a stranger to its own emotion.
  Sometimes it thinks it loves, when no love's there;
  At other times it loves quite unaware.
Philinte. I rather think Alceste is in for more
  Distress and sorrow than he's bargained for;
  Were he of my mind, Madam, his affection
  Would turn in quite a different direction,
  And we would see him more responsive to
  The kind regard which he receives from you.
Éliante. Sir, I believe in frankness, and I'm inclined,
  In matters of the heart, to speak my mind.
  I don't oppose his love for her; indeed,
  I hope with all my heart that he'll succeed,
  And were it in my power, I'd rejoice
  In giving him the lady of his choice.
  But if, as happens frequently enough
  In love affairs, he meets with a rebuff —
  If Célimène should grant some rival's suit —

I'd gladly play the role of substitute;
    Nor would his tender speeches please me less
    Because they'd once been made without success.
Philinte. Well, Madam, as for me, I don't oppose
    Your hopes in this affair; and heaven knows
    That in my conversations with the man
    I plead your cause as often as I can.
    But if those two should marry, and so remove
    All chance that he will offer you his love,
    Then I'll declare my own, and hope to see
    Your gracious favor pass from him to me.
    In short, should you be cheated of Alceste,
    I'd be most happy to be second best.
Éliante. Philinte, you're teasing.
Philinte.   Ah, Madam, never fear;
    No words of mine were ever so sincere,
    And I shall live in fretful expectation
    Till I can make a fuller declaration.

SCENE 2. [*Alceste, Éliante, Philinte*]

Alceste. Avenge me, Madam! I must have satisfaction,
    Or this great wrong will drive me to distraction!
Éliante. Why, what's the matter? What's upset you so?
Alceste. Madam, I've had a mortal, mortal blow.
    If Chaos repossessed the universe,
    I swear I'd not be shaken any worse.
    I'm ruined. . . . I can say no more. . . . My soul . . .
Éliante. Do try, Sir, to regain your self-control.
Alceste. Just heaven! Why were so much beauty and grace
    Bestowed on one so vicious and so base?
Éliante. Once more, Sir, tell us. . . .
Alceste.   My world has gone to wrack;
    I'm — I'm betrayed; she's stabbed me in the back:
    Yes, Célimène (who would have thought it of her?)
    Is false to me, and has another lover.
Éliante. Are you quite certain? Can you prove these things?
Philinte. Lovers are prey to wild imaginings
    And jealous fancies. No doubt there's some mistake. . . .
Alceste. Mind your own business, Sir, for heaven's sake.

    (*To Éliante.*)

Madam, I have the proof that you demand
Here in my pocket, penned by her own hand.
Yes, all the shameful evidence one could want
Lies in this letter written to Oronte —
Oronte! whom I felt sure she couldn't love,
And hardly bothered to be jealous of.

Philinte. Still, in a letter, appearances may deceive;
This may not be so bad as you believe.

Alceste. Once more I beg you, Sir, to let me be;
Tend to your own affairs; leave mine to me.

Éliante. Compose yourself; this anguish that you feel . . .

Alceste. Is something, Madam, you alone can heal.
My outraged heart, beside itself with grief,
Appeals to you for comfort and relief.
Avenge me on your cousin, whose unjust
And faithless nature has deceived my trust;
Avenge a crime your pure soul must detest.

Éliante. But how, Sir?

Alceste.   Madam, this heart within my breast
Is yours; pray take it; redeem my heart from her,
And so avenge me on my torturer.
Let her be punished by the fond emotion,
The ardent love, the bottomless devotion,
The faithful worship which this heart of mine
Will offer up to yours as to a shrine.

Éliante. You have my sympathy, Sir, in all you suffer;
Nor do I scorn the noble heart you offer;
But I suspect you'll soon be mollified,
And this desire for vengeance will subside.
When some belovèd hand has done us wrong
We thirst for retribution — but not for long;
However dark the deed that she's committed,
A lovely culprit's very soon acquitted.
Nothing's so stormy as an injured lover,
And yet no storm so quickly passes over.

Alceste. No, Madam, no — this is no lovers' spat;
I'll not forgive her; it's gone too far for that;
My mind's made up; I'll kill myself before
I waste my hopes upon her any more.
Ah, here she is. My wrath intensifies.
I shall confront her with her tricks and lies,
And crush her utterly, and bring you then
A heart no longer slave to Célimène.

SCENE 3. [*Célimène, Alceste*]

Alceste (*aside*). Sweet heaven, help me to control my passion.
Célimène (*aside*). Oh, Lord.

(*To Alceste.*)

                  Why stand there staring in that fashion?
And what d'you mean by those dramatic sighs,
And that malignant glitter in your eyes?
Alceste. I mean that sins which cause the blood to freeze
Look innocent beside your treacheries;
That nothing Hell's or Heaven's wrath could do
Ever produced so bad a thing as you.
Célimène. Your compliments were always sweet and pretty.
Alceste. Madam, it's not the moment to be witty.
No, blush and hang your head; you've ample reason,
Since I've the fullest evidence of your treason.
Ah, this is what my sad heart prophesied;
Now all my anxious fears are verified;
My dark suspicion and my gloomy doubt
Divined the truth, and now the truth is out.
For all your trickery, I was not deceived;
It was my bitter stars that I believed.
But don't imagine that you'll go scot-free;
You shan't misuse me with impunity.
I know that love's irrational and blind;
I know the heart's not subject to the mind,
And can't be reasoned into beating faster;
I know each soul is free to choose its master;
Therefore had you but spoken from the heart,
Rejecting my attentions from the start,
I'd have no grievance, or at any rate
I could complain of nothing but my fate.
Ah, but so falsely to encourage me —
That was a treason and a treachery
For which you cannot suffer too severely,
And you shall pay for that behavior dearly.
Yes, now I have no pity, not a shred;
My temper's out of hand; I've lost my head;
Shocked by the knowledge of your double-dealings,
My reason can't restrain my savage feelings;
A righteous wrath deprives me of my senses,
And I won't answer for the consequences.

Célimène. What does this outburst mean? Will you please explain?
  Have you, by any chance, gone quite insane?
Alceste. Yes, yes, I went insane the day I fell
  A victim to your black and fatal spell,
  Thinking to meet with some sincerity
  Among the treacherous charms that beckoned me.
Célimène. Pooh. Of what treachery can you complain?
Alceste. How sly you are, how cleverly you feign!
  But you'll not victimize me any more.
  Look: here's a document you've seen before.
  This evidence, which I acquired today,
  Leaves you, I think, without a thing to say.
Célimène. Is this what sent you into such a fit?
Alceste. You should be blushing at the sight of it.
Célimène. Ought I to blush? I truly don't see why.
Alceste. Ah, now you're being bold as well as sly;
  Since there's no signature, perhaps you'll claim . . .
Célimène. I wrote it, whether or not it bears my name.
Alceste. And you can view with equanimity
  This proof of your disloyalty to me!
Célimène. Oh, don't be so outrageous and extreme.
Alceste. You take this matter lightly, it would seem.
  Was it no wrong to me, no shame to you,
  That you should send Oronte this billet-doux?
Célimène. Oronte! Who said it was for him?
Alceste.   Why, those
  Who brought me this example of your prose.
  But what's the difference? If you wrote the letter
  To someone else, it pleases me no better.
  My grievance and your guilt remain the same.
Célimène. But need you rage, and need I blush for shame,
  If this was written to a *woman* friend?
Alceste. Ah! Most ingenious. I'm impressed no end;
  And after that incredible evasion
  Your guilt is clear. I need no more persuasion.
  How dare you try so clumsy a deception?
  D'you think I'm wholly wanting in perception?
  Come, come, let's see how brazenly you'll try
  To bolster up so palpable a lie:
  Kindly construe this ardent closing section
  As nothing more than sisterly affection!
  Here, let me read it. Tell me, if you dare to,
  That this is for a woman . . .

Célimène.   I don't care to.
   What right have you to badger and berate me,
   And so highhandedly interrogate me?
Alceste. Now, don't be angry; all I ask of you
   Is that you justify a phrase or two . . .
Célimène. No, I shall not. I utterly refuse,
   And you may take those phrases as you choose.
Alceste. Just show me how this letter could be meant
   For a woman's eyes, and I shall be content.
Célimène. No, no, it's for Oronte; you're perfectly right.
   I welcome his attentions with delight,
   I prize his character and his intellect,
   And everything is just as you suspect.
   Come, do your worst now; give your rage free rein;
   But kindly cease to bicker and complain.
Alceste (*aside*). Good God! Could anything be more inhuman?
   Was ever a heart so mangled by a woman?
   When I complain of how she has betrayed me,
   She bridles, and commences to upbraid me!
   She tries my tortured patience to the limit;
   She won't deny her guilt; she glories in it!
   And yet my heart's too faint and cowardly
   To break these chains of passion, and be free,
   To scorn her as it should, and rise above
   This unrewarded, mad, and bitter love.

   (*To Célimène.*)

   Ah, traitress, in how confident a fashion
   You take advantage of my helpless passion,
   And use my weakness for your faithless charms
   To make me once again throw down my arms!
   But do at least deny this black transgression;
   Take back that mocking and perverse confession;
   Defend this letter and your innocence,
   And I, poor fool, will aid in your defense.
   Pretend, pretend, that you are just and true,
   And I shall make myself believe in you.
Célimène. Oh, stop it. Don't be such a jealous dunce,
   Or I shall leave off loving you at once.
   Just why should I *pretend*? What could impel me
   To stoop so low as that? And kindly tell me
   Why, if I loved another, I shouldn't merely

Inform you of it, simply and sincerely!
I've told you where you stand, and that admission
Should altogether clear me of suspicion;
After so generous a guarantee,
What right have you to harbor doubts of me?
Since women are (from natural reticence)
Reluctant to declare their sentiments,
And since the honor of our sex requires
That we conceal our amorous desires,
Ought any man for whom such laws are broken
To question what the oracle has spoken?
Should he not rather feel an obligation
To trust that most obliging declaration?
Enough, now. Your suspicions quite disgust me;
Why should I love a man who doesn't trust me?
I cannot understand why I continue,
Fool that I am, to take an interest in you.
I ought to choose a man less prone to doubt,
And give you something to be vexed about.

Alceste. Ah, what a poor enchanted fool I am;
These gentle words, no doubt, were all a sham,
But destiny requires me to entrust
My happiness to you, and so I must.
I'll love you to the bitter end, and see
How false and treacherous you dare to be.

Célimène. No, you don't really love me as you ought.

Alceste. I love you more than can be said or thought;
Indeed, I wish you were in such distress
That I might show my deep devotedness.
Yes, I could wish that you were wretchedly poor,
Unloved, uncherished, utterly obscure;
That fate had set you down upon the earth
Without possessions, rank, or gentle birth;
Then, by the offer of my heart, I might
Repair the great injustice of your plight;
I'd raise you from the dust, and proudly prove
The purity and vastness of my love.

Célimène. This is a strange benevolence indeed!
God grant that I may never be in need. . . .
Ah, here's Monsieur Dubois, in quaint disguise.

SCENE 4. [*Célimène, Alceste, Dubois*]

Alceste. Well, why this costume? Why those frightened eyes?
  What ails you?
Dubois.   Well, Sir, things are most mysterious.
Alceste. What do you mean?
Dubois.   I fear they're very serious.
Alceste. What?
Dubois.   Shall I speak more loudly?
Alceste.   Yes; speak out.
Dubois. Isn't there someone here, Sir?
Alceste.   Speak, you lout!
  Stop wasting time.
Dubois.   Sir, we must slip away.
Alceste. How's that?
Dubois.   We must decamp without delay.
Alceste. Explain yourself.
Dubois.   I tell you we must fly.
Alceste. What for?
Dubois.   We mustn't pause to say good-by.
Alceste. Now what d'you mean by all of this, you clown?
Dubois. I mean, Sir, that we've got to leave this town.
Alceste. I'll tear you limb from limb and joint from joint
  If you don't come more quickly to the point.
Dubois. Well, Sir, today a man in a black suit,
  Who wore a black and ugly scowl to boot,
  Left us a document scrawled in such a hand
  As even Satan couldn't understand.
  It bears upon your lawsuit, I don't doubt;
  But all hell's devils couldn't make it out.
Alceste. Well, well, go on. What then? I fail to see
  How this event obliges us to flee.
Dubois. Well, Sir, an hour later, hardly more,
  A gentleman who's often called before
  Came looking for you in an anxious way.
  Not finding you, he asked me to convey
  (Knowing I could be trusted with the same)
  The following message. . . . Now, what *was* his name?
Alceste. Forget his name, you idiot. What did he say?
Dubois. Well, it was one of your friends, Sir, anyway.
  He warned you to begone, and he suggested
  That if you stay, you may well be arrested.

Alceste. What? Nothing more specific? Think, man, think!
Dubois. No, Sir. He had me bring him pen and ink,
  And dashed you off a letter which, I'm sure,
  Will render things distinctly less obscure.
Alceste. Well — let me have it!
Célimène.   What *is* this all about?
Alceste. God knows; but I have hopes of finding out.
  How long am I to wait, you blitherer?
Dubois (*after a protracted search for the letter*). I must have left it
  on your table, Sir.
Alceste. I ought to . . .
Célimène.   No, no, keep your self-control;
  Go find out what's behind his rigmarole.
Alceste. It seems that fate, no matter what I do,
  Has sworn that I may not converse with you;
  But, Madam, pray permit your faithful lover
  To try once more before the day is over.

ACT V

SCENE 1. [*Alceste, Philinte*]

Alceste. No, it's too much. My mind's made up, I tell you.
Philinte. Why should this blow, however hard, compel you . . .
Alceste. No, no, don't waste your breath in argument;
  Nothing you say will alter my intent;
  This age is vile, and I've made up my mind
  To have no further commerce with mankind.
  Did not truth, honor, decency, and the laws
  Oppose my enemy and approve my cause?
  My claims were justified in all men's sight;
  I put my trust in equity and right;
  Yet, to my horror and the world's disgrace,
  Justice is mocked, and I have lost my case!
  A scoundrel whose dishonesty is notorious
  Emerges from another lie victorious!
  Honor and right condone his brazen fraud,
  While rectitude and decency applaud!
  Before his smirking face, the truth stands charmed,
  And virtue conquered, and the law disarmed!

His crime is sanctioned by a court decree!
And not content with what he's done to me,
The dog now seeks to ruin me by stating
That I composed a book now circulating,
A book so wholly criminal and vicious
That even to speak its title is seditious!
Meanwhile Oronte, my rival, lends his credit
To the same libelous tale, and helps to spread it!
Oronte! a man of honor and of rank,
With whom I've been entirely fair and frank;
Who sought me out and forced me, willy-nilly,
To judge some verse I found extremely silly;
And who, because I properly refused
To flatter him, or see the truth abused,
Abets my enemy in a rotten slander!
There's the reward of honesty and candor!
The man will hate me to the end of time
For failing to commend his wretched rhyme!
And not this man alone, but all humanity
Do what they do from interest and vanity;
They prate of honor, truth, and righteousness,
But lie, betray, and swindle nonetheless.
Come then: man's villainy is too much to bear;
Let's leave this jungle and this jackal's lair.
Yes! treacherous and savage race of men,
You shall not look upon my face again.

Philinte. Oh, don't rush into exile prematurely;
  Things aren't as dreadful as you make them, surely.
  It's rather obvious, since you're still at large,
  That people don't believe your enemy's charge.
  Indeed, his tale's so patently untrue
  That it may do more harm to him than you.

Alceste. Nothing could do that scoundrel any harm:
  His frank corruption is his greatest charm,
  And, far from hurting him, a further shame
  Would only serve to magnify his name.

Philinte. In any case, his bald prevarication
  Has done no injury to your reputation,
  And you may feel secure in that regard.
  As for your lawsuit, it should not be hard
  To have the case reopened, and contest
  This judgment . . .

Alceste.   No, no, let the verdict rest.
  Whatever cruel penalty it may bring,
  I wouldn't have it changed for anything.
  It shows the times' injustice with such clarity
  That I shall pass it down to our posterity
  As a great proof and signal demonstration
  Of the black wickedness of this generation.
  It may cost twenty thousand francs; but I
  Shall pay their twenty thousand, and gain thereby
  The right to storm and rage at human evil,
  And send the race of mankind to the devil.
Philinte. Listen to me . . .
Alceste.   Why? What can you possibly say?
  Don't argue, Sir; your labor's thrown away.
  Do you propose to offer lame excuses
  For men's behavior and the times' abuses?
Philinte. No, all you say I'll readily concede:
  This is a low, conniving age indeed;
  Nothing but trickery prospers nowadays,
  And people ought to mend their shabby ways.
  Yes, man's a beastly creature; but must we then
  Abandon the society of men?
  Here in the world, each human frailty
  Provides occasion for philosophy,
  And that is virtue's noblest exercise;
  If honesty shone forth from all men's eyes,
  If every heart were frank and kind and just,
  What could our virtues do but gather dust
  (Since their employment is to help us bear
  The villainies of men without despair)?
  A heart well-armed with virtue can endure. . . .
Alceste. Sir, you're a matchless reasoner, to be sure;
  Your words are fine and full of cogency;
  But don't waste time and eloquence on me.
  My reason bids me go, for my own good.
  My tongue won't lie and flatter as it should;
  God knows what frankness it might next commit,
  And what I'd suffer on account of it.
  Pray let me wait for Célimène's return
  In peace and quiet. I shall shortly learn,
  By her response to what I have in view,
  Whether her love for me is feigned or true.

Philinte. Till then, let's visit Éliante upstairs.
Alceste. No, I am too weighed down with somber cares.
  Go to her, do; and leave me with my gloom
  Here in the darkened corner of this room.
Philinte. Why, that's no sort of company, my friend;
  I'll see if Éliante will not descend.

SCENE 2. [*Célimène, Oronte, Alceste*]

Oronte. Yes, Madam, if you wish me to remain
  Your true and ardent lover, you must deign
  To give me some more positive assurance.
  All this suspense is quite beyond endurance.
  If your heart shares the sweet desires of mine,
  Show me as much by some convincing sign;
  And here's the sign I urgently suggest:
  That you no longer tolerate Alceste,
  But sacrifice him to my love, and sever
  All your relations with the man forever.
Célimène. Why do you suddenly dislike him so?
  You praised him to the skies not long ago.
Oronte. Madam, that's not the point. I'm here to find
  Which way your tender feelings are inclined.
  Choose, if you please, between Alceste and me,
  And I shall stay or go accordingly.
Alceste (*emerging from the corner*). Yes, Madam, choose; this gentle-
  man's demand
  Is wholly just, and I support his stand.
  I too am true and ardent; I too am here
  To ask you that you make your feelings clear.
  No more delays, now; no equivocation;
  The time has come to make your declaration.
Oronte. Sir, I've no wish in any way to be
  An obstacle to your felicity.
Alceste. Sir, I've no wish to share her heart with you;
  That may sound jealous, but at least it's true.
Oronte. If, weighing us, she leans in your direction . . .
Alceste. If she regards you with the least affection . . .
Oronte. I swear I'll yield her to you there and then.
Alceste. I swear I'll never see her face again.
Oronte. Now, Madam, tell us what we've come to hear.
Alceste. Madam, speak openly and have no fear.

Oronte. Just say which one is to remain your lover.
Alceste. Just name one name, and it will all be over.
Oronte. What! Is it possible that you're undecided?
Alceste. What! Can your feelings possibly be divided?
Célimène. Enough: this inquisition's gone too far:
  How utterly unreasonable you are!
  Not that I couldn't make the choice with ease;
  My heart has no conflicting sympathies;
  I know full well which one of you I favor,
  And you'd not see me hesitate or waver.
  But how can you expect me to reveal
  So cruelly and bluntly what I feel?
  I think it altogether too unpleasant
  To choose between two men when both are present;
  One's heart has means more subtle and more kind
  Of letting its affections be divined,
  Nor need one be uncharitably plain
  To let a lover know he loves in vain.
Oronte. No, no, speak plainly; I for one can stand it.
  I beg you to be frank.
Alceste.   And I demand it.
  The simple truth is what I wish to know,
  And there's no need for softening the blow.
  You've made an art of pleasing everyone,
  But now your days of coquetry are done:
  You have no choice now, Madam, but to choose,
  For I'll know what to think if you refuse;
  I'll take your silence for a clear admission
  That I'm entitled to my worst suspicion.
Oronte. I thank you for this ultimatum, Sir,
  And I may say I heartily concur.
Célimène. Really, this foolishness is very wearing:
  Must you be so unjust and overbearing?
  Haven't I told you why I must demur?
  Ah, here's Éliante; I'll put the case to her.

SCENE 3. [*Éliante, Philinte, Célimène, Oronte,
Alceste*]

Célimène. Cousin, I'm being persecuted here
  By these two persons, who, it would appear,
  Will not be satisfied till I confess

Which one I love the more, and which the less,
And tell the latter to his face that he
Is henceforth banished from my company.
Tell me, has ever such a thing been done?
Éliante. You'd best not turn to me; I'm not the one
    To back you in a matter of this kind:
    I'm all for those who frankly speak their mind.
Oronte. Madam, you'll search in vain for a defender.
Alceste. You're beaten, Madam, and may as well surrender.
Oronte. Speak, speak, you must; and end this awful strain.
Alceste. Or don't, and your position will be plain.
Oronte. A single word will close this painful scene.
Alceste. But if you're silent, I'll know what you mean.

SCENE 4. [*Arsinoé, Célimène, Éliante, Alceste,*
            Philinte, Acaste, Clitandre, Oronte]

Acaste (to Célimène). Madam, with all due deference, we two
    Have come to pick a little bone with you.
Clitandre (to Oronte and Alceste). I'm glad you're present, Sirs, as
        you'll soon learn,
    Our business here is also your concern.
*Arsinoé (to Célimène).*Madam, I visit you so soon again
    Only because of these two gentlemen,
    Who came to me indignant and aggrieved
    About a crime too base to be believed.
    Knowing your virtue, having such confidence in it,
    I couldn't think you guilty for a minute,
    In spite of all their telling evidence;
    And, rising above our little difference,
    I've hastened here in friendship's name to see
    You clear yourself of this great calumny.
Acaste. Yes, Madam, let us see with what composure
    You'll manage to respond to this disclosure.
    You lately sent Clitandre this tender note.
Clitandre. And this one, for Acaste, you also wrote.
Acaste (to Oronte and Alceste). You'll recognize this writing, Sirs, I
        think;
    The lady is so free with pen and ink
    That you must know it all too well, I fear.
    But listen: this is something you should hear.
        "How absurd you are to condemn my lightheartedness in society,
    and to accuse me of being happiest in the company of others. Noth-

ing could be more unjust; and if you do not come to me instantly
and beg pardon for saying such a thing, I shall never forgive you as
long as I live. Our big bumbling friend the Viscount . . ."
What a shame that he's not here.

"Our big bumbling friend the Viscount, whose name stands first
in your complaint, is hardly a man to my taste; and ever since the
day I watched him spend three-quarters of an hour spitting into a
well, so as to make circles in the water, I have been unable to think
highly of him. As for the little Marquess . . ."
In all modesty, gentlemen, that is I.

"As for the little Marquess, who sat squeezing my hand for such
a long while yesterday, I find him in all respects the most trifling
creature alive; and the only things of value about him are his cape
and his sword. As for the man with the green ribbons . . ."
(*To Alceste.*) It's your turn now, Sir.

"As for the man with the green ribbons, he amuses me now and
then with his bluntness and his bearish ill-humor; but there are
many times indeed when I think him the greatest bore in the world.
And as for the sonneteer . . ."
(*To Oronte.*) Here's your helping.

"And as for the sonneteer, who has taken it into his head to be
witty, and insists on being an author in the teeth of opinion, I
simply cannot be bothered to listen to him, and his prose wearies
me quite as much as his poetry. Be assured that I am not always so
well-entertained as you suppose; that I long for your company, more
than I dare to say, at all these entertainments to which people drag
me; and that the presence of those one loves is the true and perfect
seasoning to all one's pleasures."
Clitandre. And now for me.

"Clitandre, whom you mention, and who so pesters me with his
saccharine speeches, is the last man on earth for whom I could feel
any affection. He is quite mad to suppose that I love him, and so are
you, to doubt that you are loved. Do come to your senses; exchange
your suppositions for his; and visit me as often as possible, to help
me bear the annoyance of his unwelcome attentions."
It's sweet character that these letters show,
And what to call it, Madam, you well know.
Enough. We're off to make the world acquainted
With this sublime self-portrait that you've painted.
Acaste. Madam, I'll make you no farewell oration;
No, you're not worthy of my indignation.
Far choicer hearts than yours, as you'll discover,
Would like this little Marquess for a lover.

SCENE 5. [*Célimène, Éliante, Arsinoé, Alceste,*
Oronte, Philinte]

Oronte. So! After all those loving letters you wrote,
   You turn on me like this, and cut my throat!
   And your dissembling, faithless heart, I find,
   Has pledged itself by turns to all mankind!
   How blind I've been! But now I clearly see;
   I thank you, Madam, for enlightening me.
   My heart is mine once more, and I'm content;
   The loss of it shall be your punishment.

   (*To Alceste.*)

   Sir, she is yours; I'll seek no more to stand
   Between your wishes and this lady's hand.

SCENE 6. [*Célimène, Éliante, Arsinoé, Alceste,*
Philinte]

Arsinoé (*to Célimène*). Madam, I'm forced to speak. I'm far too
      stirred
   To keep my counsel, after what I've heard.
   I'm shocked and staggered by your want of morals.
   It's not my way to mix in others' quarrels;
   But really, when this fine and noble spirit,
   This man of honor and surpassing merit,
   Laid down the offering of his heart before you,
   How *could* you . . .
Alceste.   Madam, permit me, I implore you,
   To represent myself in this debate.
   Don't bother, please, to be my advocate.
   My heart, in any case, could not afford
   To give your services their due reward;
   And if I chose, for consolation's sake,
   Some other lady, 'twould not be you I'd take.
Arsinoé. What makes you think you could, Sir? And how dare you
   Imply that I've been trying to ensnare you?
   If you can for a moment entertain
   Such flattering fancies, you're extremely vain.
   I'm not so interested as you suppose
   In Célimène's discarded gigolos.
   Get rid of that absurd illusion, do.

Women like me are not for such as you.
Stay with this creature, to whom you're so attached;
I've never seen two people better matched.

SCENE 7. [*Célimène, Éliante, Alceste, Philinte*]

Alceste (*to Célimène*). Well, I've been still throughout this exposé,
 Till everyone but me has said his say.
 Come, have I shown sufficient self-restraint?
 And may I now . . .
Célimène.   Yes, make your just complaint.
 Reproach me freely, call me what you will;
 You've every right to say I've used you ill.
 I've wronged you, I confess it; and in my shame
 I'll make no effort to escape the blame.
 The anger of those others I could despise;
 My guilt toward you I sadly recognize.
 Your wrath is wholly justified, I fear;
 I know how culpable I must appear,
 I know all things bespeak my treachery,
 And that, in short, you've grounds for hating me.
 Do so; I give you leave.
Alceste.   Ah, traitress — how,
 How should I cease to love you, even now?
 Though mind and will were passionately bent
 On hating you, my heart would not consent.

 (*To Éliante and Philinte.*)

 Be witness to my madness, both of you;
 See what infatuation drives one to;
 But wait; my folly's only just begun,
 And I shall prove to you before I'm done ⌣
 How strange the human heart is, and how far
 From rational we sorry creatures are.

 (*To Célimène.*)

 Woman, I'm willing to forget your shame,
 And clothe your treacheries in a sweeter name;
 I'll call them youthful errors, instead of crimes,
 And lay the blame on these corrupting times.
 My one condition is that you agree
 To share my chosen fate, and fly with me

To that wild, trackless, solitary place
In which I shall forget the human race.
Only by such a course can you atone
For those atrocious letters; by that alone
Can you remove my present horror of you,
And make it possible for me to love you.

Célimène. What! I renounce the world at my young age,
And die of boredom in some hermitage?

Alceste. Ah, if you really loved me as you ought,
You wouldn't give the world a moment's thought;
Must you have me, and all the world beside?

Célimène. Alas, at twenty one is terrified
Of solitude. I fear I lack the force
And depth of soul to take so stern a course.
But if my hand in marriage will content you,
Why, there's a plan which I might well consent to,
And . . .

Alceste. No, I detest you now. I could excuse
Everything else, but since you thus refuse
To love me wholly, as a wife should do,
And see the world in me, as I in you,
Go! I reject your hand, and disenthrall
My heart from your enchantments, once for all.

SCENE 8. [*Éliante, Alceste, Philinte*]

Alceste (to Éliante). Madam, your virtuous beauty has no peer;
Of all this world you only are sincere;
I've long esteemed you highly, as you know;
Permit me ever to esteem you so,
And if I do not now request your hand,
Forgive me, Madam, and try to understand.
I feel unworthy of it; I sense that fate
Does not intend me for the married state,
That I should do you wrong by offering you
My shattered heart's unhappy residue,
And that in short . . .

Éliante. Your argument's well taken:
Nor need you fear that I shall feel forsaken.
Were I to offer him this hand of mine,
Your friend Philinte, I think, would not decline.

Philinte. Ah, Madam, that's my heart's most cherished goal,
  For which I'd gladly give my life and soul.
Alceste (*to Éliante and Philinte*). May you be true to all you now
    profess,
  And so deserve unending happiness.
  Meanwhile, betrayed and wronged in everything,
  I'll flee this bitter world where vice is king,
  And seek some spot unpeopled and apart
  Where I'll be free to have an honest heart.
Philinte. Come, Madam, let's do everything we can
  To change the mind of this unhappy man.

The introduction to this volume (pp. xx–xxii) makes the rather obvious point that in both tragedy and comedy we have characters who are motivated by some ideal, and that (for example) the tragic hero who hunts out the polluted man in Thebes or who kills his wife because he thinks she is unfaithful is neither more nor less impassioned than the comic lover who writes sonnets to his mistress' eyebrow. Whether the passion is noble or comic depends not on its depth, or its persistence, but on its context, and especially on its object.

The passion for honesty that drives Molière's misanthrope, Alceste, is said by the equable Éliante to have "its noble, heroic side," and her view has found wide acceptance among audiences and readers. Alceste is sometimes seen as a tragic figure caught in a comic world, and the play is sometimes said to be a sort of tragic comedy. Alceste demands honesty, and he fulminates against flattery and other forms of insincerity that apparently compose the entire life of the other figures. Surrounded by trimmers and gossips and worse, he alone (if we except the gentle Éliante) seems to hold to a noble ideal. The only other ideal given much prominence is Philinte's, a code of such easy tolerance that it is at times almost indistinguishable from mere passive acceptance of everything.

What case can be made that Alceste is comic, not tragic? A few points suggest themselves. First, this champion of honesty is in love (or thinks he is) with a coquette. What can be more comic than the apostle of plain-dealing being himself in the power of the irrational, especially when this power deposits him at the feet of Célimène, a woman who employs all the devices that in others infuriate him? Second, his demand for honesty is indiscriminate; he is as offended at trivial courtesies as at the law's injustice. Philinte "ought to die of self-disgust" for his "crime" of effusively greeting a casual acquaintance whose name he cannot even recall. So disproportionate is Alceste's passion that when he pops onstage in IV. ii, saying to Éliante, "Avenge me, Madame," he is funny, though the words in themselves are scarcely amusing. It is worth comparing a few other lines in this scene with some roughly similar lines in *Othello*. Alceste (still talking to Éliante about Célimène's letter to a rival suitor) says, "My world has gone to wrack" ("Ah! tout est ruiné!"). When, early in the play, Brabantio had cautioned Othello that Desdemona might deceive him, Othello had said, "My life upon her faith," and, in the middle of the play "Perdition catch my soul/But I do love thee! And when I love thee not,/Chaos is come again." Later, poisoned by Iago's insinuations, he believes Desdemona is faithless, and chaos comes again as he calls her a devil, banishes her from his sight, and finally suffocates her. But Othello is "the noble Moor," whose nobility is demonstrated early in the play by his language and his actions. And Desdemona, "the divine Desdemona," "the grace of heaven," and "the sweetest innocent/That e'er did lift up eye," demonstrates her worth in every line and deed. On the other hand, Alceste, lacking all sense of proportion, is at the outset surly and evidently funny. In the very first scene his tirade against Philinte's "loving demonstrations" offered to one who is almost a stranger evokes Philinte's good-natured

> It hardly seems a hanging matter to me;
> I hope that you will take it graciously
> If I extend myself·a slight reprieve,
> And live a little longer, by your leave;

but this droll reply acerbates Alceste:

> How dare you joke about a crime so grave?

Alceste is thus laughably introduced; his passion is comic because it is disproportionate — and also because it leads to no action; Othello is heroically introduced (after an initial scene in which he is slandered), and his passion is tragic because it is frightening and pitiable, especially because it leads him to murder an innocent woman who, as he has said, is the center of his being.

Alceste's remark about joking provides a thread that may be followed usefully. He cannot take a joke. Whenever he is laughed at, he becomes indignant, but indignation (when motivated by a desire to protect the self from criticism) itself evokes further laughter because of the gap between the indignant man's presentation of himself and his real worth. Comedy does not allow people to strike attitudes. The man who protests that his argument *is* valid, dammit, or that he *has* a sense of humor, or that his opponent is a fool, is likely to evoke laughter by his monolithic insistence on his merit. When Philinte laughs at the old poem Alceste quotes, Alceste resorts to bitter irony, and when told that his frankness has made him ridiculous, he irritably replies:

> So much the better; just what I wish to hear.
> No news could be more grateful to my ear.
> All men are so detestable in my eyes.
> I should be sorry if they thought me otherwise.

He hopes that he will lose his lawsuit, just to prove that the world *is* as bad as he thinks it is. (An odd psychological state, resembling Master Ford's in Shakespeare's *Merry Wives of Windsor*, whose "God be praised for my jealousy" reveals the comic figure's infatuation with his abnormality.) And when Alceste is told that his hope that he will lose his law suit would reduce all hearers to laughter and would make his name a jest, he ill-humoredly replies, "So much the worse for jesters." When his persistent refusal to praise a trivial poem moves two auditors to laughter, he again employs frigid irony, and concludes the scene ominously:

> By heaven, Sirs, I really didn't know
> That I was being humorous.
> *Célimène.* Go, Sir; go;
> Settle your business.
> *Alceste.* I shall, and when I'm through,
> I shall return to settle things with you.

Alceste, unable to laugh at the folly of others, cannot, of course, tolerate laughter at himself. When Philinte puts into practice the frankness Alceste stormily advocates, Alceste's response is the indignation we have been commenting on. A sense of humor (as distinct from derisive laughter) involves the ability to laugh at what one values, and among the things one values is the self. Children can laugh at surprises and at the distress of other children, but they cannot laugh at themselves because they cannot see themselves in perspective, at a distance, as it were. The mature man can laugh at (for example) mimicry of himself, but the child or the immature adult will, like Alceste, sulk or fly into a rage.

In *The Misanthrope* it is entirely possible that Molière is in some degree mimicking himself. In 1662 Molière at forty married Armande Béjart, a woman less than half his age. The marriage seems to have been unhappy, apparently because his wife enjoyed attracting the attentions of other men. Some critics, pressing this point, assume that if the play is autobiographical, Alceste must be expressing Molière's point of view, and therefore he cannot be a comic figure. If anything, the autobiographic origin shows only that Molière had (which no one has doubted) a sense of humor. He could laugh at himself. Alceste's courtship of Célimène may in some degree represent Molière's unhappy marriage to a flirtatious and unappreciative woman, but the point is that Molière apparently could stand back and laugh at his own exasperation, which Alceste cannot do. (Molière sub-titled the play "The Atrabilious Man in Love"; one cannot hear Alceste speaking thus of himself. Alceste can only, rather childishly, try to maintain his way, and demand that his special merit be noted and rewarded:

> However high the praise, there's nothing worse
> Than sharing honors with the universe.
> Esteem is founded on comparison:
> To honor all men is to honor none.
> Since you embrace this indiscriminate vice,
> Your friendship comes at far too cheap a price;
> I spurn the easy tribute of a heart
> Which will not set the worthy man apart:
> I choose, Sir, to be chosen; and in fine,
> The friend of mankind is no friend of mine.

Once or twice, when he confesses that his love for Célimène is irrational, he seems to have some perspective, but mostly the scenes of Alceste as lover serve to reveal again and again his consuming egotism. His love is so great, he tells Célimène, that he wishes she were in some peril so that he could prove his love by saving her. Célimène aptly replies that Alceste's is "a strange benevolence indeed."

The argument thus far has tried to make the point that Alceste is funny — funny because (among other things) his anger is indiscriminate and disproportionate, because he is a sort of philosopher and yet is in love, and because his *idée fixe*, frankness, when turned against him, exasperates him. But when we return to Éliante's reference to his "noble, heroic side," and we recall his passion for honesty and his passionate desire to be himself, and when we see the hollowness all about him, the comic figure begins to take on a tragic aspect; and when at the end he departs from the stage unrepentant and bitter, banishing himself from the company of men, we feel that the usual comic plot too has taken on a tragic aspect. But this is hardly to say that Alceste is tragic and *The Misanthrope* a tragedy. One cannot, for example, imagine Alceste commiting suicide. He is not an Othello.

Major Barbara

GEORGE BERNARD SHAW

George Bernard Shaw (1856–1950), later famous as Bernard Shaw, was born in Dublin of Anglo-Irish stock. His father drank too much, his mother — something of an Ibsenite "new woman" — went to London to make her way as singer and voice teacher. Shaw worked in a Dublin real estate office for a while (he did not attend a college or university), and then followed his mother to London, where he wrote critical reviews, and five novels (1879–83) before turning playwright. His first play, begun with William Archer (playwright and translator of Ibsen), was abandoned in 1885, and then entirely revised by Shaw into Widowers' Houses (1892). He had already shown, in a critical study entitled The Quintessence of Ibsenism *(1891), that he regarded the stage as a pulpit and soap box; before the nineteenth century was over, he wrote nine more plays, in order (he said) to espouse socialism effectively.* Major Barbara *(1905) is his comic masterpiece, but at least a dozen of his plays have established themselves in the repertoire, including one tragedy,* Saint Joan *(1924).*

ACT I

It is after dinner in January 1906, in the library in Lady Britomart Undershaft's house in Wilton Crescent. A large and comfortable settee is in the middle of the room, upholstered in dark leather. A person sitting on it (it is vacant at present) would have, on his right, Lady Britomart's writing table, with the lady herself busy at it; a smaller writing table behind him on his left; the door behind him on Lady Britomart's side; and a window with a window seat directly on his left. Near the window is an armchair.

Lady Britomart is a woman of fifty or thereabouts, well dressed and yet careless of her dress, well bred and quite reckless of her breeding, well mannered and yet appallingly outspoken and indifferent to the opinion of her interlocutors, amiable and yet peremptory, arbitrary, and high-tempered to the last bearable degree, and withal a very typical managing matron of the upper class, treated as a naughty child until she grew into a scolding mother, and finally settling down with plenty of practical ability and worldly experience, limited in the oddest way with domestic and class limitations, conceiving the universe exactly as if it were a large house in Wilton Crescent, though handling her corner of it very effectively on that assumption, and being quite enlightened and liberal as to the books in the library, the pictures on the walls, and the music in the portfolios, and the articles in the papers.

Her son, Stephen, comes in. He's a gravely correct young man under 25, taking himself very seriously, but still in some awe of his

Major Barbara by Bernard Shaw is reprinted with the permission of the Public Trustee and The Society of Authors.

mother, from childish habit and bachelor shyness rather than from any weakness of character.

Stephen. Whats the matter?
Lady Britomart. Presently, Stephen.

(*Stephen submissively walks to the settee and sits down. He takes up a Liberal weekly called The Speaker.*)

Lady Britomart. Dont begin to read, Stephen. I shall require all your attention.

Stephen. It was only while I was waiting —

Lady Britomart. Dont make excuses, Stephen. (*He puts down The Speaker*). Now! (*She finishes her writing; rises; and comes to the settee*). I have not kept you waiting very long, I think.

Stephen. Not at all, mother.

Lady Britomart. Bring me my cushion. (*He takes the cushion from the chair at the desk and arranges it for her as she sits down on the settee*). Sit down. (*He sits down and fingers his tie nervously*). Don't fiddle with your tie, Stephen: there is nothing the matter with it.

Stephen. I beg your pardon. (*He fiddles with his watch chain instead*).

Lady Britomart. Now are you attending to me, Stephen?

Stephen. Of course, mother.

Lady Britomart. No: it's not of course. I want something much more than your everyday matter-of-course attention. I am going to speak to you very seriously, Stephen. I wish you would let that chain alone.

Stephen (*hastily relinquishing the chain*) Have I done anything to annoy you, mother? If so, it was quite unintentional.

Lady Britomart (*astonished*) Nonsense! (*With some remorse*) My poor boy, did you think I was angry with you?

Stephen. What is it, then, mother? You are making me very uneasy.

Lady Britomart (*squaring herself at him rather aggressively*) Stephen: may I ask how soon you intend to realize that you are a grown-up man, and that I am only a woman?

Stephen (*amazed*) Only a —

Lady Britomart. Dont repeat my words, please: it is a most aggravating habit. You must learn to face life seriously, Stephen. I really cannot bear the whole burden of our family affairs any longer. You must advise me: you must assume the responsibility.

Stephen. I!

Lady Britomart. Yes, you, of course. You were 24 last June. Youve been at Harrow and Cambridge. Youve been to India and Japan.

You must know a lot of things, now; unless you have wasted your time most scandalously. Well, advise me.

Stephen (*much perplexed*) You know I have never interfered in the household —

Lady Britomart. No: I should think not. I dont want you to order the dinner.

Stephen. I mean in our family affairs.

Lady Britomart. Well, you must interfere now; for they are getting quite beyond me.

Stephen (*troubled*) I have thought sometimes that perhaps I ought; but really, mother, I know so little about them; and what I do know is so painful! it is so impossible to mention some things to you — (*he stops, ashamed*).

Lady Britomart. I suppose you mean your father.

Stephen (*almost inaudibly*) Yes.

Lady Britomart. My dear: we cant go on all our lives not mentioning him. Of course you were quite right not to open the subject until I asked you to; but you are old enough now to be taken into my confidence, and to help me to deal with him about the girls.

Stephen. But the girls are all right. They are engaged.

Lady Britomart (*complacently*) Yes: I have made a very good match for Sarah. Charles Lomax will be a millionaire at 35. But that is ten years ahead and in the meantime his trustees cannot under the terms of his father's will allow him more than £800 a year.

Stephen. But the will says also that if he increases his income by his own exertions, they may double the increase.

Lady Britomart. Charles Lomax's exertions are much more likely to decrease his income than to increase it. Sarah will have to find at least another £800 a year for the next ten years; and even then they will be as poor as church mice. And what about Barbara? I thought Barbara was going to make the most brilliant career of all of you. And what does she do? Joins the Salvation Army; discharges her maid; lives on a pound a week; and walks in one evening with a professor of Greek whom she has picked up in the street, and who pretends to be a Salvationist, and actually plays the big drum for her in public because he has fallen head over ears in love with her.

Stephen. I was certainly rather taken aback when I heard they were engaged. Cusins is a very nice fellow, certainly: nobody would ever guess that he was born in Australia; but —

Lady Britomart. Oh, Adolphus Cusins will make a very good husband. After all, nobody can say a word against Greek: it stamps a man at once as an educated gentleman. And my family, thank Heaven, is not a pig-headed Tory one. We are Whigs, and believe in liberty. Let snobbish people say what they please: Barbara shall marry, not the man they like, but the man *I* like.

Stephen. Of course I was thinking only of his income. However, he is not likely to be extravagant.

Lady Britomart. Dont be too sure of that, Stephen. I know your quiet, simple, refined, poetic people like Adolphus: quite content with the best of everything! They cost more than your extravagant people, who are always as mean as they are second rate. No: Barbara will need at least £2000 a year. You see it means two additional households. Besides, my dear, you must marry soon. I dont approve of the present fashion of philandering bachelors and late marriages; and I am trying to arrange something for you.

Stephen. It's very good of you, mother; but perhaps I had better arrange that for myself.

Lady Britomart. Nonsense! you are much too young to begin matchmaking: you would be taken in by some pretty little nobody. Of course I dont mean that you are not to be consulted: you know that as well as I do. (*Stephen closes his lips and is silent*). Now dont sulk, Stephen.

Stephen. I am not sulking, mother. What has all this got to do with — with — my father?

Lady Britomart. My dear Stephen: where is the money to come from? It is easy enough for you and the other children to live on my income as long as we are in the same house; but I cant keep four families in four separate houses. You know how poor my father is: he has barely seven thousand a year now; and really, if he were not the Earl of Stevenage, he would have to give up society. He can do nothing for us. He says, naturally enough, that it is absurd that he should be asked to provide for the children of a man who is rolling in money. You see, Stephen, your father must be fabulously wealthy, because there is always a war going on somewhere.

Stephen. You need not remind me of that, mother. I have hardly ever opened a newspaper in my life without seeing our name in it. The Undershaft torpedo! The Undershaft quick firers! The Undershaft ten inch! the Undershaft disappearing rampart gun! the Undershaft submarine! and now the Undershaft aerial battleship! At Harrow they called me the Woolwich Infant. At Cambridge it was the same. A little brute at King's who was always trying to get up revivals, spoilt my Bible — your first birthday present to me — by writing under my name, 'Son and heir to Undershaft and Lazarus, Death and Destruction Dealers: address Christendom and Judea.'

But that was not so bad as the way I was kowtowed to everywhere because my father was making millions by selling cannons.

Lady Britomart. It is not only the cannons, but the war loans that Lazarus arranges under cover of giving credit for the cannons. You know, Stephen, it's perfectly scandalous. Those two men, Andrew Undershaft and Lazarus, positively have Europe under their thumbs. That is why your father is able to behave as he does. He is above the law. Do you think Bismarck or Gladstone or Disraeli could have openly defied every social and moral obligation all their lives as your father has? They simply wouldnt have dared. I asked Gladstone to take it up. I asked The Times to take it up. I asked the Lord Chamberlain to take it up. But it was just like asking them to declare war on the Sultan. They wouldnt. They said they couldnt touch him. I believe they were afraid.

Stephen. What could they do? He does not actually break the law.

Lady Britomart. Not break the law! He is always breaking the law. He broke the law when he was born: his parents were not married.

Stephen. Mother! Is that true?

Lady Britomart. Of course it's true: that was why we separated.

Stephen. He married without letting you know this!

Lady Britomart (*rather taken aback by this inference*) Oh no. To do Andrew justice, that was not the sort of thing he did. Besides, you know the Undershaft motto: Unashamed. Everybody knew.

Stephen. But you said that was why you separated.

Lady Britomart. Yes, because he was not content with being a foundling himself: he wanted to disinherit you for another foundling. That was what I couldnt stand.

Stephen (*ashamed*) Do you mean for — for — for —

Lady Britomart. Dont stammer, Stephen. Speak distinctly.

Stephen. But this is so frightful to me, mother. To have to speak to you about such things!

Lady Britomart. It's not pleasant for me, either, especially if you are still so childish that you must make it worse by a display of embarrassment. It is only in the middle classes, Stephen, that people get into a state of dumb helpless horror when they find that there are wicked people in the world. In our class, we have to decide what is to be done with wicked people; and nothing should disturb our self-possession. Now ask your question properly.

Stephen. Mother: have you no consideration for me? For Heaven's sake either treat me as a child, as you always do, and tell me nothing at all; or tell me everything and let me take it as best I can.

Lady Britomart. Treat you as a child! What do you mean? It is most unkind and ungrateful of you to say such a thing. You know I have never treated any of you as children. I have always made you my companions and friends, and allowed you perfect freedom to do and say whatever you liked, so long as you liked what I could approve of.

Stephen (*desperately*) I daresay we have been the very imperfect children of a very perfect mother; but I do beg you to let me alone for once, and tell me about this horrible business of my father wanting to set me aside for another son.

Lady Britomart (*amazed*) Another son! I never said anything of the kind. I never dreamt of such a thing. This is what comes of interrupting me.

Stephen. But you said —

Lady Britomart (*cutting him short*) Now be a good boy, Stephen, and listen to me patiently. The Undershafts are descended from a foundling in the parish of St Andrew Undershaft in the city. That was long ago, in the reign of James the First. Well this foundling was adopted by an armorer and gun-maker. In the course of time the foundling succeeded to the business; and from some notion of gratitude, or some vow or something, he adopted another foundling, and left the business to him. And that foundling did the same. Ever since that, the cannon business has always been left to an adopted foundling named Andrew Undershaft.

Stephen. But did they never marry? Were there no legitimate sons?

Lady Britomart. Oh yes: they married just as your father did; and they were rich enough to buy land for their own children and leave them well provided for. But they always adopted and trained some foundling to succeed them in the business; and of course they always quarrelled with their wives furiously over it. Your father was adopted in that way; and he pretends to consider himself bound to keep up the tradition and adopt somebody to leave the business to. Of course I was not going to stand that. There may have been some reason for it when the Undershafts could only marry women in their own class, whose sons were not fit to govern great estates. But there could be no excuse for passing over my son.

Stephen (*dubiously*) I am afraid I should make a poor hand of managing a cannon foundry.

Lady Britomart. Nonsense! you could easily get a manager and pay him a salary.

Stephen. My father evidently had no great opinion of my capacity.

Lady Britomart. Stuff, child! you were only a baby: it had nothing to do with your capacity. Andrew did it on principle, just as he did every perverse and wicked thing on principle. When my father remonstrated, Andrew actually told him to his face that history tells us of only two successful institutions: one the Undershaft firm, and the other the Roman Empire under the Antonines. That was because the Antonine emperors all adopted their successors. Such rubbish! The Stevenages are as good as the Antonines, I hope; and you are a Stevenage. But that was Andrew all over. There you have the man! Always clever and unanswerable when he was defending nonsense and wickedness: always awkward and sullen when he had to behave sensibly and decently!

Stephen. Then it was on my account that your home life was broken up, mother. I am sorry.

Lady Britomart. Well, dear, there were other differences. I really cannot bear an immoral man. I am not a Pharisee, I hope; and I should not have minded his merely doing wrong things: we are none of us perfect. But your father didnt exactly do wrong things: he said them and thought them: that was what was so dreadful. He really had a sort of religion of wrongness. Just as one doesnt mind men practising immorality so long as they own that they are in the wrong by preaching morality; so I couldn't forgive Andrew for preaching immorality while he practised morality. You would all have grown up without principles, without any knowledge of right and wrong, if he had been in the house. You know, my dear, your father was a very attractive man in some ways. Children did not dislike him; and he took advantage of it to put the wickedest ideas into their heads, and make them quite unmanageable. I did not dislike him myself: very far from it; but nothing can bridge over moral disagreement.

Stephen. All this simply bewilders me, mother. People may differ about matters of opinion, or even about religion; but how can they differ about right and wrong? Right is right; and wrong is wrong; and if a man cannot distinguish them properly, he is either a fool or a rascal: thats all.

Lady Britomart (*touched*) Thats my own boy (*she pats his cheek*)! Your father never could answer that: he used to laugh and get out of it under cover of some affectionate nonsense. And now that you understand the situation, what do you advise me to do?

Stephen. Well, what can you do?

Lady Britomart. I must get the money somehow.

Stephen. We cannot take money from him. I had rather go and live in some cheap place like Bedford Square or even Hampstead than take a farthing of his money.

Lady Britomart. But after all, Stephen, our present income comes from Andrew.

Stephen (shocked) I never knew that.

Lady Britomart. Well, you surely didnt suppose your grandfather had anything to give me. The Stevenages could not do everything for you. We gave you social position. Andrew had to contribute something. He had a very good bargain, I think.

Stephen (bitterly) We are utterly dependent on him and his cannons, then?

Lady Britomart. Certainly not: the money is settled. But he provided it. So you see it is not a question of taking money from him or not: it is simply a question of how much. I don't want any more for myself.

Stephen. Nor do I.

Lady Britomart. But Sarah does; and Barbara does. That is, Charles Lomax and Adolphus Cusins will cost them more. So I must put my pride in my pocket and ask for it, I suppose. That is your advice, Stephen, is it not?

Stephen. No.

Lady Britomart (sharply) Stephen!

Stephen. Of course if you are determined —

Lady Britomart. I am not determined: I ask your advice; and I am waiting for it. I will not have all the responsibility thrown on my shoulders.

Stephen (obstinately) I would die sooner than ask him for another penny.

Lady Britomart (resignedly) You mean that *I* must ask him. Very well, Stephen: it shall be as you wish. You will be glad to know that your grandfather concurs. But he thinks I ought to ask Andrew to come here and see the girls. After all, he must have some natural affection for them.

Stephen. Ask him here!!!

Lady Britomart. Do not repeat my words, Stephen. Where else can I ask him?

Stephen. I never expected you to ask him at all.

Lady Britomart. Now dont tease, Stephen. Come! you see that it is necessary that he should pay us a visit, dont you?

Stephen (reluctantly) I suppose so, if the girls cannot do without his money.

Lady Britomart. Thank you, Stephen: I knew you would give me the right advice when it was properly explained to you. I have asked your father to come this evening. (*Stephen bounds from his seat*). Dont jump, Stephen: it fidgets me.

Stephen (in utter consternation) Do you mean to say that my father is coming here tonight — that he may be here at any moment?

Lady Britomart (*looking at her watch*) I said nine. (*He gasps. She rises*). Ring the bell, please. (*Stephen goes to the smaller writing table; presses a button on it; and sits at it with his elbows on the table and his head in his hands, outwitted and overwhelmed*). It is ten minutes to nine yet; and I have to prepare the girls. I asked Charles Lomax and Adolphus to dinner on purpose that they might be here. Andrew had better see them in case he should cherish any delusions as to their being capable of supporting their wives. (*The butler enters: Lady Britomart goes behind the settee to speak to him*). Morrison: go up to the drawing room and tell everybody to come down here at once. (*Morrison withdraws. Lady Britomart turns to Stephen*). Now remember, Stephen: I shall need all your countenance and authority. (*He rises and tries to recover some vestige of these attributes*). Give me a chair, dear. (*He pushes a chair forward from the wall to where she stands, near the smaller writing table. She sits down; and he goes to the armchair, into which he throws himself*). I dont know how Barbara will take it. Ever since they made her a major in the Salvation Army she has developed a propensity to have her own way and order people about which quite cows me sometimes. It's not ladylike: I'm sure I dont know where she picked it up. Anyhow, Barbara shant bully me; but still it's just as well that your father should be here before she has time to refuse to meet him or make a fuss. Dont look nervous, Stephen: it will only encourage Barbara to make difficulties. *I* am nervous enough, goodness knows; but I dont shew it.

(*Sarah and Barbara come in with their respective young men, Charles Lomax and Adolphus Cusins. Sarah is slender, bored, and mundane. Barbara is robuster, jollier, much more energetic. Sarah is fashionably dressed: Barbara is in Salvation Army uniform. Lomax, a young man about town, is like many other young men about town. He is afflicted with a frivolous sense of humor which plunges him at the most inopportune moments into paroxysms of imperfectly suppressed laughter. Cusins is a spectacled student, slight, thin haired, and sweet voiced, with a more complex form of Lomax's complaint. His sense of humor is intellectual and subtle, and is complicated by an appalling temper. The lifelong struggle of a benevolent temperament and a high conscience against impulses of inhuman ridicule and fierce impatience has set up a chronic strain which has visibly wrecked his constitution. He is a most implacable, determined, tenacious, intolerant person who by mere force of character presents himself as — and indeed actually is — considerate, gentle, explanatory, even mild and apologetic, capable possibly of* murder, but not of cruelty or coarseness. *By the operation of some instinct which is not merciful enough to blind him with the illusions of love, he is obstinately bent on marrying Barbara. Lomax likes Sarah and thinks it will be rather a lark to marry her. Consequently he has not attempted to resist Lady Britomart's arrangements to that end.*

All four look as if they had been having a good deal of fun in the drawing room. The girls enter first, leaving the swains outside. Sarah comes to the settee. Barbara comes in after her and stops at the door.)

Barbara. Are Cholly and Dolly to come in?

Lady Britomart (forcibly) Barbara: I will not have Charles called Cholly: the vulgarity of it positively makes me ill.

Barbara. It's all right, mother: Cholly is quite correct nowadays. Are they to come in?

Lady Britomart. Yes, if they will behave themselves.

Barbara (through the door) Come in, Dolly; and behave yourself.

(*Barbara comes to her mother's writing table. Cusins enters smiling, and wanders towards Lady Britomart.*)

Sarah (calling) Come in, Cholly. (*Lomax enters, controlling his features very imperfectly, and places himself vaguely between Sarah and Barbara*).

Lady Britomart (peremptorily) Sit down, all of you. (*They sit. Cusins crosses to the window and seats himself there. Lomax takes a chair. Barbara sits at the writing table and Sarah on the settee*). I dont in the least know what you are laughing at, Adolphus. I am surprised at you, though I expected nothing better from Charles Lomax.

Cusins (in a remarkably gentle voice) Barbara has been trying to teach me the West Ham Salvation March.

Lady Britomart. I see nothing to laugh at in that; nor should you if you are really converted.

Cusins (sweetly) You were not present. It was really funny, I believe.

Lomax. Ripping.

Lady Britomart. Be quiet, Charles. Now listen to me, children. Your father is coming here this evening.

(*General stupefaction. Lomax, Sarah, and Barbara rise: Sarah scared, and Barbara amused and expectant.*)

Lomax (remonstrating) Oh I say!

Lady Britomart. You are not called on to say anything, Charles.

Sarah. Are you serious, mother?

Lady Britomart. Of course I am serious. It is on your account, Sarah, and also on Charles's. (*Silence. Sarah sits, with a shrug. Charles looks painfully unworthy*). I hope you are not going to object, Barbara.

Barbara. I! why should I? My father has a soul to be saved like anybody else. He's quite welcome as far as I am concerned. (*She sits on the table, and softly whistles 'Onward, Christian Soldiers'*).

Lomax (*still remonstrant*) But really, dont you know! Oh I say!

Lady Britomart (*frigidly*) What do you wish to convey, Charles?

Lomax. Well, you must admit that this is a bit thick.

Lady Britomart (*turning with ominous suavity to Cusins*) Adolphus: you are a professor of Greek. Can you translate Charles Lomax's remarks into reputable English for us?

Cusins (*cautiously*) If I may say so, Lady Brit, I think Charles has rather happily expressed what we all feel. Homer, speaking of Autolycus, uses the same phrase. πυκινὸν δόμον ἐλθεῖν means a bit thick.

Lomax (*handsomely*) Not that I mind, you know, if Sarah dont. (*He sits*).

Lady Britomart (*crushingly*) Thank you. Have I your permission, Adolphus, to invite my own husband to my own house?

Cusins (*gallantly*) You have my unhesitating support in everything you do.

Lady Britomart. Tush! Sarah: have you nothing to say?

Sarah. Do you mean that he is coming regularly to live here?

Lady Britomart. Certainly not. The spare room is ready for him if he likes to stay for a day or two and see a little more of you; but there are limits.

Sarah. Well, he cant eat us, I suppose. *I* dont mind.

Lomax (*chuckling*) I wonder how the old man will take it.

Lady Britomart. Much as the old woman will, no doubt, Charles.

Lomax (*abashed*) I didnt mean — at least —

Lady Britomart. You didnt think, Charles. You never do; and the result is, you never mean anything. And now please attend to me, children. Your father will be quite a stranger to us.

Lomax. I suppose he hasnt seen Sarah since she was a little kid.

Lady Britomart. Not since she was a little kid. Charles, as you express it with that elegance of diction and refinement of thought that seem never to desert you. Accordingly — er — (*impatiently*) Now I have forgotten what I was going to say. That comes of your provoking me to be sarcastic, Charles. Adolphus: will you kindly tell me where I was.

Cusins (*sweetly*) You were saying that as Mr Undershaft has not seen his children since they were babies, he will form his opinion of the way you have brought them up from their behavior tonight, and that therefore you wish us all to be particularly careful to conduct ourselves well, especially Charles.

Lady Britomart (*with emphatic approval*) Precisely.

Lomax. Look here, Dolly: Lady Brit didnt say that.

Lady Britomart (*vehemently*) I did, Charles. Adolphus's recollection is perfectly correct. It is most important that you should be good; and I do beg you for once not to pair off into opposite corners and giggle and whisper while I am speaking to your father.

Barbara. All right, mother. We'll do you credit. (*She comes off the table, and sits in her chair with ladylike elegance*).

Lady Britomart. Remember, Charles, that Sarah will want to feel proud of you instead of ashamed of you.

Lomax. Oh I say! theres nothing to be exactly proud of, dont you know.

Lady Britomart. Well, try and look as if there was.

(*Morrison, pale and dismayed, breaks into the room in unconcealed disorder.*)

Morrison. Might I speak a word to you, my lady?

Lady Britomart. Nonsense! Shew him up.

Morrison. Yes, my lady. (*He goes*).

Lomax. Does Morrison know who it is?

Lady Britomart. Of course. Morrison has always been with us.

Lomax. It must be a regular corker for him, dont you know.

Lady Britomart. Is this a moment to get on my nerves, Charles, with your outrageous expressions?

Lomax. But this is something out of the ordinary, really —

Morrison (*at the door*) The — er — Mr Undershaft. (*He retreats in confusion*).

(*Andrew Undershaft comes in. All rise. Lady Britomart meets him in the middle of the room behind the settee.*

Andrew is, on the surface, a stoutish, easygoing elderly man, with kindly patient manners, and an engaging simplicity of character. But he has a watchful, deliberate, waiting, listening face, and formidable reserves of power, both bodily and mental, in his capacious chest and long head. His gentleness is partly that of a strong man who has learnt by experience that his natural grip hurts ordinary people unless he handles them very carefully, and partly the mellowness of age and success. He is also a little shy in his present very delicate situation.)

Lady Britomart. Good evening, Andrew.

Undershaft. How d'ye do, my dear.

Lady Britomart. You look a good deal older.

Undershaft (apologetically) I am somewhat older. (*Taking her hand with a touch of courtship*) Time has stood still with you.

Lady Britomart (throwing away his hand) Rubbish! This is your family.

Undershaft (surprised) Is it so large? I am sorry to say my memory is failing very badly in some things. (*He offers his hand with paternal kindness to Lomax*).

Lomax (jerkily shaking his hand) Ahdedoo.

Undershaft. I can see you are my eldest. I am very glad to meet you again, my boy.

Lomax (remonstrating) No, but look here dont you know — (*Overcome*) Oh I say!

Lady Britomart (recovering from momentary speechlessness) Andrew: do you mean to say that you dont remember how many children you have?

Undershaft. Well, I am afraid I —. They have grown so much — er. Am I making any ridiculous mistake? I may as well confess: I recollect only one son. But so many things have happened since, of course — er —

Lady Britomart (decisively) Andrew: you are talking nonsense. Of course you have only one son.

Undershaft. Perhaps you will be good enough to introduce me, my dear.

Lady Britomart. That is Charles Lomax, who is engaged to Sarah.

Undershaft. My dear sir, I beg your pardon.

Lomax. Notatall. Delighted, I assure you.

Lady Britomart. This is Stephen.

Undershaft (bowing) Happy to make your acquaintance, Mr Stephen. Then (*going to Cusins*) you must be my son. (*Taking Cusins' hands in his*) How are you, my young friend? (*To Lady Britomart*) He is very like you, my love.

Cusins. You flatter me, Mr Undershaft. My name is Cusins: engaged to Barbara. (*Very explicitly*) That is Major Barbara Undershaft, of the Salvation Army. That is Sarah, your second daughter. This is Stephen Undershaft, your son.

Undershaft. My dear Stephen, I beg your pardon.

Stephen. Not at all.

Undershaft. Mr Cusins: I am much indebted to you for explaining so precisely. (*Turning to Sarah*) Barbara, my dear —

Sarah (prompting him) Sarah.

Undershaft. Sarah, of course. (*They shake hands. He goes over to Barbara*) Barbara — I am right this time, I hope?

Barbara. Quite right. (*They shake hands*).

Lady Britomart (*resuming command*) Sit down, all of you. Sit down, Andrew. (*She comes forward and sits on the settee. Cusins also brings his chair forward on her left. Barbara and Stephen resume their seats. Lomax gives his chair to Sarah and goes for another*).

Undershaft. Thank you, my love.

Lomax (*conversationally, as he brings a chair forward between the writing table and the settee, and offers it to Undershaft*) Takes you some time to find out exactly where you are, dont it?

Undershaft (*accepting the chair, but remaining standing*) That is not what embarrasses me, Mr Lomax. My difficulty is that if I play the part of a father, I shall produce the effect of an intrusive stranger; and if I play the part of a discreet stranger, I may appear a callous father.

Lady Britomart. There is no need for you to play any part at all, Andrew. You had much better be sincere and natural.

Undershaft (*submissively*) Yes, my dear: I daresay that will be best. (*He sits down comfortably*). Well, here I am. Now what can I do for you all?

Lady Britomart. You need not do anything, Andrew. You are one of the family. You can sit with us and enjoy yourself.

(*A painfully conscious pause. Barbara makes a face at Lomax, whose too long suppressed mirth immediately explodes in agonized neighings.*)

Lady Britomart (*outraged*) Charles Lomax: if you can behave yourself, behave yourself. If not, leave the room.

Lomax. I'm awfully sorry, Lady Brit; but really you know, upon my soul! (*He sits on the settee between Lady Britomart and Undershaft, quite overcome*).

Barbara. Why dont you laugh if you want to, Cholly? It's good for your inside.

Lady Britomart. Barbara: you have had the education of a lady. Please let your father see that; and dont talk like a street girl.

Undershaft. Never mind me, my dear. As you know, I am not a gentleman; and I was never educated.

Lomax (*encouragingly*) Nobody'd know it, I assure you. You look all right, you know.

Cusins. Let me advise you to study Greek, Mr Undershaft. Greek scholars are privileged men. Few of them know Greek; and none of them know anything else; but their position is unchallengeable. Other languages are the qualifications of waiters and commercial travellers: Greek is to a man of position what the hallmark is to silver.

Barbara. Dolly: dont be insincere. Cholly: fetch your concertina and play something for us.

Lomax (jumps up eagerly, but checks himself to remark doubtfully to Undershaft) Perhaps that sort of thing isnt in your line, eh?

Undershaft. I am particularly fond of music.

Lomax (delighted) Are you? Then I'll get it. (*He goes upstairs for the instrument*).

Undershaft. Do you play, Barbara?

Barbara. Only the tambourine. But Cholly's teaching me the concertina.

Undershaft. Is Cholly also a member of the Salvation Army?

Barbara. No: he says it's bad form to be a dissenter. But I dont despair of Cholly. I made him come yesterday to a meeting at the dock gates, and take the collection in his hat.

Undershaft (looks whimsically at his wife)!!

Lady Britomart. It is not my doing, Andrew. Barbara is old enough to take her own way. She has no father to advise her.

Barbara. Oh yes she has. There are no orphans in the Salvation Army.

Undershaft. Your father there has a great many children and plenty of experience, eh?

Barbara (looking at him with quick interest and nodding) Just so. How did you come to understand that? (*Lomax is heard at the door trying the concertina*).

Lady Britomart. Come in, Charles. Play us something at once.

Lomax. Righto! (*He sits down in his former place, and preludes*).

Undershaft. One moment, Mr Lomax. I am rather interested in the Salvation Army. Its motto might be my own: Blood and Fire.

Lomax (shocked) But not your sort of blood and fire, you know.

Undershaft. My sort of blood cleanses: my sort of fire purifies.

Barbara. So do ours. Come down tomorrow to my shelter — the West Ham shelter — and see what we're doing. We're going to march to a great meeting in the Assembly Hall at Mile End. Come and see the shelter and then march with us: it will do you a lot of good. Can you play anything?

Undershaft. In my youth I earned pennies, and even shillings occasionally, in the streets and in public house parlors by my natural talent for stepdancing. Later on, I became a member of the Undershaft orchestral society, and performed passably on the tenor trombone.

Lomax (scandalized — putting down the concertina) Oh I say!

Barbara. Many a sinner has played himself into heaven on the trombone, thanks to the Army.

Lomax (to Barbara, still rather shocked) Yes; but what about the cannon business, dont you know? (*To Undershaft*) Getting into heaven is not exactly in your line, is it?

Lady Britomart. Charles!!!

Lomax. Well; but it stands to reason, dont it? The cannon business may be necessary and all that: we cant get on without cannons; but it isnt right, you know. On the other hand, there may be a certain amount of tosh about the Salvation Army — I belong to the Established Church myself — but still you cant deny that it's religion; and you cant go against religion, can you? At least unless youre downright immoral, dont you know.

Undershaft. You hardly appreciate my position, Mr Lomax —

Lomax (hastily) I'm not saying anything against you personally —

Undershaft. Quite so, quite so. But consider for a moment. Here I am, a profiteer in mutilation and murder. I find myself in a specially amiable humor just now because, this morning, down at the foundry, we blew twenty-seven dummy soldiers into fragments with a gun which formerly destroyed only thirteen.

Lomax (leniently) Well, the more destructive war becomes, the sooner it will be abolished, eh?

Undershaft. Not at all. The more destructive war becomes the more fascinating we find it. No, Mr Lomax: I am obliged to you for making the usual excuse for my trade; but I am not ashamed of it. I am not one of those men who keep their morals and their business in watertight compartments. All the spare money my trade rivals spend on hospitals, cathedrals, and other receptacles for conscience money, I devote to experiments and researches in improved methods of destroying life and property. I have always done so; and I always shall. Therefore your Christmas card moralities of peace on earth and goodwill among men are of no use to me. Your Christianity, which enjoins you to resist not evil, and to turn the other cheek, would make me a bankrupt. My morality — my religion — must have a place for cannons and torpedoes in it.

Stephen (coldly — almost sullenly) You speak as if there were half a dozen moralities and religions to choose from, instead of one true morality and one true religion.

Undershaft. For me there is only one true morality; but it might not fit you, as you do not manufacture aerial battleships. There is only one true morality for every man; but every man has not the same true morality.

Lomax (*overtaxed*) Would you mind saying that again? I didnt quite follow it.

Cusins. It's quite simple. As Euripides says, one man's meat is another man's poison morally as well as physically.

Undershaft. Precisely.

Lomax. Oh, that! Yes, yes, yes. True. True.

Stephen. In other words, some men are honest and some are scoundrels.

Barbara. Bosh! There are no scoundrels.

Undershaft. Indeed? Are there any good men?

Barbara. No. Not one. There are neither good men nor scoundrels: there are just children of one Father; and the sooner they stop calling one another names the better. You neednt talk to me: I know them. Ive had scores of them through my hands: scoundrels, criminals, infidels, philanthropists, missionaries, county councillors, all sorts. Theyre all just the same sort of sinner; and theres the same salvation ready for them all.

Undershaft. May I ask have you ever saved a maker of cannons?

Barbara. No. Will you let me try?

Undershaft. Well, I will make a bargain with you. If I go to see you tomorrow in your Salvation Shelter, will you come the day after to see me in my cannon works?

Barbara. Take care. It may end in your giving up the cannons for the sake of the Salvation Army.

Undershaft. Are you sure it will not end in your giving up the Salvation Army for the sake of the cannons?

Barbara. I will take my chance of that.

Undershaft. And I will take my chance of the other. (*They shake hands on it*). Where is your shelter?

Barbara. In West Ham. At the sign of the cross. Ask anybody in Canning Town. Where are your works?

Undershaft. In Perivale St Andrews. At the sign of the sword. Ask anybody in Europe.

Lomax. Hadnt I better play something?

Barbara. Yes. Give us Onward, Christian Soldiers.

Lomax. Well, thats rather a strong order to begin with, dont you know. Suppose I sing Thourt passing hence, my brother. It's much the same tune.

Barbara. It's too melancholy. You get saved, Cholly; and youll pass hence, my brother, without making such a fuss about it.

Lady Britomart. Really, Barbara, you go on as if religion were a pleasant subject. Do have some sense of propriety.

Undershaft. I do not find it an unpleasant subject, my dear. It is the only one that capable people really care for.

Lady Britomart (*looking at her watch*) Well, if you are determined to have it, I insist on having it in a proper and respectable way. Charles: ring for prayers.

(*General amazement. Stephen rises in dismay.*)

Lomax (*rising*) Oh I say!

Undershaft (*rising*) I am afraid I must be going.

Lady Britomart. You cannot go now, Andrew: it would be most improper. Sit down. What will the servants think?

Undershaft. My dear: I have conscientious scruples. May I suggest a compromise? If Barbara will conduct a little service in the drawing room, with Mr Lomax as organist, I will attend it willingly. I will even take part, if a trombone can be procured.

Lady Britomart. Dont mock, Andrew.

Undershaft (*shocked — to Barbara*) You dont think I am mocking, my love, I hope.

Barbara. No, of course not; and it wouldnt matter if you were: half the Army came to their first meeting for a lark. (*Rising*) Come along. (*She throws her arm round her father and sweeps him out, calling to the others from the threshold*) Come, Dolly. Come, Cholly.

(*Cusins rises.*)

Lady Britomart. I will not be disobeyed by everybody. Adolphus: sit down. (*He does not*). Charles: you may go. You are not fit for prayers: you cannot keep your countenance.

Lomax. Oh I say! (*He goes out*).

Lady Britomart (*continuing*) But you, Adolphus, can behave yourself if you choose to. I insist on your staying.

Cusins. My dear Lady Brit: there are things in the family prayer book that I couldnt bear to hear you say.

Lady Britomart. What things, pray?

Cusins. Well, you would have to say before all the servants that we have done things we ought not to have done, and left undone things we ought to have done, and that there is no health in us. I cannot bear to hear you doing yourself such an injustice, and Barbara such an injustice. As for myself, I flatly deny it: I have done my best. I shouldnt dare to marry Barbara — I couldnt look you in the face — if it were true. So I must go to the drawing room.

Lady Britomart (*offended*) Well, go. (*He starts for the door*). And remember this, Adolphus (*he turns to listen*): I have a very strong suspicion that you went to the Salvation Army to worship Barbara and nothing else. And I quite appreciate the very clever way in which you systematically humbug me. I have found you out. Take care Barbara doesnt. Thats all.

Cusins (*with unruffled sweetness*) Dont tell on me. (*He steals out*).

Lady Britomart. Sarah: if you want to go, go. Anything's better than to sit there as if you wished you were a thousand miles away.

Sarah (*languidly*) Very well, mamma. (*She goes*).

(*Lady Britomart, with a sudden flounce, gives way to a little gust of tears.*)

Stephen (*going to her*) Mother: whats the matter?

Lady Britomart (*swishing away her tears with her handkerchief*) Nothing. Foolishness. You can go with him, too, if you like, and leave me with the servants.

Stephen. Oh, you mustnt think that, mother. I — I dont like him.

Lady Britomart. The others do. That is the injustice of a woman's lot. A woman has to bring up her children; and that means to restrain them, to deny them things they want, to set them tasks, to punish them when they do wrong, to do all the unpleasant things. And then the father, who has nothing to do but pet them and spoil them, comes in when all her work is done and steals their affection from her.

Stephen. He has not stolen our affection from you. It is only curiosity.

Lady Britomart (*violently*) I wont be consoled, Stephen. There is nothing the matter with me. (*She rises and goes towards the door*).

Stephen. Where are you going, mother?

Lady Britomart. To the drawing room, of course. (*She goes out. Onward, Christian Soldiers, on the concertina, with tambourine accompaniment, is heard when the door opens*). Are you coming, Stephen?

Stephen. No. Certainly not. (*She goes. He sits down on the settee, with compressed lips and an expression of strong dislike*).

ACT II

The yard of the West Ham shelter of the Salvation Army is a cold place on a January morning. The building itself, an old warehouse, is newly whitewashed. Its gabled end projects into the yard in the middle, with a door on the ground floor, and another in the loft above it without any balcony or ladder, but with a pulley rigged over it for hoisting sacks. Those who come from this central gable end into the yard have the gateway leading to the street on their left, with a stone horse-trough just beyond it, and, on the right, a penthouse shielding a table from the weather. There are forms at the table; and on them are seated a man and a woman, both much down on their luck, finish-

ing a meal of bread (one thick slice each, with margarine and golden syrup) and diluted milk.

The man, a workman out of employment, is young, agile, a talker, a poser, sharp enough to be capable of anything in reason except honesty or altruistic considerations of any kind. The woman is a commonplace old bundle of poverty and hard-worn humanity. She looks sixty and probably is forty-five. If they were rich people, gloved and muffed and well wrapped up in furs and overcoats, they would be numbed and miserable; for it is a grindingly cold raw January day; and a glance at the background of grimy warehouses and leaden sky visible over the whitewashed walls of the yard would drive any idle rich person straight to the Mediterranean. But these two, being no more troubled with visions of the Mediterranean than of the moon, and being compelled to keep more of their clothes in the pawnshop, and less on their persons, in winter than in summer, are not depressed by the cold: rather are they stung into vivacity, to which their meal has just now given an almost jolly turn. The man takes a pull at his mug, and then gets up and moves about the yard with his hands deep in his pockets, occasionally breaking into a stepdance.

The Woman. Feel better arter your meal, sir?

The Man. No. Call that a meal! Good enough for you, praps; but wot is it to me, an intelligent workin man.

The Woman. Workin man! Wot are you?

The Man. Painter.

The Woman (*sceptically*) Yus, I dessay.

The Man. Yus, you dessay! I know. Every loafer that cant do nothink calls isself a painter. Well, I'm a real painter: grainer, finisher, thirty-eight bob a week when I can get it.

The Woman. Then why dont you go and get it?

The Man. I'll tell you why. Fust: I'm intelligent — fffff! it's rotten cold here (*he dances a step or two*) — yes: intelligent beyond the station o life into which it has pleased the capitalists to call me; and they dont like a man that sees through em. Second, an intelligent bein needs a doo share of appiness; so I drink somethink cruel when I get the chawnce. Third, I stand by my class and do as little as I can so's to leave arf the job for me fellow workers. Fourth, I'm fly enough to know wots inside the law and wots outside it; and inside it I do as the capitalists do: pinch wot I can lay me ands on. In a proper state of society I am sober, industrious and honest: in Rome, so to speak, I do as the Romans do. Wots the consequence? When trade is bad — and it's rotten bad just now — and the employers az to sack arf their men, they generally start on me.

The Woman. Whats your name?

The Man. Price. Bronterre O'Brien Price. Usually called Snobby Price, for short.

The Woman. Snobby's a carpenter, aint it? You said you was a painter.

Price. Not that kind of snob, but the genteel sort. I'm too uppish, owing to my intelligence, and my father being a Chartist and a reading, thinking man: a stationer, too. I'm none of your common hewers of wood and drawers of water; and dont you forget it. (*He returns to his seat at the table, and takes up his mug*). Wots your name?

The Woman. Rummy Mitchens, sir.

Price (*quaffing the remains of his milk to her*) Your elth, Miss Mitchens.

Rummy (*correcting him*) Missis Mitchens.

Price. Wot! Oh Rummy, Rummy! Respectable married woman, Rummy, gittin rescued by the Salvation Army by pretendin to be a bad un. Same old game!

Rummy. What am I to do? I cant starve. Them Salvation lasses is dear good girls; but the better you are, the worse they likes to think you were before they rescued you. Why shouldnt they av a bit o credit, poor loves? theyre worn to rags by their work. And where would they get the money to rescue us if we was to let on we're no worse than other people? You know what ladies and gentlemen are.

Price. Thievin swine! Wish I ad their job, Rummy, all the same. Wot does Rummy stand for? Pet name praps?

Rummy. Short for Romola.

Price. For wot!?

Rummy. Romola. It was out of a new book. Somebody me mother wanted me to grow up like.

Price. We're companions in misfortune, Rummy. Both on us got names that nobody cawnt pronounce. Consequently I'm Snobby and youre Rummy because Bill and Sally wasnt good enough for our parents. Such is life!

Rummy. Who saved you, Mr Price? Was it Major Barbara?

Price. No: I come here on my own. I'm going to be Bronterre O'Brien Price, the converted painter. I know wot they like. I'll tell em how I blasphemed and gambled and wopped my poor old mother —

Rummy (*shocked*) Used you to beat your mother?

Price. Not likely. She used to beat me. No matter: you come and listen to the converted painter, and youll hear how she was a pious woman that taught me me prayers at er knee, an how I used to come home drunk and drag her out o bed be er snow white airs, an lam into er with the poker.

Rummy. Thats whats so unfair to us women. Your confessions is just as big lies as ours: you dont tell what you really done no more than us; but you men can tell your lies right out at the meetins and be made much of for it; while the sort o confessions we az to make az to be wispered to one lady at a time. It ain't right, spite of all their piety.

Price. Right! Do you spose the Army'd be allowed if it went and did right? Not much. It combs our air and makes us good little blokes to be robbed and put upon. But I'll play the game as good as any of em. I'll see somebody struck by lightnin, or hear a voice sayin 'Snobby Price: where will you spend eternity?' I'll av a time of it, I tell you.

Rummy. You wont be let drink, though.

Price. I'll take it out in gorspellin, then. I dont want to drink if I can get fun enough any other way.

(*Jenny Hill, a pale, overwrought, pretty Salvation lass of 18, comes in through the yard gate, leading Peter Shirley, a half hardened, half worn-out elderly man, weak with hunger.*)

Jenny (*supporting him*) Come! pluck up. I'll get you something to eat. Youll be all right then.

Price (*rising and hurrying officiously to take the old man off Jenny's hands*) Poor old man! Cheer up, brother: youll find rest and peace and appiness ere. Hurry up with the food, miss: e's fair done. (*Jenny hurries into the shelter*). Ere, buck up, daddy! she's fetchin y'a thick slice o breadn treacle, an a mug o skyblue. (*He seats him at the corner of the table*).

Rummy (*gaily*) Keep up your old art! Never say die!

Shirley. I'm not an old man. I'm ony 46. I'm as good as ever I was. The grey patch come in my hair before I was thirty. All it wants is three pennorth o hair dye: am I to be turned on the streets to starve for it? Holy God! Ive worked ten to twelve hours a day since I was thirteen, and paid my way all through; and now am I to be thrown into the gutter and my job given to a young man that can do it no better than me because Ive black hair that goes white at the first change?

Price (*cheerfully*) No good jawrin about it. Youre ony a jumped-up, jerked-off, orspittle-turned-out incurable of an ole workin man: who cares about you? Eh? Make the thievin swine give you a meal: theyve stole many a one from you. Get a bit o your own back. (*Jenny returns with the usual meal*). There you are, brother. Awsk a blessin an tuck that into you.

Shirley (looking at it ravenously but not touching it, and crying like a child) I never took anything before.

Jenny (petting him) Come, come! the Lord sends it to you: he wasnt above taking bread from his friends; and why should you be? Besides, when we find you a job you can pay us for it if you like.

Shirley (eagerly) Yes, yes: thats true. I can pay you back: it's only a loan. *(Shivering)* Oh Lord! oh Lord! *(He turns to the table and attacks the meal ravenously)*.

Jenny. Well, Rummy, are you more comfortable now?

Rummy. God bless you, lovely! youve fed my body and saved my soul, havnt you? *(Jenny, touched, kisses her)*. Sit down and rest a bit: you must be ready to drop.

Jenny. Ive been going hard since morning. But theres more work than we can do. I mustnt stop.

Rummy. Try a prayer for just two minutes. Youll work all the better after.

Jenny (her eyes lighting up) Oh isnt it wonderful how a few minutes prayer revives you! I was quite lightheaded at twelve o'clock, I was so tired; but Major Barbara just sent me to pray for five minutes; and I was able to go on as if I had only just begun. *(To Price)* Did you have a piece of bread?

Price (with unction) Yes, miss; but Ive got the piece that I value more; and thats the peace that passeth hall hannerstennin.

Rummy (fervently) Glory Hallelujah!

(Bill Walker, a rough customer of about 25, appears at the yard gate and looks malevolently at Jenny.)

Jenny. That makes me so happy. When you say that, I feel wicked for loitering here. I must get to work again.

(She is hurrying to the shelter, when the new-comer moves quickly up to the door and intercepts her. His manner is so threatening that she retreats as he comes at her truculently, driving her down the yard.)

Bill. Aw knaow you. Youre the one that took awy maw girl. Youre the one that set er agen me. Well, I'm gowin to ev er aht. Not that Aw care a carse for er or you: see? Bat Aw'll let er knaow; and Aw'll let you knaow. Aw'm gowing to give her a doin thatll teach er to cat awy from me. Nah in wiv you and tell er to cam aht afore Aw cam in and kick er aht. Tell er Bill Walker wants er. She'll knaow wot thet means; and if she keeps me witin itll be worse. You stop to jawr beck at me; and Aw'll stawt on you: d'ye eah? Theres your wy. In you gow. *(He takes her by the arm and slings her towards the door of the shelter. She falls on her hand and knee. Rummy helps her up again).*

Price (*rising, and venturing irresolutely towards Bill*) Easy there, mate. She aint doin you no arm.

Bill. Oo are you callin mite? (*Standing over him threateningly*) Youre gowing to stend ap for er, aw yer? Put ap your ends.

Rummy (*running indignantly to him to scold him*) Oh, you great brute — (*He instantly swings his left hand back against her face. She screams and reels back to the trough, where she sits down, covering her bruised face with her hands and rocking herself and moaning with pain).*

Jenny (*going to her*) Oh, God forgive you! How could you strike an old woman like that?

Bill (*seizing her by the hair so violently that she also screams, and tearing her away from the old woman*) You Gawd forgimme again an Aw'll Gawk forgive you one on the jawr thetll stop you pryin for a week. (*Holding her and turning fiercely on Price*) ·Ev you ennything to sy agen it?

Price (*intimidated*) No, matey: she aint anything to do with me.

Bill. Good job for you! Aw'd pat two meals into you and fawt you with one finger arter, you stawved cur. (*To Jenny*) Nah are you gowin to fetch aht Mog Ebbijem; or em Aw to knock your fice off you and fetch her meself?

Jenny (*writhing in his grasp*) Oh please someone go in and tell Major Barbara — (*she screams again as he wrenches her head down; and Price and Rummy flee into the shelter).*

Bill. You want to gow in and tell your Mijor of me, do you?

Jenny. Oh please dont drag my hair. Let me go.

Bill. Do you or downt you? (*She stifles a scream*). Yus or nao?

Jenny. God give me strength —

Bill (*striking her with his fist in the face*) Gow an shaow her thet, and tell her if she wants one lawk it to cam and interfere with me. (*Jenny, crying with pain, goes into the shed. He goes to the form and addresses the old man*). Eah: finish your mess; an git aht o maw wy.

Shirley (*springing up and facing him fiercely, with the mug in his hand*) You take a liberty with me, and I'll smash you over the face with the mug and cut your eye out. Aint you satisfied — young whelps like you — with takin the bread out o the mouths of your elders that have brought you up and slaved for you, but you must come shovin and cheekin and bullyin in here, where the bread o charity is sickenin in our stummicks?

Bill (*contemptuously, but backing a little*) Wot good are you, you aold palsy mag? Wot good are you?

Shirley. As good as you and better. I'll do a day's work agen you or any fat young soaker of your age. Go and take my job at Horrockses, where I worked for ten year. They want young men there: they cant afford to keep men over forty-five. Theyre very sorry — give you a character and happy to help you to get anything suited to your years — sure a steady man wont be long out of a job. Well, let em try you. Theyll find the differ. What do you know? Not as much as how to beeyave yourself — layin your dirty fist across the mouth of a respectable woman!

Bill. Downt provowk me to ly it acrost yours: d'ye eah?

Shirley (*with blighting contempt*) Yes: you like an old man to hit, dont you, when youve finished with the women. I aint seen you hit a young one yet.

Bill (*stung*) You loy, you aold soupkitchener, you. There was a yang menn eah. Did Aw offer to itt him or did Aw not?

Shirley. Was he starvin or was he not? Was he a man or only a crosseyed thief an a loafer? Would you hit my son-in-law's brother?

Bill. Oo's ee?

Shirley. Todger Fairmile o Balls Pond. Him that won £20 off the Japanese wrastler at the music hall by standin out 17 minutes 4 seconds agen him.

Bill (*sullenly*) Aw'm nao music awl wrastler. Ken he box?

Shirley. Yes: an you cant.

Bill. Wot! Aw cawnt, cawnt Aw? Wots thet you sy (*threatening him*)?

Shirley (*not budging an inch*) Will you box Todger Fairmile if I put him on to you? Say the word.

Bill (*subsiding with a slouch*) Aw'll stend ap to enny menn alawy, if he was ten Todger Fairmawls. But Aw dont set ap to be a perfeshnal.

Shirley (*looking down on him with unfathomable disdain*) You box! Slap an old woman with the back o your hand! You hadnt even the sense to hit her where a magistrate couldnt see the mark of it, you silly young lump of conceit and ignorance. Hit a girl in the jaw and ony make her cry! If Todger Fairmile'd done it, she wouldnt a got up inside o ten minutes, no more than you would if he got on to you. Yah! I'd set about you myself if I had a week's feedin in me instead o two months' starvation. (*He turns his back on him and sits down moodily at the table*).

Bill (*following him and stooping over him to drive the taunt in*) You loy! youve the bread and treacle in you that you cam eah to beg.

Shirley (*bursting into tears*) Oh God! it's true: I'm only an old pauper on the scrap heap. (*Furiously*) But youll come to it yourself; and then youll know. Youll come to it sooner than a teetotaller like me, fillin yourself with gin at this hour o the mornin!

Bill. Aw'm nao gin drinker, you oald lawr; bat wen Aw want to give my girl a bloomin good awdin Aw lawk to ev a bit o devil in me: see? An eah Aw emm, talkin to a rotten aold blawter like you sted o givin her wot for. (*Working himself into a rage*) Aw'm gowin in there to fetch her aht. (*He makes vengefully for the shelter door*).

Shirley. Youre going to the station on a stretcher, more likely; and theyll take the gin and the devil out of you there when they get you inside. You mind what youre about: the major here is the Earl o Stevenage's granddaughter.

Bill (*checked*) Garn!

Shirley. Youll see.

Bill (*his resolution oozing*) Well, Aw aint dan nathin to er.

Shirley. Spose she said you did! who'd believe you?

Bill (*very uneasy, skulking back to the corner of the penthouse*) Gawd! theres no jastice in this cantry. To think wot them people can do! Aw'm as good as er.

Shirley. Tell her so. It's just what a fool like you would do.

(*Barbara, brisk and businesslike, comes from the shelter with a note book, and addresses herself to Shirley. Bill, cowed, sits down in the corner of a form, and turns his back on them.*)

Barbara. Good morning.

Shirley (*standing up and taking off his hat*) Good morning, miss.

Barbara. Sit down: make yourself at home. (*He hesitates; but she puts a friendly hand on his shoulder and makes him obey*). Now then! since youve made friends with us, we want to know all about you. Names and addresses and trades.

Shirley. Peter Shirley. Fitter. Chucked out two months ago because I was too old.

Barbara (*not at all surprised*) Youd pass still. Why didnt you dye your hair?

Shirley. I did. Me age come out at a coroner's inquest on me daughter.

Barbara. Steady?

Shirley. Teetotaller. Never out of a job before. Good worker. And sent to the knackers like an old horse!

Barbara. No matter: if you did your part God will do his.

Shirley (*suddenly stubborn*) My religion's no concern of anybody but myself.

Barbara (*guessing*) I know. Secularist?

Shirley (*hotly*) Did I offer to deny it?

Barbara. Why should you? My own father's a Secularist, I think. Our Father — yours and mine — fulfills himself in many ways; and I daresay he knew what he was about when he made a Secularist of you. So buck up, Peter! we can always find a job for a steady man like you. (*Shirley, disarmed and a little bewildered, touches his hat. She turns from him to Bill*). Whats your name?

Bill (*insolently*) Wots thet to you?

Barbara (*calmly making a note*) Afraid to give his name. Any trade?

Bill. Oo's afride to give is nime? (*Doggedly, with a sense of heroically defying the House of Lords in the person of Lord Stevenage*) If you want to bring a chawge agen me, bring it. (*She waits, unruffled*). Moy nime's Bill Walker.

Barbara (*as if the name were familiar: trying to remember how*) Bill Walker? (*Recollecting*) Oh, I know: youre the man that Jenny Hill was praying for inside just now. (*She enters his name in her note book*).

Bill. Oo's Jenny Ill? And wot call as she to pry for me?

Barbara. I dont know. Perhaps it was you that cut her lip.

Bill (*defiantly*) Yus, it was me that cat her lip. Aw aint afride o you.

Barbara. How could you be, since youre not afraid of God? Youre a brave man, Mr Walker. It takes some pluck to do our work here; but none of us dare lift our hand against a girl like that, for fear of her father in heaven.

Bull (*sullenly*) I want nan o your kentin jawr. I spowse you think Aw cam eah to beg from you, like this demmiged lot eah. Not me. Aw downt want your bread and scripe and ketlep. Aw dont blieve in your Gawd, no more than you do yourself.

Barbara (*sunnily apologetic and ladylike, as on a new footing with him*) Oh, I beg your pardon for putting your name down, Mr Walker. I didnt understand. I'll strike it out.

Bill (*taking this as a slight, and deeply wounded by it*) Eah! you let maw nime alown. Aint it good enaff to be in your book?

Barbara (*considering*) Well, you see, theres no use putting down your name unless I can do something for you, is there? Whats your trade?

Bill (*still smarting*) Thets nao concern o yours.

Barbara. Just so. (*Very businesslike*) I'll put you down as (*writing*) the man who — struck — poor little Jenny Hill — in the mouth.

Bill (*rising threateningly*) See eah. Awve ed enaff o this.

Barbara (*quite sunny and fearless*) What did you come to us for?

Bill. Aw cam for maw gel, see? Aw cam to tike her aht o this and to brike er jawr for er.

Barbara (*complacently*) You see I was right about your trade. (*Bill, on the point of retorting furiously, finds himself, to his great shame and terror, in danger of crying instead. He sits down again sud-denly*). Whats her name?

Bill (*dogged*) Er nime's Mog Ebbijem: thets wot her nime is.

Barbara. Mog Habbijam! Oh, she's gone to Canning Town, to our barracks there.

Bill (*fortified by his resentment of Mog's perfidy*) Is she? (*Vindic-tively*) Then Aw'm gowing to Kennintahn arter her. (*He crosses to the gate; hesitates; finally comes back at Barbara*). Are you loyin to me to git shat o me?

Barbara. I dont want to get shut of you. I want to keep you here and save your soul. Youd better stay: youre going to have a bad time today, Bill.

Bill. Oo's gowing to give it to me? You, preps?

Barbara. Someone you dont believe in. But youll be glad afterwards.

Bill (*slinking off*) Aw'll gow to Kennintahn to be aht o reach o your tangue. (*Suddenly turning on her with intense malice*) And if Aw dSwnt fawnd Mog there, Aw'll cam beck and do two years for you, selp me Gawd if Aw downt!

Barbara (*a shade kindlier, if possible*) It's no use, Bill. She's got an-other bloke.

Bill. Wot!

Barbara. One of her own converts. He fell in love with her when he saw her with her soul saved, and her face clean, and her hair washed.

Bill (*surprised*) Wottud she wash it for, the carroty slat? It's red.

Barbara. It's quite lovely now, because she wears a new look in her eyes with it. It's a pity youre too late. The new bloke has put your nose out of joint, Bill.

Bill. Aw'll put his nowse aht o joint for him. Not that Aw care a carse for er, mawnd thet. But Aw'll teach her to drop me as if Aw was dirt. And Aw'll teach him to meddle with maw judy. Wots iz bleedin nime?

Barbara. Sergeant Todger Fairmile.

Shirley (*rising with grim joy*) I'll go with him, miss. I want to see them two meet. I'll take him to the infirmary when it's over.

Bill (*to Shirley, with undissembled misgiving*) Is thet im you was speakin on?

Shirley. Thats him.

Bill. Im that wrastled in the music awl?

Shirley. The competitions at the National Sportin Club was worth nigh a hundred a year to him. He's gev em up now for religion; so he's a bit fresh for want of the exercise he was accustomed to. He'll be glad to see you. Come along.

Bill. Wots is wight?

Shirley. Thirteen four. (*Bill's last hope expires*).

Barbara. Go and talk to him, Bill. He'll convert you.

Shirley. He'll convert your head into a mashed potato.

Bill (*sullenly*) Aw aint afride of im. Aw aint afride of ennybody. Bat e can lick me. She's dan me. (*He sits down moodily on the edge of the horse trough*).

Shirley. You aint going. I thought not. (*He resumes his seat*).

Barbara (*calling*) Jenny!

Jenny (*appearing at the shelter door with a plaster on the corner of her mouth*) Yes, Major.

Barbara. Send Rummy Mitchens out to clear away here.

Jenny. I think she's afraid.

Barbara (*her resemblance to her mother flashing out for a moment*) Nonsense! she must do as she's told.

Jenny (*calling into the shelter*) Rummy: the Major says you must come.

(*Jenny comes to Barbara, purposely keeping on the side next Bill, lest he should suppose that she shrank from him or bore malice.*)

Barbara. Poor little Jenny! Are you tired? (*Looking at the wounded cheek*) Does it hurt?

Jenny. No: it's all right now. It was nothing.

Barbara (*critically*) It was as hard as he could hit, I expect. Poor Bill! You dont feel angry with him, do you?

Jenny. Oh no, no, no: indeed I dont, Major, bless his poor heart!

(*Barbara kisses her; and she runs away merrily into the shelter. Bill writhes with an agonizing return of his new and alarming symptoms, but says nothing. Rummy Mitchens comes from the shelter*).

Barbara (*going to meet Rummy*) Now Rummy, bustle. Take in those mugs and plates to be washed; and throw the crumbs about for the birds.

(*Rummy takes the three plates and mugs; but Shirley takes back his mug from her, as there is still some milk left in it.*)

Rummy. There aint any crumbs. This aint a time to waste good bread on birds.

Price (*appearing at the shelter door*) Gentleman come to see the shelter, Major. Says he's your father.

Barbara. All right. Coming. (*Snobby goes back into the shelter, followed by Barbara*).

Rummy (*stealing across to Bill and addressing him in a subdued voice, but with intense conviction*) I'd av the lor of you, you flat eared

pignosed potwalloper, if she'd let me. Youre no gentleman, to hit
a lady in the face. (*Bill, with greater things moving in him, takes no
notice*).

Shirley (*following her*) Here! in with you and dont get yourself into
more trouble by talking.

Rummy (*with hauteur*) I aint ad the pleasure o being hintroduced to
you, as I can remember. (*She goes into the shelter with the plates*).

Shirley. Thats the —

Bill (*savagely*) Downt you talk to me, d'ye eah? You lea me alown,
or Aw'll do you a mischief. Aw'm not dirt under your feet, ennywy.

Shirley (*calmly*) Dont you be afeerd. You aint such prime company
that you need expect to be sought after. (*He is about to go into the
shelter when Barbara comes out, with Undershaft on her right*).

Barbara. Oh, there you are, Mr Shirley! (*Between them*) This is my
father: I told you he was a Secularist, didn't I? Perhaps youll be
able to comfort one another.

Undershaft (*startled*) A Secularist! Not the least in the world: on the
contrary, a confirmed mystic.

Barbara. Sorry, I'm sure. By the way, papa, what is your religion? in
case I have to introduce you again.

Undershaft. My religion? Well, my dear, I am a Millionaire. That is
my religion.

Barbara. Then I'm afraid you and Mr Shirley wont be able to comfort
one another after all. Youre not a Millionaire, are you, Peter?

Shirley. No; and proud of it.

Undershaft (*gravely*) Poverty, my friend, is not a thing to be proud of.

Shirley (*angrily*) Who made your millions for you? Me and my like.
Whats kep us poor? Keepin you rich. I wouldnt have your conscience, not for all your income.

Undershaft. I wouldnt have your income, not for all your conscience,
Mr Shirley. (*He goes to the penthouse and sits down on a form*)

Barbara (*stopping Shirley adroitly as he is about to retort*) You
wouldnt think he was my father, would you, Peter? Will you go
into the shelter and lend the lasses a hand for a while: we're worked
off our feet.

Shirley (*bitterly*) Yes: I'm in their debt for a meal, aint I?

Barbara. Oh, not because youre in their debt, but for love of them,
Peter, for love of them. (*He cannot understand, and is rather scandalized*) There! dont stare at me. In with you; and give that conscience of yours a holiday (*bustling him into the shelter*).

Shirley (*as he goes in*) Ah! it's a pity you never was trained to use
your reason, miss. Youd have been a very taking lecturer on
Secularism.

(*Barbara turns to her father.*)

Undershaft. Never mind me, my dear. Go about your work; and let me watch it for a while.

Barbara. All right.

Undershaft. For instance, whats the matter with that outpatient over there?

Barbara (*looking at Bill, whose attitude has never changed, and whose expression of brooding wrath has deepened*) Oh, we shall cure him in no time. Just watch. (*She goes over to Bill and waits. He glances up at her and casts his eyes down again, uneasy, but grimmer than ever*). It would be nice to just stamp on Mog Habbijam's face, wouldnt it, Bill?

Bill (*starting up from the trough in consternation*) It's a loy: Aw never said so. (*She shakes her head*). Oo taold you wot was in moy mawnd?

Barbara. Only your new friend.

Bill. Wot new friend?

Barbara. The devil, Bill. When he gets round people they get miserable, just like you.

Bill (*with a heartbreaking attempt at devil-may-care cheerfulness*) Aw aint miserable. (*He sits down again, and stretches his legs in an attempt to seem indifferent*).

Barbara. Well, if youre happy, why dont you look happy, as we do?

Bill (*his legs curling back in spite of him*) Aw'm eppy enaff, Aw tell you. Woy cawnt you lea me alown? Wot ev I dan to you? Aw aint smashed your fice, ev Aw?

Barbara (*softly: wooing his soul*) It's not me thats getting at you, Bill.

Bill. Oo else is it?

Barbara. Somebody that doesnt intend you to smash women's faces, I suppose. Somebody or something that wants to make a man of you.

Bill (*blustering*) Mike a menn o me! Aint Aw a menn? eh? Oo sez Aw'm not a menn?

Barbara. Theres a man in you somewhere, I suppose. But why did he let you hit poor little Jenny Hill? That wasnt very manly of him, was it?

Bill (*tormented*) Ev dan wiv it, Aw tell you. Chack it. Aw'm sick o your Jenny Ill and er silly little fice.

Barbara. Then why do you keep thinking about it? Why does it keep coming up against you in your mind? Youre not getting converted, are you?

Bill (*with conviction*) Not ME. Not lawkly.

Barbara. Thats right, Bill. Hold out against it. Put out your strength.

Dont lets get you cheap. Todger Fairmile said he wrestled for three nights against his salvation harder than he ever wrestled with the Jap at the music hall. He gave in to the Jap when his arm was going to break. But he didnt give in to his salvation until his heart was going to break. Perhaps youll escape that. You havnt any heart, have you?

Bill. Wot d'ye mean? Woy aint Aw got a awt the sime as ennybody else?

Barbara. A man with a heart wouldnt have bashed poor little Jenny's face, would he?

Bill (almost crying) Ow, will you lea me alown? Ev Aw ever offered to meddle with you, that you cam neggin and provowkin me lawk this? (*He writhes convulsively from his eyes to his toes*).

Barbara (with a steady soothing hand on his arm and a gentle voice that never lets him go) It's your soul thats hurting you, Bill, and not me. Weve been through it all ourselves. Come with us, Bill. (*He looks wildly round*). To brave manhood on earth and eternal glory in heaven. (*He is on the point of breaking down*). Come. (*A drum is heard in the shelter; and Bill, with a gasp, escapes from the spell as Barbara turns quickly. Adolphus enters from the shelter with a big drum*). Oh! there you are, Dolly. Let me introduce a new friend of mine, Mr Bill Walker. This is my bloke, Bill: Mr Cusins. (*Cusins salutes with his drumstick*).

Bill. Gowin to merry im?

Barbara. Yes.

Bill (fervently) Gawd elp im! Gaw-aw-aw-awd elp im!

Barbara. Why? Do you think he wont be happy with me?

Bill. Awve aony ed to stend it for a mawnin: e'll ev to stend it for a lawftawm.

Cusins. That is a frightful reflection, Mr Walker. But I cant tear myself away from her.

Bill. Well, Aw ken. (*To Barbara*) Eah! do you knaow where Aw'm gowin to, and wot Aw'm gowin to do?

Barbara. Yes: youre going to heaven; and youre coming back here before the week's out to tell me so.

Bill. You loy. Aw'm gowin to Kennintahn, to spit in Todger Fairmawl's eye. Aw beshed Jenny Ill's fice; an nar Aw'll git me aown fice beshed and cam beck and shaow it to er. Ee'll itt me ardern Aw itt her. Thatll mike us square. (*To Adolphus*) Is thet fair or is it not? Youre a genlmn: you oughter knaow.

Barbara. Two black eyes wont make one white one, Bill.

Bill. Aw didnt awst you. Cawnt you never keep your mahth shat? Oy awst the genlmn.

Cusins (*reflectively*) Yes: I think youre right, Mr Walker. Yes: I should do it. It's curious: it's exactly what an ancient Greek would have done.

Barbara. But what good will it do?

Cusins. Well, it will give Mr Fairmile some exercise; and it will satisfy Mr Walker's soul.

Bill. Rot! there aint nao sach a thing as a saoul. Ah kin you tell wevver Awve a saoul or not? You never seen it.

Barbara. Ive seen it hurting you when you went against it.

Bill (*with compressed aggravation*) If you was maw gel and took the word aht o me mahth lawk thet, Aw'd give you sathink youd feel urtin, Aw would. (*To Adolphus*) You tike maw tip, mite. Stop er jawr; or youll doy afoah your tawm (*With intense expression*) Wore aht: thets wot youll be: wore aht. (*He goes away through the gate*).

Cusins (*looking after him*) I wonder!

Barbara. Dolly! (*indignant, in her mother's manner*).

Cusins. Yes, my dear, it's very wearing to be in love with you. If it lasts, I quite think I shall die young.

Barbara. Should you mind?

Cusins. Not at all. (*He is suddenly softened, and kisses her over the drum, evidently not for the first time, as people cannot kiss over a big drum without practice. Undershaft coughs*).

Barbara. It's all right papa, weve not forgotten you. Dolly: explain the place to papa: I havnt time. (*She goes busily into the shelter*).

(*Undershaft and Adolphus now have the yard to themselves. Undershaft, seated on a form, and still keenly attentive, looks hard at Adolphus. Adolphus looks hard at him.*)

Undershaft. I fancy you guess something of what is in my mind, Mr Cusins. (*Cusins flourishes his drumsticks as if in the act of beating a lively rataplan, but makes no sound*). Exactly so. But suppose Barbara finds you out!

Cusins. You know, I do not admit that I am imposing on Barbara. I am quite genuinely interested in the views of the Salvation Army. The fact is, I am a sort of collector of religions; and the curious thing is that I find I can believe them all. By the way, have you any religion?

Undershaft. Yes.

Cusins. Anything out of the common?

Undershaft. Only that there are two things necessary to Salvation.

Cusins (*disappointed, but polite*) Ah, the Church Catechism. Charles Lomax also belongs to the Established Church.

Undershaft. The two things are —

Cusins. Baptism and —

Undershaft. No. Money and gunpowder.

Cusins (*surprised, but interested*) That is the general opinion of our governing classes. The novelty is in hearing any man confess it.

Undershaft. Just so.

Cusins. Excuse me: is there any place in your religion for honor, justice, truth, love, mercy and so forth?

Undershaft. Yes: they are the graces and luxuries of a rich, strong, and safe life.

Cusins. Suppose one is forced to choose between them and money or gunpowder?

Undershaft. Choose money and gunpowder; for without enough of both you cannot afford the others.

Cusins. That is your religion?

Undershaft. Yes.

(*The cadence of this reply makes a full close in the conversation, Cusins twists his face dubiously and contemplates Undershaft. Undershaft contemplates him.*)

Cusins. Barbara wont stand that. You will have to choose between your religion and Barbara.

Undershaft. So will you, my friend. She will find out that that drum of yours is hollow.

Cusins. Father Undershaft: you are mistaken: I am a sincere Salvationist. You do not understand the Salvation Army. It is the army of joy, of love, of courage: it has banished the fear and remorse and despair of the old hell-ridden evangelical sects: it marches to fight the devil with trumpet and drum, with music and dancing, with banner and palm, as becomes a sally from heaven by its happy garrison. It picks the waster out of the public house and makes a man of him: it finds a worm wriggling in a back kitchen, and lo! a woman! Men and women of rank too, sons and daughters of the Highest. It takes the poor professor of Greek, the most artificial and self-suppressed of human creatures, from his meal of roots, and lets loose the rhapsodist in him; reveals the true worship of Dionysos to him; sends him down the public street drumming dithyrambs (*he plays a thundering flourish on the drum*).

Undershaft. You will alarm the shelter.

Cusins. Oh, they are accustomed to these sudden ecstasies. However, if the drum worries you — *he pockets the drumsticks; unhooks the drum; and stands it on the ground opposite the gateway*).

Undershaft. Thank you.

Cusins. You remember what Euripides says about your money and gunpowder?

Undershaft. No.

Cusins (*declaiming*)   One and another
    In money and guns may outpass his brother;
    And men in their millions float and flow
    And seethe with a million hopes as leaven;
    And they win their will; or they miss their will;
    And their hopes are dead or are pined for still;
        But who'er can know
        As the long days go
    That to live is happy, has found his heaven.

My translation: what do you think of it?

Undershaft. I think, my friend, that if you wish to know, as the long days go, that to live is happy, you must first acquire money enough for a decent life, and power enough to be your own master.

Cusins. You are damnably discouraging. (*He resumes his declamation*).   Is it so hard a thing to see
    That the spirit of God — whate'er it be —
    The law that abides and changes not, ages long,
    The Eternal and Nature-born: these things be strong?
    What else is Wisdom? What of Man's endeavor,
    Or God's high grace so lovely and so great?
    To stand from fear set free? to breathe and wait?
    To hold a hand uplifted over Fate?
    And shall not Barbara be loved for ever?

Undershaft. Euripides mentions Barbara, does he?

Cusins. It is a fair translation. The word means Loveliness.

Undershaft. May I ask — as Barbara's father — how much a year she is to be loved for ever on?

Cusins. As for Barbara's father, that is more your affair than mine. I can feed her by teaching Greek: that is about all.

Undershaft. Do you consider it a good match for her?

Cusins (*with polite obstinacy*) Mr Undershaft: I am in many ways a weak, timid, ineffectual person; and my health is far from satisfactory. But whenever I feel that I must have anything, I get it, sooner or later. I feel that way about Barbara. I dont like marriage: I feel intensely afraid of it; and I dont know what I shall do with Barbara or what she will do with me. But I feel that I and nobody else must marry her. Please regard that as settled. — Not that I wish to be arbitrary; but why should I waste your time in discussing what is inevitable?

Undershaft. You mean that you will stick at nothing: not even the conversion of the Salvation Army to the worship of Dionysos.

Cusins. The business of the Salvation Army is to save, not to wrangle about the name of the pathfinder. Dionysos or another: what does it matter?

Undershaft (*rising and approaching him*) Professor Cusins: you are a young man after my own heart.

Cusins. Mr Undershaft: you are, as far as I am able to gather, a most infernal old rascal; but you appeal very strongly to my sense of ironic humor.

(*Undershaft mutely offers his hand. They shake.*)

Undershaft (*suddenly concentrating himself*) And now to business.

Cusins. Pardon me. We are discussing religion. Why go back to such an uninteresting and unimportant subject as business?

Undershaft. Religion is our business at present, because it is through religion alone that we can win Barbara.

Cusins. Have you, too, fallen in love with Barbara?

Undershaft. Yes, with a father's love.

Cusins. A father's love for a grown-up daughter is the most dangerous of all infatuations. I apologize for mentioning my own pale, coy, mistrustful fancy in the same breath with it.

Undershaft. Keep to the point. We have to win her; and we are neither of us Methodists.

Cusins. That doesnt matter. The power Barbara wields here — the power that wields Barbara herself — is not Calvinism, not Presbyterianism, not Methodism —

Undershaft. Not Greek Paganism either, eh?

Cusins. I admit that. Barbara is quite ŏriginal in her religion.

Undershaft (*triumphantly*) Aha! Barbara Undershaft would be. Her inspiration comes from within herself.

Cusins. How do you suppose it got there?

Undershaft (*in towering excitement*) It is the Undershaft inheritance. I shall hand on my torch to my daughter. She shall make my converts and preach my gospel —

Cusins. What! Money and gunpowder!

Undershaft. Yes, money and gunpowder. Freedom and power. Command of life and command of death.

Cusins (*urbanely: trying to bring him down to earth*) This is extremely interesting, Mr Undershaft. Of course you know that you are mad.

Undershaft (*with redoubled force*) And you?

Cusins. Oh, mad as a hatter. You are welcome to my secret since I have discovered yours. But I am astonished. Can a madman make cannons?

Undershaft. Would anyone else than a madman make them? And now (*with surging energy*) question for question. Can a sane man translate Euripides?

Cusins. No.

Undershaft (*seizing him by the shoulder*) Can a sane woman make a man of a waster or a woman of a worm?

Cusins (*reeling before the storm*) Father Colossus — Mammoth Millionaire —

Undershaft (*pressing him*) Are there two mad people or three in this Salvation shelter today?

Cusins. You mean Barbara is as mad as we are?

Undershaft (*pushing him lightly off and resuming his equanimity suddenly and completely*) Pooh, Professor! let us call things by their proper names. I am a millionaire; you are a poet: Barbara is a savior of souls. What have we three to do with the common mob of slaves and idolators? (*He sits down again with a shrug of contempt for the mob*).

Cusins. Take care! Barbara is in love with the common people. So am I. Have you never felt the romance of that love?

Undershaft (*cold and sardonic*) Have you ever been in love with Poverty, like St Francis? Have you ever been in love with Dirt, like St Simeon! Have you ever been in love with disease and suffering, like our nurses and philanthropists? Such passions are not virtues, but the most unnatural of all the vices. This love of the common people may please an earl's granddaughter and a university professor; but I have been a common man and a poor man; and it has no romance for me. Leave it to the poor to pretend that poverty is a blessing: leave it to the coward to make a religion of his cowardice by preaching humility: we know better than that. We three must stand together above the common people: how else can we help their children to climb up beside us? Barbara must belong to us, not to the Salvation Army.

Cusins. Well, I can only say that if you think you will get her away from the Salvation Army by talking to her as you have been talking to me, you don't know Barbara.

Undershaft. My friend: I never ask for what I can buy.

Cusins (*in a white fury*) Do I understand you to imply that you can buy Barbara?

Undershaft. No; but I can buy the Salvation Army.

Cusins. Quite impossible.

Undershaft. You shall see. All religious organizations exist by selling themselves to the rich.

Cusins. Not the Army. That is the Church of the poor.

Undershaft. All the more reason for buying it.

Cusins. I don't think you quite know what the Army does for the poor.

Undershaft. Oh yes I do. It draws their teeth: that is enough for me as a man of business.

Cusins. Nonsense! It makes them sober —

Undershaft. I prefer sober workmen. The profits are larger.

Cusins — honest —

Undershaft. Honest workmen are the most economical.

Cusins — attached to their homes —

Undershaft. So much the better: they will put up with anything sooner than change their shop.

Cusins — happy —

Undershaft. An invaluable safeguard against revolution.

Cusins — unselfish —

Undershaft. Indifferent to their own interests, which suits me exactly.

Cusins — with their thoughts on heavenly things —

Undershaft (*rising*) And not on Trade Unionism nor Socialism. Excellent.

Cusins (*revolted*) You really are an infernal old rascal.

Undershaft (*indicating Peter Shirley, who has just come from the shelter and strolled dejectedly down the yard between them*) And this is an honest man!

Shirley. Yes; and what av I got by it? (*he passes on bitterly and sits on the form, in the corner of the penthouse*).

(*Snobby Price, beaming sanctimoniously, and Jenny Hill, with a tambourine full of coppers, come from the shelter and go to the drum, on which Jenny begins to count the money.*)

Undershaft (*replying to Shirley*) Oh, your employers must have got a good deal by it from first to last. (*He sits on the table, with one foot on the side form. Cusins, overwhelmed, sits down on the same form nearer the shelter. Barbara comes from the shelter to the middle of the yard. She is excited and a little overwrougt*).

Barbara. Weve just had a splendid experience meeting at the other gate in Cripps's lane. I've hardly ever seen them so much moved as they were by your confession, Mr Price.

Price. I could almost be glad of my past wickedness if I could believe that it would elp to keep hathers stright.

Barbara. So it will, Snobby. How much, Jenny?

Jenny. Four and tenpence, Major.

Barbara. Oh Snobby, if you had given your poor mother just one more kick, we should have got the whole five shillings!

Price. If she heard you say that, miss, she'd be sorry I didnt. But I'm glad. Oh what a joy it will be to her when she hears I'm saved!

Undershaft. Shall I contribute the odd twopence, Barbara? The millionaire's mite, eh? (*He takes a couple of pennies from his pocket*).

Barbara. How did you make that twopence?

Undershaft. As usual. By selling cannons, torpedoes, submarines, and my new patent Grand Duke hand grenade.

Barbara. Put it back in your pocket. You cant buy your salvation here for twopence: you must work it out.

Undershaft. Is twopence not enough? I can afford a little more, if you press me.

Barbara. Two million millions would not be enough. There is bad blood on your hands; and nothing but good blood can cleanse them. Money is no use. Take it away. (*She turns to Cusins*). Dolly: you must write another letter for me to the papers. (*He makes a wry face*). Yes: I know you dont like it; but it must be done. The starvation this winter is beating us: everybody is unemployed. The General says we must close this shelter if we cant get more money. I force the collections at the meetings until I am ashamed: dont I, Snobby?

Price. It's a fair treat to see you work it, miss. The way you got them up from three-and-six to four-and-ten with that hymn, penny by penny and verse by verse, was a caution. Not a Cheap Jack on Mile End Waste could touch you at it.

Barbara. Yes; but I wish we could do without it. I am getting at last to think more of the collection than of the people's souls. And what are those hatfuls of pence and halfpence? We want thousands! tens of thousands! hundreds of thousands! I want to convert people, not to be always begging for the Army in a way I'd die sooner than beg for myself.

Undershaft (*in profound irony*) Genuine unselfishness is capable of anything, my dear.

Barbara (*unsuspectingly, as she turns away to take the money from the drum and put it in a cash bag she carries*) Yes, isnt it? (*Undershaft looks sardonically at Cusins*).

Cusins (*aside to Undershaft*) Mephistopheles! Machiavelli!

Barbara (*tears coming into her eyes as she ties the bag and pockets it*) How are we to feed them? I cant talk religion to a man with bodily hunger in his eyes. (*Almost breaking down*) It's frightful.

Jenny (*running to her*) Major, dear —

Barbara (rebounding) No: dont comfort me. It will be all right. We shall get the money.

Undershaft. How?

Jenny. By praying for it, of course. Mrs Baines says she prayed for it last night; and she has never prayed for it in vain: never once. (*She goes to the gate and looks out into the street*).

Barbara (who has dried her eyes and regained her composure) By the way, dad, Mrs Baines has come to march with us to our big meeting this afternoon; and she is very anxious to meet you, for some reason or other. Perhaps she'll convert you.

Undershaft. I shall be delighted, my dear.

Jenny (at the gate: excitedly) Major! Major! heres that man back again.

Barbara. What man?

Jenny. The man that hit me. Oh, I hope he's coming back to join us.

(*Bill Walker, with frost on his jacket, comes through the gate, his hands deep in his pockets and his chin sunk between his shoulders, like a cleaned-out gambler. He halts between Barbara and the drum.*)

Barbara. Hullo, Bill! Back already!

Bill (nagging at her) Bin talkin ever sence, ev you?

Barbara. Pretty nearly. Well, has Todger paid you out for poor Jenny's jaw?

Bill. Nao e aint.

Barbara. I thought your jacket looked a bit snowy.

Bill. Sao it is snaowy. You want to knaow where the snaow cam from, downt you?

Barbara. Yes.

Bill. Well, it cam from orf the grahnd in Pawkinses Corner in Kennintahn. It got rabbed orf be maw shaoulders: see?

Barbara. Pity you didnt rub some off with your knees, Bill! That would have done you a lot of good.

Bill (with sour mirthless humor) Aw was sivin anather menn's knees at the tawm. E was kneelin on moy ed, e was.

Jenny. Who was kneeling on your head?

Bill. Todger was. E was pryin for me: pryin camfortable wiv me as a cawpet. Sow was Mog. Sao was the aol bloomin meetin. Mog she sez 'Ow Lawd brike is stabborn sperrit; bat downt urt is dear art.' Thet was wot she said. 'Downt urt is dear art'! An er blowk — thirteen stun four! — kneelin wiv all is wight on me. Fanny, aint it?

Jenny. Oh no. We're so sorry, Mr Walker.

Barbara (*enjoying it frankly*) Nonsense! of course it's funny. Served you right, Bill! You must have done something to him first.

Bill (*doggedly*) Aw did wot Aw said Aw'd do. Aw spit in is eye. E looks ap at the skoy and sez, 'Ow that Aw should be fahnd worthy to be spit upon for the gospel's sike!' e sez; an Mog sez 'Glaory Allelloolier!'; an then e called me Braddher, an dahned me as if Aw was a kid and e was me mather worshin me a Setterda nawt. Aw ednt jast nao shaow wiv im at all. Arf the street pryed; an the tather arf larfed fit to split theirselves. (*To Barbara*) There! are you settisfawd nah?

Barbara (*her eyes dancing*) Wish I'd been there, Bill.

Bill. Yus: youd a got in a hextra bit o talk on me, wouldnt you?

Jenny. I'm so sorry, Mr Walker.

Bill (*fiercely*) Downt you gow being sorry for me: youve no call. Listen eah. Aw browk your jawr.

Jenny. No, it didn't hurt me: indeed it didnt, except for a moment. It was only that I was frightened.

Bill. Aw downt want to be forgive be you, or be ennybody. Wot Aw did Aw'll py for. Aw trawd to gat me aown jawr browk to settisfaw you —

Jenny (*distressed*) Oh no —

Bill (*impatiently*) Tell y' Aw did: cawnt you listen to wots bein taold you? All Aw got be it was bein mide a sawt of in the pablic street for me pines. Well, if Aw cawnt settisfaw you one wy, Aw ken anather. Listen eah! Aw ed two quid sived agen the frost; an Awve a pahnd of it left. A mite o mawn last week ed words with the judy e's gowing to merry. E give er wot-for; an e's bin fawnd fifteen bob. E ed a rawt to itt er cause they was gowin to be merrid; but Aw ednt nao rawt to itt you! sao put anather fawv bob on an call it a pahnd's worth. (*He produces a sovereign*). Eahs the manney. Tike it; and lets ev no more o your forgivin an prying and your Mijor jawrin me. Let wot Aw dan be dan an pide for; and let there be a end of it.

Jenny. Oh, I couldnt take it, Mr Walker. But if you would give a shilling or two to poor Rummy Mitchens! you really did hurt her; and she's old.

Bill (*contemptuously*) Not lawkly. Aw'd give her anather as soon as look at er. Let her ev the lawr o me as she threatened! She aint forgiven me: not mach. Wot Aw dan to er is not on me mawnd — wot she (*indicating Barbara*) mawt call on me conscience — no more than stickin a pig. It's this Christian gime o yours that Aw wownt ev plyed agen me: this bloomin forgivin an neggin an jawrin that mikes a menn thet sore that iz lawf's a burdn to im. Aw wownt ev it, Aw tell you; sao tike your manney and stop thraowin your silly beshed fice hap agen me.

Jenny. Major: may I take a little of it for the Army?

Barbara. No: the Army is not to be bought. We want your soul, Bill; and we'll take nothing less.

Bill (bitterly) Aw knaow. Me an maw few shillins is not good enaff for you. Youre a earl's grendorter, you are. Nathink less than a andered pahnd for you.

Undershaft. Come Barbara! you could do a great deal of good with a hundred pounds. If you will set this gentleman's mind at ease by taking his pound, I will give the other ninety-nine.

(*Bill, dazed by such opulence, instinctively touches his cap.*)

Barbara. Oh, youre too extravagent, papa. Bill offers twenty pieces of silver. All you need offer is the other ten. That will make the standard price to buy anybody who's for sale. I'm not; and the Army's not. (*To Bill*) Youll never have another quiet moment, Bill, until you come round to us. You cant stand out against your salvation.

Bill (sullenly) Aw cawnt stend aht agen music awl wrastlers and awtful tangued women. Awve offered to py. Aw can do no more. Tike it or leave it. There it is. (*He throws the sovereign on the drum, and sits down on the horse-trough. The coin fascinates Snobby Price, who takes an early opportunity of dropping his cap on it*).

(*Mrs. Baines comes from the shelter. She is dressed as a Salvation Army Commissioner. She is an earnest looking woman of about 40, with a caressing, urgent voice, and an appealing manner.*)

Barbara. This is my father, Mrs Baines. (*Undershaft comes from the table, taking his hat off with marked civility*). Try what you can do with him. He wont listen to me, because he remembers what a fool I was when I was a baby. (*She leaves them together and chats with Jenny*).

Mrs Baines. Have you been shewn over the shelter, Mr Undershaft? You know the work we're doing, of course.

Undershaft (very civilly) The whole nation knows it, Mrs Baines.

Mrs Baines. No, sir: the whole nation does not know it, or we should not be crippled as we are for want of money to carry our work through the length and breadth of the land. Let me tell you that there would have been rioting this winter in London but for us.

Undershaft. You really think so?

Mrs Baines. I know it. I remember 1886, when you rich gentlemen hardened your hearts against the cry of the poor. They broke the windows of your clubs in Pall Mall.

Undershaft (*gleaming with approval of their method*) And the Mansion House Fund went up next day from thirty thousand pounds to seventy-nine thousand! I remember quite well.

Mrs Baines. Well, wont you help me to get at the people? They wont break windows then. Come here, Price. Let me shew you to this gentleman (*Price comes to be inspected*). Do you remember the window breaking?

Price. My ole father thought it was the revolution, maam.

Mrs Baines. Would you break windows now?

Price. Oh no, maam. The windows of eaven av bin opened to me. I know now that the rich man is a sinner like myself.

Rummy (*appearing above at the loft door*) Snobby Price!

Snobby. Wot is it?

Rummy. Your mother's askin for you at the other gate in Cripps's Lane. She's heard about your confession (*Price turns pale*).

Mrs Baines. Go, Mr Price; and pray with her.

Jenny. You can go through the shelter, Snobby.

Price (*to Mrs Baines*) I couldnt face her now, maam, with all the weight of my sins fresh on me. Tell her she'll find her son at ome, waitin for her in prayer. (*He skulks off through the gate, incidentally stealing the sovereign on his way out by picking up his cap from the drum*).

Mrs Baines (*with swimming eyes*) You see how we take the anger and the bitterness against you out of their hearts, Mr Undershaft.

Undershaft. It is certainly most convenient and gratifying to all large employers of labor, Mrs Baines.

Mrs Baines. Barbara: Jenny: I have good news: most wonderful news. (*Jenny runs to her*). My prayers have been answered. I told you they would, Jenny, didnt I?

Jenny. Yes, yes.

Barbara (*moving nearer to the drum*) Have we got money enough to keep the shelter open?

Mrs Baines. I hope we shall have enough to keep all the shelters open. Lord Saxmundham has promised us five thousand pounds —

Barbara. Hooray!

Jenny. Glory!

Mrs Baines. — if —

Barbara. 'If!' If what?

Mrs Baines. — if five other gentlemen will give a thousand each to make it up to ten thousand.

Barbara. Who is Lord Saxmundham? I never heard of him.

Undershaft (*who has pricked up his ears at the peer's name, and is now watching Barbara curiously*) A new creation, my dear. You have heard of Sir Horace Bodger?

Barbara. Bodger! Do you mean the distiller? Bodger's whiskey!

Undershaft. That is the man. He is one of the greatest of our public benefactors. He restored the cathedral at Hakington. They made him a baronet for that. He gave half a million to the funds of his party: they made him a baron for that.

Shirley. What will they give him for the five thousand?

Undershaft. There is nothing left to give him. So the five thousand, I should think, is to save his soul.

Mrs Baines. Heaven grant it may! O Mr Undershaft, you have some very rich friends. Cant you help us towards the other five thousand? We are going to hold a great meeting this afternoon at the Assembly Hall in the Mile End Road. If I could only announce that one gentleman had come forward to support Lord Saxmundham, others would follow. Dont you know somebody? couldnt you? wouldnt you? (*her eyes fill with tears*) oh, think of those poor people, Mr Undershaft: think of how much it means to them, and how little to a great man like you.

Undershaft (*sardonically gallant*) Mrs Baines: you are irresistible. I cant disappoint you; and I cant deny myself the satisfaction of making Bodger pay up. You shall have your five thousand pounds.

Mrs Baines. Thank God!

Undershaft. You dont thank me?

Mrs Baines. Oh sir, dont try to be cynical: dont be ashamed of being a good man. The Lord will bless you abundantly; and our prayers will be like a strong fortification round you all the days of your life. (*With a touch of caution*) You will let me have the cheque to shew at the meeting, wont you? Jenny: go in and fetch a pen and ink. (*Jenny runs to the shelter door*).

Undershaft. Do not disturb Miss Hill: I have a fountain pen (*Jenny halts. He sits at the table and writes the cheque. Cusins rises to make room for him. They all watch him silently*).

Bill (*cynically, aside to Barbara, his voice and accent horribly debased*) Wot prawce selvytion nah?

Barbara. Stop. (*Undershaft stops writing: they all turn to her in surprise*). Mrs Baines: are you really going to take this money?

Mrs Baines (*astonished*) Why not, dear?

Barbara. Why not! Do you know what my father is? Have you forgotten that Lord Saxmundham is Bodger the whiskey man? Do you remember how we implored the County Council to stop him from writing Bodger's Whiskey in letters of fire against the sky; so that the poor drink-ruined creatures on the Embankment could not wake up from their snatches of sleep without being reminded of their deadly thirst by that wicked sky sign? Do you know that the worst thing I have had to fight here is not the devil, but Bodger, Bodger, Bodger, with his whiskey, his distilleries, and his tied houses? Are you going to make our shelter another tied house for him, and ask me to keep it?

Bill. Rotten dranken whisky it is too.

Mrs Baines. Dear Barbara: Lord Saxmundham has a soul to be saved like any of us. If heaven has found the way to make a good use of his money, are we to set ourselves up against the answer to our prayers?

Barbara. I know he has a soul to be saved. Let him come down here; and I'll do my best to help him to his salvation. But he wants to send his cheque down to buy us, and go on being as wicked as ever.

Undershaft (*with a reasonableness which Cusins alone perceives to be ironical*) My dear Barbara: alcohol is a very necessary article. It heals the sick —

Barbara. It does nothing of the sort.

Undershaft. Well, it assists the doctor: that is perhaps a less questionable way of putting it. It makes life bearable to millions of people who could not endure their existence if they were quite sober. It enables Parliament to do things at eleven at night that no sane person would do at eleven in the morning. Is it Bodger's fault that this inestimable gift is deplorably abused by less than one per cent of the poor? (*He turns again to the table; signs the cheque; and crosses it*).

Mrs Baines. Barbara: will there be less drinking or more if all those poor souls we are saving come tomorrow and find the doors of our shelters shut in their faces? Lord Saxmundham gives us the money to stop drinking — to take his own business from him.

Cusins (*impishly*) Pure self-sacrifice on Bodger's part, clearly! Bless dear Bodger! (*Barbara almost breaks down as Adolphus, too, fails her*).

Undershaft (*tearing the cheque and pocketing the book as he rises and goes past Cusins to Mrs Baines*) I also, Mrs Baines, may claim a little disinterestedness. Think of my business! think of the widows and orphans! the men and lads torn to pieces with shrapnel and poisoned with lyddite! (*Mrs Baines shrinks; but he goes on remorselessly*) the oceans of blood, not one drop of which is shed in a really just cause! the ravaged crops! the peaceful peasants forced, women and men, to till their fields under the fire of opposing armies on pain of starvation! the bad blood of the fierce little cowards at home who egg on others to fight for the gratification of their national vanity! All this makes money for me: I am never richer, never busier than when the papers are full of it. Well, it is your work to preach peace on earth and good will to men. (*Mrs Baines's face lights up again*). Every convert you make is a vote against war. (*Her lips move in prayer*). Yet I give you this money to help you to hasten my own commercial ruin. (*He gives her the cheque*).

Cusins (*mounting the form in an ecstasy of mischief*) The millennium will be inaugurated by the unselfishness of Undershaft and Bodger. Oh be joyful! (*He takes the drum-sticks from his pocket and flourishes them*).

Mrs Baines (*taking the cheque*) The longer I live the more proof I see that there is an Infinite Goodness that turns everything to the work of salvation sooner or later. Who would have thought that any good could have come out of war and drink? And yet their profits are brought today to the feet of salvation to do its blessed work. (*She is affected to tears*).

Jenny (*running to Mrs Baines and throwing her arms round her*) Oh dear! how blessed, how glorious it all is!

Cusins (*in a convulsion of irony*) Let us seize this unspeakable moment. Let us march to the great meeting at once. Excuse me just an instant. (*He rushes into the shelter. Jenny takes her tambourine from the drum head*).

Mrs Baines. Mr Undershaft: have you ever seen a thousand people fall on their knees with one impulse and pray? Come with us to the meeting. Barbara shall tell them that the Army is saved, and saved through you.

Cusins (*returning impetuously from the shelter with a flag and a trombone, and coming between Mrs Baines and Undershaft*) You shall carry the flag down the first street, Mrs Baines (*he gives her the flag*). Mr Undershaft is a gifted trombonist: he shall intone an Olympian diapason to the West Ham Salvation March. (*Aside to Undershaft, as he forces the trombone on him*) Blow, Machiavelli, blow.

Undershaft (*aside to him, as he takes the trombone*) The trumpet in Zion! (*Cusins rushes to the drum, which he takes up and puts on. Undershaft continues, aloud*) I will do my best. I could vamp a bass if I knew the tune.

Cusins. It is a wedding chorus from one of Donizetti's operas; but we have converted it. We convert everything to good here, including Bodger. You remember the chorus. 'For thee immense rejoicing —

immenso giubilo — immenso giubilo.' (*With drum obbligato*) Rum
tum ti tum tum, tum tum ti ta —

Barbara. Dolly: you are breaking my heart.

Cusins. What is a broken heart more or less here? Dionysos Undershaft has descended. I am possessed.

Mrs Baines. Come, Barbara: I must have my dear Major to carry the
flag with me.

Jenny. Yes, yes, Major darling.

Cusins (*snatches the tambourine out of Jenny's hand and mutely
offers it to Barbara*).

Barbara (*coming forward a little as she puts the offer behind her with
a shudder, whilst Cusins recklessly tosses the tambourine back to
Jenny and goes to the gate*) I cant come.

Jenny. Not come!

Mrs Baines (*with tears in her eyes*) Barbara: do you think I am wrong
to take the money?

Barbara (*impulsively going to her and kissing her*) No, no: God help
you, dear, you must: you are saving the Army. Go; and may you
have a great meeting!

Jenny. But arnt you coming?

Barbara. No. (*She begins taking off the silver S brooch from her
collar*).

Mrs Baines. Barbara: what are you doing?

Jenny. Why are you taking your badge off? You cant be going to leave
us, Major.

Barbara (*quietly*) Father: come here.

Undershaft (*coming to her*) My dear! (*Seeing that she is going to pin
the badge on his collar, he retreats to the penthouse in some alarm*).

Barbara (*following him*) Dont be frightened. (*She pins the badge on
and steps back towards the table, shewing him to the others*)
There! It's not much for £5000, is it?

Mrs Baines. Barbara: if you wont come and pray with us, promise me
you will pray for us.

Barbara. I cant pray now. Perhaps I shall never pray again.

Mrs Baines. Barbara!

Jenny. Major!

Barbara (*almost delirious*) I cant bear any more. Quick march!

Cusins (*calling to the procession in the street outside*) Off we go.
Play up, there! Immenso giubilo. (*He gives the time with his drum;
and the band strikes up the march, which rapidly becomes more
distant as the procession moves briskly away*).

Mrs Baines. I must go, dear. Youre overworked: you will be all right
tomorrow. We'll never lose you. Now Jenny: step out with the old

flag. Blood and Fire! (*She marches out through the gate with her flag*).

Jenny. Glory Hallelujah! (*flourishing her tambourine and marching*).

Undershaft (*to Cusins, as he marches out past him easing the slide of his trombone*) 'My ducats and my daughter'!

Cusins (*following him out*) Money and gunpowder!

Barbara. Drunkenness and Murder! My God: why hast thou forsaken me?

(*She sinks on the form with her face buried in her hands. The march passes away into silence. Bill Walker steals across to her.*)

Bill (*taunting*) Wot prawce selvytion nah?

Shirley. Dont you hit her when she's down.

Bill. She itt me wen aw wiz dahn. Waw shouldnt Aw git a bit o me aown beck?

Barbara (*raising her head*) I didnt take your money, Bill.

(*She crosses the yard to the gate and turns her back on the two men to hide her face from them*).

Bill (*sneering after her*) Naow, it warnt enaff for you. (*Turning to the drum, he misses the money*) Ellow! If you aint took it sammun else ez. Weres it gorn? Bly me if Jenny Ill didnt tike it arter all!

Rummy (*screaming at him from the loft*) You lie, you dirty blackguard! Snobby Price pinched it off the drum when he took up his cap. I was up here all the time an see im do it.

Bill. Wot! Stowl maw manney! Waw didnt you call thief on him, you silly aold macker you?

Rummy. To serve you aht for ittin me acrost the fice. It's cost y'pahnd, that az. (*Raising a pæan of squalid triumph*) I done you. I'm even with you. Uve ad it aht o y — (*Bill snatches up Shirley's mug and hurls it at her. She slams the loft door and vanishes. The mug smashes against the door and falls in fragments*).

Bill (*beginning to chuckle*) Tell us, aol menn, wot o'clock this mawnin was it wen im as they call Snobby Prawce was sived?

Barbara (*turning to him more composedly, and with unspoiled sweetness*) About half past twelve, Bill. And he pinched your pound at a quarter to two. I know. Well, you cant afford to lose it. I'll send it to you.

Bill (*his voice and accent suddenly improving*) Not if Aw wiz to stawve for it. Aw aint to be bought.

Shirley. Aint you? Youd sell yourself to the devil for a pint o beer; only there aint no devil to make the offer.

Bill (*unashamed*) Sao Aw would, mite, and often ev, cheerful. But she cawnt baw me. (*Approaching Barbara*) You wanted maw saoul, did you? Well, you aint got it.

Barbara. I nearly got it, Bill. But weve sold it back to you for ten thousand pounds.

Shirley. And dear at the money!

Barbara. No, Peter: it was worth more than money.

Bill (*salvationproof*) It's nao good: you cawnt get rahnd me nah. Aw downt blieve in it; and Awve seen tody that Aw was rawt. (*Going*) Sao long, aol soupkitchener! Ta, ta, Mijor Earl's Grendorter! (*Turning at the gate*) Wot prawce selvytion nah? Snobby Prawce! Ha! ha!

Barbara (*offering her hand*) Goodbye, Bill.

Bill (*taken aback, half plucks his cap off; then shoves it on again defiantly*) Git aht. (*Barbara drops her hand, discouraged. He has a twinge of remorse*). But thets aw rawt, you knaow. Nathink pasnl. Naow mellice. Sao long, Judy. (*He goes*).

Barbara. No malice. So long, Bill.

Shirley (*shaking his head*) You make too much of him, miss, in your innocence.

Barbara (*going to him*) Peter: I'm like you now. Cleaned out, and lost my job.

Shirley. Youve youth an hope. Thats two better than me.

Barbara. I'll get you a job, Peter. Thats hope for you: the youth will have to be enough for me. (*She counts her money*). I have just enough left for two teas at Lockharts, a Rowton doss for you, and my tram and bus home. (*He frowns and rises with offended pride. She takes his arm*). Dont be proud, Peter: it's sharing between friends. And promise me youll talk to me and not let me cry. (*She draws him towards the gate*).

Shirley. Well, I'm not accustomed to talk to the like of you —

Barbara (*urgently*) Yes, yes: you must talk to me. Tell me about Tom Paine's books and Bradlaugh's lectures. Come along.

Shirley. Ah, if you would only read Tom Paine in the proper spirit, miss! (*They go out through the gate together*).

ACT III

Next day after lunch Lady Britomart is writing in the library in Wilton Crescent. Sarah is reading in the armchair near the window. Barbara, in ordinary fashionable dress, pale and brooding, is on the settee. Charles Lomax enters. He starts on seeing Barbara fashionably attired and in low spirits.

Lomax. Youve left off your uniform!

(*Barbara says nothing; but an expression of pain passes over her face*).

Lady Britomart (*warning him in low tones to be careful*) Charles!

Lomax (*much concerned, coming behind the settee and bending sympathetically over Barbara*) I'm awfully sorry, Barbara. You know I helped you all I could with the concertina and so forth. (*Momentously*) Still, I have never shut my eyes to the fact that there is a certain amount of tosh about the Salvation Army. Now the claims of the Church of England —

Lady Britomart. Thats enough, Charles. Speak of something suited to your mental capacity.

Lomax. But surely the Church of England is suited to all our capacities.

Barbara (*pressing his hand*) Thank you for your sympathy, Cholly. Now go and spoon with Sarah.

Lomax (*dragging a chair from the writing table and seating himself affectionately by Sarah's side*) How is my ownest today?

Sarah. I wish you wouldnt tell Cholly to do things, Barbara. He always comes straight and does them. Cholly: we're going to the works this afternoon.

Lomax. What works?

Sarah. The cannon works.

Lomax. What? your governor's shop!

Sarah. Yes.

Lomax. Oh I say!

(*Cusins enters in poor condition. He also starts visibly when he sees Barbara without her uniform.*)

Barbara. I expected you this morning, Dolly. Didnt you guess that?

Cusins (*sitting down beside her*) I'm sorry. I have only just breakfasted.

Sarah. But weve just finished lunch.

Barbara. Have you had one of your bad nights?

Cusins. No: I had rather a good night: in fact, one of the most remarkable nights I have ever passed.

Barbara. The meeting?

Cusins. No: after the meeting.

Lady Britomart. You should have gone to bed after the meeting. What were you doing?

Cusins. Drinking.

Lady Britomart.	⎫	⎧ Adolphus!
Sarah.	⎬ ⎨	Dolly!
Barbara.	⎬ ⎨	Dolly!
Lomax.	⎭	⎩ Oh I say!

Lady Britomart. What were you drinking, may I ask?

Cusins. A most devilish kind of Spanish burgundy, warranted free from added alcohol: a Temperance burgundy in fact. Its richness in natural alcohol made any addition superfluous.

Barbara. Are you joking, Dolly?

Cusins (*patiently*) No. I have been making a night of it with the nominal head of this household: that is all.

Lady Britomart. Andrew made you drunk!

Cusins. No: he only provided the wine. I think it was Dionysos who made me drunk. (*To Barbara*) I told you I was possessed.

Lady Britomart. Youre not sober yet. Go home to bed at once.

Cusins. I have never before ventured to reproach you, Lady Brit; but how could you marry the Prince of Darkness?

Lady Britomart. It was much more excusable to marry him than to get drunk with him. That is a new accomplishment of Andrew's, by the way. He usent to drink.

Cusins. He doesnt now. He only sat there and completed the wreck of my moral basis, the rout of my convictions, the purchase of my soul. He cares for you, Barbara. That is what makes him so dangerous to me.

Barbara. That has nothing to do with it, Dolly. There are larger loves and diviner dreams than the fireside ones. You know that, dont you?

Cusins. Yes: that is our understanding. I know it. I hold to it. Unless he can win me on that holier ground he may amuse me for a while; but he can get no deeper hold, strong as he is.

Barbara. Keep to that; and the end will be right. Now tell me what happened at the meeting?

Cusins. It was an amazing meeting. Mrs Baines almost died of emotion. Jenny Hill simply gibbered with hysteria. The Prince of Darkness played his trombone like a madman: its brazen roarings were like the laughter of the damned. 117 conversions took place then and there. They prayed with the most touching sincerity and gratitude for Bodger, and for the anonymous donor of the £5000. Your father would not let his name be given.

Lomax. That was rather fine of the old man, you know. Most chaps would have wanted the advertisement.

Cusins. He said all the charitable institutions would be down on him like kites on a battle-field if he gave his name.

Lady Britomart. Thats Andrew all over. He never does a proper thing without giving an improper reason for it.

Cusins. He convinced me that I have all my life been doing improper things for proper reasons.

Lady Britomart. Adolphus: now that Barbara has left the Salvation
Army, you had better leave it too. I will not have you playing that
drum in the streets.

Cusins. Your orders are already obeyed, Lady Brit.

Barbara. Dolly: were you ever really in earnest about it? Would you
have joined if you had never seen me?

Cusins (*disingenuously*) Well — er — well, possibly, as a collector of
religions —

Lomax (*cunningly*) Not as a drummer, though, you know. You are
a very clearheaded brainy chap, Dolly; and it must have been apparent to you that there is a certain amount of tosh about —

Lady Britomart. Charles: if you must drivel, drivel like a grown-up man
and not like a schoolboy.

Lomax (*out of countenance*) Well, drivel is drivel, dont you know,
whatever a man's age.

Lady Britomart. In good society in England, Charles, men drivel at all
ages by repeating silly formulas with an air of wisdom. Schoolboys
make their own formulas out of slang, like you. When they reach
your age, and get political private secretaryships and things of that
sort, they drop slang and get their formulas out of The Spectator or
The Times. You had better confine yourself to The Times. You will
find that there is a certain amount of tosh about The Times; but
at least its language is reputable.

Lomax (*overwhelmed*) You are so awfully strong-minded, Lady Brit —

Lady Britomart. Rubbish! (*Morrison comes in*). What is it?

Morrison. If you please, my lady, Mr Undershaft has just drove up
to the door.

Lady Britomart. Well, let him in. (*Morrison hesitates*). Whats the
matter with you?

Morrison. Shall I announce him, my lady; or is he at home here, so to
speak, my lady?

Lady Britomart. Announce him.

Morrison. Thank you, my lady. You wont mind my asking, I hope.
The occasion is in a manner of speaking new to me.

Lady Britomart. Quite right. Go and let him in.

Morrison. Thank you, my lady. (*He withdraws*).

Lady Britomart. Children: go and get ready. (*Sarah and Barbara go
upstairs for their out-of-door wraps*). Charles: go and tell Stephen
to come down here in five minutes: you will find him in the drawing room. (*Charles goes*). Adolphus: tell them to send round the
carriage in about fifteen minutes. (*Adolphus goes*).

Morrison (*at the door*) Mr Undershaft.

(*Undershaft comes in. Morrison goes out.*)

Undershaft. Alone! How fortunate!

Lady Britomart (*rising*) Dont be sentimental, Andrew. Sit down. (*She sits on the settee: he sits beside her, on her left. She comes to the point before he has time to breathe*). Sarah must have £800 a year until Charles Lomax comes into his property. Barbara will need more, and need it permanently, because Adolphus hasnt any property.

Undershaft (*resignedly*) Yes, my dear: I will see to it. Anything else? for yourself, for instance?

Lady Britomart. I want to talk to you about Stephen.

Undershaft (*rather wearily*) Dont, my dear. Stephen doesnt interest me.

Lady Britomart. He does interest me. He is our son.

Undershaft. Do you really think so? He has induced us to bring him into the world; but he chose his parents very incongruously, I think. I see nothing of myself in him, and less of you.

Lady Britomart. Andrew: Stephen is an excellent son, and a most steady, capable, highminded young man. You are simply trying to find an excuse for disinheriting him.

Undershaft. My dear Biddy: the Undershaft tradition disinherits him. It would be dishonest of me to leave the cannon foundry to my son.

Lady Britomart. It would be most unnatural and improper of you to leave it to anyone else, Andrew. Do you suppose this wicked and immoral tradition can be kept up for ever? Do you pretend that Stephen could not carry on the foundry just as well as all the other sons of the big business houses?

Undershaft. Yes: he could learn the office routine without understanding the business, like all the other sons; and the firm would go on by its own momentum until the real Undershaft — probably an Italian or a German — would invent a new method and cut him out.

Lady Britomart. There is nothing that any Italian or German could do that Stephen could not do. And Stephen at least has breeding.

Undershaft. The son of a foundling! Nonsense!

Lady Britomart. My son, Andrew! And even you may have good blood in your veins for all you know.

Undershaft. True. Probably I have. That is another argument in favor of a foundling.

Lady Britomart. Andrew: dont be aggravating. And dont be wicked. At present you are both.

Undershaft. This conversation is part of the Undershaft tradition, Biddy. Every Undershaft's wife has treated him to it ever since the house was founded. It is mere waste of breath. If the tradition be ever broken it will be for an abler man than Stephen.

Lady Britomart (pouting) Then go away.

Undershaft (deprecatory) Go away!

Lady Britomart. Yes: go away. If you will do nothing for Stephen, you are not wanted here. Go to your foundling, whoever he is; and look after him.

Undershaft. The fact is, Biddy —

Lady Britomart. Dont call me Biddy. I dont call you Andy.

Undershaft. I will not call my wife Britomart: it is not good sense. Seriously, my love, the Undershaft tradition has landed me in a difficulty. I am getting on in years; and my partner Lazarus has at last made a stand and insisted that the succession must be settled one way or the other; and of course he is quite right. You see, I havent found a fit successor yet.

Lady Britomart (obstinately) There is Stephen.

Undershaft. Thats just it: all the foundlings I can find are exactly like Stephen.

Lady Britomart. Andrew!

Undershaft. I want a man with no relations and no schooling: that is, a man who would be out of the running altogether if he were not a strong man. And I cant find him. Every blessed foundling nowadays is snapped up in his infancy by Barnardo homes, or School Board officers, or Boards of Guardians; and if he shews the least ability he is fastened on by schoolmasters; trained to win scholarships like a racehorse; crammed with secondhand ideas; drilled and disciplined in docility and what they call good taste; and lamed for life so that he is fit for nothing but teaching. If you want to keep the foundry in the family, you had better find an eligible foundling and marry him to Barbara.

Lady Britomart. Ah! Barbara! Your pet! You would sacrifice Stephen to Barbara.

Undershaft. Cheerfully. And you, my dear, would boil Barbara to make soup for Stephen.

Lady Britomart. Andrew: this is not a question of our likings and dislikings: it is a question of duty. It is your duty to make Stephen your successor.

Undershaft. Just as much as it is your duty to submit to your husband. Come, Biddy! these tricks of the governing class are of no use with me. I am one of the governing class myself; and it is waste of time giving tracts to a missionary. I have the power in this matter; and I am not to be humbugged into using it for your purposes.

Lady Britomart. Andrew: you can talk my head off; but you cant change wrong into right. And your tie is all on one side. Put it straight.

Undershaft (*disconcerted*) It wont stay unless it's pinned (*he fumbles at it with childish grimaces*) —

(*Stephen comes in.*)

Stephen (*at the door*) I beg your pardon (*about to retire*).

Lady Britomart. No: come in, Stephen. (*Stephen comes forward to his mother's writing table*).

Undershaft (*not very cordially*) Good afternoon.

Stephen (*coldly*) Good afternoon.

Undershaft (*to Lady Britomart*) He knows all about the tradition, I suppose?

Lady Britomart. Yes. (*To Stephen*) It is what I told you last night, Stephen.

Undershaft (*sulkily*) I understand you want to come into the cannon business.

Stephen. I go into the trade! Certainly not.

Undershaft (*opening his eyes, greatly eased in mind and manner*) Oh! in that case —

Lady Britomart. Cannons are not trade, Stephen. They are enterprise.

Stephen. I have no intention of becoming a man of business in any sense. I have no capacity for business and no taste for it. I intend to devote myself to politics.

Undershaft (*rising*) My dear boy: this is an immense relief to me. And I trust it may prove an equally good thing for the country. I was afraid you would consider yourself disparaged and slighted. (*He moves towards Stephen as if to shake hands with him*).

Lady Britomart (*rising and interposing*) Stephen: I cannot allow you to throw away an enormous property like this.

Stephen (*stiffly*) Mother: there must be an end of treating me as a child, if you please. (*Lady Britomart recoils, deeply wounded by his tone*). Until last night I did not take your attitude seriously, because I did not think you meant it seriously. But I find now that you left me in the dark as to matters which you should have explained to me years ago. I am extremely hurt and offended. Any further discussion of my intentions had better take place with my father, as between one man and another.

Lady Britomart. Stephen! (*She sits down again, her eyes filling with tears*).

Undershaft (*with grave compassion*) You see, my dear, it is only the big men who can be treated as children.

Stephen. I am sorry, mother, that you have forced me —

Undershaft (*stopping him*) Yes, yes, yes, yes: thats all right, Stephen. She wont interfere with you any more: your independence is achieved: you have won your latchkey. Dont rub it in; and above all, dont apologize. (*He resumes his seat*). Now what about your future, as between one man and another — I beg your pardon, Biddy: as between two men and a woman.

Lady Britomart (*who has pulled herself together strongly*) I quite understand, Stephen. By all means go your own way if you feel strong enough. (*Stephen sits down magisterially in the chair at the writing table with an air of affirming his majority*).

Undershaft. It is settled that you do not ask for the succession to the cannon business.

Stephen. I hope it is settled that I repudiate the cannon business.

Undershaft. Come, come! dont be so devilishly sulky: it's boyish. Freedom should be generous. Besides, I owe you a fair start in life in exchange for disinheriting you. You cant become prime minister all at once. Havnt you a turn for something? What about literature, art, and so forth?

Stephen. I have nothing of the artist about me, either in faculty or character, thank Heaven!

Undershaft. A philosopher, perhaps? Eh?

Stephen. I make no such ridiculous pretension.

Undershaft. Just so. Well, there is the army, the navy, the Church, the Bar. The Bar requires some ability. What about the Bar?

Stephen. I have not studied law. And I am afraid I have not the necessary push — I believe that is the name barristers give to their vulgarity — for success in pleading.

Undershaft. Rather a difficult case, Stephen. Hardly anything left but the stage, is there? (*Stephen makes an impatient movement*). Well, come! is there anything you know or care for?

Stephen (*rising and looking at him steadily*) I know the difference between right and wrong.

Undershaft (*hugely tickled*) You dont say so! What! no capacity for business, no knowledge of law, no sympathy with art, no pretension to philosophy; only a simple knowledge of the secret that has puzzled all the philosophers, baffled all the lawyers, muddled all the men of business, and ruined most of the artists: the secret of right and wrong. Why, man, youre a genius, a master of masters, a god! At twentyfour, too!

Stephen (*keeping his temper with difficulty*) You are pleased to be facetious. I pretend to nothing more than any honorable English gentleman claims as his birthright (*he sits down angrily*).

Undershaft. Oh, thats everybody's birthright. Look at poor little Jenny Hill, the Salvation lassie! she would think you were laughing at her if you asked her to stand up in the street and teach grammar or geography or mathematics or even drawing room dancing; but it never occurs to her to doubt that she can teach morals and religion. You are all alike, you respectable people. You cant tell me the bursting strain of a ten-inch gun, which is a very simple matter; but you all think you can tell me the bursting strain of a man under temptation. You darent handle high explosives; but youre all ready to handle honesty and truth and justice and the whole duty of man, and kill one another at that game. What a country! What a world!

Lady Britomart (*uneasily*) What do you think he had better do, Andrew?

Undershaft. Oh, just what he wants to do. He knows nothing and he thinks he knows everything. That points clearly to a political career. Get him a private secretaryship to someone who can get him an Under Secretaryship; and then leave him alone. He will find his natural and proper place in the end on the Treasury Bench.

Stephen (*springing up again*) I am sorry, sir, that you force me to forget the respect due to you as my father. I am an Englishman and I will not hear the Government of my country insulted. (*He thrusts his hands in his pockets, and walks angrily across to the window*).

Undershaft (*with a touch of brutality*) The government of your country! *I* am the government of your country: I, and Lazarus. Do you suppose that you and half a dozen amateurs like you, sitting in a row in that foolish gabble shop, can govern Undershaft and Lazarus? No, my friend: you will do what pays *us*. You will make war when it suits us, and keep peace when it doesnt. You will find out that trade requires certain measures when we have decided on those measures. When I want anything to keep my dividends up, you will discover that my want is a national need. When other people want something to keep my dividends down, you will call out the police and military. And in return you shall have the support and applause of my newspapers, and the delight of imagining that you are a great statesman. Government of your country! Be off with you, my boy, and play with your caucuses and leading articles and historical parties and great leaders and burning questions and the rest of your toys. I am going back to my counting-house to pay the piper and call the tune.

Stephen (*actually smiling, and putting his hand on his father's shoulder with indulgent patronage*) Really, my dear father, it is impossible to be angry with you. You dont know how absurd all this sounds to me. You are very properly proud of having been industrious enough to make money; and it is greatly to your credit that you have made so much of it. But it has kept you in circles where you are valued for your money and deferred to for it, instead of in the doubtless very old-fashioned and behind-the-times public school and university where I formed my habits of mind. It is natural for you to think that money governs England; but you must allow me to think I know better.

Undershaft. And what does govern England, pray?

Stephen. Character, father, character.

Undershaft. Whose character? Yours or mine?

Stephen. Neither yours nor mine, father, but the best elements in the English national character.

Undershaft. Stephen: Ive found your profession for you. Youre a born journalist. I'll start you with a high-toned weekly review. There!

(*Before Stephen can reply Sarah, Barbara, Lomax, and Cusins come in ready for walking. Barbara crosses the room to the window and looks out. Cusins drifts amiably to the armchair. Lomax remains near the door, whilst Sarah comes to her mother.*

Stephen goes to the smaller writing table and busies himself with his letters.)

Sarah. Go and get ready, mamma: the carriage is waiting. (*Lady Britomart leaves the room*).

Undershaft (*to Sarah*) Good day, my dear. Good afternoon, Mr Lomax.

Lomax (*vaguely*) Ahdedoo.

Undershaft (*to Cusins*) Quite well after last night, Euripides, eh?

Cusins. As well as can be expected.

Undershaft. Thats right. (*To Barbara*) So you are coming to see my death and devastation factory, Barbara?

Barbara (*at the window*) You came yesterday to see my salvation factory. I promised you a return visit.

Lomax (*coming forward between Sarah and Undershaft*) Youll find it awfully interesting. Ive been through the Woolwich Arsenal; and it gives you a ripping feeling of security, you know, to think of the lot of beggars we could kill if it came to fighting. (*To Undershaft, with sudden solemnity*) Still, it must be rather an awful reflection for you, from the religious point of view as it were. Youre getting on, you know, and all that.

Sarah. You dont mind Cholly's imbecility, papa, do you?

Lomax (*much taken aback*) Oh I say!

Undershaft. Mr Lomax looks at the matter in a very proper spirit, my dear.

Lomax. Just so. Thats all I meant, I assure you.

Sarah. Are you coming, Stephen?

Stephen. Well, I am rather busy — er — (*Magnanimously*) Oh well, yes: I'll come. That is, if there is room for me.

Undershaft. I can take two with me in a little motor I am experimenting with for field use. You wont mind its being rather unfashionable. It's not painted yet; but it's bullet proof.

Lomax (*appalled at the prospect of confronting Wilton Crescent in an unpainted motor*) Oh I say!

Sarah. The carriage for me, thank you. Barbara doesnt mind what she's seen in.

Lomax. I say, Dolly, old chap: do you really mind the car being a guy? Because of course if you do I'll go in it. Still —

Cusins. I prefer it.

Lomax. Thanks awfully, old man. Come, my ownest. (*He hurries out to secure his seat in the carriage. Sarah follows him*).

Cusins (*moodily walking across to Lady Britomart's writing table*) Why are we two coming to this Works Department of Hell? that is what I ask myself.

Barbara. I have always thought of it as a sort of pit where lost creatures with blackened faces stirred up smoky fires and were driven and tormented by my father? Is it like that, dad?

Undershaft (*scandalized*) My dear! It is a spotlessly clean and beautiful hillside town.

Cusins. With a Methodist chapel? Oh do say theres a Methodist chapel.

Undershaft. There are two: a Primitive one and a sophisticated one. There is even an Ethical Society; but it is not much patronized, as my men are all strongly religious. In the High Explosives Sheds they object to the presence of Agnostics as unsafe.

Cusins. And yet they dont object to you!

Barbara. Do they obey all your orders?

Undershaft. I never give them any orders. When I speak to one of them it is 'Well, Jones, is the baby doing well? and has Mrs Jones made a good recovery?' 'Nicely, thank you, sir.' And thats all.

Cusins. But Jones has to be kept in order. How do you maintain discipline among your men?

Undershaft. I dont. They do. You see, the one thing Jones wont stand is any rebellion from the man under him, or any assertion of social equality between the wife of the man with 4 shillings a week less than himself, and Mrs Jones! Of course they all rebel against me, theoretically. Practically, every man of them keeps the man just below him in his place. I never meddle with them. I never bully them. I dont even bully Lazarus. I say that certain things are to be done; but I dont order anybody to do them. I dont say, mind you, that there is no ordering about and snubbing and even bullying. The men snub the boys and order them about; the carmen snub the sweepers; the artisans snub the unskilled laborers; the foremen drive and bully both the laborers and artisans; the assistant engineers find fault with the foremen; the chief engineers drop on the assistants; the departmental managers worry the chiefs; and the clerks have tall hats and hymnbooks and keep up the social tone by refusing to associate on equal terms with anybody. The result is a colossal profit, which comes to me.

Cusins (revolted) You really are a — well, what I was saying yesterday.

Barbara. What was he saying yesterday?

Undershaft. Never mind, my dear. He thinks I have made you unhappy. Have I?

Barbara. Do you think I can be happy in this vulgar silly dress? I! who have worn the uniform. Do you understand what you have done to me? Yesterday I had a man's soul in my hand. I set him in the way of life with his face to salvation. But when we took your money he turned back to drunkenness and derision. (*With intense conviction*) I will never forgive you that. If I had a child, and you destroyed its body with your explosives — if you murdered Dolly with your horrible guns — I could forgive you if my forgiveness would open the gates of heaven to you. But to take a human soul from me, and turn it into the soul of a wolf! that is worse than any murder.

Undershaft. Does my daughter despair so easily? Can you strike a man to the heart and leave no mark on him?

Barbara (her face lighting up) Oh, you are right: he can never be lost now: where was my faith?

Cusins. Oh, clever clever devil!

Barbara. You may be a devil; but God speaks through you sometimes. (*She takes her father's hands and kisses them*). You have given me back my happiness: I feel it deep down now, though my spirit is troubled.

Undershaft. You have learnt something. That always feels at first as if you had lost something.

Barbara. Well, take me to the factory of death; and let me learn something more. There must be some truth or other behind all this frightful irony. Come, Dolly. (*She goes out*).

Cusins. My guardian angel! (*To Undershaft*) Avaunt! (*He follows Barbara*).

Stephen (*quietly, at the writing table*) You must not mind Cusins, father. He is a very amiable good fellow; but he is a Greek scholar and naturally a little eccentric.

Undershaft. Ah, quite so, Thank you, Stephen. Thank you. (*He goes out*).

(*Stephen smiles patronizingly; buttons his coat responsibly; and crosses the room to the door. Lady Britomart, dressed for out-of-doors, opens it before he reaches it. She looks round for others; looks at Stephen; and turns to go without a word.*)

Stephen (*embarrassed*) Mother —

Lady Britomart. Dont be apologetic, Stephen. And dont forget that you have outgrown your mother. (*She goes out*).

Perivale St Andrews lies between two Middlesex hills, half climbing the northern one. It is an almost smokeless town of white walls, roofs of narrow green slates or red tiles, tall trees, domes, campaniles, and slender chimney shafts, beautifully situated and beautiful in itself. The best view of it is obtained from the crest of a slope about half a mile to the east, where the high explosives are dealt with. The foundry lies hidden in the depths between, the tops of its chimneys sprouting like huge skittles into the middle distance. Across the crest runs an emplacement of concrete, with a firestep, and a parapet which suggests a fortification, because there is a huge cannon of the obsolete Woolwich Infant pattern peering across it at the town. The cannon is mounted on an experimental gun carriage: possibly the original model of the Undershaft disappearing rampart gun alluded to by Stephen. The firestep, being a convenient place to sit, is furnished here and there with straw disc cushions; and at one place there is the additional luxury of a fur rug.

Barbara is standing on the firestep, looking over the parapet towards the town. On her right is the cannon; on her left the end of a shed raised on piles, with a ladder of three or four steps up to the door, which opens outwards and has a little wooden landing at the threshold, with a fire bucket in the corner of the landing. Several dummy soldiers more or less mutilated, with straw protruding from their gashes, have been shoved out of the way under the landing. A few others are nearly upright against the shed; and one has fallen forward and lies, like a grotesque corpse, on the emplacement. The parapet stops short of the shed, leaving a gap which is the beginning of the path down the hill through the foundry to the town. The rug is on the firestep near this gap. Down on the emplacement behind the cannon is a trolley carrying a huge conical bombshell with a red band painted on it. Further to the right is the door of an office, which, like the sheds, is of the lightest possible construction.

Cusins arrives by the path from the town.

Barbara. Well?

Cusins. Not a ray of hope. Everything perfect! wonderful! real! It only needs a cathedral to be a heavenly city instead of a hellish one.

Barbara. Have you found out whether they have done anything for old Peter Shirley?

Cusins. They have found him a job as gatekeeper and timekeeper. He's frightfully miserable. He calls the time-keeping brainwork, and says he isnt used to it; and his gate lodge is so splendid that he's ashamed to use the rooms, and skulks in the scullery.

Barbara. Poor Peter!

(*Stephen arrives from the town. He carries a fieldglass.*)

Stephen (*enthusiastically*) Have you two seen the place? Why did you leave us?

Cusins. I wanted to see everything I was not intended to see; and Barbara wanted to make the men talk.

Stephen. Have you found anything discreditable?

Cusins. No. They call him Dandy Andy and are proud of his being a cunning old rascal; but it's all horribly, frightfully, immorally, unanswerably perfect.

(*Sarah arrives.*)

Sarah. Heavens! what a place! (*She crosses to the trolley*). Did you see the nursing home!? (*She sits down on the shell*).

Stephen. Did you see the libraries and schools!?

Sarah. Did you see the ball room and the banqueting chamber in the Town Hall!?

Stephen. Have you gone into the insurance fund, the pension fund, the building society, the various applications of cooperation!?

(*Undershaft comes from the office, with a sheaf of telegrams in his hand.*)

Undershaft. Well, have you seen everything? I'm sorry I was called away. (*Indicating the telegrams*) Good news from Manchuria.

Stephen. Another Japanese victory?

Undershaft. Oh, I dont know. Which side wins does not concern us here. No: the good news is that the aerial battleship is a tremendous success. At the first trial it has wiped out a fort with three hundred soldiers in it.

Cusins (*from the platform*) Dummy soldiers?

Undershaft (*striding across to Stephen and kicking the prostrate dummy brutally out of his way*) No: the real thing.

(*Cusins and Barbara exchange glances. Then Cusins sits on the step and buries his face in his hands. Barbara gravely lays her hand on his shoulder. He looks up at her in whimsical desperation.*)

Undershaft. Well, Stephen, what do you think of the place?

Stephen. Oh, magnificent. A perfect triumph of modern industry. Frankly, my dear father, I have been a fool: I had no idea of what it all meant: of the wonderful forethought, the power of organization, the administrative capacity, the financial genius, the colossal capital it represents. I have been repeating to myself as I came through your streets 'Peace hath her victories no less renowned than War.' I have only one misgiving about it all.

Undershaft. Out with it.

Stephen. Well, I cannot help thinking that all this provision for every want of your workmen may sap their independence and weaken their sense of responsibility. And greatly as we enjoyed our tea at that splendid restaurant — how they gave us all that luxury and cake and jam and cream for threepence I really cannot imagine! — still you must remember that restaurants break up home life. Look at the continent, for instance! Are you sure so much pampering is really good for the men's characters?

Undershaft. Well you see, my dear boy, when you are organizing civilization you have to make up your mind whether trouble and anxiety are good things or not. If you decide that they are, then, I take it, you simply dont organize civilization; and there you are, with trouble and anxiety enough to make us all angels! But if you decide the other way, you may as well go through with it. However, Stephen, our characters are safe here. A sufficient dose of anxiety is always provided by the fact that we may be blown to smithereens at any moment.

Sarah. By the way, papa, where do you make the explosives?

Undershaft. In separate little sheds, like that one. When one of them blows up, it costs very little; and only the people quite close to it are killed.

(*Stephen, who is quite close to it, looks at it rather scaredly, and moves away quickly to the cannon. At the same moment the door of the shed is thrown abruptly open; and a foreman in overalls and list slippers comes out on the little landing and holds the door for Lomax, who appears in the doorway.*)

Lomax (*with studied coolness*) My good fellow: you neednt get into a state of nerves. Nothing's going to happen to you; and I suppose it wouldnt be the end of the world if anything did. A little bit of British pluck is what you want, old chap. (*He descends and strolls across to Sarah*).

Undershaft (*to the foreman*) Anything wrong, Bilton?

Bilton (*with ironic calm*) Gentleman walked into the high explosives shed and lit a cigaret, sir: thats all.

Undershaft. Ah, quite so. (*Going over to Lomax*) Do you happen to remember what you did with the match?

Lomax. Oh come! I'm not a fool. I took jolly good care to blow it out before I chucked it away.

Bilton. The top of it was red hot inside, sir.

Lomax. Well, suppose it was! I didnt chuck it into any of your messes.

Undershaft. Think no more of it, Mr Lomax. By the way, would you mind lending me your matches.

Lomax (*offering his box*) Certainly.

Undershaft. Thanks. (*He pockets the matches*).

Lomax (*lecturing to the company generally*) You know, these high explosives dont go off like gunpowder, except when theyre in a gun. When theyre spread loose, you can put a match to them without the least risk: they just burn quietly like a bit of paper. (*Warming to the scientific interest of the subject*) Did you know that, Undershaft? Have you ever tried?

Undershaft. Not on a large scale, Mr Lomax. Bilton will give you a sample of gun cotton when you are leaving if you ask him. You can experiment with it at home. (*Bilton looks puzzled*).

Sarah. Bilton will do nothing of the sort, papa. I suppose it's your business to blow up the Russians and Japs; but you might really stop short of blowing up poor Cholly. (*Bilton gives it up and retires into the shed*).

Lomax. My ownest, there is no danger. (*He sits beside her on the shell*).

(*Lady Britomart arrives from the town with a bouquet.*)

Lady Britomart (*impetuously*) Andrew: you shouldnt have let me see this place.

Undershaft. Why, my dear?

Lady Britomart. Never mind why: you shouldnt have: thats all. To think of all that (*indicating the town*) being yours! and that you have kept it to yourself all these years!

Undershaft. It does not belong to me. I belong to it. It is the Undershaft inheritance.

Lady Britomart. It is not. Your ridiculous cannons and that noisy banging foundry may be the Undershaft inheritance; but all that plate and linen, all that furniture and those houses and orchards and gardens belong to us. They belong to me: they are not a man's business. I wont give them up. You must be out of your senses to throw them all away; and if you persist in such folly, I will call in a doctor.

Undershaft (*stooping to smell the bouquet*) Where did you get the flowers, my dear?

Lady Britomart. Your men presented them to me in your William Morris Labor Church.

Cusins. Oh! It needed only that. A Labor Church! (*he mounts the firestep distractedly, and leans with his elbows on the parapet, turning his back to them*).

Lady Britomart. Yes, with Morris's words in mosaic letters ten feet high round the dome. NO MAN IS GOOD ENOUGH TO BE ANOTHER MAN'S MASTER. The cynicism of it!

Undershaft. It shocked the men at first, I am afraid. But now they take no more notice of it than of the ten commandments in church.

Lady Britomart. Andrew: you are trying to put me off the subject of the inheritance by profane jokes. Well, you shant. I dont ask it any longer for Stephen: he has inherited far too much of your perversity to be fit for it. But Barbara has rights as well as Stephen. Why should not Adolphus succeed to the inheritance? I could manage the town for him; and he can look after the cannons, if they are really necessary.

Undershaft. I should ask nothing better if Adolphus were a foundling. He is exactly the sort of new blood that is wanted in English business. But he's not a foundling; and theres an end of it. (*He makes for the office door*).

Cusins (*turning to them*) Not quite. (*They all turn and stare at him*). I think — Mind! I am not committing myself in any way as to my future course — but I think the foundling difficulty can be got over. (*He jumps down to the emplacement*).

Undershaft (*coming back to him*) What do you mean?

Cusins. Well, I have something to say which is in the nature of a confession.

Sarah.
Lady Britomart.
Barbara. } Confession!
Stephen.

Lomax. Oh I say!

Cusins. Yes, a confession. Listen, all. Until I met Barbara I thought myself in the main an honorable, truthful man, because I wanted the approval of my conscience more than I wanted anything else. But the moment I saw Barbara, I wanted her far more than the approval of my conscience.

Lady Britomart. Adolphus!

Cusins. It is true. You accused me yourself, Lady Brit, of joining the Army to worship Barbara; and so I did. She bought my soul like a flower at a street corner; but she bought it for herself.

Undershaft. What! Not for Dionysos or another?

Cusins. Dionysos and all the others are in herself. I adored what was divine in her, and was therefore a true worshipper. But I was romantic about her too. I thought she was a woman of the people, and that a marriage with a professor of Greek would be far beyond the wildest social ambitions of her rank.

Lady Britomart. Adolphus!!

Lomax. Oh I say!!!

Cusins. When I learnt the horrible truth —

Lady Britomart. What do you mean by the horrible truth, pray?

Cusins. That she was enormously rich; that her grandfather was an earl; that her father was the Prince of Darkness —

Undershaft. Chut!

Cusins. — and that I was only an adventurer trying to catch a rich wife, then I stooped to deceive her about my birth.

Barbara (rising) Dolly!

Lady Britomart. Your birth! Now Adolphus, dont dare to make up a wicked story for the sake of these wretched cannons. Remember: I have seen photographs of your parents; and the Agent General for South Western Australia knows them personally and has assured me that they are most respectable married people.

Cusins. So they are in Australia; but here they are outcasts. Their marriage is legal in Australia, but not in England. My mother is my father's deceased wife's sister; and in this island I am consequently a foundling. (*Sensation*).

Barbara. Silly! (*She climbs to the cannon, and leans, listening, in the angle it makes with the parapet*).

Cusins. Is the subterfuge good enough, Machiavelli?

Undershaft (*thoughtfully*) Biddy: this may be a way out of the difficulty.

Lady Britomart. Stuff! A man cant make cannons any the better for being his own cousin instead of his proper self (*she sits down on the rug with a bounce that expresses her downright contempt for their casuistry*).

Undershaft (*to Cusins*) You are an educated man. That is against the tradition.

Cusins. Once in ten thousand times it happens that the schoolboy is a born master of what they try to teach him. Greek has not destroyed my mind: it has nourished it. Besides, I did not learn it at an English public school.

Undershaft. Hm! Well, I cannot afford to be too particular: you have cornered the foundling market. Let it pass. You are eligible, Euripides: you are eligible.

Barbara. Dolly: yesterday morning, when Stephen told us all about the tradition, you became very silent; and you have been strange and excited ever since. Were you thinking of your birth then?

Cusins. When the finger of Destiny suddenly points at a man in the middle of his breakfast, it makes him thoughtful.

Undershaft. Aha! You have had your eye on the business, my young friend, have you?

Cusins. Take care! There is an abyss of moral horror between me and your accursed aerial battleships.

Undershaft. Never mind the abyss for the present. Let us settle the practical details and leave your final decision open. You know that you will have to change your name. Do you object to that?

Cusins. Would any man named Adolphus — any man called Dolly! — object to be called something else?

Undershaft. Good. Now, as to money! I propose to treat you handsomely from the beginning. You shall start at a thousand a year.

Cusins (*with sudden heat, his spectacles twinkling with mischief*) A thousand! You dare offer a miserable thousand to the son-in-law of a millionaire! No, by Heavens, Machiavelli! you shall not cheat me. You cannot do without me; and I can do without you. I must have two thousand five hundred a year for two years. At the end of that time, if I am a failure, I go. But if I am a success, and stay on, you must give me the other five thousand.

Undershaft. What other five thousand?

Cusins. To make the two years up to five thousand a year. The two thousand five hundred is only half pay in case I should turn out a failure. The third year I must have ten per cent on the profits.

Undershaft (*taken aback*) Ten per cent! Why, man, do you know what my profits are?

Cusins. Enormous, I hope: otherwise I shall require twenty-five per cent.

Undershaft. But, Mr Cusins, this is a serious matter of business. You are not bringing any capital into the concern.

Cusins. What! no capital! Is my mastery of Greek no capital? Is my access to the subtlest thought, the loftiest poetry yet attained by humanity, no capital? My character! my intellect! my life! my career! what Barbara calls my soul! are these no capital? Say another word; and I double my salary.

Undershaft. Be reasonable —

Cusins (*peremptorily*) Mr Undershaft: you have my terms. Take them or leave them.

Undershaft (*recovering himself*) Very well. I note your terms; and I offer you half.

Cusins (*disgusted*) Half!

Undershaft (*firmly*) Half.

Cusins. You call yourself a gentleman; and you offer me half!!

Undershaft. I do not call myself a gentleman; but I offer you half.

Cusins. This to your future partner! your successor! your son-in-law!

Barbara. You are selling your own soul, Dolly, not mine. Leave me out of the bargain, please.

Undershaft. Come! I will go a step further for Barbara's sake. I will give you three fifths; but that is my last word.

Cusins. Done!

Lomax. Done in the eye! Why, *I* get only eight hundred, you know.

Cusins. By the way, Mac, I am a classical scholar, not an arithmetical one. Is three fifths more than half or less?

Undershaft. More, of course.

Cusins. I would have taken two hundred and fifty. How you can succeed in business when you are willing to pay all that money to a University don who is obviously not worth a junior clerk's wages! — well! What will Lazarus say?

Undershaft. Lazarus is a gentle romantic Jew who cares for nothing but string quartets and stalls at fashionable theatres. He will be blamed for your rapacity in money matters, poor fellow! as he has hitherto been blamed for mine. You are a shark of the first order, Euripides. So much the better for the firm!

Barbara. Is the bargain closed, Dolly? Does your soul belong to him now?

Cusins. No: the price is settled: that is all. The real tug of war is still to come. What about the moral question?

Lady Britomart. There is no moral question in the matter at all, Adolphus. You must simply sell cannons and weapons to people whose cause is right and just, and refuse them to foreigners and criminals.

Undershaft (determined) No: none of that. You must keep the true faith of an Armorer, or you dont come in here.

Cusins. What on earth is the true faith of an Armorer?

Undershaft. To give arms to all men who offer an honest price for them, without respect of persons or principles: to aristocrat and republican, to Nihilist and Tsar, to Capitalist and Socialist, to Protestant and Catholic, to burglar and policeman, to black man, white man and yellow man, to all sorts and conditions, all nationalities, all faiths, all follies, all causes and all crimes. The first Undershaft wrote up in his shop IF GOD GAVE THE HAND, LET NOT MAN WITHHOLD THE SWORD. The second wrote up ALL HAVE THE RIGHT TO FIGHT: NONE HAVE THE RIGHT TO JUDGE. The third wrote up TO MAN THE WEAPON: TO HEAVEN THE VICTORY. The fourth had no literary turn; so he did not write up anything; but he sold cannons to Napoleon under the nose of George the Third. The fifth wrote up PEACE SHALL NOT PREVAIL SAVE WITH A SWORD IN HER HAND. The sixth, my master, was the best of all. He wrote up NOTHING IS EVER DONE IN THIS WORLD UNTIL MEN ARE PREPARED TO KILL ONE ANOTHER IF IT IS NOT DONE. After that, there was nothing left for the seventh to say. So he wrote up, simply, UNASHAMED.

Cusins. My good Machiavelli, I shall certainly write something up on the wall; only, as I shall write it in Greek, you wont be able to read it. But as to your Armorer's faith, if I take my neck out of the noose of my own morality I am not going to put it into the noose of yours. I shall sell cannons to whom I please and refuse them to whom I please. So there!

Undershaft. From the moment when you become Andrew Undershaft, you will never do as you please again. Dont come here lusting for power, young man.

Cusins. If power were my aim I should not come here for it. You have no power.

Undershaft. None of my own, certainly.

Cusins. I have more power than you, more will. You do not drive this place: it drives you. And what drives the place?

Undershaft (enigmatically) A will of which I am a part.

Barbara (startled) Father! Do you know what you are saying; or are you laying a snare for my soul?

Cusins. Dont listen to his metaphysics, Barbara. The place is driven by the most rascally part of society, the money hunters, the pleasure hunters, the military promotion hunters; and he is their slave.

Undershaft. Not necessarily. Remember the Armorer's Faith. I will take an order from a good man as cheerfully as from a bad one. If you good people prefer preaching and shirking to buying my weapons and fighting the rascals, dont blame me. I can make cannons: I cannot make courage and conviction. Bah! you tire me, Euripides, with your morality mongering. Ask Barbara: she understands. (*He suddenly reaches up and takes Barbara's hands, looking powerfully into her eyes*) Tell him, my love, what power really means.

Barbara (*hypnotized*) Before I joined the Salvation Army, I was in my own power; and the consequence was that I never knew what to do with myself. When I joined it, I had not time enough for all the things I had to do.

Undershaft (*approvingly*) Just so. And why was that, do you suppose?

Barbara. Yesterday I should have said, because I was in the power of God. (*She resumes her self-possession, withdrawing her hands from his with a power equal to his own*). But you came and shewed me that I was in the power of Bodger and Undershaft. Today I feel — oh! how can I put it into words? Sarah: do you remember the earthquake at Cannes, when we were little children? — how little the surprise of the first shock mattered compared to the dread and horror of waiting for the second? That is how I feel in this place today. I stood on the rock I thought eternal; and without a word of warning it reeled and crumbled under me. I was safe with an infinite wisdom watching me, an army marching to Salvation with me; and in a moment, at a stroke of your pen in a cheque book, I stood alone; and the heavens were empty. That was the first shock of the earthquake: I am waiting for the second.

Undershaft. Come, come, my daughter! dont make too much of your tinpot tragedy. What do we do here when we spend years of work and thought and thousands of pounds of solid cash on a new gun or an aerial battleship that turns out just a hairsbreadth wrong after all? Scrap it. Scrap it without wasting another hour or another pound on it. Well, you have made for yourself something that you call a morality or a religion or what not. It doesn't fit the facts. Well, scrap it. Scrap it and get one that does fit. That is what is wrong with the world at present. It scraps its obsolete steam engines and dynamos; but it wont scrap its old prejudices and its old moralities and its old religions and its old political constitutions. Whats the result? In machinery it does very well; but in morals and religion and politics it is working at a loss that brings it nearer bankruptcy every year. Dont persist in that folly. If your old religion broke down yesterday, get a newer and a better one for tomorrow.

Barbara. Oh how gladly I would take a better one to my soul! But you offer me a worse one. (*Turning on him with sudden vehemence*). Justify yourself: shew me some light through the darkness of this dreadful place, with its beautifully clean workshops, and respectable workmen, and model homes.

Undershaft. Cleanliness and respectability do not need justification, Barbara: they justify themselves. I see no darkness here, no dreadfulness. In your Salvation shelter I saw poverty, misery, cold and hunger. You gave them bread and treacle and dreams of heaven. I give from thirty shillings a week to twelve thousand a year. They find their own dreams; but I look after the drainage.

Barbara. And their souls?

Undershaft. I save their souls just as I saved yours.

Barbara (*revolted*) You saved my soul! What do you mean?

Undershaft. I fed you and clothed you and housed you. I took care that you should have money enough to live handsomely — more than enough; so that you could be wasteful, careless, generous. That saved your soul from the seven deadly sins.

Barbara (*bewildered*) The seven deadly sins!

Undershaft. Yes, the deadly seven. (*Counting on his fingers*) Food, clothing, firing, rent, taxes, respectability and children. Nothing can lift those seven millstones from Man's neck but money; and the spirit cannot soar until the millstones are lifted. I lifted them from your spirit. I enabled Barbara to become Major Barbara; and I saved her from the crime of poverty.

Cusins. Do you call poverty a crime?

Undershaft. The worst of crimes. All the other crimes are virtues beside it: all the other dishonors are chivalry itself by comparison. Poverty blights whole cities; spreads horrible pestilences; strikes dead the very souls of all who come within sight, sound, or smell of it. What you call crime is nothing: a murder here and a theft there, a blow now and a curse then: what do they matter? they are only the accidents and illnesses of life: there are not fifty genuine professional criminals in London. But there are millions of poor people, abject people, dirty people, ill fed, ill clothed people. They poison us morally and physically: they kill the happiness of society: they force us to do away with our own liberties and to organize unnatural cruelties for fear they should rise against us and drag us down into their abyss. Only fools fear crime: we all fear poverty. Pah! (*turning on Barbara*) you talk of your half-saved ruffian in West Ham: you accuse me of dragging his soul back to perdition.

Well, bring him to me here; and I will drag his soul back again to salvation for you. Not by words and dreams; but by thirtyeight shillings a week, a sound house in a handsome street, and a permanent job. In three weeks he will have a fancy waistcoat; in three months a tall hat and a chapel sitting; before the end of the year he will shake hands with a duchess at a Primrose League meeting, and join the Conservative Party.

Barbara. And will he be the better for that?

Undershaft. You know he will. Dont be a hypocrite, Barbara. He will be better fed, better housed, better clothed, better behaved; and his children will be pounds heavier and bigger. That will be better than an American cloth mattress in a shelter, chopping firewood, eating bread and treacle, and being forced to kneel down from time to time to thank heaven for it: knee drill, I think you call it. It is cheap work converting starving men with a Bible in one hand and a slice of bread in the other. I will undertake to convert West Ham to Mahometanism on the same terms. Try your hand on my men: their souls are hungry because their bodies are full.

Barbara. And leave the east end to starve?

Undershaft (*his energetic tone dropping into one of bitter and brooding remembrance*) I was an east ender. I moralized and starved until one day I swore that I would be a full-fed free man at all costs; that nothing should stop me except a bullet, neither reason nor morals nor the lives of other men. I said 'Thou shalt starve ere I starve'; and with that word I became free and great. I was a dangerous man until I had my will: now I am a useful, beneficent, kindly person. That is the history of most self-made millionaires, I fancy. When it is the history of every Englishman we shall have an England worth living in.

Lady Britomart. Stop making speeches, Andrew This is not the place for them.

Undershaft (*punctured*) My dear: I have no other means of conveying my ideas.

Lady Britomart. Your ideas are nonsense. You got on because you were selfish and unscrupulous.

Undershaft. Not at all. I had the strongest scruples about poverty and starvation. Your moralists are quite unscrupulous about both: they make virtues of them. I had rather be a thief than a pauper. I had rather be a murderer than a slave. I dont want to be either; but if you force the alternative on me, then, by Heaven, I'll chose the braver and more moral one. I hate poverty and slavery worse than any other crimes whatsoever. And let me tell you this. Poverty and slavery have stood up for centuries to your sermons and leading articles: they will not stand up to my machine guns. Dont preach at them: dont reason with them. Kill them.

Barbara. Killing. Is that your remedy for everything?

Undershaft. It is the final test of conviction, the only lever strong enough to overturn a social system, the only way of saying Must. Let six hundred and seventy fools loose in the streets; and three policemen can scatter them. But huddle them together in a certain house in Westminster; and let them go through certain ceremonies and call themselves certain names until at last they get the courage to kill; and your six hundred and seventy fools become a government. Your pious mob fills up ballot papers and imagines it is governing its masters; but the ballot paper that really governs is the paper that has a bullet wrapped up in it.

Cusins. That is perhaps why, like most intelligent people, I never vote.

Undershaft. Vote! Bah! When you vote, you only change the names of the cabinet. When you shoot, you pull down governments, inaugurate new epochs, abolish old orders and set up new. Is that historically true, Mr Learned Man, or is it not?

Cusins. It is historically true. I loathe having to admit it. I repudiate your sentiments. I abhor your nature. I defy you in every possible way. Still, it is true. But it ought not to be true.

Undershaft. Ought! ought! ought! ought! ought! Are you going to spend your life saying ought, like the rest of our moralists? Turn your oughts into shalls, man. Come and make explosives with me. Whatever can blow men up can blow society up. The history of the world is the history of those who had courage enough to embrace this truth. Have you the courage to embrace it, Barbara?

Lady Britomart. Barbara: I positively forbid you to listen to your father's abominable wickedness. And you, Adolphus, ought to know better than to go about saying that wrong things are true. What does it matter whether they are true if they are wrong?

Undershaft. What does it matter whether they are wrong if they are true?

Lady Britomart (*rising*) Children: come home instantly. Andrew: I am exceedingly sorry I allowed you to call on us. You are wickeder than ever. Come at once.

Barbara (*shaking her head*) It's no use running away from wicked people, mamma.

Lady Britomart. It is every use. It shews your disapprobation of them.

Barbara. It does not save them.

Lady Britomart. I can see that you are going to disobey me. Sarah: are you coming home or are you not?

Sarah. I daresay it's very wicked of papa to make cannons; but I dont think I shall cut him on that account.

Lomax (*pouring oil on the troubled waters*) The fact is, you know, there is a certain amount of tosh about this notion of wickedness. It doesnt work. You must look at facts. Not that I would say a word in favor of anything wrong; but then, you see, all sorts of chaps are always doing all sorts of things; and we have to fit them in somehow, dont you know. What I mean is that you cant go cutting everybody; and thats about what it comes to. (*Their rapt attention to his eloquence makes him nervous*). Perhaps I dont make myself clear.

Lady Britomart. You are lucidity itself, Charles. Because Andrew is successful and has plenty of money to give to Sarah, you will flatter him and encourage him in his wickedness.

Lomax (*unruffled*) Well, where the carcase is, there will the eagles be gathered, dont you know. (*To Undershaft*) Eh? What?

Undershaft. Precisely. By the way, may I call you Charles?

Lomax. Delighted. Cholly is the usual ticket.

Undershaft (*to Lady Britomart*) Biddy —

Lady Britomart (*violently*) Dont dare call me Biddy. Charles Lomax: you are a fool. Adolphus Cusins: you are a Jesuit. Stephen: you are a prig. Barbara: you are a lunatic. Andrew: you are a vulgar tradesman. Now you all know my opinion; and my conscience is clear, at all events (*she sits down with a vehemence that the rug fortunately softens*).

Undershaft. My dear: you are the incarnation of morality. (*She snorts*). Your conscience is clear and your duty done when you have called everybody names. Come, Euripides! It is getting late; and we all want to go home. Make up your mind.

Cusins. Understand this, you old demon —

Lady Britomart. Adolphus!

Undershaft. Let him alone, Biddy. Proceed, Euripides.

Cusins. You have me in a horrible dilemma. I want Barbara.

Undershaft. Like all young men, you greatly exaggerate the difference between one young woman and another.

Barbara. Quite true, Dolly.

Cusins. I also want to avoid being a rascal.

Undershaft (*with biting contempt*) You lust for personal righteousness, for self-approval, for what you call a good conscience, for what Barbara calls salvation, for what I call patronizing people who are not so lucky as yourself.

Cusins. I do not: all the poet in me recoils from being a good man. But there are things in me that I must reckon with. Pity —

Undershaft. Pity! The scavenger of misery.

Cusins. Well, love.

Undershaft. I know. You love the needy and the outcast: you love the oppressed races, the negro, the Indian ryot, the underdog everywhere. Do you love the Japanese? Do you love the English?

Cusins. No. Every true Englishman detests the English. We are the wickedest nation on earth; and our success is a moral horror.

Undershaft. That is what comes of your gospel of love, is it?

Cusins. May I not love even my father-in-law?

Undershaft. Who wants your love, man? By what right do you take the liberty of offering it to me? I will have your due heed and respect, or I will kill you. But your love! Damn your impertinence!

Cusins (grinning) I may not be able to control my affections, Mac.

Undershaft. You are fencing, Euripides. You are weakening: your grip is slipping. Come! try your last weapon. Pity and love have broken in your hand: forgiveness is still left.

Cusins. No: forgiveness is a beggar's refuge. I am with you there: we must pay our debts.

Undershaft. Well said. Come! you will suit me. Remember the words of Plato.

Cusins (starting) Plato! You dare quote Plato to me!

Undershaft. Plato says, my friend, that society cannot be saved until either the Professors of Greek take to making gunpowder, or else the makers of gunpowder become Professors of Greek.

Cusins. Oh, tempter, cunning tempter!

Undershaft. Come! choose, man, choose.

Cusins. But perhaps Barbara will not marry me if I make the wrong choice.

Barbara. Perhaps not.

Cusins (desperately perplexed) You hear!

Barbara. Father: do you love nobody?

Undershaft. I love my best friend.

Lady Britomart. And who is that, pray?

Undershaft. My bravest enemy. That is the man who keeps me up to the mark.

Cusins. You know, the creature is really a sort of poet in his way. Suppose he is a great man, after all!

Undershaft. Suppose you stop talking and make up your mind, my young friend.

Cusins. But you are driving me against my nature. I hate war.

Undershaft. Hatred is the coward's revenge for being intimidated. Dare you make war on war? Here are the means: my friend Mr Lomax is sitting on them.

Lomax (*springing up*) Oh I say! You dont mean that this thing is loaded, do you? My ownest: come off it.

Sarah (*sitting placidly on the shell*) If I am to be blown up, the more thoroughly it is done the better. Dont fuss, Cholly.

Lomax (*to Undershaft, strongly remonstrant*) Your own daughter, you know!

Undershaft. So I see. (*To Cusins*) Well, my friend, may we expect you here at six tomorrow morning?

Cusins (*firmly*) Not on any account. I will see the whole establishment blown up with its own dynamite before I will get up at five. My hours are healthy, rational hours: eleven to five.

Undershaft. Come when you please: before a week you will come at six and stay until I turn you out for the sake of your health. (*Calling*) Bilton! (*He turns to Lady Britomart, who rises*). My dear: let use leave these two young people to themselves for a moment. (*Bilton comes from the shed*). I am going to take you through the gun cotton shed.

Bilton (*barring the way*) You cant take anything explosive in here, sir.

Lady Britomart. What do you mean? Are you alluding to me?

Bilton (*unmoved*) No, maam. Mr Undershaft has the other gentleman's matches in his pocket.

Lady Britomart (*abruptly*) Oh! I beg your pardon. (*She goes into the shed*).

Undershaft. Quite right, Bilton, quite right: here you are. (*He gives Bilton the box of matches*). Come, Stephen. Come, Charles. Bring Sarah. (*He passes into the shed*).

(*Bilton opens the box and deliberately drops the matches into the fire-bucket.*)

Lomax. Oh! I say (*Bilton stolidly hands him the empty box*). Infernal nonsense! Pure scientific ignorance! (*He goes in*).

Sarah. Am I all right, Bilton?

Bilton. Youll have to put on list slippers, miss: thats all. Weve got em inside. (*She goes in*).

Stephen (*very seriously to Cusins*) Dolly, old fellow, think. Think before you decide. Do you feel that you are a sufficiently practical man? It is a huge undertaking, an enormous responsibility. All this mass of business will be Greek to you.

Cusins. Oh, I think it will be much less difficult than Greek.

Stephen. Well, I just want to say this before I leave you to yourselves. Dont let anything I have said about right and wrong prejudice you against this great chance in life. I have satisfied myself that the business is one of the highest character and a credit to our country. (*Emotionally*) I am very proud of my father. I — (*Unable to proceed, he presses Cusins' hand and goes hastily into the shed, followed by Bilton*).

(*Barbara and Cusins, left alone together, look at one another silently.*)

Cusins. Barbara: I am going to accept this offer.

Barbara. I thought you would.

Cusins. You understand, dont you, that I had to decide without consulting you. If I had thrown the burden of the choice on you, you would sooner or later have despised me for it.

Barbara. Yes: I did not want you to sell your soul for me any more than for this inheritance.

Cusins. It is not the sale of my soul that troubles me: I have sold it too often to care about that. I have sold it for a professorship. I have sold it for an income. I have sold it to escape being imprisoned for refusing to pay taxes for hangmen's ropes and unjust wars and things that I abhor. What is all human conduct but the daily and hourly sale of our souls for trifles? What I am now selling it for is neither money nor position nor comfort, but for reality and for power.

Barbara. You know that you will have no power, and that he has none.

Cusins. I know. It is not for myself alone. I want to make power for the world.

Barbara. I want to make power for the world too; but it must be spiritual power.

Cusins. I think all power is spiritual: these cannons will not go off by themselves. I have tried to make spiritual power by teaching Greek. But the world can never be really touched by a dead language and a dead civilization. The people must have power; and the people cannot have Greek. Now the power that is made here can be wielded by all men.

Barbara. Power to burn women's houses down and kill their sons and tear their husbands to pieces.

Cusins. You cannot have power for good without having power for evil too. Even mother's milk nourishes murderers as well as heroes. This power which only tears men's bodies to pieces has never been so horribly abused as the intellectual power, the imaginative power, the poetic, religious power that can enslave men's souls. As a teacher of Greek I gave the intellectual man weapons against the common man. I now want to give the common man weapons against the intellectual man. I love the common people. I want to arm them against the lawyers, the doctors, the priests, the literary men, the professors, the artists, and the politicians, who, once in authority, are more disastrous and tyrannical than all the fools, rascals, and impostors. I want a power simple enough for common men to use, yet strong enough to force the intellectual oligarchy to use its genius for the general good.

Barbara. Is there no higher power than that (*pointing to the shell*)?

Cusins. Yes; but that power can destroy the higher powers just as a tiger can destroy a man: therefore Man must master that power first. I admitted this when the Turks and Greeks were last at war. My best pupil went out to fight for Hellas. My parting gift to him was not a copy of Plato's Republic, but a revolver and a hundred Undershaft cartridges. The blood of every Turk he shot — if he shot any — is on my head as well as on Undershaft's. That act commited me to this place for ever. Your father's challenge has beaten me. Dare I make war on war? I must. I will, And now, is it all over between us?

Barbara (*touched by his evident dread of her answer*) Silly baby Dolly! How could it be!

Cusins (*overjoyed*) Then you — you — you — Oh for my drum! (*He flourishes imaginary drumsticks*).

Barbara (*angered by his levity*) Take care, Dolly, take care. Oh, if only I could get away from you and from father and from it all! if I could have the wings of a dove and fly away to heaven!

Cusins. And leave me!

Barbara. Yes, you, and all the other naughty mischievous children of men. But I cant. I was happy in the Salvation Army for a moment. I escaped from the world into a paradise of enthusiasm and prayer and soul saving; but the moment our money ran short, it all came back to Bodger: it was he who saved our people: he, and the Prince of Darkness, my papa. Undershaft and Bodger: their hands stretch everywhere: when we feed a starving fellow creature, it is with their bread, because there is no other bread; when we tend the sick, it is in the hospitals they endow; if we turn from the churches they build, we must kneel on the stones of the streets they pave. As long as that lasts, there is no getting away from them. Turning our backs on Bodger and Undershaft is turning our backs on life.

Cusins. I thought you were determined to turn your back on the wicked side of life.

Barbara. There is no wicked side: life is all one. And I never wanted to shirk my share in whatever evil must be endured, whether it be sin or suffering. I wish I could cure you of middle-class ideas, Dolly.

Cusins (*gasping*) Middle cl—! A snub! A social snub to me! from the daughter of a foundling!

Barbara. That is why I have no class, Dolly: I come straight out of the heart of the whole people. If I were middle-class I should turn my back on my father's business; and we should both live in an artistic drawing room, with you reading the reviews in one corner, and I in the other at the piano, playing Schumann: both very superior persons, and neither of us a bit of use. Sooner than that, I would sweep out the guncotton shed, or be one of Bodger's barmaids. Do you know what would have happened if you had refused papa's offer?

Cusins. I wonder!

Barbara. I should have given you up and married the man who accepted it. After all, my dear old mother has more sense than any of you. I felt like her when I saw this place — felt that I must have it — that never, never, never could I let it go; only she thought it was the houses and the kitchen ranges and the linen and china, when it was really all the human souls to be saved: not weak souls in starved bodies, sobbing with gratitude for a scrap of bread and treacle, but fullfed, quarrelsome, snobbish, uppish creatures, all standing on their little rights and dignities, and thinking that my father ought to be greatly obliged to them for making so much money for him — and so he ought. That is where salvation is really wanted. My father shall never throw it in my teeth again that my converts were bribed with bread. (*She is transfigured*). I have got rid of the bribe of bread. I have got rid of the bribe of heaven. Let God's work be done for its own sake: the work he had to create us to do because it cannot be done except by living men and women. When I die, let him be in my debt, not I in his; and let me forgive him as becomes a woman of my rank.

Cusins. Then the way of life lies through the factory of death?

Barbara. Yes, through the raising of hell to heaven and of man to God, through the unveiling of an eternal light in the Valley of The Shadow. (*Seizing him with both hands*) Oh, did you think my courage would never come back? did you believe that I was a deserter? that I, who have stood in the streets, and taken my people to my heart, and talked of the holiest and greatest things with them, could ever turn back and chatter foolishly to fashionable people about nothing in a drawing room? Never, never, never, never: Major Barbara will die with the colors. Oh! and I have my dear little Dolly boy still; and he has found me my place and my work. Glory Hallelujah! (*She kisses him*).

Cusins. My dearest: consider my delicate health. I cannot stand as much happiness as you can.

Barbara. Yes: it is not easy work being in love with me, is it? But it's good for you. (*She runs to the shed, and calls, childlike*) Mamma! Mamma! (*Bilton comes out of the shed, followed by Undershaft*). I want Mamma.

Undershaft. She is taking off her list slippers, dear. (*He passes on to Cusins*). Well? What does she say?

Cusins. She has gone right up into the skies.

Lady Britomart (*coming from the shed and stopping on the steps, obstructing Sarah, who follows with Lomax. Barbara clutches like a baby at her mother's skirt*) Barbara: when will you learn to be independent and to act and think for yourself? I know as well as possible what that cry of 'Mamma, Mamma,' means. Always running to me!

Sarah (*touching Lady Britomart's ribs with her finger tips and imitating a bicycle horn*) Pip! pip!

Lady Britomart (*highly indignant*) How dare you say Pip! pip! to me, Sarah? You are both very naughty children. What do you want, Barbara?

Barbara. I want a house in the village to live in with Dolly. (*Dragging at the skirt*) Come and tell me which one to take.

Undershaft (*to Cusins*) Six o'clock tomorrow morning, Euripides.

THE END

One of the earliest English remarks about comedy, Sir Philip Sidney's written about 1580, runs thus:

> Comedy is an imitation of the common errors of our life, which he representeth in the most ridiculous and scornful sort that may be; so that it is impossible that any beholder can be content to be such a one.

Sidney is indebted to Italian commentators, who in turn are indebted to Roman commentators, and behind them are the Greeks, notably Aristotle. Along the way, of course, there are lots of variations, but the basic ideas may fairly be said to constitute the "classical" theory of comedy:

1) the characters are ignoble
2) their actions arouse derision (rather than, say, terror or pity)
3) the spectators, if they have resembled the dramatis personae, leave the theater morally improved after seeing the absurdity of such behavior.

The "classical" theory, often stated before Sidney, has since been restated at least as often. Almost every comic dramatist who has commented on his work has offered it as his justification. Shaw, in a preface to his *Complete Plays*, put it thus:

> If I make you laugh at yourself, remember that my business as a classic writer of comedies is "to chasten morals with ridicule"; and if I sometimes make you feel like a fool, remember that I have by the same action cured your folly, just as the dentist cures your toothache by pulling out your tooth. And I never do it without giving you plenty of laughing gas.

To begin with the laughing gas in *Major Barbara*: the first act suggests that the play is a drawing-room comedy, full of aristocratic people bouncing elegant lines off each other. (Lady Brit, of course, affects innocence, but she is accomplished at getting what she wants.) Sample:

> I am not a Pharisee, I hope; and I should not have minded his merely doing wrong things: we are none of us perfect. But your father didnt exactly do wrong things: he said them and thought them: that was what was so dreadful. He really had a sort of religion of wrongness. Just as one doesnt mind men practising immorality so long as they own that they are in the wrong by preaching morality; so I couldnt forgive Andrew for preaching immorality while he practised morality.

Another sample:

> *Cusins.* Let me advise you to study Greek, Mr. Undershaft. Greek scholars are privileged men. Few of them know Greek; and none of them know anything else; but their position is unchallengeable. Other languages are the qualifications of waiters and commercial travellers: Greek is to a man of position what the hallmark is to silver.

If Shaw had been content to write a comedy in the classical tradition, he would have contrived a plot which would probably have involved an unsuitable wooer of Barbara, maybe a rich old aristocrat, maybe a parvenu, maybe a fortune hunter, who would finally be unmasked and then displaced by an appropriately young and charming and socially acceptable bridegroom. But Shaw turned to comedy as a propagandist. He had been deeply impressed by Ibsen's plays, and he saw in the drama an opportunity to preach his economic ideas to a wider audience than is normally reached by the pamphleteer. For Shaw, the heart of Ibsen's plays lies in such a "discussion" as the one in *A Doll's House*, where Nora explains to her husband that things are all wrong in their apparently happy marriage. (The interested reader is advised to look at Shaw's *The Quintessence of Ibsenism*, especially the next to the last chapter, "The Technical Novelty," which insists that post-Ibsen plays must replace the old formula of exposition-situation-unraveling with "exposition, situation, and discussion; and the discussion is the test of the playwright. . . . The serious playwright recognizes not only the main test of his highest powers, but also the real center of his play's interest.")

What Shaw does, then, is introduce massive discussions into a comedy that at first seems to be doing little more than spoofing Lady Brit and holding her son Stephen up to rather obvious ridicule. Stephen is not merely an ass; he is made to serve as a sort of straightman for Undershaft, who expounds at length unconventional ideas about munitions, sin, power, and poverty. These ideas require discussion because Shaw, unlike most comic writers, is not content with the traditional views. Comic playwrights usually criticize eccentric behavior, and at least implicitly suggest that there is a reasonable norm, known to all men of sense, from which fools depart. But because Shaw believed that society's norm is itself foolish, he devotes much of his play to expounding a new creed. Shaw reverses the old joke about the entire platoon being out of step except Johnny; for Shaw, the deviant, Johnny, *is* in step, and the rest of the platoon is laughably out of step. During the central part of *Major Barbara*, then, Undershaft, the eccentric, is for Shaw the least laughable character. Even Barbara, the heroine, is exposed as a fool, though with great tenderness, and is forced to shed her conventional illusions. So great is the tenderness that as we see her world collapse, she seems almost a tragic figure:

> I stood on the rock I thought eternal; and without a word of warning it reeled and crumbled under me.

But Undershaft dispels the tragedy, harshly but necessarily, with, "Come, come, my daughter! dont make too much of your little tinpot tragedy. . . . Dont persist in that folly. If your old religion broke down yesterday, get a newer and a better one for tomorrow."

Enough has been said to give some idea of the novelty of Shaw's comic practice, however conventional his theory. But one should note, too, that in one important way his practice is conventional: his plays have the stock quack doctors, pompous statesmen, dragonlike matrons, and young lovers of traditional comedy. And in *Major Barbara* he even uses the ancient motif of the foundling who proves to be a suitable husband for the heroine.

Something more, however, must be said of Undershaft. Having allowed Undershaft to triumph over Barbara, Shaw does not stop; very late in the play Undershaft himself is threatened with the loss of *his* illusions when Barbara and Adolphus Cusins will make their presence felt in the munitions factory. The play ends with the usual marriage, joy, and promise of a newly organized society; in its suggestion, however, that this new society is not a return to a sensible world that was lost before the play began (think, for example, of the end of *As You Like It*, where the duke is restored to his realm), but rather is the beginning of a totally new sort of world, it marks a departure from comic practice. Maybe that is why the end of the play has seemed to most audiences the least amusing part.

The Matchmaker

A Farce in Four Acts

THORNTON WILDER

Thornton Wilder (1897–   ) was born in Madison, Wisconsin, the son of an editor and publisher. When his father was appointed consul general in Hong Kong, Wilder accompanied him, but he returned to the United States for some of his high school years, and for college. He attended Oberlin, was graduated from Yale (1918), did further study in Rome, and received a master's degree from Princeton (1926). His novel, The Bridge of San Luis Rey (1928) brought him a Pulitzer prize and fame; two of his plays, Our Town (1938) and The Skin of Our Teeth (1942) also won Pulitzer prizes. The Matchmaker (1954), which has been turned into a musical comedy, Hello, Dolly (1964), is a revision of Wilder's The Merchant of Yonkers, which is an adaptation of an Austrian play that itself was adapted from an English play. Possibly Wilder's years in China, where the dramatic conventions are markedly different from those of the Western world, helped to establish his interest in a highly unrealistic theater.

CHARACTERS

Horace Vandergelder, a merchant of Yonkers, New York

Cornelius Hackl
Barnaby Tucker } clerks in his store
Malachi Stack

Ambrose Kemper, an artist
Joe Scanlon, a barber
Rudolph
August } waiters

A Cabman
Mrs. Dolly Levi } friends of Vandergelder's
Miss Flora Van Huysen } late wife

Mrs. Irene Molloy, a milliner
Minnie Fay, her assistant
Ermengarde, Vandergelder's niece
Gertrude, Vandergelder's housekeeper
Miss Van Huysen's Cook

TIME: The early 80's.

Act I. Vandergelder's house in Yonkers, New York.

Act II. Mrs. Molloy's hat shop, New York.

Act III. The Harmonica Gardens Restaurant on the Battery, New York.

Act IV. Miss Van Huysen's house, New York.

This play is based upon a comedy by Johann Nestroy, *Einen Jux will es sich Machen* (Vienna, 1842), which was in turn based upon an English original, *A Day Well Spent* (London, 1835) by John Oxenford.

664

ACT I

Living room of Mr. Vandergelder's house, over his hay, feed and provision store in Yonkers, fifteen miles north of New York City. Articles from the store have overflowed into this room; it has not been cleaned for a long time and is in some disorder, but it is not sordid or gloomy.

There are three entrances. One at the center back leads into the principal rooms of the house. One on the back right (all the directions are from the point of view of the actors). opens on steps which descend to the street door. One on the left leads to Ermengarde's room.

In the center of the room is a trap door; below it is a ladder descending to the store below.

Behind the trap door and to the left of it is a tall accountant's desk; to the left of it is an old-fashioned stove with a stovepipe going up into the ceiling. Before the desk is a tall stool. On the right of the stage is a table with some chairs about it.

The Matchmaker from Three Plays by Thornton Wilder. Copyright © 1955, 1957 by Thornton Wilder. Copyright 1939 by Thornton Wilder, an earlier version under the title of "The Merchant of Yonkers." Reprinted by permission of Harper & Row, Publishers.

Mr. Vandergelder's Gladstone bag, packed for a journey, is beside the desk.

It is early morning.

(*Vandergelder, sixty, choleric, vain and sly, wears a soiled dressing gown. He is seated with a towel about his neck, in a chair beside the desk, being shaved by Joe Scanlon. Vandergelder is smoking a cigar and holding a hand mirror. Ambrose Kemper is angrily striding about the room.*)

Vandergelder (*loudly*). I tell you for the hundredth time you will never marry my niece.

Ambrose (*thirty; dressed as an "artist"*). And I tell you for the thousandth time that I will marry your niece; and right soon, too.

Vandergelder. Never!

Ambrose. Your niece is of age, Mr. Vandergelder. Your niece has consented to marry me. This is a free country, Mr. Vandergelder — not a private kingdom of your own.

Vandergelder. There are no free countries for fools, Mr. Kemper. Thank you for the honor of your visit — good morning.

Joe (*fifty; lanky, mass of gray hair falling into his eyes*). Mr. Vandergelder, will you please sit still one minute? If I cut your throat it'll be practically unintentional.

Vandergelder. Ermengarde is not for you, nor for anybody else who can't support her.

Ambrose. I tell you I can support her. I make a very good living.

Vandergelder. No, sir! A living is made, Mr. Kemper, by selling something that everybody needs at least once a year. Yes, sir! And a million is made by producing something that everybody needs every day. You artists produce something that nobody needs at any time. You may sell a picture once in a while, but you'll make no living. Joe, go over there and stamp three times. I want to talk to Cornelius. (*Joe crosses to trap door and stamps three times.*)

Ambrose. Not only can I support her now, but I have considerable expectations.

Vandergelder. *Expectations!* We merchants don't do business with them. I don't keep accounts with people who promise somehow to pay something someday, and I don't allow my niece to marry such people.

Ambrose. Very well, from now on you might as well know that I regard any way we can find to get married is right and fair. Ermengarde is of age, and there's no law . . . (*Vandergelder rises and crosses*

*toward Ambrose. Joe Scanlon follows him complainingly and tries to
find a chance to cut his hair even while he is standing.*)

Vandergelder. Law? Let me tell you something, Mr. Kemper: most
of the people in the world are fools. The law is there to prevent
crime; we men of sense are there to prevent foolishness. It's I, and
not the law, that will prevent Ermengarde from marrying you, and
I've taken some steps already. I've sent her away to get this nonsense
out of her head.

Ambrose. Ermengarde's . . . not here?

Vandergelder. She's gone — east, west, north, south. I thank you for
the honor of your visit. (*Enter Gertrude — eighty; deaf; half blind;
and very pleased with herself.*)

Gertrude. Everything's ready, Mr. Vandergelder. Ermengarde and I
have just finished packing the trunk.

Vandergelder. Hold your tongue! (*Joe is shaving Vandergelder's throat,
so he can only wave his hands vainly.*)

Gertrude. Yes, Mr. Vandergelder, Ermengarde's ready to leave. Her
trunk's all marked. Care Miss Van Huysen, 8 Jackson Street, New
York.

Vandergelder (*breaking away from Joe*). Hell and damnation! Didn't
I tell you it was a secret?

Ambrose (*picks up hat and coat — kisses Gertrude*). Care Miss Van
Huysen, 8 Jackson Street, New York. Thank you very much. Good
Morning, Mr. Vandergelder. (*Exit Ambrose, to the street.*)

Vandergelder. It won't help you, Mr. Kemper — (*To Gertrude.*) Deaf!
And blind! At least you can do me the favor of being dumb!

Gertrude. Chk — chk! Such a temper! Lord save us! (*Cornelius puts
his head up through the trap door. He is thirty-three; mock-deferen-
tial — he wears a green apron and is in his shirt-sleeves.*)

Cornelius. Yes, Mr. Vandergelder?

Vandergelder. Go in and get my niece's trunk and carry it over to the
station. Wait! Gertrude, has Mrs. Levi arrived yet? (*Cornelius comes
up the trap door, steps into the room and closes the trap door behind
him.*)

Gertrude. Don't shout. I can hear perfectly well. Everything's clearly
marked. (*Exit left.*)

Vandergelder. Have the buggy brought round to the front of the store
in half an hour.

Cornelius. Yes, Mr. Vandergelder.

Vandergelder. This morning I'm joining my lodge parade and this
afternoon I'm going to New York. Before I go, I have something
important to say to you and Barnaby. Good news. Fact is — I'm
going to promote you. How old are you?

Cornelius. Thirty-three, Mr. Vandergelder.

Vandergelder. What?

Cornelius. Thirty-three.

Vandergelder. That all? That's a foolish age to be at. I thought you were forty.

Cornelius. Thirty-three.

Vandergelder. A man's not worth a cent until he's forty. We just pay 'em wages to make mistakes — don't we, Joe?"

Joe. You almost lost an ear on it, Mr. Vandergelder.

Vandergelder. I was thinking of promoting you to chief clerk.

Cornelius. What am I now, Mr. Vandergelder?

Vandergelder. You're an impertinent fool, that's what you are. Now, if you behave yourself, I'll promote you from impertinent fool to chief clerk, with a raise in your wages. And Barnaby may be promoted from idiot apprentice to incompetent clerk.

Cornelius. Thank you, Mr. Vandergelder.

Vandergelder. However, I want to see you again before I go. Go in and get my niece's trunk.

Cornelius. Yes, Mr. Vandergelder. (*Exit Cornelius, left.*)

Vandergelder. Joe — the world's getting crazier every minute. Like my father used to say: the horses'll be taking over the world soon.

Joe (*presenting mirror*). I did what I could, Mr. Vandergelder, what with you flying in and out of the chair. (*He wipes the last of the soap from Vandergelder's face.*)

Vandergelder. Fine, fine, Joe, you do a fine job, the same fine job you've done me for twenty years. Joe . . . I've got special reasons for looking my best today . . . isn't there something a little extry you could do, something a little special? I'll pay you right up to fifty cents — see what I mean? Do some of those things you do to the young fellas. Touch me up; smarten me up a bit.

Joe. All I know is fifteen cents' worth, like usual, Mr. Vandergelder; and that includes everything that's decent to do to a man.

Vandergelder. Now hold your horses, Joe — all I meant was . . .

Joe. I've shaved you for twenty years and you never asked me no such question before.

Vandergelder. Hold your horses, I say, Joe! I'm going to tell you a secret. But I don't want you telling it to that riffraff down to the barbershop what I'm going to tell you now. All I ask of you is a little extry because I'm thinking of getting married again; and this very afternoon I'm going to New York to call on my intended, a very refined lady.

Joe. Your gettin' married is none of my business, Mr. Vandergelder.

I done everything to you I know, and the charge is fifteen cents like it always was, and . . . (*Cornelius crosses, left to right, and exit, carrying a trunk on his shoulder. Ermengarde and Gertrude enter from left.*) I don't dye no hair, not even for fifty cents I don't!

Vandergelder. Joe Scanlon, get out!

Joe. And lastly, it looks to me like you're pretty rash to judge which is fools and which isn't fools, Mr. Vandergelder. People that's et onions is bad judges of who's et onions and who ain't. Good morning, ladies; good morning, Mr. Vandergelder. (*Exit Joe.*)

Vandergelder. Well, what do you want?

Ermengarde (*twenty-four; pretty, sentimental*). Uncle! You said you wanted to talk to us.

Vandergelder. Oh yes. Gertrude, go and get my parade regalia — the uniform for my lodge parade.

Gertrude. What? Oh yes. Lord have mercy! (*Exit Gertrude, back center.*)

Vandergelder. I had a talk with that artist of yours. He's a fool. (*Ermengarde starts to cry.*) Weeping! weeping! You can go down and weep for a while in New York where it won't be noticed. (*He sits on desk chair, puts tie round neck and calls her over to tie it for him.*) Ermengarde! I told him that when you were old enough to marry you'd marry someone who could support you. I've done you a good turn. You'll come and thank me when you're fifty.

Ermengarde. But Uncle, I love him!

Vandergelder. I tell you you don't.

Ermengarde. But I *do!*

Vandergelder. And I tell you you don't. Leave those things to me.

Ermengarde. If I don't marry Ambrose I know I'll die.

Vandergelder. What of?

Ermengarde. A broken heart.

Vandergelder. Never heard of it. Mrs. Levi is coming in a moment to take you to New York. You are going to stay two or three weeks with Miss Van Huysen, an old friend of your mother's. (*Gertrude re-enters with coat, sash and sword. Enter from the street, right, Malachi Stack.*) You're not to receive any letters except from me. I'm coming to New York myself today and I'll call on you tomorrow. (*To Malachi.*) Who are you?

Malachi (*fifty. Sardonic. Apparently innocent smile; pretense of humility*). Malachi Stack, your honor. I heard you wanted an apprentice in the hay, feed, provision and hardware business.

Vandergelder. An apprentice at your age?

Malachi. Yes, your honor; I bring a lot of experience to it.

Vandergelder. Have you any letters of recommendation?

Malachi (*extending a sheaf of soiled papers*). Yes, indeed, your honor! First-class recommendation.

Vandergelder. Ermengarde! Are you ready to start?

Ermengarde. Yes.

Vandergelder. Well, go and get ready some more. Ermengarde! Let me know the minute Mrs. Levi gets here.

Ermengarde. Yes, Uncle Horace. (*Ermengarde and Gertrude exit. Vandergelder examines the letters, putting them down one by one.*)

Vandergelder. I don't want an able seaman. Nor a typesetter. And I don't want a hospital cook.

Malachi. No, your honor, but it's all experience. Excuse me! (*selects a letter.*) This one is from your former partner, Joshua Van Tuyl, in Albany. (*He puts letters from table back into pocket.*)

Vandergelder. ". . . for the most part honest and reliable . . . occasionally willing and diligent." There seems to be a certain amount of hesitation about these recommendations.

Malachi. Businessmen aren't writers, your honor. There's only one businessman in a thousand that can write a good letter of recommendation, your honor. Mr. Van Tuyl sends his best wishes and wants to know if you can use me in the provision and hardware business.

Vandergelder. Not so fast, not so fast! What's this "your honor" you use so much?

Malachi. Mr. Van Tuyl says you're President of the Hudson River Provision Dealers' Recreational, Musical and Burial Society.

Vandergelder. I am; but there's no "your honor" that goes with it. Why did you come to Yonkers?

Malachi. I heard that you'd had an apprentice that was a good-for-nothing, and that you were at your wit's end for another.

Vandergelder. Wit's end, wit's end! There's no dearth of good-for-nothing apprentices.

Malachi. That's right, Mr. Vandergelder. It's employers there's a dearth of. Seems like you hear of a new one dying every day.

Vandergelder. What's that? Hold your tongue. I see you've been a barber, and a valet too. Why have you changed your place so often?

Malachi. Changed my place, Mr. Vandergelder? When a man's interested in experience . . .

Vandergelder. Do you drink?

Malachi. No, thanks. I've just had breakfast.

Vandergelder. I didn't ask you whether — Idiot! I asked you if you were a drunkard.

Malachi. No, sir! No! Why, looking at it from all sides I don't even like liquor.

Vandergelder. Well, if you keep on looking at it from all sides, out you go. Remember that. Here. (*Gives him remaining letters.*) With all your faults, I'm going to give you a try.

Malachi. You'll never regret it, Mr. Vandergelder. You'll never regret it.

Vandergelder. Now today I want to use you in New York. I judge you know your way around New York?

Malachi. Do I know New York? Mr. Vandergelder, I know every hole and corner in New York.

Vandergelder. Here's a dollar. A train leaves in a minute. Take that bag to the Central Hotel on Water Street, have them save me a room. Wait for me. I'll be there about four o'clock.

Malachi. Yes, Mr. Vandergelder. (*Picks up the bag, starts out, then comes back.*) Oh, but first, I'd like to meet the other clerks I'm to work with.

Vandergelder. You haven't time. Hurry now. The station's across the street.

Malachi. Yes, sir. (*Away — then back once more.*) You'll see, sir, you'll never regret it. . . .

Vandergelder. I regret it already. Go on. Off with you. (*Exit Malachi, right. The following speech is addressed to the audience. During it Mr. Vandergelder takes off his dressing gown, puts on his scarlet sash, his sword and his bright-colored coat. He is already wearing light blue trousers with a red stripe down the sides.*)

Vandergelder. Ninety-nine per cent of the people in the world are fools and the rest of us are in great danger of contagion. But I wasn't always free of foolishness as I am now. I was once young, which was foolish; I fell in love; and for a while I was poor, which was more foolish than all the other things put together. Then my wife died, which was foolish of her; I grew older, which was sensible of me; then I became a rich man, which is as sensible as it is rare. Since you see I'm a man of sense, I guess you were surprised to hear that I'm planning to get married again. Well, I've two reasons for it. In the first place, I like my house run with order, comfort and economy. That's a woman's work; but even a woman can't do it well if she's merely being paid for it. In order to run a house well, a woman must have the feeling that she owns it. Marriage is a bribe to make a housekeeper think she's a householder. Did you ever watch an ant carry a burden twice its size? What excitement! What patience! What will! Well, that's what I think of when I see a woman running a house. What giant passions in those little bodies — what quarrels with the butcher for the best cut — what fury at discovering a moth in a cupboard! Believe me! — if women could harness their natures to something bigger than a house and a baby carriage — tck! tck! — they'd change the world. And the second reason, ladies and gentlemen? Well, I see by your faces you've guessed it already. There's nothing like mixing with women to bring out all the foolishness in a man of sense. And that's a risk I'm willing to take. I've just turned sixty, and I've just laid side by side the last dollar of my first half million. So if I should lose my head a little, I still have enough money to buy it back. After many years' caution and hard work, I have earned a right to a little risk and adventure, and I'm thinking of getting married. Yes, like all you other fools, I'm willing to risk a little security for a certain amount of adventure. Think it over. (*Exit back center. Ambrose enters from the street, crosses left, and whistles softly. Ermengarde enters from left.*)

Ermengarde. Ambrose! If my uncle saw you!

Ambrose. Sh! Get your hat.

Ermengarde. My hat!

Ambrose. Quick! Your trunk's at the station. Now quick! We're running away.

Ermengarde. Running away!

Ambrose. Sh!

Ermengarde. Where?

Ambrose. To New York. To get married.

Ermengarde. Oh, Ambrose, I can't do that. Ambrose dear — it wouldn't be proper!

Ambrose. Listen. I'm taking you to my friend's house. His wife will take care of you.

Ermengarde. But, Ambrose, a girl can't go on a train with a man. I can see you don't know anything about girls.

Ambrose. But I'm telling you we're going to get married!

Ermengarde. Married! But what would *Uncle* say?

Ambrose. We don't care what Uncle'd say — we're eloping.

Ermengarde. Ambrose Kemper! How can you use such an awful word!

Ambrose. Ermengarde, you have the soul of a field mouse.

Ermengarde (crying). Ambrose, why do you say such cruel things to me? (*Enter Mrs. Levi, from the street, right. She stands listening.*)

Ambrose. For the last time I beg you — get your hat and coat. The train leaves in a few minutes. Ermengarde, we'll get married tomorrow. . . .

Ermengarde. Oh, Ambrose! I see you don't understand anything about weddings. Ambrose, don't you *respect* me? . . .

Mrs. Levi (*uncertain age; mass of sandy hair; impoverished elegance; large, shrewd but generous nature, an assumption of worldly cynicism conceals a tireless amused enjoyment of life. She carries a handbag and a small brown paper bag*). Good morning, darling girl — how are you? (*They kiss.*)

Ermengarde. Oh, good morning, Mrs. Levi.

Mrs. Levi. And who is this gentleman who is so devoted to you?

Ermengarde. This is Mr. Kemper, Mrs. Levi. Ambrose, this is . . . Mrs. Levi . . . she's an old friend. . . .

Mrs. Levi. Mrs. Levi, born Gallagher. Very happy to meet you, Mr. Kemper.

Ambrose. Good morning, Mrs. Levi.

Mrs. Levi. Mr. Kemper, *the artist!* Delighted! Mr. Kemper, may I say something very frankly?

Ambrose. Yes, Mrs. Levi.

Mrs. Levi. This thing you were planning to do is a very great mistake.

Ermengarde. Oh, Mrs. Levi, please explain to Ambrose — of *course!* I want to marry him, but to *elope!* . . . How . . .

Mrs. Levi. Now, my dear girl, you go in and keep one eye on your uncle. I wish to talk to Mr. Kemper for a moment. You give us a warning when you hear your Uncle Horace coming. . . .

Ermengarde. Ye-es, Mrs. Levi. (*Exit Ermengarde, back center.*)

Mrs. Levi. Mr. Kemper, I was this dear girl's mother's oldest friend. Believe me, I am on your side. I hope you two will be married very soon, and I think I can be of real service to you. Mr. Kemper, I always go right to the point.

Ambrose. What is the point, Mrs. Levi?

Mrs. Levi. Mr. Vandergelder is a very rich man, Mr. Kemper, and Ermengarde is his only relative.

Ambrose. But I am not interested in Mr. Vandergelder's money. I have enough to support a wife and family.

Mrs. Levi. Enough? How much is enough when one is thinking about children and the future? The future is the most expensive luxury in the world, Mr. Kemper.

Ambrose. Mrs. Levi, what is the point.

Mrs. Levi. Believe me, Mr. Vandergelder wishes to get rid of Ermengarde, and if you follow my suggestions he will even permit her to marry you. You see, Mr. Vandergelder is planning to get married himself.

Ambrose. What? That monster!

Mrs. Levi. Mr. Kemper!

Ambrose. Married! To you, Mrs. Levi?

Mrs. Levi (taken aback). Oh, no, no . . . NO! I am merely arranging it. I am helping him find a suitable bride.

Ambrose. For Mr. Vandergelder there are no suitable brides.

Mrs. Levi. I think we can safely say that Mr. Vandergelder will be married to someone by the end of next week.

Ambrose. What are you suggesting, Mrs. Levi?

Mrs. Levi. I am taking Ermengarde to New York on the next train. I shall not take her to Miss Van Huysen's, as is planned; I shall take her to my house. I wish you to call for her at my house at five thirty. Here is my card.

Ambrose. "Mrs. Dolly Gallagher Levi. Varicose veins reduced."

Mrs. Levi (trying to take back card). I beg your pardon . . .

Ambrose (holding card). I beg *your* pardon. "Consultations free."

Mrs. Levi. I meant to give you my other card. Here.

Ambrose. "Mrs. Dolly Gallagher Levi. Aurora Hosiery. Instruction in the guitar and mandolin." You do all these things, Mrs. Levi?

Mrs. Levi. Two and two make four, Mr. Kemper — always did. So you will come to my house at five thirty. At about six I shall take you both with me to the Harmonia Gardens Restaurant on the Battery; Mr. Vandergelder will be there and everything will be arranged.

Ambrose. How?

Mrs. Levi. Oh, I don't know. One thing will lead to another.

Ambrose. How do I know that I can trust you, Mrs. Levi? You could easily make our situation worse.

Mrs. Levi. Mr. Kemper, your situation could not possibly be worse.

Ambrose. I wish I knew what you get out of this, Mrs. Levi.

Mrs. Levi. That is a very proper question. I get two things: profit and pleasure.

Ambrose. How?

Mrs. Levi. Mr. Kemper, I am a woman who arranges things. At present I am arranging Mr. Vandergelder's domestic affairs. Out of it I get — shall we call it: little pickings? I need little pickings, Mr. Kemper, and especially just now, when I haven't got my train fare back to New York. You see: I am frank with you.

Ambrose. That's your profit, Mrs. Levi; but where do you get your pleasure?

Mrs. Levi. My pleasure? Mr. Kemper, when you artists paint a hillside or a river you change everything a little, you make thousands of little changes, don't you? Nature is never completely satisfactory and must be corrected. Well, I'm like you artists. Life as it is is never quite interesting enough for me — I'm bored, Mr. Kemper, with life as it is — and so I do things. I put my hand in here, and I put my hand in there, and I watch and I listen — and often I'm very much amused.

Ambrose (rises). Not in my affairs, Mrs. Levi.

Mrs. Levi. Wait, I haven't finished. There's another thing. I'm very interested in this household here — in Mr. Vandergelder and all that idle, frozen money of his. I don't like the thought of it lying in great piles, useless, motionless, in the bank, Mr. Kemper. Money should circulate like rain water. It should be flowing down among the people, through dressmakers and restaurants and cabmen, setting up a little business here, and furnishing a good time there. Do you see what I mean?

Ambrose. Yes, I do.

Mrs. Levi. New York should be a very happy city, Mr. Kemper, but it isn't. My late husband came from Vienna; now there's a city that understands this. I want New York to be more like Vienna and less like a collection of nervous and tired ants. And if you and Ermengarde get a good deal of Mr. Vandergelder's money, I want you to see that it starts flowing in and around a lot of people's lives. And for that reason I want you to come with me to the Harmonia Gardens Restaurant tonight. (*Enter Ermengarde.*)

Ermengarde. Mrs. Levi, Uncle Horace is coming.

Mrs. Levi. Mr. Kemper, I think you'd better be going. . . . (*Ambrose crosses to trap door and disappears down the ladder, closing trap as he goes.*) Darling girl, Mr. Kemper and I have had a very good talk. You'll see: Mr. Vandergelder and I will be dancing at your wedding very soon — (*Enter Vandergelder at back. He has now added a splendid plumed hat to his costume and is carrying a standard or small flag bearing the initials of his lodge.*) Oh, Mr. Vandergelder, how handsome you look! You take my breath away. Yes, my dear girl, I'll see you soon. (*Exit Ermengarde back center.*) Oh, Mr. Vandergelder, I wish Irene Molloy could see you now. But then! I don't know what's come over you lately. You seem to be growing younger every day.

Vandergelder. Allowing for exaggeration, Mrs. Levi. If a man eats careful there's no reason why he should look old.

Mrs. Levi. You never said a truer word.

Vandergelder. I'll never see fifty-five again.

Mrs. Levi. Fifty-five! Why, I can see at a glance that you're the sort that will be stamping about at a hundred — and eating five meals a day, like my Uncle Harry. At fifty-five my Uncle Harry was a mere boy. I'm a judge of hands, Mr. Vandergelder — show me your hand. (*Looks at it.*) Lord in heaven! What a life line!

Vandergelder. Where?

Mrs. Levi. From *here* to *here*. It runs right off your hand. I don't know where it goes. They'll have to hit you on the head with a mallet. They'll have to stifle you with a sofa pillow. You'll bury us all! However, to return to our business — Mr. Vandergelder, I suppose you've changed your mind again. I suppose you've given up all idea of getting married.

Vandergelder (complacently). Not at all, Mrs. Levi. I have news for you.

Mrs. Levi. News?

Vandergelder. Mrs. Levi, I've practically decided to ask Mrs. Molloy to be my wife.

Mrs. Levi (taken aback). You have?

Vandergelder. Yes, I have.

Mrs. Levi. Oh, you have! Well, I guess that's just about the best news I ever heard. So there's nothing more for me to do but wish you every happiness under the sun and say goodbye. (*Crosses as if to leave.*)

Vandergelder (stopping her). Well — Mrs. Levi — Surely I thought —

Mrs. Levi. Well, I did have a little suggestion to make — but I won't. You're going to marry Irene Molloy, and that closes the matter.

Vandergelder. What suggestion was that, Mrs. Levi?

Mrs. Levi. Well — I *had* found *another* girl for you.

Vandergelder. Another?

Mrs. Levi. The most wonderful girl, the ideal wife.

Vandergelder. Another, eh? What's her name?

Mrs. Levi. Her name?

Vandergelder. Yes!

Mrs. Levi (groping for it). Err . . . er . . . her *name?* — Ernestina — Simple. *Miss* Ernestina Simple. But now of course all that's too late. After all, you're engaged — you're practically engaged to marry Irene Molloy.

Vandergelder. Oh, I ain't engaged to Mrs. Molloy!

Mrs. Levi. Nonsense! You can't break poor Irene's heart now and change to another girl. . . . When a man at your time of life calls four times on an attractive widow like that — and sends her a pot of geraniums — that's practically an engagement!

Vandergelder. That ain't an engagement!

Mrs. Levi. And yet — ! If only you were free! I've found this treasure of a girl. Every moment I felt like a traitor to Irene Molloy — but let me tell you: I couldn't help it. I told this girl all about you, just as though you were a free man. Isn't that dreadful? The fact is: she has fallen in love with you already.

Vandergelder. Ernestina?

Mrs. Levi. Ernestina Simple.

Vandergelder. Ernestina Simple.

Mrs. Levi. Of course she's a very different idea from Mrs. Molloy, Ernestina is. Like her name — simple, domestic, practical.

Vandergelder. Can she cook?

Mrs. Levi. Cook, Mr. Vandergelder? I've had two meals from her hands, and — as I live — I don't know what I've done that God should reward me with such meals.

Mrs. Levi (*continues*). Her duck! Her steak!

Vandergelder. Eh! Eh! In this house we don't eat duck and steak every day, Mrs. Levi.

Mrs. Levi. But didn't I tell you? — that's the wonderful part about it. Her duck — what was it? Pigeon! I'm alive to tell you. I don't know how she does it. It's a secret that's come down in her family. The greatest chefs would give their right hands to know it. And the steaks? Shoulder of beef — four cents a pound. Dogs wouldn't eat. But when Ernestina passes her hands over it — !!

Vandergelder. Allowing for exaggeration, Mrs. Levi.

Mrs. Levi. No exaggeration. I'm the best cook in the world myself, and I *know* what's good.

Vandergelder. Hm. How old is she, Mrs. Levi?

Mrs. Levi. Nineteen, well — say twenty.

Vandergelder. Twenty, Mrs. Levi? Girls of twenty are apt to favor young fellows of their own age.

Mrs. Levi. But you don't listen to me. And you don't know the girl. Mr. Vandergelder, she has a positive horror of flighty, brainless young men. A fine head of gray hair, she says, is worth twenty shined up with goose grease. No, sir. "I like a man that's *settled*" — in so many words she said it.

Vandergelder. That's . . . that's not usual, Mrs. Levi.

Mrs. Levi. Usual? I'm not wearing myself to the bone hunting up *usual* girls to interest you, Mr. Vandergelder. Usual, indeed. Listen to me. Do you know the sort of pictures she has on her wall? Is it any of these young Romeos and Lochinvars? No — it's Moses on the Mountain — that's what she's got. If you want to make her happy, you give her a picture of Methuselah surrounded by his grandchildren. That's my advice to you.

Vandergelder. I hope . . . hm . . . that she has some means, Mrs. Levi. I have a large household to run.

Mrs. Levi. Ernestina? She'll bring you five thousand dollars a year.

Vandergelder. Eh! Eh!

Mrs. Levi. Listen to me, Mr. Vandergelder. You're a man of sense, I hope. A man that can reckon. In the first place, she's an orphan.

She's been brought up with a great saving of food. What does she eat herself? Apples and lettuce. It's what she's been used to eat and what she likes best. She saves you two thousand a year right there. Secondly, she makes her own clothes — out of old tablecloths and window curtains. And she's the best-dressed woman in Brooklyn this minute. She saves you a thousand dollars right there. Thirdly, her health is of iron —

Vandergelder. But, Mrs. Levi, that's not money in the pocket.

Mrs. Levi. We're talking about marriage, aren't we, Mr. Vandergelder? The money she saves while she's in Brooklyn is none of your affair — but if she were your wife that would be *money*. Yes, sir, that's money."

Vandergelder. What's her family?

Mrs. Levi. Her father — God be good to him! He was the best — what am I trying to say? — the best undertaker in Brooklyn, respected, esteemed. He knew all the best people — knew them well, even before they died. So — well, that's the way it is. (*Lowering her voice, intimately.*) Now let me tell you a little more of her appearance. Can you hear me: as I say, a beautiful girl, beautiful, I've seen her go down the street — you know what I mean? — the young men get dizzy. They have to lean against lampposts. And she? Modest, eyes on the ground — I'm not going to tell you any more. . . . Couldn't you come to New York today?

Vandergelder. I was thinking of coming to New York this afternoon. . . .

Mrs. Levi. You were? Well now, I wonder if something could be arranged — oh, she's so eager to see you! Let me see . . .

Vandergelder. Could I . . . Mrs. Levi, could I give you a little dinner, maybe?

Mrs. Levi. Really, come to think of it, I don't see where I could get the time. I'm so busy over that wretched lawsuit of mine. Yes. If I win it, I don't mind telling you, I'll be what's called a very rich woman. I'll own half of Long Island, that's a fact. But just now I'm at my wit's end for a little help, just enough money to finish it off. My wit's end! (*She looks in her handbag. In order not to hear this, Vandergelder has a series of coughs, sneezes and minor convulsions.*) But perhaps I could arrange a little dinner; I'll see. Yes, for that lawsuit all I need is fifty dollars, and Staten Island's as good as mine. I've been trotting all over New York for you, trying to find you a suitable wife.

Vandergelder. Fifty dollars! !

Mrs. Levi. Two whole months I've been . . .

Vandergelder. Fifty dollars, Mrs. Levi . . . is no joke. (*Producing purse.*) I don't know where money's gone to these days. It's in hiding. . . . There's twenty . . . well, there's twenty-five. I can't spare no more, not now I can't.

Mrs. Levi. Well, this will help — will help somewhat. Now let me tell you what we'll do. I'll bring Ernestina to that restaurant on the Battery. You know it: the Harmonia Gardens. It's good, but it's not flashy. Now, Mr. Vandergelder, I think it'd be nice if just this once you'd order a real nice dinner. I guess you can afford it.

Vandergelder. Well, just this once.

Mrs. Levi. A chicken wouldn't hurt.

Vandergelder. Chicken! ! — Well, just this once.

Mrs. Levi. And a little wine.

Vandergelder. Wine? Well, just this once.

Mrs. Levi. Now about Mrs. Molloy — what do you think? Shall we call that subject closed?

Vandergelder. No, not at all, Mrs. Levi, I want to have dinner with Miss . . . with Miss . . .

Mrs. Levi. Simple.

Vandergelder. With Miss Simple; but first I want to make another call on Mrs. Molloy.

Mrs. Levi. Dear, dear, dear! And Miss Simple? What races you make me run! Very well; I'll meet you on one of those benches in front of Mrs. Molloy's hat store at four thirty, as usual. (*Trap door rises, and Cornelius' head appears.*)

Cornelius. The buggy's here, ready for the parade, Mr. Vandergelder.

Vandergelder. Call Barnaby. I want to talk to both of you.

Cornelius. Yes, Mr. Vandergelder. (*Exit Cornelius down trap door. Leaves trap open.*)

Mrs. Levi. Now do put your thoughts in order, Mr. Vandergelder. I can't keep upsetting and disturbing the finest women in New York City unless you mean business.

Vandergelder. Oh, I mean business all right!

Mrs. Levi. I hope so. Because, you know, you're playing a very dangerous game.

Vandergelder. Dangerous? — Dangerous, Mrs. Levi?

Mrs. Levi. Of course, it's dangerous — and there's a name for it! You're tampering with these women's affections, aren't you? And the only way you can save yourself now is to be married to *someone* by the end of next week. So think that over! (*Exit center back. Enter Cornelius and Barnaby, by the trap door.*)

Vandergelder. This morning I'm joining my lodge parade, and this afternoon I'm going to New York. When I come back, there are going to be some changes in the house here. I'll tell you what the change is, but I don't want you discussing it amongst yourselves: you're going to have a mistress.

Barnaby (*seventeen; round-faced, wide-eyed innocence; wearing a green apron*). I'm too young, Mr. Vandergelder! !

Vandergelder. Not yours! Death and damnation! Not yours, idiot — mine! (*Then realizing*) Hey! Hold your tongue until you're spoken to! I'm thinking of getting married.

Cornelius (*crosses, hand outstretched*). Many congratulations, Mr. Vandergelder, and my compliments to the lady.

Vandergelder. That's none of your business. Now go back to the store. (*The boys start down the ladder, Barnaby first.*) Have you got any questions you want to ask before I go?

Cornelius. Mr. Vandergelder — er — Mr. Vandergelder, does the chief clerk get one evening off every week?

Vandergelder. So that's the way you begin being chief clerk, is it? When I was your age I got up at five; I didn't close the shop until ten at night, and then I put in a good hour at the account books. The world's going to pieces. You elegant ladies lie in bed until six and at nine o'clock at night you rush to close the door so fast the line of customers bark their noses. No, sir — you'll attend to the store as usual, and on Friday and Saturday nights you'll remain open until ten — now hear what I say! This is the first time I've been away from the store overnight. When I come back I want to hear that you've run the place perfectly in my absence. If I hear of any foolishness, I'll discharge you. An evening free! Do you suppose that I had evenings free? (*At the top of his complacency.*) If I'd had evenings free I wouldn't be what I am now! (*He marches out, right.*)

Barnaby (*watching him go*). The horses nearly ran away when they saw him. What's the matter, Cornelius?

Cornelius (*sits in dejected thought*). Chief clerk! Promoted from chief clerk to chief clerk.

Barnaby. Don't you like it?

Cornelius. Chief clerk! — and if I'm good, in ten years I'll be promoted to chief clerk again. Thirty-three years old and I still don't get an evening free? When am I going to begin to live?

Barnaby. Well — ah . . . you can begin to live on Sundays, Cornelius.

Cornelius. That's not living. Twice to church, and old Wolf-trap's eyes on the back of my head the whole time. And as for holidays! What did we do last Christmas? All those canned tomatoes went bad and exploded. We had to clean up the mess all afternoon. Was that living?

Barnaby (*holding his nose at the memory of the bad smell*). No ! ! !

Cornelius (*rising with sudden resolution*). Barnaby, how much money
    have you got — where you can get at it?

Barnaby. Oh — three dollars. Why, Cornelius?

Cornelius. You and I are going to New York.

Barnaby. Cornelius! ! ! We can't! Close the store?

Cornelius. Some more rotten-tomato cans are going to explode.

Barnaby. Holy cabooses! How do you know?

Cornelius. I know they're rotten. All you have to do is to light a match
    under them. They'll make such a smell that customers can't come
    into the place for twenty-four hours. That'll get us an evening free.
    We're going to New York too, Barnaby, we're going to live! I'm
    going to have enough adventures to last me until I'm *partner.* So go
    and get your Sunday clothes on.

Barnaby. Wha-a-a-t?

Cornelius. Yes, I mean it. We're going to have a good meal; and we're
    going to be in danger; and we're going to get almost arrested; and
    we're going to spend all our money.

Barnaby. Holy cabooses! !

Cornelius. And one more thing: we're not coming back to Yonkers
    until we've kissed a girl.

Barnaby. Kissed a girl! Cornelius, you can't do that. You don't know
    any girls.

Cornelius. I'm thirty-three. I've got to begin sometime.

Barnaby. I'm only seventeen, Cornelius. It isn't so urgent for me.

Cornelius. Don't start backing down now — if the worst comes to the
    worst and we get discharged from here we can always join the Army.

Barnaby. Uh — did I hear you say that you'd be old Wolf-trap's
    partner?

Cornelius. How can I help it? He's growing old. If you go to bed at
    nine and open the store at six, you get promoted upward whether
    you like it or not.

Barnaby. My! Partner.

Cornelius. Oh, there's no way of getting away from it. You and I
    will be Vandergelders.

Barnaby. I? Oh, no — I may rise a little, but I'll never be a Vander-
    gelder.

Cornelius. Listen — everybody thinks when he gets rich he'll be a
    different kind of rich person from the rich people he sees around
    him, later on he finds out there's only one kind of rich person, and
    he's it.

Barnaby. Oh, but I'll —

Cornelius. No. The best of all would be a person who has all the good
    things a poor person has, and all the good meals a rich person has,

but that's never been known. No, you and I are going to be Vandergelders; all the more reason, then, for us to try and get some living and some adventure into us now — will you come, Barnaby?

Barnaby (in a struggle with his fears, a whirlwind of words). But Wolf-trap — KRR-pt, Gertrude-KRR-pt — (*With a sudden cry of agreement.*) Yes, Cornelius! (*Enter Mrs. Levi, Ermengarde and Gertrude from back center. The boys start down the ladder, Cornelius last.*)

Mrs. Levi. Mr. Hackl, is the trunk waiting at the station?

Cornelius. Yes, Mrs. Levi. (*Closes the trap door.*)

Mrs. Levi. Take a last look, Ermengarde.

Ermengarde. What?

Mrs. Levi. Take a last look at your girlhood home, dear. I remember when I left my home. I gave a whinny like a young colt, and off I went. (*Ermengarde and Gertrude exit.*)

Ermengarde (as they go). Oh, Gertrude, do you think I ought to get married this way? A young girl has to be so careful! (*Mrs. Levi is alone. She addresses the audience.*)

Mrs. Levi. You know, I think I'm going to have this room with *blue wallpaper,* — yes, in blue! (*Hurries out after the others. Barnaby comes up trap door, looks off right, then lies on floor, gazing down through the trap door.*)

Barnaby. All clear up here, Cornelius! Cornelius — hold the candle steady a minute — the bottom row's all right — but try the top now . . . they're swelled up like they are ready to bust! (*BANG.*) Holy CABOOSES! (*BANG, BANG.*) Cornelius! I can smell it up here! (*Rises and dances about, holding his nose.*)

Cornelius (rushing up the trap door). Get into your Sunday clothes, Barnaby. We're going to New York! (*As they run out . . . there is a big explosion. A shower of tomato cans comes up from below, as —*

THE CURTAIN FALLS)

ACT II

Mrs. Molloy's hat shop, New York City.

There are two entrances. One door at the extreme right of the back wall, to Mrs. Molloy's workroom; one at the back left corner, to the street. The whole left wall is taken up with the show windows, filled with hats. It is separated from the shop by a low brass rail, hung with

*net; during the act both Mrs. Molloy and Barnaby stoop under the
rail and go into the shop window. By the street door stands a large
cheval glass. In the middle of the back wall is a large wardrobe or
clothes cupboard, filled with ladies' coats, large enough for Cornelius
to hide in. At the left, beginning at the back wall, between the wardrobe and the workroom door, a long counter extends toward the
audience, almost to the footlights. In the center of the room is a
large round table with a low-hanging red cloth. There are a small gilt
chair by the wardrobe and two chairs in front of the counter. Over the
street door and the workroom door are bells which ring when the
doors are opened.*

*As the curtain rises, Mrs. Molloy is in the window, standing on a
box, reaching up to put hats on the stand. Minnie Fay is sewing by
the counter. Mrs. Molloy has a pair of felt overshoes, to be removed
later.*

Mrs. Molloy. Minnie, you're a fool. Of course I shall marry Horace
   Vandergelder.
Minnie. Oh, Mrs. Molloy! I didn't ask you. I wouldn't dream of
   asking you such a personal question.
Mrs. Molloy. Well, it's what you meant, isn't it? And there's your
   answer. I shall certainly marry Horace Vandergelder if he asks me.
   (*Crawls under window rail, into the room, singing loudly.*)
Minnie. I know it's none of my business . . .
Mrs. Molloy. Speak up, Minnie, I can't hear you.
Minnie. . . . but do you . . . do you . . . ?
Mrs. Molloy (*having crossed the room, is busy at the counter*). Min-
   nie, you're a fool. Say it: Do I love him? Of course, I don't love
   him. But I have two good reasons for marrying him just the same.
   Minnie, put something on that hat. It's not ugly enough. (*Throws
   hat over counter.*)
Minnie (*catching and taking hat to table*). Not ugly enough!
Mrs. Molloy. I couldn't sell it. Put a . . . put a sponge on it.
Minnie. Why, Mrs. Molloy, you're in such a *mood* today.
Mrs. Molloy. In the first place I shall marry Mr. Vandergelder to get
   away from the millinery business. I've hated it from the first day I
   had anything to do with it. Minnie, I hate hats. (*Sings loudly
   again.*)
Minnie. Why, what's the matter with the millinery business?
Mrs. Molloy (*crossing to window with two hats*). I can no longer
   stand being suspected of being a wicked woman, while I have
   nothing to show for it. I can't stand it. (*She crawls under rail into
   window.*)

Minnie. Why, no one would dream of suspecting you —

Mrs. Molloy (on her knees, she looks over the rail). Minnie, you're a fool. All millineresses are suspected of being wicked women. Why, half the time all those women come into the shop merely to look at me.

Minnie. Oh!

Mrs. Molloy. They enjoy the suspicion. But they aren't certain. If they were *certain* I was a wicked woman, they wouldn't put foot in this place again. Do I go to restaurants? No, it would be bad for business. Do I go to balls, or theatres, or operas? No, it would be bad for business. The only men I ever meet are feather merchants. (*Crawls out of window, but gazes intently into the street.*) What are those two young men doing out there on that park bench? Take my word for it, Minnie, either I marry Horace Vandergelder, or I break out of this place like a fire engine. I'll go to every theatre and ball and opera in New York City. (*Returns to counter, singing again.*)

Minnie. But Mr. Vandergelder's not . . .

Mrs. Molloy. Speak up, Minnie, I can't hear you.

Minnie. . . . I don't think he's attractive.

Mrs. Molloy. But what I think he is — and it's very important — I think he'd make a good fighter.

Minnie. Mrs. Molloy!

Mrs. Molloy. Take my word for it, Minnie: the best part of married life is the fights. The rest is merely so-so.

Minnie (fingers in ears). I won't listen.

Mrs. Molloy. Peter Molloy — God rest him! — was a fine arguing man. I pity the woman whose husband slams the door and walks out of the house at the beginning of an argument. Peter Molloy would stand up and fight for hours on end. He'd even throw things, Minnie, and there's no pleasure to equal that. When I felt tired I'd start a good bloodwarming fight and it'd take ten years off my age; now Horace Vandergelder would put up a good fight; I know it. I've a mind to marry him.

Minnie. I think they're just awful, the things you're saying today.

Mrs. Molloy. Well, I'm enjoying them myself, too.

Minnie (at the window). Mrs. Molloy, those two men out in the street —

Mrs. Molloy. What?

Minnie. Those men. It looks as if they meant to come in here.

Mrs. Molloy. Well now, it's time some men came into this place. I give you the younger one, Minnie.

Minnie. Aren't you terrible! (*Mrs. Molloy sits on center table, while Minnie takes off her felt overshoes.*)

Mrs. Molloy. Wait till I get my hands on that older one! Mark my words, Minnie, we'll get an adventure out of this yet. Adventure, adventure! Why does everybody have adventures except me, Minnie? Because I have no spirit, I have no gumption. Minnie, they're coming in here. Let's go into the workroom and make them wait for us for a minute.

Minnie. Oh, but Mrs. Molloy . . . my work! . . .

Mrs. Molloy (*running to workroom*). Hurry up, be quick now, Minnie! (*They go out to workroom. Barnaby and Cornelius run in from street, leaving front door open. They are dressed in the stiff discomfort of their Sunday clothes. Cornelius wears a bowler hat, Barnaby a straw hat too large for him.*)

Barnaby. No one's here.

Cornelius. Some women were here a minute ago. I saw them. (*They jump back to the street door and peer down the street.*) That's Wolf-trap all right! (*Coming back.*) Well, we've got to hide here until he passes by.

Barnaby. He's sitting down on that bench. It may be quite a while.

Cornelius. When these women come in, we'll have to make conversation until he's gone away. We'll pretend we're buying a hat. How much money have you got now?

Barnaby (*counting his money*). Forty cents for the train — seventy cents for dinner — twenty cents to see the whale — and a dollar I lost — I have seventy cents.

Cornelius. And I have a dollar seventy-five. I wish I knew how much hats cost!

Barnaby. Is this an adventure, Cornelius?

Cornelius. No, but it may be.

Barnaby. I think it is. There we wander around New York all day and nothing happens; and then we come to the quietest street in the whole city and suddenly Mr. Vandergelder turns the corner. (*Going to door.*) I think that's an adventure. I think . . . Cornelius! That Mrs. Levi is there now. She's sitting down on the bench with him.

Cornelius. What do you know about that! We know only one person in all New York City, and there she is!

Barnaby. Even if our adventure came along now I'd be too tired to enjoy it. Cornelius, why isn't this an adventure?

Cornelius. Don't be asking that. When you're in an adventure, you'll know it all right.

Barnaby. Maybe I wouldn't. Cornelius, let's arrange a signal for you to give me when an adventure's really going on. For instance, Cornelius, you say . . . uh . . . uh . . . *pudding;* you say *pudding* to me as if it's an adventure we're in.

Cornelius. I wonder where the lady who runs this store is? What's her name again?

Barnaby. Mrs. Molloy, hats for ladies.

Cornelius. Oh yes. I must think over what I'm going to say when she comes in. (*To counter.*) "Good afternoon, Mrs. Molloy, wonderful weather we're having. We've been looking everywhere for some beautiful hats."

Barnaby. That's fine, Cornelius!

Cornelius. "Good afternoon, Mrs. Molloy; wonderful weather . . ." We'll make her think we're very rich. (*One hand in trouser pocket, the other on back of chair.*) "Good afternoon, Mrs. Molloy . . ." You keep one eye on the door the whole time. "We've been look-ing everywhere for . . ." (*Enter Mrs. Molloy from the workroom.*)

Mrs. Molloy (*behind the counter*). Oh, I'm sorry. Have I kept you waiting? Good afternoon, gentlemen.

Cornelius (*hat off*). Here, Cornelius Hackl.

Barnaby (*hat off*). Here, Barnaby Tucker.

Mrs. Molloy. I'm very happy to meet you. Perhaps I can help you. Won't you sit down?

Cornelius. Thank you, we will. (*The boys place their hats on the table, then sit down at the counter facing Mrs. Molloy.*) You see, Mrs. Molloy, we're looking for hats. We've looked everywhere. Do you know what we heard? Go to Mrs. Molloy's, they said. So we came here. Only place we *could* go . . .

Mrs. Molloy. Well, now, that's *very* complimentary.

Cornelius. . . . and we were right. Everybody was right.

Mrs. Molloy. You wish to choose some hats for a friend?

Cornelius. Yes, exactly. (*Kicks Barnaby.*)

Barnaby. Yes, exactly.

Cornelius. We were thinking of five or six, weren't we, Barnaby?

Barnaby. Er — five.

Cornelius. You see, Mrs. Molloy, money's no object with us. None at all.

Mrs. Molloy. Why, Mr. Hackl . . .

Cornelius (*rises and goes toward street door*). . . . I beg your pardon, what an interesting street! Something happening every minute. Passers-by, and . . . (*Barnaby runs to join him.*)

Mrs. Molloy. You're from out of town, Mr. Hackl?

Cornelius (*coming back*). Yes, ma-am — Barnaby, just keep your eye

on the street, will you? You won't see that in Yonkers every day.
(*Barnaby remains kneeling at street door.*)

Barnaby. Oh yes, I will.

Cornelius. Not all of it.

Mrs. Molloy. Now this friend of yours — couldn't she come in with you someday and choose her hats herself?

Cornelius (sits at counter). No. Oh, no. It's a surprise for her.

Mrs. Molloy. Indeed? That may be a little difficult, Mr. Hackl. It's not entirely customary. — Your friend's very interested in the street, Mr. Hackl.

Cornelius. Oh yes. Yes. He has reason to be.

Mrs. Molloy. You said you were from out of town?

Cornelius. Yes, we're from Yonkers.

Mrs. Molloy. Yonkers?

Cornelius. Yonkers . . . yes, Yonkers. (*He gazes rapt into her eyes.*) You should know Yonkers, Mrs. Molloy. Hudson River; Palisades; drives; some say it's the most beautiful town in the world; that's what they say.

Mrs. Molloy. Is that so!

Cornelius (rises). Mrs. Molloy, if you ever had a Sunday free, I'd . . . we'd like to show you Yonkers. Y'know, it's very historic, too.

Mrs. Molloy. That's very kind of you. Well, perhaps . . . now about those hats. (*Takes two hats from under counter, and crosses to back center of the room.*)

Cornelius (following). Is there . . . Have you a . . . Maybe Mr. Molloy would like to see Yonkers too?

Mrs. Molloy. Oh, I'm a widow, Mr. Hackl.

Cornelius (joyfully). You are! (*With sudden gravity.*) Oh, that's too bad. Mr. Molloy would have enjoyed Yonkers.

Mrs. Molloy. Very likely. Now about these hats. Is your friend dark or light?

Cornelius. Don't think about that for a minute. Any hat you'd like would be perfectly all right with her.

Mrs. Molloy. Really! (*She puts one on.*) Do you like this one?

Cornelius (in awe-struck admiration). Barnaby! (*In sudden anger.*) Barnaby! Look! (*Barnaby turns; unimpressed, he laughs vaguely, and turns to door again.*) Mrs. Molloy, that's the most beautiful hat I ever saw. (*Barnaby now crawls under the rail into the window.*)

Mrs. Molloy. Your friend is acting very strangely, Mr. Hackl.

Cornelius. Barnaby, stop acting strangely. When the street's quiet and empty, come back and talk to us. What was I saying? Oh yes: Mrs. Molloy, you should know Yonkers.

Mrs. Molloy (hat off). The fact is, I have a friend in Yonkers. Perhaps you know him. It's always so foolish to ask in cases like that, isn't it? (*They both laugh over this with increasing congeniality. Mrs. Molloy goes to counter with hats from table. Cornelius follows.*) It's a Mr. Vandergelder.

Cornelius (*stops abruptly*). What was that you said?

Mrs. Molloy. Then you do know him?

Cornelius. Horace Vandergelder?

Mrs. Molloy. Yes, that's right.

Cornelius. Know him! (*Look to Barnaby.*) Why, no. No!

Barnaby. No! No!

Cornelius (*starting to glide about the room, in search of a hiding place*). I beg your pardon, Mrs. Molloy — what an attractive shop you have! (*Smiling fixedly at her he moves to the workshop door.*) And where does this door lead to? (*Opens it, and is alarmed by the bell which rings above it.*)

Mrs. Molloy. Why, Mr. Hackl, that's my workroom.

Cornelius. Everything here is so interesting. (*Looks under counter.*) Every corner. Every door, Mrs. Molloy. Barnaby, notice the interesting doors and cupboards. (*He opens the cupboard door.*) Deeply interesting. Coats for ladies. (*Laughs.*) Barnaby, make a note of the table. Precious piece of furniture, with a low-hanging cloth, I see. (*Stretches his leg under table.*)

Mrs. Molloy (*taking a hat from box left of wardrobe*). Perhaps your friend might like some of this new Italian straw. Mr. Vandergelder's a substantial man and very well liked, they tell me.

Cornelius. A lovely man, Mrs. Molloy.

Mrs. Molloy. Oh yes — charming, charming!

Cornelius (*smiling sweetly*). Has only one fault, as far as I know; he's hard as nails; but apart from that, as you say, a charming nature, ma'am.

Mrs. Molloy. And a large circle of friends — ?

Cornelius. Yes, indeed, yes indeed — five or six.

Barnaby. Five!

Cornelius. He comes and calls on you here from time to time, I suppose.

Mrs. Molloy (*turns from mirror where she has been putting a hat on*). This summer we'll be wearing ribbons down our back. Yes, as a matter of fact I am expecting a call from him this afternoon. (*Hat off.*)

Barnaby. I think . . . Cornelius! I think . . . !!

Mrs. Molloy. Now to show you some more hats —

Barnaby. Look out! (*He takes a flying leap over the rail and flings himself under the table.*)

Cornelius. Begging your pardon, Mrs. Molloy. (*He jumps into the cupboard.*)

Mrs. Molloy. Gentlemen! Mr. Hackl! Come right out of there this minute!

Cornelius (*sticking his head out of the wardrobe door*). Help us just this once, Mrs. Molloy! We'll explain later!

Mrs. Molloy. Mr. Hackl!

Barnaby. We're as innocent as can be, Mrs. Molloy.

Mrs. Molloy. But really! Gentlemen! I can't have this! What are you doing?

Barnaby. Cornelius! Cornelius! Pudding?

Cornelius (*a shout*). Pudding! (*They disappear. Enter from the street Mrs. Levi, followed by Mr. Vandergelder. Vandergelder is dressed in a too-bright checked suit, and wears a green derby — or bowler — hat. He is carrying a large ornate box of chocolates in one hand, and a cane in the other.*)

Mrs. Levi. Irene, my darling child, how are you? Heaven be good to us, how well you look! (*They kiss.*)

Mrs. Molloy. But what a surprise! And Mr. Vandergelder in New York — what a pleasure!

Vandergelder (*swaying back and forth on his heels complacently*). Good afternoon, Mrs. Molloy. (*They shake hands. Mrs. Molloy brings chair from counter for him. He sits at left of table.*)

Mrs. Levi. Yes, Mr. Vandergelder's in New York. Yonkers lies up there — *decimated* today. Irene, we thought we'd pay you a very short call. Now you'll tell us if it's inconvenient, won't you?

Mrs. Molloy (*placing a chair for Mrs. Levi at right of table*). Inconvenient, Dolly! The idea! Why, it's sweet of you to come. (*She notices the boys' hats on the table — sticks a spray of flowers into crown of Cornelius' bowler and winds a piece of chiffon round Barnaby's panama.*)

Vandergelder. We waited outside a moment.

Mrs. Levi. Mr. Vandergelder thought he saw two customers coming in — two men.

Mrs. Molloy. Men! Men, Mr. Vandergelder? Why, what will you be saying next?

Mrs. Levi. Then we'll sit down for a minute or two. . . .

Mrs. Molloy (*wishing to get them out of the shop into the workroom*). Before you sit down — (*She pushes them both.*) Before you sit down, there's something I want to show you. I want to show Mr. Vandergelder my workroom, too.

Mrs. Levi. I've seen the workroom a hundred times. I'll stay right here and try on some of these hats.

Mrs. Molloy. No, Dolly, you come too. I have something for you.
Come along, everybody. (*Exit Mrs. Levi to workroom.*) Mr. Vandergelder, I want your advice. You don't know how helpless a woman
in business is. Oh, I feel I need advice every minute from a fine
business head like yours. (*Exit Vandergelder to workroom. Mrs.
Molloy shouts this line and then slams the workroom door.*) Now
I shut the door!! (*Exit Mrs. Molloy. Cornelius puts his head out
of the wardrobe door and gradually comes out into the room, leaving
door open.*)

Cornelius. Hsst!

Barnaby (*pokes his head out from under the table*). Maybe she wants
us to go, Cornelius?

Cornelius. Certainly I won't go. Mrs. Molloy would think we were just
thoughtless fellows. No, all I want is to stretch a minute.

Barnaby. What are you going to do when he's gone, Cornelius? Are
we just going to run away?

Cornelius. Well . . . I don't know yet. I like Mrs. Molloy a lot. I
wouldn't like her to think badly of me. I think I'll buy a hat. We
can walk home to Yonkers, even if it takes us all night. I wonder
how much hats cost. Barnaby, give me all the money you've got.
(*As he leans over to take the money, he sneezes. Both return to
their hiding places in alarm; then emerge again.*) My, all those per-
fumes in that cupboard tickle my nose! But I like it in there . . . it's
a woman's world, and very different.

Barnaby. I like it where I am, too; only I'd like it better if I had a
pillow.

Cornelius (*taking coat from wardrobe*). Here, take one of these coats.
I'll roll it up for you so it won't get mussed. Ladies don't like to
have their coats mussed.

Barnaby. That's fine. Now I can just lie here and hear Mr. Vandergelder talk. (*Cornelius goes slowly above table towards cheval mirror, repeating Mrs. Molloy's line dreamily.*)

Cornelius. "This summer we'll be wearing ribbons down our back. . . ."

Barnaby. Can I take off my shoes, Cornelius? (*Cornelius does not reply.
He comes to the footlights and addresses the audience, in completely
simple naïve sincerity:*)

Cornelius. Isn't the world full of wonderful things. There we sit cooped
up in Yonkers for years and years and all the time wonderful people
like Mrs. Molloy are walking around in New York and we don't
know them at all. I don't know whether — from where you're sitting — you can see — well, for instance, the way (*He points to the
edge of his right eye.*) her eye and forehead and cheek come together, up here. Can you? And the kind of fireworks that shoot out

of her eyes all the time. I tell you right now: a fine woman is the greatest work of God. You can talk all you like about Niagara Falls and the Pyramids; they aren't in it at all. Of course, up there at Yonkers they came into the store all the time, and bought this and that, and I said, "Yes, ma'am," and "That'll be seventy-five cents, ma'am"; and I *watched* them. But today I've talked to one, equal to equal, equal to equal, and to the finest one that ever existed, in my opinion. They're so different from men! Everything that they say and do is so different that you feel like laughing all the time. (*He laughs.*) Golly, they're different from men. And they're awfully mysterious, too. You never can be really sure what's going on in their heads. They have a kind of wall around them all the time — of pride and a sort of play-acting: I bet you could know a woman a hundred years without ever being really sure whether she liked you or not. This minute I'm in danger. I'm in danger of losing my job and my future and everything that people think is important; but I don't care. Even if I have to dig ditches for the rest of my life, I'll be a ditch digger who once had a wonderful day.

    Barnaby!

Barnaby. Oh, you woke me up!

Cornelius (*kneels*). Barnaby, we can't go back to Yonkers yet and you know why.

Barnaby. Why not?

Cornelius. We've had a good meal. We've had an adventure. We've been in danger of getting arrested. There's only one more thing we've got to do before we go back to be successes in Yonkers.

Barnaby. Cornelius! You're never going to kiss Mrs. Molloy!

Cornelius. Maybe.

Barnaby. But she'll scream.

Cornelius. Barnaby, you don't know anything at all. You might as well know right now that everybody except us goes through life kissing right and left all the time.

Barnaby (*pauses for reflection: humbly*). Well, thanks for telling me, Cornelius. I often wondered. (*Enter Mrs. Levi from workroom.*)

Mrs. Levi. Just a minute, Irene. I must find my handkerchief. (*Cornelius, caught by the arrival of Mrs. Levi, drops to his hands and knees, and starts very slowly to crawl back to the wardrobe, as though the slowness rendered him visible. Mrs. Levi, leaning over the counter, watches him. From the cupboard he puts his head out of it and looks pleadingly at her.*) Why, Mr. Hackl, I thought you were up in Yonkers.

Cornelius. I almost always am, Mrs. Levi. Oh, Mrs. Levi, don't tell Mr. Vandergelder! I'll explain everything later.

Barnaby (*puts head out*). We're terribly innocent, Mrs. Levi.

Mrs. Levi. Why, who's that?

Barnaby. Barnaby Tucker — just paying a call.

Mrs. Levi (*looking under counter and even shaking out her skirts*). Well, who else is here?

Cornelius. Just the two of us, Mrs. Levi, that's all.

Mrs. Levi. Old friends of Mrs. Molloy's, is that it?

Cornelius. We never knew her before a few minutes ago, but we like her a lot — don't we, Barnaby? In fact, I think she's . . . I think she's the finest person in the world. I'm ready to tell that to anybody.

Mrs. Levi. And does she think *you're* the finest person in the world?

Cornelius. Oh, no. I don't suppose she even notices that I'm alive.

Mrs. Levi. Well, I think she must notice that you're alive in that cupboard, Mr. Hackl. Well, if I were you, I'd get back into it right away. Somebody could be coming in any minute. (*Cornelius disappears. She sits unconcernedly in chair right. Enter Mrs. Molloy.*)

Mrs. Molloy (*leaving door open and looking about in concealed alarm*). Can I help you, Dolly?

Mrs. Levi. No, no, no. I was just blowing my nose. (*Enter Vandergelder from workroom.*)

Vandergelder. Mrs. Molloy, I've got some advice to give you about your business. (*Mrs. Molloy comes to the center of the room and puts Barnaby's hat on floor in window, then Cornelius' hat on the counter.*)

Mrs. Levi. Oh, advice from Mr. Vandergelder! The whole city should hear this.

Vandergelder (*standing in the workroom door, pompously*). In the first place, the aim of business is to make profit.

Mrs. Molloy. Is that so?

Mrs. Levi. I never heard it put so clearly before. Did you hear it?

Vandergelder (*crossing the room to the left*). You pay those girls of yours too much. You pay them as much as men. Girls like that enjoy their work. Wages, Mrs. Molloy, are paid to make people do work they don't want to do.

Mrs. Levi. Mr. Vandergelder thinks so ably. And that's exactly the way his business is run up in Yonkers.

Vandergelder (*patting her hand*). Mrs. Molloy, I'd like for you to come up to Yonkers.

Mrs. Molloy. That would be very nice. (*He hands her the box of chocolates.*) Oh, thank you. As a matter of fact, I know someone from Yonkers, someone else.

Vandergelder (*hangs hat on the cheval mirror*). Oh? Who's that?

(*Mrs. Molloy puts chocolates on table and brings gilt chair forward and sits center at table facing the audience.*)

Mrs. Molloy. Someone quite well-to-do, I believe, though a little free and easy in his behavior. Mr. Vandergelder, do you know Mr. Cornelius Hackl in Yonkers?

Vandergelder. I know him like I know my own boot. He's my head clerk.

Mrs. Molloy. Is that so?

Vandergelder. He's been in my store for ten years.

Mrs. Molloy. Well, I never!

Vandergelder. Where would you have known him? (*Mrs. Molloy is in silent confusion. She looks for help to Mrs. Levi, seated at right end of table.*)

Mrs. Levi (*groping for means to help Mrs. Molloy*). Err . . . blah . . . err . . . bl . . . er . . . Oh, just one of those chance meetings, I suppose.

Mrs. Molloy. Yes, oh yes! One of those chance meetings.

Vandergelder. What? Chance meetings? Cornelius Hackl has no right to chance meetings. Where was it?

Mrs. Molloy. Really, Mr. Vandergelder, it's very unlike you to question me in such a way. I think Mr. Hackl is better known than you think he is.

Vandergelder. Nonsense.

Mrs. Molloy. He's in New York often, and he's very well liked.

Mrs. Levi (*having found her idea, with decision*). Well, the truth might as well come out now as later. Mr. Vandergelder, Irene is quite right. Your head clerk is often in New York. Goes everywhere; has an army of friends. Everybody knows Cornelius Hackl.

Vandergelder (*laughs blandly and sits in chair at left of table*). He never comes to New York. He works all day in my store and at nine o'clock at night he goes to sleep in the bran room.

Mrs. Levi. So you think. But it's not true.

Vandergelder. Dolly Gallagher, you're crazy.

Mrs. Levi. Listen to me. You keep your nose so deep in your account books you don't know what goes on. Yes, by day, Cornelius Hackl is your faithful trusted clerk — that's true; but by night! Well, he leads a double life, that's all! He's here at the opera; at the great restaurants; in all the fashionable homes . . . why, he's at the Harmonia Gardens Restaurant three nights a week. The fact is, he's the wittiest, gayest, naughtiest, most delightful man in New York. Well, he's just *the* famous Cornelius Hackl!

Vandergelder (*sure of himself*). It ain't the same man. If I ever thought Cornelius Hackl came to New York, I'd discharge him.

Mrs. Levi. Who took the horses out of Jenny Lind's carriage and pulled her through the streets?

Mrs. Molloy. Who?

Mrs. Levi. Cornelius Hackl! Who dressed up as a waiter at the Fifth Avenue Hotel the other night and took an oyster and dropped it right down Mrs. . . . (*Rises.*) No, it's too wicked to tell you!

Mrs. Molloy. Oh yes, Dolly, tell it! Go on!

Mrs. Levi. No. But it *was* Cornelius Hackl.

Vandergelder (*loud*). It ain't the same man. Where'd he get the money?

Mrs. Levi. But he's very rich.

Vandergelder (*rises*). Rich! I keep his money in my own safe. He has a hundred and forty-six dollars and thirty-five cents.

Mrs. Levi. Oh, Mr. Vandergelder, you're killing me! Do come to your senses. He's one of *the* Hackls. (*Mrs. Molloy sits at chair right of table where Mrs. Levi has been sitting.*)

Vandergelder. *The* Hackls?

Mrs. Levi. They built the Raritan Canal.

Vandergelder. Then why should he work in my store?

Mrs. Levi. Well, I'll tell you. (*Sits at the center of the table, facing the audience.*)

Vandergelder (*striding about*). I don't want to hear! I've got a headache! I'm going home. *It ain't the same man!!* He sleeps in my bran room. You can't get away from facts. I just made him my chief clerk.

Mrs. Levi. If you had any sense you'd make him partner. (*Rises, crosses to Mrs. Molloy.*) Now Irene, I can see you were as taken with him as everybody else is.

Mrs. Molloy. Why, I only met him once, very hastily.

Mrs. Levi. Yes, but I can see that you were taken with him. Now don't you be thinking of marrying him!

Mrs. Molloy (*her hands on her cheeks*). Dolly! What are you saying! Oh!

Mrs. Levi. Maybe it'd be fine. But think it over carefully. He breaks hearts like hickory nuts.

Vandergelder. Who?

Mrs. Levi. Cornelius Hackl!

Vandergelder. Mrs. Molloy, how often has he called on you?

Mrs. Molloy. Oh, I'm telling the truth. I've only seen him once in my life. Dolly Levi's been exaggerating so, I don't know where to look! (*Enter Minnie from workroom and crosses to window.*)

Minnie. Excuse me, Mrs. Molloy. I must get together that order for Mrs. Parkinson.

Mrs. Molloy. Yes, we must get that off before closing.

Minnie. I want to send it off by the errand girl. (*Having taken a hat from the window.*) Oh, I almost forgot the coat. (*She starts for the wardrobe.*)

Mrs. Molloy (*running to the wardrobe to prevent her*). Oh, oh! I'll do that, Minnie! (*But she is too late. Minnie opens the right-hand cupboard door and falls back in terror, and screams:*)

Minnie. Oh, Mrs. Molloy! Help! There's a man! (*Mrs. Molloy with the following speech pushes her back to the workroom door. Minnie walks with one arm pointing at the cupboard. At the end of each of Mrs. Molloy's sentences she repeats — at the same pitch and degree — the words:*) There's a man!ʼ

Mrs. Molloy (*slamming cupboard door*). Minnie, you imagined it. You're tired, dear. You go back in the workroom and lie down. Minnie, you're a fool; hold your tongue! ·

Minnie. There's a man! (*Exit Minnie to workroom. Mrs. Molloy returns to the front of the stage. Vandergelder raises his stick threateningly.*)

Vandergelder. If there's a man there, we'll get him out. Whoever you are, come out of there! (*Strikes table with his stick.*)

Mrs. Levi (*goes masterfully to the cupboard — sweeps her umbrella around among the coats and closes each door as she does so*). Nonsense! There's no man there. See! Miss Fay's nerves have been playing tricks on her. Come now, let's sit down again. What were you saying, Mr. Vandergelder? (*They sit, Mrs. Molloy right, Mrs. Levi center, Vandergelder left. A sneeze is heard from the cupboard. They all rise, look towards cupboard, then sit again.*) Well now . . . (*Another tremendous sneeze. With a gesture that says,*) "I can do no more: God bless you!" (*They all rise. Mrs. Molloy stands with her back to the cupboard.*)

Mrs. Molloy (*to Vandergelder*). Yes, there is a man in there. I'll explain it all to you another time. Thank you very much for coming to see me. Good afternoon, Dolly. Good afternoon, Mr. Vandergelder.

Vandergelder. You're protecting a man in there!

Mrs. Molloy (*with back to cupboard*). There's a very simple explanation, but for the present, good afternoon. (*Barnaby now sneezes twice, lifting the table each time. Vandergelder, right of table, jerks off the tablecloth. Barnaby pulls cloth under table and rolls himself up in it. Mrs. Molloy picks up the box of chocolates, which has rolled on the floor.*)

Mrs. Levi. Lord, the whole room's *crawling* with men! I'll never get over it.

Vandergelder. The world is going to pieces! I can't believe my own eyes!

Mrs. Levi. Come, Mr. Vandergelder. Ernestina Simple is waiting for us.

Vandergelder (finds his hat and puts it on). Mrs. Molloy, I shan't trouble you again, and *vice versa.* (*Mrs. Molloy is standing trans-fixed in front of cupboard, clasping the box of chocolates. Vander-gelder snatches the box from her and goes out.*)

Mrs. Levi (crosses to her). Irene, when I think of all the interesting things you have in this room! (*Kisses her.*) Make the most of it, dear. (*Raps cupboard.*) Good-by! (*Raps on table with umbrella.*) Good-by! (*Exit Mrs. Levi, Mrs. Molloy opens door of cupboard. Cornelius steps out.*)

Mrs. Molloy. So that was one of your practical jokes, Mr. Hackl?

Cornelius. No, no, Mrs. Molloy!

Mrs. Molloy. Come out from under that, Barnaby Tucker, you trouble-maker! (*She snatches the cloth and spreads it back on table. Minnie enters.*) There's nothing to be afraid of, Minnie, I know all about these gentlemen.

Cornelius. Mrs. Molloy, we realize that what happened here —

Mrs. Molloy. You think because you're rich you can make up for all the harm you do, is that it?

Cornelius. No, no!

Barnaby (on the floor-putting shoes on). No, no!

Mrs. Molloy. Minnie, this is the famous Cornelius Hackl who goes round New York tying people into knots; and that's Barnaby Tucker, another troublemaker.

Barnaby. How d'you do?

Mrs. Molloy. Minnie, choose yourself any hat and coat in the store. We're going out to dinner. If this Mr. Hackl is so rich and gay and charming, he's going to be rich and gay and charming to us. He dines three nights a week at the Harmonia Gardens Restaurant, does he? Well, he's taking us there now.

Minnie. Mrs. Molloy, are you sure it's safe?

Mrs. Molloy. Minnie, hold your tongue. We're in a position to put these men into jail if they so much as squeak.

Cornelius. Jail, Mrs. Molloy?

Mrs. Molloy. Jail, Mr. Hackl. Officer Cogarty does everything I tell him to do. Minnie, you and I have been respectable for years; now we're in disgrace, we might as well make the most of it. Come into the workroom with me; I know some ways we can perk up our appearances. Gentlemen, we'll be back in a minute.

Cornelius. Uh — Mrs. Molloy, I hear there's an awfully good restaurant at the railway station.

Mrs. Molloy (high indignation). Railway station? Railway station? Certainly not! No, sir! You're going to give us a good dinner in the heart of the fashionable world. Go on in, Minnie! Don't you boys forget that you've made us lose our reputations, and now the fashionable world's the only place we can eat. *(Mrs. Molloy exits to workroom.)*

Barnaby. She's angry at us, Cornelius. Maybe we'd better run away now.

Cornelius. No, I'm going to go through with this if it kills me. Barnaby, for a woman like that a man could consent to go back to Yonkers and be a success.

Barnaby. All I know is no woman's going to make a success out of me.

Cornelius. Jail or no jail, we're going to take those ladies out to dinner. So grit your teeth. *(Enter Mrs. Molloy and Minnie from workroom dressed for the street.)*

Mrs. Molloy. Gentlemen, the cabs are at the corner, so forward march! *(She takes a hat — which will be Barnaby's at the end of Act III — and gives it to Minnie.)*

Cornelius. Yes, ma'am. *(Barnaby stands shaking his empty pockets warningly.)* Oh, Mrs. Molloy . . . is it far to the restaurant? Couldn't we walk?

Mrs. Molloy (pauses a moment, then). Minnie, take off your things. We're not going.

Others. Mrs. Molloy!

Mrs. Molloy. Mr. Hackl, I don't go anywhere I'm not wanted. Good night. I'm not very happy to have met you. *(She crosses the stage as though going to the workroom door.)*

Others. Mrs. Molloy!

Mrs. Molloy. I suppose you think we're not fashionable enough for you? Well, I won't be a burden to you. Good night, Mr. Tucker. *(The others follow her behind counter: Cornelius, Barnaby, then Minnie.)*

Cornelius. We want you to come with us more than anything in the world, Mrs. Molloy. *(Mrs. Molloy turns and pushes the three back. They are now near the center of the stage, to the right of the table, Mrs. Molloy facing the audience.)*

Mrs. Molloy. No, you don't! Look at you! Look at the pair of them, Minnie! Scowling, both of them!

Cornelius. Please, Mrs. Molloy!

Mrs. Molloy. Then smile. (*To Barnaby*) Go on, smile! No, that's not enough. Minnie, you come with me and we'll get our own supper.

Cornelius. Smile, Barnaby, you lout!

Barnaby. My face can't smile any stronger than that.

Mrs. Molloy. Then do something! Show some interest. Do something lively: sing!

Cornelius. I can't sing, really I can't.

Mrs. Molloy. We're wasting our time, Minnie. They don't want us.

Cornelius. Barnaby, what can you sing? Mrs. Molloy, all we know are sad songs.

Mrs. Molloy. That doesn't matter. If you want us to go out with you, you've got to sing something. (*All this has been very rapid; the boys turn up to counter, put their heads together, confer and abruptly turn, stand stiffly and sing "Tenting tonight; tenting tonight; tenting on the old camp ground." The four of them now repeat the refrain, softly harmonizing. At the end of the song, after a pause, Mrs. Molloy, moved, says:*)

Mrs. Molloy. We'll come! (*The boys shout joyfully.*) You boys go ahead. (*Cornelius gets his hat from counter; as he puts it on he discovers the flowers on it. Barnaby gets his hat from window. They go out whistling. Minnie turns and puts her hat on at the mirror.*) Minnie, get the front door key — I'll lock the workroom. (*Mrs. Molloy goes to workroom. Minnie takes key from hook left of wardrobe and goes to Mrs. Molloy, at the workroom door. She turns her around.*)

Minnie. Why, Mrs. Molloy, you're crying! (*Mrs. Molloy flings her arms round Minnie.*)

Mrs. Molloy. Oh, Minnie, the world is full of wonderful things. Watch me, dear, and tell me if my petticoat's showing. (*She crosses to door, followed by Minnie, as —*

THE CURTAIN FALLS)

ACT III

Veranda at the Harmonia Gardens Restaurant on the Battery, New York.

This room is informal and rustic. The main restaurant is indicated to be off stage back right.

There are three entrances: swinging double doors at the center of the back wall leading to the kitchen; one on the right wall (perhaps up a few steps and flanked by potted palms) to the street; one on the left wall to the staircase leading to the rooms above.

On the stage are two tables, left and right, each with four chairs. It is now afternoon and they are not yet set for dinner.

Against the back wall is a large folding screen. Also against the back wall are hat and coat racks.

As the curtain rises, Vandergelder is standing, giving orders to Rudolph, a waiter. Malachi Stack sits at table left.

Vandergelder. Now, hear what I say. I don't want you to make any mistakes. I want a table for three.

Rudolph (*tall "snob" waiter, alternating between cold superiority and rage. German accent*). For three.

Vandergelder. There'll be two ladies and myself.

Malachi. It's a bad combination, Mr. Vandergelder. You'll regret it.

Vandergelder. And I want a chicken.

Malachi. A chicken! You'll regret it.

Vandergelder. Hold your tongue. Write it down: chicken.

Rudolph. Yes, sir. Chicken Esterhazy? Chicken cacciatore? Chicken à la crème — ?

Vandergelder (*exploding*). A chicken! A chicken like everybody else has. And with the chicken I want a bottle of wine.

Rudolph. Moselle? Chablis? Vouvray?

Malachi. He doesn't understand you, Mr. Vandergelder. You'd better speak louder.

Vandergelder (*spelling*). W-I-N-E.

Rudolph. Wine.

Vandergelder. Wine! And I want this table removed. We'll eat at that table alone. (*Exit Rudolph through service door at back.*)

Malachi. There are some people coming in here now, Mr. Vandergelder. (*Vandergelder goes to back right to look at the newcomers.*)

Vandergelder. What! Thunder and damnation! It's my niece Ermengarde! What's she doing here?! — Wait till I get my hands on her.

Malachi (*running up to him*). Mr. Vandergelder! You must keep your temper!

Vandergelder. And there's that rascal artist with her. Why, it's a plot. I'll throw them in jail.

Malachi. Mr. Vandergelder! They're old enough to come to New York. You can't throw people into jail for coming to New York.

Vandergelder. And there's Mrs. Levi! What's she doing with them? It's a plot. It's a conspiracy! What's she saying to the cabman? Go up and hear what she's saying.

Malachi (*listening at entrance, right*). She's telling the cabman to wait, Mr. Vandergelder. She's telling the young people to come in and have a good dinner, Mr. Vandergelder.

Vandergelder. I'll put an end to this.

Malachi. Now, Mr. Vandergelder, if you lose your temper, you'll make matters worse. Mr. Vandergelder, come here and take my advice.

Vandergelder. Stop pulling my coat. What's your advice?

Malachi. Hide, Mr. Vandergelder. Hide behind this screen, and listen to what they're saying.

Vandergelder (*being pulled behind the screen*). Stop pulling at me. (*They hide behind the screen as Mrs. Levi, Ermengarde and Ambrose enter from the right. Ambrose is carrying Ermengarde's luggage.*)

Ermengarde. But I don't want to eat in a restaurant. It's not proper.

Mrs. Levi. Now, Ermengarde, dear, there's nothing wicked about eating in a restaurant. There's nothing wicked, even, about being in New York. Clergymen just make those things up to fill out their sermons.

Ermengarde. Oh, I wish I were in Yonkers, where *nothing* ever happens!

Mrs. Levi. Ermengarde, you're hungry. That's what's troubling you.

Ermengarde. Anyway, after dinner you must promise to take me to Aunt Flora's. She's been waiting for me all day and she must be half dead of fright.

Mrs. Levi. All right but of course, you know at Miss Van Huysen's you'll be back in your uncle's hands.

Ambrose (*hands raised to heaven*). I can't stand it.

Mrs. Levi (*to Ambrose*). Just keep telling yourself how pretty she is. Pretty girls have very little opportunity to improve their other advantages.

Ambrose. Listen, Ermengarde! You don't want to go back to your uncle. Stop and think! That old man with one foot in the grave!

Mrs. Levi. And the other three in the cashbox.

Ambrose. Smelling of oats —

Mrs. Levi. And axle grease.

Malachi. That's not true. It's only partly true.

Vandergelder (*loudly*). Hold your tongue! I'm going to teach them a lesson.

Malachi (*whisper*). Keep your temper, Mr. Vandergelder. Listen to what they say.

Mrs. Levi (hears this; throws a quick glance toward the screen; her whole manner changes). Oh, dear, what was I saying? The Lord be praised, how glad I am that I found you two dreadful children just as you were about to break poor dear Mr. Vandergelder's heart.

Ambrose. He's got no heart to break!

Mrs. Levi (vainly signaling). Mr. Vandergelder's a much kinder man than you think.

Ambrose. Kinder? He's a wolf.

Mrs. Levi. Remember that he leads a very lonely life. Now you're going to have dinner upstairs. There are some private rooms up there, — just meant for shy timid girls like Ermengarde. Come with me. (*She pushes the young people out left, Ambrose carrying the luggage.*)

Vandergelder (coming forward). I'll show them! (*He sits at table right.*)

Malachi. Everybody should eavesdrop once in a while, I always say. There's nothing like eavesdropping to show you that the world outside your head is different from the world inside your head.

Vandergelder (producing a pencil and paper). I want to write a note. Go and call that cabman in here. I want to talk to him.

Malachi. No one asks advice of a cabman, Mr. Vandergelder. They see so much of life that they have no ideas left.

Vandergelder. Do as I tell you.

Malachi. Yes, sir. Advice of a cabman! (*Exit right. Vandergelder writes his letter.*)

Vandergelder. "My dear Miss Van Huysen" (*To audience.*) Everybody's dear in a letter. It's enough to make you give up writing 'em. "My dear Miss Van Huysen. This is Ermengarde and that rascal Ambrose Kemper. They are trying to run away. Keep them in your house until I come." (*Malachi returns with an enormous Cabman in a high hat and a long coat. He carries a whip.*)

Cabman (entering). What's he want?

Vandergelder. I want to talk to you.

Cabman. I'm engaged. I'm waiting for my parties.

Vandergelder (folding letter and writing address). I know you are. Do you want to earn five dollars?

Cabman. Eh?

Vandergelder. I asked you, do you want to earn five dollars?

Cabman. I don't know. I never tried.

Vandergelder. When those parties of yours come downstairs, I want you to drive them to this address. Never mind what they say, drive them to this address. Ring the bell: give this letter to the lady of the house: see that they get in the door and keep them there.

Cabman. I can't make people go into a house if they don't want to.

Vandergelder (producing purse). Can you for ten dollars?

Cabman. Even for ten dollars, I can't do it alone.

Vandergelder. This fellow here will help you.

Malachi (sitting at table left). Now I'm pushing people into houses.

Vandergelder. There's the address: Miss Flora Van Huysen, 8 Jackson Street.

Cabman. Even if I get them in the door I can't be sure they'll stay there.

Vandergelder. For fifteen dollars you can.

Malachi. Murder begins at twenty-five.

Vandergelder. Hold your tongue! *(To cabman.)* The lady of the house will help you. All you have to do is to sit in the front hall and see that the man doesn't run off with the girl. I'll be at Miss Van Huysen's in an hour or two and I'll pay you then.

Cabman. If they call the police, I can't do anything.

Vandergelder. It's perfectly honest business. Perfectly honest.

Malachi. Every man's the best judge of his own honesty.

Vandergelder. The young lady is my niece. *(The Cabman laughs, skeptically.)* The young lady is my niece!! *(The Cabman looks at Malachi and shrugs.)* She's trying to run away with a good-for-nothing and we're preventing it.

Cabman. Oh, I know them, sir. They'll win in the end. Rivers don't run uphill.

Malachi. What did I tell you, Mr. Vandergelder? Advice of a cabman.

Vandergelder (hits table with his stick). Stack! I'll be back in half an hour. See that the table's set for three. See that nobody else eats here. Then go and join the cabman on the box.

Malachi. Yes, sir. *(Exit Vandergelder right.)*

Cabman. Who's your friend?

Malachi. Friend!! That's not a friend; that's an employer I'm trying out for a few days.

Cabman. You won't like him.

Malachi. I can see you're in business for yourself because you talk about liking employers. No one's ever liked an employer since business began.

Cabman. AW — !

Malachi. No, sir. I suppose you think *your horse* likes you?

Cabman. My old Clementine? She'd give her right feet for me.

Malachi. That's what all employers think. You imagine it. The streets of New York are full of cab horses winking at one another. Let's go in the kitchen and get some whiskey. I can't push people into houses when I'm sober. No, I've had about fifty employers in my life, but this is the most employer of them all. He talks to everybody as though he were paying them.

Cabman. I had an employer once. He watched me from eight in the morning until six at night — just sat there and watched me. Oh, dear! Even my mother didn't think I was as interesting as that. (*Cabman exits through service door.*)

Malachi (*following him off*). Yes, being employed is like being loved: you know that somebody's thinking about you the whole time. (*Exits. Enter right, Mrs. Molloy, Minnie, Barnaby and Cornelius.*)

Mrs. Molloy. See! Here's the place I meant! Isn't it fine? Minnie, take off your things; we'll be here for hours.

Cornelius (*stopping at door*). Mrs. Molloy, are you sure you'll like it here? I think I feel a draught.

Mrs. Molloy. Indeed, I do like it. We're going to have a fine dinner right in this room; it's private, and it's elegant. Now we're all going to forget our troubles and call each other by our first names. Cornelius! Call the waiter.

Cornelius. Wait — wait — I can't make a sound. I must have caught a cold on that ride. Wai — No! It won't come.

Mrs. Molloy. I don't believe you. Barnaby, you call him.

Barnaby (*boldly*). Waiter! Waiter! (*Cornelius threatens him. Barnaby runs left.*)

Minnie. I never thought I'd be in such a place in my whole life. Mrs. Molloy, is this what they call a "cafe"?

Mrs. Molloy (*sits at table left, facing audience*). Yes, this a café. Sit down, Minnie. Cornelius, Mrs. Levi gave us to understand that every waiter in New York knew you.

Cornelius. They will. (*Barnaby sits at chair left; Minnie in chair back to audience. Enter Rudolph from service door.*)

Rudolph. Good evening, ladies and gentlemen.

Cornelius (*shaking his hand*). How are you, Fritz? How are you, my friend?

Rudolph. I am Rudolph.

Cornelius. Of course. Rudolph, of course. Well, Rudolph, these ladies want a little something to eat — you know what I mean? Just if you can find the time — we know how busy you are.

Mrs. Molloy. Cornelius, there's no need to be so familiar with the waiter. (*Takes menu from Rudolph.*)

Cornelius. Oh, yes, there is.

Mrs. Molloy (*passing menu across*). Minnie, what do you want to eat?

Minnie. Just anything, Irene.

Mrs. Molloy. No, speak up, Minnie. What do you want?

Minnie. No, really, I have no appetite at all. (*Swings round in her chair and studies the menu, horrified at the prices.*) Oh . . . Oh . . . I'd like some sardines on toast and a glass of milk.

Cornelius (*takes menu from her*). Great grindstones! What a sensible girl. Barnaby, shake Minnie's hand. She's the most sensible girl in the world. Rudolph, bring us gentlemen two glasses of beer, a loaf of bread and some cheese.

Mrs. Molloy (*takes menu*). I never heard such nonsense. Cornelius, we've come here for a good dinner and a good time. Minnie, have you ever eaten pheasant?

Minnie. Pheasant? No-o-o-o!

Mrs. Molloy. Rudolph, have you any pheasant?

Rudolph. Yes, ma'am. Just in from New Jersey today.

Mrs. Molloy. Even the pheasants are leaving New Jersey. (*She laughs loudly, pushing Cornelius, then Rudolph; not from menu.*) Now, Rudolph, write this down: mock turtle soup; pheasant; mashed chestnuts; green salad; and some nice red wine. (*Rudolph repeats each item after her.*)

Cornelius (*losing all his fears, boldly*). All right, Barnaby, you watch me. (*He reads from the bill of fare.*) Rudolph, write this down: Neapolitan ice cream; hothouse peaches; champagne . . .

All. Champagne! (*Barnaby spins round in his chair.*)

Cornelius (*holds up a finger*). . . . and a German band. Have you got a German band?

Mrs. Molloy. No, Cornelius, I won't let you be extravagant. Champagne, but no band. Now, Rudolph, be quick about this. We're hungry. (*Exit Rudolph to kitchen. Mrs. Molloy crosses to right.*) Minnie, come upstairs. I have an idea about your hair. I think it'd be nice in two wee horns —

Minnie (*hurrying after her, turns and looks at the boys*). Oh! Horns! (*They go out right. There is a long pause. Cornelius sits staring after them.*)

Barnaby. Cornelius, in the Army, you have to peel potatoes all the time.

Cornelius (*not turning*). Oh, that doesn't matter. By the time we get out of jail we can move right over to the Old Men's Home. (*Another waiter, August, enters from service door bearing a bottle of champagne in cooler, and five glasses. Mrs. Molloy re-enters right, followed by Minnie, and stops August.*)

Mrs. Molloy. Waiter! What's that? What's that you have?

August (*young waiter; baby face; is continually bursting into tears.*) It's some champagne, ma'am.

Mrs. Molloy. Cornelius; it's our champagne. (*All gather round August.*)

August. No, no. It's for His Honor the Mayor of New York and he's very impatient.

Mrs. Molloy. Shame on him! The Mayor of New York has more important things to be impatient about. Cornelius, open it. (*Cornelius takes the bottle, opens it and fills the glasses.*)

August. Ma'am, he'll kill me.

Mrs. Molloy. Well, have a glass first and die happy.

August (*sits at table right, weeping*). He'll kill me. (*Rudolph lays the cloth on the table, left.*)

Mrs. Molloy. I go to a public restaurant for the first time in ten years and all the waiters burst into tears. There, take that and stop crying, love. (*She takes a glass to August and pats his head, then comes back.*) Barnaby, make a toast!

Barnaby (*center of the group, with naïve sincerity*). I? . . . uh . . . To all the ladies in the world . . . may I get to know more of them . . . and . . . may I get to know them better. (*There is a hushed pause.*)

Cornelius (*softly*). To the ladies!

Mrs. Molloy. That's *very* sweet and *very* refined. Minnie, for that I'm going to give Barnaby a kiss.

Minnie. Oh!

Mrs. Molloy. Hold you tongue, Minnie. I'm old enough to be his mother, and — (*Indicating a height three feet from the floor.*) a dear wee mother I would have been too. Barnaby, this is for you from all the ladies in the world. (*She kisses him. Barnaby is at first silent and dazed, then:*)

Barnaby. Now I can go back to Yonkers, Cornelius. Pudding. Pudding! Pudding! (*He spins round and falls on his knees.*)

Mrs. Molloy. Look at Barnaby. He's not strong enough for a kiss. His head can't stand it. (*Exit August, right service door, with tray and cooler. The sound of "Les Patineurs" waltz comes from off left. Cornelius sits in chair facing audience, top of table. Minnie at left. Barnaby at right and Mrs. Molloy back to audience.*) Minnie, I'm enjoying myself. To think that this goes on in hundreds of places every night, while I sit at home darning my stockings. (*Mrs. Molloy rises and dances, alone, slowly about the stage.*) Cornelius, dance with me.

Cornelius (*rises*). Irene, the Hackls don't dance. We're Presbyterian.

Mrs. Molloy. Minnie, you dance with me. (*Minnie joins her. Cornelius sits again.*)

Minnie. Lovely music.

Mrs. Molloy. Why, Minnie, you dance beautifully.

Minnie. We girls dance in the workroom when you're not looking, Irene.

Mrs. Molloy. You thought I'd be angry! Oh dear, no one in the world understands anyone else in the world. (*The girls separate. Minnie dances off to her place at the table. Mrs. Molloy sits thoughtfully at table right. The music fades away.*) Cornelius! Jenny Lind and all those other ladies — do you see them all the time?

Cornelius (*rises and joins her at table right*). Irene, I've put them right out of my head. I'm interested in . . . (*Rudolph has entered by the service door. He now flings a tablecloth between them on table.*)

Mrs. Molloy. Rudolph, what are you doing?

Rudolph. A table's been reserved here. Special orders.

Mrs. Molloy. Stop right where you are. That party can eat inside. This veranda's ours.

Rudolph. I'm very sorry. This veranda is open to anybody who wants it. Ah, there comes the man who brought the order. (*Enter Malachi from the kitchen, drunk.*)

Mrs. Molloy (*to Malachi*). Take your table away from here. We got here first, Cornelius, throw him out.

Malachi. Ma'am, my employer reserved this room at four o'clock this afternoon. You can go and eat in the restaurant. My employer said it was very important that he have a table alone.

Mrs. Molloy. No, sir. We got here first and we're going to stay here — alone, too. (*Minnie and Barnaby come forward.*)

Rudolph. Ladies and gentlemen!

Mrs. Molloy. Shut up, you! (*To Malachi.*) You're an impertinent, idotic kill-joy.

Malachi (*very pleased*). That's an insult!

Mrs. Molloy. All the facts about you are insults. (*To Cornelius.*) Cornelius, do something. Knock it over! The table.

Cornelius. Knock it over. (*After a shocked struggle with himself Cornelius calmly overturns the table. August rights the table and picks up cutlery, weeping copiously.*)

Rudolph (*in cold fury*). I'm sorry, but this room can't be reserved for anyone. If you want to eat alone, you must go upstairs. I'm sorry, but that's the rule.

Mrs. Molloy. We're having a nice dinner alone and we're going to stay here. Cornelius, knock it over. (*Cornelius overturns the table again. The girls squeal with pleasure. The waiter August again scrambles for the silver.*)

Malachi. Wait till you see my employer!

Rudolph (*bringing screen down*). Ladies and gentlemen! I'll tell you what we'll do. There's a big screen here. We'll put the screen up between the tables. August, come and help me.

Mrs. Molloy. I won't eat behind a screen. I won't. Minnie, make a noise. We're not animals in a menagerie. Cornelius, no screen. Minnie, there's a fight. I feel ten years younger. No screen! No screen! (*During the struggle with the screen all talk at once.*)

Malachi (*loud and clear and pointing to entrance at right*). Now you'll learn something. There comes my employer now, getting out of that cab.

Cornelius (*coming to him, taking off his coat*). Where? I'll knock him down too. (*Barnaby has gone up to right entrance. He turns and shouts clearly:*)

Barnaby. Cornelius, it's Wolf-trap. Yes, it is!

Cornelius. Wolf-trap! Listen, everybody. I think the screen's a good idea. Have you got any more screens, Rudolph? We could use three or four. (*He pulls the screen forward again.*)

Mrs. Molloy. Quiet down, Cornelius, and stop changing your mind. Hurry up, Rudolph, we're ready for the soup. (*During the following scene Rudolph serves the meal at the table left, as unobtrusively as possible. The stage is now divided in half. The quartet's table is at the left. Enter Vandergelder from the right. Now wears overcoat and carries the box of chocolates.*)

Vandergelder. Stack! What's the meaning of this? I told you I wanted a table alone. What's that? (*Vandergelder hits the screen twice with his stick. Mrs. Molloy hits back twice with a spoon. The four young people sit: Barnaby facing audience; Mrs. Molloy right, Minnie left, and Cornelius back to audience.*)

Malachi. Mr. Vandergelder, I did what I could. Mr. Vandergelder, you wouldn't believe what wild savages the people of New York are. There's a woman over there, Mr. Vandergelder — civilization hasn't touched her.

Vandergelder. Everything's wrong. You can't even manage a thing like that. Help me off with my coat. Don't kill me, Don't kill me. (*During the struggle with the overcoat Mr. Vandergelder's purse flies out of his pocket and falls by the screen. Vandergelder goes to the coat tree and hangs his coat up.*)

Mrs. Molloy. Speak up! I can't hear you.

Cornelius. My voice again. Barnaby, how's your throat? Can you speak?

Barnaby. Can't make a sound.

Mrs. Molloy. Oh, all right. Bring your heads together, and we'll whisper.

Vandergelder. Who are those people over there?

Malachi. Some city sparks and their girls, Mr. Vandergelder. What goes on in big cities, Mr. Vandergelder — best not think of it.

Vandergelder. Has that couple come down from upstairs yet? I hope they haven't gone off without your seeing them.

Malachi. No, sir. Myself and the cabman have kept our eyes on everything.

Vandergelder (*sits at right of table, profile to the audience*). I'll sit here and wait for my guests. You go out to the cab.

Malachi. Yes, sir. (*Vandergelder unfurls newspaper and starts to read. Malachi sees the purse on the floor and picks it up.*) Eh, What's that? A purse. Did you drop something, Mr. Vandergelder?

Vandergelder. No. Don't bother me any more. Do as I tell you.

Malachi (*stooping over. Coming center*). A purse. That fellow over there must have let it fall during the misunderstanding about the screen. No, I won't look inside. Twenty-dollar bills, dozens of them. I'll go over and give it to him. (*Starts toward Cornelius, then turns and says to audience:*) You're surprised? You're surprised to see me getting rid of this money so quickly, eh? I'll explain it to you. There was a time in my life when my chief interest was picking up money that didn't belong to me. The law is there to protect property, but — sure, the law doesn't care whether a property owner deserves his property or not, and the law has to be corrected. There are several thousands of people in this country engaged in correcting the law. For a while, I too was engaged in the redistribution of superfluities. A man works all his life and leaves a million to his widow. She sits in hotels and eats great meals and plays cards all afternoon and evening, with ten diamonds on her fingers. Call in the robbers! Call in the robbers! Or a man leaves it to his son who stands leaning against bars all night boring a bartender. Call in the robbers! Stealing's a weakness. There are some people who say you shouldn't have any weaknesses at all — no vices. But if a man has no vices, he's in great danger of making vices out of his virtues, and there's a spectacle. We've all seen them: men who were monsters of philanthropy and women who were dragons of purity. We've seen people who told the truth, though the Heavens fall, — and the Heavens fell. No, no — nurse one vice in your bosom. Give it the attention it deserves and let your virtues spring up modestly around it. Then you'll have the miser who's no liar; and the drunkard who's the benefactor of a whole city. Well, after I'd had that weakness of stealing for a while, I found another: I took to whisky — whisky took to me. And then I discovered an important rule that I'm going to pass on to you: Never support two weaknesses at the same time. It's your combination sinners — your lecherous liars and your miserly drunkards — who dishonor the vices and bring them into bad repute. So now you see why I want to get rid of this money: I want to keep my mind free to do the credit to whisky that it deserves. And my last word to you, ladies and gentlemen, is this: one vice at a time. (*Goes over to Cornelius.*) Can I speak to you for a minute?

Cornelius (*rises*). You certainly can. We all want to apologize to you about that screen — that little misunderstanding. (*They all rise, with exclamations of apology.*) What's your name, sir?

Malachi. Stack, sir. Malachi Stack. If the ladies will excuse you, I'd like to speak to you for a minute. (*Draws Cornelius down to front of stage.*) Listen, boy, have you lost . . . ? Come here . . . (*Leads him further down, out of Vandergelder's hearing.*) Have you lost something?

Cornelius. Mr. Stack, in this one day I've lost everything I own.

Malachi. There it is. (*Gives him purse.*) Don't mention it.

Cornelius. Why, Mr. Stack . . . you know what it is? It's a miracle. (*Looks toward the ceiling.*)

Malachi. Don't mention it.

Cornelius. Barnaby, come here a minute. I want you to shake hands with Mr. Stack. (*Barnaby, napkin tucked into his collar, joins them.*) Mr. Stack's just found the purse I lost, Barnaby. You know — the purse full of money.

Barnaby (*shaking his hand vigorously*). You're a wonderful man, Mr. Stack.

Malachi. Oh, it's nothing — nothing.

Cornelius. I'm certainly glad I went to church all these years. You're a good person to know, Mr. Stack. In a way. Mr. Stack, where do you work?

Malachi. Well, I've just begun. I work for a Mr. Vandergelder in Yonkers. (*Cornelius is thunderstruck. He glances at Barnaby and turns to Malachi with awe. All three are swaying slightly, back and forth.*)

Cornelius. You do? It's a miracle. (*He points to the ceiling.*) Mr. Stack, I know you don't need it — but can I give you something for . . . for the good work?

Malachi (*putting out his hand*). Don't mention it. It's nothing. (*Starts to go left.*)

Cornelius. Take that. (*Hands him a note.*)

Malachi (*taking note*). Don't mention it.

Cornelius. And that. (*Another note.*)

Malachi (*takes it and moves away*). I'd better be going.

Cornelius. Oh, here. And that.

Malachi (*hands third note back*). No . . . I might get to like them. (*Exit left. Cornelius bounds exultantly back to table.*)

Cornelius. Irene, I feel a lot better about everything. Irene, I feel so well that I'm going to tell the truth.

Mrs. Molloy. I'd forgotten that, Minnie. Men get drunk so differently from women. All right, what is the truth?

Cornelius. If I tell the truth, will you let me . . . will you let me put my arm around your waist? (*Minnie screams and flings her napkin over her face.*)

Mrs. Molloy. Hold your tongue, Minnie. All right, you can put your arm around my waist just to show it can be done in a gentlemanly way; but I might as well warn you: a corset is a corset.

Cornelius (*his arm around her; softly*). You're a wonderful person, Mrs. Molloy.

Mrs. Molloy. Thank you. (*She removes his hand from around her waist.*) All right, now that's enough. What is the truth?

Cornelius. Irene, I'm not as rich as Mrs. Levi said I was.

Mrs. Molloy. Not rich!

Cornelius. I almost never came to New York. And I'm not like she said I was, — bad. And I think you ought to know that at this very minute Mr. Vandergelder's sitting on the other side of that screen.

Mrs. Molloy. What! Well, he's not going to spoil any party of mine. So *that's* why we have been whispering? Let's forget all about Mr. Vandergelder and have some more wine. (*They start to sing softly: "The Sidewalks of New York." Enter Mrs. Levi, from the street, in an elaborate dress, Vandergelder rises.*)

Mrs. Levi. Good evening, Mr. Vandergelder.

Vandergelder. Where's — where's Miss Simple?

Mrs. Levi. Mr. Vandergelder, I'll never trust a woman again as long as I live.

Vandergelder. Well? What is it?

Mrs. Levi. She ran away this afternoon and got married!

Vandergelder. She did?

Mrs. Levi. Married, Mr. Vandergelder, to a young boy of fifty.

Vandergelder. She did?

Mrs. Levi. Oh, I'm as disappointed as you are. I-can't-eat-a-thing-what-have-you-ordered?

Vandergelder. I ordered what you told me to, a chicken. (*Enter August. He goes to Vandergelder's table.*)

Mrs. Levi. I don't think I could face a chicken. Oh, waiter. How do you do? What's your name?

August. August, ma'am.

Mrs. Levi. August, this is Mr. Vandergelder of Yonkers — Yonkers' most influential citizen, in fact. I want you to see that he's served with the best you have and served promptly. And there'll only be the two of us. (*Mrs. Levi gives one set of cutlery to August. Vandergelder puts chocolate box under table.*) Mr. Vandergelder's been through some trying experiences today — what with men hidden all over Mrs. Molloy's store — like Indians in ambush.

Vandergelder (between his teeth). Mrs. Levi, you don't have to tell him everything about me. (*The quartet commences singing again very softly.*)

Mrs. Levi. Mr. Vandergelder, if you're thinking about getting married, you might as well learn right now you have to let women be women. Now, August, we want excellent service.

August. Yes, ma'am. (*Exits to kitchen.*)

Vandergelder. You've managed things very badly. When I plan a thing it takes place. (*Mrs. Levi rises.*) Where are you going?

Mrs. Levi. Oh, I'd just like to see who's on the other side of that screen. (*Mrs. Levi crosses to the other side of the stage and sees the quartet. They are frightened and fall silent.*)

Cornelius (rising). Good evening, Mrs. Levi. (*Mrs. Levi takes no notice, but, taking up the refrain where they left off, returns to her place at the table right.*)

Vandergelder. Well, who was it?

Mrs. Levi. Oh, just some city sparks entertaining their girls, I guess.

Vandergelder. Always wanting to know everything; always curious about everything; always putting your nose into other people's affairs. Anybody who lived with you would get as nervous as a cat.

Mrs. Levi. What? What's that you're saying.

Vandergelder. I said anybody who lived with you would —

Mrs. Levi. Horace Vandergelder, get that idea right out of your head this minute. I'm surprised that you even mentioned such a thing. Understand once and for all that I have no intention of marrying you.

Vandergelder. I didn't mean that.

Mrs. Levi. You've been hinting around at such a thing for some time, but from now on put such ideas right out of your head.

Vandergelder. Stop talking that way. That's not what I meant at all.

Mrs. Levi. I hope not. I should hope not. Horace Vandergelder, you go your way. (*Points a finger.*) and I'll go mine. (*Points in same direction.*) I'm not some Irene Molloy, whose head can be turned by a pot of geraniums. Why, the idea of you even suggesting such a thing.

Vandergelder. Mrs. Levi, you misunderstood me.

Mrs. Levi. I certainly hope I did. If I had any intention of marrying again it would be to a far more pleasure-loving man than you. Why I'd marry Cornelius Hackl before I'd marry you. (*Cornelius raises his head in alarm. The others stop eating and listen.*) However, we won't discuss it any more. (*Enter August with a tray.*) Here's August with our food. I'll serve it, August.

August. Yes, ma'am. (*Exit August.*)

Mrs. Levi. Here's some white meat for you, and some giblets, very tender and very good for you. No, as I said before, you go your way and I'll go mine. — Start right in on the wine. I think you'll feel better at once. However, since you brought the matter up, there's one more thing I think I ought to say."

Vandergelder (*rising in rage*). I didn't bring the matter up at all.

Mrs. Levi. We'll have forgotten all about it in a moment, but — sit down, sit down, we'll close the matter forever in just a moment, but there's one more thing I ought to say. (*Vandergelder sits down.*) It's true, I'm a woman who likes to know everything that's going on; who likes to manage things, you're perfectly right about that. But I wouldn't like to manage anything as disorderly as your household, as out of control, as untidy. You'll have to do that yourself, God helping you.

Vandergelder. It's not out of control.

Mrs. Levi. Very well, let's not say another word about it. Take some more of that squash, it's good. No, Horace, a complaining, quarrelsome, friendless soul like you is no sort of companion for me. You go your way (*Peppers her own plate.*) and I'll go mine. (*Peppers his plate.*)

Vandergelder. Stop saying that.

Mrs. Levi. I won't say another word.

Vandergelder. Besides . . . I'm not those things you said I am.

Mrs. Levi. What? — Well, I guess you're friendless, aren't you? Ermengarde told me this morning you'd even quarreled with your barber — a man who's held a razor to your throat for twenty years! Seems to me that's sinking pretty low.

Vandergelder. Well, . . . but . . . my clerks, they . . .

Mrs. Levi. They like you? Cornelius Hackl and that Barnaby? Behind your back they call you Wolf-trap. (*Quietly the quartet at the other table have moved up to the screens — bringing chairs for Mrs. Mol-*

loy and Minnie. Wine glasses in hand, they overhear this conversation.)

Vandergelder (*blanching*). They don't.

Mrs. Levi. No, Horace. It looks to me as though I were the last person in the world that liked you, and even I'm just so-so. No, for the rest of my life I intend to have a good time. You'll be able to find some housekeeper who can prepare you three meals for a dollar a day — it can be done, you know, if you like cold baked beans. You'll spend your last days listening at keyholes, for fear someone's cheating you. Take some more of that.

Vandergelder. Dolly, you're a damned exasperating woman.

Mrs. Levi. There! You see? That's the difference between us. I'd be nagging you all day to get some spirit into you. You could be a perfectly charming, witty, amiable man, if you wanted to.

Vandergelder (*rising, bellowing*). I don't want to be charming.

Mrs. Levi. But you are. Look at you now. You can't hide it.

Vandergelder (*sits*). Listen at keyholes! Dolly, you have no right to say such things to me.

Mrs. Levi. At your age you ought to enjoy hearing the honest truth.

Vandergelder. My age! My age! You're always talking about my age.

Mrs. Levi. I don't know what your age is, but I do know that up at Yonkers with bad food and bad temper you'll double it in six months. Let's talk of something else; but before we leave the subject there's one more thing I *am* going to say.

Vandergelder. Don't!

Mrs. Levi. Sometimes, just sometimes, I think I'd be tempted to marry you out of sheer pity; and if the confusion in your house gets any worse I may *have* to.

Vandergelder. I haven't asked you to marry me.

Mrs. Levi. Well, *please don't.*

Vandergelder. And my house is not in confusion.

Mrs. Levi. What? With your niece upstairs in the restaurant right now?

Vandergelder. I've fixed that better than you know.

Mrs. Levi. And your clerks skipping around New York behind your back?

Vandergelder. They're in Yonkers where they always are.

Mrs. Levi. Nonsense!

Vandergelder. What do you mean, nonsense?

Mrs. Levi. Cornelius Hackl's the other side of that screen this very minute.

Vandergelder. It ain't the same man!

Mrs. Levi. All right. Go on. Push it, knock it down. Go and see.

Vandergelder (*goes to screen, pauses in doubt, then returns to his chair again*). I don't believe it.

Mrs. Levi. All right. All right. Eat your chicken. Of course, Horace, if your affairs went from bad to worse and you became actually miserable, I might feel that it was my duty to come up to Yonkers and be of some assistance to you. After all, I was your wife's oldest friend.

Vandergelder. I don't know how you ever got any such notion. Now understand, once and for all, I have *no intention of marrying anybody.* Now, I'm tired and I don't want to talk. (*Cornelius crosses to extreme left, Mrs. Molloy following him.*)

Mrs. Levi. I won't say another word, either.

Cornelius. Irene, I think we'd better go. You take this money and pay the bill. Oh, don't worry, it's not mine.

Mrs. Molloy. No, no, I'll tell you what we'll do. You boys put on our coats and veils, and if he comes stamping over here, he'll think you're girls.

Cornelius. What! Those things!

Mrs. Molloy. Yes. Come on. (*She and Minnie take the clothes from the stand.*)

Vandergelder (*rises*). I've got a headache. I've had a bad day. I'm going to Flora Van Huysen's, and then I'm going back to my hotel. (*Reaches for his purse.*) So, here's the money to pay for the dinner. (*Searching another pocket.*) Here's the money to pay for the . . . (*Going through all his pockets.*) Here's the money . . . I've lost my purse!!

Mrs. Levi. Impossible! I can't imagine you without your purse.

Vandergelder. It's been stolen. (*Searching overcoat.*) Or I left it in the cab. What am I going to do? I'm new at the hotel; they don't know me. I've never been here before . . . Stop eating the chicken, I can't pay for it!

Mrs. Levi (*laughing gaily*). Horace, I'll be able to find some money. Sit down and calm yourself.

Vandergelder. Dolly Gallagher, I gave you twenty-five dollars this morning.

Mrs. Levi. I haven't a cent. I gave it to my lawyer. We can borrow it from Ambrose Kemper, upstairs.

Vandergelder. I wouldn't take it.

Mrs. Levi. Cornelius Hackl will lend it to us.

Vandergelder. He's in Yonkers. — Waiter! (*Cornelius comes forward dressed in Mrs. Molloy's coat, thrown over his shoulder like a cape.*

Mrs. Levi is enjoying herself immensely. Vandergelder again goes to back wall to examine the pockets of his overcoat.)

Mrs. Molloy. Cornelius, is that Mr. Vandergelder's purse?

Cornelius. I didn't know it myself. I thought it was money just wandering around loose that didn't belong to anybody.

Mrs. Molloy. Goodness! That's what politicians think!

Vandergelder. Waiter! (*A band off left starts playing a polka. Barnaby comes forward dressed in Minnie's hat, coat and veil.*)

Minnie. Irene, doesn't Barnaby make a lovely girl? He just ought to stay that way. (*Mrs. Levi and Vandergelder move their table upstage while searching for the purse.*)

Mrs. Molloy. Why should we have our evening spoiled? Cornelius, I can teach you to dance in a few minutes. Oh, he won't recognize you.

Minnie. Barnaby, it's the easiest thing in the world. (*They move their table up against the back wall.*)

Mrs. Levi. Horace, you danced with me at your wedding and you danced with me at mine. Do you remember?

Vandergelder. No. Yes.

Mrs. Levi. Horace, you were a good dancer then. Don't confess to me that you're too old to dance.

Vandergelder. I'm not too old. I just don't want to dance.

Mrs. Levi. Listen to that music. Horace, do you remember the dances in the firehouse at Yonkers on Saturday nights? You gave me a fan. Come, come on! (*Vandergelder and Mrs. Levi start to dance. Cornelius, dancing with Mrs. Molloy, bumps into Vandergelder, back to back. Vandergelder, turning, fails at first to recognize him, then does and roars:*)

Vandergelder. You're discharged! Not a word! You're fired! Where's that idiot, Barnaby Tucker? He's fired too. (*The four young people, laughing, start rushing out the door to the street. Vandergelder, pointing at Mrs. Molloy, shouts:*) You're discharged!

Mrs. Molloy (*pointing at him*). You're discharged! (*Exit.*)

Vandergelder. You're discharged! (*Enter from left, Ambrose and Ermengarde. To Ermengarde.*) I'll lock you up for the rest of your life, young lady.

Ermengarde. Uncle! (*She faints in Ambrose's arms.*)

Vandergelder (*to Ambrose*). I'll have you arrested. Get out of my sight. I never want to see you again.

Ambrose (*carrying Ermengarde across to exit right*). You can't do anything to me, Mr. Vandergelder. (*Exit Ambrose and Ermengarde.*)

Mrs. Levi (*who has been laughing heartily, follows the distraught Vandergelder about the stage as he continues to hunt for his purse*). Well, there's your life, Mr. Vandergelder! Without niece — without clerks — without bride — and without your purse. *Will you marry me now?*

Vandergelder. No! (*To get away from her, he dashes into the kitchen. Mrs. Levi, still laughing exclaims to the audience.*)

Mrs. Levi. Damn!! (*And rushes off right.*

THE CURTAIN FALLS)

ACT IV

Miss Flora Van Huysen's house.

This is a prosperous spinster's living room and is filled with knick-knacks, all in bright colors, and hung with family portraits, bird cages, shawls, etc.

There is only one entrance — a large double door in the center of the back wall. Beyond it one sees the hall which leads left to the street door and right to the kitchen and the rest of the house. On the left are big windows hung with lace curtains on heavy draperies. Front left is Miss Van Huysen's sofa, covered with bright-colored cushions, and behind it a table. On the right is another smaller sofa. Miss Van Huysen is lying on the sofa. The cook is at the window, left, Miss Van Huysen, fifty, florid, stout and sentimental, is sniffing at smelling salts. Cook (enormous) holds a china mixing bowl.

Cook. No, ma'am. I could swear I heard a cab drawing up to the door.

Miss Van H. You imagined it. Imagination. Everything in life . . . like that . . . disappointment . . . illusion. Our plans . . . our hopes . . . what becomes of them? Nothing. The story of my life. (*She sings for a moment.*)

Cook. Pray God nothing's happened to the dear girl. Is it a long journey from Yonkers?

Miss Van H. No; but long enough for a thousand things to happen.

Cook. Well, we've been waiting all day. Don't you think we ought to call the police about it?

Miss Van H. The police! If it's God's will, the police can't prevent it. Oh, in three days, in a week, in a year, we'll know what's happened. . . . And if anything *has* happened to Ermengarde, it'll be a lesson to *him* — that's what it'll be.

Cook. To who?

Miss Van H. To that cruel uncle of hers, of course, — to Horace Vandergelder, and to everyone else who tries to separate young lovers. Young lovers have enough to contend with as it is. Who should know that better than I? No one. The story of my life. (*Sings for a moment, then.*) There! Now I hear a cab. Quick!

Cook. No. No, ma'am. I don't see anything.

Miss Van H. There! What did I tell you? Everything's imagination — illusion.

Cook. But surely, if they'd changed their plans Mr. Vandergelder would have sent you a message.

Miss Van H. Oh, I know what's the matter. That poor child probably thought she was coming to another prison — to another tyrant. If she'd known that I was her friend, and a friend of all young lovers, she'd be here by now. Oh, yes, she would. Her life shall not be crossed with obstacles and disappointments as . . . Cook, a minute ago my smelling salts were on this table. Now they've completely disappeared.

Cook. Why, there they are, ma'am, right there in your hand.

Miss Van H. Goodness! How did they get there? I won't inquire. Stranger things have happened!

Cook. I suppose Mr. Vandergelder was sending her down with someone?

Miss Van H. Two can go astray as easily as . . . (*She sneezes.*)

Cook. God bless you! (*Runs to window.*) Now, here's a carriage stopping. (*The doorbell rings.*)

Miss Van H. Well, open the door, Cook. (*Cook exits.*) It's probably some mistake. (*Sneezes again.*) God bless you! (*Sounds of altercation off in hall.*) It almost sounds as though I heard voices.

Cornelius (*off*). I don't want to come in. This is a free country, I tell you.

Cabman (*off*). Forward march!

Malachi (*off*). In you go. We have orders.

Cornelius (*off*). You can't make a person go where he doesn't want to go. (*Enter Malachi, followed by Cook. The Cabman bundles Barnaby and Cornelius into the room, but they fight their way back into the hall. Cornelius has lost Mrs. Molloy's coat, but Barnaby is wearing Minnie's clothes.*)

Malachi. Begging your pardon, ma'am, are you Miss Van Huysen?

Miss Van H. Yes, I am, unfortunately. What's all this noise about?

Malachi. There are two people here that Mr. Vandergelder said must be brought to this house and kept here until he comes. And here's his letter to you.

Miss Van H. No one has any right to tell me whom I'm to keep in my house if they don't want to stay.

Malachi. You're right, ma'am. Everybody's always talking about people breaking into houses, ma'am; but there are more people in the world who want to break out of houses, that's what I always say. — Bring them in, Joe. (*Enter Cornelius and Barnaby being pushed by the Cabman.*)

Cornelius. This young lady and I have no business here. We jumped into a cab and asked to be driven to the station and these men brought us to the house and forced us to come inside. There's been a mistake.

Cabman. Is your name Miss Van Huysen?

Miss Van H. Everybody's asking me if my name's Miss Van Huysen. I think that's a matter I can decide for myself. Now will you all be quiet while I read this letter? . . . "This is Ermengarde and that rascal Ambrose Kemper . . ." Now I know who you two are, anyway. "They are trying to run away . . ." Story of my life. "Keep them in your house until I come." Mr. Kemper, you have nothing to fear. (*To Cabman.*) Who are you?

Cabman. I'm Joe. I stay here until the old man comes. He owes me fifteen dollars.

Malachi. That's right, Miss Van Huysen, we must stay here to see they don't escape.

Miss Van H. (*to Barnaby*). My dear child, take off your things. We'll all have some coffee. (*To Malachi and Cabman.*) You two go out and wait in the hall. I'll send coffee out to you. Cook, take them. (*Cook pushes Malachi and Cabman into the hall.*)

Cornelius. Ma'am, we're not the people you're expecting, and there's no reason . . .

Miss Van H. Mr. Kemper, I'm not the tyrant you think I am. . . . You don't have to be afraid of me. . . . I know you're trying to run away with this innocent girl. . . . All my life I have suffered from the interference of others. You shall not suffer as I did. So put yourself entirely in my hands. (*She lifts Barnaby's veil.*) Ermengarde! (*Kisses him on both cheeks.*) Where's your luggage?

Barnaby. It's — uh — uh — it's . . .

Cornelius. Oh, I'll find it in the morning. It's been mislaid.

Miss Van H. Mislaid! How like life! Well, Ermengarde; you shall put on some of my clothes.

Barnaby. Oh, I know I wouldn't be happy, really.

Miss Van H. She's a shy little thing, isn't she? Timid little darling! . . . Cook! Put some gingerbread in the oven and get the coffee ready . . .

Cook. Yes, ma'am. (*Exits to kitchen.*)

Miss Van H. . . . while I go and draw a good hot bath for Ermengarde.

Cornelius. Oh, oh — Miss Van Huysen . . .

Miss Van H. Believe me, Ermengarde, your troubles are at an end. You two will be married tomorrow. (*To Barnaby.*) My dear, you look just like I did at your age, and your sufferings have been as mine. While you're bathing, I'll come and tell you the story of my life.

Barnaby. Oh, I don't want to take a bath. I always catch cold.

Miss Van H. No, dear, you won't catch cold. I'll slap you all over. I'll be back in a minute. (*Exit.*)

Cornelius (*looking out of window*). Barnaby, do you think we could jump down from this window?

Barnaby. Yes — we'd kill ourselves.

Cornelius. We'll just have to stay here and watch for something to happen. Barnaby, the situation's desperate.

Barnaby. It began getting desperate about half-past four and it's been getting worse ever since. Now I have to take a bath and get slapped all over. (*Enter Miss Van Huysen from kitchen.*)

Miss Van H. Ermengarde, you've still got those wet things on. Your bath's nearly ready. Mr. Kemper, you come into the kitchen and put you feet in the oven. (*The doorbell rings. Enter Cook.*) What's that? It's the doorbell. I expect it's your uncle.

Cook. There's the doorbell. (*At window.*) It's *another* man and a girl in a cab!

Miss Van H. Well, go and let them in, Cook. Now, come with me, you two. Come, Ermengarde. (*Exit Cook. Miss Van Huysen drags Cornelius and the protesting Barnaby off into the kitchen.*)

Cook (*off*). No, that's impossible. Come in, anyway. (*Enter Ermengarde, followed by Ambrose, carrying the two pieces of luggage.*) There's some mistake. I'll tell Miss Van Huysen, but there's some mistake.

Ermengarde. But, I tell you, I *am* Mr. Vandergelder's niece; I'm Ermengarde.

Cook. Beg your pardon, Miss, but you *can't* be Miss Ermengarde.

Ermengarde. But — but — here I *am*. And that's my baggage.

Cook. Well, I'll tell Miss Van Huysen who you *think* you are, but she won't like it. (*Exits.*)

Ambrose. You'll be all right now, Ermengarde. I'd better go before she sees me.

Ermengarde. Oh, no. You must stay. I feel so strange here.

Ambrose. I know, but Mr. Vandergelder will be here in a minute. . . .

Ermengarde. Ambrose, you can't go. You can't leave me in this crazy house with those drunken men in the hall. Ambrose . . . Ambrose, let's say you're someone else that my uncle sent down to take care of me. Let's say you're — you're Cornelius Hackl!

Ambrose. Who's Cornelius Hackl?

Ermengarde. You know. He's chief clerk in Uncle's store.

Ambrose. I don't want to be Cornelius Hackl. No, no, Ermengarde, come away with me now, I'll take you to my friend's house. Or I'll take you to Mrs. Levi's house.

Ermengarde. Why, it was Mrs. Levi who threw us right at Uncle Horace's face. Oh, I wish I were back in Yonkers where nothing ever happens. (*Enter Miss Van Huysen.*)

Miss Van H. What's all this I hear? Who do you say you are?

Ermengarde. Aunt Flora . . . don't you remember me? I'm Ermengarde.

Miss Van H. And you're Mr. Vandergelder's niece?

Ermengarde. Yes, I am.

Miss Van H. Well, that's very strange indeed, because he has just sent me another niece named Ermengarde. She came with a letter from him, explaining everything. Have you got a letter from him?

Ermengarde. No . . .

Miss Van H. Really! — And who is this?

Ermengarde. This is Cornelius Hackl, Aunt Flora.

Miss Van H. Never heard of him.

Ermengarde. He's chief clerk in Uncle's store.

Miss Van H. Never heard of him. The other Ermengarde came with the man she's in love with, and that *proves* it. She came with Mr. Ambrose Kemper.

Ambrose (*shouts*). Ambrose Kemper!

Miss Van H. Yes, Mr. Hackl, and Mr. Ambrose Kemper is in the kitchen there now with his feet in the oven. (*Ermengarde starts to cry. Miss Van Huysen takes her to the sofa. They both sit.*) Dear child, what is your trouble?

Ermengarde. Oh, dear. I don't know what to do.

Miss Van H. (*in a low voice*). Are you in love with this man?

Ermengarde. Yes, I am.

Miss Van H. I could see it — and are people trying to separate you?

Ermengarde. Yes, they are.

Miss Van H. I could see it — who? Horace Vandergelder?

Ermengarde. Yes.

Miss Van H. That's enough for me. I'll put a stop to Horace Vandergelder's goings on. (*Miss Van Huysen draws Ambrose down to sit on her other side.*) Mr. Hackl, think of me as your friend. Come in the kitchen and get warm. . . . (*She rises and starts to go out.*) We can decide later who everybody is. My dear, would you like a good hot bath?

Ermengarde. Yes, I would.

Miss Van H. Well, when Ermengarde comes out you can go in. (*Enter Cornelius from the kitchen.*)

Cornelius. Oh, Miss Van Huysen . . .

Ermengarde. Why, Mr. Hack — !!

Cornelius (*sliding up to her, urgently*). Not yet! I'll explain. I'll explain everything.

Miss Van H. Mr. Kemper! — Mr. Kemper! This is Mr. Cornelius Hackl. (*To Ambrose*) Mr. Hackl, this is Mr. Ambrose Kemper. (*Pause, while the men glare at one another.*) Perhaps you two know one another?

Ambrose. No!

Cornelius. No, we don't.

Ambrose (*hotly*). Miss Van Huysen, I know that man is not Ambrose Kemper.

Cornelius (*ditto*). And he's not Cornelius Hackl.

Miss Van H. My dear young men, what does it matter what your names are? The important thing is that you are you. (*To Ambrose.*) You are alive and breathing, aren't you, Mr. Hackl? (*Pinches Ambrose's left arm.*)

Ambrose. Ouch, Miss Van Huysen.

Miss Van H. This dear child imagines she is Horace Vandergelder's niece Ermengarde.

Ermengarde. But I am.

Miss Van H. The important thing is that you're all in love. Everything else is illusion. (*She pinches Cornelius' arm.*)

Cornelius. Ouch! Miss Van Huysen!

Miss Van H. (*comes down and addresses the audience*). Everybody keeps asking me if I'm Miss Van Huys . . . (*She seems suddenly to be stricken with doubt as to who she is; her face shows bewildered alarm. She pinches herself on the upper arm and is abruptly and happily relieved.*) Now, you two gentlemen sit down and have a nice chat while this dear child has a good hot bath. (*The doorbell rings. Ermengarde exit, Miss Van Huysen about to follow her, but stops. Enter cook.*)

Cook. There's the doorbell again.

Miss Van H. Well, answer it. (*She and Ermengarde exit to kitchen.*)

Cook (*at window, very happy about all these guests*). It's a cab and three ladies. I never saw such a night. (*Exit to front door.*)

Miss Van H. Gentlemen, you can rest easy. I'll see that Mr. Vandergelder lets his nieces marry you both. (*Enter Mrs. Levi.*)

Mrs. Levi. Flora, how are you?

Miss Van H. Dolly Gallagher! What brings you here?

Mrs. Levi. Great Heavens, Flora, what are those two drunken men doing in your hall?

Miss Van H. I don't know. Horace Vandergelder sent them to me.

Mrs. Levi. Well, I've brought you two girls in much the same condition. Otherwise they're the finest girls in the world. (*She goes up to the door and leads in Mrs. Molloy. Minnie follows.*) I want you to meet Irene Molloy and Minnie Fay.

Miss Van H. Delighted to know you.

Mrs. Levi. Oh, I see you two gentlemen are here, too. Mr. Hackl, I was about to look for you (*Pointing about the room.*) somewhere here.

Cornelius. No, Mrs. Levi. I'm ready to face anything now.

Mrs. Levi. Mr. Vandergelder will be here in a minute. He's downstairs trying to pay for a cab without any money.

Mrs. Molloy (*holding Vandergelder's purse*). Oh, I'll help him.

Mrs. Levi. Yes, will you, dear? You had to pay the restaurant bills. You must have hundreds of dollars there it seems.

Mrs. Molloy. This is his own purse he lost. I can't give it back to him without seeming . . .

Mrs. Levi. I'll give it back to him. — There, you help him with this now. (*She gives Mrs. Molloy a bill and puts the purse airily under her arm.*)

Vandergelder (*off*). Will somebody please pay for this cab? (*Mrs. Molloy exits to front door.*)

Mrs. Molloy (*off stage*). I'll take care of that, Mr. Vandergelder. (*As Mr. Vandergelder enters, Malachi and the Cabman follow him in. Vandergelder carries overcoat, stick and box of chocolates.*)

Cabman. Fifteen dollars, Mr. Vandergelder.

Malachi. Hello, Mr. Vandergelder.

Vandergelder (*to Malachi*). You're discharged! (*To Cabman.*) You too! (*Malachi and Cabman go out and wait in the hall.*) So I've caught up with you at last! (*To Ambrose.*) I never want to see you again! (*To Cornelius.*) You're discharged! Get out of the house, both of you. (*He strikes sofa with his stick; a second after, Miss Van Huysen strikes him on the shoulder with a folded newspaper or magazine.*)

Miss Van H. (*forcefully*). Now then you. Stop ordering people out of my house. You can shout and carry on in Yonkers, but when you're in my house you'll behave yourself.

Vandergelder. They're both dishonest scoundrels.

Miss Van H. Take your hat off. Gentlemen, you stay right where you are.

Cornelius. Mr. Vandergelder, I can explain —

Miss Van H. There aren't going to be any explanations. Horace, stop scowling at Mr. Kemper and forgive him.

Vandergelder. That's not Kemper, that's a dishonest rogue named Cornelius Hackl.

Miss Van H. You're crazy. (*Points to Ambrose.*) That's Cornelius Hackl.

Vandergelder. I guess I know my own chief clerk.

Miss Van H. I don't care what their names are. You shake hands with them both, or out you go.

Vandergelder. Shake hands with those dogs and scoundrels!

Mrs. Levi. Mr. Vandergelder, you've had a hard day. You don't want to go out in the rain now. Just for form's sake, you shake hands with them. You can start quarreling with them tomorrow.

Vandergelder (*gives Cornelius one finger to shake*). There! Don't regard that as a handshake. (*He turns to Ambrose, who mockingly offers him one finger.*) Hey! I never want to see you again. (*Mrs. Molloy enters from front door.*)

Mrs. Molloy. Miss Van Huysen.

Miss Van H. Yes, dear?

Mrs. Molloy. Do I smell coffee?

Miss Van H. Yes, dear.

Mrs. Molloy. Can I have some, good and black?

Miss Van H. Come along, everybody. We'll all go into the kitchen and have some coffee. (*As they all go:*) Horace, you'll be interested to know there are two Ermengardes in there. . . .

Vandergelder. Two!! (*Last to go is Minnie, who revolves about the room dreamily waltzing, a finger on her forehead. Mrs. Levi has been standing at one side. She now comes forward, in thoughtful mood. Minnie continues her waltz round the left sofa and out to the kitchen. Mrs. Levi, left alone, comes to the front, addressing an imaginary Ephraim.*)

Mrs. Levi. Ephraim Levi, I'm going to get married again. Ephraim, I'm marrying Horace Vandergelder for his money. I'm going to send his money out doing all the things you taught me. Oh, it won't be a marriage in the sense that we had one — but I shall certainly make him happy, and Ephraim — I'm tired. I'm tired of living from hand to mouth, and I'm asking your permission, Ephraim — will you give me away? (*Now addressing the audience, she holds up the purse.*) Money! Money! — it's like the sun we walk under; it can kill or cure. — Mr. Vandergelder's money! Vandergelder's never tired of saying most of the people in the world are fools, and in a way he's right, isn't he? Himself, Irene, Cornelius, myself! But there comes a moment in everybody's life when he must decide whether he'll live among human beings or not — a fool among fools or a fool alone.

As for me, I've decided to live among them.

I wasn't always so. After my husband's death I retired into myself. Yes, in the evenings, I'd put out the cat, and I'd lock the door, and I'd make myself a little rum toddy; and before I went to bed I'd say a little prayer, thanking God that I was independent — that no one else's life was mixed up with mine. And when ten o'clock sounded from Trinity Church tower, I fell off to sleep and I was a perfectly contented woman. And one night, after two years of this, an oak leaf fell out of my Bible. I had placed it there on the day my husband asked me to marry him; a perfectly good oak leaf — but without color and without life. And suddenly I realized that for a long time I had not shed one tear; nor had I been filled with the wonderful hope that something or other would turn out well. I saw that I was like that oak leaf, and on that night I decided to rejoin the human race.

Yes, we're all fools and we're all in danger of destroying the world with our folly. But the surest way to keep us out of harm is to give us the four or five human pleasures that are our right in the world, — and that takes a little *money!*

The difference between a little money and no money at all is enormous — and can shatter the world. And the difference between a little money and an enormous amount of money is very slight — and that, also, can shatter the world.

Money, I've always felt, money — pardon my expression — is like manure; it's not worth a thing unless it's spread about encouraging young things to grow.

Anyway, — that's the opinion of the second Mrs. Vandergelder. (*Vandergelder enters with two cups of coffee. With his back, he closes both doors.*)
Vandergelder. Miss Van Huysen asked me to bring you this.

Mrs. Levi. Thank you both. Sit down and rest yourself. What's been going on in the kitchen?

Vandergelder. A lot of foolishness. Everybody falling in love with everybody. I forgave 'em; Ermengarde and that artist.

Mrs. Levi. I knew you would.

Vandergelder. I made Cornelius Hackl my partner.

Mrs. Levi. You won't regret it.

Vandergelder. Dolly, you said some mighty unpleasant things to me in the restaurant tonight . . . all that about my house . . . and everything.

Mrs. Levi. Let's not say another word about it.

Vandergelder. Dolly, you have a lot of faults —

Mrs. Levi. Oh, I know what you mean.

Vandergelder. You're bossy, scheming, inquisitive . . .

Mrs. Levi. Go on.

Vandergelder. But you're a wonderful woman. Dolly, marry me.

Mrs. Levi. Horace! (*Rises.*) Stop right there.

Vandergelder. I know I've been a fool about Mrs. Molloy, and that other woman. But, Dolly, forgive me and marry me. (*He goes on his knees.*)

Mrs. Levi. Horace, I don't dare. No. I don't dare.

Vandergelder. What do you mean?

Mrs. Levi. You know as well as I do that you're the first citizen of Yonkers. Naturally, you'd expect your wife to keep open house, to have scores of friends in and out all the time. Any wife of yours should be used to that kind of thing.

Vandergelder (after a brief struggle with himself). Dolly, you can live any way you like.

Mrs. Levi. Horace, you can't deny it, your wife would have to be a *somebody.* Answer me: am I a somebody?

Vandergelder. You are . . . you are. Wonderful woman.

Mrs. Levi. Oh, you're partial. (*She crosses, giving a big wink at the audience, and sits on sofa right. Vandergelder follows her on his knees.*) Horace, it won't be enough for you to load your wife with money and jewels; to insist that she be a benefactress to half the town. (*He rises and, still struggling with himself, coughs so as not to hear this.*) No, she must be a somebody. Do you really think I have it in me to be a credit to you?

Vandergelder. Dolly, everybody knows that you could do anything you wanted to do.

Mrs. Levi. I'll try. With your help, I'll try — and by the way, I found your purse. (*Holds it up.*)

Vandergelder. Where did you — ! Wonderful woman!

Mrs. Levi. It just walked into my hand. I don't know how I do it. Sometimes I frighten myself. Horace, take it. Money walks out of my hands, too.

Vandergelder. Keep it. Keep it.

Mrs. Levi. Horace! (*Half laughing, half weeping, and with an air of real affection for him.*) I never thought . . . I'd ever . . . hear you say a thing like that! (*Barnaby dashes in from the kitchen in great excitement. He has discarded Minnie's clothes.*)

Barnaby. Oh! Excuse me. I didn't know anybody was here.

Vandergelder (*bellowing*). Didn't know anybody was here. Idiot!

Mrs. Levi (*putting her hand on Vandergelder's arm; amiably*). Come in Barnaby. Come in. (*Vandergelder looks at her a minute; then says, imitating her tone.*)

Vandergelder. Come in, Barnaby. Come in.

Barnaby. Cornelius is going to marry Mrs. Molloy!!

Mrs. Levi. Isn't that fine! Horace! . . . (*Mrs. Levi rises, and indicates that he has an announcement to make.*)

Vandergelder. Barnaby, go in and tell the rest of them that Mrs. Levi has consented —

Mrs. Levi. *Finally* consented!

Vandergelder. Finally consented to become my wife.

Barnaby. Holy cabooses. (*Dashes back to the doorway.*) Hey! Listen, everybody! Wolf-trap — I mean — Mr. Vandergelder is going to marry Mrs. Levi. (*Miss Van Huysen enters followed by all the people in this act. She is now carrying the box of chocolates.*)

Miss Van H. Dolly, that's the best news I ever heard. (*She addresses the audience.*) There isn't any more coffee; there isn't any more gingerbread; but there are three couples in my house and they're all going to get married. And do you know, one of those Ermengardes wasn't a dear little girl at all — she was a boy! Well, that's what life is: disappointment, illusion.

Mrs. Levi (*to audience*). There isn't any more coffee; there isn't any more gingerbread, and there isn't any more play — but there is one more thing we have to do. . . . Barnaby, come here. (*She whispers to him, pointing to the audience. Then she says to the audience.*) I think the youngest person here ought to tell us what the moral of the play is. (*Barnaby is reluctantly pushed forward to the footlights.*)

Barnaby. Oh, I think it's about . . . I think it's about adventure. The test of an adventure is that when you're in the middle of it, you say to yourself, "Oh, now I've got myself into an awful mess; I wish I were sitting quietly at home." And the sign that something's wrong with you is when you sit quietly at home wishing you were out having lots of adventure. What we would like for you is that you have just the right amount of sitting quietly at home and just the right amount of — adventure! So that now we all want to thank you for coming tonight, and we all hope that in your lives you have just the right amount of — adventure!

(THE CURTAIN FALLS)

Just beneath the title of his play, Wilder put "A Farce in Four Acts." When we think of the low esteem in which farce is held, it is almost pedantic to mention that *The Matchmaker* is a slight revision of an earlier play by Wilder, *The Merchant of Yonkers* (1938), which in turn is derived from an Austrian play, Johann Nestroy's *Einen Jux will er sich machen* (*Out for a Good Time*, 1842), which itself is an adaptation of an English comedy, John Oxenford's *A Day Well Spent; or, Three Adventures* (1836). A long lineage for a play in what is thought to be a humble genre.

A few words about farce may be useful. It is generally considered a kind of comedy that depends more heavily on physical action than on wit, or, to put it somewhat differently, on plot rather than on subtlety of character. But no good playwright scorns plot, and subtlety of character is not a *sine qua non* of good comedy. Perhaps what identifies farce is amusing overt desperation. In a way, all drama — comedy and tragedy — deals with desperate people: Othello falls into a fit; Hedda fires pistols; Major Barbara is (for a while) heartbroken; even Undershaft meets his match in Cusins, who at one point is said to be "desperately perplexed." But the desperation is usually intermittent, and rarely unsettles the dramatis personae in comedy, where pressures are most often released in the civilized form of banter, and where all but a few crabby fathers or foolish wooers usually preserve good manners. In farce the desperation bursts to the surface, and characters are driven about the stage, hiding under tables, inventing grotesque lies, and leaping into outlandish disguises. (In one of his films Charlie Chaplin escapes his ardent pursuers by standing rigid, a shade on his head, disguising himself as a floor lamp.)

And this is the sort of thing we get in *The Matchmaker*. Wilder contrives — or, rather, adapts — a plot that reveals engaging desperation all around. Cornelius Hackl, Horace Vandergelder's clerk, wants to spend a day in New York, to have a good dinner, to be in danger, to almost get arrested, and to kiss a girl (he is thirty-three); Mrs. Irene

Molloy wants to escape the monotonous life of a widowed milliner ("I can no longer stand being suspected of being a wicked woman, while I have nothing to show for it. I can't stand it."), and Dolly Levi wants a husband and the fun that distributing his money will bring. Even Horace Vandergelder, despite his grumblings and his sermons, despite his dreary "caution and hard work," wants "a little risk and adventure." Wilder gives us four acts in which people are taxed to their uttermost, and respond in entertaining zany ways. Small sample: Horace Vandergelder, about to marry, is informing his junior clerk of his plans:

> *Vandergelder.* When I come back, there are going to be some changes in the house here. I'll tell you what the change is, but I don't want you discussing it amongst yourselves: you're going to have a mistress.

> *Barnaby.* (*Seventeen; round-faced, wide-eyed innocence; wearing a green apron*) I'm too young, Mr. Vandergelder!!

What does it add up to? We can, of course, hunt through a play and find some scraps of a message. There are, for instance, a few lines that glance at the underpaid working class: Vandergelder says to Mrs. Molloy, "You pay those girls of yours too much. You pay them as much as men. Girls like that enjoy their work. Wages, Mrs. Molloy, are paid to make people do work they don't want to do." Malachi's suggestion that thieves are engaged in the useful task of redistributing wealth might fit here too, but we hardly take seriously these criticisms of bourgeois morality. They may appeal briefly to our anarchic impulses, but we laugh at them rather than think hard about them. There is, of course, the larger, more pervasive theme, which Wilder summarized thus: "My play is about the aspirations of the young (and not only of the young) for a fuller, freer participation in life." Any number of speeches could be cited as evidence, but perhaps the most explicit is one of Dolly's: "And suddenly I realized that for a long time I had not shed one tear; nor had I been filled with the wonderful hope that something or other would turn out well. . . . And on that night I decided to rejoin the human race . . . . Money, I've always felt, money — pardon my expression — is like manure; it's not worth a thing unless it's spread about encouraging young things to grow."

Yet the play's value is surely not entirely dependent upon such speeches, or upon its theme. For one thing, the theme is that of almost all comedy, and we can scarcely value Wilder for presenting a stock theme. In an interview (printed in *Writers at Work*, ed. Malcolm Cowley) Wilder remarked that the didactic content of a literary work probably has two origins. It is there because it gave the author his initial impetus, but it tends to disappear. It "starts the motor. Or let us say: many of the things we eat are cooked over a gas stove, but there is no taste of gas in the food." It gives the author a sense that he is doing something respectable, and, Wilder added, it also gives the audience something that audiences normally expect. But the didactic content is paradoxically, a sugar coating, both for author and audience. Shaw had said that the heart of his plays was a message, and he found the audience would accept the message only when it was sugar-coated with an amusing plot. But for Wilder the heart of a play is its presentation of "the pure event," "experience for experience's sake — rather than for moral improvement's sake." Those who want a moral will find it in *The Matchmaker;* those who want an experience, an adventure (as Cornelius Hackl and Horace Vandergelder do) will find it there too.

A GLOSSARY OF
DRAMATIC TERMS

act. A main division in drama or opera. Act divisions probably arose in Roman theory and derive ultimately from the Greek practice of separating episodes in a play by choral interludes, but Greek (and probably Roman) plays were performed without interruption, for the choral interludes were part of the plays themselves. The division of Elizabethan plays into five acts is often the work of editors rather than authors. No play of Shakespeare's was published in his lifetime with divisions into five acts. Today an act division is commonly indicated by lowering the curtain and turning up the house-lights. A **scene** is a smaller unit, either: (i) a division with no change of locale or abrupt shift of time, or (ii) a division consisting of an actor or a group of actors on the stage; according to the second definition, the departure or entrance of an actor changes the composition of the group and thus produces a new scene. In an entirely different sense, the scene is the locale where a work is set. The first speech in *Romeo and Juliet* informs the audience of the play's locale: "In fair Verona, where we lay our scene. . . ." Often the décor lets the spectator know where the play is set, but during the last hundred years playwrights have tended, for the convenience of readers, to write long stage directions describing the scene. Here is the beginning of the first stage direction in Shaw's *Candida*: "A fine morning in October 1894 in the north east quarter of London, a vast district miles away from the London of Mayfair and St James's, and much less narrow, squalid, fetid and airless in its slums. . . ."

action. (1) The physical movement of an actor, whether he is leaping into Ophelia's grave or speaking softly to himself. That talk is action is easily seen in the Bastard's remark (*King John*, II.i.466):

731

"Zounds! I was never so bethumped with words/ Since I first called my brother's father dad." (2) An incident in the plot, an episode. (3) Aristotle's statement that a drama is an "imitation of an action" (*praxis*) has provoked considerable controversy; recently there has been a tendency to regard this action as the motive underlying the outward deeds of the plot. Francis Fergusson says (in *The Human Image in Dramatic Literature*, p. 116), for example, that the action of *Oedipus the King* "is the quest for Laius's slayer, . . . which persists through the changing circumstances of the play." See above, pp. xiv–xvi.

aesthetic distance, or **physical distance.** The detachment between the receptor and the work of art. The concept is chiefly associated with Edward Bullough (see the essay in his *Aesthetics*, reprinted in Melvin Rader, *A Modern Book of Aesthetics*). Bullough explains that there must be some sort of psychical "distance" (gap) between our practical self (our personal needs) and the work of art. Thus, a jealous man who suspects his wife may be unable to divorce his personal feelings from *Othello*. He may be too involved with the piece as life to see it as art. But "distance" does not mean that the receptor is totally detached or objective. Rather, he is detached from his usual personal involvements, and because of this detachment he can look with a new vigorous interest — he can look with a new sort of passion born of his new personality — at the work of art as art. Persons who do not understand the need for distance between themselves and a work, Bullough explains, commonly say that they do not wish to see a tragedy because there is enough suffering in real life. But the more sophisticated spectator at a tragedy realizes that as a picture is distanced by the frame, a play is distanced (the characters may speak verse, they perform behind footlights, and their deeds cohere to make a unified harmonious pattern); the feelings it evokes in him are not the feelings evoked by a roughly similar event in real life. In the theater we feel "rapturous awe" at what in life would be depressing. See also dramatic illusion, empathy, epic drama.

agon (Greek: contest). A debate in a Greek comedy. See p. 436. In the last few decades the term has been used (*e.g.*, by Francis Fergusson, *The Idea of a Theater*) to designate a scene of conflict in tragedy, such as the agonizing struggle between Oedipus and Teiresias.

agroikos. See character.

alazon. See character.

alienation effect. See epic drama.

allegory. When St. Augustine noted that we derive pleasure from thinking of holy men as sheep, he was commenting on the pleasure afforded by allegory. Frequently an allegory is a narrative wherein abstractions (*e.g.*, virtue, fear) are made concrete (Mr. Virtue, Giant Fear), for the purpose of effectively communicating a moral, but in essence an allegory is merely a system of equivalents. Though allegory need not personify abstractions, allegoric drama almost always does. *Everyman* (c. 1500), an allegoric morality play includes among its dramatis personae Death, Good Deeds, Beauty, and of course, Everyman. But morality plays may also include allegoric castles (standing for strength or chastity), roses (standing for love or virtue), etc. Consult Bernard Spivack, *Shakespeare and the Allegory of Evil*.

anagnorisis (or **disclosure, discovery, recognition**). For Aristotle the "recognition" or "disclosure" seems to be merely a recognition of who is who, by such tokens as birthmarks, clothes, etc., but the term has been extended to include the tragic hero's recognition of himself and/or the essence of life. Thus Othello, having murdered his faithful wife, learns he was beguiled into thinking her dishonest, and finally recognizes himself as "one not easily jealous, but being wrought/ Perplexed in the extreme"; and he exacts justice from himself by suicide. See p. xix.

antecedent action. See plot.

anticlimax. A descent, the lines or happenings being markedly less important or less impressive than their predecessors. In melodrama, a decrease in tension may cause disappointment and loss of interest; in comedy, a sharp descent (the beautiful princess opens her mouth and sounds like a burlesque queen) may get a desirable laugh. On the desirability of a gradual decrease in tension in tragedy (*i.e.*, a "quiet ending"), consult Max Beerbohm, "Last Acts," in *Around Theatres*.

antimasque. See masque.

arena stage. (1) In British usage, a stage with a back wall and with an audience on three sides. (2) In American usage, a playing space surrounded by spectators, **theater-in-the-round.** Proponents of arena staging (in the American sense) stress the intimacy afforded by having actors in the midst of the audience, but opponents suggest that at least for some plays the intimacy ought not to be very great. (See aesthetic distance.) It has been noted, too, that even in arena staging the audience normally feels set apart from the actors, for the audience is in the dark while the actors are in an illuminated playing area. Critics of arena staging cite the following difficulties: soliloquies, asides, and direct addresses are hard to deliver in such a theater; directors, aware that the back of an actor's head is not very expressive, tend to have the actors gyrate disturbingly and meaninglessly; entrances and exits are cumbersome; little use can be made of elevation and of groupings of actors.

arras. See Elizabethan playhouse.

aside. See soliloquy, convention.

bombast. From a word meaning "cotton stuffing"; rant, speech that is too inflated for the occasion. In Marlowe's *Tamburlaine* (c. 1587), Tamburlaine brags thus:

> Our quivering lances, shaking in the air,
> And bullets, like Jove's dreadful thunderbolts,
> Enrolled in flames and fiery smoldering mists,
> Shall threat the gods more than Cyclopian wars:
> And with our sun-bright armor as we march,
> Will chase the stars from Heaven and dim their eyes
> That stand and muse at our admirèd arms.

bomolochos. See character.

bourgeois drama. A serious play with middle-class dramatis personae. There are a few Elizabethan tragedies of middle-class life, but bourgeois drama, with its emphasis on pathos, is more or less an eighteenth-century invention. Bourgeois dramas were written in the eighteenth and nineteenth centuries, apparently in response to the middle class's desire to see itself on the stage; the bourgeois by the eighteenth century regarded himself as a suitable replacement for the nobleman of earlier tragedy. Speaking generally, the characteristics of these plays are: middle-class dramatis personae, virtue in distress, sentimentality, and an unreasonably high moral tone. Eighteenth-century critics, not sure what to do with pathetic plays on middle-class life, used the terms *drame*, *drame bourgeois*, *comédie larmoyante* (tearful comedy), *tragédie bourgeoise*, *bürgerliches Trauerspiel* (bourgeois tragedy) interchangeably. (Note that a *comédie larmoyante* need not end happily, nor a *tragédie bourgeoise* end sadly.) In England, George Lillo's *The London Merchant* (1731), "a tale of private woe. A London 'prentice ruined," depicted an apprentice who murdered his benefactor. In France, Diderot compared *The London Merchant* to plays by Sophocles and Euripides. In Germany, it moved Lessing to write *Miss Sara Sampson* (1755), a play set in England: Sara, inveigled into eloping with a blackguard, is poisoned by his former mistress, causing him to repent his villainy in the presence of Sara's lamenting father. Unlike Miss Sara, bourgeois drama does not die in the eighteenth century; it lives on into the nineteenth century to become melodrama in many hands and tragedy in Ibsen's hands. Consult Fred O. Nolte, *Early Middle Class Drama*; and Eric Auerbach, *Mimesis*, Ch. 17. On Ibsen as a bourgeois dramatist, consult Eric Bentley, *The Playwright as Thinker*. See domestic tragedy, sentimental, and pp. 220n., 365–366.

burlesque. Any imitation which, by distortion, aims to amuse. Its subject matter is sometimes said to be faults rather than vices, and its tone is neither shrill nor savage. Thus, in distinction from satire it can be defined as a comic imitation of a mannerism or a minor fault (either in style or subject-matter), contrived to arouse amusement rather than indignation. In the theater, a burlesque may be a play that amusingly criticizes another play by grotesquely imitating aspects of it, as Gay's *The Beggar's Opera* (1728) mimicked serious operas, Buckingham's *The Rehearsal* (1671) mimicked heroic drama, and Sheridan's *The Critic* (1779) mimicked (among other things) sentimental drama. In England, a burlesque may be a musical extravaganza in which fantasy has almost entirely ousted criticism. In America, burlesque (especially popular in the late nineteenth and first half of the twentieth century) is usually a sort of vaudeville or variety show stressing bawdy humor and sex. The sexual theme is most fully revealed in the striptease, introduced about 1920. Consult V. C. Clinton-Baddeley, *The Burlesque Tradition in the English Theater after 1660*; Gypsy Rose Lee, *The G-String Murders*. See comedy, satire.

catastrophe. See plot.

catharsis. Aristotle and countless followers said that tragedy evokes pity and fear, and that it produces in the spectator a catharsis (purgation, or, some scholars hold, purification) of these emotions: it drains or perhaps refines or modifies these emotions, and thus tragedy is socially useful. (Aristotle's *Poetics* is the subject of much controversy; one cannot with security assert that Aristotle said anything, without a counter-argument being offered. For various views of catharsis, consult F. L. Lucas, *Tragedy*, and Gerald F. Else's monumental *Aristotle's Poetics*.)

character. (1) One of the dramatis personae, *e.g.*, Hamlet. (2) The personality of such a figure. Characters are sometimes divided into **flat** and **round characters.** The former have only one "side," representing a single trait (*e.g.*, the faithful wife, the genial drunkard); the latter have many traits and are seen, as it were, from all sides, in the round. The behavior of flat characters is thoroughly predictable, that of round characters is sometimes unexpected though credible. The term "flat" is not necessarily pejorative, for it is sometimes desirable to show only one aspect of a single character, but E. M. Forster suggests (*Aspects of the Novel*) that "flat people are not in themselves as big achievements as round ones, and also . . . they are best when they are comic." See comedy of humors. A **stock character** is a type that recurs in many works. For example, from Greek comedy to the present there have been numerous braggart soldiers, stubborn fathers, jealous husbands. Northrop Frye finds four chief types of comic figures: (i) the *alazon*, the impostor, boaster, hypocrite; (ii) the *eiron* (see irony), the man who deprecates himself and exposes the boaster; (iii) the *bomolochos*, the buffoon, or more generally, the man who entertains by his mannerisms and talk; (iv) the *agroikos*, the straightman who is the unwitting butt of humor. Each of these types appears in many dresses; the *alazon*, for example, is most commonly the braggart soldier (*miles gloriosus*), but he is also the pedant, the crank, or anyone who is full of ideas that have no relation to reality. (See commedia dell' arte; consult Northrop Frye, *Anatomy of Criticism*, pp. 171–176.) Stock characters are not limited to comedy: the proud tragic hero is a stock character, as are, for example, the cruel stepmother and the son who wishes to avenge his father. See also motivation, plot. Consult J. L. Styan, *The Elements of Drama*, Ch. 8.

chorus. In Greek drama, a group of performers who play a role, *e.g.*, Old Men of Corinth. (The chorus leader is the *koryphaeus*.) In Aeschylus' *The Suppliants* (c. 490 B.C.), perhaps the earliest extant play, the chorus consists of the heroines, but in most Greek plays the chorus consists of subsidiary figures who comment rather helplessly on what is happening to the important people. Aeschylus reduced the chorus of fifty to twelve; Sophocles increased it to fifteen, where it remained. The Greek chorus, it is often said, is a sort of middle-man between the unusual main figures and the humdrum spectators. Elizabethan dramas occasionally had a chorus of one actor who, not a participant in the story, commented on it. The Chorus (or prologue) in Shakespeare's *Henry* V urges the audience to

> Think when we talk of horses that you see them
> Printing their proud hoofs i' the receiving earth;
> For 'tis your thoughts that now must deck our kings,
> Carry them here and there, jumping o'er times,
> Turning the accomplishment of many years
> Into an hour-glass: for the which supply,
> Admit me Chorus to this history:
> Who prologue-like your humble patience pray,
> Gently to hear, kindly to judge, our play.

A **chorus character** (or *raisonneur*), however, such as Enobarbus in *Antony and Cleopatra*, is a character who participates in the story yet seems to be the author's mouthpiece, intelligently commenting (often with irony) on the actions of the other characters. But Alfred Harbage, in *As They Liked It*, skeptically and aptly calls such a figure "The Unreliable Spokesman." The use of the chorus, in one form or another, continues into our times, for example in T.S. Eliot's *Murder in the Cathedral*, whose "Chorus of Women of Canterbury," like a Greek chorus and like the audience, "are forced to bear witness"; and in Tennessee Williams' *The Glass Menagerie*, whose Tom Wingfield tells the audience he is "the narrator of the play, and also a character in it."

climax. See plot.

closet drama. A play suited only for reading, not for acting. Most nineteenth-century English poetic dramas (*e.g.*, Coleridge's, Shelley's, Tennyson's) fit into this category, although Byron's plays have recently been moving out of the closet. Consult Moody Prior, *The Language of Tragedy*.

comedy. Most broadly, anything amusing — a literary work or a situation — is a comedy. More specifically, comedy is (in Dr. Johnson's words) "such a dramatic representation of human life, as may excite mirth." Dramatic comedies generally depict a movement from unhappiness to happiness, from (for example) young lovers frustrated by their parents to young lovers happily married. The unhappy situation is so presented that it entertains rather than distresses the spectator; it is ridiculous and/or diverting rather than painful.

Comic drama seems related to fertility rituals; it celebrates generation, renewal, variety (laughing away any narrow-minded persons who seek to limit life's abundance), and it celebrates man's triumphs over the chances of life. Irate parents and shipwrecks cannot prevent journeys from ending with lovers meeting. Consult C. Hoy, *The Hyacinth Room; Theories of Comedy*, ed. P. Lauter; L. J. Potts, *Comedy*.

Comedy of humors. A term sometimes applied to plays — notably those of Ben Jonson — wherein the characters, though somewhat individualized, obviously represent types or moods (the jealous husband, the witless pedant). A humor was a bodily liquid (blood [Latin: *sanguis*], phlegm, yellow bile, black bile) thought to control one's behavior. Allegedly, a proper mixture produced a well adjusted man, but a preponderance of any one humor produced a distorted personality. The old sense of the word survives in the phrase, "He is in a bad humor"; "sanguine," "choleric," "phlegmatic," and "bilious" are also modern survivals of the old psychology of humors. **Humor characters** are common in **situational comedy**; they are engineered by a clever plot into a situation that displays their absurdity: the man who craves silence is confronted with a talkative woman; the coward is confronted by the braggart; the hypochondriacal lady meets a veterinarian and asks for medical advice.

comic relief. Humorous episodes in tragedy, alleged to alleviate or lighten the tragic effect. Some comic scenes in tragedy, however, not only provide "relief" but enlarge the canvas of tragedy, showing us a fuller picture of life. The clown who brings Cleopatra the poisonous asp sets her tragedy against the daily world. Critics have increasingly noted that the comic scenes (such as the macabre comments of the grave-diggers in *Hamlet*) often deepen rather than alleviate the tragic effect. See tragicomedy. Although Aristotle stressed "unity of action," some Greek tragedies include figures that seem comic to us, *e.g.*, Okeanos in Aeschylus' *Prometheus Bound*. Consult A. P. Rossiter, *Angel with Horns*, Ch. 14.

commedia dell' arte. Italian drama, more or less improvised, performed by professionals in Italy and abroad, mostly in the sixteenth century but still alive in the early eighteenth century. In contrast to the classically-inspired written drama (*commedia erudita*) performed by actors who memorized their lines, *commedia dell' arte* (perhaps best translated as "professional drama") employed sketches of plots (*scenario*; pl. *scenarii*) specifying entrances and exits and the gist of the dialogue; in performance these *scenarii* were fleshed out with stock bits of comic stage business (*lazzi*) or larger pieces of business (**burle**) such as practical jokes. (The singulars are *lazzo* and **burla**.) Thus a *scenario* may call for the *lazzo* of anger, or the *burla* of chasing a fly, and leave it to the actor to work out the swats and the smile when at last he munches the fly. Though these plays are said to have been improvised, the stock characters, stock situations, and stock stage business make them something more — or less — than improvised. The origin of the *commedia dell' arte* is much disputed. It may be a reflowering of the mimes who, through the Dark Ages, perhaps carried on the tradition of the ancient *fabula Atellana* (ancient rustic farces), which used masked characters. In any case, the chief characters — most of whom wore masks — in the *commedia dell' arte* are Pantalone, an elderly Venetian merchant wearing a little cap, a red jacket, loose trousers (hence our word "pants"), and slippers: his age, amours, and avarice make him ridiculous; Dottore, a Bolognese doctor wearing a black academic gown: his age and his pedantry make him ridiculous; Capitano, a soldier, ridiculous because a braggart and a coward; several servants called *zanne* (singular: *zanni*, from *Gianni*, "Johnny") including Arlecchino (later Harlequin), who in the sixteenth century wore patches that in the next century were represented by triangles or diamonds; Brighella, a rather cruel and crafty rogue; Pulcinella, noted for his resourcefulness and his disguises; Pedrolino, a naive valet who becomes the melancholy Pagliacci and Pierrot; Colombina, who later becomes Columbine and loves Harlequin. Further, there are usually four lovers, children of the two Old Men. Consult Allardyce Nicoll, *Masks, Mimes and Miracles*, and *The World of Harlequin*; and K. M. Lea, *Italian Popular Comedy*.

   complication. See plot.

   confidant (feminine: **confidante**). A character in whom a principal character confides, revealing his state of mind and often furthering the exposition. Horatio is Hamlet's confidant; Oenone is Phèdre's. Although Horatio and Oenone are memorable, the confidant is sometimes absurdly vapid; though the French defended the device as more plausible than the soliloquy, the confidant may be more trouble than he is worth. In *The Critic* (1779), Sheridan ridiculed it thus: "Enter Tilburina stark mad in white satin, and her confidante stark mad in white linen."

   conflict. See plot.

   convention. An unrealistic device that the public agrees to tolerate. Thus, a character in a drama may express his thoughts aloud and not be heard by other characters (the **aside**), or he may speak his thoughts aloud on the empty stage (the **soliloquy**). Italian characters (*e.g.*, Desdemona and Iago) speak English, yet are understood to be speaking Italian. On the Roman comic stage, a character entering at the left was conventionally understood to be coming from the harbor, and one entering at the right from the forum. In motion pictures, one image fades out, another fades in, and through this convention the audience knows that there is a shift in time or place. More generally any character-type, any theme, or motif (*e.g.*, the suspected butler) widely used in literature or drama is a convention. Consult Harry Levin, *Contexts of Criticism*; M. C. Bradbrook, *Themes and Conventions of Elizabethan Tragedy*.

   coup de théatre. A surprise, especially a striking turn of events in the plot. Consult Alan R. Thompson, *The Anatomy of Drama*.

   denouement. See plot.

   deus ex machina. Literally, a god out of a machine. (1) In Greek drama a god who descends by a crane-like arrangement and solves a problem in the story, thus allowing the play to end. It was much used by Euripides; Sophocles in his old age borrowed the idea and introduced Heracles at the end of *Philoctetes* to induce the title-character to go to Troy. (2) Any unexpected and improbable device (*e.g.*, an unexpected inheritance from a long-lost uncle in Australia) used to unknot a problem and thus conclude the work.

   deuteragonist. See protagonist.

dialogue. The speech exchanged between characters, or, loosely, even the speech of a single character. Dialogue is sometimes contrasted to action, but Elizabeth Bowen aptly says that dialogue is what the characters *do* to each other, and Shaw aptly says that his plays are all talk just as Beethoven's symphonies are all music. **Stichomythia** is a special form of dialogue, wherein two speakers in a verbal duel thrust and parry in alternating lines. Example:

Queen.   Hamlet, thou hast thy father much offended.
Hamlet.   Mother, you have my father much offended.
Queen.   Come, come, you answer with an idle tongue.
Hamlet.   Go, go, you question with a wicked tongue.

The Elizabethans probably got stichomythia from Seneca (4 B.C.– A.D. 65), who doubtless got it from the Greeks. In Greek tragedy it often consists of questions and answers. See action, soliloquy. Consult J. L. Styan, *The Elements of Drama*, Chs. 1–2.

diction. (1) Choice of words, wording. Dr. Johnson objected to the "knife" ("an instrument used by butchers and cooks," he said) which Lady Macbeth says she will use to murder the King. "Words too familiar, or too remote," Johnson said, "defeat the purpose of a poet." Consult Moody Prior, *The Language of Tragedy*. (2) A performer's manner or style of speaking, including pronunciation and phrasing.

Dionysus. Greek god of wine, the phallus, the surge of growth, and (to join all these) irrational impulse. It is commonly held that Greek tragedy grew from choral celebrations in his honor; in any case, from the sixth century B.C. tragedies were performed in Athens at the **Great** (or **Greater**, or **City**) **Dionysia**, a festival in Dionysus' honor. (The Dionysiac origin is interestingly rejected by H. D. F. Kitto, in *Theatre Survey*, I [1960], 3–17.) Friedrich Nietzsche suggested in *The Birth of Tragedy* (1872) that Greek tragedy, usually considered calm and poised, was not the product of quiet minds. If tragedy, Nietzsche said, showed light and beauty (over which the god **Apollo** presided), it was nevertheless also indebted to Dionysus, who represented the frenzied, buried self-assertions of the mind. That is, Greek tragedy was the product of **Dionysian** ecstatic and violent self-assertion tamed by (or fused with) the **Apollonian** sense of reason, of moderation, and of external order. "Apollonian" is often associated with classicism, and "Dionysian" with romanticism.

domestic tragedy. A serious play showing the misfortunes (especially within the family) of a private citizen rather than of a man of high rank who is involved in events that shake a realm. See bourgeois drama. Consult Henry H. Adams, *English Domestic or Homiletic Tragedy 1575 to 1642*.

drama (from Greek *dran:* to do). (1) A play, a work that tells a story by means of impersonators. (2) The whole body of work written for the theater. (3) A serious but untragic play (see drame). (4) Events containing conflict, tension, surprise ("life is full of drama"; "the first act lacks drama"). See closet drama, comedy, melodrama, tragedy. A play is written by a **dramatist;** the art of writing plays is **dramaturgy.** A man who writes plays is also a **playwright.** (Note that the last syllable is not "-write" but "-wright," denoting a maker, as a shipwright is a maker of ships.) Consult Kenneth T. Rowe, *Write That Play;* Walter Kerr, *How Not to Write a Play;* Bernard Grebanier, *Playwriting.*

dramatic illusion. The notion that the reader or spectator voluntarily enters into the world of the piece of literature, disclaiming (as Coleridge says in *Biographia Literaria*, Ch. 22) "denial or affirmation." This state, between delusion (the spectator thinks the world on the stage is real), and full awareness (the spectator never forgets he is looking at scenery and actors), Coleridge characterized (Ch. 14) as "that willing suspension of disbelief for the moment, which constitutes poetic faith." In *A Midsummer Night's Dream*, Bottom fears that delusion will occur unless the audience is carefully warned: "Write me a prologue, and let the prologue seem to say we will do no harm with our swords, and that Pyramus is not killed indeed. And, for the more better assurance, tell them that I Pyramus am not Pyramus, but Bottom the Weaver. This will put them out of fear." See aesthetic distance.

George Henry Lewes (1817–1878) introduced into English dramatic criticism the term *optique du théâtre,* taken from the French actor François René Molé (1734–1802). A spectator must have this "theater view," this understanding of "scenic illusion," if he is to enjoy the theater; if he lacks it, he will complain that Hamlet ought to be speaking Danish (see convention). *Optique du théâtre* requires that we be given not reality but a symbolic representation of it. A stage miser should finger his gold differently from a real miser; a stage character must be heard, even though in real life the character he is playing might speak softly.

Staging that aims at delusion or a high degree of illusion is **representational staging.** Here the stage-characters eat real food on stage, speak with their backs to the audience, etc. (See naturalism, realism.) When David Belasco staged *The Governor's Lady* in 1912, he was representational, placing on the stage an exact duplicate of a particular (Child's) restaurant. On the other hand, **presentational staging** is antirealistic; in Thornton Wilder's *Our Town* (1938), a drugstore counter, for example, consisted of a board across the backs of two chairs. The staging in musical comedies, ballets, and puppet shows is, of course, presentational. Presentational staging is sometimes called **theatrical staging. Theatricalism,** by its unreality, continually reminds us that we are in the theater, not in the street. On theatricalism, see style. A derogatory way of saying a work is theatrical is to say it is **stagy.**

drame. A solemn but untragic play, especially an eighteenth-century play that, quietly glorifying the bourgeois virtues, preaches and appeals to the audience's emotions. See bourgeois drama. Consult Alan R. Thompson, *The Anatomy of Drama*, which classifies most naturalistic and realistic plays (*e.g.*, Ibsen's and Chekhov's) as drames.

Elizabethan playhouse. The first permanent structure built in England for plays was The Theater, built outside the city limits of London in 1576 by James Burbage. It soon had several competitors, but little is known about any of these playhouses. The contract for one, The Fortune (built in 1600), survives; it tells us that the three-storied building was square, 80′ on the outside, 55′ on the inside. The stage was 43′ broad and 27½′ deep. It has been calculated that about 800 people (the **groundlings**) could stand around the three sides of the stage on the ground that was called the **yard**, and another 1500 could be seated in the three galleries. The other chief pieces of evidence concerning the physical nature of the theater are (i) the "De Witt drawing," which is really a copy of a sketch made by a visitor (c. 1596) to The Swan, and (ii) bits of evidence that can be gleaned from the plays themselves, such as "Enter a Fairy at one door, and Robin Goodfellow at another." Conclusions vary and scholarly tempers run high; the following statements are not indisputable. Most theaters were polygonal or round structures (Shakespeare calls the theater a "wooden O") with three galleries; the yard was open to the sky. From one side a raised stage (or open **platform**) jutted into the middle. A sort of wooden canopy (the **heavens,** or the **shadow**) projected over the stage and in some theaters rested on two pillars; these pillars could conveniently serve as a hiding place for an actor supposed to be unseen by the other characters. At the rear of the stage was probably a curtained alcove or booth or pavilion, which when uncurtained might represent a room or a cave. The curtain is often called an **arras,** and it was probably behind this curtain that Polonius hid, only to be stabbed. (John Cranford Adams, in *The Globe Playhouse,* assumes a permanent alcove or **inner stage;** the Swan drawing, however, is against him. But because there are some clear references to a sort of chamber at the rear, a temporary curtained booth, erected for some performances, has intelligently been conjectured.) At the rear of the stage (flanking the curtained space?) there were perhaps also two or three doors, through which entrances and exits were made. Probably the **tiring house** ("attiring house," *i.e.,* dressing room) was behind the rear of the stage. Above the alcove or booth was an **upper stage** (used, for example, in scenes of people standing on a city's walls); flanking the upper stage were windows, one of which may have served Juliet for her misnamed balcony scene. Some scholars argue that in a yet higher place were musicians, and at the very top — called the **top** — was an opening from which an actor could look; in *Henry VI, Part I,* Joan of Arc appears "on the top, thrusting out a torch burning." Most of the acting was done on the main stage (the platform), but the "inner stage," "upper stage," "windows," and "top" must have been useful occasionally (if they existed); and there is some evidence that actors occasionally vaulted off the platform stage into the audience. The **cellar** (beneath the stage) was used, for example for the voice of the ghost in *Hamlet,* and for Ophelia's grave. Though some scenery was used, the absence of a front curtain precluded many elaborate scenic effects (much, however, could be done by carrying banners) and encouraged continuous action. The stage that was a battlefield could in an instant, by the introduction of a throne, become a room in a palace. Two readable books are A. M. Nagler, *Shakespeare's Stage*, and C. Walter Hodges, *The Globe Restored*. Nagler (Ch. 12) also gives information about a second kind of Elizabethan theater — basically a platform at one end of a hall — that catered to a courtly group. Interesting specialized items on playhouses are in *Shakespeare Survey* I and XII, ed. Allardyce Nicoll.

   empathy. The projection of one's feelings into a perceived object. The Germans call it *Einfühlung* — "a feeling into." Vernon Lee, one of the formulators of the idea, claimed that when we say "the mountain rises" we do so not because the mountain rises (it doesn't) but because we have often raised our eyes, head, and total muscular structure to look at mountains or other tall objects. In perceiving a mountain, we merge (unawares) its image with the previously accumulated idea of rising. We are said to empathize with a character if we flinch at a blow directed at him, or if we feel bowed with his grief; if, in short, we *experience* as well as *see* his behavior. Empathy is often distinguished from **sympathy**: we empathize if we feel *with* the character; we sympathize if we feel *for* the character. See aesthetic distance. Consult Vernon Lee's essay in *A Modern Book of Aesthetics*, ed. Melvin Rader; Herbert S. Langfeld, *The Aesthetic Attitude*.

   epic drama. Bertolt Brecht (1898–1956) labeled "Aristotelian" most drama before his own. He held that it aimed at enthralling the spectators by building up to a climax, thus arousing and then purging their emotions. In contrast, Brecht said, epic drama (he borrowed the phrase from Erwin Piscator) aims at arousing the audience's detached thought; it teaches, keeping the spectators alert by preventing any emotional involvement. The epic drama (probably so-called because it resembles the epic in its abundance of loosely connected scenes and its tendency to deal with a society rather than merely with a few individuals) achieves this estrangement or **alienation effect** (German: *Verfremdungseffekt*) by many means: the epic play (*e.g.*, Brecht's *Puntilla*, or his *Mother Courage*) commonly consists of a series of loosely connected scenes rather than a tightly organized plot with a climax; the settings are not realistic but merely suggest the locale, and they are often changed in full view of the audience, preventing any entrancing illusion (a night scene may be done on an illuminated stage, again to prevent the audience from emotionally entering into the play); the actor may address the audience directly, sometimes in song, and he aims not at becoming the character but at presenting him, or, to put it differently, at making a comment on him, as we might do when we put aside a cigarette and say, "He said to me, '. . . .' "; loudspeakers, films, and placards may be used, and the whole is something of a lecture-demonstration, aimed not at arousing and then quieting the audience's emotions, but at making things somewhat strange to the audience so that the audience will look sharply and will think. Consult Bertolt Brecht, "A Short Organum," in *Playwrights on Playwriting*, ed. Toby Cole; John Willett, *The Theatre of Bertolt Brecht*; Ronald Gray, *Brecht*; *The Tulane Drama Review*, VI, No. 1 (September 1961).

epilogue. (1) An appendix (usually a concluding address) to a play; (2) the actor who recites such an appendix (*e.g.*, Rosalind, at the close of Shakespeare's *As You Like It*).

expressionism. An anti-naturalistic movement chiefly associated with Germany just after World War I, but which was foreshadowed by Strindberg, notably in his trilogy, *To Damascus* (1898–1904), and in his *A Dream Play* (1902). Expressionism does not seek to present reality dispassionately imitated, but reality passionately felt. Thus, when Mr. Zero shakes his employer (in Elmer Rice's *The Adding Machine* [1923]), the office spins; when he is on trial, the walls of the courtroom veer crazily. Speaking broadly, expressionist plays (in addition to being unrealistic) usually (i) depict types or classes (Rice's Mr. Zero; the Man, the Woman, the Nameless One in Ernst Toller's *Man and Masses* [1921]), (ii) employ dream sequences, often making concrete and obvious the forces working on the protagonist (in Kaufman and Connelly's *Beggar on Horseback* [1924] the young composer who is about to marry for money dreams that his bride's bouquet consists of banknotes), (iii) assume that man is responsible for his troubles, and can remake the world if he frees himself from his self-enslavement. Though Arthur Miller's *Death of a Salesman* (1949) is in many ways "realistic," it also is indebted to expressionism, especially in the scenes involving Ben. Consult Richard Samuel and R. Hinton Thomas, *Expressionism in German Life, Literature, and the Theatre*; H. F. Garten, *Modern German Drama*; John Gassner, *The Theatre in Our Times*.

exposition. See plot.

Farce. A sort of comedy based not on clever language or subtleties of character, but on broadly humorous situations (a man mistakenly enters the ladies' locker room), is lucidly defended by Eric Bentley in his introduction to *"Let's Get a Divorce" and Other Plays*, where he suggests that farce, like dreams, shows "the disguised fulfillment of repressed wishes." Farce is usually filled with surprise, with swift physical action, and with assault; character is unsubtle, being subordinated to plot. See the afterword to Thornton Wilder's *The Matchmaker*, p. 727. **Slapstick** (named for an implement made of two slats which resound when slapped against a posterior) is farce that relies on physical assault. Farce and slapstick are **low comedy**, as is comedy that depends on obscenity.

foil. A character who sets off another, as Laertes and Fortinbras — young men who, like Hamlet, have lost a father — help to set off Hamlet, or as a braggart soldier helps to set off a courageous one.

Greek and **Hellenistic theater.** The great age of the Greek drama was the fifth century B.C. The audience sat on wooden benches in tiers on a hillside, looking down at a flat circular dancing-place (the **orchestra**), in the middle of which was an altar to Dionysus; behind the dancing place was a playing-area, which logic (but no concrete evidence) suggests may have been slightly elevated; visible behind the playing-area was the **skene**, a wooden "scene-building" introduced about 458 B.C. that served as a background, as a place for actors to make entrances from and exits to, and as a dressing room. To speak of these elements in a little more detail: the seating-area, which held as many as 16,000 people, was the **theatron** ("seeing-place"); fan-shaped or horseshoe shaped, it swept around the orchestra in a segment a little greater than a semicircle. The chorus, entering by an aisle (**parodos**) at each side of the *theatron*, danced in the orchestra. The front (*i.e.*, the façade) of the *skene* (or perhaps a temporary screen) and sometimes the playing-area in front of it seem to have been called the **proskenion**. Though the *skene's* façade perhaps suggested the front of a palace, there were further efforts at indicating locale: Sophocles is said to have invented scene-painting (a painted cloth or screen in front of the *skene?*), and there are allusions to **periaktoi**, upright prisms bearing a different decoration on each side. Apparently when a new locality in the same town was to be indicated, the *periaktos* at the right was turned, when an entirely new locality was to be indicated, both *periaktoi* were turned. Other machines were the **eccyclema**, a platform that was rolled out of the *skene* to indicate a scene indoors, and the **mechane**, a crane from which a god could descend or by means of which a character could soar through the air. (See *deus ex machina*.)

It should be added that plays were put on chiefly during two holidays, the **Lenaea** (Feast of the Wine-press) in January, and the **Great** (or **Greater**, or **City**) **Dionysia** in March or April. The Lenaea was chiefly associated with comedy, the Great Dionysia with tragedy. At the latter, on each of three mornings a tragic dramatist presented three tragedies and one satyr-play. The expense was born by a *choregus*, a wealthy citizen ordered by the state to assume the financial burden. See comedy, satyr-play, tragedy.

The **Hellenistic theater** (*i.e.*, theaters of, say, the third and second centuries B.C. erected in towns to which Greek culture had been spread by Alexander's conquests) seems to have been much like the Greek theater, though now the *proskenion* is apparently more highly decorated, having pillars a few feet in front of it and being fitted with painted panels called *pinakes*. And the *skene*, now of stone rather than of wood, may have had projections at the sides (*paraskenia*) and an upper story (*episkenion*). The playing-area on this upper level is the **logeion**. Consult Margarete Bieber, *The History of the Greek and Roman Theater*.

hamartia. This Greek word is variously translated as "tragic flaw" or "error" or "shortcoming" or "weakness," and in many plays it *is* a flaw or even a vice such as *hubris* (also *hybris*) — Greek for overweening pride, arrogance, excessive confidence. But in other plays it is merely a misstep, such as a choice that turns out badly. Indeed, the tragic hero may be undone by his virtue — his courage, for example, when others are not merely prudent but cowardly. It is a serious misconception to insist that a tragic hero necessarily has a moral fault (*e.g.*, to attribute lust or rashness to Romeo and Juliet). See pp. 13–14.

High comedy. Intellectual rather than physical, it requires the close attention of a sophisticated audience, flourishing (says George Meredith in his *Essay on Comedy* [1877]) in a "society of cultivated men and women . . . wherein ideas are current, and the perceptions quick." Etherege, Wycherley, Congreve, and other playwrights of the decades following the Restoration of Charles II to the throne of England (1660) wrote **Restoration comedy,** high comedy of a particular sort, often called **comedy of manners** or **comedy of wit.** Their plays abound in witty **repartee** (what Dr. Johnson called "gay remarks and unexpected answers"), and often strike modern audiences as cynical. Example (from Congreve's *The Way of the World* [1700]): "Marriage is honorable, as you say; and if so, wherefore should cuckoldom be a discredit, being derived from so honorable a root?" The common assumption in much comedy of wit, that love, marriage, and conventional notions of romance are humbug, caused George Meredith to speak of "our so-called Comedy of Manners, or comedy of the manners of South-Sea islanders under city veneer." Recently, however, it has been seen that the Restoration dramatists were not merely flippant and without values, but were forcefully presenting a view of man as selfish, pleasure-loving, and skeptical of irrational traditions. Furthermore, in *The Way of the World*, Congreve satirizes the "affected wit" of most of his characters, and rejects the view that love is a fiction. Restoration comedy has no precise terminal date, but can be said to end about 1700, when satire came to be directed against heartless cleverness rather than against deviations from manners. Coincident with the decline of comedy of manners is the development of sentimental comedy, plays of venerable parents and middle-class dutiful sons who love pure young things. Example: Richard Steele's *The Conscious Lovers* (1722). Consult Thomas H. Fujimura, *The Restoration Comedy of Wit*; Louis Kronenberger, *The Thread of Laughter*; Norman N. Holland, *The First Modern Comedies.*

hubris. See *hamartia.*

hybris. See *hamartia.*

imitation (Greek: *mimesis*). Not a pejorative term in much criticism, for it often implies a "making" or "re-creating" or "re-presenting" of a form in a substance not natural to it. Thus Michelangelo reproduced or imitated the form of Moses, in stone. For Aristotle, tragedy is the imitation (*i.e.*, representation, re-creation) by means of words, gesture, music, and scenery, of an important action.

induction. An Elizabethan word for a prologue or introductory scene, especially one in which the characters are presented to the audience and their relationships established, or in which the theme or atmosphere of the play is quickly set forth. The beginning of *Macbeth*, showing the witches, can be considered an induction.

interlude. (1) A light entertainment, usually musical, introduced into a play, sometimes while scenery is being shifted. (2) In mid-sixteenth-century England, the word is used to describe so many sorts of short plays, from farces to moralities, that it is virtually equivalent to "play," though some scholars hold that it describes a professionally performed play, or a play (*ludus*) put on between (*inter*) halves of a banquet. Consult E. K. Chambers, *The Mediaeval Stage*, Volume II, Book IV; T. W. Craik, *The Tudor Interlude*.

irony. Irony is of several sorts. **Socratic irony,** named for Socrates, who commonly feigned more ignorance than he possessed, denotes understatement. The *eiron* (see character) is the cunning fellow who plays the underdog. **Dramatic irony,** or **Sophoclean irony,** or **tragic irony** refers to a condition of affairs which is the tragic reverse of what the participants think. Thus, it is ironic that Macbeth kills Duncan, thinking he will achieve happiness; he later finds he loses all that makes life worth living. Oedipus accuses the blind prophet of corruption, but by the end of the play Oedipus learns (as the audience knew at the outset) that he himself is corrupt, that he has been mentally blind (ignorant) and that the prophet has had vision (knowledge). Oedipus meant what he said, but his words have proved to be ironic. (Aristotle's word for reversal is *peripeteia*.) We have dramatic irony, it can be said, when a speech or action is more fully understood by the spectators than by the characters. This sort of irony, based on misunderstanding, or partial knowledge, is common in tragedy, but comedy too has its misunderstandings; comic speeches or actions are ironic if they bring about the opposite of what is intended. More generally, the contrast implied in "irony" need be neither tragic nor comic; it is "ironic" that the strong man is overthrown by the weak man and that the liar unknowingly tells the truth.

Irony of fate (a phrase which H. W. Fowler's *Modern English Usage* aptly says is hackneyed), or **cosmic irony,** denotes the view that God, or fate, or some sort of supernatural figure, is amused to manipulate human beings as a puppeteer manipulates his puppets. Thus, by an irony of fate the messenger delivers the prisoner's pardon an instant too late. Consult Garnett G. Sedgewick, *Of Irony*; Alan R. Thompson, *The Dry Mock*.

low comedy. See farce.

masque, mask, disguising. An entertainment (apparently derived from an ancient ritual) in the Renaissance court, wherein noblemen performed a dignified playlet, usually allegorical and mythological. The masque was lavishly produced, but its basic structure was generally simple: the masquers (costumed and masked noble performers) enter, supposedly having come from afar, they dance with the ladies of the court, and then they depart. Because the masquers are of the same rank as the ladies, and because performers and audience join in a dance, the masque is very close to the masked ball. Shakespeare's *Henry VIII*, I.iv, dramatizes the masque at which in fact the king met his second wife, Anne Boleyn, but Renaissance England's greatest writer of masques was Ben Jonson, who collaborated with the architect Inigo Jones. Jonson popularized what he called the **antimasque** (a grotesque dance of monsters or clowns), performed by professionals representing chaos, who are dispelled by the courtly performers. ("Anti," from "antic," meaning "a grotesque caper" or "a fool," is sometimes written "ante" because the antimasque precedes the masque.) Consult Enid Welsford, *The Court Masque*; E. K. Chambers, *The Mediaeval Stage* and *The Elizabethan Stage*.

medieval drama. Though the Christian church strongly opposed the Roman theater and suppressed theatrical performances during the Dark Ages, in the tenth century the churchmen themselves put on a playlet of a few lines as part of the Easter liturgy. A tenth-century manuscript preserves the text, which is based on Mark 16: 1–7: clerics dressed as the Three Marys approach the "tomb" of Christ (the altar) and are asked by a cleric, disguised as an angel, whom they seek. When they reply that they seek Christ, he tells them that Christ has risen and shows them the empty "tomb." This playlet — it has impersonation, dialogue, and action — is part of the service or liturgy and therefore is a **liturgical drama;** it has been entitled *Quem Quaeritis* (Whom do you seek), from its opening line. The performers were all male, and the dialogue (in Latin) was chanted or sung; probably the gestures were stylized. The *Quem Quaeritis* was later amplified (*e.g.*, the Apostles Peter and John were added, hymns were added, etc.) and detached from the liturgy. As characters were added, calling for several locales, the performance spread out over the church; here might be the booth of a man who sells ointment to the Marys, there might be a tomb, further over there might be the garden in which Mary Magdalene met the risen Christ. These settings, called **mansions** or *loca* or *sedes* or *domus* or *houses,* were all on the floor at one time, and the performers moved from one to the other, as the plot demanded. The system is called **multiple setting** or **simultaneous staging,** and it continued for centuries, even when the drama left the church. Neutral (*i.e.*, un-localized) ground was the *platea* (playing-space). By the mid-twelfth century some plays were done outside of the church, perhaps because they took too much space. In many places, however, drama continued to be performed undisturbed within the church up to the Reformation. The notable Anglo-Norman *Adam* (twelfth century) seems to have been staged outside the cathedral because the play called for demons, who could not be admitted into sacred ground. Laymen now did the acting, in the vernacular (though *Adam* contains some passages in Latin). By the mid-fourteenth century there had grown up in various communities great cycles of playlets: a **cycle** normally showed the history of existence from Lucifer's fall, through the creation and fall of man, to the Judgment Day. At York, for example, the cycle had forty-eight plays, and probably took a full day to perform; in some places the plays took several days. Various guilds (associations of merchants and craftsmen) acted in these **craft cycles,** performing plays appropriate to their trade: in some places the bakers did the Last Supper, the shipwrights Noah's Ark, the plasterers the Creation of the World. These plays of Biblical episodes and of saints' lives are commonly called **miracle plays,** or **mystery plays,** but some historians reserve "miracle plays" exclusively for plays about saints. ("Mystery" is derived ultimately from Latin *ministerium*, "office," "occupation." More immediately it comes either from *misterium*, "liturgical office," because the plays derived from part of the liturgy, or from *mysterie*, "trade," "craft," because the plays were performed by craftsmen. Cf. the modern French word, *métier*.) A play might also be called a *ludus* (Latin), a *repraesentatio* (Latin), an *auto sacramental* (Spanish), a *sacra rappresentazione* (Italian), or even a play. The plays were popular throughout the Catholic world, but they were especially splendid in France. A witness of the performances at Valenciennes in 1547 reported that angels descended from impressive heights, Lucifer wonderfully arose from a depth, water was changed into wine, and five loaves and two fish were miraculously multiplied into an abundance that was distributed among more than a thousand spectators. The Spanish *auto* had a long life; in the seventeenth century Calderón wrote them, and he had successors in the eighteenth century.

Though *Quem Quaeritis* had been performed at Easter, after plays moved outdoors they attached themselves in the fourteenth century to Corpus Christi day in June (hence such a play can also be called a **Corpus Christi play**), partly because of the favorable weather and partly to give a visible representation of the story of man's fall and redemption. In some cities the plays were given in several places; a spectator went to a convenient playing place, and waited for the first wagon (called a **pageant**) to roll up and perform the first play. Then this pageant rolled on to the next playing-place, while a second pageant rolled up and performed the second play. And so on. But even on a single wagon there might be a multiple set of, say, a pasture, a house, and a stable. These plays were at their height in the late fourteenth century; by 1500 they had seriously declined in England, though they were immensely popular on the Continent. The causes of the decline are uncertain; some scholars suggest that the guilds found the plays burdensome, some suggest that Protestantism found the plays idolatrous and stifled them, and some suggest that the rise of professional drama offered severe competition. Consult E. K. Chambers, *The Mediaeval Stage*; Grace Frank, *The Medieval French Drama*; F. M. Salter, *Medieval Drama at Chester*; Harold Gardiner, *Mysteries' End*; for a good short discussion of the drama in the church, consult Mary H. Marshall, "Aesthetic Values of the Liturgical Drama," *English Institute Essays, 1950*, pp. 89–115; for a collection of plays see *Everyman and Medieval Miracle Plays*, ed. A. C. Cawley.

The **morality play,** a later medieval development that remained popular well into the sixteenth century, was an allegorical drama on some aspect of the moral life, including such characters as Everyman, Good Deeds, and Avarice. It usually showed the conflict between good and evil, or the way in which the Christian faces death. One of its characters is commonly the **Vice,** descended either from the jester or from a combination of the Seven Deadly Sins; in any case, he is a mischief-maker who, with considerable foolery, attempts to seduce the character who represents man. Consult E. K. Chambers, *The Mediaeval Stage;* Karl J. Holzknecht, *The Backgrounds of Shakespeare's Plays;* A. P. Rossiter, *English Drama from Early Times to the Elizabethans;* for the morality play and its influence, especially on *Othello,* consult Bernard Spivack, *Shakespeare's Allegory of Evil.* There were in the Middle Ages also plays of a less literate sort than those discussed above. Doubtless in England there were secular farces, but only a few puzzling scraps remain, and in France there was the *sottie.* For a study of medieval dramatic foolery, consult Allardyce Nicoll, *Masks, Mimes and Miracles.* For a study of pageants, consult George R. Kernodle, *From Art to Theatre.*

melodrama. Originally, in Renaissance Italy, an opera; later, a drama with occasional songs, or with music (*melos* is Greek for "song") expressing a character's thoughts, much as in films today. In the early nineteenth century plays with musical accompaniment became so stereotyped that the word acquired a second (and now dominant) meaning: a play wherein characters clearly virtuous or vicious are pitted against each other in sensational situations filled with suspense, until justice triumphs. The situations, not the characters, are exciting. The exotic horror (castles with dungeons) dominant in early nineteenth-century melodramas was often replaced later in the century by local horror (the cruel landlord), but whether exotic or local, melodrama is improbable, and virtue — unsullied by any touch of guilt — triumphs over unlikely circumstances. Melodrama is sometimes said to be tragedy with character left out (*i.e.,* it contains serious happenings), but by virtue of its happy ending and its one-sided characters it can better be described as comedy with good-nature left out. Some critics use "melodrama" without any pejorative connotation to describe such serious, often sensational, plays as Emlyn Williams' *Night Must Fall* (1935), Robert Ardrey's *Thunder Rock* (1939), and Arthur Miller's *All My Sons* (1947).

motivation. Grounds in character and situation that make behavior plausible. Such grounds are not always present, even in great drama: when Othello asks why Iago "hath thus ensnared my soul," Iago replies, "Demand me nothing: what you know, you know." See character. Consult J. I. M. Stewart, *Character and Motive in Shakespeare.*

myth. Defined by Mark Schorer (in his *William Blake*) as "a large, controlling image that gives philosophical meaning to the facts of ordinary life. . . . All real convictions involve a mythology. . . . Wars may be described as the clash of mythologies." A myth, then, in the broadest usage is any idea, true or false, to which people subscribe. Thus, one can speak of the "myth" of democracy or of totalitarianism. Because the myths that were sacred truths for pagans were falsehoods for Christians, "myth" sometimes means any imaginary person, place, thing, or idea, such as the myth that the majority is necessarily right. A myth has sometimes been defined as a narrative, usually anonymous, of the origins of life and/or of the deeds (present or future) of supra-mortal creatures, often explaining the whys and wherefores of natural phenomena. For example, a Zulu myth explains that rain is the tears of the rain-god weeping for a beloved slain bird. Myths in the sense of primitive legends about gods, heroes, external nature, etc., have often been regarded by modern men as mere fantasies and legends, or as primitive explanations of natural phenomena, inferior to the explanations supplied by reason and experiment. But in recent years myth has been increasingly dignified, partly because Freud and Jung regarded it as akin to dreams — that is, as a "language" which, properly understood, tells us things otherwise unrevealed. Eric Fromm (see below) says that myths and dreams are "a language in which inner experiences feelings and thoughts are expressed as if they were sensory experiences, events in the outer world."

Because most Greek tragedies were based on the traditional legends of gods and godlike men, it is often said that the Greek audience knew the happenings in the play and concentrated on seeing how the dramatist would handle this familiar material. But Aristotle says that in fact the stories were not known to many. In the present century, French dramatists have displayed a marked tendency to re-interpret the Greek myths (*e.g.*, Cocteau's *The Infernal Machine*, on the Oedipus legend; Sartre's *The Flies*, on the Orestes legend; Gide's *Theseus*). In Germany, Hofmannsthal wrote a notable *Electra*, and in America O'Neill reused the Orestes legend in his *Mourning Becomes Electra*. Consult H. J. Rose, *A Handbook of Greek Mythology*; Eric Fromm, *The Forgotten Language*; Gilbert Highet, *The Classical Tradition*, Ch. 23; Francis Fergusson, *The Idea of a Theater*, Ch. 1.

naturalism. Sometimes defined, like realism, as the portrayal of "a scientifically accurate, detached picture of life, including everything and selecting nothing." The spectator looking through the peephole of the proscenium, as a scientist looks through the eyepiece of a microscope, is to feel he is witnessing life rather than a symbolic representation of life. More commonly, however, "naturalism" alludes neither to a panoramic view nor to the detailed presentation of a narrow **slice of life** (French: *tranche de vie*), but to a particular attitude held by some writers since the middle of the nineteenth century. Though claiming to be dispassionate observers, they were influenced by evolutionary thought, and regarded man not as possessed of a soul and of free will, but as a creature determined by his heredity and environment. The movement in drama can be said to begin with the Goncourt Brothers' unsuccessful *Henriette Maréchal* (1865), but it is usual to say that the opening gun in the battle for naturalism was fired in Émile Zola's dramatization (1873) of his novel, *Thérèse Raquin.* Thérèse and her lover drown her husband, but are then so guilt-ridden that they poison themselves. In his preface Zola urged that the theater be brought "into closer relation with the great movement toward truth and experimental science which has since the last century been on the increase. . . . I have chosen characters who were completely dominated by their nerves and blood." In Paris, André Antoine opened his Thêâtre Libre in 1887, devoting it mostly to plays showing the power of instincts and the influence of heredity and environment. These plays were staged as untheatrically as possible; for example, the actors turned their backs to the audience. In Germany, Otto Brahm opened the Freie Bühne in 1889, and in England J. T. Grein opened the Independent Theatre in 1891, both with Ibsen's *Ghosts* (1881), a play showing the destruction of a young man by inherited syphilis. Ibsen's greatness does not allow him to be pinned down by the label "naturalist," but he can be said to be naturalistic (among other things) by virtue of his serious interest in the effects of heredity and environment. Other dramatists who wrote naturalistic plays include August Strindberg (*e.g.*, his *Miss Julie* [1888]) and Gerhart Hauptmann (early in his career, say, through *The Weavers* [1892]), and Eugene O'Neill (again, the early plays such as *The Rope* [1918] and *Diff'rent* [1920]). Note, however, that the major naturalistic writers usually are more than naturalistic; Strindberg's *Miss Julie*, for example, has a preface that talks about the influence of heredity and environment, and it deals with sordid aspects of reality, but it also has symbolic overtones, notably in Julie's and Jean's dreams. Consult Mordecai Gorelik, *New Theatres for Old*; and (for Strindberg, O'Neill, and the sources of their ideas) Oscar Cargill, *Intellectual America*.

obligatory scene. See *scène à faire*.

pathos. The quality that evokes pity. The pathetic is often distinguished from the tragic; in the former, the suffering is experienced by the passive and the innocent (especially women and children), while in the latter it is experienced by persons who act, struggle, and are in some measure responsible for their sufferings. Discussing Aeschylus' *The Suppliants*, H. D. F. Kitto says in *Greek Tragedy* (2nd ed.): "The Suppliants are not only pathetic, as the victims of outrage, but also tragic, as the victims of their own misconceptions." See bourgeois drama, and the afterword to Tennessee Williams' *A Streetcar Named Desire*, pp. 364–365.

peripeteia (anglicized to **peripety,** meaning **reversal**). The reversal occurs when an action produces the opposite of what was intended or expected, and it is therefore a kind of irony. In *Oedipus the King*, the messenger from Corinth tries to cheer up Oedipus, but the words have the reverse effect, and terrify Oedipus. In *Macbeth*, Macbeth kills Duncan to gain happiness, but his deed brings the reverse, unhappiness. (See irony, plot.)

pièce à thèse. A play with a thesis, a play in which the dramatist argues a point. Commonly the thesis is not about, say, the benevolence of God, but about the merits or defects of some social institution; a play dealing with a social institution may also be called a **problem play** or a **drama of ideas.** Some critics distinguish between the terms, saying that a problem play merely poses a social problem, as Galsworthy does in *Strife* (1909), while a thesis play propounds a solution. Shaw says that "The material of the dramatist is always some conflict of human feeling with circumstances"; when the circumstances are "human institutions" (*e.g.*, divorce laws, penal codes) rather than unchanging facts of life (*e.g.*, death), and the audience is forced to meditate on the value of the institutions, we have a problem play. Shaw's essay, "The Play of Ideas," is in *Shaw on Theatre*, ed. E. J. West. Consult also Walter Kerr, *How Not to Write a Play*, Ch. 5.

pièce bien faite, or **well-made play.** A play, with much suspense and with little depth of characterization, that relies on a cleverly constructed plot, first developing a situation, then building the crisis to a climax, and then resolving the business. The type, which perhaps can be described as melodrama with the fisticuffs left out, is chiefly associated with Victorien Sardou (1831–1908), but Sardou was indebted to Eugène Scribe (1791–1861). Shaw called their plays clockwork mice, and Sardoodledom, but the influence of Sardou on Shaw's hero, Ibsen, is undeniable. See plot, and consult Walter Kerr, *How Not to Write a Play*, Ch. 10; Eric Bentley, "Homage to Scribe," *What is Theatre?*; C. E. Montague, *Dramatic Values*, pp. 63–74; *Camille and Other Plays*, ed. Stephen S. Stanton.

plot and **character.** The plot is sometimes the "story," the "narrative," but usually it is the happenings *as the author arranges them.* In *Hamlet*, for example, the story involves the poisoning of Hamlet's father, but Shakespeare omits this scene from his plot. Aristotle, in Chapter 6 of the *Poetics*, calls plot "the whole structure of the incidents," and he speaks of plot as the "soul of tragedy," thus making it more important than character. By character he means the personalities of the figures in the story. For Aristotle, the aspects of personality (whether a warrior is brave or cowardly, gentle or harsh, etc.) arise out of the action the writer has in mind. Menander (a Greek comic dramatist) is said to have told a friend that he had finished a comedy, though he had not yet written a line of dialogue; the anecdote implies that Menander had completed his idea of *what happens* (action) and in *what order* (plot), and he would find it easy then to write the lines of the characters necessary to this plot. The separation, however, between plot and character is misleading, for the two usually interplay. Although it is true that there may be much plot and little character (as in a thriller), in most great plays there is such a fusion between what is done and the personality of the doer that we feel the truth of Henry James's questions: "What is character but the determination of incident? What is incident but the illustration of character?" (See also character.)

Most plots entail a **conflict,** wherein the protagonist is somehow opposed. If he is opposed chiefly by another person rather than by a force such as Fate or God or by an aspect of himself, the opposing figure is the antagonist. The German critic, Gustav Freytag, in *Technique of the Drama* (1863), held that a play dramatizes "the rushing forth of will power from the depths of man's soul toward the external world," and "the coming into being of a deed and its consequences on the human soul." The five-act play, he said, commonly arranged such an action into a **pyramidal structure,** consisting of a **rising action,** a **climax,** and a **falling action.** The rising action begins with the **exposition,** in which is given essential information, especially about the **antecedent action** (what has occurred before this piece of action begins). The two gossiping servants who tell each other that after a year away in Paris the young master is coming home today with his new wife are giving the audience the exposition. The exposition in Shakespeare's *The Tempest* is almost ruthlessly direct: Prospero tells his naïve daughter "I should inform thee farther," and for about one hundred and fifty lines he proceeds to tell her why she is on an almost uninhabited island. The action rises through a **complication** (the protagonist is opposed) to a high point or **crisis** or **climax** (a moment at which tension is high, and which is a decisive turning point). The falling action goes through a **reversal** (if a tragedy, the protagonist loses power), and then into a **catastrophe,** also called a **denouement** (unknotting) or resolution. (Aristotle's word for the reversal is *peripeteia,* anglicized to **peripety,** and translated as "irony of events," would in a comedy be a change from bad fortune to good, and the catastrophe would thus be happy.) The denouement frequently involves what Aristotle called an *anagnorisis* (**recognition, disclosure, discovery**). This recognition may be as simple as the identification of a long-lost brother by a birth mark, or it may involve a character's recognition of his own true condition. Shakespeare sometimes used a pyramidal structure, placing his climax neatly in the middle of what seems to us to be the third of five acts. In *Julius Caesar,* Brutus rises in the first half of the play, reaching his height in III. i, with the death of Caesar; but later in this scene he gives Marc Antony permission to speak at Caesar's funeral and thus sets in motion his own fall, which occupies the second half of the play. In *Macbeth,* the protagonist attains his height in III. i. ("Thou hast it now: King"), but he soon perceives that he is going downhill:

> I am in blood
> Stepped in so far that, should I wade no more,
> Returning were as tedious as go o'er.

Some works have a **double plot,** that is, two plots, usually with some sort of relation. For example, the **subplot** or **underplot** (the secondary narrative) might be a grotesque version of the serious main plot. In Shakespeare's *The Tempest,* the main plot and subplot both deal with usurpation. In *King Lear,* the main plot concerns Lear's relation to his daughters, while the parallel subplot concerns Gloucester's relation to his sons. For another aspect of the subplot, see comic relief; consult William Empson, *Some Versions of Pastoral,* Ch. 2. On plotting see *pièce bien faite* and *scène à faire;* consult John H. Lawson, *Theory and Technique of Playwriting.*

poetic justice. A term coined by Thomas Rymer in 1678, denoting the reward of the virtuous and the punishment of the vicious. Aristotle had said or implied that the tragic hero is undone partly by some sort of personal flaw — *i.e.,* he is at least partly responsible for the suffering he later encounters. (See *hamartia,* and pp. xvii–xviii.) "Poetic justice," with its idea that all characters reap the harvest of their just deserts, is a hardening of Aristotle's suggestion. Consult Alfred Harbage, "Justice in Comic Fable," in his *As They Liked It;* M. A. Quinlan, *Poetic Justice in the Drama.*

problem play. See *pièce à thèse.*

prologue. (1) A preface or introduction. For the Greeks the *prologos* was the first scene, which gave the exposition. Elizabethan prologues commonly summarize the plot, as the Chorus does in this prologue to *Romeo and Juliet:*

> Two households, both alike in dignity,
> In fair Verona, where we lay our scene,
> From ancient grudge break to new mutiny,
> Where civil blood makes civil hands unclean.
> From forth the fatal loins of these two foes
> A pair of star-crossed lovers take their life. . . .

But in the English theater of the late seventeenth century, the prologue was almost an independent verse essay spoken before the play began. Consult Autrey N. Wiley, *Rare Prologues and Epilogues 1642–1700.* (2) The actor who speaks a piece of the sort described above.

proscenium stage, or **picture-frame stage.** A playing-area framed in the front, and thus separated from the audience. This frame is the **proscenium arch** or the **proscenium;** the empty space it contains, sometimes filled with a curtain, is the **proscenium opening.** Basically a **proscenium theater** has two rooms, one for the audience and another (with a hole in the mutual wall) for the performers. Such a theater is at least as old as the early seventeenth century, when the Farnese Theater was built in Parma. Consult Allardyce Nicoll, *The Development of the Theatre.*

protagonist. The chief figure in a play. In Greek the word means literally the "first contender," *i.e.,* the chief actor (*protos:* first). The second role was given to the **deuteragonist,** the third to the **tritagonist.** The protagonist is commonly opposed by the **antagonist,** played by the deuteragonist. For the relationship between the protagonist and the antagonist, see plot.

realism. The reproduction of life, especially as it appears to the eye and ear; the illusion of nature. Usually it deals with ordinary men in ordinary situations, moving in scenery that closely imitates reality. In England, T. W. Robertson (1829–1871) insisted, for example, that doorknobs not be painted on the doors but be three-dimensional. Wings and a backcloth (*i.e.*, projecting flats at the sides and a painted cloth at the rear) were increasingly replaced by the box set (a room with the front wall missing, containing real furniture) for interior scenes. Gas lighting, introduced to the stage about 1820, soon became capable of producing effects of sunlight, moonlight, etc. The dialogue, as well as the sets, came closer to what the senses perceive. Realistic plays (in prose, of course) avoided soliloquies, asides, and declamation. The great playwrights of the movement are Ibsen and Chekhov, but W. Somerset Maugham has somewhat impatiently described the little world in which Ibsen's figures move: "It is not a gross exaggeration to say that his only gambit is the sudden arrival of a stranger who comes into a stuffy room and opens the windows; whereupon the people who were sitting there catch their death of cold and everything ends unhappily." That realism shades into naturalism is clear; that in Ibsen it shades into symbolism is less obvious but is well demonstrated by John Northam, *Ibsen's Dramatic Method*. A simple example of Ibsen's symbolism: in *Hedda Gabler*, Hedda's hair is "not particularly ample," but Thea's is "unusually rich and wavy," suggesting Hedda's barrenness and Thea's fertility. Consult Mordecai Gorelik, *New Theatres for Old*; A. Nicholas Vardac, *Stage to Screen*, Chs. 4, 9; Ernest B. Watson, *Sheridan to Robertson*. In **selective realism,** some of the scenery (*e.g.*, a window and a door) closely reproduces reality, but some (*e.g.*, a framework *suggesting* a roof) does not.

ritual. A ceremonial act, an observance or customary procedure, especially by worshipers. Primitive people perform ritual dances to induce rain, to drive out sickness, etc. Rituals, that is, often attempt to order seemingly chaotic experiences. We have rituals at most critical moments — birth, commencement, marriage, death — marking the importance of these moments and sometimes (as in some prayers for the dead) to induce a desired effect. Much literature seems to have originated in ritual — Greek tragedy, for example. The precise ritual behind it is uncertain, but it is perhaps descended from some ritual imitating growth and death, or mutability. A common theory holds that it imitates the decline of a vegetation god from spring to winter; the potent tragic hero moves from power to weakness, allegedly a remote descendant of rituals imitating the Year-Spirit who annually died. A ritual inducing the rebirth of the Year-Spirit (spring comes again) is often said to be behind the ancient comic pattern, which moves from threats to joyous feasts and marriages (*i.e.*, to fertility). Consult Jane E. Harrison, *Ancient Art and Ritual*; Herbert Weisinger, *Tragedy and the*

Paradox of the Fortunate Fall; Francis Fergusson, *The Idea of a Theater*.

Roman theater. A permanent theater was not built at Rome until the first century B.C. The plays of Plautus (254?–184 B.C.) and Terence (190?–159? B.C.) were performed on temporary stages erected in the Circus Maximus and the Forum during holidays. In the permanent Roman theater, the enormous audience (40,000 or more) sat in a semicircle around a level space that was a vestige of what had been called the "orchestra" ("dancing place") of the Greek theater. Behind this vestige was the stage, running through what would have been the diameter of the circle. The long, slightly elevated stage was backed by a façade (painted to resemble two or three houses) with several doors through which actors made some of their exits and entrances, the others being made at the ends of the stage. Behind the façade was the dressing-room. The Roman theater, unlike the Greek and Hellenistic theaters, was a self-enclosed structure, built on level ground, not against a hillside. Consult Margarete Bieber, *The History of the Greek and Roman Theater*.

satire. A work ridiculing aspects of human behavior and seeking to arouse in the audience contempt for its object. Satirists almost always justify their attacks by claiming that satire is therapeutic. Shaw says, in the preface to his *Complete Plays*, "If I make you laugh at yourself, remember that my business as a classic writer of comedies is to 'chasten morals with ridicule'; and if I sometimes make you feel like a fool, remember that I have by the same action cured your folly." Satire, however, is sometimes distinguished from comedy on the grounds that satire aims to correct by ridiculing, while comedy aims simply to evoke amusement. Among notable satires (in addition to those discussed under burlesque) are the plays of Aristophanes; Gay's *The Beggar's Opera* (1728); Brecht's *The Three-Penny Opera* (1928); Kaufman, Ryskind, and Gershwin's *Of Thee I Sing* (1931) — though Kaufman himself has defined satire as "that which closes on Saturday night." See burlesque, comedy. Consult Dane F. Smith, *Plays about the Theatre in England from "The Rehearsal" in 1671 to the Licensing Act in 1737*; Northrop Frye, *Anatomy of Criticism*.

satyr-play. A piece in which there is a chorus of lewd satyrs (creatures half-man, the other half either horse or goat). The Greek tragic playwright of the fifth century B.C. presented three tragedies and a satyr-play for the dramatic festival. Apparently the satyr-play often burlesqued a hero, showing him in a ludicrous situation. Only one complete satyr-play (Euripides' *The Cyclops*) is extant; it travesties the legend of Odysseus' encounter with Polyphemus. Consult Philip W. Harsh, *A Handbook of Classical Drama*.

scene. See act.

scenery. The carpentry and painted cloths (and projected images) used on a stage. Scenery may be used to conceal parts of the stage, to decorate, to imitate or suggest locales, to establish time or to evoke mood. For comments on early scenery, see Greek theater, medieval drama, and Elizabethan playhouse. The Elizabethan public theater did not use much scenery. In *Twelfth Night*, when Viola asks "What country, friends, is this?" she is told "This is Illyria, lady," and the audience knows all that carpenters and painters can tell them. But even before Shakespeare's birth, Renaissance Italians had placed buildings, probably of lath and cloth, at the right and left of the stage. Behind the buildings, which were three-dimensional and were embellished with moldings, projected flat pieces cut and painted to look like other buildings at a distance, and behind these flat pieces were yet other flats, still smaller. By means of such a **perspective set,** the spectator seemed to be looking into a street or a square. A performer might enter a door in either of the houses at the front, but he could not, of course, go toward the rear of the stage lest he suddenly appear gigantic. (On the perspective sets designed by Sebastiano Serlio [1475–1554], consult E. K. Chambers, *The Elizabethan Stage*, III, 10–11, IV, 353–365; Allardyce Nicoll, *The Development of the Theatre*, Ch. 4; George R. Kernodle, *From Art to Theatre*, Ch. 6.

scène à faire, or (in William Archer's translation of Francisque Sarcey's term) **obligatory scene.** "An obligatory scene [Archer says] is one which the audience (more or less clearly and consciously) foresees and desires, and the absence of which it may with reason resent." For example, a familiar legend may make a scene obligatory, or a dramatist may cause the audience to expect a certain scene. In *Hamlet* the play-within-the-play (III.ii) has been called such a scene: Hamlet has doubted the ghost, and we must see the ghost's words verified. Consult William Archer, *Play-making*.

Senecan tragedy. Any of the serious plays by the Roman author Seneca (4 B.C.–65 A.D.), or imitations of them. Of the ten extant Roman tragedies, nine are attributed to Seneca, and these were probably written not for the stage but for private readings. The heroes seem to us to be almost madmen, but perhaps they are to be regarded sympathetically as people overwhelmed by passion. Seneca's influence on the Elizabethan dramatists was considerable; the **revenge play,** with its ghosts and its deranged hero who seeks vengeance, doubtless would have been different had Seneca not existed. Among the signs of Seneca's influence are: ghosts, revenge, deeds of horror (*e.g.*, children stewed and served to their parents), occasional stoical speeches but a predominance of passionate speeches, use of stichomythia (see dialogue), a *nuntius* (messenger) who recites in a heightened style an off-stage happening (*e.g.*, the wounded soldier in *Macbeth*, I.i.). But, of course, not every use of any of these characteristics is necessarily attributable to Seneca's influence. And there are differences: *e.g.*, the horrors in Seneca are narrated, but in *King Lear* Gloucester is blinded on the stage. Consult F. L. Lucas, *Seneca and Elizabethan Tragedy*; Madeleine Doran, *Endeavors of Art*; Willard Farnham, *The Medieval Heritage of Elizabethan Tragedy*; Fredson Bowers, *Elizabethan Re-*

venge Tragedy 1587–1642. Howard Baker, *Induction to Tragedy*, minimizes Seneca's influence.

sentimental. Generally a pejorative word in literary criticism, indicating a superabundance of tender emotion, a disproportionate amount of sentiment (feeling). It is sentimental to be intensely distressed because one has stepped on a flower. A character, say Hamlet, may display deep emotions, but they are sentimental only if they are in excess of what the situation warrants. More specifically, "sentimental" writing refers to writing wherein evil is facilely conquered, denied, overlooked, or bathed in a glow of forgiving tenderness. In the eighteenth century the ability to respond emotionally (usually tearfully) to acts of benevolence or malevolence was called **sensibility.** In its **sentimental drama** there is at the expense of reason an emphasis on tearful situations; man's benevolent emotions are overestimated, for he is assumed to be innately good, and villains reform, usually in bursts of repenting tears. There is little wit, the characters are usually of the middle class, and they demonstrate their virtue by weeping at the sight of distress. In his "Comparison between Sentimental and Laughing Comedy" (1772), Oliver Goldsmith attacked sentimental comedy, saying that in it:

> "the virtues of private life are exhibited, rather than the vices exposed; and the distresses rather than the faults of mankind make our interest in the piece. . . . Almost all the characters are good, . . . and though they want humor, have abundance of sentiment and feeling. If they happen to have faults or foibles, the spectator is taught, not only to pardon, but to applaud them, in consideration of the goodness of their hearts; so that folly, instead of being ridiculed, is commended, and the comedy aims at touching our passions, without the power of being truly pathetic."

See bourgeois drama. Consult Ernest Bernbaum, *The Drama of Sensibility*; Arthur Sherbo, *English Sentimental Drama*.

slice of life. See naturalism.

sock and **buskin.** Performers of Latin comedy wore a light slipper or sandal called the *soccus*. The sock is either this piece of footwear or comedy itself. In "L'Allegro" Milton says:

> Then to the well-trod stage anon,
> If Jonson's learned sock be on.

The high boot worn by Greek tragic actors was the **cothurnus** or *kothurnus.* In Hellenistic times it acquired a very thick sole, giving the performer the height appropriate to a great man. In English this footgear (or tragic drama in general) is called the **buskin,** apparently from Old French *broissequin*, from Middle Dutch *brosekin*, a small leather boot. Consult Margarete Bieber, *The History of the Greek and Roman Theater.*

soliloquy. A speech wherein a character utters his thoughts aloud while alone. An **aside** is a speech wherein a character expresses his thoughts in words audible to the spectators but supposedly unheard by the other stage characters present. Both were important conventions in Elizabethan drama and, later, in melodrama, but the late nineteenth century sought so vigorously to present on the stage the illusion of real life that both techniques were banished. They have, however, been revived in the twentieth century, *e.g.*, in Eugene O'Neill's *Strange Interlude*, where the asides represent the characters' thoughts and unspoken desires. In **direct address**, a character turns from the world on the stage and speaks directly to the audience, telling it, for instance to watch closely. Because the character thus seems to leave the play, direct address is sometimes (unfortunately) called **extra-dramatic speech**. Consult Una Ellis-Fermor, *The Frontiers of Drama*, Ch. 6; George E. Duckworth, *The Nature of Roman Comedy*; Max Beerbohm, "Soliloquies in Drama," *Around Theatres*. The soliloquy, the aside, and direct address are all monologues, but more often a **monologue** is either a long speech delivered by one character, which may be heard but not interrupted by others in his presence, or a performance by a single actor.

sound effect. An imitative noise, usually produced by simple machinery. Though a sound effect may be a mere imitation of nature, it may also be a richly symbolic suggestion. Chekhov's *The Cherry Orchard* (1904) concludes: "A sound is heard that seems to come from the sky, like a breaking harp-string, dying away mournfully. All is still again, and there is heard nothing but the strokes of the axe far away in the orchard." Consult Frank Napier, *Noises Off*.

spectacle. The last of Aristotle's six elements of drama, spectacle denotes what appeals to the eye, *e.g.*, costume and scenery. Greek drama was splendidly costumed and made some use of scenery. Aeschylus especially seems to have contrived moments that caught the eye, such as Agamemnon's entrance in a chariot. The Elizabethan stage, though sparse in scenery, apparently was architecturally impressive, and doubtless military scenes were embellished with waving banners. In the Restoration, spectacle sometimes got the upper hand. Alexander Pope complained:

> The play stands still; damn action and discourse,
> Back fly the scenes, and enter foot and horse;
> Pageants on pageants, in long order drawn,
> Peers, heralds, bishops, ermine, gold, and lawn.

In the nineteenth century the development of gas light and then electric light made possible elaborate sunrises and twilights, and at the end of the century (especially in Russia) there was an emphasis on ensemble acting which gave a tableau-effect. Pictorial effects in late-nineteenth-century productions of Shakespeare were often achieved at the cost of Shakespeare's lines. At the very end of the century William Poel rejected spectacle and helped establish a trend to stage Shakespeare in what was thought to be an Elizabethan manner: an uncluttered stage, allowing the action to proceed rapidly. Consult James Laver, *Drama*; A. Nicholas Vardac, *Stage to Screen*, Chs. 3–4.

stage business. Minor physical action — including posture and facial expression — by a performer. Business ranges from head-scratching to an addition Henry Irving made to *The Merchant of Venice*, II.vi: in Shakespeare's scene, Jessica and Lorenzo elope and the scene ends quietly; Irving added business in which Shylock entered, and knocked on the door of his empty house while the curtain fell. His successors amplified this business; Shylock entered the house, cried out, and re-appeared, etc. Consult Arthur C. Sprague, *Shakespeare and the Actors*.

style. The mode of expression. Newman, talking of the writer's style, called it "a thinking out into language." This idea of "a thinking out" (but not into language) is applicable also to the style of the scene designer, the costume designer, etc. Kenneth Tynan in *Curtains* defines good style as "a happy consonance of manner with matter, of means with end, of tools with job." To **stylize** a play commonly means to present it with a noticeable artful manner rather than to present it realistically, though in fact realism itself is a style. A **stylized production** usually is presentational or anti-illusionistic rather than representational (see dramatic illusion). Consult George R. Kernodle, "Style, Stylization, and Styles of Acting," *Educational Theatre Journal*, XII (1960), 251–261.

surrealism. A literary movement, especially vigorous in France in the 1920's and 1930's, that insisted that reality is grasped by the un-conscious, the irrational, rather than by the conscious. The best art, it is held, is the dream. Among the forerunners were Alfred Jarry, whose *Ubu Roi* (1896) combined grotesque farce with anti-bourgeois satire, August Strindberg, whose *To Damascus* (three parts, 1898–1904) and *The Dream Play* (1902) had presented dream-like worlds, and Guil-laume Apollinaire, whose *Breasts of Tiresias* (1917) was called a *"drame surréaliste"* (the first use of the word) by the author. Perhaps the chief surrealist dramatist is Jean Cocteau, notably in his *Orpheus* (1926), in which a glazier is an angel and a horse dictates prophetic words. Consult Georges E. Lemaître, *From Cubism to Surrealism in French Literature*.

suspense. Uncertainty, often characterized by anxiety. Suspense is usually a curious mixture of pain and pleasure, as Gwendolen, in Oscar Wilde's *The Importance of Being Earnest*, implies: "This suspense is terrible. I hope it will last." Most great art relies more heavily on sus-pense than on **surprise** (the unexpected). One can rarely sit twice through a play depending on surprise; the surprise gone, the interest is gone. Suspense is usually achieved in part by **foreshadowing** — hints of what is to come. Dumas *fils* put it this way: "The art of the theater is the art of preparations." Coleridge, who held that Shakespeare gives us not surprise but expectation and then the satisfaction of perfect knowledge, once wrote: "As the feeling with which we startle at a shooting star, compared with that of watching the sunrise at the pre-established moment, such and so low is surprise compared with expecta-tion." Thus, in *Hamlet*, the ghost does not pop up surprisingly, but satisfies the eager expectations that have been aroused by references to "this thing," "this dreaded sight," and "this apparition." Often, in fact, Shakespeare — like the Greek dramatists — used traditional stories; the audience presumably was not surprised by the deaths of Caesar and Brutus, and it enjoyed the suspense of anticipating them. Suspense is thus related to tragic irony. The tragic character moves closer and closer to his doom, and though he may be surprised by it, we are not; we are held by suspense. If, in fact, he is suddenly and unexpectedly saved (as is a hero of a melodrama), we may feel cheated. On surprise, consult David L. Grossvogel, *The Self-Conscious Stage in Modern French Drama* (reprinted in paperback as *Twentieth-Century French Drama*).

symbolism. Derived from Greek *symballein*, "to throw together," which thus suggests the essential quality of symbolism, the drawing together of two worlds; it presents the concrete material world of roses, toads, caves, stars, etc., and through them reveals an otherwise invisible world. As a noun, the original Greek word denoted half of something broken in two, and thus the word suggests not something that stands for something else, but something that is part of a larger unit.

Symbolism is often distinguished from allegory. Where the allegorist commonly invents a world (the author of *Everyman* [c. 1500] invents a figure called Everyman, who seeks aid from figures called Goods, Kindred, etc.) in order to talk about the real world, the symbolist commonly presents the phenomena of what we usually call the real world in order to reveal a "higher," eternal world of which the symbol is a part. The allegorist is free to invent any number of imaginary worlds to talk about the real world, but the symbolist feels that there is only one way by which he can present the "higher" real world he envisions. The everyday world is often considered by symbolists as a concrete but transient version of a more important realm, and the symbolist who presents, say, a rose, is (he might hold) speaking about a rose and also about the eternal beauty of womanhood in the only possible way. The allegorist, who can invent half a dozen ways of embodying his idea, does not insist on the reality of his invented world. An allegory can with relative ease be paraphrased; but a symbol, because it not only stands for something else which cannot otherwise be expressed, but also is *part of something else and is itself too*, cannot be clearly explained. As Carlyle says in *Sartor Resartus*, in a symbol "the Infinite is made to blend itself with the Finite, to stand visible, and as it were, attainable there." The symbol (which may be a situation, character, setting — *e.g.*, birth, an infant, a manger) is given unusual stress, perhaps by repetition within the play, or from one of the author's plays to another, and so it is highly potent, richly suggestive.

In the second half of the nineteenth century there arose in France the so-called **Symbolist Movement,** but it must be emphasized that symbolism of a sort is probably as old as literature. An author's insistence on some object may cause us to regard it as more than its apparent nature. For example, the forest or greenwood in *As You Like It* suggests a benevolent nature that restores man to his best part. But on the whole Shakespeare's plays do not leave the world of sensible reality. The plays of the Symbolists do. The Symbolic writer presents a world that seems to be a dream world, a world that is not the usual world enriched, but a new world. In his preface to *The Dream Play* (1902), Strindberg says he "has tried to imitate the disconnected but seemingly logical form of the dream. Anything may happen. . . . The characters split, double, multiply, vanish, solidify, blur, clarify." See surrealism.

The best naturalists (Ibsen, Chekhov, Strindberg, and Hauptmann) at times wrote symbolic works, but the chief Symbolic dramatists are the French (if we include the Belgian Maurice Maeterlinck) and William Butler Yeats. In Maeterlinck's *The Intruder* (1890) a blind old man sees with his soul the approach of Death. In *The Blind* (1890) a group of blind men are lost in a forest; their leader was a priest, but he has died. Maeterlinck occasionally said some of his plays were for marionettes, and though his statement is sometimes held to be a mildly self-deprecating joke, in fact there is much in the plays that belongs to the realm of impassive, other-worldly dolls, not surprising in the work of a writer who said he wished to study "man . . . in the presence of eternity and mystery." Paul Claudel's *Tidings Brought to Mary* (written in 1892, revised in 1899 and 1912) was acted in 1912. Claudel, who said he had gained from Arthur Rimbaud (one of the leading Symbolists) "an almost physical impression of the supernatural," in this play envelops his medieval characters in a divine world, and dramatizes salvation. In Ireland, Yeats, who compared an artistic work to a magic talisman ("it entangles . . . a part of the Divine essence") wrote verse plays of Irish supernatural creatures and heroes. In *On Baile's Strand* (1903), for instance, Cuchulain, the protagonist, is said to have been sired by a hawk. The bird imagery is insisted on; Cuchulain's associates are chicks and nestlings, and the Fool (who represents Cuchulain on another level) is delighted with feathers. Near the conclusion of the play, Cuchulain rushes out to fight the waves, literally doing what Hamlet spoke metaphorically of doing.

In Russia, Meyerhold in 1906 staged Ibsen's *Hedda Gabler* (1890) as symbolically as possible, turning what had been a naturalistic play into a vision suggestive of another world, something (in the words of a hostile critic) "halfway between metaphysics and ballet." (Consult Nikolai Gorchakov, *The Theater in Soviet Russia.*) For symbolism in the sense of richly suggestive images, consult Alan S. Downer, "The Life of Our Design: the Function of Imagery in the Poetic Drama," *The Hudson Review*, II (Summer 1949), 242–260. On the Symbolist Movement, consult William Butler Yeats, *Essays and Introductions;* Arthur Symons, *The Symbolist Movement in Literature; Yale French Studies*, No. 9; Eric Bentley, *The Playwright as Thinker;* John Gassner, *Form and Idea in the Modern Theatre.*

tragedy. For Aristotle, tragedy was a dramatic imitation (representation) of an "action of high importance." A Greek tragedy was serious, but it did not necessarily end unhappily. Aeschylus' *Eumenides,* for example, ends on a note of solemn joy. For us a tragedy is generally a play that faces evil, depicts suffering, and ends with death or (especially in the naturalistic tragedies since the latter part of the nineteenth century) ends with the hero alive but spiritually crushed. Tragedy's essence, Alfred North Whitehead says (*Science and the Modern World,* Ch. 1), resides not in unhappiness but "in the solemnity of the remorseless working of things." H. D. F. Kitto says (*The Greeks,* Ch. 4) that Greek tragedy — and perhaps one might add the great tragedy of other countries — was in part the product of intellectualism and humanism. Intellectualism let the Greeks see that human life must be lived within a great framework of what might be called the will of the gods, or Necessity: "Actions must have their consequences; ill-judged actions must have uncomfortable results." Humanism denied the Greeks an easy view of a heavenly life, and gave them an "almost fierce joy in life, the exultation in human achievement and in human personality." The tragic note, Kitto suggests, is produced by a tension between this unalterable framework and this passionate delight in life. Consult R. Sewall, *The Vision of Tragedy.*

tragicomedy. Renaissance critical theorists, embroidering on Aristotle's *Poetics,* assumed that tragedies dealt with noble (important) figures and ended with a death; comedies dealt with trivial (laughable) figures and ended with a celebration. A tragi-comedy was some sort of mixture: high characters in a play ending happily, or a mingling of deaths and feasts, or, most often (as in many American films) threats of death which are happily — and unconvincingly — evaded. John Fletcher (1579–1625), who with his collaborator Francis Beaumont, wrote graceful dramas relying heavily on passionate outbursts and surprising turns of plot, defined a tragicomedy as a play that lacks deaths (and thus is no tragedy) but "brings some near it, which is enough to make it no comedy." One of the speakers in John Dryden's *Essay of Dramatick Poesie* (1668) says: "There is no theater in the world has anything so absurd as the English tragi-comedy; . . . here a course of mirth, there another of sadness and passion, and a third of honor and a duel: thus, in two hours and a half, we run through all the fits of Bedlam." Consult Eugene Waith, *The Pattern of Tragi-Comedy.* On what can roughly be called the bitter or ironic comedy of the nineteenth and twentieth centuries, consult K. S. Guthke, *Modern Tragicomedy,* and C. Hoy, *The Hyacinth Room.*

trilogy. A unit of three works. Though Greek tragic dramatists submitted three tragedies at a time, the plays are only a trilogy if they have an internal unity. Aeschylus' *Oresteia* (458 B.C.) is the only extant complete Greek trilogy; Sophocles' three plays on the Oedipus legend — *Antigone* (c. 422 B.C.), *Oedipus the King* (c. 425), and *Oedipus at*

Colonus (c. 406) are not properly a trilogy because they were written at widely separated times and do not cohere into a consistent, unified whole. A modern trilogy: O'Neill's *Mourning Becomes Electra* (1931).

unity. Generally means something like "coherence," "congruence"; in a unified piece the parts work together and jointly contribute to the whole. The subplot of a play may parallel the main plot, or one character may be a foil to another. In any case, unity suggests "completeness" or "pattern" resulting from a controlling intelligence. A current metaphor, **organic unity,** likens an artistic creation to an organism (*i.e.,* a living thing) rather than to a mechanism. A watch consists of parts stuck together; its total is the sum of its separable parts, and it can be analyzed by being dissected. A living organism, however, allegedly consists of parts so inseparable that none can without fundamental damage be separated from the others, for, as Henry James says, "in each of the parts there is something of each of the other parts." The whole (some critics say) must be grasped as a totality, rather than as a collection of mechanically joined parts. In the *Poetics*, Aristotle had said that a tragedy should have a unified action, and he had mentioned that most tragedies cover a period of twenty-four hours. Italian critics, making his comments rigid, in the late sixteenth century established the **Three Unities** of Time, Place, and Action: a play (1) must not cover more than twenty-four hours, (2) must be set in one locale only, or, at worst, in various parts of a single city, and (3) must be either entirely tragic or entirely comic, rather than a mixture of (as Sir Philip Sidney said) "hornpipes and funerals." (Consult H. B. Charlton, *Castelvetro's Theory of Poetry*.) Actually, the time covered by Greek tragedies is vague; characters come from distant places in the space of relatively few lines. For example, in *Oedipus the King*, a shepherd, who lives in the "farthest" fields from Corinth, is sent for in line 863 and arrives in line 1108. Nor is unity of place invariable in Greek tragedy; there are violations of it in, for example, Aeschylus' *The Eumenides* and Sophocles' *Ajax*.

well-made play. See *pièce bien faite*.